# Florida

50 miles
50 km

W9-BOO-114

**Waycross** · **Savannah** · St Simons Island
**Brunswick**

page 214

Fernandina Beach

Callahan

Jacksonville

Jacksonville Beach

page 216
St Augustine

Starke
Waldo

Gainesville · Palatka · Flagler Beach

Bunnell

page 212mond Beach
Daytona Beach

Ocala
De Land
Deltona · New Smyrna Beach

Belleview

Eustis

Canaveral Nat'l Seashore

Leesburg

Sanford
Titusville

page 258
Orlando
Bellwood
★Kennedy Space Center
Cape Canaveral

Walt Disney World★
Clinton Heights
Kissimmee page 234
St Cloud
page 198
Cocoa
Holo

A T L A N T I C

Lakeland
Winter Haven

Melbourne

Bartow
Lake Wales

page 186
Sebastian

O C E A N

Zolfo Springs
Sebring

Yeeh Junct.
Vero Beach

Fort Drum
Fort Pierce
Port Saint Lucie

Myakka River State Park
Arcadia
keechobee
Stuart

North Port · Port Charlotte
Palmdale
Lake Okeechobee
Canal Point
Jupiter

Little Abaco Island

Cape Coral
La Belle
Clewiston
Belle Glade
Boynton
page 218
North Palm Beach
page 184
m Beach Shores
st Palm Beach

Grand Bahama Island

Great Abaco Island

Fort Myers
Immokalee
Loxahatchee Nat'l Wildl. Refuge
page 176
Palm Beach
Delray Beach
Boca Raton

Sambel Island

Freeport

B A H A M A S

Plantation
page 174
Pompano Beach
Fort Lauderdale

Naples
Big Cypress Swamp
Big Cypress Nat'l Preserve
Carol City
Hollywood
page 120
Collier-Seminole St. Pk.
Marco Island
page 308
page 100
Hia
Miami
Miami Beach

Ten Thousand Islands
Chokoloskee
Kendall
Coral Gables

The Everglades
Perrine

Homestead
Cutler Ridge

Everglades National Park

Cape Sable
page 134

New Providence Island

Key Largo

Florida Bay

Key West
page 160
Marathon
Andros Island

Marquesas Keys

F l o r i d a   K e y s

Straits of Florida

# INSIGHT GUIDES
# FLORIDA

APA PUBLICATIONS L

Part of the Langenscheidt Publishing Group

# ✱ INSIGHT GUIDE

# FLORIDA

### Editorial
Project Editor
**John Gattuso**
Managing Editor
**Brian Bell**
Picture Editor
**Steven Lawrence**
Series Editor
**Dorothy Stannard**

### Distribution

North America
**Langenscheidt Publishers, Inc.**
36–36 33rd Street 4th Floor
Long Island City, NY 11106
Fax: 1 (718) 784 0640

UK & Ireland
**GeoCenter International Ltd**
Meridian House, Churchill Way West
Basingstoke, Hampshire RG21 6YR
Fax: (44) 1256 817988

Australia
**Universal Publishers**
1 Waterloo Road
Macquarie Park, NSW 2113
Fax: (61) 2 9888 9074

New Zealand
**Hema Maps New Zealand Ltd (HNZ)**
Unit D, 24 Ra ORA Drive
East Tamaki, Auckland
Fax: (64) 9 273 6479

Worldwide
**Apa Publications GmbH & Co.
Verlag KG (Singapore branch)**
38 Joo Koon Road, Singapore 628990
Tel: (65) 6865 1600. Fax: (65) 6861 6438

### Printing

**Insight Print Services (Pte) Ltd**
38 Joo Koon Road, Singapore 628990
Tel: (65) 6865 1600. Fax: (65) 6861 6438

©2009 Apa Publications GmbH & Co.
Verlag KG (Singapore branch)
All Rights Reserved

First Edition 1982
Eleventh Edition 2009

### CONTACTING THE EDITORS
We would appreciate it if readers
would alert us to errors or out-
dated information by writing to:
**Insight Guides, P.O. Box 7910,
London SE1 1WE, England.
Fax: (44) 20 7403 0290.
insight@apaguide.co.uk**

**www.insightguides.com**

# ABOUT THIS BOOK

The first Insight Guide pioneered the use of creative full-color photography in travel guides in 1970. Since then, we have ex-panded our range to cater to our readers' need not only for reliable information about their chosen des-tination but also for a real under-standing of the culture and workings of that destination. Now, when the internet can supply inexhaustible (but not always reliable) facts, our books marry text and pictures to provide those much more elusive qualities: knowledge and discernment.

## How to use this book

Insight Guide: Florida is structured to convey an understanding of the state and its people as well as to guide readers through its attractions:

◆ The **Features** section, indicated by a pink bar at the top of each page, covers the natural and cultural history of the region as well as illu-minating essays on Florida history, culture, sports, and food as well as an exploration of the theme park business.

◆ The main **Places** section, indi-cated by a blue bar, is a complete guide to all the sights and areas worth visiting. Places of special interest are coordinated by number with the maps.

◆ The **Travel Tips** listings section, with a yellow bar, provides full infor-mation on transportation, hotels, activities from culture and shopping to sports, an A–Z section of essen-tial practical information. An easy-to-find contents list for Travel Tips is printed on the back flap, which also serves as a bookmark.

## The contributors

With a destination as dynamic as Florida, it's not enough to simply

**LEFT:** high-rise hotels and condos overlook the ocean at South Beach in Miami.

glades and the Gulf Coast cities of Naples, Sarasota, St Petersburg, and Tampa to Gainesville, Ocala, and the often overlooked "Nature Coast."

Vermont-based writers **William and Kay Scheller** left chilly New England in order to rework chapters on Palm Springs, Fort Lauderdale, and the Florida Keys as well as pen new essays on Florida's rich and varied cuisine and cultural scene. They also took a behind-the-scenes look at the running of a theme park, which they share in "The Business of Pleasure."

**Joann Biondi**, a resident of Coconut Grove, dipped into a deep well of local knowledge in her pieces on vibrant, multicultural Miami and Miami Beach. **Jason Dehart**, a staff writer for *Tallahassee* magazine, leads readers on a tour of Tallahassee, Pensacola, and Panama City Beach as well as the lightly traveled "Forgotten Coast" of the Florida Panhandle.

**Martha Bayne**, whose work recently appeared in *Insight Guide: Chicago*, took a welcome break from the Windy City to explore Florida's northeast coast, including Daytona Beach, St Augustine, and Jacksonville. **Jason Mitchell**, editor of the Insight Guides' latest titles on the Orlando area, revamped chapters on Walt Disney World, greater Orlando, and the Space Coast. **Edward A. Jardim** freshened up the history chapters and provided invaluable editorial assistance.

Most of the spectacular photography is the work of **Richard and Abraham Nowitz**, father and son, whose recent work for the Insight Guides has taken them to China, Peru, and Arizona, among other far-flung places.

**Isobel McLean** indexed the book. The map editor was **Zoë Goodwin**.

update a travel guide – you need to rewrite and rephotograph large portions of it. That's what we've done for this major new edition, bringing together a team of expert writers and photographers who combine inside knowledge with the investigative skills of seasoned journalists.

This latest edition was managed by **John Gattuso**, a veteran Insight Guide editor and writer whose earlier books include a guide to Orlando and Walt Disney World. Gattuso built upon the foundations laid down by the title's previous editors, **Martha Ellen Zenfell** and **Emily Hatchwell**.

Among the first people Gattuso contacted was **Nicky Leach**, an award-winning travel writer and long-time Insight Guide contributor whose work appears in guides to Orlando, Arizona, New Mexico, and numerous other Insight Guides. For this book, her travels took her from the Ever-

## Map Legend

| | |
|---|---|
| ━ ·· ━ | International Boundary |
| ━ ━ ━ ━ | State Boundary |
| ━·━·━ | National Park/Reserve |
| ━ ━ ━ ━ | Ferry Route |
| ⊖ | Border Crossing |
| ✈ ✈ | Airport: International/Regional |
| 🚌 | Bus Station |
| Ⓜ | Metromover station |
| ❶ | Tourist Information |
| ✝ † ✝ | Church/Ruins |
| † | Monastery |
| ∴ | Archaeological Site |
| ∩ | Cave |
| ⚊ | Statue/Monument |
| ★ | Place of Interest |
| ↟ | Beach |
| ⌘ | Lighthouse |

The main places of interest in the Places section are coordinated by number with a full-colour map (e.g. ❶), and a symbol at the top of every right-hand page tells you where to find the map.

# Contents

**LEFT:** live oaks festooned with Spanish moss near St Augustine.

## Maps

## Travel Tips

# THE BEST OF FLORIDA: TOP ATTRACTIONS

With more than 300 sunny days a year, 1,800 miles of gorgeous coastline, and no fewer than nine state-of-the-art theme parks, Florida is America's top vacation destination

△ The Conch Republic, Margaritaville, Mañanaland – call it what you like, **Key West** is always up for a party. Perched at the end of the Florida Keys, the southernmost city is – like many end-of-the-line towns – a hub of colorful nonconformity where free spirits find refuge from the mainstream and the rest of us can drop in for a couple of drinks. *Pages 159–67*

▽ Encompassing more than 1¹⁄₂ million acres of subtropical wilderness, **Everglades National Park** sustains hundreds of plant and animal species, including endangered Florida panthers and West Indian manatees. *Pages 133–43*

△ Disney, Universal, SeaWorld, and Busch Gardens operate no less than nine **theme parks** in Florida, and each would be considered a major destination in its own right if located anywhere else. At the center of the theme-park galaxy is Orlando, home of Walt Disney World Resort, which claims more than 45 million visitors each year. *Pages 233–55, 257–62, 287–9*

△ Had enough of the crowds? The **Florida Panhandle** has miles of undeveloped beaches and quiet seaside towns. *Pages 344–53*

◁ History and science are brought vividly to life at the **Kennedy Space Center**, where, if your timing is right, you might even see a rocket launch. *Page 197–205*

△ The buff, bronze, and beautiful gather at the red-hot nightclubs and glorious Art Deco hotels of Miami's **South Beach** – the new American Riviera. *Pages 119–22*

△ White "sugar sand" and warm azure waters are the key ingredients of Florida's **beautiful beaches**. With 1,800 miles of coastline, there's a beach for every taste and occasion. *Pages 304–5*

△ Let your imagination run wild at St Petersburg's **Salvador Dalí Museum**, one of the country's finest museums dedicated to a single artist. *Pages 296–7*

◁ NASCAR's most prestigious race – and one of the country's biggest sporting events – the **Daytona 500** is a blistering, 500-mile contest of driving skill and mechanical prowess. *Pages 211–2*

▷ A palazzo packed with priceless European art, the **John and Mable Ringling Museum of Art** is a tribute to a man better known for creating the "Greatest Show on Earth." *Pages 312–3*

# THE BEST OF FLORIDA: EDITOR'S CHOICE

**Sun-drenched beaches, high-tech thrill rides, romantic hideaways, historic sites, cultural attractions, and the great outdoors ... here, at a glance, are our top recommendations for a visit**

## BEST BEACHES

● **Bill Baggs Cape Florida State Park.** Regularly rated as one of the best in the US, this pristine beach on Key Biscayne soothes the weary soul. *See page 127.*

● **Bradenton Beach.** At the south end of Anna Maria Key, Bradenton has walkable streets and white beaches that attract nesting sea turtles in summer. *See page 309.*

● **Caladesi Island State Park.** Florida's No. 1 white-sand beach is a boat-in-only experience with a mangrove kayak trail and glimpses of ospreys in the pines. *See page 293.*

● **Cayo Costa Island State Park.** This boat-in beach offers rustic lodging and campsites away from crowds for self-sufficient, outdoorsy types. *See page 316.*

● **Fort de Soto County Park.** The largest park in Pinellas County, this former fort has white-sand beaches and shoreline campsites with boat launches, and can be reached by car from the mainland. *See page 293.*

● **Sanibel Island.** Do the "Sanibel Stoop" to collect lovely shells washed up on the shores of this beautifully preserved island. *See page 315.*

● **St Joseph Peninsula State Park.** This Panhandle park has miles of beautiful beaches and an excellent hiking trail, plus rental cabins and a basic campground. *See page 347.*

## BEST THRILL RIDES

● **Amazing Adventures of Spider-Man.** The most sophisticated ride in Orlando is part simulator, part 3-D cinema, part dark ride. *See page 259.*

● **Dueling Dragons.** It's a fine line between terror and exhilaration as twin coasters zoom past each other at a "fly-by" speed of 120 mph. *See page 260.*

● **Incredible Hulk Coaster.** From 0 to 40 mph in two seconds, followed by three rolls, two loops, and the world's highest inversion. *See page 260.*

● **Kraken.** A floorless coaster with speeds in excess of 60 mph. *See page 261.*

● **Montu.** One of the world's tallest and longest inverted coasters. *See page 289.*

● **Mission: SPACE** The newest attraction at Epcot is by far the best. You feel you've earned your wings after this simulated trip to the red planet. Barf bag included. *See page 241.*

● **Rock 'n' Roller Coaster** An indoor coaster with a 60 mph launch, plus dips, inversions, and blaring rock music. *See page 246.*

● **Twilight Zone Tower of Terror.** This elaborately themed ride is based on a simple formula: Climb up. Plummet down. Scream. Repeat. *See page 246.*

**LEFT:** Fort de Soto Beach. **ABOVE:** Dueling Dragons.

## BEST ROADSIDE ATTRACTIONS

● **Cypress Gardens Adventure Park.** Time hasn't diminished the charms of this pre-Disney "theme park," with water rides, animal exhibits, a famous water-skiing show, gardens, and strolling southern belles. *See page 270–1.*

● **Gatorland.** Gator wrestling is one of the big attractions at this old-time Orlando tourist

**ABOVE:** Weeki Wachee.

draw. *See page 269–70.*

● **Henry the Pole-Vaulting Fish.** In this case, the fish is a lark. The real attraction is the glass-bottom boat ride in crystal-clear Wakulla Springs. *See page 343.*

● **Holy Land Experience.** A Christian theme park with historical re-creations, shows, and museums *See page 263.*

● **Theater of the Sea.** Watch dolphins perform – or even swim with them – in this realm of blue lagoons and coral grottoes. *See page 149–50.*

● **Weeki Wachee Springs.** A gloriously retro attraction where beautiful young "mermaids" perform underwater shows in crystal waters. *See page 300.*

**ABOVE:** Cà d'Zan at the Ringling Museum of Art.

## MUST-SEE MUSEUMS

● **Charles Hosmer Morse Museum of American Art.** A sumptuous collection of Tiffany leaded glass and other artworks, including his chapel interior for the 1893 World's Columbian Exposition in Chicago. *See pages 267–8.*

● **Flagler Museum.** Railroad baron and developer Henry Flagler's Palm Beach mansion defined "over the top" in a city that loves excess. *See page 185.*

● **Florida Museum of Natural History.** A light, bright, kid-friendly museum with well-interpreted exhibits on Florida's life zones and native cultures, plus an awesome butterfly pavilion. *See page 331.*

● **Salvador Dalí Museum.** The location is almost as bizarre as the

large-scale psycho-drama paintings, but early Impressionist-inspired works show a sweeter side to the surrealist master. *See page 296.*

● **John and Mable Ringling Museum of Art.** The circus impresario's over-the-top estate includes a gorgeous Venetian-style home, a theater, a circus museum, landscaped grounds, and Baroque masterpieces by Rubens. *See page 312.*

● **Norton Museum of Art.** French Impressionists, Post-Impressionists, and modern American masters put the Norton on a par with institutions many times its size. *See page 188.*

● **Vizcaya.** With 70 rooms of European antiques, Vizcaya is a rare example of opulent life lived long ago. *See pages 113 and 116–7.*

## BEST PLACE TO PARTY

● **CityWalk.** Universal's "nightclub district" caters to grown-up tastes with food, drink, dancing, and live entertainment designed for an over-21 clientele. The scene heats up after 10pm and stays open to 2am. *See page 260.*

● **Key West.** A year-round party at the end of the road, the "Conch Republic" is always up for a good time. *See page 159–67.*

● **Panama City Beach and Daytona Beach.** Though some towns have cracked

down on Spring Break revelry, the girls – and boys – still go wild at these student favorites. *See pages 347 and 211–12.*

● **South Beach.** With pulsating neon lights and scantily clad buff bodies, Ocean Drive is party central all night long. The same bodies can be seen stretched out on the sand during the day. *See pages 121–22.*

**RIGHT:** CityWalk.

## BEST OF THE OUTDOORS

- **Anhinga and Gumbo Limbo Trails, Everglades National Park.** Nose-to-nose encounters with spread-winged anhingas, freeze-framed herons and egrets, rambunctious alligators, and the red-peeling gumbo limbo, aka the "tourist tree." *See page 138.*
- **Crystal River National Wildlife Refuge.** View an archaeological site and swim with wild manatees in the spring-fed river at this popular refuge south of Cedar Key. *See pages 300–1.*
- **Fakahatchee Strand State Park.** The Big Cypress Bend Boardwalk Trail is a perfect western Everglades stroll, with lush vegetation, tinkling birdsong, and glimpses of the world's rarest orchids. *See page 142.*
- **J.N. "Ding" Darling National Wildlife Refuge.** Early mornings in winter bring roseate spoonbills, flamingos, pelicans, and thousands of other birds to this birder's paradise. *See page 315.*
- **John Pennekamp Coral Reef State Park.** The only living coral reef in the continental US reveals its riot of color to snorkelers, divers, and glass-bottom boat tours. *See pages 148–9.*
- **Merrit Island National Wildlife Refuge.** See manatees and sea turtles in the shadow of the Kennedy Space Center. *See page 205.*
- **Myakka River State Park.** A former ranch, Florida's largest state park offers rustic cabins, campsites, hiking, and horseback riding. *See page 312.*
- **Wilderness Waterway, Ten Thousand Islands.** The 99-mile (160-km) classic Everglades experience for seasoned kayakers meanders through islands offering solitude and "chickee-style" campsites. *See page 133.*
- **St Marks National Wildlife Refuge.** Birders come from far and wide to view some 300 bird species. *See page 344.*

**ABOVE:** Universal's Seuss Landing is a family favorite.

## BEST FOR FAMILIES

- **Busch Gardens.** Conservation is job one at this top-drawer zoo and theme park, which educates as it entertains, particularly on the theme of gorillas and African animals. *See page 287.*
- **Discovery Cove.** Sea World's resort gives visitors a chance to interact with a dolphin. Give it a smooch, and it will give you a lift back to the beach. *See page 261.*
- **Florida and Mote Marine Aquariums.** Kids can scuba dive with sharks or swim with fishes in a large tank at Florida Aquarium while, across Tampa Bay, Mote Aquarium offers encounters with recuperating dolphins, sharks, and manatees. *See page 286 and 310.*
- **Kennedy Space Center.** Even jaded kids will be enthralled by the human quest to leave the home planet. *See pages 197–205.*
- **Magic Kingdom.** Quintessential Disney. *See pages 235–41.*
- **Seuss Landing.** Perhaps the most imaginative children's play area in Orlando is this Seuss-themed area at Universal. *See page 259.*

**LEFT:** kayaking in the Ten Thousand Islands.

## BEST EVENTS

● **Calle Ocho.** The largest Hispanic heritage festival in the US is a sizzling, salsa-fueled street party in Miami. *See pages 106–7.*

● **Goombay Festival.** A grand Caribbean carnival celebrates the Bahamian roots of Coconut Grove. *See page 111.*

● **Hemingway Look-Alike Contest.** Calling all burly whitebeards: a new Papa wannabe is crowned each year. *See page 377.*

● **Kissimmee Rodeo.** Harken back to the good old days when the only thing treated like cattle in Orlando was, well, cattle. *See page 379.*

● **Miami Book Fair.** The event brings over 400 authors to downtown Miami for a weeklong celebration of the written word. *See page 101.*

● **St George Island Mullet Toss.** This beach party gives new meaning to the term "flying fish." *See page 346.*

● **Space Shuttle launch.** The ground shakes as rockets blast the 4.5-million-pound vessel into the stratosphere. *See page 203.*

● **Sunset Celebration at Mallory Square.** Why applaud a sunset? Because in Key West the sun doesn't just set, it hits the Gulf in a blaze of glory. *See page 161.*

**ABOVE:** Amelia Island Plantation.

## ROMANTIC GETAWAYS

● **Amelia Island and Fernandina Beach.** This gracious seaside community has modern first-class resorts with every conceivable amenity, plus a touch of laid-back Old Florida style. *See pages 223–4.*

● **Anna Maria Key.** This pedestrian-friendly island has both Gulf and bayfront beaches, nesting sea turtles, superb restaurants, and vacation rentals for sunset watching. *See page 309.*

● **Biltmore Hotel.** This historic hotel in Coral Gables has it all: Spanish Mediterranean ambience, lush tropical gardens, and a swimming pool that has known more than a few movie stars. *See page 108.*

● **Honeymoon Island State Park.** Its popular palm-thatched huts for newlyweds are gone, but the ambience is pure romance and the birding is excellent on this sandy key adjoining Dunedin *See page 298.*

**ABOVE:** the Goombay Festival is a Bahamian carnival.

## BEST HISTORIC SITES

● **Edison and Ford Winter Estates.** This popular estate offers the inside scoop on the great men and their work and includes rare plants and trees, two riverfront homes, and Edison's lab. *See page 314.*

● **Fort Jefferson.** A fortress that never fired in anger, this massive masonry pile 68 miles (109km) off Key West broods over one of the US's loneliest national parks. *See page 165.*

● **Little White House.** Time stopped around 1950 at this unpretentious Key West retreat, where you can picture Harry S. Truman in his Hawaiian shirt at the poker table. *See page 160.*

● **Castillo de San Marcos.** The 17th-century Spanish fort still guards the oldest continuously occupied city in the US. *See pages 215–6.*

**RIGHT:** Castillo de San Marcos, St Augustine.

# LET THE SUN SHINE

Florida's population has almost doubled in the past 30 years. There are plenty of reasons for its enduring popularity

In his 1962 novel *Travels with Charley*, John Steinbeck writes of Florida's allure: "As I went farther and farther north and it got colder I was aware of more and more advertising for Florida real estate and, with the approach of the long and bitter winter, I could see why Florida is a golden world. As I went along I found that more and more people lusted toward Florida and that thousands had moved there and that more thousands wanted to and would. The advertising… made few claims except for the fact that what they were selling was in Florida. Some of them went out on a limb and promised that it was above tide level. But that didn't matter; the very name Florida carried the message of warmth and ease and comfort. It was irresistible."

Florida's climate and image as a place where dreams come true have lost none of their appeal, and about 1,000 newcomers a day arrive in the state. People joke that most of Florida's inhabitants were born elsewhere – anywhere from upstate New York to Cuba.

In addition, tourists regard it as an unbeatable vacation destination – and with good reason. Nature has played a major role, providing everything from the tropical Keys and wild Everglades to miles and miles of shimmering beaches. And when nature isn't enough, man-made attractions fill the gap at such places as Orlando, theme park capital of the world, and Miami, where the ice-cream-colored Art Deco buildings provide the backdrop for posing and partying in trendy South Beach.

It is easy to get around Florida so long as you're comfortable behind the wheel, with rental cars easy to come by and reasonably priced. Accommodations are plentiful, ranging from affordable roadside motels to quaint bed-and-breakfasts and beachside resorts. The weather is unlikely to disappoint, though summers can be oppressively hot and humid.

Comparing the state with California, Walt Disney said: "Here in Florida, we have something special we never enjoyed at Disneyland – the blessing of size. There's enough land here to hold all the ideas and plans we can possibly imagine." Visitors, their plans made, are just as unlikely to be disappointed.     ❑

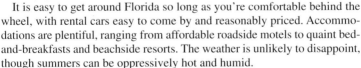

**PRECEDING PAGES:** the view from a St Augustine lighthouse; shooting the rapids at a Universal water ride in Orlando; Ybor City, Tampa. **LEFT:** playing in the surf near the Naples Pier. **TOP:** flying the flag of the "Conch Republic" in Key West. **ABOVE RIGHT:** the beach at Taylor State Park, Key West.

# DECISIVE DATES

## INDIGENOUS PEOPLE

### circa 8000 BC
Nomadic tribes reach Florida.

### 5000 BC
Nomadic peoples begin to settle and plant maize.

### AD 300–1000
Native tribes inhabit much of Florida. About 10,000 people are living in the region by the time the Spanish arrive.

## CONQUEST

### 1492
Christopher Columbus arrives in the New World, landing first on Hispaniola.

### 1513
Spanish conquistador Ponce de León is the first European to set foot on the peninsula, near present-day St Augustine.

### 1521
Ponce de León returns to Florida with 200 settlers, but the expedition is later abandoned.

### 1539
Hernando de Soto organizes a treasure-hunting trip to Florida, but he is unsuccessful and dies three years later.

### 1562
The French arrive in Florida to challenge the Spanish, who then strengthen their hold.

### 1565
The Spaniard Pedro Menéndez de Avilés founds St Augustine – the first perma-

nent settlement in Florida and the oldest city in the US.

### 1586
The English explorer Francis Drake attacks St Augustine and sets the town on fire. Further attacks follow. For the next two centuries Florida is disputed among Britain, France, and Spain.

### 1670
The British use Indians in their colonies to the north to help them fight the Spanish in Florida.

### circa 1710
Fleeing pressure from British settlers, Creek Indians from Georgia (later

known as Seminoles) start moving south into Florida.

### 1763
After the Seven Years' War, the English receive Florida from Spain in exchange for Havana, capital of Cuba.

### 1783
Florida is returned to Spain after the Revolutionary War.

## 1803

The Spanish cede the Panhandle to Napoleon. In 1805 he sells the region, together with Louisiana, to the Americans.

## 1817–18

Pressure from white settlers, plus attempts by plantation owners from nearby states to recover their runaway slaves, result in violent clashes with Indian tribes in northern Florida and lead to the outbreak of the First Seminole War. General Andrew Jackson overcomes Seminole resistance, then sets about taking control of Florida on behalf of the US government.

## 1819

Spain cedes Florida to the US government to clear $5 million of claims against it by Anmerican citizens.

**Left Top:** an impression of Florida Indians c.1564 by French artist and explorer Jacques le Moyne. **Left Middle::** Osceola rejects an American treaty. **Left Bottom:** native Florida woman. **Above:** early map of Florida. **Right:** alligator wrestling in Orlando c.1900.

## STATEHOOD

## 1821

Andrew Jackson, future US president, becomes the first governor of Florida.

## 1824

The newly founded town of Tallahassee is declared capital of Florida Territory.

## 1832

Under the Treaty of Payne's Creek, 15 Seminole chiefs agree to move west.

## 1835–42

Seminole leader Osceola launches a campaign against the US Army. The Second Seminole War ends in 1842 when most of the Indians surrender and are deported to Arkansas and Oklahoma.

## 1845

Florida becomes the 27th state of the Union.

## 1855–58

More Indians are deported as a result of the Third Seminole War, though some manage to hide in the Everglades.

## 1861

As a major slave-holding state (around 39,000 of its population of 87,000 are black slaves), Florida secedes from the Union and joins forces with the Confederate States in the US Civil War.

## 1865

The Civil War ends, costing Florida $20 million in damages and over 5,000 lives.

## RECONSTRUCTION

## 1868

Following a revolt against Spain in Cuba, the first wave of Cubans arrives in Florida. Many settle in Key West, where they build a cigar industry.

## 1883

The great railroad-building era begins. Railroad magnate Henry Flagler begins to build the East Coast Rail-

road along the Atlantic coast via Palm Beach and Miami, while his rival Henry B. Plant builds the Atlantic Coast Line linking Richmond, Virginia, with Tampa. More settlers, and also tourists, head south.

**1898**
Revolution erupts in Cuba and the US joins in to drive Spain off the island. Tampa is the main departure point for soldiers bound for Cuba.

**1912**
Completion of the final section of the East Coast Railroad to Key West.

**1924**
The first property boom of the 20th century begins. Thousands of settlers and tourists arrive. The population reaches one million.

**1926**
A powerful hurricane devastates Miami, killing 250.

**1928**
Another massive hurricane leaves over 2,000 dead near Lake Okeechobee.

**1929**
The stock market crash adds to Florida's misery as the US enters the Great Depression.

**1930s**
Miami Beach's Art Deco hotels are built and tourism thrives in South Florida.

**1939–45**
During World War II Florida is used as a training ground for soldiers.

## POSTWAR BOOM
**1949**
Missle test site is established at Cape Canaveral.

**1950s**
Large-scale tourism begins, partly thanks to soldiers who trained in Florida returning with their families.

**1959**
Fidel Castro leads a revolution in Cuba and later embraces communism.

**1960s**
In the years following the revolution, thousands of Cubans flee and settle in the Miami region. More emigrés from Central and South America follow.

**1961**
The first rockets soar from Cape Canaveral at the start of the space race.

**1964**
The US Civil Rights Act is passed. Blacks in Florida begin to overcome severe racial discrimination.

**1969**
The first moonshot is launched from Florida.

**1970s**
An economic recession badly hurts Florida. Thousands of Haitians sail rickety boats to Miami.

**1971**
Walt Disney World, Florida's first major theme park, opens near Orlando.

## MODERN TIMES

### 1980
Cuban refugees arrive during the Mariel boatlift, increasing Miami's population by around 125,000.

### 1980s
Campaign to restore the Art Deco district of Miami Beach launches the area's renaissance.

### 1981
The maiden voyage of the Space Shuttle is launched at the Kennedy Space Center.

### 1984
The influential TV series *Miami Vice* premieres. It ran to five series, changing the public image of the city.

### 1985
Xavier Suarez is Miami's first Cuban mayor.

### 1990
Manuel Noriega, former head of state of Panama, is tried in Miami on drug charges.

### 1992
Andrew, the biggest hurricane for decades, devastates southeast Florida. The damage is estimated at $30 billion.

### 1994
Economic collapse in Cuba brings another wave of refugees to South Florida.

### 1996
The city of Miami is declared bankrupt. A motion to merge the city into Dade County is not passed.

### 1997
Designer Gianni Versace is shot and killed on Ocean Drive in South Beach.

### 2000
Florida is at the center of a vote recount controversy following the presidential campaign between Al Gore and George W. Bush.

### 2003
The Space Shuttle Columbia, launched from Kennedy Space Center, burns up on re-entry into the earth's atmosphere. All seven astronauts die.

### 2004
Four hurricanes pummel the coastline over a 48-day period, breaking a record set in 1964.

### 2005
The 50th anniversary of Disneyland in Anaheim, California, is celebrated at Disney World in Orlando.

### 2008
Governor Charlie Crist announces that the state of Florida has agreed to spend $1.7 billion to buy nearly 200,000 acres (80,000 hectares) of land from a sugar producer to help restore the Everglades. ❑

**LEFT TOP:** postcard from the early 20th century. **LEFT MIDDLE:** Walt Disney and Mickey Mouse in a publicity photo from 1935. **LEFT BOTTOM:** hurricane destruction in Pensacola. **ABOVE:** trick photos were a popular tourist souvenir.
**RIGHT:** South Beach condos under construction.

# NATIVE FLORIDA

This land was their land long before
European invaders arrived and
altered the course of history

Florida's first "snowbirds" were Paleo-Indians fleeing the frozen north during the Ice Age, when the Florida peninsula was a dry desert with a land mass twice the size of what it is today. The hunters were attracted by the warm climate and abundant game, among them now-extinct ground sloths, mastodons, camels, and giant bison. They camped along coastal areas, then, as the glaciers melted and the climate grew wetter, moved inland. Paleo-era remains have been uncovered at Silver Springs and other central Florida water sources.

## Ancient hunters

By 6000 BC, these ancient Floridians had coalesced into hunter-gatherers associated with particular territories, where they hunted otters, rats, squirrels, turtles, alligators, and opossums, fished in lakes, and gathered cactus fruit and other delicacies. Early Archaic people invented tools made from animal teeth and bone fastened to wooden handles. They ceremonially interred their dead wrapped in woven palmettos. The swampy land preserved the corpses so well that archaeologists

*A sinkhole in Dade County contains evidence of human habitation dating back about 10,000 years. Found at the site were the bones of extinct Ice Age mammals as well as stone tools and human remains.*

excavating Windover Ponder near Titusville were able to extract human brain DNA – a first on the continent. As the climate got wetter, more water sources appeared, supporting larger populations.

**LEFT:** Indian leader of the upper St John's River.
**RIGHT:** Calusa Indians inhabited Florida's Gulf coast.

The people consumed oysters and conchs in coastal areas as well as mussels and snails at freshwater sites, and used large shells as tools for fashioning dugout canoes. The shell mounds were a distinguishing feature of camps and may still be seen beside inland rivers and the mouths of estuaries.

As early as 1500 BC, Archaic people were making the first ceramics in North America, which they strengthened with Spanish moss and palmetto fibers. They grew corn and squash and traded for carved stearite from Alabama and Georgia. People living along the St John's River created distinctive effigy pots, stamped with corncob patterns.

Archaeologists are particularly fascinated by the more than 14,000 burial mounds, probably influenced by the Hopewell cultures of Ohio and

Illinois, found throughout Florida. They occur in Matecumbe in the Keys, Bear Lake in the Everglades, Safety Harbor on the Gulf, and at dozens of sites in the Panhandle, and have yielded insight into religious rituals among these ancient people.

By the time Spanish conquistador Juan Ponce de Leon landed at Cape Canaveral in 1513, more than 150,000 native people were living on the peninsula. The eastern Panhandle was the province of the Apalachee. Their neighbors in the western Panhandle were the Pensacola, Apalachicola, and Chtot. The Mayaimi people lived on the shores of Lake Okeechobee. Modern-day Miami and Palm Beach were home to the

thatched huts. Chiefs and female nobles were lavishly tattooed and wore feather capes, shell beads, and metal belts. Males wore breechcloths of deerskin, while women dressed in skirts of Spanish moss so tightly woven it shone like silk.

Powerful astronomer priests lived in temples and residences atop large sand mounds. They read the movements of the sun, moon, and planets and predicted when ceremonies should be held to ensure bountiful harvests of corn, squash, and other crops. Ceremonies lasted all night and involved dancing and drinking (and vomiting) black holly berry tea for purification – rituals still performed by Seminole Indians today.

Tequesta. Southwestern Florida was the territory of the fierce Calusa, whose shell-tipped arrows took Ponce de Leon's life in 1521. The largest group were direct descendants of the agricultural St John's culture who called themselves the Timucua. A related tribe called the Tocobaga lived in the Tampa Bay area.

## Chiefs and nobles

The first European to document Florida's Indians was Frenchman Jacques Le Moyne. He made watercolors of Indians after surviving the 1565 massacre at Fort Caroline on the St John's River by Spanish conquistador Pedro Menendez de Aviles. Le Moyne's drawings show a tall, handsome people ruled by chiefs and nobles in villages of palm-

## The Seminoles

By the early 1700s, Florida's Indian population had been drastically reduced by warfare and European diseases. Between 1613 and 1617, half of the 16,000 converted Indians in Spanish missions in northern Florida had died of the plague and other infectious diseases. British colonists raiding from the coast of Carolina seized 1,000 Apalachee between 1702 and 1704, emptying villages in the north.

In Georgia, meanwhile, Creek Indians had formed an uneasy alliance with the British, bartering deerskins and furs for guns and joining British raids. When that alliance collapsed, Spain seized the opportunity to invite Creeks into depopulated areas of northern Florida. Sometime between 1716 and 1767, Creeks began colonizing former Apalachee towns, spreading into the center of the state, where they took over former Timucuan farmlands, reestablished trading networks, and lived alongside escaped slaves granted sanctuary by the Spanish since 1693.

In Florida, the powerful Creek Indians transformed themselves into a new people: the Seminoles. Their name was derived from the Spanish word *cimarron*, meaning "wild and unruly." Always great traders, Seminoles traveled as far as Cuba in dugout canoes and bartered with ships sailing along the Atlantic Coast. They hunted deer and other game in forested islands in the Everglades and grew corn, rice, watermelons, peaches, potatoes, and pumpkins in fertile central Florida.

In 1764, Spain gave up Florida to the British, and many Indians and blacks left with the Spanish for Cuba rather than risk being forced into slavery on British plantations. Creeks in Georgia and Florida Seminoles fared better. They used their alliance with the British to continue trading through the powerful Panton, Leslie Company, owned by Scotsman William Panton, a friend of Alexander McGillivray, the half-English headman of the Creek Confederacy.

By the time Florida was returned to Spain by the American government in 1783, much of the place was settled by Seminoles and blacks and Spanish cattle ranchers and farmers. Many blacks chose to live just outside Seminole villages, where they enjoyed the protection of their Indian neighbors in exchange for labor and goods.

## The long war

American ire over Spain's sanctuary policy for runaway slaves and its own agenda of Indian removal led to clashes along the Florida-Georgia border between 1785 and 1821. In 1818, Andrew Jackson, who would become Florida's first territorial governor under US rule, instigated the First Seminole War in northern Florida. His ruthless pursuit of Indian removal and extermination led the Seminoles to call him "Sharp Knife."

After spending $20 million to fight a long and difficult Second Seminole War between 1835 and 1842, the US government coerced 3,824 Seminoles and runaway black slaves onto reservations west of the Mississippi. They abandoned the forts they had built, leaving only citizen-soldiers to defend new settlements like Orlando and Tampa. Skirmishes between settlers and Seminoles led to

the Third Seminole War, which lasted from 1855 to 1858. At its close, the last Seminole holdouts, led by Chief Billy Bowlegs, were rounded up and sent to reservations in the Everglades and near Tampa Bay, where their descendants live today.

During this period, Florida's Seminoles proved themselves to be brave, implacable foes, well suited to guerilla warfare in the swamps. The era's best known Indian leader, Osceola, born Billy Powell in 1804 to an English father and Creek mother in Alabama, was neither Seminole nor a chief. But after moving with his mother to Florida early in the Second Seminole War, he grew to prominence as a war leader of ruthless daring. In 1837, he was cap-

tured under a white flag of truce by US Major General Thomas Jessup, a treacherous action that elevated Osceola to the level of martyr and legend in the public imagination.

Also legendary was Coacoochee, son of Miccosukee chief Philip and nephew of Micanopy, head of the Alachua Seminole near modern Gainesville. Coacoochee united these two main groups of Florida Indians and fought tirelessly during the Second Seminole War. But in 1842, even he acknowledged defeat, telling his captors: "The white men are as thick as the leaves in the hammock; they come upon us thicker every year. They may shoot us, drive our women and children night and day; they may chain our hands and feet, but the red man's heart will always be free." ❏

---

**LEFT:** a diorama at the South Florida Museum depicts a Paleo-Indian hunting an ancient bison.
**RIGHT:** Osceola, a Seminole war leader.

# NEW SPAIN

The first of the Iberian explorers stopped by in 1513, thirsty for a taste of magical waters, before conquistadors and others began seeking their own place in the sun

Florida's calendar of official holidays salutes such notables as social reformers Martin Luther King Jr and Susan B. Anthony, Confederate patriots Robert E. Lee and Jefferson Davis (Florida was early among the Southern states to secede from the Union), and of course Presidents Washington and Lincoln.

And then there's Pascua Florida Day.

The latter occasion, known also as Florida State Day, is observed annually on April 2, and it reminds us once again of what lies beneath a good part of the American historical experience. What lies beneath is "the Spanish tinge," as Jelly Roll Morton once said famously when describing the cultural flavors that went into the making of jazz. There's a Spanish substratum undergirding the Florida saga, as with a good part of the entire American South and Southwest, and it represents more than just a blur in the historical timeline. It represents altogether some three centuries of contact and conflict, adventure and achievement, mixing and matching the Spanish heritage with Native American and Anglo-American protagonists, as well as English, French and Dutch rivals.

> Ponce de León called the Florida Keys Los Mártires because the low rocky islands reminded him of a line of martyred men.

## Land of flowers

The timeline vis-à-vis the Spanish chapter in the Florida saga begins on March 27, 1513. That date saw the appearance of a Spanish ship bearing explorer Juan Ponce de León and crew. They spot-

ted land that at first was mistaken for an island but turned out to be a peninsula, thick with vegetation. Ponce de León christened it La Florida because he and his men landed there during Eastertime, or "Pascua Florida" – Feast of Flowers. The tag stuck, and La Florida would be applied initially to all Spanish holdings on the North American continent.

It is widely believed among scholars, it should be noted, that Ponce de León may have been preceded to Florida by earlier European pathfinders. One such might have been John Cabot, who had voyaged to Labrador and northern locales years earlier, while Portuguese mariners had begun thrusting into the Atlantic nearly a full century earlier. Still, credit has traditionally gone to Ponce de León.

---

**LEFT:** Castillo de San Marcos.
**RIGHT:** Juan Ponce de León, "discoverer" of Florida.

## Soldier of fortune

Just who was this reputed discoverer of Florida, the "Sunshine State" that would someday be represented by the 27th star emblazoned on the American flag? His beginnings are somewhat shadowy. Ponce de León may have been the illegitimate son, born in 1460, of a Seville nobleman. As a young man, he fought the Moors as they made their last stand at Granada. He took part in the second of Christopher Columbus's epochal voyages to the New World, and he became the first governor of Puerto Rico, in 1509.

Given an opportunity by Spain's King Ferdinand I to become governor of a fabled island called Bimini – reputed to be a paradise flowing with waters of Viagra-like potency that could perpetuate youthful vigor – the fiftyish adventurer and his expedition had set forth on March 3, 1513, to find his Fountain of Youth. Bimini and that magically regenerative fountain would prove elusive, but Ponce de León made his fortune nonetheless.

Promised virtual ownership of the fabled island and anything else he might discover, including gold or other precious metals, the explorer and his crew poked about in the Bahamas for about 25 days aboard the *Santa Maria de la Consolación* and the *Santiago*. There was no trace of Bimini, but they did locate the Bahama Channel, a short-

cut to the Caribbean from the Atlantic Ocean. Ponce de León and his crew celebrated Pascua Florida aboard ship. Six days later, on April 2, the unknown shore was sighted.

The expedition made landfall several days later, somewhere between the site that would soon become the first permanent settlement in the continental United States – St Augustine – and a river now known as the St John's.

## Unfriendly natives

Further exploration led the expedition north to the mouth of the St John's River and south around the Florida Keys. After rounding the Keys, Ponce de León sailed up the west coast, possibly as far as Pensacola Bay, and it became apparent to him that he had found more than a mythical island. He made at least one more stop at Charlotte Harbor, once called Bahía Juan Ponce, near the modern city of Fort Myers. There, he encountered Florida's native inhabitants. They were tall and powerful – and intensely hostile.

Ponce de León returned to Puerto Rico from that maiden voyage to plot his conquest of La Florida. But it wasn't until 1521 that he had managed to scrape together two ships, 200 men, 50 horses, and all the equipment he needed. The king commissioned him and a contingent of missionary priests to settle the "island of Florida," taking care to treat the Indians well, "seeking in every possible way to

blood stained the newly consecrated soil. By some accounts, the Spanish even set snarling greyhounds on their attackers.

Despite heavy losses, the Indians never retreated. An arrow hewn from swamp reed tore into Ponce de León's flesh. Six of his men, wounded, collapsed along with him. Survivors managed to get him and the others into a boat. They reached Cuba, where he expired. Puerto Rico became the final resting place for this discoverer of Florida.

## The conquistadors

Three major expeditions and several smaller ones followed Ponce de León into La Florida during the

convert them to our Holy Catholic faith."

Ponce de León again put ashore near Charlotte Harbor, an event Catholic scholars consider the first authenticated instance of priests landing on the soil of the future United States. Unfortunately for the ill-fated entourage, their collective prayers proved fruitless.

While laying foundations for the first shelters of the settlement, the newcomers were surprised by a group of Calusas or Mayaimis, who attacked with a barrage of stones and arrows. De León vainly tried to lead a counterattack. He and his men fought pitched battles with daggers. Already,

**LEFT AND ABOVE:** Jacques le Moyne's drawings depict Florida Indians at prayer and at war.

next 40 years, seeking to tame the hostile new land and its unfriendly inhabitants. All failed. About 2,000 Spaniards lost their lives in the process.

One such failed expedition was led by Pánfilo de Narváez, who waded ashore at Tampa Bay with about 400 men on Good Friday in 1528. A redbearded soldier, Narváez had earned his reputation when he lost an argument and an eye to Hernando Cortéz in Mexico. He firmly warned the Indians that if they did not obey him, and thus the King of Spain and the Pope, "I will take your goods, doing you all the evil and injury that I may be able… and I declare to you that the deaths and damages that arise therefrom, will be your fault and not that of His Majesty, nor mine, nor of these cavaliers who came with me." The Indians told

Narváez exactly what he wanted to hear: there existed a land to the north called Apalachee, where they would find the treasure sought by every self-respecting conquistador – gold. Pánfilo de Narváez set out for Apalachee on foot, ordering his ships to rendezvous with him there. He found tall forests of longleaf pine, vast plains of cabbage palm, and sparkling springs and rivers. But no gold.

Occasional Indian raids and mosquito attacks took their toll. The dwindling party arrived in the Panhandle land of Apalachee exhausted and starving. Indian villagers offered them some small rations, and they butchered their horses for meat. The ships never showed up. Narváez and his men

were forced to construct six makeshift vessels, in which they set off for Mexico.

Alas, the ships vanished, Narváez never being heard from again. Years later, four survivors of the expedition turned up in Mexico with an amazing story. Led by Alvar Nuñez Cabeza de Vaca, they had survived a shipwreck, then wandered in the American Southwest for eight years before finding their way to Mexico.

## De Soto's cavaliers

Hernando de Soto, the conquistador *par excellence* of his time, headed a more ambitious assault on Florida with only slightly better results than

Narváez. In an 1836 narrative *Notices of Florida and the Campaigns*, M.M. Cohen described the escapades of the adventurous 36-year-old as "poetry put in action; it was the knight errantry of the Old World carried into the depths of the American wilderness …"

De Soto landed at Tampa Bay in May 1539 with an army of 1,000 knights and fortune-hunters. They killed and enslaved Indians and penetrated the thick brush of the interior. Puzzled by the absence of gold and magnificent cities such as those he had seen in Peru and Mexico, De Soto pushed on through the Panhandle to Georgia and North Carolina before turning west to Alabama to continue his search.

Three years and thousands of miles after his

arrival in North America, De Soto died of a fever. His men submerged his body in the Mississippi River. Most of the conquistadors returned to Spain empty-handed.

Unfortunately, the precise details of De Soto's historic expedition died along with him. As Garcilaso Inca de la Vega, the son of a Spanish nobleman and a Peruvian Inca princess, wrote in his 1609 *History of the Conquest of Florida*, "the Spaniards did not think so much of learning the situation of places, as of hunting for gold and silver in Florida."

One lasting legend came out of De Soto's trip, however. On Tampa Bay, the conquistadors curi-

ously scrutinized one Indian who greeted their arrival in fluent Spanish. Under his paint, the man turned out to be Juan Ortiz, a soldier who had landed with Narváez and survived capture by Indians in a remarkable manner.

Garcilaso described Ortiz' ordeal at the hands of a Timucuan chief – or cacique – named Harriga: "He ate and slept very little, and was tormented … he began to run at sunrise, and did not stop till night; and even during the dining of the cacique they would not suffer him to interrupt his course, so that at the end of the day he was in a pitiable

FAR LEFT: a reconstruction of Spanish Mission San Luis de Apalachee, built in 1633. LEFT: Hernando de Soto. ABOVE : Pedro Menéndez de Avilés.

condition … The wife and daughters of Harriga, touched with compassion, then threw some clothes upon him, and assisted him so opportunely that they prevented him from dying."

Ortiz finally escaped with the aid of the chief's eldest daughter. Many years later, upon reading of the adventures of Ortiz, a biographer of Captain John Smith "borrowed" the scenario for his own subject and an Indian girl named Pocahontas. Smith then perpetuated the plagiarism by putting it into his own history.

Tristan de Luna y Arellano, a rich Spanish nobleman, tried to conquer Florida next. He was undismayed by his predecessors' failures and undeterred by the slaying of three missionaries by Indians at Tampa Bay in 1549. Ten years later, his party of more than 1,500 tried to establish a settlement on Pensacola Bay. Devastated by a hurricane, desperate for food and disillusioned by Luna's quixotic leadership, the Spaniards abandoned the attempt in 1561.

## A foothold in Florida

Emboldened by Spain's preoccupation with pirates and its inability to colonize La Florida, a certain Jean Ribaut captained a French effort to establish a settlement on the St John's River in 1562. Ribaut constructed an arrowhead-shaped fort, Caroline, near the modern metropolis of Jacksonville.

That move intensified Spain's own efforts. Their purpose now was not just to gain a foothold but also to expel the French trespassers, whom they considered tantamount to pirates. A great armada under the command of Pedro Menéndez de Avilés established a site at a promising spot on the east coast, south of the French outpost, from which to mount its defense.

The day was August 28, 1565, the Feast of St Augustine. On September 8, Pedro Menéndez formally broke ground for a settlement that to this day bears the name of that patron saint. It was the first permanent settlement, and is still the oldest continuous settlement, on United States soil, founded more than 50 years before the Pilgrims showed up at Plymouth Rock in New England.

Well aware that Menéndez planned to attack, Jean Ribaut rushed back to Fort Caroline, assembled his forces, and tried to surprise the Spanish. But again nature played a role in molding Florida's destiny. A hurricane grounded the French ships before they reached St Augustine. Meanwhile, Menéndez had marched up the coast and seized the French fort, killing all the residents except Catholics, women, and children. On the way back to St Augustine, he encountered remnants of Jean Ribaut's assault party and had all but 16 of the total of 150 men put to death, including Ribaut himself, who was beheaded. The location of that bloody meeting became known as Matanzas – in Spanish, the "place of slaughter."

With the French out of the way, Menéndez tried to guarantee Spain's Florida claims by befriending various Indian tribes, aiding Jesuit mission development, and trying to colonize other parts of the peninsula. Of the settlements, only St Augustine would survive, and somewhat shakily at that. England's Sir Francis Drake leveled the city in 1585. Another killer hurricane flooded the rebuilt colony in 1599. Despite everything, St Augustine has managed to hang on for more than 400 years.

Menéndez died in 1574 in Spain, an ocean away from his beloved Florida. An epitaph on his grave, penned by José-Maria de Heredia, serves as a fitting tribute to him and the other conquistadors who found Florida their most formidable challenge:

> *Glory has grooved the furrows on thy brow,*
> *And seamed thy cheek, illustrious cavalier;*
> *The scars of wars and scorching suns appear*
> *On that bold front that none could force to bow.*

## LE MOYNE'S VIEW OF FLORIDA

Jacques le Moyne described the customs of the natives with both pictures and words. He wrote, for example, that the east coast groups were generally more hospitable than those on Florida's west coast. He said that they cultivated fields of beans and maize which they stored in granaries; that they worshiped the sun and scalped and mutilated their enemies. He also praised the Indians' success in hunting deer by skillfully disguising themselves in deerskins and antlers. "I do not believe," he wrote, "that any European could do it as well."

He vividly portrayed the heavily tattooed chiefs and queens, who grew their fingernails long and sharpened them to points, and who

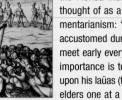

painted the skin around their mouths blue. He said their striking attire included deer skin capes, belts made of Spanish moss, and earrings fashioned from fish-bladders inflated and dyed red.

Describing their social institutions, le Moyne also said that the Florida Indians practiced what could be thought of as a form of representative parliamentarianism: "The chief and his nobles are accustomed during certain days of the year to meet early every morning... If any question of importance is to be discussed, the chief calls upon his laüas (that is, his priests) and upon the elders one at a time to deliver their opinions."

## Lifestyle of the Indians

Ribaut and his mapmaker, Jacques le Moyne, provided future generations with a meticulous word-and-picture portrait of the Indian tribes they encountered in Florida. Ribaut wrote graphically in 1563: "The most parte of them cover their raynes and pryvie partes with faire hartes skins, paynted cunyngly with sondry collours, and the fore parte of there bodye and armes paynted with pretye devised workes of azure, redd, and black, so well and so properly don as the best paynter of Europe could not amend yt. The wemen have there bodies covered with a certen herbe like onto moste, whereof the cedertrees and all other trees

"The people of Florida are idolaters, and have the sun and moon for divinities, which they adore without offering them either prayers or sacrifices ... [T]hey have temples, but they make use of them only to inter those who die, and to shut up their treasures. They erect also at … these temples, in the form of a trophy, the spoils of their enemies."

Contact with the Europeans was eventually the fatal blow to the aboriginal cultures. Some fell victim to diseases like chicken pox, measles, and colds. Slave traders spirited away as many as 12,000 Indians. Many of those who resisted the European invasion died defending the lands their tribes had occupied for 10,000 years.

be alwaies covered. The men for pleasure do always tryme themselves therwith, after sundry fasshions. They be of tawny colour, hawke nosed and of a pleasaunt countenaunce. The women be well favored and modest and will not suffer that one approche them to nere, but we were not in theire howses, for we sawe none at that tyme."

Garcilaso de la Vega also provided insights into the customs and lifestyle of the Florida Indians. He noted many similarities in customs to the Incas, especially in their practice of putting their temples on artificial mounds mounted by wooden stairways.

---

**FAR LEFT:** 16th-century map of St Augustine.
**LEFT:** Sir Francis Drake. **ABOVE:** Timucua hunters use camouflage to stalk deer.

## Coming of the Seminoles

Historians estimate that by the mid-16th century, the native population had dwindled to less than one-fourth of its original size of about 25,000. Jesuit and Franciscan missionaries labored in Florida's humid conditions in their thick woolen robes, winning converts among the aboriginals of northern Florida with a string of about 50 missions in the 17th century. But British raiders leveled all at the turn of the 18th century, driving the few remaining Timucuans and Apalachees farther south. Spaniards took the last remaining 200 aboriginals to Cuba with them when they handed Florida over to the British in 1763.

By then, the Oconee Creeks had migrated into the peninsula from Georgia. In Florida, they would become known as Seminoles. ❏

# TURF WARS

Spain loses its grip, Native Americans are elbowed aside, and the United States takes control, only to plunge headlong into a military conflagration that tears the nation apart

Although the Spanish presence in Florida was long in years overall, it was limited in scope – largely precarious, sporadic, fragmented. For one thing, the peninsula lacked the cache of precious metals found in places like Mexico and Peru that in Spanish eyes glittered like gold. And, too, Florida's soil was incapable of yielding any particularly rich blessing of agricultural fruits.

What mostly kept the Iberian occupiers hanging on to their peninsular possession for so long was the region's strategic location. For the overlords of New Spain, the Straits of Florida represented a vital corridor through which treasure ships laden with riches could make their way relatively safely en route back to the homeland's overflowing coffers. For such riches, too, could the occupiers put up with the persistent hostility exhibited by Native Americans, who were none too happy with the Spaniards' presence in their homeland.

## Britain's territorial ambitions

In actuality, Spain managed only to settle St Augustine and Pensacola and to man a small garrison at St Marks in the Panhandle. To the north,

*Dr John Gorrie of Apalachicola in the Florida Pan-handle changed the course of domestic life in 1848 when he invented an ice machine, the forerunner of modern refrigerators and air conditioners.*

with its growing colonies, Great Britain cast a covetous eye on Florida, prompting Spanish authorities to build Castillo de San Marcos to

**LEFT:** Billy Bowlegs, leader of the Seminoles during the Third Seminole War.
**RIGHT:** a member of the Confederate 1st Florida Cavalry.

defend St Augustine. Defend it they did.

The castle's mass of earthworks and cannon repelled repeated assaults by the Brits, including a major attack by General James Edward Oglethorpe in 1742. As it turned out, England acquired Florida with the pen rather than the sword. That took place in 1763 via the first Treaty of Paris. Britain had captured Cuba during the Seven Years War (known in America as the French and Indian War) and agreed to give Havana back to Spain in return for Florida.

Remnants of the Spanish quickly evaporated. The Creek tribes of Alabama and Georgia, who were generally on friendly terms with the British, speeded up their migration southward. Slicing the territory into East Florida (from the Atlantic coast to the Apalachicola River in the Panhandle) and West Florida (from there to the Mississippi River) made British administration easier, and the Brits virtually transformed the new territory into their 14th and 15th American colonies.

Under Redcoat rule, Florida for the first time experienced ties with the rest of the North American continent. Spain had always operated from its flourishing base in Havana. New plantations of indigo, rice, and citrus, a subsequent increase in the slave trade from Africa and the West Indies, and a wave of new immigrants with Cork and Cockney accents also marked British rule in frontier Florida.

## Breaking away

The rumblings in Britain's original 13 colonies never reached Florida. British subjects there remained loyal to London when rebellion-minded American colonists turned their backs on King George III and declared independence on July 4, 1776. Angry residents of St Augustine even strung up effigies of American revolutionary leaders John Hancock and John Adams and burned them.

Capitalizing on Britain's preoccupation with fighting the American Revolution, Spain recaptured Pensacola and regained control of all West Florida. Over in East Florida, it remained Tory territory, its citizens donning red woolen coats and

## CROSSING CULTURES

Turmoil between the various ethnic groups and political powers that inhabited Florida in the late 18th and early 19th centuries gave rise to a host of colorful characters who were adept at forging links between cultures.

Take, for example, Alexander McGillivray, the son of a Scotsman and a woman of Creek and French blood, who is remembered for his diplomatic skill. He cultivated a working relationship between Florida's Spanish governors, English traders, the US Army, and a confederation he organized among 45,000 Indians of several tribes. The alliance endured until his death in 1793.

William Augustus Bowles had no Indian blood, but he lived among the Creeks and married an Indian after emi-

grating from England. When the Spanish returned to power, he contacted McGillivray and offered to supply the Creeks with weapons to wage war against the Georgians. His adventures included an attack on the St Marks garrison near Tallahassee, before the Spaniards captured him and sent him to Havana, where he died.

Zephaniah Kingsley was a flamboyant Scot who made his fortune from the slave trade. He imported thousands from Africa and the West Indies in the early 1800s, trained them in the servile arts, then resold them for a vast profit. He became a legend by defending the slave system, even marrying one of his servants and raising the children to be his heirs.

brandishing muskets to beat back three incursions by American Whigs from the North.

Then, 20 years after acquiring Florida, the British gave it back to Spain in 1783 under the terms of the Second Treaty of Paris. The fact that the territory had resisted falling into the American column was small consolation.

## A cultural stew

Florida's reputation as a magnet for the homeless, the displaced, and the runaway predates 20th-century influxes of "boat people" from Cuba and Haiti. At the time of the American Revolution, Florida already sheltered a cross-section of the

world's populations. There were Africans and West Indians, English and Spanish, Germans and Greeks, Sicilians and Minorcans, Creek and Choctaw Indians. All put down roots that would flourish in the bright glare of Florida's subtropical sunshine.

The second Spanish occupation of Florida fared little better than the first. British, black, and Indian refugees from the newly formed United States continued to trickle into the state. Georgians stirred up trouble along the northern border, forcing Spain to withdraw to the 31st parallel, the modern Florida-Georgia boundary.

**LEFT:** Fort Brooke at Tampa Bay, 1835. **ABOVE:** United States soldiers setting fire to an Indian camp during the Seminole War. **ABOVE RIGHT:** Andrew Jackson.

## Who's in charge here?

In 1800, Spain ceded the Louisiana Territory to France, which in turn sold the territory to the US – foreshadowing the imminent acquisition of the Florida peninsula by the Americans. The US extended its claim in 1813 to Mobile in Alabama, Florida's present western boundary. Americans in West Florida instigated a movement for independence. So, in yet another twist, the British – with whom the Spanish were allied in the War of 1812 – sent troops to Pensacola reputedly to reinforce Spain's claim.

This sparked concern about the return of the Redcoats. Tennessee's Andrew Jackson, nick-named "Old Hickory" because of his stern reputation, took it upon himself to stop the British rebuilding their forces in Florida. He used a Creek Indian uprising in Alabama as a pretext for advancing toward Florida. He defeated the Indians at the Battle of Horseshoe Bend, then marched on Pensacola and drove out the British.

A subsequent skirmish between Americans and Indians sparked the First Seminole War of 1817–18. Spain then accepted an offer by the US to cancel $5 million in debts to Washington in exchange for ownership of the entire peninsula. Jackson returned to Pensacola in 1821. There, on July 17, he witnessed the raising of the Stars and Stripes over this old Spanish capital. Old Hickory was now Florida's first American governor.

## The road to conflict

Andrew Jackson remained only three months as governor before returning to Washington, where later he would exercise influence over the new territory directly from the White House. The officials he left behind soon realized that the distance between Pensacola and St Augustine was too great to manage the territory effectively, so they consolidated government in a village of Talasi Indians, and thus Tallahassee became Florida's capital in 1823.

White settlers pushed aside the Indians when founding Tallahassee, as so often happened when land was seized for farming or for carving out a highway. The migration of Indian tribes, who were mostly associated with the Creek confederation, had started in the 1700s. It continued steadily as the native people disappeared from Florida. They took over the deserted farmlands and hunted in the forests where their ancestors had pursued game. These Indians collectively came to be known as Se-mi-no-lee, meaning "wild ones." Some spoke variations of the Hitchiti language, others Nuskogee.

As white settlers and Indians trickled into the new territory, Florida's population practically doubled, from 34,370 in 1830 to 66,500 in 1845. Jackson's initial clash with the Seminoles proved to be only a taste of bloodier days ahead. Pres-

### SHIFTING FORTUNES

The story behind the Adams-Onís Treaty of 1819 is the shifting fortunes of national power – Spain in decline, the US in flower. The treaty reconfigured the geographical dividing line in North America between the two domains, with Florida as a chief bargaining chip, and it drew on diplomatic precedents dating as far back as the papal bull of 1493 that granted Spain colonial rights in north-western America.

For Spain, the slate was wiped clean of $5 million in debt claims while the US got Florida. The treaty was ironed out in 1819 in Washington, DC, by John Quincy Adams, the American Secretary of State, and Luis de Onís, the Spanish foreign minister. It went into effect in 1821.

sure mounted for the government to remove Florida's native people to reservations in the West.

## Removal and retaliation

In 1823, Seminole tribes massed at Moultrie Creek near St Augustine. Led by Neamathla, chief of a group called Miccosukees, the Indians agreed to a compromise with the American government. Thirty-two chiefs signed a treaty calling for them to move their people and their black slaves to a 4-million-acre (1.6-million-hectare) reserve in west-central Florida, in return for payment for abandoned lands and financial aid to help them live on the new lands. Neither side abided by the provisions of the agreement. The Seminoles found the land unsuitable for agriculture and migrated there slowly, if at all. Drought conditions aggravated food shortages on the reservation. The US government reneged on payments. In 1830, Congress passed a removal act requiring all Indians in the east to be sent west.

The two sides met again at Payne's Landing on the Oklawaha River running through the rugged Green Swamp of central Florida. This time, US officials managed to coax only seven chiefs into signing a new agreement, which canceled the Moultrie Creek Treaty and required the Seminoles to move to reservations in the Arkansas Territory (part of present-day Oklahoma). Most of the Seminole nation reacted angrily when the seven

into the document and cried, "The only treaty I will ever make is this!"

With that act, Osceola became an American hero. Though his great-grandfather was a Scotsman, he publicly disavowed any white ancestry and fervently pursued the Creek culture. Historian Marjory Stoneman Douglas considered Osceola "unquestionably the greatest Floridian of his day."

Inspired by Osceola's act of defiance at Fort King, the Seminoles rebelled. A party of warriors ambushed Major Francis Langhorne Dade while he was en route from Fort Brooke (at Tampa Bay) to Fort King. The Indians killed Dade with their first bullet and massacred all but three of his 111 men.

chiefs returned from a visit to the new reservations and reported that they had been coerced into agreeing to the move. But President Jackson issued an edict to the Seminoles in which he warned: "I tell you that you must go and that you will go."

Flanked by 10 companies of soldiers, General Duncan L. Clinch ordered Seminole chiefs at Fort King, near modern Ocala, to sign away their Florida lands. He managed to get the "X" of Micanopy, the timid chief of the nation, but few others. Florida tradition holds that an indignant young brave named Osceola plunged his knife

**LEFT:** Seminoles attack a US blockhouse on the Withlacoochee River in 1835. **ABOVE:** bloodhounds were used to hunt Indians during the Second Seminole War.

## The capture of Osceola

The incident touched off the Second Seminole War, a bloody seven-year struggle (1835–42) in which the outmanned but determined Seminoles fought the better-armed white soldiers to a stalemate. They used the wilderness of the Green Swamp to their advantage, striking at American settlements, then melting back into the marshes. The waters of the Withlacoochee and Oklawaha rivers ran red with blood. The war cost the US $40 million and nearly 1,500 dead. In order to protect themselves, the settlers built defensive forts like Lauderdale, Jupiter, Myers, and Pierce.

Deception contributed to the defeat of the Seminoles. In 1837, Osceola rode into St Augustine under a white flag of truce sent to him by General Thomas S. Jessup. The general violated his own flag by arresting Osceola. He imprisoned the now legendary warrior, his wives, children, and 116 others at Fort Moultrie in Charleston.

Suffering from malaria and a broken spirit, Osceola died just a year after his capture. The attending doctor cut off his head, supposedly in retribution for an incident in which Osceola had severed his brother-in-law's head early in the war. The doctor's great-granddaughter recalled that he hung Osceola's head on a bedpost in the room of his three little boys whenever they misbehaved and also exhibited the head in circus sideshows.

Osceola's capture broke the spirit of the Semi-noles. Jessup continued his trickery, capturing another 400 Indians and Chief Alligator after promising to meet with them for truce discussions. General Zachary Taylor didn't pull any under-handed punches, however, when he defeated a party of Seminole braves on the Kissimmee River in the last major battle of the war. The army rounded up Seminole men, women, and children and in 1842 shipped 3,000 of them west of the Mississippi River.

## The return of war

Some Seminoles managed to avoid deportation by disappearing into the Everglades. There, under

### OSCEOLA

Osceola, the great Indian military leader (pictured), was, said an Army surgeon, diminutive and refined in appearance: "His person… was elegantly formed, with hands and feet effeminately small. He had a countenance expressive of much thought and cunning… His eyes were black and pierc-ing; and when animated were full of dark fire, but when in repose they were softer than the soft eye of woman. His mouth, when relieved by a smile, wore an expression of great sweetness."

Chief Billy Bowlegs, they regrouped – and in 1855 massacred a camp of surveyors whom they considered trespassers. That ignited the Third Seminole War. Soldiers and settlers hunted the Seminoles like dogs for the next three years. They offered huge rewards for the capture of Indians. Chief Bowlegs surrendered with a group of warriors in 1858 and was sent west. Others stubbornly refused to leave and evaded capture. The Floridians eventually gave up the search, enabling about 300 Seminoles to remain beyond the impenetrable sawgrass rivers of the Ever-glades and, thus, in safety.

The Seminoles were really never defeated. As Coacoochee so eloquently stated in a speech to his people during the war: "The white men …

may shoot us, drive our women and children night and day; they may chain our hands and feet, but the red man's heart will always be free."

## From statehood to civil war

After two decades of successful politicking by forces that saw benefits in joining the Union, Florida became an American state on March 3, 1845. But the romance ended just 16 years later. A man's wealth in Florida was measured by the number of slaves he owned. Influential planters and landowners opposed the abolition of slavery and convinced their legislators to secede from the Union on January 10, 1861. Florida joined forces

Such progress, modest as it was, was stunted by the Civil War. Florida mustered its minuscule population and even smaller budget to join the Confederate cause. Its participation in the war was both brief and limited, but devastating nonetheless. Union forces invaded the busy northeastern port of Jacksonville four times. They seized most of Florida's forts. The town of Fernandina Beach, at one time a haven for slave-smuggling after the United States banned the practice, fell to the Union.

Florida's Confederate soldiers fought back valiantly. Their biggest battle occurred on February 20, 1864, when 10,000 soldiers representing

with the Confederate States and went, with some zeal, to war against the North.

The Civil War proved particularly disastrous for Florida. The state had only barely recovered from the wasteful Seminole Wars, which had stunted its growth for decades. Agriculture had just begun making an impact with multiplying acres of cotton, indigo, rice, sugar, and tobacco. The rugged interior of the state had begun to open by 1861, when a railroad sliced through the forests of scrub and pine and linked Tallahassee to Cedar Key on the Gulf Coast.

---

**LEFT:** US troops capturing Seminole Indians.
**ABOVE:** Confederate soldiers repelled Union troops at the Battle of Olustee in 1864.

both sides, North and South, clad in blue and gray, clashed at Olustee, east of Lake City. The Floridians suffered nearly 100 men killed and over 800 wounded, but the survivors held their ground. They stopped the advance of the Union army, which suffered twice as many casualties.

The "Cradle and Grave Company," consisting of teenagers and old men, later fell to a Union brigade in another Panhandle battle. But the "Baby Corp," mainly schoolboys, bravely turned back Union soldiers – who were wearing hats inscribed "To Tallahassee or Hell" – at a natural bridge over the St Marks River on March 5, 1865. Union soldiers never did reach Florida's capital city. But this was a hollow triumph for the Floridians. Only a month after the battle at Natural Bridge, General Robert E. Lee surrendered on behalf of Florida and the rest of the Confederacy.

## Reconstruction

The Civil War cost Florida about 5,000 lives and $20 million in damage to its smoldering cities. The slaves were freed only in principle. The anti-slavery novel *Uncle Tom's Cabin*, published in 1852 and written by Harriet Beecher Stowe – who would spend her later years in a cottage in Mandarin on the St John's River near Jacksonville – inspired abolitionists at the time. However, hooded Ku Klux Klansmen and gun-toting "reg-ulators" continued to oppress the black population. In fact, until the Civil Rights Act of 1964, blacks in most of Florida still rode in the backs of buses and used segregated "public" drinking facilities and washrooms.

The American flag flew over Tallahassee again on May 30, 1865. Political and economic reconstruction got off to a hesitant start. Florida remained a wild frontier where the strong and the armed prevailed. Yellow fever, malaria, and cholera also slowed the flow of settlers. Still, the sun began to lure northerners in large numbers. Florida's population nearly doubled in the two decades immediately after 1860, from 140,000 to 270,000.

### TOUTING THE SUNSHINE STATE

American affluence was on the rise after the Civil War, in that period generally known as the Gilded Age. Pleasure-seekers began widening their gaze beyond such standard enticements as Newport and Saratoga Springs, becoming attracted in particular in the latter part of the 19th century by Florida's natural beauty and mild climate.

Luring them on was a growing number of descriptive guides touting the charms of the Sunshine State and various of its locales. One of the earliest was by no less a literary superstar than Harriet Beecher Stowe, author of *Uncle Tom's Cabin*, the blockbuster novel that helped trigger the Civil War. Her guide, *Palmetto-Leaves*, published in Boston in 1873, glowingly evoked the sunshine springs and green forests of the northeastern Florida region where she would spend her winters in the 1870s and 1880s. One of its chapters was entitled "Buying Land in Florida."

Singling out just two others in this early manifestation of the travelogue genre, George M. Barbour's *Florida for Tourists, Invalids, and Settlers* was first published in 1884, while the poet-critic Sidney Lanier's *Florida: Its Scenery, Climate and History* appeared even earlier, in 1875. Florida, in Lanier's florid prose, represented "an indefinite enlargement of many people's pleasures" as opposed to "that universal killing ague of modern life – the fever of the unrest of trade throbbing through the long chill of a seven-months' winter."

Among those attracted to the Sunshine State were developers, entrepreneurs, agriculturalists, inventors, and writers. Swampland in the Caloosahatchee and Kissimmee valleys was drained, clearing the rivers for navigation and making soggy South Florida solid enough for settlement and farming. Cubans followed Vicente Martínez Ybor to Tampa in the 1880s to roll tobacco, helping to make the name of the city synonymous with cigars.

On the state's east coast, a Chinese immigrant, Lue Gim Gong, developed a frostproof orange that began to flourish along the Indian River, laying the basis for Florida's citrus industry.

minarets that still dominate the city's skyline. Tourists soon began to come, and Plant then offered the option of continuing by steamer from Tampa to Cuba.

Flagler's Florida East Coast Railroad had an even bigger impact on the state's growth. Beginning in 1885, he sank about $50 million into a series of hotels at locations connected by his railroad line, from the posh Ponce de León in St Augustine to the Ormond north of Daytona Beach. In 1894, his rail line abruptly ended on a desolate slip of land by the sea. Flagler dubbed it Palm Beach, erected the venerable Breakers Hotel, and thereby created a haughty haunt for the extremely

## Railroads and tourists

The far-sightedness of two men of that period in particular laid the groundwork for the boom that occurred in the 20th century. They were Henry Morrison Flagler (1830–1913), one of the founders of Standard Oil, and Henry B. Plant (1819–99), president of a number of railroad and shipping companies. The latter constructed the Atlantic Coastline Railroad that linked Richmond, Virginia, with Tampa on the Gulf Coast. At the end of the line, Plant built the ostentatious but luxurious Tampa Bay Hotel, complete with Moorish

wealthy. Palm Beach became one of the nation's storied resorts.

A freeze nearly wiped out the state's fledgling citrus industry in the winter of 1894–95. Mrs Julia D. Tuttle, a wealthy refugee from Cleveland, Ohio, managed to convince Flagler to extend his railroad farther south to a strip of scrub on Biscayne Bay in 1896. Thus did Miami come into being, rivaling even the Palm Beach phenomenon. Then, in 1903, Flagler laid tracks south first to Homestead, then all the way along the Florida Keys to Key West by 1912, a year before his death.

Wherever Flagler went, more hotels were sure to follow. And in their wake came a flood of tourists and immigrants. ❑

**LEFT:** railroad and hotel baron Henry Morrison Flagler.
**ABOVE:** the Ponce de León was one of several hotels built to lure tourists, and train passengers, to Florida.

# MODERN TIMES

**They came from near and far in the 20th century, fun-seekers and refugees seeking new lives in a Sunshine State that was undergoing its own form of extreme makeover**

U p and down Florida's east and west coasts, cities sprang up toward the end of the 19th century along the railroad tracks laid by Messrs Plant and Flagler. The state's growth was further stimulated by the Spanish-American War of 1898, a situation different from past occasions when conflict tended to depress economic activity.

Florida's role in the war grew out of the cigar factories and Spanish cafés of the community founded by Vicente Martínez Ybor in Tampa in the 1880s. Cuban immigrants here cheered on efforts by their compatriots back home to free the island of Spanish overlordship. Huge crowds turned out in Tampa to hear Cuban freedom fighter José Martí plead for contributions to the cause. The cause was so popular that a rising political star named Napoleon Bonaparte Broward achieved notoriety for surreptitiously supplying weapons and ammunition to Cuban rebels before the United States officially entered the war. Broward soon after became one of Florida's most progressive governors.

The sinking of the battleship USS *Maine* in Havana's harbor on February 15, 1898, gave America an excuse to join the revolutionaries in

> When John Ringling was first buying land around Sarasota, he managed to acquire 66,000 acres (26,700 hectares) during a game of poker.

the war against Spain that broke out at the end of April (although the Spanish almost certainly had nothing to do with it). American troops poured into Florida, setting up tent cities while waiting to sail to Cuba.

## Good times

Tampa became a command post for the army. Theodore Roosevelt stormed into town with his Rough Riders en route to glory at San Juan Hill near the Cuban city of Santiago. Red Cross founder Clara Barton established a hospital in Tampa, while a young British journalist named Winston Churchill checked into the Tampa Bay Hotel to report a bloody good story. At the very place where it began its conquest four centuries earlier, Spain was being driven from the New World.

The victorious Americans returned to points north with accounts of their exploits – and glowing depictions of Tampa, Miami, Key West, and other Florida ports and their attractive ambience. Some returned home only long enough to gather up their belong-

---

**LEFT:** an Art Deco high-rise in South Beach.
**RIGHT:** postcard images helped fuel a boom in tourism.

ings, and perhaps a few friends and intimates, before heading back to Florida. By 1920, the Sunshine State's first major boom was under way.

Many of the characters who wheeled-and-dealed in real estate were interested only in fast fortunes, and they plundered Florida much as the Spanish and British had done earlier. Others came, made money, stayed, and formed the first solid core of state leaders. One who struck it rich was Walter Fuller. He carved up St Petersburg, a sun-kissed Gulf Coast city founded by Russian railroad czar Peter Demens. In his book *This Was Florida's Boom*, Fuller tells how he paid $50,000 for land he resold for $270,000, a hefty sum at the time.

Sarasota, while Dave Davis dredged up islands that became enclaves for Tampa's elite.

## Onward and downward

In 1926, a cold winter slowed spiraling prices. Then a hurricane whipped across the peninsula, killing hundreds and bulldozing some of the flimsy housing developments. This brought the madness hastily but temporarily to an end. But it was nothing compared to the Wall Street crash of 1929 and the Great Depression that followed. Overnight, as it were, Davis and Fuller and dozens of other millionaires became paupers. Still, the groundwork had been laid. When the effects of

Fast-talking salesmen sold swamp-like tracts at auction. Even the golden-tongued William Jennings Bryan, that perennial presidential wannabe, got into the act, peddling real estate at George Merrick's development in Coral Gables. That site was the nation's first planned community, replete with regal entrance gates, pools, hotels, golf courses, zoned business districts, and alluring lots on palm-lined boulevards and canals.

Carl Fisher, meanwhile, dredged sand from the bottom of Biscayne Bay and transformed tangles of mangroves off the coast of Miami into a beach. In 1925 alone, 481 hotels and apartment buildings rose in the fabulous makeover that was Miami Beach. And over on Florida's west coast, circus tycoon John Ringling created the city of

the Depression were played out, Florida's growth resumed and happy days were here again.

Between 1920 and 1940, the state's population doubled to nearly two million. By the start of World War II, tourists numbering upward of $2\frac{1}{2}$ million came to visit annually – a phenomenal figure when compared with other states in the Union. Florida's population was growing increasingly urban. By 1940, more than 55 percent of the people were living in towns and cities, compared to 37 percent in 1920. Tampa attracted industry; Miami received the sun-worshipers. More hotel rooms were built in Greater Miami between 1945 and 1954 than in the rest of the state combined.

Pari-mutuel betting on greyhounds and horses was legalized in 1931, bringing in additional revenues for the state's coffers – and an incentive for organized-crime rings to enter the field, especially in the big urban centers. Members of the syndicate shuttled between profitable rackets in Miami. The notorious mobster Al "Scarface" Capone found the location so convenient that he moved into a fortified estate on Palm Island in the bay off Miami Beach.

## Space Age

Florida's greatest contribution to future shock began to take shape after World War II, when the War Department started testing missiles at Cape Canaveral. Florida was host to the world's first scheduled airline service – a short hop between St Petersburg and Tampa – and in 1959 the first domestic jet flights in the US were launched. By that time, Cape Canaveral was well on its way to becoming the site of Kennedy Space Center. The last steps Neil Armstrong took on Mother Earth before his "giant step" on the moon in 1969 were made on the sandy soil of Florida.

Some well-known personalities brought a measure of fame to the state during the 1960s. Jackie Gleason's hit television show enhanced Miami Beach's renown, this time under the rubric of "sun and fun capital of the world." Tennessee Williams, author of such major dramatic works as *The Glass Menagerie* and *A Streetcar Named Desire*, made Key West his winter home. He died there in 1983.

## The new Floridians

Florida's reputation as a haven for refugees was heightened by the Cuban revolution engineered by Fidel Castro and his socialist compatriots in 1959. It sent a wave of anti-Castro and anti-communist Cubans to these shores throughout the 1960s. During the 1970s a slow but steady exodus continued, and in 1980 another big influx of Cubans landed in the Key West region as part of the so-called Mariel boatlift. Most of those 125,000 refugees eventually made their way to the Miami area where an intricate immigrant network was already in place.

The 1980s also brought to South Florida some 75,000 Nicaraguans fleeing their country and its communist regime, and about 125,000 Haitians. Coming in rough-hewn boats, the Haitians made the perilous journey to escape economic deprivation in their Caribbean homeland.

**Left:** new roads and bridges, such as the Gandy Bridge across Tampa Bay, encouraged development. **Above Right:** Cuban refugees arrive in Florida during the 1980 Mariel boatlift.

In addition, the 1980s saw sharp increases in population in Palm Beach County, the Orlando area, and the Gulf Coast, as many Northerners continued to stream into the state in search of the Sun Belt lifestyle enlivening much of the South and Southwest. Many of the nation's largest companies moved their headquarters south to Florida, and the international banking industry bloomed, particularly in Miami, well-situated for trading with Latin America and the Caribbean. For Florida, it was an invigorating period of steady growth, both economic and demographic.

Unhappily, growth came as well from opportunists dealing in extra-legal and plainly illicit

### BUILDING AMBITION

Architecture is indicative of the state's ability to take setbacks in stride. After a hurricane shredded Flagler's railroad through the Keys in 1935, engineers transformed it into the Overseas Highway. Miami Beach, which sprouted Art Deco hotels in the 1930s and '40s, was one of few cities in the US to undergo a building boom during the Depression. Construction of Florida Southern College, designed by Frank Lloyd Wright *(pictured)*, began in 1938 in Lakeland and is still a fitting monument to Wright's supreme originality.

pursuits. With revenue from drug sales, the so-called Cocaine Cowboys left their mark on South Florida along with a trail of violence. Buying luxury homes and fancy sports cars with suitcases full of cash, drug smugglers pumped billions of dollars into Florida's economy.

Along with the influx of immigrants and relocated Northerners, the 1980s brought both good times and bad times for the southern regions of the state. The slick, action-packed television series *Miami Vice*, first broadcast in 1984, transformed the international image of Miami permanently – from retirement haven to sexy and sleek pastel paradise. Syndicated in over 130 countries, *Miami Vice* glam-

investment opportunity. Tourism, the golden egg for the Sunshine State's economy, continued to grow at astonishing rates, with the result that Florida now lures a phenomenal number of tourists every year. The total is variously estimated at 50 million to 80 million, roughly one-fourth of them from overseas.

Above all, it was the arrival of entertainment magnate Walt Disney and his theme parks, the first of which opened in 1971, that decisively transformed tourism in the state.

Theme parks and other forms of wholesome family entertainment have proliferated in Orlando and now attract far more tourists than the magnificent beaches that line much of the coast.

orized the city's crime-ridden reputation and made mayhem in the tropics a fashionable trend.

And there were bad times. Fueled by economic hardship and ethnic tensions, some residents of Miami's African-American community engaged in violent protest, first in the neighborhood of Liberty City in 1980 and again in Overtown in 1982. The two civil disturbances caused millions of dollars worth of damage and forced municipal leaders to confront urban decay and socioeconomic problems.

## A flood of tourists

As the 1990s began, Florida was still growing rapidly. This time around, the influx of newcomers included Europeans, South Americans, and Japanese, who saw Florida as one great sunny

### ANDREW'S LEGACY

Between August and September 2004, four major hurricanes – Charley, Frances, Ivan, Jeanne – hammered the state. Pensacola, Punta Gorda, Orlando, and Stuart were all hit hard, and many other towns suffered as well. When the devastating images of docks crumbling and roofs blowing away landed in newspapers across the USA, state tourism officials got worried. But fortunately, when the sun came back, so did the tourists. Although the four storms killed 117 people and caused $60 billion in damages, the fallout was nowhere near the damage caused in 1992 when Hurricane Andrew ravaged South Florida. Even today, Andrew remains one of the costliest natural disasters ever to hit US soil.

Tourism in all its forms, however, is vital to the economy of many counties. After years of development, Florida has at last learned the importance of preserving its natural heritage. The state has numerous parks and preserves, from the vast Everglades National Park to small recreation areas tucked in among the urban sprawl. They have enhanced Florida's appeal. And the cruise industry is booming, adding billions of dollars to the state's revenue every year.

## Stormy weather

While much of Florida follows a fairly stable course, the southern half of the state continues its roller-coaster existence, especially topsy-turvy Miami. In 1992, Hurricane Andrew's four-hour devastation through southern Florida left half of Miami-Dade County in a shambles. Two years later, southern Florida received another great wave of refugees. Images of Cubans arriving aboard homemade rafts made headlines around the world. Tensions inevitably resulted as the state, and Miami in particular, struggled to cope with the influx.

Then, in 1996, came the news that Miami was bankrupt. The crisis publicized the fact that many among Miami's wealthy residents were feeling frustrated by the city's crime problem and its expanding Hispanic culture. Observers perceived a growing tendency at resettlement away from Miami to booming areas such as Orlando.

One area to have been consistently upwardly mobile is the Art Deco district of South Beach, which has undergone a renaissance that can only be described as spectacular. Fashion models, tourists, and trendsetters elbow each other for table space at Ocean Drive's bars and cafés, while convertibles and stretch limos compete for space on the road.

## What made headlines

Florida today ranks fourth in population in the Union, a number that is expected to total 19.6 million by the year 2010. If it is not lacking in people, it is also not lacking in headline-making notoriety.

Much attention was focused in the year 2000, for example, on the plight of a Cuban boy named Elian Gonzalez. Not quite six years of age when he left Cuba, he had survived a harrowing voyage in a small boat and an inner tube across the Florida Straits before being rescued; his mother and ten oth-

ers had perished in the attempt. Following a protracted legal tug-of-war over his custody that involved relatives, the courts, federal officials, and the Miami-based Cuban-American community, Elian returned with his father to Cuba in June.

There was widespread grief on February 1, 2003, when seven astronauts aboard the *Columbia* space shuttle died when it disintegrated during re-entry into the Earth's atmosphere. The cause: a piece of the apparatus had broken off during its launch from Cape Canaveral two weeks earlier.

In the summer of 2004, the region sustained 50 deaths and billions of dollars in damage from four successive hurricanes. And the following year

brought a "right-to-die" controversy when doctors petitioned to remove feeding tubes that had sustained life for a 41-year-old brain-damaged woman, Terry Sciavo, at a hospice in Pinellas Park. She died two weeks after the tubes were taken away.

The grandest controversy of all was the legal struggle waged to decide the victor in the 2000 presidential campaign between George W. Bush, the Republican governor of Texas, and Al Gore, the Democratic vice president. The tally in the contest for Florida's 25 electoral votes was exceedingly close, and the legal jockeying by cadres of high-powered attorneys that resulted over the issue of a recount was unprecedented. A 5–4 decision of the US Supreme Court decided the election in Bush's favor. The ruling remains highly contentious. ❏

**LEFT:** George W. Bush supporters demonstrate during the controversial presidential recount in 2000.
**ABOVE:** Hurricane Andrew devastated South Florida.

# THE CULTURAL LANDSCAPE

**Florida has been dismissed as the "land of the newlyweds and the nearly dead." But the influx of newcomers has created a lively market for both the visual and the performing arts**

Like its history, the development of Florida's cultural character unfolded in a distinctly different pattern than that of the rest of the American South. During its initial period of Spanish rule, which lasted from the early 16th century until the acquisition of the peninsula by Britain in 1763, Florida was held primarily for strategic reasons and was sparsely colonized, with only a few Spanish residents. Consequently, the long colonial period left only a scant legacy of an indigenous Hispanic culture, such as developed in California and the Southwest.

Most of the Spanish settlers left after the British occupation, during which land grants and other inducements to settlement resulted in an influx of other European emigrants, primarily from Italy and Greece. On St George Street in St Augustine, there is a Greek Orthodox shrine that serves as a vivid reminder of the religion and culture of these early arrivals to the region. (The Greek heritage of Tarpon Springs dates to a much more recent migration of sponge divers to the west coast town.)

There was, of course, an indigenous culture in the Florida peninsula long before the arrival of

*The top American states feeding Florida's population boom are New York, New Jersey, Ohio, Michigan, and Illinois. Some might say that Yankees have remade South Florida in the image of the Northeast.*

the Spanish or any other European newcomers. The Seminole Indians, with their sub-tribe the

Miccosukees, survived the bitter Seminole Wars of the early 19th century – a protracted struggle against United States authority in which the natives have never conceded defeat – and continue to practice their traditional crafts and rituals, as evidenced at the Miccosukee Cultural Center in the Everglades, along the Tamiami Trail, and at the annual Seminole tribal fair in Hollywood.

## Slow start

The second period of Spanish rule over Florida, which lasted from 1783 until the peninsula was ceded to the United States in 1821, likewise saw little cultural influence on the part of the old colonial power; in fact, of the approximately 5,000 residents of the territory at the time Spanish

**LEFT:** a replica of Michelangelo's *David* at the Ringling Museum of Art in Sarasota. **RIGHT:** *Young Shepherdess* by William Bouguereau at the Appleton Museum of Art. **PRECEDING PAGES:** bar dancers, South Beach.

rule ended, a significant number were Americans. These emigrants from neighboring southern states, and those who followed in the years after American control became official, settled primarily in northern Florida, bringing with them a system of plantation agriculture based in large part on slavery. When Florida became a state, in 1845, nearly half of its population of 60,000 were African-American slaves working on cotton and sugar plantations. Many of them were rooted in the Gullah culture of the Carolina Low Country and carried with them a West African tradition of music and storytelling. Among whites – most of whom had also come to Florida from Georgia and the Carolinas – a "Cracker" folk culture, akin to that of the southern Appalachians, predominated. There were only 140,000 Floridians – still, nearly half of them slaves – at the time of the Civil War. Any cultural awakening in the state would clearly have to wait for a significant increase in population, and for the growth of cities.

## Culture matters

The population increase began with the discovery of Florida as a winter retreat for northerners, beginning with the arrival of railroads along the state's east coast in the 1880s. But it wasn't until

### HEAVEN'S WAITING ROOM

After World War II, Florida experienced a surge in northern retirees wanting to spend their golden years in the Sunshine State. The influx of senior citizens reshaped Florida, transforming former villages like Clearwater and Fort Myers into metropolises and making pension checks one of the state's major sources of cold cash. Nearly one in every six Floridians is a senior citizen. In 15 of Florida's 67 counties, more than a third of the populace is over 60, and senior citizens number over 40 percent of the residents in several of those counties. This distinction, when combined with the influx of honeymooners, has earned Florida a reputation as a "land of the newlywed and the nearly dead."

the boom of the 1920s that the state's year-round numbers began to climb significantly, creating the critical mass for culture. It was during this period that wealthy winter sojourners such as circus king John Ringling gave a tremendous boost to the Florida arts scene. Ringling, who built his Venetian-inspired fantasy home Cà d'Zan in Sarasota, opened the John and Mable Ringling Museum of Art in the west coast city in 1931. Another overwintering magnifico, James Deering, created Miami's lavish Vizcaya estate, although its transition to a public museum did not occur until the 1950s.

Prior to the 1960s, Florida's cultural atmosphere reflected its traditional mix of Southern whites and African-Americans, émigrés from the North, and local populations of Cubans around the cigar-making centers of Tampa and Key West. But the political sea change that overtook Cuba in 1959, following the socialist revolution led by Fidel Castro, brought the arts and traditions of Florida's island neighbor into the mainstream. The great migration of Cubans – abetted by a smaller influx of Haitians, Dominicans, and natives of other Caribbean nations – made a Latin American capital of Miami and transformed the cultural flavor of all but the northernmost portions of the peninsula. For a sample of the Cuban performing-arts scene, take in one of the programs offered by IFÉ-ILÉ Afro-Cuban Dance and Music, a Miami-based organization that presents traditional and contem-

rollicks with music, dancing, and street performers. Miami's Haitian community, too, highlights its music and dance traditions with the annual Compas Festival, held in Bayfront Park each May.

## Visual arts

The visual and performing-arts scene in Florida revolves around venues, museums, and festivals scattered among a half-dozen or so important population centers. In metropolitan Miami, two must-visit museums are the Bass Museum of Art, which is strong in European painting and sculpture from the Renaissance through the 19th century, and Wolfsonian-Florida International University, which

porary dances, concerts, and poetry readings (in Spanish), and sponsors a dance and music festival each July. There's also a Cuban-American Heritage Festival in Key West each June.

You don't have to visit Florida in the warmer months to enjoy the biggest of all Cuban celebrations: Miami's Calle Ocho (that's Eighth Street) Festival, held in March, draws 1 million visitors to a bash that concludes with a massive block party featuring 30 music stages. If March is too far off, head to Calle Ocho on the last Friday of each month, when the Viernes Culturales street party

**LEFT:** the Cummer Museum of Art in Jacksonville.
**ABOVE:** modern masters are the specialty of the Boca Raton Museum of Art.

features revolving exhibitions drawn from a vast trove whose outstanding component is a collection of late 19th- to early 20th-century European and American decorative arts. The Lowe Art Museum, at the University of Miami in Coral Gables, has a splendid collection of Native American art, as well as pre-Columbian Latin American pieces, although western works, particularly from the 15th through 17th centuries, are not neglected.

In Fort Lauderdale, the city's Museum of Art has chosen as a major focus the works of northern European Expressionists of the mid-20th century. Jacksonville's Cummer Museum of Art has the best collection in the northern part of the state, with a collection that ranges from the early Renaissance through the 18th century and beyond.

Orlando boasts three respectable art museums. The Orlando Museum of Art, in the city's Loch Haven park culture cluster, is strong in pre-Columbian American art, traditional African art, and American painters. Rollins College, in Winter Park just north of Orlando, is home to the Cornell Museum of Fine Arts, which has amassed a collection of amazing breadth ranging from the Renaissance to the American Hudson River School to modern and postmodern works. And there is the Charles Hosmer Morse Museum of American Art, where the star attraction – among a superb collection of 19th- and 20th-century American art – is an entire chapel designed for the 1893 Chicago World Columbian Exposition by the incomparable Louis Comfort Tiffany.

## Gulf Coast museums

Over on the west coast, the Tampa Museum of Art stresses ancient Greek and Roman sculptures and a 20th-century American collection; while the city's Museum of African-American Art has holdings that encapsulate the careers of America's finest 19th- and 20th-century black artists. In nearby St Petersburg, one of the nation's finest museums devoted to the work of a single artist chronicles the unusual career of Spanish surrealist Salvador Dalí. The Salvador Dalí Museum

comprises the collection of tycoon A. Reynolds Morse and his wife, Eleanor, who amassed one of the world's great collections of work by their friend Dalí over nearly a half-century of determined collecting. The city is also home to the Museum of Fine Arts, housed in a building that might pass for the villa of a wealthy collector. French Impressionists and pre-Columbian American art are standouts here, but there is much, much more, including an archive of historic photographs.

Sarasota, where John Ringling put down his winter roots, remains the great beneficiary of his largesse. His Cà d'Zan ("John's house," in Venetian dialect) is itself a magnificent work of art, with a Venetian Gothic exterior derived from the Palace of the Doges. The premier attraction of the Ringling

### CHORAL CAPITAL

Residents of Palm Beach have a special love for choral music. Six fine choral groups flourish within the city and its environs, including the Master Chorale of South Florida; the Masterworks Chorus; the Choral Society of the Palm Beaches; the Boca Raton Singers; and Voices of Pride, a gay chorus. Performing at venues throughout Palm Beach County and Florida's east coast, these polished vocalists – most local residents – offer a repertory ranging from classical oratorios to Gilbert and Sullivan, and from spirituals to Broadway show tunes. Among favorite annual performances is the Masterworks Chorus's rendition of Handel's *Messiah*, now in its fourth decade. The concert is held in December at the Royal Poinciana Chapel in Palm Beach.

compound is the Ringling Museum of Art, which he built to house the treasures amassed during a lifetime spent pursuing great art as well as great circus acts. Baroque art is a special focus, with a world-renowned collection of paintings by Peter Paul Rubens at its heart.

## Performing arts

For classical music, the most important Miami area institutions are the Miami Symphony Orchestra, which performs at the University of Miami's Gusman Hall and at Miami Beach's Lincoln Theater; the New World Symphony, directed by Michael Tilson Thomas, also making its home at Lincoln Theater; Florida Grand Opera, based at the Carnival Center for the Performing Arts (also with performances in Fort Lauderdale); and the Miami Lyric Opera, offering performances at the Colony Theater in Miami Beach and, once a year, outdoors at Flamingo Park.

Sarasota, which bills itself as the heart of the "Cultural Coast," is home to the Florida West Coast Symphony, performing at several venues in and around the city; the annual La Musica International Chamber Music Festival; and the Sarasota Opera, whose home is the city's beautifully restored 1926 Opera House. Visiting orchestras, dance troupes, and pop artists perform at Sarasota's Van Wezel Performing Arts Hall, one of Florida's most spacious and handsome concert venues.

In Palm Beach, the Palm Beach Symphony performs at the Henry Morrison Flagler Museum, the Society of the Four Arts, and the Church of Bethesda by the Sea. The Palm Beach Opera offers an annual program of four operas, as well as a vocal competition, at the Kravis Center for the Performing Arts. The city also hosts the annual Palm Beach Chamber Music Festival each summer.

Fort Lauderdale's Broward Center for the Performing Arts, anchoring the city's Riverwalk Arts and Entertainment District, hosts the Symphony of the Americas, along with a diverse series of guest artists. This is the venue for local performances by Florida Grand Opera.

Northeastern Florida's classical music scene revolves around the Jacksonville Symphony Orchestra. The 60-year-old ensemble, and its affiliated Youth Orchestra, perform in an acoustic gem, the Robert E. Jacoby Symphony Hall at the Times-Union Center for the Performing Arts.

---

**LEFT:** sculpture garden at the Ringling Museum.
**RIGHT:** part of the Rubell Family Collection, Miami.

The Tampa Bay Performing Arts Center, the largest center of its kind south of Washington, DC's Kennedy Center, is a complex of five theaters that serve as home to the Tampa Bay Symphony and Opera Tampa. Also on the state's west coast, the Naples Philharmonic Orchestra performs at the city's Philharmonic Center for the Arts, which also hosts a broad array of visiting artists. And in Orlando, a city far better known for its theme parks than for classical music, the Orlando Philharmonic Orchestra makes its home at the Bob Carr Performing Arts Center and the Margeson Theater. The Carr is also the venue for the Orlando Opera and the Florida Symphony Youth orchestra.

## On your toes

Dance troupes abound in Florida. The Miami City Ballet, whose founding director is Edward Villella, is one of America's largest ballet companies. Its principal performance facility is the spectacular Ophelia and Juan Jr Roca Center in Miami Beach, although it also stages ballets at various other South Florida venues, including the Naples Philharmonic Center. Headquartered at the Colony Theater in Miami Beach, the Miami Contemporary Dance Company schedules its performances throughout the fall and winter. And in late summer, the International Ballet Festival of Miami presents five performances at locations in the Miami and Palm Beach areas and at Fort Lauderdale's Broward Center for the Performing Arts. For enthusiasts of modern dance, the Dance Now! Ensemble, based in Miami Beach, performs in both proscenium theater and informal studio surroundings.

The premier dance ensemble of the "Cultural Coast" is the Sarasota Ballet of Florida, which presents its fall/winter program performances at the Van Wezel Performing Arts Center. The West Coast Civic Ballet, an accomplished non-professional troupe, presents one ballet and a spring dance festival each year, and also offers classes. Ballet Florida is Palm Beach's professional dance organization, offering an ambitious annual schedule of repertoire and premier ballets at the city's Kravis Center, and has enrolled thousands of stu-

dents in its Academy of Ballet Florida. Orlando Ballet, headquartered at the city's Bob Carr Performing Arts Center, stages four ballets each year, at least two of which are also performed in Tampa – the west coast city, unfortunately, no longer has a resident ballet company of its own. Modern dance thrives in Orlando as well, with the city's Voci Dance staging performances at locations throughout the city during winter and spring.

## On stage

Miami is the live theater capital of Florida, with dozens of stages small and large, as well as several locally-based drama companies. Among them are

## THE SOUTHERNMOST SYMPHONY

It's a rare town with a population of fewer than 30,000 that can support a professional symphony orchestra, but for more than a decade, the citizens of Key West have done just that.

The Key West Symphony Orchestra was founded by Sebrina Maria Alfonso, a fifth-generation "Conch" of Cuban ancestry, who has served since the orchestra's inception as its conductor and music director. Beginning in 1997, Maestra Alfonso marshaled support for the project among Key West businesses and individuals, and set about recruiting musicians from around the United States for the orchestra's premiere concert in December 1998.

Each year, the director – herself an accomplished professional who has conducted throughout the US and Europe –

draws upon a list of between 100 and 150 instrumentalists to assemble a group of up to 70 that can commit to performing in Key West during the orchestra's four-concert winter series at the Performing Arts Centers for Key West, which is supplemented by occasional free outdoor "Community Concerts," children's programs, master classes, and a popular annual Christmas season revival of Gian Carlo Menotti's *Amahl and the Night Visitors*. The Key West Symphony players all have careers with other orchestras, including several of the nation's most prestigious organizations, but enjoy making room in their busy schedules to bring classical music to the arts-loving little town at the end of the Overseas Highway.

the Actors' Playhouse at the Miracle Theater in Coral Gables, offering professionally staged theater for children and adults; and City Theater, specializing in new shorter drama presented at the Jerry Herman Ring Theater in Coral Gables and at the Broward Center for the Performing Arts in Fort Lauderdale. Plays bound for Broadway often stop at the Coconut Grove Playhouse in Coconut Grove. And for Spanish language performances, try the Teatro de Bellas Artes, in Miami's Little Havana neighborhood, where drama, comedy, and musical performances fill out the bill of fare.

The unquestioned star of Sarasota's theater scene is the Asolo Repertory Theatre, possessor of the state's most exquisite venue for live dramatic performances. The Asolo is an 18th-century theater purchased by the John and Mable Ringling Museum of Art more than a half century ago and moved to the grounds of the museum and the Ringlings' Cà d'Zan Venetian palazzo. As the repertory company – founded under the aegis of Florida State University – has grown, so have its audiences, and it now stages its performances in three venues: the Asolo Theater itself, where one Repertory play and one training conservatory play are presented each year; the Mertz Theater, a 1903 Scottish opera house moved to Sarasota; and the contemporary Cook Theater.

Other Sarasota-area theater venues include The Players of Sarasota, a community group staging comedy acts and dramas; and the Venice Little Theater, 20 miles (32km) south of Sarasota in Venice, with a varied and ambitious schedule of comedy, drama, and musicals.

In the Palm Beach area, Palm Beach Dramaworks, in West Palm Beach, mounts four productions each year. Elsewhere in Palm Beach County, the Caldwell Theatre Company, in Boca Raton, has recently moved to its sumptuous new Count de Hoernle Theatre. In addition to its dramatic presentations, the Caldwell also offers an acclaimed Adult Storytelling Series. Fort Lauderdale's Parker Playhouse, operating under the umbrella of the Broward Center for the Performing Arts, is a lovely neoclassical-style theater where visiting musical acts and Broadway plays as well as local productions are staged.

Orlando and environs are richly endowed with live theater organizations. The Orlando Repertory

Theatre, housed in a three-theater facility in Loch Haven Park, operates in conjunction with the University of Central Florida to present an ambitious program of children's and adult plays; the Repertory's American Classic Theatre specializes in the work of American playwrights. The Orlando Shakespeare Theater, also affiliated with UCF, mounts ten productions each year, including several of the Bard's works. In downtown Orlando, Mad Cow Theatre presents stagings of classic and modern dramas and a cabaret festival in May; and Theatre Downtown is a repertory company that spotlights the work of local playwrights as well as acknowledged masters.

## Key West theater

In Key West, lively Duval Street is home to the intimate Red Barn Theatre, where offerings run to comedy, drama, musical theater, and cabaret; a half-dozen shows fill the bill between December and March, drawing on the considerable talent residing right in Key West.

Nearby, the Performing Arts Centers for Key West operates the Tennessee Williams Theatre, named for the distinguished playwright who was a sometime resident of the southernmost city. The Centers are also home to Island Opera Theatre of the Florida Keys, dedicated to musical theater of all kinds as well as classical opera and the Key West Symphony Orchestra *(see box on opposite page)*.    ❑

**LEFT:** patrons await a performance at the Kravis Center for the Performing Arts in West Palm Beach.
**ABOVE RIGHT:** Mary Carmen Catoya, Miami City Ballet.

# EXTREME WEATHER

**Florida does nothing by halves. Famously, it boasts more sun than most corners of the United States, but it also has more than its fair share of rain and thunderstorms**

In her book *Cross Creek*, Marjorie Kinnan Rawlings said that in Florida the seasons "move in and out like nuns in soft clothing, making no rustle in their passing." It is, indeed, hard to tell spring from summer here, and fall slips into winter almost without notice. Temperatures drop in winter but rarely approach freezing. And Florida has the advantage of being sunny all year round: the coldest temperature ever recorded was a frosty −2°F (−19°C) in Tallahassee in 1899.

"Sunshine State" isn't merely a catchy slogan dreamed up by a PR company to lure tourists but an official name that demonstrates the importance of the sun in raising billions of dollars for Florida by attracting tourists, baseball squads, and fashion photographers, who revel in the fact that in winter their models can pose in next to nothing against a blue sky while most of the nation is bundled up in sweaters. Furthermore, many crops, including vegetables and tropical fruit from oranges to mangoes, thrive in the warm and wet climate.

## THUNDER AND LIGHTNING

Florida is a place of extremes. It is the lightning capital of the United States, and ranks fourth in the world in the frequency of lightning strikes, which have killed more than 425 and injured over 2,000 people in the state since 1960. A so-called "lightning belt" extends from Jacksonville to Fort Myers, with Fort Myers averaging 100 lightning-packed days a year. Even reality-defying Walt Disney World has to come to a standstill when lightning strikes.

**ABOVE:** A hurricane can lift boats out of the water, flatten houses and rip the facades off apartment buildings. Hurricane Andrew, which buffeted Florida in 1992, was hardly the strongest on record but devastating nonetheless, leaving 250,000 temporarily homeless.

**ABOVE:** The Gulf Coast between St Pete Beach and Clearwater Beach enjoys an average of 363 sunny days a year. From 1967 to 1969 an amazing 768 consecutive days of sunshine were recorded here.

**LEFT:** Seven of the 10 hottest US cities are in Florida. Key West ranks first, then Miami, with a year-round average of 75.6°F (24.2°C). In the sultry summer months, Miami Beach's Art Deco thermometer simply cannot cope.

**LEFT:** For many visitors from the northern hemisphere, spending Christmas in the heat of Florida can be a positively bizarre experience.

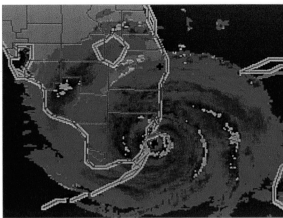

## THE DEVELOPMENT OF A HURRICANE

A tropical storm is called a hurricane when its wind speed exceeds 74 miles (119km) per hour. The hurricane is then classified from one to five according to the Saffir-Simpson Scale, which measures the winds and expected flooding. Category 5 is the worst, with winds of over 155 miles (249km) per hour.

Many of the hurricanes that hit Florida move across the Atlantic from the coast of Africa. Several factors contribute to the formation of a hurricane, above all heat and wind. The key ingredient is the heat of the summer sun, which warms the surface of the ocean enough for water to evaporate. As the warm air rises, it condenses into thunderclouds, which are sent spinning by the rotation of the earth. The hurricane moves forward at 7–30 miles (11–48km) per hour and can measure hundreds of miles across.

The National Hurricane Center in Miami tracks a hurricane's progress using radar and satellites, and pilots, known as Hurricane Hunters, also fly in and out of the storm in order to gather data. Such warning of the severity of a hurricane can greatly reduce the damage done if it eventually makes landfall. While the winds can be devastating, most damage and deaths are caused by flooding from the storm surge – a wall of water that can reach a height of 20ft (6 meters).

See *Travel Tips* for more information on hurricanes.

**RIGHT:** snow is so rare that merely a touch of it can cripple even north Florida. The highest recorded snowfall in the state was on February 13, 1899, when 4 inches (10cm) fell at Lake Butler near Jacksonville.

**BELOW:** Florida is wetter than anywhere else in the US. Over half the average total rainfall is recorded from June to September, when the state can be subjected to as much rainfall as some European cities get in a whole year. Key West is the driest city and still has 40 inches (100cm).

**RIGHT:** Ever since Florida's boom of the 1920s and the arrival of advertising, graphic images of Florida's warm and sunny weather have been used to draw northerners to the state, as demonstrated in this early poster of Greater Miami.

# FLORIDA CUISINE

It's not all shrimp, alligator tail steak and Key lime pie.
The state's multi-ethnic population is reflected in
its cuisine, and the strong Caribbean influence
can add a tangy flavor when least expected

For centuries, Florida cooks have charted a splendidly varied culinary course, drawing not only upon a bounty of local ingredients but upon a broad range of regional and international influences. There's no single Florida cuisine but rather a panoply of down-home Southern, Anglo, Caribbean, and Latin American trends that enliven an ever-changing food culture, one of the most exciting in the US.

In the beginning, Floridians – natives and Europeans alike – dined sumptuously off the peninsula's abundance drawn from land and sea. One passionate chronicler of old Floridian cuisine was the late Marjorie Kinnan Rawlings, Pulitzer-Prize-winning author of *The Yearling*, whose books *Cross Creek* and *Cross Creek Cookery* documented her life and kitchen adventures in her adopted home of Cross Creek, a tiny village in the northern part of the state where she lived in the 1930s and '40s. In *Cross Creek Cookery*, Rawlings set down her neighbors' recipes for old-time dishes such as hush puppies, pecan pie, cream of peanut soup, and the more exotic coot surprise and alligator tail steak. One of Rawlings' favorite dishes was turtle eggs (not from sea turtles), whose "fine and

> *Florida's early explorers dined on boar, venison, and even bear, which the native people sometimes bartered with the settlers. The tribes also simmered turtle, duck eggs, frog legs, eels, and alligator in herbs.*

distinct flavor" she praised, noting that "a dozen turtle eggs, with plain bread and butter and a glass of ale, make all I ask of a light luncheon or supper."

**LEFT:** Columbia Restaurant in Ybor City, Tampa.
**RIGHT:** a taste of lobster from Caretta on the Gulf at the Sandpearl Resort in Clearwater Beach.

## Hotel fare

Many of these dishes, of course, are representative not only of Florida but of the coastal South in general. Before it was discovered by winter-weary northerners, Florida was much more a typical Southern state than it is today, and Southern culinary folkways were predominant. When the outsiders did arrive, via Henry Flagler's railway, their tastes ran to the conventionally substantial hotel menus of the era. The table d'hôte offerings at the big Atlantic coast hotels might have been perked up with fresh local orange juice and locally caught seafood, but they were essentially what a traveler might expect at posh hostelries from Cleveland to New York and Philadelphia to Boston.

Later, when Miami and environs began to

attract not only hotel-bound vacationers but retirees from the North who came to stay, one of the greatest culinary influences became the Jewish delicatessen cuisine of the New York metropolitan area. In Miami Beach, you'll never look far for a bagel with cream cheese and lox or a pastrami sandwich. And in Florida's cities and resorts as in any cosmopolitan environment, Italian, French, Chinese, Thai, and a host of other international dining choices are always available.

## Florida orange

Despite rivers, lakes, and offshore waters that teemed with fish and shellfish, the food that first drew the attention of the outside world to Florida was the orange. Oranges are not native to Florida; they were first brought to the peninsula by the Spanish explorers Ponce de León and Hernando de Soto and soon grew wild throughout what remained of Spanish territory (except for a brief period under the British flag) until American sovereignty was established in 1821.

The orange industry in Florida got its start as early as the 1770s. A century later, thousands of acres of groves had been planted, and Florida oranges were heading north by train just as the tourists were traveling south. The region around the Indian River, not a river but a saltwater lagoon

### OYSTER BAR

Apalachicola Bay, one of the world's richest estuarine systems, is famous for its oysters, providing Florida with 90 percent of its annual oyster harvest. Oyster farmers in the bay, poised on their small boats, use tongs fashioned from two giant rakes to pincer their "crop," which is cultivated in carefully selected water (neither too salty nor too fresh) in nurseries known as "oyster bars." They can be fished year-round, but the catch tends to be smaller during summer.

120 miles (190km) long and seldom more than 2 miles (3km) wide, became a prime growing area and still is, despite the encroachment of residential development. Indian River is also famous for its grapefruit, a citrus family member that originated in the West Indies and was first planted in Florida in 1823. Shipments of grapefruit didn't reach the northeastern US until the 1880s, when Americans began to develop a taste for their tart, juicy flesh. The grapefruit that James Cagney squished into Mae Clarke's face in 1931's *The Public Enemy* was almost surely grown in Florida.

## Key lime and conch

One Florida crop that is indelibly linked with one of the state's most distinctive regions is, ironically, no longer grown commercially there. This is the Key lime, a small, yellowish lime known to most visitors as the main ingredient in Key lime pie. Even in the Keys, when you order a slice of Key lime pie, you'll be savoring fruit grown in Mexico – unless you've lucked into a mom-and-pop bakery or coffee shop where the proprietors, or one of the help, has a Key lime tree or two in the back yard. Like the Keys' pygmy deer (which are emphatically not on any menus), Key limes are far more famous than they are abundant.

Any mention of Keys cuisine brings to mind another of the island chain's iconic dishes: conch (pronounced "konk"). Conch is so indelibly linked

based; as "cracked conch," strips that have been tenderized by pounding and lightly breaded or battered and fried; and in conch fritters, the best of which have a high ratio of conch to batter and have been fried at just the right temperature to avoid greasiness. There are some terrific conch fritters served by street vendors in Mallory Square, Key West, around the time when the inevitable tourist throng applauds the sunset.

## Fresh seafood

But Florida waters still yield a delicious array of seafood. Key West pink shrimp are a succulent alternative to the farm-raised supermarket vari-

with the culinary traditions of Key West that its native-born residents call themselves "conchs," but the mollusk itself, at least as far as local tables go, is a native no longer. Restrictions on harvesting the now-depleted shellfish in Florida waters mean that all conch served in the state are imported from the Bahamas. When you do order conch, it's the queen conch that you will be served. Its flesh, which is similar to that of calamari, is most frequently prepared in one of four ways: as conch salad, sort of a seviche with a hot pepper kick; in a chowder, either tomato or cream-

**FAR LEFT:** Key lime pie is a classic tropical dessert.
**ABOVE LEFT AND ABOVE:** fresh local shrimp and stone crab are Florida specialties.

ety, especially when tossed with pasta or fried and tucked into that New Orleans import, the "po'boy" sandwich. Stone crabs – there's a famous and eponymously named restaurant in Miami Beach that built its reputation on them – are unique among sustainable shellfish resources in that their big, sweet claws, where all the meat is, grow back after they are removed and the crab is returned to the sea. Claws, however, don't figure at all as part of the lobsters harvested in South Florida waters. These are a different species from the cold-water specimens in New England. More properly called spiny lobster or langouste, they aren't armed with fat pincers but instead are nearly all tail meat. They're most often served broiled; just tell your server to make sure they don't spend too much time under the flame, which can make the flesh dry.

Fin fish found on Florida menus include several members of the snapper clan – yellowtail, hog, and mutton snapper are predominant – as well as mahi-mahi, the name given to the fish once commonly known as dolphin but rechristened to avoid confusion with those other dolphins, the mammals visitors can get up close and personal with at several Florida dolphin education centers. Grouper turns up on quite a few Florida restaurant tables as well. Like conch, it's a versatile and delectable ocean denizen that's a dietary mainstay of the nearby Bahamas. But again, as with conch, fishing pressure on grouper

has caused a worrisome decline in stocks, so it's best to save it for the occasional meal.

## A taste of the islands

But by far the biggest news on the Florida food scene over the past few decades has been the impact made by the variegated cuisines of Latin America. Given the close proximity of the peninsula to the West Indies – Grand Bahama Island is a scant 60 miles (95km) from Florida, Cuba only 90 miles (140km) – it would seem to have been natural for Bahamian and Caribbean influences to have shown up earlier. But for centuries, mainland American tastes prevailed, and foreign flavors

### SUSTAINABLE SEAFOOD

Given the extensive variety of seafood on Florida menus, it's a good idea to be aware of which species are relatively abundant and which have been negatively affected by fishing pressure. Grouper is a long-lived species that is particularly vulnerable to overfishing, and management of the fishery has been spotty. Orange roughy is another species with a long reproductive cycle – they don't mature until 20 years old – and their stocks have been significantly depleted by trawler fishing, which also damages their deep-water spawning habitat. Sharks, too, are slow-growing and do not reproduce prolifically and are overfished in international waters.

Among the least threatened commercially caught fish is mahi-mahi, which reproduces quickly and can sustain high fishing pressure – especially when the method used is trolling, as opposed to longline fishing. Albacore, yellowfin, and skipjack tuna stocks also stand up to commercial harvest, as long as pole and troll methods are used, although longline and purse-seine fishing for tuna takes a heavy toll and causes the collateral destruction of sharks and marine mammals.

Among sustainable shellfish species, Florida hard clams are a particular standout. The clams, which are farmed commercially off Brevard County on the Atlantic and along the Gulf Coast, grow to maturity in suspended nets, which eliminates the need for harmful dredging, and do not require feeding with fishmeal or other potential pollutants, as the mollusks filter nutrients from seawater.

intruded primarily in the Keys, particularly Key West. One very old neighborhood in that city has long been imbued with the tastes of its Bahamian-descended inhabitants and their way with conch, grouper, pork, chicken, and the ubiquitous side dish of pigeon peas with rice. During the late 19th century, though, Cuban cigar makers began migrating to Key West, as they did to Tampa on Florida's west coast, and they brought with them the harbingers of the cuisine that has since become part of the cultural signature of all of South Florida, especially Miami and its Little Havana neighborhood. The Miami-area Cuban population, of course, burgeoned suddenly in the early 1960s as the result of Cuba's drastic political shift, and another great wave of Cuban immigrants came in the early 1980s.

The recipes the Cubans brought with them included *ropa vieja* ("old clothes"), a long-simmered stew of shredded beef; the slow-roasted pork called *lechon*; plantains fried in butter until they caramelize; and *picadillo*, a mélange of ground meat and potatoes seasoned with onions, tomatoes, pimientos, green olives, and capers. Black beans and rice are a universal accompaniment, and a mainstay throughout the day is strong Cuban coffee, usually well sweetened and served in the morning with hot milk as *café con leche*. The one Cuban dish nearly every visitor can find, even without seeking out Cuban restaurants, is the sandwich Cubano, stuffed with ham, roast pork, cheese, and pickles, served hot from a press. The *medianoche* version (named for its popularity as a midnight snack) is usually made with a sweeter variety of the thin-crusted Cuban bread that has a soft, flaky inside.

## Florribean flavors

Other kinds of Caribbean cuisine have also followed the waves of immigrants that have come to Florida from the islands. A sizable Dominican community brought *pastelitos*, turnovers filled with meat or cheese; the hearty stew called *sancocho*, made with chicken or beef melded with the flavors of green plantains and any combination of cassava (yucca), the similar but creamier yautia, and potatoes, and invariably served with rice; and fish poached in coconut milk. *Buñuelos*, sweet donuts, are a popular accompaniment to strong coffee.

From Jamaica come spicy meat pasties

(turnovers) and jerk chicken and pork, the time-honored street foods of Kingston and Montego Bay, along with curried goat, chicken, and shrimp. The tamarind and ginger native to the island season many Jamaican dishes, and cassava bread is always a favorite.

Haitians, one of the most recent émigré groups, carried with them their fondness for fish boiled with lime juice, onion and garlic, and hot pepper. Highly seasoned beef patties and corn fritters are also reminders of the creole cuisine of their homeland. In the larger cities, Florida's new generation of star chefs experiment with all of these traditions, adding locally fresh produce and especially seafood to cre-

ate a fusion "Florribean" repertoire all their own.

The wonderful thing about the dishes of Florida is that they haven't supplanted each other either through the passing of time or the arrival of ethnic newcomers. The flavors of Florida exist side by side, admittedly more traditionally Southern in the north and Latin in the South, but always in close enough proximity so that a single sojourn in the state can supply a visitor with savory memories of Dixie barbecue, luminously fresh shellfish, a hefty *medianoche* sandwich properly consumed in the wee hours ... and that sack of Honeybell oranges, so juicy that they should have been sold with a roll of paper towels.

The coot surprise and turtle eggs may be a little harder to come by.  ❑

**LEFT:** pasta with shrimp and mussels at the Naples Tomato. **ABOVE RIGHT:** chef James King presents dinner at the Grill Room Restaurant at Amelia Island Plantation.

# THE BUSINESS OF PLEASURE

It takes a heap of logistics to keep theme parks
up and running and ahead of the competition.
Lots of toilet paper helps, too

Each evening, after approximately 117,000 guests exit through the turnstiles at Walt Disney World, the park's night crew swings into action. Almost 25,000 people work until morning to refresh the cobwebs and "antique" grime in the Magic Kingdom's Haunted Mansion, mowing more than 2,000 acres (810 hectares) of grass, distributing over three tons of food to more than 1,000 animals at Animal Kingdom, even refilling the toilet tissue holders that will dispense 19,000 miles (31,000km) of paper in a year. This crew is about half of the "cast" of 55,000 hired by central Florida's largest employer to help keep Disney World "the happiest place on earth" – and also perhaps the best maintained.

For the Disney Company, Mickey and the gang are big business: the estimated 47 million people – that's one and a half times the population of Canada – who pass through the gates every year will spend more than $100 each on tickets, meals, refreshments, and souvenirs. It's no wonder so much hard work goes into assuring that everyone has fun.

The Disney folks produce and package pleasure. They provide a safe, clean, and controlled

> Every day an average of 100 pairs of sunglasses are turned into the Lost and Found at the Magic Kingdom. That's more than 1.2 million pairs since the park opened in 1971.

environment staffed by cast members (the Disney term for employees) who are always neat and well-groomed, and who never sport beards, long

**LEFT:** lifeguard on duty at Wet 'n Wild; theme parks are Orlando's biggest employers.
**RIGHT:** A Busch Gardens staff member is ready to help.

nails, tattoos, or visible body piercings. They buff and polish a place where youngsters can frolic and parents can relive their childhood fantasies alongside Cinderella, Peter Pan, and a host of cartoon characters that by now seem part of the American family. And the cast does it well: Walt Disney World is the most visited vacation destination on earth.

## Day-to-day Disney

Disney World functions well because it was planned that way from the beginning. When Walt and his brother Roy began scouting sites for an East Coast theme park, they wanted to avoid mistakes they'd made in building Disneyland in California. One mistake was not purchasing a piece of land large enough to accommodate a self-contained vacation resort that could offer visitors everything they would want or need, so that they wouldn't have to go off-property to spend their money. Under a blind trust, Disney purchased 27,300 acres (11,000 hectares) of rural central Florida for an average of $200 an acre. Although it was mostly swamp, the 43-square-mile (111-sq-km) parcel – a piece of land twice the size of Manhattan – would allow Disney to create a buffer large enough to keep competition well at bay.

## A home of its own

Equally important as having enough land was having the authority to develop and manage the prop-

## Beneath the kingdom

From the outset, Disney's plan was to retain complete control of its environment. With an initial investment of $400 million, the company built an energy plant, Reedy Creek Utilities Company, which generates approximately 35 percent of the electricity needed to operate the park. (Each year, Disney World uses about half as many kilowatt hours as the entire state of Maine.)

Disney also set up its own waste disposal system, which now handles a daily load of up to 50 tons of trash – much of it generated at the park's restaurants. Each day more than 500 employees prepare and distribute 8,000 different menu items,

erty as the Disney people saw fit. The Florida legislature knew that the park would be a cash cow for the state: it was estimated that during construction and the first ten years of operation it would generate $6.6 billion. A sizable cut of that amount would go to the state, before new construction and permanent service jobs were added in.

The legislature thus approved a bill granting Disney permission to establish the Reedy Creek Improvement District, an area some wags have dubbed "the Florida Vatican." The legislation gave Disney authority to develop and manage every aspect of its property, including decisions about zoning, establishing building codes, levying taxes, and even building an airport or nuclear power plant if and when the need arises.

a gigantic enterprise that incorporates the services of bakers (more than 40,000 pounds/18,000kg of flour go into each week's supply of bread, rolls, and pastries); people to oversee machines, including automated pizza makers that pump out pies at the rate of one every two seconds; and delivery personnel to service 450 food vendor locations throughout the property.

The heart of the disposal system is a giant underground vacuum called an AVAC (automated vacuum-assisted collection), which sucks refuse from points scattered throughout the park and scoots it at 60 miles per hour (97kph) through tubes leading to a central repository, where it is compacted and transported to a landfill. Enormous amounts of material, including 6,500 pounds

(3,000kg) of aluminum cans each day, are processed at the park's recycling center.

When the Magic Kingdom was in its planning stage, designers came up with an elegant way to hide from guests the day-to-day operations necessary to run the park. They built a 2.8-mile (4.5-km) utility corridor, or "utilidor," with 15-ft-high (5-meter) tunnels at ground level, covered it with 8 million cubic yards (6 million cubic meters) of soil dug to create the Seven Seas Lagoon, and built the park over it. The utilidor houses the park's computer operations, the AVAC tubes, wires, offices, makeup operations, and costuming rooms. Color-coded connecting corridors lead to each of the Kingdom's four themed areas, permitting Mickey and the gang a quick and easy way to suit up and then scoot to different parts of the park. A smaller utilidor is used at Epcot, where the central computer bank is located 20ft (6 meters) under the Innovations east pavilion.

## Vying for dollars

The Orlando Convention and Visitors Bureau estimates that more than 45 million people visit the city annually. The hundreds of area hotels (with a combined total of more than 110,000 rooms), restaurants, stores, and attractions all want a share of the money these visitors will spend, and most of them pool a portion of their advertising budgets to get it. Theme parks, including Universal Orlando, SeaWorld, and Gatorland, offer discounts in a myriad of free coupon books and offer substantial discounts through programs including the Convention & Visitors Bureau's MagiCard and the Orlando Flexticket.

Disney managers have taken a different route. Not only do they decline to advertise cooperatively with other businesses, they've pursued a policy of building attractions in an attempt to monopolize tourist dollars: hence the additions in recent years of Typhoon Lagoon (to compete with Wet 'n Wild), Hollywood Studios (to combat Universal Studios), and Animal Kingdom (to draw clientele from Busch Gardens and SeaWorld). The building of Downtown Disney to compete with Universal's CityWalk and downtown Orlando's Church Street Station was so effective that the latter closed its doors early in 2002. The $100 million Wide World of Sports Complex – a 200-acre

(80-hectare) development that includes an 8,000-seat baseball stadium, four major-league practice fields, and a 5,000-seat fieldhouse with six basketball courts – is Disney's attempt to capture yet another giant segment of the tourist market.

Disney does offer a few discounts – generally on packages that include the purchase of multiday "park hopper" tickets and through its own Disney Club, as well as in cooperation with AAA. In an unusual move for a company that retains ironfisted control over its marketing, Disney has entered a distribution agreement with Travelocity.com giving the travel website authority to book theme park tickets, onsite hotels, and cruises for its customers.

## Disney World, here I come

The Travelocity deal may well be an acknowledgment of the fact that there is more competition than ever for tourist dollars, and Disney is aggressively protective of its market share. Competition may also be the reason that Orlando theme parks, and Disney in particular, have stepped up their advertising campaigns. In fact, "stepped up" may be an understatement for a company that, until 1984, did no direct advertising. Until then the company relied on word of mouth and co-advertising: when Epcot opened, in 1982, corporations such as Kraft and General Motors paid a total of $300 million to have their companies associated with Disney, which, of course, was the recipient of all that free advertising.

LEFT: a food vendor at Busch Gardens. ABOVE RIGHT: a souvenir shop at Universal Orlando; food concessions and gift shops are a major revenue stream.

For more than 20 years, celebrity athletes have gazed into a TV camera at the moment of their greatest victories and uttered the five words that confirm their status as superstars: "I'm going to Disney World." Even former president George W. Bush got into the act, exhorting the American public, after September 11, 2001, to "Get down to Disney World in Florida ... take your families and enjoy life the way we want it to be enjoyed."

The slogan is the foundation of the enormously successful "What's Next" campaign launched in 1987, designed to present Disney World as the place for people – especially winning athletes – to go when they're celebrating. President Bush used the park as a metaphor for America's ultimate vacation ideal, just as astronaut Sally Ride evoked Disney when she described her journey into space as an "E-ticket ride" (referring to the early days when the best rides in the park went by that designation).

Lately, Disney has been scoring big with its "Year of a Million Dreams" ad campaign, which featured megastars like David Beckham, Beyoncé Knowles, and Scarlett Johansson costumed as familiar Disney characters and photographed by no less than Annie Leibovitz. And what did quaterback Eli Manning say after leading the New York Giants to an unexpected victory in the

## MOB MANAGEMENT: FOLLOW THE WIENIE

Crowd control designed to keep guests docile, mannerly and patient in lengthy queues starts at Walt Disney World before visitors even enter the park. It begins as cars funnel into lanes at parking toll booths and drivers thread their way through the cones to assigned spaces. It continues as visitors listen to a barrage of instructions on the tram ride to the ticket booth, then wait in line to buy an admission ticket, pass through security, and, finally, clear a park turnstile.

Inside, guests are moved along with what the Disney people call "wienies": lures like Cinderella's Castle and Big Thunder Mountain that draw them from one spot to another. As Walt said, "you've got to have a wienie at the end of every street." Other controls include peppy music to keep guests moving and a "flow-through" ride protocol, whereby passengers enter on one side and leave on another, reducing loading time.

Many attractions have "hidden lines": no one is waiting outside, but once inside, guests are channeled into winding corridors and wend slowly toward the loading zone. Because the scenery changes as they move, they sense progress. A variation is the pre-show – usually presented on video screens – that keep guests entertained and fills them in on the ride's story line. In essence, the queue becomes an extension of the ride – yet another Disney innovation.

2008 Super Bowl? "Living the dream … I'm going to Disney World."

## Staying on top

Despite the growth of competing attractions, Disney World remains the 800-pound gorilla of Orlando theme parks, outdistancing its nearest competitor by more than four times. In 2007, 47.1 million people paid admission to Disney World's four major theme parks, 11.6 million went to Universal Orlando, and 5.8 million flocked to SeaWorld.

But management knows that to stay on top, the park has to continue to meet – better yet, to exceed – the expectations of its guests, approximately 70

designed dark ride. Disney has also announced that it will be scrapping the Pleasure Island "night-club district" to meet the demand for more family-friendly diversions.

But there's grumbling among some Disney aficionados that these new entries don't measure up to the latest generation of high-tech rides that are being developed at other theme parks. Indeed, that's what the folks at Universal and SeaWorld might well be counting on to boost their own attendance figures in the years ahead. Since it opened its Orlando venue in 1990, Universal's East Coast working studio has evolved into an entertainment empire, with two distinct theme

percent of whom are repeat customers. So in a business climate in which fuel costs are prohibitively high, the US economy is in a funk, and tourists are rethinking the whole idea of a family vacation to Florida or anywhere else, quality must be maintained and image burnished even more aggressively. Efforts include the unveiling of new rides like Epcot's Mission: SPACE, which is a state-of-the-art simulator ride, and Animal Kingdom's Expedition Everest, which combines a roller coast experience with an elaborately

parks, a water park, the CityWalk entertainment complex, and three huge theme hotels.

## On the edge

The words most often used to compare Universal with Disney are "hipper," "edgier" ... and "newer." It's hard to imagine two more different experiences than listening to a calm, carefully-scripted presentation at, say, the Magic Kingdom's Jungle Cruise (ad-libbing by Disney cast members is forbidden) and hearing a sweating, frantic "guide" at Universal's Poseidon's Fury scream in terror, "open the friggin' door." And there's no Disney equivalent to Universal's Horror Make-Up Show, a raucous, pun-filled comedy whose hosts aren't above taking a potshot at the Mouse next door.

**LEFT:** a SeaWorld audience waits for Shamu; theme parks have turned crowd control into a science.
**ABOVE LEFT:** a billboard lures tourists into the parks.
**ABOVE RIGHT:** park maps are available at the gate.

Because it's so much newer than much of Disney and is not as concerned with overall family image, Universal's rides and attractions tend to be much more state-of-the-art and hair-raising. Even a fairly mild ride like Men in Black: Alien Invasion, a ride-through, interactive "shooting gallery," makes its Disney equivalent, Buzz Lightyear, feel almost quaint by comparison. Terminator 2: 3-D, which combines live action with a 3-D film, is a wild and violent extravaganza that assaults the senses with explosions, gunfire, billowing smoke, and ear-splitting volume. This is emphatically not the sort of show you want a young child to experience, especially those who

Kraken is the pièce de résistance at SeaWorld. Although SeaWorld has been rated the world's best marine life park, management realized that it would have to introduce several thrill rides to keep attendance figures up. Its response to the challenge was Kraken, the tallest, fastest and steepest roller coaster in the South. Also in SeaWorld is Journey to Atlantis, described as part water ride, part roller coaster – a white-knuckle combination that includes two of the steepest, wettest, and fastest drops of any ride in the world.

SeaWorld also offers a very un-Disney-like attraction: free beer. The drink that is banned in the Magic Kingdom flows at the marine park's

may not fully understand the difference between playacting and real life (a distinction that some adults may be uncertain about, especially if they've never experienced this type of attraction).

## A will to thrill

In 1999 Universal opened its 110-acre (45-hectare) Islands of Adventure, laying to rest any debate as to which Orlando park offers the best thrill rides. In addition to gut-twisting roller coasters like the Incredible Hulk, Dueling Dragons, and the Revenge of the Mummy (an indoor coaster clearly designed to compete with Disney's popular Rock 'n' Roller Coaster at Hollywood Studios), there are innovative 3-D and simulator rides like the Amazing Adventures of Spider-Man and the Simpsons Ride.

Hospitality House, where customers can sample the wares of its parent company, Anheuser-Busch.

Alcohol, in fact, was forbidden at Disney World for years, because Walt didn't feel that it was appropriate in a family environment. (This policy almost sank Disneyland Paris when it first opened: Parisians, incredulous that they couldn't have a glass of wine when they relaxed between rides, boycotted the park until management gave in and began serving alcohol.) It was only in 1984, when Epcot opened, that beer, wine, and spirits were approved for sale at restaurants in the World Showcase. Management realized that customers did not want to wash down bangers and mash with ginger ale at the Rose & Crown Pub or sip Coke while dining on sumptuous French cuisine. Alcohol is also available at Universal Orlando – for a price, of course – and it's not unusual to see visitors strolling the park with a tall glass of beer in hand.

## The war of more

Orlando is a land of superlatives. "Universal Orlando Resort is a spectacular vacation destination which includes the world's two most amazing theme parks ... a dazzling entertainment complex, and magnificently themed on-site hotels," proclaims that park's brochure. SeaWorld boasts of the Kraken roller coaster, "Nothing like it in Orlando ... The highest, fastest, longest and only floorless coaster" and touts, at its Atlantis

pied by theme restaurants and hip nightclubs as well as high-profile live shows like Blue Man Group.

SeaWorld, vying with Disney's Animal Kingdom to be the No. 1 park for live animal acts, opened Discovery Cove, where visitors can swim with dolphins and snorkel through coral reefs. It's new water park, Aquatica, which opened to positive reviews in 2008, puts a spin on the traditional panoply of flumes and slides by introducing dolphins and other sea creatures into the mix.

Universal and Disney are also locked in a battle to keep tourists from leaving their properties. Guests who stay at one of Universal's resort hotels enjoy a variety of special privileges,

Bayside Stadium, "the best water athletes in the world pour it on." Downtown Disney is "the epicenter of excitement ... a waterfront 'wanderland' of top-notch, world-famous shopping, entertainment, and dining."

Every attraction in the Orlando area wages a daily battle for tourist dollars. But the big three are engaged in a war of "more." Universal's answer to Downtown Disney, an entertainment complex anchored by DisneyQuest (a center for virtual-reality amusements), Cirque du Soleil, and Planet Hollywood, is CityWalk, a similar complex occu-

**LEFT AND ABOVE :** The Adventures of Spider-Man and Terminator 2, both at Universal Orlando, dazzle audiences with 3-D effects.

including complimentary on-site transportation, priority restaurant seating, and, most important at a park where lines for major attractions can be up to 90 minutes long, express access on most rides. Not to be outdone, Disney offers similar perks to guests at its hotels, most notably its Extra Magic Hours program, which allows resort guests to enter a designated park an hour before the offical opening time and stay as long as three hours after closing.

Each year the parks raise their admission fees: as of 2008, the average cost for a one-day visit to the big three parks was $68. So it's important for each of them to continue to make their customers believe they are the biggest and the best. That's only good business. ❑

# Thrill Machines

**Hold on tight! The roller coasters at Florida's biggest theme parks are faster, wilder, and more imaginative than ever before**

When you get right down to it, we don't really visit theme parks for the themes. There's no denying that much of the lure of Walt Disney World is the familiarity of the Disney characters and the Disney way of storytelling. But beneath

the story lines, the reason we flock by the millions through the gates of theme parks is the same as it was for our grandparents when they frolicked at Coney Island in Brooklyn or on midway rides at county fairs. We simply want to be tossed around until our insides can barely stand it, shot through space at traffic-ticket speeds, plummeted earthwards with harrowing abandon. When we surrender ourselves to the untender mercies of the best thrill rides, what we really want is to feel like we are about to die … forgetting for just a moment that the brakes will work, the tracks will turn from the abyss, just in the nick of time.

The marquee thrill rides at the big Florida parks are close cousins to the great amusement park roller coasters, and they use the same tricks of physics and physiology to make you delightfully terrified.

## G-force and air time

If roller coasters traveled downhill in a straight line, the only thrills would be those of speed and forward motion. The most exciting sensations on a coaster are the result of shifting G-forces, which lessen and magnify the force of gravity upon the riders.

A force of 1G is what we feel under normal circumstances. At 1G, a 170-pound (77-kg) man feels like he weighs 170 pounds. Double the G-force and gravity's apparent effect is doubled: in other words, our 170-pounder feels like he's packing 340 pounds (154 kg). Most American coasters exert forces under 3Gs. A scant few pin riders back into their seats with 5Gs. The G-force effect also works in the opposite direction. At less than 1G, there is a sensation of lightness; at zero Gs is a feeling of weightlessness.

The initial descent from the top of the lift hill and down subsequent inclines lessens G-force. Whipping quickly uphill increases it, while sharp turns exert G-force in a lateral direction. Much of the thrill occurs at the points where there is a sudden transfer from positive to negative G-force, such as at the top of a hill in the moment before a drop. This is the coaster enthusiast's treasured "air time," achieved on Universal's Incredible Hulk Coaster in the roll that immediately follows a lightning ascent through a 150-ft (46-meter) tunnel. Air time should not be confused with "hang time" – that mini-eternity of suspended motion at the crest of a lift hill before the plummet begins. Coaster designers often deliberately prolong hang time in order to enhance anticipation and make the payoff all the more delicious.

All of these external effects focus on a tiny but crucial component of our anatomies, contributing not only to exhilaration but to the disorientation and outright nausea that make rapid, twisting rides less than appealing for many theme-park patrons. The inner ear is our gyroscope, an apparatus that enables us to walk upright and react to changing spatial circumstances. But when those circumstances are manipulated as quickly and unnaturally as they are on a coaster ride, the fluid in the inner ear and the nerves leading to the brain simply can't keep up. The result is dizziness, occasionally nausea, compounded by the sloshing and squeezing of the stomach.

## The steel age

The classic, clattering wooden coaster is a favorite of thrill-ride aficionados and, in some cases, can deliver much the same impact as its high-tech cousins. One example is Gwazi, unveiled in 1999 at Busch Gardens in Tampa. Built of more than 1.25 million ft (400,000 meters) of lumber, it's actually two coasters on intertwining tracks that hurtle past each other at 50 miles per hour (80kmh) or, as the park likes to boast, a "fly-by" speed of 100 miles per hour.

Coaster design was revolutionized by the development of the tubular steel track, first introduced in 1959 at California's Disneyland. Steel liberates coaster cars from having to remain right side up and made possible rides with corkscrews, helixes, barrel rolls, and other gravity-defying effects. Steel tubes also enabled the construction of "suspended" coasters, in which seats hang from the tracks rather than ride upon them, and swing from hinges. Since the connection to the track is out of sight, riders have the sensation of flying through space.

65 miles per hour (105kmh) and a drop of 144ft (44 meters), is the faster and taller of the two, but Montu wins plaudits for overall design, with huge inversions, tight corkscrews, and G-forces of 3.85.

## Kick start

As if all this weren't thrilling enough, new propulsion systems are replacing the old chain-lift approach to launching a coaster, delivering more explosive acceleration and higher speeds. Among the methods now in use are blasts of compressed air and – in the case of Universal's Incredible Hulk Coaster – a tire-driven launch. The Hulk climbs 150ft (46 meters) and reaches a launch speed of 67mph (108kmh), more

On "inverted" coasters, seats are suspended but not hinged. This setup allows the maneuvers that turn passengers upside down. Universal Orlando's Dueling Dragons compounds the topsy-turvy routine with sheer terror, as dual coasters careen towards each other at 60 miles per hour (96kmh) – only to loop out of the way at the very last moment. Conventional coasters with their wheels on the bottom can also turn upside down on steel tracks, as they do on Universal's Incredible Hulk. For sheer muscle, however, it's hard to beat Busch Gardens' Montu or SeaWorld's Kraken, both floorless coasters with hairy drops and multiple loops. Kraken, at a top speed of

**ABOVE:** Busch Gardens' Kumba (left) and Gwazi (right) are among the wildest rides in Florida.

than enough to fire passengers through seven subsequent inversions on a 3,700-ft (1,130-meter) track.

Many engineers feel that the future of coaster propulsion lies in the use of linear synchronous motors (LSM) – the same devices associated with magnetic-levitation trains. Disney World's entry in the LSM derby is the Rock 'n' Roller Coaster at Hollywood Studios. Themed around a rock 'n' roll story involving the rock band Aerosmith – which created the pulsing theme music – the electromagnetic motors launch riders from zero to 57mph (92kmh) in 2.8 seconds, with a force of nearly 5Gs. This coaster may not climb 400ft (120 meters), but it is hardly tame. The entire ride takes place on 3,400ft (1,040 meters) of indoor track, incorporating two rollovers and a corkscrew.  ❑

# HIGH-STAKES SPORTS

**In addition to professional and collegiate baseball, football, and basketball, Florida has a variety of alternative sports like auto racing and jai alai, some of which offer the added thrill of legalized gambling**

Florida can be a very dangerous place for sports-junkie gamblers. But if you admit that you're hooked, and just can't say no, give in to one of the three big vices, and promise you'll quit in the morning.

## Speed demons

On a crisp February day in 1959, a race was held at Daytona International Speedway, and the world of stock car racing changed forever.

Since then, headlines in newspapers the world over have chronicled car racing in Florida, but no story has ever approached that first race at Daytona in significance. It was the contest to beat all contests, which took Florida stock car racing out of the proverbial backwoods and brought with it a following that had previously been reserved for classic American race cities like Indianapolis.

Not that stock car racing was new here. William H.G. "Bill" France, seeking his fortune in the South years before, transformed a group of grease-covered speed demons into the National Association for Stock Car Auto Racing, now better known as NASCAR. If the popular open-wheel cars could

*The sport of jai alai originated in the Basque country and reached the US in the early 20th century. It came via Cuba, so it is no surprise that Florida has more jai alai arenas than anywhere else in the country.*

have a showplace like the Indianapolis Speedway, France speculated, why couldn't stock cars have a similar showplace?

**LEFT:** Philadelphia Phillies play the Tampa Bay Rays during spring training in Clearwater. **RIGHT:** jai alai has the added thrill of pari-mutuel betting.

Daytona International Speedway made its debut on that February day in 1959. Its "D"-shaped speedway and ultra-high banking turns were designed for blazing speeds, and first-day fans were left enthralled – stock car racing, born in the north Florida hill country decades before, had been born again in Daytona.

Today, spectators are still enthralled by the course and even more enthralled by the speeds. The patch of land in suburban Daytona Beach has since become the second most famous racecourse in the United States, next to Indianapolis. Names like Richard Petty and Mario Andretti have established Daytona as one of the greatest fuel-guzzling, engine-blasting, high-excitement speedways in the world.

It is estimated that between 150,000 and

200,000 fans jam the speedway each February for the Daytona 500, its premier race.

Shortly after Daytona is the famous 12 Hours of Sebring endurance race at Sebring International Speedway about 80 miles (130km) south of Orlando. Sebring is known for its less-than-smooth track, but drivers seem to relish the rough and rugged conditions. For the 35,000 or so spectators who converge on this small Florida town each March, the 12 Hours – like the Daytona 500 – is a good excuse to throw a party. The land surrounding the course turns into a huge campground, and during the race it looks like a giant cookout.

casual gambler betting for fun rather than profit.

Florida is one of the few states in the US where you can wager on human beings – as long as they are playing jai alai. Once again, Florida takes first place in this sport; with numerous jai alai arenas (known as frontons), including those in Miami, West Palm Beach, Tampa, and Daytona Beach. Connecticut and Rhode Island are the only other states in the nation where you can watch jai alai.

The wagers common to other pari-mutuel sports hold for jai alai: win, place, show, quinela, perfecta, and trifecta. All apply to the men who play this version of handball.

Also vying for attention in the racing world is the Homestead-Miami Speedway, which is host to an annual NASCAR race with all the excitement of Daytona. The speedway also puts on Indy car racing and specialty events.

## Taking a gamble

If the incessant roar of engines isn't enough to sate a craving for a sports-induced high, Florida offers the intoxicating thrill of legalized gambling. Over 15 million people a year wage over $1.6 billion on jai alai and on greyhound and horse racing in Florida. Generally, pari-mutuel sports attract two distinct types of fans: the serious player who approaches his or her wager of choice with a steadfast dedication and desire to win, and the

## And they're off!

Thoroughbred racing, however, is still a major force in the state's gambling industry, though legalized gambling on Indian reservations has certainly cut into the sport's revenue stream. Horse racing's high-society tradition is known throughout the world and earned it the sobriquet the "Sport of Kings." The Miami area has been a winter mecca for the nation's best horses and jockeys for years, and in a routine winter season, every important thoroughbred in training east of the Mississippi River is likely to be stabled somewhere in South Florida.

Years ago, prominent sports, entertainment, and political figures made South Florida's horse tracks a place to see and be seen. These days, those memories still have a hold over some of the more elaborate tracks, but for the most part the crowds are more pedestrian than genteel. Gulfstream Park, north of Miami Beach and once one of the state's premier racing venues, is now more urban and sits in the middle of a high-rise condo community. Tracks are situated in Pompano Beach and Tampa as well.

Between October and April, South Florida is also the focal point of the nation's harness racing. The opening of Pompano Park in Pompano Beach about 30 years ago served as the catalyst for what has become an annual southern migration of big-name harness horsemen to Florida. Virtually all of the sport's superstars ship their stables to Pompano for winter racing. They also prepare young horses being developed for the next summer's races in the North.

## Dog races

Along with horses, Florida's greyhound racing industry is without peer. The state is by far the most important greyhound area in the nation if for no other reason than sheer volume. Annual paid attendance statewide is about 8 million people who wager, with zeal, some $900 million per year.

All major metropolitan areas have at least one track nearby, where the sleek canines can be watched as they are lured by an artificial rabbit around the track to the cheers of the crowd. The modern version of greyhound racing is believed to have evolved from a coursing meet held in 1904 in North Dakota. Anthropologists claim that Cleopatra fancied greyhounds, a trait she shared with most Egyptian royalty. In England, the sport reached its great popularity during the Tudor period, in the reign of Queen Elizabeth I, who inspired the slogan the "Sport of Queens."

## The boys of spring

Another spectacular spectator sport that lures fans in droves to Florida is the all-American, apple-pie institution of baseball.

Careers are reborn every spring in Florida as baseball blossoms all over the state, when many of the country's major league teams head south for training (*see pages 322–3*). Like polar bears awakening from winter hibernation, the boys of baseball stretch, yawn, and try to get in shape. Stiff pitching arms are loosened and catchers' hands burn at the first pop of a 96-mph (154-kmh) fastball.

It begins in early March, when most of the country is still scraping ice off their driveways, and lasts for two months. The skies are clear blue and temperatures seem locked at a pleasant 70°F (21°C). Author Pat Jordan captured the spirit of the season when he obsereved that "Spring training is like a big summer picnic, where everyone's playing softball and eating barbecue. It's like a big country fair with people all around the ballpark."

And even though none of the games are "official," the multimillion-dollar players attract tens of thousands of fans from across the country who chow down mediocre hot dogs, slurp warm beer,

and scream and shout with excitement at the thought of scoring a foul ball or an autographed baseball cap. While ballpark seats aren't free for spring games, they cost considerably less than for regular-season games.

Along with being fun to watch, spring training is also big business. Television crews and news organizations from around the country and the world shine a spotlight on the prospects of various teams and players. Hotels fill up and rates climb, and restaurants require reservations. A spring training camp can mean as much as $30 million to a local economy and several mayors have tried to lure teams away from other cities in order to get their own two-month joy ride … and infusion of cash. Who says it's just a game? ❏

**LEFT:** the Daytona 500 Experience, an "interactive motorsports attraction," captures the thrill of auto racing. **RIGHT:** a close finish at a Florida racetrack.

# PLACES

A detailed guide to the entire state, arranged
by region and with all main sites clearly
cross-referenced by number to the maps

*There's just too much to see waiting in front of me,
And I know that I just can't go wrong
With these changes in latitudes, changes in attitudes.*
– Jimmy Buffett

With those words, the Florida-based balladeer Jimmy Buffett put his guitar-pickin' finger on a fundamental reason for Florida's popularity as a retreat for routine-weary travelers. No other place in the continental United States lies in more southern latitudes. Some folks have become so addicted to the tranquilizing effects of Florida's balmy climes, they return year after year for another dose.

Nature laid the groundwork for this annual people invasion by providing the beaches and forests. Then entrepreneurs added hotels and theme parks. Now, it's a rare corner of Florida that doesn't have at least a gator farm or an orange juice stand within jogging distance.

Florida is much too big and diverse to swallow in one gulp. The following pages are designed to help you find your way around the state in smaller sips.

● **South Florida** is anchored by Metropolitan Miami and Miami Beach, with its famous Art Deco District. It extends west to take in the wild expanse of the Everglades and Big Cypress Swamp, then south to the Florida Keys.

● **The Atlantic Coast** stretches from Fort Lauderdale, within easy reach of Miami, right up to Jacksonville in the far north – taking in en route Palm Beach, the Space Coast, Daytona Beach, and historic St Augustine.

● **Central Florida** revolves around Orlando and the crowd-pulling attractions such as Walt Disney World Resort.

● **The Gulf Coast** has Tampa-St Petersburg as its nucleus, with Marco Island at its southern end and Cedar Key at its northern tip. Sarasota and Fort Myers are the other major cities in this region.

● **North Florida** encompasses the Panhandle region – anchored by Tallahassee, the state capital, in the east, and Pensacola in the far west. It also takes in the "Forgotten Coast," a strip of lightly developed barrier islands in Florida's Big Bend region known for its natural beauty, bountiful seafood, and old-time seaside villages. ❏

---

**PRECEDING PAGES:** Miami Beach; kayak trip into Everglades National Park; Gulf Islands National Seashore near Pensacola in the Florida Panhandle.
**LEFT:** a relaxing afternoon at the Don CeSar Beach Resort in St Pete Beach.
**TOP:** the Florida Aquarium, Tampa. **ABOVE RIGHT:** fishing on Amelia Island.

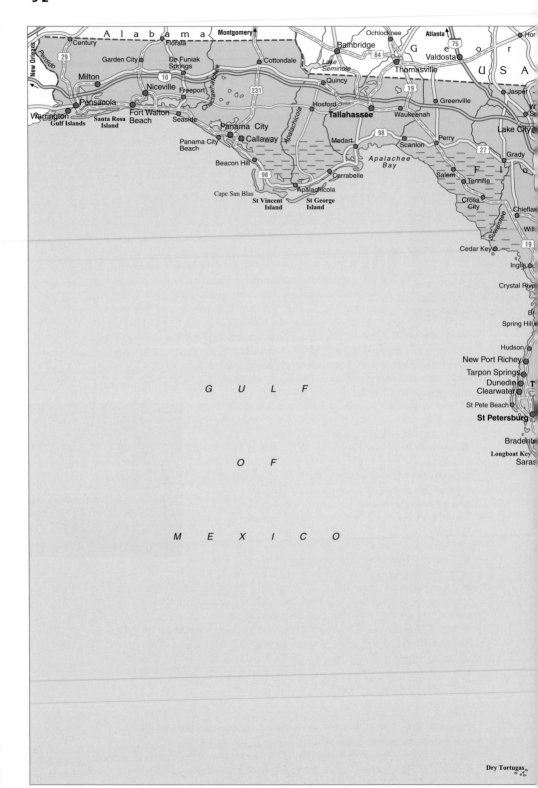

Alabama

Montgomery

Atlanta

Ochlocknee

New Orleans

Century

Florala

Bainbridge

Georgia

Garden City

De Funiak Springs

Cottondale

Valdosta

USA

Milton

Niceville

Freeport

Quincy

Greenville

Jasper

Pensacola

Fort Walton Beach

Seaside

Hosford

Tallahassee

Waukeenah

Warrington

Santa Rosa Island

Panama City

Callaway

Lake City

Gulf Islands

Panama City Beach

Medart

Scanlon

Perry

Beacon Hill

Apalachee Bay

Salem

Grady

Carrabelle

Tennille

FlO

Cape San Blas

Apalachicola

Cross City

Chiefla

St Vincent Island

St George Island

Will

Cedar Key

Inglis

Crystal River

Br

Spring Hill

Hudson

GULF

New Port Richey

Tarpon Springs

Dunedin

Clearwater

St Pete Beach

St Petersburg

OF

Bradent

Longboat Key

Saras

MEXICO

Dry Tortugas

Florida

0                    50 miles
0            50 km

N

Savannah
Cumberland
Island
Fernandina
Beach
allahan
ne
a
1
Jacksonville
Beach
ksonville
Starke
d
St Augustine
a
aldo
esville
Palatka
Flagler Beach
Bunnell
Ormond Beach
Ocala
L.
George
Daytona Beach
Barberville
Belleview
De Land
New Smyrna Beach
Deltona
Eustis
95
sburg
Sanford
Pine
Hills
Ocoee
Titusville
Kennedy Space Center
Bellwood
Walt Disney World
Orlando
Cape
Canaveral
linton
eights
27
Kissimmee
St Cloud
Cocoa
Holopaw
4
Winter Haven
Melbourne
sland
Bartow
Lake
Wales
Yeehaw
Junction
95
Sebastian
Peace
Vero Beach
ifo Springs
Sebring
Fort
Drum
Fort Pierce
Arcadia
Okeechobee
Port Saint Lucie
Stuart
75
Palmdale
Lake
Okeechobee
Jupiter
Port Charlotte
Canal
Point
North Palm Beach
41
Caloosahatchee
Palm Beach Shores
La
Belle
Clewiston
27
Belle
Glade
West Palm Beach
Cape
Coral
Fort Myers
Boynton Beach
Delray Beach
d
Immokalee
Boca Raton
27
Pompano Beach
Naples
Plantation
Fort Lauderdale
75
Hollywood
Big Cypress
Swamp
Carol City
Miami
Marco Island
41
Hialeah
Miami Beach
Ten Thousand
Islands
Chokoloskee
Kendall
Coral Gables
The Everglades
Perrine
Homestead
Cutler
Ridge
Everglades
National Park
Cape Sable
Key
Largo
esas
Keys
Pine Island
Key West
Marathon

A T L A N T I C
O C E A N

B A H A M A S

Little Abaco
Island
Grand Bahama Island
Great Abaco
Island
Freeport

New
Providence
Island

Andros
Island

Straits of Florida
Florida Bay
F l o r i d a   K e y s

## SOUTHBEACH

↑ Post Office

↑ Española Way

← Police Station

← Old City Hall

← Flamingo Park

→ Collins Avenue Shopping District

→ Ocean Drive

MIAMIBEACH

# SOUTH FLORIDA

Miami offers urban thrills, with the Everglades just a short drive away and, to the south, the alluring, tropical Florida Keys

outh Florida is a region of extremes. In Miami you will find one of the most cosmopolitan cities in the United States – a great metropolis with a distinctly Caribbean flavor. In South Beach, the Art Deco architecture, swank shops, sizzling nightlife, and throngs of beautiful people (including quite a few actors and models) are the very height of celebrity chic.

Just beyond the superhighways and skyscrapers of metropolitan Miami are the swamps of the Everglades – an alligator-inhabited area of 1.4 million acres (565,000 hectares). This "river of grass" encompasses a fascinating blend of tropical and temperate environments, a laboratory where nature experiments with the ever-changing cycles of life and death.

Emblematic of Florida's physical and cultural connection to the Caribbean, the state's southern boundary doesn't simply come to an abrupt end but trickles gently away in a necklace of coral and limestone islands known as the Keys. The archipelago stretches 180 miles (290km) from Miami's Biscayne Bay to the Dry Tortugas, just 86 miles (140km) north of Havana. The dozens of islands are sewn together by 113-mile-long (182-km) US Highway 1, the Overseas Highway, stretching across 43 bridges from Key Largo to Key West.

From the scuba culture of the Upper Keys to the Bohemian counterculture of Key West, each island maintains its own identity. Even the people are different from one key to the next: disillusioned Gold Coasters populate the upper islands, while natives of the lower keys proudly call themselves Conchs and have removed themselves emphatically from the 9-to-5 hustle of mainstream life. Mañanaland, Margaritaville, the American Riviera – the Keys have been called many things. Whatever the appellation, they are a place to take off your watch and kick back.                ❑

---

**LEFT:** a favorite of celebrities, models, and other "beautiful people," South Beach is a hub of sizzling nightlife and stylish shops. **TOP:** lounging on Smathers Beach in Key West. **ABOVE RIGHT:** sunset reddens the horizon at Key Largo.
**FOLLOWING PAGES:** the Atlantic breaks on Miami Beach.

# METROPOLITAN MIAMI

**South Florida's urban hub is a crossroads of Latin American, Caribbean, and Yankee cultures with a vibrant arts scene, great restaurants, and a distinctly tropical ambience**

**M**iami is the big dot on the Florida map. Brash, beautiful, exotic, and vibrant, it is the state's most complex and multifaceted city, large in size as well as personality. Made up of over 30 municipalities, "Greater Miami" is situated within Miami-Dade County and encompasses over 500 sq miles (1,300 sq km) that contain a rich and diverse ethnic stew. About 60 percent of the area's population is foreign born, which means the city speaks with many accents – Spanish, French, Hebrew, Portuguese, Russian, Creole, and Jamaican, to name just a few.

With a population of over 2.4 million, Greater Miami has its share of big-city problems and downtrodden neighborhoods, but it also has a stunningly beautiful natural landscape, a cutting-edge art community, the best Latin music this side of the Gulf Stream, and a restaurant scene that has finally come of age. Throughout its many incarnations of the past 20 years – from Paradise Lost to the New Riviera – it has always fascinated visitors and for good reason. It is full of energy yet laid-back and casual. It embraces all things shiny and new but remains a few steps behind other major American cities. It boasts world-class sophistication but is riddled with Third World insecurities.

None of this is more apparent than in downtown Miami where dozens of new skyscrapers – many of them unfinished and empty – reach for the sky as well as status on the world stage. The building boom of the past decade has been phenomenal, fueled by get-rich-quick speculators and foreign investors. But it has also created an urban core that's jam-packed with construction sites and road detours that will likely be around for years to come. This congested mess, however, has in no way dampened the excitement and new-blood enthusiasm that permeates the neighborhood.

## Downtown

As it curves northward along Biscayne Bay, Brickell Avenue eases into down-

**LEFT:** Biltmore Hotel.
**BELOW:** Bayfront Park.

*Waterfront shopping and dining at Bayside Marketplace.*

town Miami and is studded with futuristic buildings, many of them banks, that sparkle at night with colorful neon lights. Once there, Brickell crosses over the Miami River and becomes the major thoroughfare of **Biscayne Boulevard.** On the south bank of the Miami River and the east side of Brickell Avenue sits a controversial piece of land. Here, in 1989, construction workers unexpectedly uncovered a circle of stones that turned out to be the remnants of a Tequesta Indian settlement dating back over a

thousand years. After years of battles between historians and the developers who owned the land, the site – now deemed the Miami Circle – is slated to be turned into an urban park that will preserve the stones and contain an interpretive center placing them in their historical context.

## By the bay

Anchoring much of the downtown tourist traffic on Biscayne Boulevard is **Bayside Marketplace** ❶ (401 Biscayne Blvd; tel: 305-577-3344; Mon–Sat 10am–11pm, Sun 11am–8pm; free), a 16-acre (6-hectare) waterfront extravaganza of over 100 shops, restaurants, and attractions that

often hosts free live concerts. Within walking distance of Bayside to the south is **Bayfront Park**, a verdant and peaceful waterfront public space.

At the southern end of the park is a memorial designed by the late Japanese sculptor Isamu Noguchi and dedicated to the astronauts and crew who lost their lives aboard the space shuttle *Challenger* when it exploded over Florida in 1986. At night, Bayfront Park often puts on laser-light shows that throw beams of bright colors into the Miami sky.

A few steps to the north of Bayside is the **American Airlines Arena**, home to the Miami Heat basketball team and a venue for major pop, rock, and Latin music events. Just beyond it is **Bicentennial Park**, a lush greenway that often hosts outdoor concerts and is scheduled to be turned into a new museum complex in the next decade. Nearby is the entrance to the **Port of Miami**, a major marine commerce hub as well as the busiest port for cruise ships in the world, funneling over 3 million passengers a year to all points in the Caribbean.

Across the street is the **Freedom Tower ❷**, one of the more significant historic buildings in the downtown area. Built in 1925, the peach-colored Mediterranean Revival building was the home of the now defunct *Miami News* and served as a processing center in the 1960s for Cuban immigrants who fled the communist takeover of their country, hence the name. Today, the perfectly preserved 17-story building occasionally hosts art shows and cultural events.

## Art and culture

Behind the Tower are a series of dense streets filled with electronic and jewelry shops, and the downtown campus of **Miami-Dade College**, site of the **Miami Book Fair International** held every November. Nearby on Flagler Street is the **Gusman Cultural Center**, a glorious baroque-style theater that hosts the **Miami International Film Festival** each winter. Named after railroad magnate Henry Flagler, Flagler Street is one of the busiest downtown, packed with

small stores catering to South American shoppers who arrive in Miami with large empty suitcases.

At 101 W. Flagler is the **Metro-Dade Cultural Plaza ❸**. A popular lunch site for downtown lawyers and office workers, the Plaza has an expansive tiled courtyard graced with flowing pools of water. It is also home to the **Miami-Dade Main Library**; the **Historical Museum of Southern Florida** (tel: 305-375-1492; Mon–Sat 10am–5pm; charge), which maintains a permanent exhibit depicting 10,000 years of South Florida history; and the **Miami Art Museum** (tel: 305-375-3000; Tue–Fri 10am–5pm, Sat–Sun noon–5pm; charge), where rotating exhibits range from American modern to European classical art.

The most recent addition to downtown's cultural hub and a major element in the city's revitalization plan is the **Arsht Center for the Performing Arts ❹** (1350 Biscayne Blvd; tel: 305-949-6722, www.arshtcenter.com). The $461 million Cesar Pelli-designed center was intended to elevate Miami's ranking among "the world's great cities" and prove that it's no longer a cultural wasteland.

*Many Miami addresses are given according to their location relative to Miami Avenue and Flagler Street: eg 1200 NW 26th Street is 12 blocks west of Miami Avenue and 26 blocks north of Flagler Street.*

**BELOW:** the County Courthouse near the Metro-Dade Cultural Plaza.

*Artist Carlos Betancourt with some of his work in Wynwood.*

**BELOW:** the Public Library at the Metro-Dade Cultural Plaza.

## The Upper East Side

Continuing north on Biscayne Boulevard, the urban atmosphere becomes more gritty but also more interesting and artsy. In recent years this area has been tagged the Upper East Side by hip young developers (many from New York) who see the neighborhood as an evolving work of art.

Also known as the **Biscayne Corridor**, this bustling area includes the neighborhood of **Buena Vista**, the **Wynwood Art District**, and the **Miami Design District**. A Bohemian frontier, it's where many enterprising artistic types have settled after fleeing the mainstreaming of South Beach in the last few years. Some are hard at work breathing new life into old MiMo (Miami Modern architecture) motels built in the 1950s or transforming shabby bungalows and small apartment buildings into hipster enclaves where emerging young artists in worn-out jeans mingle with interior decorators in designer clothes. With dozens of sleek Greenwich Village-like lofts popping up all over, it's a thriving area quickly rising in prominence in the

Spectacularly beautiful, the venue includes a state-of-the-art concert hall and a separate ballet house that host major cultural events, including those of four resident companies – the **Concert Association of Florida**, **Florida Grand Opera**, **Miami City Ballet**, and **New World Symphony**. The smaller "black box" theater is where more offbeat and intimate productions are held. On weekends, the center has free events on the plaza, such as flamenco dance classes, Caribbean steel bands, and Latin jazz ensembles.

MIAMI-DADE PUBLIC LIBRARY

*Recommended Restaurants and Bars on pages 114–5*

international art world where intrepid visitors can view impressive private art collections during the day or dodge the lingering drug dealers late at night.

## Wynwood

From 19th to 37th streets is the neighborhood of Wynwood, where funky galleries are sandwiched between auto repair shops that also share the streets with two highly regarded private collections – the **Rubell Family Collection ❺** (95 NW 29th St; tel: 305-573-6090; Wed–Sun 10am–6pm; closed summer; charge) and the **Margulies Collection ❻** (591 NW 27th St; tel: 305-576-1051; Fri–Sat 11am–4pm; closed summer; free). Housed in enormous warehouses, both collections contain a broad representation of contemporary art, sculpture, and photography.

The Rubell site is owned by New Yorkers Don and Mera Rubell, relatives of the late Steve Rubell, who owned the famous Studio 54 nightclub. Other respected art venues include the **Cisneros Fontanals Arts Foundation** and the **Frederic Snitzer**, **Diana Lowenstein**, **Spinello**, **Gary Nader**, and **World**

**Class Boxing** galleries. On the second Saturday of every month, Wynwood – in conjunction with the Design District – hosts a Gallery Walk when art lovers stroll from gallery to gallery and enjoy complimentary wine, champagne, and hors d'oeuvres.

## Design District

Although the Wynwood Art District is the sassy new kid on the block, it would not have been possible if it weren't for the more dignified **Design District** (www.miamidesigndistrict.net) a few blocks to the north. About 16 square blocks that run from NE 36th to NE 41st streets between NE 2nd and N. Miami avenues, the Design District is a dense cluster of all things divine in the design world. In the 1920s the area was called Decorator's Row and has since gone through various periods of boom and bust. These days represent another boom period, and the compact village is once again an example of tropical splendor.

Easily explored in a few hours, it's full of high-end furniture importers, interior design showrooms, art galleries, and kitchen and garden boutiques. Anchor-

*An art installation at the Rubell Family Collection.*

**BELOW:** a show opening at the Rubell Family Collection.

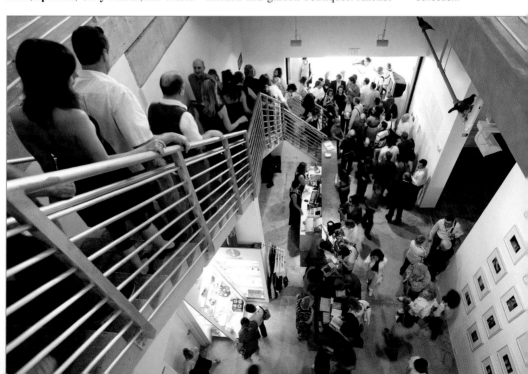

*A mural adorns a Little Haiti building.*

**BELOW:** ceramic saints and other figures at a Little Haiti botanica.

ing the cluster is the historic **Moore Building** ❼ (4040 NE 2nd Ave), a gleaming white four-story gem that has an outdoor bamboo garden lounge and a nonprofit art gallery that consistently exhibits internationally acclaimed artists. The Moore serves as home base for **Design Miami**, the design offshoot of the phenomenally successful Art Basel Miami Beach, held each December. During the event, the Moore Building and many other venues in the Upper East Side have satellite art and design shows, parties, films, and seminars that compliment the main schedule of events at the Miami Beach Convention Center.

Most shops in the Design District are open to the public Monday through Saturday from 11am to 5pm. As the area has grown in popularity, a few clever restaurants have shown up as well. Among them: **Sheeba**, an exotic Ethiopian eatery; **Grass**, a sophisticated al fresco dining space; and **Michael's Genuine Food and Drink**, an unpretentious but highly rated bistro *(see listings, page 115).*

## Little Haiti

One of the great things about Miami is its ethnic enclaves, and Little Haiti is no doubt among the more fascinating. Beginning a few blocks north of the Design District, it lies within the boundaries of 79th Street to the north, 46th Street to the south, Biscayne Boulevard to the east, and I-95 to the west.

Like many big-city ethnic neighborhoods, it is a juxtaposition of immigrant optimism and inner-city decay, and it offers an intimate encounter with a rich Caribbean culture. Although perhaps not as economically successful as their Cuban-immigrant counterparts, Miami's Haitian community has prospered in the local arts scene and now plays an active roll in city politics. Many Miami Haitians have moved into the middle-class suburbs, but the heart of the community is still in Little Haiti.

Here mom-and-pop grocery stores and small restaurants thrive as they cater to the community with heaping servings

of griot (fried pork), lambi (stewed conch), and spicy oxtail stew. There are several small botanicas in the neighborhood, and they welcome visitors for a look. Shops that specialize in religious paraphernalia and medicinal herbs for practitioners of the Afro-Caribbean religions of voodoo and Santeria, botanicas can be found in many other areas of Miami as well.

The **Haitian Catholic Center** and **Church of Notre Dame d'Haiti** ❽ (130 NE 62nd St; tel: 305-751-6289) has long been an advocate of Haitian immigrant rights in Miami. It is also a safe and welcoming venue to get to meet local Haitians, especially on Sunday mornings when thousands come out for a Mass that blends traditional Catholicism with rhythmic Haitian music.

A few blocks away is **Libreri Mapou** (5919 NE 2nd Ave; tel: 305-757-9922), one of the few bookstores in Florida that specializes in Haitian Creole books and music. Owned by Haitian writer Jan Mapou, the bookshop also stocks Haitian arts and crafts and is a popular gathering place for Haitian writers and musicians.

## North Miami

About 2 miles (3km) to the north of Little Haiti is the city of North Miami, which for a few years had a Haitian-American mayor. A very diverse middle-class neighborhood, the city is also one of the area's up-and-coming arts districts. Most of the action here is around 125th Street, where there are several cafés, restaurants, and galleries that put on poetry readings and world music concerts. The big draw, however, is the **Museum of Contemporary Art** ❾ (770 NE 125th St; tel: 305-893-6211, www.mocanomi.org; Tue–Sat 11am–5pm, Sun

*The Museum of Contemporary Art is host to changing exhibits as well as films, musical performances, and artist workshops.*

**BELOW:** a guitarist plays for passersby in Little Haiti.

**BELOW:** Don Johnson and Olivia Brown of *Miami Vice.*
**BELOW RIGHT:** a reconstructed cloister at the Ancient Spanish Monastery.

noon–5pm; charge). Known for fresh contemporary art with lots of attitude, MoCA features rotating exhibits of local and internationally recognized artists. Its permanent collection includes works by Julian Schnabel, Louise Nevelson, and Yoko Ono. On the last Friday of each month is a free outdoor concert; the audience gathers on the grass with coolers full of wine and takes in the sounds of jazz, Latin, and folk music.

The other major attraction in North Miami is the **Ancient Spanish Monastery** ⑩ (16711 W. Dixie Hwy; tel: 305-945-1461, www.spanishmonastery.com; Mon–Sat 9am–4.30pm, Sun noon–2pm; charge). Built in Segovia, Spain, in the 12th century, then dismantled and shipped to Florida in 1925, the monastery was rebuilt in this location in 1952. Tucked behind stone walls with meandering tropical gardens, it's now a peaceful oasis within a busy neighborhood that is welcoming to visitors from all walks of life.

## Little Havana

Another ethnic enclave that offers an authentic experience is Little Havana, located in the south part of Miami-Dade

County just to the west of downtown. It is here that the first wave of Cuban immigrants settled in the early 1960s, and the cultural infusion is still apparent. While the Cuban population of Greater Miami – approximately a million people – has spread throughout every corner of the city, it is in Little Havana that the passion for the lost homeland is most profound. In this neighborhood the scent of Cuban coffee and the blare of salsa trumpets permeate the air, and heated arguments about a post-Castro Cuba can be overheard on almost every corner.

Although it is still a scruffy, lower-income neighborhood, Little Havana has gone upscale in some places with the addition of new art galleries, nightclubs, and restaurants that serve as the symbolic heart of the exile community. On the last Friday of the month, the place pulsates with **Viernes Culturales** (Cultural Fridays), a street party of concerts, gallery openings, and historic walking tours of the neighborhood.

Most of the action takes place on **Calle Ocho** ⑪ (SW 8th St) between 14th and 27th avenues. This is also where the wildly flamboyant Latin street

## Miami on Screen

With its exotic ambience and endless sun, it's no surprise that Miami has served as the setting for so many films and TV shows. It started in 1941 with *Moon Over Miami*, starring the woman with the great legs, Betty Grable. Frank Sinatra came to town in 1959 to film *Hole in the Head*, followed the next year by Jerry Lewis starring in *The Bellboy*. The swinging sixties was the decade of Jackie Gleason, who filmed his weekly TV show in the "sun and fun capital of the world." It was also when American TV viewers fell in love with a friendly bottlenose dolphin named Flipper.

The 1980s brought grit and lots of it – *Scarface,* starring Al Pacino as a Cuban drug dealer, and the violent yet glamorous *Miami Vice* television series. More contemporary films include *Ace Ventura Pet Detective* (1994), *Miami Rhapsody* (1995), *The Perez Family* (1995), *Striptease* (1996), *The Birdcage* (1996), *Something About Mary* (1998), Eddie Murphy's *Holy Man* (1998); *Bad Boys II* (2003), and, of course, the resurrection of *Miami Vice* as a feature film (2006).

*Recommended Restaurants and Bars on pages 114–5*

festival known as "Calle Ocho" takes place each March.

But you don't need a festival to enjoy Calle Ocho, because the street bustles with action both day and night. At **Versailles Restaurant** *(see listing, page 115)* the Cuban food is hearty and plentiful, and the clientele ranges from power brokers and politicians to poets and musicians. Always loud and very busy, it's perhaps the most famous Cuban restaurant in the US. Directly across the street is **La Carreta** *(see listing, page 115)*, another popular Cuban eatery, open 24 hours.

Heading eastward toward the Miami River, in the 1600 block of 8th Street, there are a few good finds, including **Alfaro's**, a cozy wine and tapas lounge; **Art District Cigars,** where visitors can watch artisans hand-roll stogies while taking in live Latin music; and **Molina Fine Art**, a gallery featuring vibrant paintings that reflect tales from Afro-Cuban folklore. Around the corner is the small **Bay of Pigs Museum** (1821 SW 9th St; tel: 305-649-4719, www. bayofpigsmuseum.org; Mon–Sat 9am–4pm; charge), a crowded collection of artifacts and memorabilia honoring those who died in the failed 1961 US invasion of Cuba.

## Just like home

On the corner of 8th Street and 15th Avenue is **Domino Park** ⑫, also known as Máximo Gómez Park, a fenced-in courtyard where elderly Cuban men gather for lively games of dominoes and talk about the good old days in Havana. Park officials enforce a custom that restricts admittance to men over 55, but tourists are welcome.

Next door to the park is **Little Havana To Go**, a playful souvenir shop where visitors are treated to a complimentary *cafecito* and the shelves are brimming with all things Cuban – music, art, domino sets, cigars, and guayabera shirts. Across the street from the shop is the beautiful **Tower Theater**. Built as a movie palace in 1926, this perfectly restored Art Deco building is owned by the City of Miami and is host to film festivals, lectures, book signings, dance, and theatrical performances.

About two blocks away is **La Casa de los Trucos** (1343 8th St), a business originally founded in Cuba. Also known as House of Tricks, this neighborhood

*Cuban men engage in spirited games of dominoes at Domino Park.*

**BELOW LEFT:** Little Havana cigar shop.
**BELOW:** Calle Ocho festival.

*Smells of Havana in El Credito Cigar Factory.*

**BELOW:**
the Venetian Pool, on the National Register of Historic Places, is open to the public.

institution sells costumes, funny hats, masks, maracas, and magic tricks and is always packed in the weeks leading up to Halloween. On the corner of SW 12th Street is **La Esquina de Tejas**, a family-style Cuban restaurant that still boasts about the day that President Ronald Reagan stopped in for lunch while on the campaign trail. On the same street is **Casino Records**, a famed Latin music shop that sells an enormous selection of material, including early 20th-century Cuban danzons, Latin jazz, Afro-Cuban drumming, mambo, salsa, meringue, tango, and samba.

At 1106 8th Street is **El Credito Cigar Factory** ⓭ (tel: 305-858-4162; Mon–Sat 8am–5pm), the oldest and largest cigar factory in Miami and the producer of four distinct brands, including the famous La Gloria Cubana. Founded in 1907 in Cuba, the shop moved to Miami after the Cuban revolution, and the interior feels, smells, and looks like Havana circa 1950. Dozens of workers chop heaps of tobacco on antique tables and load them into vintage wooden presses as Spanish language radio programs blare in the background.

## Coral Gables

To the south of Little Havana is a city where many affluent Cuban exiles moved after climbing the socio-economic ladder in Miami. Designed by developer George Merrick in the 1920s, Coral Gables is an enchanting city of Mediterranean-style architecture, ornate limestone arches, and a vibrant art and culture scene. With avenues named after cities in Spain and street signs on tiny white stones, it is not easy to navigate. But it has several landmark properties that are worth seeking out.

Surrounded by palatial mansions, the old **Biltmore Hotel** ⓮ (1200 Anastasia Ave; tel: 305-445-1926) was the grand dame of South Florida hotels in the Roaring Twenties. Its swimming pool – billed as the largest in the US, was once the setting for elegant water ballets, and Johnny Weissmuller, star of Tarzan movies, set a world swimming record here in the 1930s. Today it is a playground for the international jet set and is often used for fashion shoots. The hotel offers free walking tours of the property on Sunday afternoons.

Another stunning swimming hole in Coral Gables is the **Venetian Pool** ⓯

*Recommended Restaurants and Bars on pages 114–5*

(2701 DeSoto Blvd; tel: 305-460-5306; Mon–Fri 11am–6.30pm, Sat–Sun 10am–4.30pm; charge), a freshwater coral rock lagoon with caves and waterfalls amid lush tropical gardens. The pool is drained nightly and refilled in the morning with artesian well water. Its Venetian-style architecture and soft sandy beach provide a fine setting for an afternoon swim.

## Miracle Mile

The commercial center of the Gables lies along and parallel to **Miracle Mile** ⑯, a visitor-friendly street filled with upscale boutiques, cafés and restaurants. From several points on Miracle Mile, the **Coral Gables Trolley** offers free transportation throughout the business hub of the city every day to 10pm.

The Trolley is also a convenient way to take in the **Gables Gallery Night** held on the first Friday of every month. Mostly specializing in fine Latin American art, there are many respected galleries in downtown Coral Gables such as **Virginia Miller Galleries**, **Americas Collection**, **La Boheme Fine Art**, and **Cernuda Arte**. There are several modern luxury hotels in the downtown area, including the Hyatt

Regency and Omni Colonnade, but they can't compete with the charming Old World ambience of the historic **Hotel Place St Michel** (162 Alcazar Ave), which was built during the 1920s and includes an intimate French restaurant.

Within walking distance is Miami's literary epicenter, **Books & Books** (265 Aragon Ave; tel: 305-442-4408, www.booksandbooks.com; daily 9am–11pm). Housed in a stark white Mediterranean building with an inner courtyard, this is more than a bookstore. It's a full-service restaurant and bar that also offers live music and foreign films at night. Every night the store hosts readings by some of the world's most famous authors – Nobel laureates, Pulitzer Prize winners, politicians, presidents, talk-show hosts, movie stars, and others. It also presents many local authors and readings in both English and Spanish.

## Art, history, nature

Beyond the downtown district toward the southeast of Coral Gables is the **University of Miami**, home of the **Lowe**

*Avid readers gather for books, author events, drinking, and dining at Books & Books, with three locations in the Miami area.*

**BELOW:** the Biltmore Hotel.

*Classic figurative sculpture at the Lowe Museum.*

**BELOW:**
schoolchildren take a tour of the Lowe Museum.

**Art Museum ⓱** (1301 Stanford Dr; tel: 305-284-3535, www.lowemuseum.org; Tue, Wed, Fri, Sat 10am–5pm, Thu noon–7pm, Sun noon–5pm; charge). One of Miami's finest museums, the Lowe has an impressive permanent collection that includes Renaissance and Baroque art; 19th- and 20th-century European art; Egyptian, Greek, and Roman antiquities; Latin American and Asian collections; and Native American art and artifacts.

Continuing east, near Biscayne Bay, the attractions feature the handiwork of nature instead of people. **Matheson Hammock Park ⓲** (9610 Old Cutler Road; daily 6am–sunset; charge) is a 100-acre (40-hectare) park with a marina, saltwater atoll pool, and small beach. Along with beautiful walkways and cycling trails through dense mangroves, Matheson Hammock has a restaurant, picnic facilities, barbecues, and sailboat and kite-surfing rentals.

A little farther down the road is **Fairchild Tropical Garden** (10901 Old Cutler Rd; tel: 305-667-1651; daily 9.30am–4:30pm; charge), the largest garden of its type in the continental US. Named for famed botanist David Fairchild, it has an outstanding collection of tropical flowering trees and over 5,000 species of palms, ferns, and orchids. Many species in the park are rare and endangered; others are used for medicinal purposes and some for the making of perfume – the ylang-ylang tree blossoms are the primary ingredient of Channel No. 5. Tram tours include a 40-minute narrated ride that is informative and fun. A virtual oasis in

the middle of a big city, Fairchild also has several lakes and caves that are a delight to the senses.

## Coconut Grove

Next door to Coral Gables is the Miami neighborhood of **Coconut Grove**. Formerly an art colony and hippie hangout, the Grove, as locals call it, is one of Miami's oldest and most interesting neighborhoods. Built by Bahamian laborers about a century ago, it still has much of the laid-back attitude it is famous for and at various times in its history has claimed famous American writers, musicians, and artists as residents. Each June it hosts the **Goombay Festival**, a weekend street party that pays tribute to its Bahamian roots with live Junkanoo bands, conch fritter vendors, and dancing in the streets.

Under a dense canopy of green, the houses in the Grove run the gamut from palatial pink mansions to funky old Florida cottages, and there is still a Saturday morning **farmers' market** (Grand Ave and McDonald St), where locals gather to buy organic fruits and vegetables. The main commercial activities center around Main

Highway and Commodore Plaza, where on weekend nights the pedestrian traffic is heavy. Here, restaurants such as **Greenstreets** *(see listing, page 114)* and **Cefalo's Wine Corner** are busy both day and night. Nearby is the old **Coconut Grove Playhouse**, a Mediterranean-style venue built in 1926 but currently out of commission due to financial woes.

Across the street is the **Barnacle State Historic Site ⓭** (3485 Main Hwy; tel: 305-442-6866; Fri–Mon 9am–4pm; charge), home of the Miami pioneer Commodore Ralph Munroe (1851–1933), a boat-builder, mariner, botanist, and photographer. Built in 1891, the home sits on a coral ridge overlooking Biscayne Bay and is filled with family heirlooms and period antiques. It is totally secluded from traffic and other buildings. It's possible to sit on the home's wrap-around porch and imagine what life was like in South Florida before tourism took hold of the economy. Tours of the home and grounds are given about every two hours throughout the day.

*Fairchild Tropical Garden is filled with colorful flowering plants.*

**BELOW:** dawn breaks over a lake fringed with palm trees at Fairchild Tropical Garden.

*Coconut Grove has a reputation for being an artsy, eclectic community.*

**BELOW:** special events at CocoWalk include fashion shows, live music, and ethnic festivals.

## Shop and dine

A few blocks away is **CocoWalk** ⑳ (3015 Grand Ave; www.cocowalk.net; Sun–Thu 10am–10pm, Fri–Sat 10am–11pm, bars and restaurants open later), a multi-story shopping center and entertainment complex and the Grove's busiest attraction. Popular with college students on weekends, it has an eight-screen movie theater and numerous bars.

Next door is the **Streets of Mayfair** (2911 Grand Ave; tel: 305-448-1700; Mon–Fri 10am–7pm, Thu to 8pm, Sun noon–5pm), another shopping venue but this one anchored by the **Mayfair Hotel & Spa** (tel: 305-441-0000), a tranquil and plush property with a soaring atrium, copper sculptures, and gushing fountains.

Near the entrance of CocoWalk, Grand Avenue connects with McFarlane Road, and this leads to S. Bayshore Drive. At McFarlane and Bayshore is **Peacock Park** ㉑, a large green playground that once contained South Florida's first hotel, the Peacock Inn, built in 1882. Today the waterfront park is popular with Frisbee players and sunbathers, and it occasionally hosts outdoor concerts.

Continuing north on Bayshore Drive is **Miami City Hall** ㉒, a beautifully preserved Art Deco building originally built to be a passenger terminal for Pan American Airways' seaplanes in 1934. Nearby is **Dinner Key Marina**, a popular mooring site always filled with sailboats and yachts, as well as several landmark restaurants, including **Monty's Stone Crab**, **Chart House**, and **Scotty's Landing** (*see listing, page 114*).

## Science museum

Continuing northward, Bayshore Drive becomes Miami Avenue, where you'll find the **Miami Museum of Science and Space Planetarium** ㉓ (3280 S. Miami Ave; tel: 305-646-4200, www.miamisci.org; daily 10am–6pm; charge). Dedicated to science exploration and the mysteries of outer space, this hands-on museum contains over 150 exhibits, natural specimens, and interactive games. The planetarium offers astronomy shows on Friday and Saturday evenings guided

*Recommended Restaurants and Bars on pages 114–5*

by Jack Horkheimer, well-known public television astronomer.

## Vizcaya

Tucked behind coral rock walls across the street from the science museum is Miami's grandest residence – **Vizcaya Museum and Gardens** ㉔ (3251 S. Miami Ave; tel: 305-250-9133, www.vizcayamuseum .org; daily 9.30am–4.30pm; charge; *see pages 116–7*). Built between 1914 and 1916 for industrialist James Deering and intended to resemble an Italian Renaissance villa, Vizcaya required over 10,000 laborers to complete. During its heyday it occupied 180 acres (70 hectares) and was a totally self-sufficient enclave with its own livestock and vegetable gardens.

Today, the opulent 70-room palace is a museum filled with European antiques, gold leaf furniture, oriental carpets, tapestries, and fine art. Its baroque and rococo interiors look exactly as they did when it was a private home. A few of the more dramatic rooms are the Tea House, inspired by French architecture; the Music Room, which contains an 18th-century harpsichord; and the Dining Room, which has the air

of a Renaissance-era banqueting hall.

Docent-guided tours are offered all day long, and a special "Vizcaya by Moonlight" tour is offered one evening a month during the full moon from January to April. Surrounded by manicured gardens and lushly vegetated islands connected by footbridges, the mansion also has a coral rock grotto and swimming pool, dozens of outdoor sculptures, an orchid house, and a coral rock dock on Biscayne Bay complete with a vintage gondola. ❏

*CocoWalk is a self-contained complex with more than 30 shops, restaurants, galleries, nightclubs, and movie theaters.*

**BELOW:** Vizcaya Museum and Gardens.

# RESTAURANTS AND BARS

## Restaurants

Prices for a three-course dinner per person, excluding tax, tip, and beverages:

**$** = under $20
**$$** = $20–45
**$$$** = $45–60
**$$$$** = over $60

### Coconut Grove

**Berrie's**
2884 SW 27th Ave
Tel: 305-448-2111
B, L & D daily
A popular hangout with knowledgeable locals, this little juice bar has grown into a full-fledged restaurant with salads, sandwiches, wraps, and handmade pastas as well as fresh blackened mahi mahi. The setting, with wooden tables, brick flooring, and market umbrellas, is charming

and the daily happy hour is the best in town. $$

**Bizcaya Grill at The Ritz Carlton Coconut Grove**
3300 SW 27th Ave
Tel: 305-644-4675
B, L & D daily
This Mediterranean stunner is perfect for an elegant meal in the otherwise very casual Grove. Set against a cascading waterfall with accents of wood and marble, the food and service are top-notch to match. $$$$

**Greenstreet Café**
3110 Commodore Plaza
Tel: 305-567-0662
B, L & D daily, Br Sat–Sun
This child- and dog-friendly café has great views of colorful characters gliding by one of Coconut Grove's

busiest corners. The French-Med fare includes a snapper in white wine sauce, vegetable lasagne, lamb burger with goat cheese on brioche, and divine desserts. $$

**The Original Daily Bread**
2400 SW 27th St
Tel: 305-856-5893
B, L & D Mon–Sat, L & D Sun
This Middle Eastern market and cafeteria-style eatery serves Miami's best hummus and baklava. There are seats inside among the racks of dried beans and bins of olives as well as outdoor tables. $

**Scotty's Landing**
3381 Pan American Dr
Tel: 305-854-2626
L & D daily
A salty shack with million-dollar views, this old-time Miami hangout on the marina offers grilled fish sandwiches, cole slaw, and tasty burgers. $$

### Coral Gables

**Cacao**
141 Giralda Ave
Tel: 305-445-1001
L & D Mon–Fri, D Sat
Intriguing Nuevo Latino cuisine and a stunning setting make this a popular gathering spot for foodies seeking the finer things in life. $$$$

**Fleming's Prime Steakhouse**
2525 Ponce de León Blvd
Tel: 305-569-7995
D daily
It may be a chain, but this value-priced chophouse

gives nearby steak spots a run for their money. The exceptional wine list features more than 100 labels by the glass. $$$

**Miss Saigon Bistro**
148 Giralda Ave
Tel: 305-446-8006
L Mon–Fri, D daily
Waiters in Vietnamese garb sing and sometimes dance, but they aren't the only attractions at this Restaurant Row veteran. The Vietnamese fare is fresh and tasty. $$$

**Palm d'Or at the Biltmore**
1200 Anastasia Ave
Tel: 305-445-1926
D Tue–Sat
Small plates of exquisite New French cuisine are served in one of Miami's most romantic settings. Deft wine pairings and a professional staff add to the experience. $$$$

**Pascal's on Ponce**
2611 Ponce de León Blvd
Tel: 305-444-2024
L Mon–Fri, D Mon–Sat
Magnifique French fare draws Francophiles to this pocket-size hideaway. Leave space for an exemplary dessert soufflé. $$$

### Downtown Miami

**Acqua at the Four Seasons Miami**
1435 Brickell Ave SE
Tel: 305-358-3535
B & L Mon–Sat, D daily, Br Sun
This international restaurant in the Four Seasons Hotel offers elegance

**LEFT:** artistic presentation on the Upper East Side.

unmatched in Miami. The food is excellent, and the European-trained servers know how to pamper their guests. The restaurant is reason enough to book a room. $$$$

## Caribbean Delight
236 NE 1st Ave
Tel: 305-381-9254
B, L & early D daily (closes at 6pm most nights)
Serving what may be the best Jamaican food this side of Kingston, this cheery little dive offers jerk chicken, curry goat, and much more. $

## Garcia's Seafood Grille
398 NW North River Dr
Tel: 305-375-0765
L & D daily
This seafood shack on the Miami River is great for grilled mahi-mahi, fried fish sandwiches, and stone crabs in season. $$

## Mosaico/Salero
1000 S. Miami Ave
Tel: 305-371-3473
Salero: L & D Mon–Sat
Mosaico: D Mon–Sat
A stunning refit of a 1920s firehouse, chic Spanish fare, and a romantic outdoor terrace distinguish this restaurant. Downstairs is casual tapas; upstairs is experimental cuisine with an emphasis on fresh fish. $$–$$$$

Little Havana
## Blue Sky Food by the Pound
3803 W. Flagler St
Tel: 305-642-4388
B, L & D daily
Locals love the hearty Cuban food, and they feast on it here or take it out to enjoy as a picnic. $

## Casa Juancho
2436 8th St
Tel: 305-642-2452
L & D daily
Cuban-Americans throng

this Latin spot, regarded as one of the best in Miami. $$

## La Caretta
3632 SW 8th St
Tel: 305-444-7501
Daily 24 hours
With outlets all over the city, this rustic fast-food chain offers cheap Cuban fare, especially welcome after a night on the town. $

## Islas Canarias
285 NW 27th Ave
Tel: 305-649-0440
B, L & D daily
Fast service and some of the best Cuban cooking in the neighborhood. $$

## Versailles
3555 SW 8th St
Tel: 305-444-0240
B, L & D daily
Feel the pulse of the Cuban community and enjoy traditional, hearty Cuban fare. $$

Upper East Side
## A
4582 NE 2nd Ave
Tel: 305-972-3358
D daily from 8pm
This is an artists' collective serving good food, including a range of vegetarian and vegan options. There's no liquor, so bring your own alcohol. $

## Canela Café
5132 Biscayne Blvd
Tel: 305-756-3930
L & D Mon–Sat
Excellent tapas are served at night at this Latin café. The paella is the best in town, and the lunch menu includes Cuban sandwiches, ropa vieja, and grilled meats. Great sangria, too. $$

## Dogma
7030 Biscayne Blvd
Tel: 305-759-3433
L & D daily
A real gourmet wiener

stand, this busy outlet also offers Greek salads, chicken sandwiches, thick-cut fries, and shakes. $

## Grass
28 NE 40th St
Tel: 305-573-3355
L Tue–Fri, D Wed–Sat
Dine alfresco at this cool, sophisticated restaurant and bar, with a well-deserved reputation for fresh, innovative cuisine with an Asian and Mediterranean flare. $$–$$$

## Michael's Genuine Food and Drink
130 NE 40th St
Tel: 305-573-5550
L Mon–Fri, D daily
Try fish, chicken, pizza, and other dishes prepared in the wood-fired oven at this collegial bistro and bar with seating indoors and out. $$–$$$

## Michy's
6927 Biscayne Blvd
Tel: 305-759-2001
L & D Tue–Sun
Book in advance for this charming 50-seat bistro. Celebrity chef Michelle Bernstein, with husband David running the front of the house, ensures a delicious meal. $$$

## Sheba Ethiopian Restaurant
4029 N. Miami Ave
Tel: 305-573-1819
L & D Mon–Sat, Sun D
Miami's first Ethiopian restaurant, this sexy outpost draws the artsy crowd from the nearby Design District. Low wooden tables and bright paintings make for an appealing setting. $$$

## Soyka
5556 E. 4th Court
Tel: 305-759-3117
L & D daily, Br Sat–Sun
Large portions and reasonable prices keep loyal patrons coming back to

this industrial-chic spot. Offerings like grilled salmon, big burgers, and hummus and pita make it an appealing choice for family meals, too. $$

Bars
Coconut Grove
## Café TuTu Tango
3015 Grand Ave
Tel: 305-529-2222
L & D daily
With a swinging singles scene fueled by imaginative drinks and eclectic small dishes, this is a perennial favorite in CocoWalk. All this is coupled with a killer sangria and an abundance of art, tango, belly dancing, and tarot readings. $$

Upper East Side
## Karu & Y Restaurant and Ultra Lounge
71 NW 14th St
Tel: 305-403-7850
D Tue–Sun
This multimillion-dollar lounge, club, restaurant, and performance space is a sanctuary for art, cuisine, and entertainment in lush surroundings.

## The Pawn Shop
1222 NE 2nd Ave
Tel: 305-373-3511
Wed–Sat 10pm–5am
An especially happening scene erupts here on Saturday nights with '80s music. The all-round good-time atmosphere continues until the wee small hours.

## XXI Amendment
190 NE 46th St
Tel: 305-571-7200
Tue–Sun to 3am, Sun to midnight
With a full liquor license and a bordello-like setting, this enticing space hosts live music and other cool performances. A tapas menu sates the palates of the hip young crowd.

# VIZCAYA

**A bayfront villa set in formal gardens offers an evocative glimpse of bygone days and moonlit nights**

Inspired by the opulent country estates of the Veneto region of northern Italy, James Deering – a principal of the International Harvester Company and a member of one of the wealthiest families in the US – set out to build a winter retreat in Miami. Constructed in 1916 on 180 acres (73 hectares) of spectacular bayfront, the house was designed to resemble an Italian Renaissance villa but also has baroque, rococo, and neoclassical features. The estate's name is from the Basque word for "elevated place" and is also the name of a Basque province on the Bay of Biscay, which itself inspired the name of Miami's Biscayne Bay.

Deering, his architect Burrall Hoffman Jr, and painter Paul Chafin inspired themselves by traveling to Italy to study architectural details. Along with imported doors, ceilings, and fireplaces, native Florida materials such as limestone were employed to maintain a local ambience.

The house has 70 rooms and needed a staff of 30 during the four months the Deerings were in residence. Today, half of the rooms are open to public view. Every detail is exquisite, from the black-and-white marble tub to the gold-leaf cornices, especially the swimming pool, extending from the sun-lit exterior to a grotto beneath the house, its ceiling adorned with shells and carved stone.

Sadly, Deering was able to enjoy the estate for less than a decade. He died in 1925. A hurricane severely damaged the property the following year and again in 1935. The family sold the estate to Dade County in 1952.

**ABOVE:** the villa's south side faces the Italian Renaissance-style formal gardens, featuring elaborate stonework, pools, and greenery.

**RIGHT:** The 17th-century statuary adorning the gardens include busts of such mythological figures as Neptune, Minerva, and Apollo.

**ABOVE:** The Entrance Loggia is a transitional space. Its shaded vaults and cool marble surfaces invite visitors into the cool rooms within.

## VIZCAYA BY MOONLIGHT

"Miami by Moonlight" has long been a romantic angle for poets and songwriters. Now visitors can enjoy "Vizcaya by Moonlight" on an evening spent wandering among the sweetly scented gardens, guided by a knowledgeable docent.

The tours are only once a month, on the night of the full moon, and only in the more temperate season, January through April, weather permitting. The visit begins inside the palazzo itself, with a short talk on the gardens and statuary, including tips on the sights that unfold in the moonlit grounds, and what views to look out for along the way.

Programs begin at about 6.30pm and last around 90 minutes. The tour takes in Vizcaya's subtropical forest, proceeds toward the main house along a lit walkway lined with fountains and foliage, and includes live music, views of Biscayne Bay, and the gorgeous orchids in the David A. Klein Orchidarium on the north side of the main house. Vizcaya's café and gift shop remain open on these evenings.

*Vizcaya is open every day except Christmas from 9.30am to 4.30pm. For information on tours, go to www.vizcayamuseum.org or tel: 305-250-9133.*

**ABOVE:** At one end of the sea wall, a bridge leads to the delightful Tea House, inspired by French architecture.
**BELOW:** Decorated in the lively spirit of Italian Rococo, the Music Room has an 18th-century harpsichord and a Louis XVI harp.

**RIGHT:** Deering named each guest room after the style in which it is decorated. The Cathay Bedroom is decorated with chinoiserie, popular in the 18th century.

# MIAMI BEACH

Art Deco treasures, sizzling nightlife, a sun-kissed beach, and an endless parade of the rich, famous, and beautiful have transformed this once troubled strip into the American Riviera

Miami Beach is a barrier island barely 15 miles (24km) long and a mile (1.7km) wide. Physically (and psychologically) distinct from its mainland big sister, it is a man-made paradise dedicated to the pursuit of pleasure.

Since it was incorporated as a city in 1917, countless millions have come to its shores. They have come to play, work, drink, dance, and run away from humdrum lives elsewhere. Although it has gone through several incarnations in its short lifetime – from elite playground of the rich in the 1940s and 1950s to the urban decay and rampant crime of the 1970s and then the hip New Riviera of the 1990s – Miami Beach continues to seduce visitors with its unique charms and gloriously wide beach.

Today it is a vibrant global village filled with colorful characters that include American celebrities, vanguard artists, European real-estate investors, wealthy South Americans, recent Caribbean immigrants, nouveau-riche Russians, fashion models, gays and lesbians, and world-weary New Yorkers who view it as a new and more affordable Greenwich Village.

## SoBe and Art Deco

At the southern tip of Miami Beach is the neighborhood of **South Beach**, or SoBe as some like to call it. It was here that Miami Beach's rebirth began. When the Swinging Sixties came to an end, Miami Beach slipped into a period of decline that lasted for almost two

decades. But then a few forward-thinking preservationists came to the rescue and spread the word that this thing called Art Deco was something worth saving. In 1979, the Miami Beach Art Deco National Historic District was founded, and things have been looking up ever since.

Containing more than 500 Art Deco buildings constructed mostly in the 1930s and 1940s, the Deco District is the youngest historic district in America. Since its inception it has grown and prospered and served as the cornerstone of a new wave of preservation pride that has

**Main attractions**
SOUTH BEACH
ART DECO DISTRICT
JEWISH MUSEUM
OCEAN DRIVE
WOLFSONIAN-FIU
OLD CITY HALL
ESPANOLA WAY
LINCOLN ROAD
HOLOCAUST MEMORIAL
BOTANICAL GARDEN
BASS MUSEUM OF ART

**LEFT:** Miami Beach from above.
**BELOW:** cruising Ocean Drive.

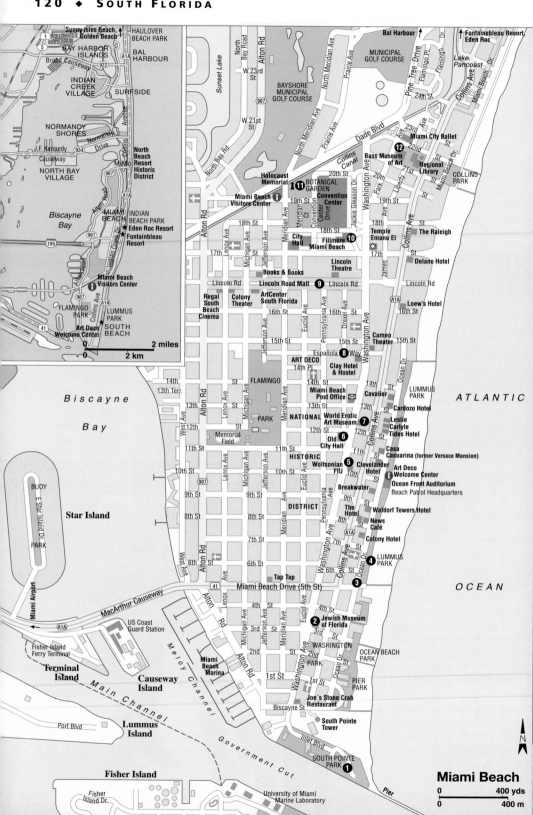

Sunny Isles Beach,
Golden Beach
HAULOVER
BEACH PARK
BAY HARBOR
ISLANDS
BAL
HARBOUR
Broad Causeway
922
INDIAN
CREEK
VILLAGE
SURFSIDE
NORMANDY
SHORES
J.F. Kennedy
Causeway
934
NORTH
BAY
VILLAGE
North
Beach
Resort
Historic
District
Biscayne
Bay
195
MIAMI
BEACH
INDIAN
BEACH PARK
Eden Roc Resort
Fontainbleau
Resort
Miami Beach
Visitors Center
FLAMINGO
PARK
LUMMUS
PARK
41
Art Deco
Welcome Center
SOUTH
BEACH
2 miles

0        2 km

Bal Harbour
Fontainebleau Resort,
Eden Roc

MUNICIPAL
GOLF COURSE

Lake
Pancoast

BAYSHORE
MUNICIPAL
GOLF COURSE

Miami City Ballet
Bass Museum
of Art
Regional
Library
COLLINS
PARK

Holocaust
Memorial
Miami Beach
Visitors Center
BOTANICAL
GARDEN
Convention
Center

Temple
Emanu El
Fillmore
Miami Beach
The Raleigh
City
Hall
Delano Hotel

Books & Books
Lincoln
Theatre
Lincoln Road Mall
ArtCenter
South Florida
Loew's Hotel

Regal
South
Beach
Cinema
Colony
Theater
Cameo
Theater

ART DECO
Clay Hotel
& Hostel
Miami Beach
Post Office
World Erotic
Art Museum
Old
City Hall
Cavalier
Cardozo Hotel
Leslie
Carlyle
Tides Hotel
Casa
Casuarina (former Versace Mansion)
Art Deco
Welcome Center
Ocean Front Auditorium
Beach Patrol Headquarters

Biscayne
Bay

Star Island

FLAMINGO
PARK

Memorial
Field

NATIONAL

HISTORIC
Wolfsonian
FIU
Clevelander
Hotel
Breakwater
The
Hotel
Waldorf Towers Hotel
News
Café
Colony Hotel

DISTRICT

LUMMUS
PARK

ATLANTIC

OCEAN

BUOY

Miami Airport

US Coast
Guard Station

Fisher Island
Ferry Terminal

Terminal
Island
Causeway
Island
Miami Beach
Marina

Tap Tap
Miami Beach Drive (5th St)

Jewish Museum
of Florida
WASHINGTON
PARK

OCEAN
BEACH
PARK

PIER
PARK

Joe's Stone Crab
Restaurant

South Pointe
Tower

Port Blvd
Lummus
Island

Fisher Island

Fisher
Island Dr

University of Miami
Marine Laboratory

SOUTH POINTE
PARK

Pier

N

# Miami Beach

0        400 yds
0        400 m

Recommended Restaurants and Bars on pages 128–9

swept the entire island. Encompassing about one square mile (2½ sq km), it runs roughly from 6th to 23rd streets and Ocean Drive to Alton Road.

After driving across the MacArthur Causeway, the main thoroughfare to SoBe, the highway becomes 5th Street. Between Jefferson and Meridian on 5th is **Tap Tap** *(see listing, page 129)*, Miami Beach's only Haitian restaurant. Along with offering classic Haitian food in a setting of bold Haitian art, Tap Tap regularly hosts live bands, author signings, and screenings of film documentaries with a socially conscious slant.

To the south of 5th Street is **South Pointe Park ❶**, a verdant 17-acre (7-hectare) playground with meandering walkways and great views of the Port of Miami. It is also one of the few vacant pieces of land left on the island. A few blocks away is the **Jewish Museum of Florida ❷** (301 Washington Ave; tel: 305-672-5044, www.jewishmuseum.com; Tue–Sun 10am–5pm; charge). Housed in a beautifully restored 1936 synagogue, the museum is full of artifacts that document the history of Jews throughout the state of Florida. A few blocks away is the

oldest restaurant on Miami Beach, **Joe's Stone Crab** *(see listing, page 129)*, which has been serving the succulent crustaceans since 1913 and lists as a former customer gangster Al Capone, who once lived nearby.

## Ocean Drive

Fifth Street ends at **Ocean Drive ❸**, the world-famous see-and-be-seen street where curvaceous Latin beauties and handsome bronzed hunks strut their stuff. Always busy, Ocean Drive is one of the prettiest streets in Miami Beach, filled with restored Art Deco hotels and dozens of outdoor bistros. One of the most popular is the **News Café** at the corner of 8th Street. A favorite for locals and visiting fashion photographers, it's the place where fashion designer Gianni Versace came to pick up an Italian newspaper just before he was gunned down a few blocks away in front of his mansion.

Across the street is **Lummus Park ❹**, a hub of beach activity with a tree-lined promenade ideal for roller-bladers, a chil-

*A bar dancer at Mango's Tropical Café in South Beach.*

**BELOW:** Tap Tap Haitian restaurant is covered with colorful murals.

*The World Erotic Art Museum.*

**BELOW:** an exhibit at the Jewish Museum celebrates Jewish comic book artists and writers like the creators of Superman, Jerry Siegel and Joe Shuster.

mation on local architecture and history.

At 1114 Ocean Drive is **Casa Casuarina**, a strikingly beautiful Mediterranean Revival mansion surrounded by pine trees. Like Miami Beach itself, the property has undergone many metamorphoses. Designed to resemble Christopher Columbus's home in the Dominican Republic, it was originally built as an apartment house called Amsterdam Palace. In 1992 Gianni Versace bought the building and transformed it into a private Italian-style villa. Following Versace's death it was sold and now functions as a private club with a VIP clientele.

A block away is the **Tides Hotel**, once owned by Island Records founder Chris Blackwell. Billed as the Diva of Ocean Drive, the Tides is a tower of luxury with a soothingly neutral palate that blends historic ambience with modern service—every guest is assigned a "personal assistant." In the next few blocks are a group of historic properties that were among the first to be restored in the late 1980s – the **Carlyle**, **Leslie**, **Cavalier**, and **Cardozo**, which is owned by Grammy Award-winning singer Gloria Estefan and her husband.

dren's playground, and volleyball nets. Several unique lifeguard stands mark this part of the beach, each in a pseudo-Deco style. In the next few blocks are some of the beach's great Art Deco darlings—the **Waldorf Towers**, **Breakwater**, and **Clevelander** hotels, all perfectly preserved architectural gems.

On the beach at 10th Street is the **Miami Beach Ocean Front Auditorium**, a public venue that hosts concerts and events. Next door in a tiny blue building is the **Art Deco Welcome Center** (daily 10am–7pm), a nucleus of infor-

## Washington Avenue

Two blocks to the west and running parallel to Ocean Drive is Washington Avenue, a less glamorous but more interesting street. While many great restaurants can be found here, there are also lots of tiny cafeterias, mom-and-pop grocery stores, tattoo parlors, and clothing boutiques selling garments that leave little to the imagination. Plenty of tourists can be found on Washington, but it is also where locals come for morning coffee or late-night snacks.

At 10th and Washington is the most impressive building on the street, the **Wolfsonian-Florida International University** ❺ (1001 Washington Ave; tel: 305-531-1001, www.wolfsonian.org; Mon–Tue and Sat–Sun noon–6pm, Thu–Fri noon–9pm; charge). Housed in a 1920s Spanish Baroque structure that once served as a storage company, the offbeat Wolfsonian-FIU museum was founded by Mitchell Wolfson Jr, heir to the Wometco movie theater chain, and contains a collection of decorative and propaganda arts from 1895 to 1945. Focusing on the social, political and aesthetic significance of design from that era, the eccentric collec-

tion includes bronze busts of Mussolini, Hitler posters, textiles, comic books, and furniture designed by Frank Lloyd Wright.

One block to the north is **Old City Hall** ❻, a beautiful Mediterranean Revival structure that was the first building in Miami Beach to be granted an historic designation. Behind City Hall is the **Miami Beach Police Station**, where officers gear up on bicycles for their daily patrols.

Nearby is the **World Erotic Art Museum** ❼ (1205 Washington Ave; tel: 305-532-9336, www.weam.com; daily 11am–midnight; charge). Founded by Naomi Wilzig, a Jewish grandmother who amassed a 4,000-piece erotica collection, the museum holds a smoldering and informative display of sculptures, prints, paintings, and other things erotic.

Between 14th and 15th Streets on Washington Avenue is the block-long **Espanola Way** ❽. A charming assortment of Spanish Mediterranean buildings, all painted bright pink and white, Espanola is one of the last true bohemian sections of South Beach. Originally built to be an artist colony in the 1920s, it became a red-light district soon after and

TIP

The pastel-painted, air-conditioned South Beach Local bus stops at numerous places from one end of the district to the other. The service runs every 10–15 minutes until 1am and costs only 25 cents.

**BELOW LEFT:** the Wolfsonian-Florida International University museum.
**BELOW:** the Art Deco District encompasses hundreds of notable buildings.

## Art Deco Walking Tours

Covering the spectrum from flamingo pink to cool turquoise, with sculpted mermaids and neon lights thrown in for fun, tropical Art Deco architecture is a whimsical sight to behold. With its small scale and many nooks and crannies, the Art Deco District is best explored on foot because there are so many details to take in.

The Miami Design Preservation League offers some of the best walking tours in all of Florida. Hosted by historians and architects, the 90-minute tours tell the story behind the style. Tours depart from the **Art Deco Welcome Center** (1001 Ocean Drive) at 10.30am Wednesday, Friday, Saturday, and Sunday and at 6.30pm Thursday. Tours focus on Art Deco as well as Mediterranean Revival structures and include fascinating tidbits of local lore. In-depth explanations are given about the buildings' design and history as well as their decline and restoration.

Reservations are not required, but a hat and comfy shoes are suggested. Self-guided audio tours in five languages are also available daily from 10am to 4pm. For information, call 305-531-3484 or go to www.mdpl.org.

*A barista awaits customers at A La Folie Café on Espanola Way.*

**BELOW:** biking past shops and restaurants on Espanola Way.

still retains a nonconformist spirit. It was here in the late 1930s that Desi Arnaz, Cuban singer and future husband of TV actress Lucille Ball, first performed in the US. With wrought-iron balconies and lots of outdoor tables, Espanola often plays host to belly-dancing shows, Cuban jazz bands, and Haitian drummers. It is also home to the **Clay Hotel and International Youth Hostel** (tel: 305-534-2988), the only real bargain accommodation left on the beach, and a favorite hangout for young European backpackers.

## Lincoln Road

Once called the Fifth Avenue of the South, **Lincoln Road** ❾ (between 16th and 17th Streets) is the prime artery for local street life in South Beach. Unlike the frenetic energy of Ocean Drive, Lincoln Road is more mellow and much easier to navigate. With roots that go back to the late 1920s, it is a storied place that was transformed into a pedestrian-only thoroughfare in the 1960s by modernist architect Morris Lapidus. Today it bustles with bars, restaurants, boutiques, galleries, coffee houses, jazz clubs and theaters. Families with strollers, beautiful women walking their toy terriers, trendy artist types, and flamboyant drag queens—who really liven the place up during Halloween—all mingle here as one.

Much of Lincoln Road's revival goes back to 1984, when **ArtCenter South Florida** (924 Lincoln Rd; tel: 305-674-8278, www.artcentersf.org; call for hours) first opened its doors. A nonprofit gallery with several working studios, it features three exhibition areas and regularly hosts cocktail parties and special arts events.

About two blocks away is the **Colony Theater** (1040 Lincoln Rd; tel: 305-674-1026), an Art Deco jewel that was once a movie theater and is now a city-owned performing-arts venue. At 541 Lincoln Road is the **Lincoln Theatre** (tel: 305-673-3330), home to the New World Symphony, America's only national orchestra training company for musicians aged 21 to 30. In a few years, the New World Symphony is scheduled to

move to a new home a few blocks away when the Frank Gehry-designed Miami Beach City Center opens.

At the western edge of Lincoln Road is the **Regal South Beach Cinema**, a modern multiscreen movie theater that hosts many of the foreign films featured during the **Miami International Film Festival** each winter. Local residents regard the cinema as a much-needed addition but are less sanguine about nearby chain stores that lack the quirky character the beach prides itself on. One place that clings to the neighborhood's independent spirit is **Books & Books** (933 Lincoln Rd; tel: 305-532-3222; daily 10am–11pm ). Like its sister store in Coral Gables, Books & Books on the beach is more than a bookstore. It's a restaurant, café, and meeting place for local literati that often hosts readings by award-wining authors and special events supported by the arts community.

## 17th Street

To the north of Lincoln Road is **17th Street**, also known as Hank Meyer Boulevard – named for the publicist who convinced Jackie Gleason to move his show to Miami Beach in 1964. On the north side of the street is the **Fillmore Miami Beach ❿** (305-673-7300), formerly the Jackie Gleason Theater. After the Arscht Center opened in downtown Miami, the old Gleason Theater underwent a renovation and now stages major rock, comedy, and pop performances. On the sidewalk along the south side of the theater is Miami Beach's version of the Walk of Stars, where handprints of famous inductees include Muhammad Ali and Ann-Margret.

On the west side of the theater is the **Miami Beach Convention Center**, home to the December art extravaganza known as **Art Basel Miami Beach** as well as dozens of other trade shows and events. Nearby is the new **Miami Beach City Hall**, and a much welcomed patch of green, the **Miami Beach Botanical Garden** (2000 Convention Center Dr; tel: 305-673-7256, www.mbgarden.org; Tue–Sun 9am–5pm; free). Full of native plants and exotic orchids, this 4-acre (1.6-

hectare) tropical garden offers classes and lectures and serves as the main environmental entity that encourages the densely built city of Miami Beach to "go green."

## Holocaust Memorial

Until about a decade ago, Miami Beach had one of the largest populations of Holocaust survivors in the US, so it made sense that the island would want to commission a testament to the tragedies of World War II. Designed by Kenneth Treister, the **Holocaust Memorial ⓫** (1933-1945 Meridian Ave; tel: 305-538-1663; daily 9am–9pm; free) is a somber reminder of those who lost their lives in the Nazi death camps. The 42-ft (13-meter) bronze sculpture is that of an outstretched hand reaching toward the heavens, with nearly 100 life-size statues of tormented people grasping for help. The memorial also has a peaceful garden and plaza, a pictorial history of the Holocaust, and a granite wall inscribed with the names of thousands of victims.

## Collins Park

In an effort to reduce some of South Beach's congestion and move the arts-

*A bit mellower than Ocean Drive, Lincoln Road is nonetheless a colorful and lively place for shopping dining, and strolling.*

**BELOW:** jazzy art at an Ocean Drive gift shop.

**TIP**

Gay and lesbian travelers can get information about accommodations, dining, events, and other services from the Miami-Dade Gay and Lesbian Chamber of Commerce (tel: 305-573-4000; www.gogaymiami.com).

**BELOW:** strolling the boardwalk near the Fontainebleau Resort.

and-culture scene a little northward, the city recently created the **Collins Park Cultural Center** between 17th and 25th Streets. Part of a project that plans on bringing affordable housing to resident artists – many of whom can no longer afford to live in Miami Beach – the Collins Park "campus" runs along Collins Avenue and is made of three components: headquarters of the **Miami City Ballet**; the **Miami Beach Regional Library**, a state-of-the-art facility and repository for books and artifacts on Miami Beach history; and the **Bass Museum of Art** ⑫ (2121 Park Ave; tel: 305-673-7530, www.bassmuseum.org; Tue–Sat 10am–5pm, Sun 11am–5pm; charge).

Built in 1930 as the city library, the Art Deco building has been a museum since the 1960s when philanthropist John Bass donated his own art collection. Enlarged in 2002 by Japanese architect Arata Isozaki, the Bass hosts visiting exhibits but is most noted for its extensive European collection, including Renaissance works, 16th-century Flemish tapestries, paintings by Peter Paul Rubens, ecclesiastical artifacts, and lithographs by Henri Toulouse-Lautrec.

## Middle Beach and MiMo

North of the Bass Museum, the beach takes on a different tone and the buildings become taller, less Deco and more futuristic in design. Stretching from 23rd to 47th Streets is an area known as **Middle Beach**, which includes a few landmark properties. Built in 1954, the **Fontainebleau Resort** (4441 Collins Ave) was where the Kings of Cool – Frank Sinatra, Sammy Davis Jr, and Dean Martin – serenaded the crowds in the 1950s and 1960s. Ostentatious to the core, it was designed by the late Morris Lapidus, who today is considered the father of MiMo (Miami Modern) architecture.

Lapidus also designed its neighbor, the **Eden Roc** (4525 Collins Ave), the other grand-dame of MiMo. Both are perfect examples of the over-the-top resort vernacular that came about during the unbridled American optimism of the 1950s. Both have also been renovated and expanded. For years MiMo buildings were considered tacky and vulgar, an embarrassment to the aesthetically inclined, but after the millennium they were elevated to historic status and praised for their naïve playfulness.

Common throughout Miami and Miami Beach, MiMo buildings are characterized by flamboyant angles and lines, accordion walls, cheese-hole masonry, massive columns, anodized aluminum, and polished terrazzo floors.

## NoBe

Once Collins Avenue passes north of 47th Street, the neighborhood becomes NoBe, **North Beach**, one of the more desirable residential areas. Formerly the realm of northern retirees, NoBe is now a hip and happening neighborhood full of young Brazilians, savvy Europeans, and other trendy newcomers. Full of MiMo architecture and a diverse group of good restaurants, it also has great beach access and an easygoing attitude.

To the west are the upscale resident islands of **Normandy Shores** and **Indian Creek**; to the north are the towns of **Surfside**, **Bal Harbour**, **Sunny Isles**, and **Golden Beach**. ❏

# Key Biscayne

Just minutes from the hustle of
Miami is an island getaway with
golden beaches, secluded coves,
plush resorts, and water sports

A tiny barrier island just a few minutes from
downtown Miami, Key Biscayne is an oasis
of tranquility. Juan Ponce de Leon claimed
the island for Spain in 1513, and President Richard
Nixon used it as a winter escape from his Washington woes in the 1970s. Although it has a sizable
residential community, the island is also an exclusive
tropical getaway that offers a serene alternative to
Miami Beach with water sports, lovely beaches, a
world-famous tennis center, and plush resorts.

After crossing the Rickenbacker Causeway
Bridge over Biscayne Bay, the atmosphere quickly
mellows. The first stop is **Virginia Key** where several outlets offer windsurfing and kiteboarding
rentals on the calm bay waters. On the left side of
the highway is a turnoff to **Virginia Key Beach
Park**, a 2-mile (3-km) stretch of sand that during
segregation served as Miami's only "black beach."
A dirt road nearby meanders down to **Jimbo's**, a
quirky Old Florida eatery that has been serving
smoked fish and cold beer since the 1950s.

## Aquatic theme park

On the opposite side of the highway is the **Miami
Seaquarium** (4400 Rickenbacker Causeway; tel:
305-361-5705; daily 9:30am–6pm; charge).
Founded in 1955, the Seaquarium is a stellar
marine research center as well as an aquatic
theme park that features enormous tanks full of
sharks, manatees, stingrays, alligators, and dolphins; exotic birds and wildlife; and spectacular
water shows starring killer whales and sea lions.
For an extra fee, the Seaquarium offers two-hour
tours of the facilities that include a half-hour of
swimming and playing with the resident dolphins.

Farther down the spine of the island is **Crandon
Park Beach**, a 3-mile-long (5-km) public park complete with a soccer field and 18-hole public golf
course. Considered one of Miami's most popular
"party beaches," Crandon tends to be very busy on
weekends. On the bay side nearby is the **Crandon
Park Tennis Center** (tel: 305-446-2200), where

RIGHT: feeding time at the Miami Seaquarium.

top-ranked tennis pros compete each spring for
prizes worth millions during the Sony Ericsson
Open. Over 200,000 spectators turn out to watch
such top-ranked players as Venus Williams and
Roger Federer compete in the weeklong event, and
then partake in the after-hours parties.

Past the tennis center is the **Village of Key Biscayne**. With a population of about 10,000, the village is definitely for the well-heeled, and the tempo
is slow and casual. Several bicycle rental shops
make it easy for tourists to tour the island by bike.

At the far end of the island is **Bill Baggs Cape
Florida State Park** (daily sunrise to sunset; charge).
Regularly rated as one of the best beaches in the
US, Bill Baggs is a unique experience for a Miami-area beach – there are no lifeguards and no buildings
within site of the sand. Dotted with endangered sea
oats and towering Australian pine trees, the beach is
broad and soft, and the water is deep close to shore.
At the park's southern end is the 95-ft-tall (30-meter)
**Cape Florida Lighthouse**. Built in 1825, it is one of
the oldest structures in South Florida and the only
lighthouse in the country to have been attacked by
American Indians (Seminoles). Park rangers offer
tours Thursday through Monday at 10am and 1pm.
A few steps away is a restaurant with good seafood
and frosty drinks. In the distance offshore are the
few remaining stilt houses that comprised a once-vibrant community known as **Stiltsville**.  ❑

# RESTAURANTS AND BARS

## Restaurants

Prices for a three-course dinner per person, excluding tax, tip, and beverages:

**$** = under $20
**$$** = $20–45
**$$$** = $45–60
**$$$$** = over $60

### A La Folie
516 Espanola Way
Tel: 305-538-4484
B, L & D daily (to midnight).
A romantic outdoor setting with the atmosphere of a Left Bank café, where handsome young waiters serve French crepes with good-value wine to accompany. $$

### Arnie & Richie's
525 41st St
Tel: 305-531-7691
B & L daily
Still Miami Beach's best deli after six decades, this is a temple to New York-style bagels, pastrami, and corned beef on rye. A recent revamp has not detracted from the authentic fare or the brusque service. $

### Café at Books & Books
933 Lincoln Rd
Tel: 305-695-8898
B, L & D daily, Br Sat–Sun
Fresh, well-composed lunches and dinners make this bookstore's New American café one of the best on Lincoln Road. Outdoor seating and sassy servers add to the literary allure. $$

### Café Ragazzi
9500 Harding Ave
Tel: 305-866-4495
L & D Mon–Sat, D Sun
You'll feel like one of the famiglia at this crowded but charming Italian ristorante. Waits are common but compensated for by a glass of house wine outside to pass the time. $$

### Carpaccio
Shops of Bal Harbour, 9700 Collins Ave
Tel: 305-867-7777
L & D daily
Armani, Fendi, and Gucci are on parade in this posh Italian restaurant for ladies who lunch. The signature carpaccio is recommended, as are the delicate, handmade pastas, the fresh salads, and extensive wine list. Prices soar, but this is Bal Harbour, after all. $$$

### Eleventh Street Diner
1065 Washington Ave
Tel: 305-534-6373
B, L & D daily
This classic diner in an aluminum trailer smack dab in the middle of South Beach clubland is a perfect spot for the "morning after" cure. Greasy grill fare, with a full bar. Best of all, the diner is open 24/7. $$

### Emeril's Miami Beach
The Loews Resort, 1601 Collins Ave
Tel: 305-695-4550
L & D daily
Effusive TV chef Emeril Lagasse may not actually be here, but his specialties like blackened pecan redfish and gumbo have a big presence. Quality can vary, but the star power is definitely in abundance. Make a reservation early and ask for an outdoor table. $$$

### Escopazzo
1311 Washington Ave
Tel: 305-674-9450
D daily
Northern Italian dishes are made with lots of local produce, accompanied by a fine, all-Italian wine list and served by knowledgeable, helpful staff. A better choice than many of the flashy South Beach eateries that cost as much but don't deliver the quality. $$$$

### The Forge
432 41st St
Tel: 305-538-8533
D daily
An institution in Miami Beach for four decades, this gilded icon is a magnet for celebrities and celeb-spotters. Tuxedoed servers give tours of the historic and well-stocked wine cellar. $$$$

### Joe's Stone Crab
11 Washington Ave
Tel: 305-673-0365
L & D Tue–Sat, limited summer hours, closed Aug–Sep
The oldest and most talked about restaurant on the beach – some might even call it a tourist trap. But Joe's is still great if you can nab a seat (reservations are not accepted). Service is brusque but worth it for the nationally-known stone crabs in season mid-Oct to mid-May. $$$$

**LEFT:** an artfully prepared dish at Emeril's, one of many restaurants owned by celebrity chef Emeril Lagasse.

## La Provence French Bakery
1629 Collins Avenue
Tel: 305 538-2406
B, L & D daily
The beach's finest French bakery has a constant carb-hungry line for baguettes and croissants. Big salads are on offer, as are yummy sandwiches with prosciutto or mozzarella, quiches, and temptingly pretty pastries. $

## Shoji
100 Collins Ave
Tel: 305-532-4245
L Mon–Fri, D daily
Sushi like you won't find elsewhere. Shoji impresses even Japanese expats with huge slabs of jewel-like fish and shellfish, as well as cooked dishes like oyster miso and grilled skirt steak with enoki mushrooms. The sexy interior attracts a great-looking crowd, so dress up. $$$

## Spris
731 Lincoln Rd
Tel: 305-673-2020
L & D daily
Roman-style pizza with paper-thin crusts charred on the edges and nearly see-through in the middle are all the rage at this busy Lincoln Road pizzeria. The good news is that you can also order from the menus of the eateries on either side of Spris, so try the mussels from le Bon or the pasta from Tiramisu; all are owned by restaurateur Graziano Sbroggi. $

## Talula
210 23rd St
Tel: 305-672-0778
Tue–Fri L & D, Sat D, Sun Br & D
Husband and wife Andrea and Frank Randazzo delight their local regulars with impressive

tartare of ahi tuna dotted with serrano chiles, cucumber, and crisped rice and conch ceviche. The rustic brick interior is romantic and cozy, while the enchanting courtyard is a dream in the cool months. $$$

## Tamarind
946 Normandy Dr
Tel: 305-861-6222
L & D Tue–Sun
A little-known Thai delight, almost lost in an area dominated by Argentinian eateries, this authentic, good-looking and moderately-priced spot is well worth a detour. Specialty dishes include tamarind duck, shrimp, and sweet corn cake, or you could opt for the fantastic pad Thai. The award-winning chef, Vatcharin Bhumichitr, never fails to deliver a delightful evening with his superb cuisine. $$

## Tap Tap
819 Fifth St
Tel: 305-672-2898
D daily
The beach's only Haitian eatery, this Caribbean restaurant is decorated with brightly colored murals and attended by equally colorful patrons. The food, including fried pork tidbits and curried goat stew, recalls the taste of the islands. Live music on weekends completes the exotic scene. $$

## Taverna Opa
36 Ocean Drive
Tel: 305-673-6730
D daily
Opa is like a souped up Greek frat party, replete with raucous plate-smashing. The lamb, squid, and moussaka make the inevitable wait worthwhile. $$

## Toni's Sushi Bar
1208 Washington Ave
Tel: 305-673-9368
D daily, L Sat
A veteran on South Beach, this Japanese pearl still pleases finicky raw fish lovers with pristine sushi served in cozy curtained booths. It's usually crowded with regulars on weekends, but always worth the wait. $$$

## Wish at the Hotel
801 Collins Ave
Tel: 305-674-9474
B & L daily, D Tue–Sun
Delightful and totally tropical, the romantic setting is enchanting in this Todd Oldham- designed restaurant. The inner garden is exotic, but the outside tables among palms and twinkling lights are truly magical, while the classic American and contemporary Asian cuisine is a perfect match for the setting. Be sure to enjoy a pre-dinner drink at the upstairs terrace bar. $$$$

## Buck 15
707 Lincoln Lane
Tel: 305-534-5488
Tue–Sat 10pm–5am
A hip, upstairs hideaway hangout where you can find the coolest DJs and club kids gathering here for drinks before hitting the South Beach scene. It's also a good after-hours haunt. Retro art hangs among the rec-room decor.

## Clarke's
840 1st St
Tel: 305-538-9885
D daily, L Mon–Fri and Sun
An Irish pub and bar that serves remarkably good food way beyond shepherd's pie and fish and chips. There's a killer wine list and, of course, a great range of beers and ales on tap.

## Kafka
1464 Washington Ave
Tel: 305-672-4526
Daily 8am–midnight
A bookstore, cyber café, and all-around excellent place to loiter, this corner spot appeals to the literary crowd as well as to their smart friends.

## Mac's Club Deuce
222 14th St
Tel: 305-531-6200
8am–5am daily
An all-day and all-night institution on South Beach, this hard-drinking Deco bar across the street from a tattoo parlor is a place not to be missed while you're in town. Everyone from bikers to bankers are made to feel welcome.

## Segafreddo Café
1040 Lincoln Rd
Tel: 305-673-0047
Daily for appetizers and drinks
Luxurious sofas with lounging Europeans line this Lincoln Road location. They come here for cocktails and even better coffees, carpaccio, and huge sandwiches, served at all hours.

## VIX and VUE at the Hotel Victor
1144 Ocean Dr
Tel: 305-779-8888
L & D daily
With glowing jellyfish tanks, thumping DJs, and an open-air lounge, the Victor plays host to one of the hottest scenes on the beach. On offer is not only the unbeatable view over South Beach's sexy oceanfront, but also the gathering of pretty young things who lounge under the stars on canopied orbit beds – all the while nibbling on tasty tapas and sipping the latest luscious libations.

# ART DECO: SOUTH BEACH STYLE

**The exotic, colorful buildings on Ocean Drive and nearby streets are the product of Miami's unique interpretation of Art Deco style**

The splendid Art Deco buildings in Miami Beach were built to raise the spirits of Americans during the Great Depression. Many decades later, preservationists say that they are among the most architecturally significant structures in the US.

The roots of Art Deco go back to 1901, when the Société des Artistes Décorateurs was formed in Paris with the goal of merging the mass production of industrial technology with the decorative arts. It was proudly introduced to the world in 1925 at the Paris Exposition Internationale des Arts Décoratifs et Industriels Modernes. The nickname "Art Deco" gained currency only in 1966, when it was dreamed up for a retrospective of the 1925 Paris show.

The Art Deco style was thoroughly evocative of the new Machine Age, which was inspired partly by the aerodynamic designs of airplanes and cars. However, Art Deco combined all kinds of influences, from the swirls of Art Nouveau to the hard lines of Cubism.

## TROPICAL DECO

In the 1930s and '40s, hundreds of Deco structures were built in South Beach. Art Deco's stark, white exteriors were already well suited to Florida's hot climate, but architects in Miami soon developed their own style, later dubbed Tropical Deco. Many features, from window design to color choice, were inspired by South Florida's weather and its seaside location. The more futuristic Art Deco style known as Streamline Moderne, which replaced some of the detail characteristic of traditional Art Deco with smoother lines and sweeping curves, was particularly popular in Miami. Several elements, such as "porthole" windows and tube railings, were borrowed from the design of ocean liners.

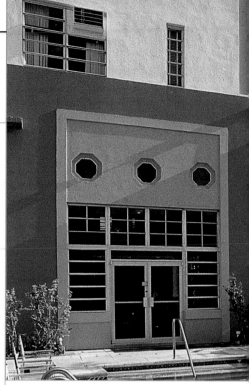

**ABOVE:** Long bands of windows, often continuing around the corner building (as seen here, on the Park Central Hotel on Ocean Drive), all in plenty of natural light and refreshing sea breezes.

**ABOVE:** This hotel on Collins is a classic Streamline building. Notice the rounded corners and "eyebrows" canopies which shade the windows against the sun. Deco roofs were generally flat but often broken by a raised central parapet or pointed finial.

**RIGHT:** Many exteriors, elevator doors, and windows feature typical Tropical Deco motifs, such as pelicans and sunbursts.

## THE FIGHT TO SAVE MIAMI DECO

The Art Deco hotels of South Beach provided a welcome refuge for visiting northerners for some time, but by the 1960s they had begun to decay. Several of the area's once-glamorous hotels became low-rent housing for the elderly, and much of the district became rundown.

In 1976, Barbara Capitman (above) set up the Miami Design Preservation League to stop the demolition of the Art Deco buildings and to encourage their restoration. In 1979, 1 sq mile (2.5 sq km) of South Beach was listed in the National Registry of Historic Places. It was the first 20th-century district to receive such recognition.

In the 1980s, designer Leonard Horowitz endowed South Beach with a new color scheme, nicknamed Deco Dazzle, by painting many of the old buildings in bright colors; originally most would have been white with color trim.

Media interest in Miami's Art Deco enclave skyrocketed after South Beach became a favorite backdrop in the hit TV series *Miami Vice*. Fashion photographers such as Bruce Weber were drawn south to Florida too. In the late 1980s, developers and other entrepreneurs moved in, opening nightclubs and model agencies, and renovating hotels.

**ABOVE:** the Breakwater Hotel, illustrated here on a postcard, has a tower like a ship's funnel and horizontal "racing stripes."

**LEFT:** The Ritz Plaza on Collins Avenue is one of several later Art Deco hotels, built in South Beach in the 1940s, whose design was influenced by the science-fiction fantasies of Buck Rogers and Flash Gordon. This is noticeable particularly in the thrust of its tower.

**RIGHT:** The Art Deco architects in Miami tried out all kinds of new materials, including chrome, glass blocks, and terrazzo – a cheap, imitation marble. Neon lighting was used for the first time and is one of the most distinctive features of South Beach. It means that the architecture can be enjoyed day and night.

*Recommended Restaurants on page 143*

# THE EVERGLADES

A two-hour drive from Miami takes visitors to
Florida's untamed heart – an ecological treasure
rich in subtropical plants and animals

I t's an unseasonably warm, humid February morning in **Everglades City ❶**, the fishing village that serves as the gateway to the Ten Thousand Islands unit of **Everglades National Park** on the Gulf of Mexico. The sun is already glinting off the sapphire waters in front of the park's **Gulf Coast Visitor Center** (tel: 239-695-2945). At the dock, a narrated boat tour of scenic Chokoloskee Bay is just pulling out, while a seasonal park ranger gets ready to guide a paddling tour to Sandfly Island, a shell-mound island that was once home to Calusa Indians and early pioneers.

## Water world

About a mile away, another kayaking trip is loading outside Ivey House, a popular eco-lodge. On the screened porch, a group of kayakers dressed in roll-down pants and shirts, closed-toe sneakers, and broad-brimmed hats lathers on sunscreen and insect repellent while listening to an orientation from the tour leader. They will drive by van north to the intersection of SR 29 and US 41, then another 6 miles (10km) east through Big Cypress National Preserve to the Turner River highway bridge. From this put-in, it's a leisurely southward paddle through the largest mangrove ecosystem in the US, a boggy place of tangled branch tunnels, estuary waters, and intimate wildlife viewing.

Day trips like these offer an enjoyable and safe introduction to the watery beauty of the **Ten Thousand Islands**, the Wild West frontier of the Everglades.

The park's signature kayaking route, the 99-mile (160-km) **Wilderness Waterway**, passes through the **Marjorie Stoneman Douglas Wilderness**, the largest wilderness east of the Mississippi, linking Ten Thousand Islands with Cape Sable and Florida Bay, the southernmost tip of the main park. You can do the challenging eight-day trip in either direction, beginning or ending at the old fishing village of **Flamingo ❷** in Florida Bay.

Currently, there are challenges for visitors using Florida Bay. In 2005, Hurricanes Katrina and Wilma blew ashore

**Main attractions**
EVERGLADES CITY
GULF COAST VISITOR CENTER
WILDERNESS WATERWAY
ERNEST COE VISITOR CENTER
ROYAL PALM VISITOR CENTER
MICCOSUKEE CULTURAL
   CENTER
SHARK VALLEY
   VISITOR CENTER
AH-TAH-THI-KI MUSEUM
BIG CYPRESS PRESERVE

**LEFT:** kayakers near Everglades City.
**BELOW:** an alligator watches for prey.

*Mosquitoes are abundant during the rainy season, roughly June through October.*

and severely damaged Flamingo Lodge, the visitor center, and marina. Self-sufficient visitors may still enjoy outdoor activities like kayaking, boat tours, birding, ranger walks, and camping in the large, semideveloped beachfront campground (reservations strongly advised in high season; tel: 800-365-CAMP). Those unprepared for roughing it will want to base themselves elsewhere.

## Orientation

Hurricanes are a fact of life in South Florida. In the 1900s, killer hurricanes devastated Ten Thousand Islands, Lake Okeechobee, Homestead, and now Flamingo. Overall, the loss of services at its major visitor hub has been a blessing in disguise for Everglades National Park. Many of the park's million annual visitors – most of whom arrive in Miami and devote a single day to the park before heading to the Florida Keys – explore farther afield and learn that the Everglades is much more than bogs, birds, and bugs. It's actually a complex mosaic of nine ecosystems, comprising ponds, sloughs, sawgrass marshes, hardwood hammocks, and forested uplands

essential to native wildlife, and covers all of South Florida from Biscayne Bay to the Gulf of Mexico.

The main part of the park is an hour south of Miami, off US 1. Homestead and adjoining Florida City, the gateway towns, were flattened by Hurricane Andrew in 1992. They still show signs of trauma today and have never regenerated as a visitor destination. Hotels and restaurants are modest. One good choice for adventurous travelers is funky Everglades Hostel in Florida City. It has dorms and private rooms, self-catering facilities, Internet, and, like Ivey House in Everglades City, specializes in kayak tours of the park.

Park headquarters is next to **Ernest Coe Visitor Center ❸** (tel: 305-242-7700, www.nps.gov/ever; daily 9am–5pm), just inside the park entrance. The visitor center is named for feisty landscape architect Ernest Coe who, starting in 1928, spearheaded the effort to get Everglades National Park authorized by Congress. It has exhibits, a film, a bookstore, and two campgrounds and trails at nearby Long Pine Key. The two most popular trails in the park are 4 miles

**Everglades**

0 ————— 30 miles
0 ————— 30 km

*Recommended Restaurants on page 143*

(6km) away at **Royal Palm Visitor Center** (exhibits, gift shop, ranger-led activities), the former state park that was the first piece of land acquired for the national park. The historic road to Flamingo is a 38-mile-long (61-km) scenic drive that winds through the peaceful landscape, with hiking trails and scenic pullouts.

The main entry to Everglades National Park along historic **Tamiami Trail** (US 41) is 30 miles (48km) west of Miami at **Shark Valley**. Biologically rich, Shark Valley is one of the three vital drainage areas for the Everglades and was added to the park in 1989. The unit's chief attractions are its proximity to US 41 and the accessible 15-mile (24km) loop road and side trails adjoining Shark River Slough. **Shark Valley Visitor Center ❹** (tel: 305-221-8776) is open daily and has ranger-led activities. You can walk or ride a bicycle or open-air tram on the paved loop year-round, although the wet season inundates many areas, making it hard to see dispersed wildlife.

Close encounters with alligators and wading birds are guaranteed in the dry season, when animals concentrate in major sloughs. Alligators have an important role to play in the functioning of this ecosystem. Their thrashing around creates wallows that fill with water used by other wildlife. A 50-ft-high (15-meter) observation tower overlooks the River of Grass.

## Native heritage

Here you are in Florida's Indian Country. Airboat rides are available on the large reservation belonging to the Miccosukee Tribe (tel: 305-223-8380), whose private chickee-hut village compounds and tourist-oriented **Miccosukee Cultural Center ❺** adjoin Shark Valley on US 41. There are about 369 enrolled tribal members living on the reservation. Information is available at the tribal offices on the north side of US 41. The Miccosukee Tribe also runs a casino-hotel at the junction of US 41 and Krome Avenue (SR 997), the closest hotel to this part of the park, and has lands near their relatives, the Big Cypress Seminoles.

The **Big Cypress Seminole Reservation** is a quiet, pastoral landscape reached from Exit 49 of I-75 (Alligator Alley) near Miami. The Seminoles are renowned for cattle ranching and maintain a big operation here, along with a rodeo stadium. There are several tourist facilities, including a casino, gas station, convenience store, restaurant, and guided outdoor activities.

By far the best interpretation of Seminole culture in Florida is available at the tribe's excellent **Ah-Tah-Thi-Ki**

*A photographer gets a close-up of the local bird life.*

**BELOW:** Miccosukee children on an airboat, the fastest way to travel in the backcountry.

*A park ranger offers advice to visitors at the Ernest Coe Visitor Center.*

**BELOW:** tourists snap photos on the Anhinga Trail.

**Museum** ❻ (tel: 863-902-1113; www.ahtahthiki.com; daily 9am–5pm; charge), an affiliate of the Smithsonian Institution. The museum has a film about Seminole history and interesting dioramas showing their distinctive chickee-hut architecture, distinctive colorful patchwork clothes, canoes, traditional foods, and seasonal ceremonies like the Green Corn Ceremony. Out back is a boardwalk trail with interpretive plaques about plants used for food and medicine. It ends at a replica Seminole Village.

## River of grass

Exhibits at its three visitor centers tell the story of Everglades National Park. It's a long, complex, cautionary tale of what happens when a unique ecosystem is misunderstood, misappropriated, and misused by human beings intent on their own agenda. The designation of the park was just the beginning; the ending is still to be decided—probably in court, if past battles are any indication.

Authorized in 1934 but only dedicated in 1947 after funds to purchase lands were approved, Everglades National Park is now recognized worldwide for its unique habitat. It protects the only subtropical preserve in North America and is a major "edge place," where northern and southern flora and fauna species mingle. A large, flat prairie whose highest point is 8 ft (2½ meters) above sea level, at Chokoloskeee Island, the park is, contrary to rumor, not a large, impenetrable swamp. It is, as author, conservationist, and park champion Marjorie Stoneman Douglas famously observed, a "River of Grass" – at 50 miles (80km) wide, the largest continuous stand of seasonally inundated sawgrass prairie in North America.

Jeopardized by the rampant development surrounding it, the Everglades is today on life support. Its subtle beauty inspires visitors who take the time to get to know it, but the Everglades is most important as a sanctuary for wildlife. Living here are more than 400 species of birds, 125 species of fish, 60 species of reptiles and amphibians, 25 species of mammals, more than 120 species of trees, 1,000 species of seed-bearing

*Recommended Restaurants on page 143*

plants, and 24 species of orchids, including the rare ghost orchid. The Everglades is the only place in the US where you'll find both crocodiles and alligators living side by side. Crocodiles (distinguished from alligators by a spade-shaped snout and two visible sets of teeth rather than one) are one of 14 endangered species protected here. Others are Florida panthers, West Indian manatees, Cable Sable sea sparrows, and wood storks. There are nine threatened species.

## Troubled waters

The headwaters of the Everglades are 80 miles (129km) to the north in the Kissimmee River Basin, now protected in the Nature Conservancy's Disney Wilderness. Disastrously channelized for ranching and agriculture, the Kissimmee River was once a wide, shallow river whose waters used to wend slowly south to Lake Okeechobee. But surrounded by the massive 1930 Hoover Dike, which controls flooding and provides irrigation for agriculture, Lake Okeechobee, Florida's largest lake, is a dying ecosystem.

The lake's historic role in the Everglades system was pivotal. Up to 60 inches (150cm) of summer rainfall caused it to seasonally overspill its margins, allowing floodwaters to slowly move south across the sawgrass prairie. This water nourished the wetlands and percolated through limestone into the Biscayne Aquifer, source of drinking water for South Florida. It then exited the mainland via the huge mangrove swamps at the salty edge of the estuaries into Biscayne and Florida Bays and the Ten Thousand Islands region of the Gulf.

Fully 50 percent of the Everglades has been been lost since the 1930s, along with 93 percent of its 2 million birds. Encroaching urban settlements, pollution by nitrate fertilizers from subsidized sugar-cane agriculture around Lake Okeechobee, subsequent invasion by exotics, and massive habitat loss have been an ecological disaster.

Recently, the world's largest environmental restoration plan, the Comprehensive Everglades Restoration Plan, was authorized by Congress. It's designed to return water to more natural patterns of quantity, timing, and distribution throughout the South Florida ecosystem. The South Florida Water Management

**TIP**

For an entertaining and informative account of the politics of Everglades protection, read *The Swamp* by *Miami Herald* journalist Michael Grunwald.

**BELOW:** thick vegetation in Big Cypress Preserve.

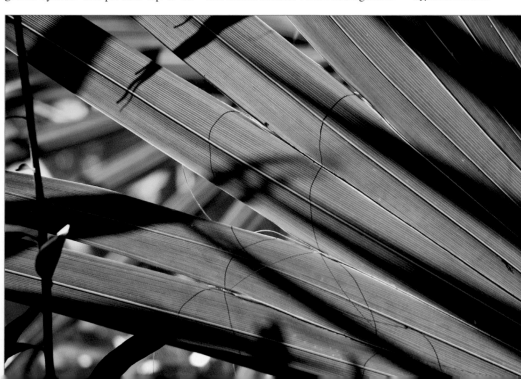

**TIP**

If time permits, stop at Clyde Butcher's Big Cypress Gallery (52388 Tamiami Trail, Ochopee; tel: 239-695-2428). Butcher's gorgeous, large-format, black-and-white images of Big Cypress and the rest of the Everglades will haunt your dreams. Look for them on the walls of many hotels and other businesses throughout southwest Florida.

**BELOW:** sunset over Chokoloskee Bay.

District, together with the US Army Corps of Engineers, is working to mimic nature with seasonal water releases south of Lake Okeechobee's agricultural areas. The effort will be given a huge boost when the state purchases some 187,000 acres (76,000 hectares) of land from the US Sugar Corporation. The deal was announced in 2008 and is estimated to cost $1.75 billion.

## The Main Park

The collision of urban environment and natural ecosystem is easy to appreciate when you visit the main park. Agricultural fields and tropical plant nurseries surround homely Homestead and Florida City, continuing all the way to the park entrance where, magically, human development disappears and the huge vistas of sawgrass prairie and tree hammocks take center stage all the way to Flamingo.

For many visitors, the highlights of a visit to the main park are the two easy trails at historic Royal Palm, east of the scenic drive. Nothing seems to perturb the lively shenanigans of alligators and anhingas and the silent predations of blue herons, snowy egrets, and other wildlife going about their daily business in the

Taylor Slough. The short **Anhinga Trail** lets you get astonishingly close to wildlife. The **Gumbo Limbo Trail**, named for the tree with the red peeling bark known as "the tourist tree," loops through a hardwood hammock forest reshaped by Hurricane Andrew in 1992.

Heading south on the scenic drive, the **Pineland Trail** leads through some of the most diverse pinelands in south Florida, ending at the campground at **Long Pine Key ❼**. The **Pa-hay-okee Overlook ❽** is a boardwalk trail that offers the best place in this part of the park to experience the more than 20 different grasses that compose the sawgrass prairie at the heart of the Everglades.

If you do decide to continue to Flamingo, you'll be rewarded by views of white and brown pelicans and other seabirds massing offshore on white sandbars in the turquoise waters of Florida Bay. Meander along the beach trail to get a closer look, or stand on the concrete breezeway at the **Flamingo Visitor Center** (tel: 239-695-2945; daily 9am–4.30pm Nov–May), binoculars in hand, and enjoy the tranquil beauty. Part of the Florida Keys is in the park, along with the Intra-

coastal Waterway. For more information, contact the Key Largo Ranger Station (tel: 305-852-0304).

## Ten Thousand Islands

Like Flamingo, Everglades City and **Chokoloskee Island ❾** are former fishing villages. Chokoloskee Island was settled by whites in the 1870s, although it had long been home to Calusa Indians. Smallwood Store, a stilted building with its own quay, is now a dusty family-run museum, open daily for a small fee. It belonged to Charles "Ted" Smallwood, who ran a trading post for homesteaders in the Ten Thousand Islands region. Supplies were shipped from Key West, Fort Myers, or Tampa by boat; local sugar cane syrup, fish, and produce were shipped in return.

In Everglades City, the "Stone Crab Capital of Florida," early 20th-century homesteader George Storter was also a merchant, as well as postmaster and a hotel owner. Hurricanes devastated Everglades City and Chokoloskee in 1909 and 1910, leveling all but the highest ground of the old Calusa shell mound, salting farm fields, and forcing many homesteaders to leave.

Tragedy gave Barron Collier an opening to buy southwest Florida on the cheap. Collier initially used Everglades City as his base for building the 1928 Tamiami Trail, later moving the county seat to Naples. The lodge that adjoins the bed-and-breakfast inn at Ivey House is Everglades City's oldest structure: a former boardinghouse for trail workers. Collier bought Storter's waterfront hotel to use as a hunting and fishing retreat. These activities, popular with Everglades

*A survivor of several hurricanes, historic Everglades City Hall remains a handsome local landmark.*

**BELOW:** the Gumbo Limbo Trail leads through a hammock of strangler figs, gumbo limbo trees, and royal palms.

## The Chokoloskee Murders

The most notorious outlaw associated with the Ten Thousand Islands was Ed Watson, who moved to Chokoloskee in the early 1880s. Watson had been suspected of murder several times: three times in Florida and in the Oklahoma Territory, where he reputedly joined forces with female outlaw Belle Starr. His luck ran out in Chokoloskee. First, he got into a fight with town patriarch Adolphus Santini and tried to slit his throat. Then two squatters turned up dead on his land. Three more corpses were found on his property, ostensibly murdered by a man named Cox. Watson threatened to kill the man, but the locals had had enough. A mob grabbed Watson and killed him. After this, the murders stopped, leading to the inevitable conclusion that Watson had been behind them.

*An airboat operator guides visitors on a tour of the Everglades.*

**BELOW:** several companies offer eco-tours, with an emphasis on low-impact modes of travel like canoes and kayaks that are excellent for spotting wildlife.

City residents and visitors today, are still a draw at the Rod and Gun Club, although the hotel has now seen better days.

## Big Cypress

Early in the history of Everglades National Park, it was clear that Big Cypress Basin, which receives much of the water flowing southwestward from Lake Okeechobee, warranted protection as a key element of the hydrologic system. These calls became urgent in the 1960s, when burgeoning land development and speculation schemes led to extensive logging and the partial draining of Big Cypress Swamp. In 1968, a proposed jetport on the swamp's eastern edge created a land rush and provoked massive opposition.

In 1974, a compromise between pro-development and pro-conservation groups was reached, when Congress authorized 720,000-acre (290,000-hectare) **Big Cypress National Preserve ❿**. It was one of the first preserves to be managed by the National Park Service

for multiple uses that include hunting, fishing, and offroad vehicles and airboats in addition to wildlife protection and low-impact activities like birdwatching, hiking, and camping.

**Oasis Visitor Center ⓫** (33100 Tamiami Trail East, Ochopee; tel: 239-695-1201, www.nps.gov/bicy; daily 9am–4.30pm) is exactly halfway between Naples and Miami, 5 miles (8km) east of SR 29, and has exhibits to help you plan a visit. All attractions are accessed off the Tamiami Trail. There are four scenic drives (The Loop, Turner River Road, Wagonwheel Road, and Birdon Road) and developed **Monument Lake** and **Midway campgrounds** along US 41.

The 27-mile (43-km) **Loop Drive**, beginning opposite the visitor center, is your best introduction to the beauty of Big Cypress. A gravel road travels among the "glades" (a term first used to describe the Everglades by an English surveyor in the 1700s). There are numerous openings in the forest that offer a peek at dwarf cypress trees (there are no "big cypress"—the name refers to the size of the forests) reflected in mirror-smooth brackish waters. Look for alligators,

snowy egrets, and other bird rookeries. There are four small primitive campgrounds, available on a first-come, first-served basis, with no water or usage fee.

A 6½-mile (10-km) one-way portion of the **Florida National Scenic Trail**, begins near the entrance to the Loop. Passing through **Roberts Lake Strand**, it's a wonderful way to find solitude among the haunting cypress and prairie. Remember: Outdoor activities are really only tolerable in the winter dry season, when temperatures average 75°F (25°C), humidity is generally low, and bugs are less pesky. In summer, when it's hot, wet, and humid, you'll have to slog through water that may rise to your chest, not to mention the millions of mosquitoes, no-see-ums, and other biting insects.

## West Tamiami Trail

All along the Tamiami Trail are places to pull off and watch egrets, herons, ibis, anhingas, cormorants, and other birds fishing in the Tamiami Canal. West of Big Cypress are several enjoyable trails and campgrounds. **Kirby Storter Roadside Park** has a pleasant boardwalk trail among the dwarf cypress. **H.P. Williams**

**Roadside Park**, on the north side of the road, adjoins the Turner River highway bridge and has picnic tables. The tiny roadside hamlet of **Ochopee** is famous for having the smallest post office in the country, a postage stamp–sized hut on the south side of the road tended by a very patient postmaster who will pose for photos, if you ask her. Ochopee is one of the few places on US 41 with a restaurant, actually a roadside shack serving seafood on paper plates.

Just past the turnoff for SR 29 is **Big Cypress Bend**, a delightful boardwalk

*The Ochopee Post Office is reputed to be the smallest in the US.*

**BELOW:** a park ranger leads a group on a nature walk along the Anhinga Trail.

*Birdwatching on the Big Cypress Bend boardwalk.*

**BELOW:** elevated boardwalks allow hikers to view the watery sections of the park.

the orchid and bromeliad capital of the US, with 44 native orchid species and 14 native bromeliad species, many epiphytes, or air plants, that grow on tree branches. Fakahatchee's orchids gained notoriety in the 1998 bestseller *The Orchid Thief*, author Susan Orlean's evocative account of the $10-billion illegal orchid trade in Florida. The exposé focused on maverick orchid collector John Laroche, a horticulture consultant for the Seminoles arrested for stealing rare ghost orchids in Fakahatchee Strand and propagating them for profit. The book was the source material for the 2002 movie *Adaptation*, starring Meryl Streep, Nicholas Cage, and Chris Cooper.

## Wildlife and wilderness

trail that offers a glimpse of **Fakahatchee Strand Preserve State Park** (tel. 239-695-4593), dubbed the "Amazon of North America." If you only have time to hike one trail on US 41, this is a great choice. Fakahatchee Strand is a very productive bird rookery, and you'll see brilliant flashes of wings and hear bird calls as you stroll this magical place. It's also the only spot where you'll see stately royal palms growing alongside dwarf cypress in "strands," the wetland forests of the Everglades.

Fakahatchee Strand is most famous as

If you have time, consider driving the **Jaynes Scenic Drive** north into the park, which takes you through open prairie that is home to Florida panthers and raptors like red-tailed hawks and vultures. Endangered panthers, which require several hundred square miles per cat, are almost never seen, although you may see their preferred prey, white-tailed deer. Naples Zoo, which has an excellent panther exhibit, works closely with Panther National Wildlife Refuge and Everglades National Park staff to radio-collar and track panther activity in the Everglades. There's not much to see at the refuge, although there is a boardwalk trail.

From Fakahatchee, its only 25 miles (40km) to Naples, a wonderful base for day trips if you want to combine a beach holiday and cultural activities with your Everglades forays *(see page 316)*. On your left as you drive north is the sparkling Gulf of Mexico. Ten Thousand Islands National Wildlife Refuge protects wildlife just north of Everglades National Park and is also a good place for kayaking. Another state park, Collier-Seminole State Park, sits at the turnoff for Marco Island across from Rookery Bay Estuarine Reserve. It has excellent camping, hiking, and picnicking. One of the "walking dredgers" used to drain the Tamiami Trail route is on display here.

# RESTAURANTS

## Restaurants

Prices for a three-course dinner per person, excluding tax, tip, and beverages:

**$** = under $20
**$$** = $20–45
**$$$** = $45–60
**$$$$** = over $60

## Chokoloskee

### Big House Coffee
238 Mamie St
Tel: 239-695-3633
L & D daily
This Floribbean restaurant is housed in the old 1890 McKinney Store on Chokoloskee Island. The menu includes hot pressed Cuban sandwiches, crab cakes and mango salsa, an organic Florida citrus salad, and a vegetarian special of portobello mushrooms broiled with goat cheese over linguine with pan fried yams, apples, and scallions. $$

## Everglades City

### Ghost Orchid Grill at the Ivey House Bed and Breakfast
107 Camellia St
Tel: 239-695-3299
B daily, closed May–Oct
Mingle with kayakers and other eco-adventurers and enjoy a basic but abundant buffet breakfast at this small historic lodge. $

### Oyster House
901 Copeland Ave E.
Tel: 239-695-2073
L & D daily, closed June–Sep
With sunset views over Chokoloskee Bay and a choice of fresh seafood and meats (the owner is a passionate hunter), Oyster House is one of the area's best dining experiences. The grilled grouper seems to have swum to your plate it's so fresh, and the stone crab can't be beat. $$–$$$

### Rod and Gun Club
205 Broadway
Tel: 239-695-2101
D daily
If only the dark paneled walls of this historic landmark could talk. A celebrity hideaway for a century, the club is a little long in the tooth, but you can still have them cook whatever you catch in the bay or enjoy stone crab, mullet, grouper, and other local seafood served with traditional hush puppies and corn on the cob. $$$$

## Homestead

### Farmers' Market Restaurant
300 N. Krome Ave
Tel: 305-242-0008
B, L & D daily
The plain appearance of this small family-run restaurant next to a farmers' market can be deceiving. People flock here for egg breakfasts and the super-fresh seafood and homemade pies. It's a great place to rub shoulders with the locals, who, understandably, like to keep this treasure to themselves. $

### Main Street Café
28 N. Krome Ave
Tel: 305-245-7575
L Tue–Sat, D Wed–Sat

Main Street Café serves deli sandwiches, soups, vegan sandwiches, and Caribbean specialties right on the main drag in Homestead. The café is popular for its excellent homemade soups, which are ladled from a "soup bar" at the rear of the restaurant. You'll also find conch salad, chicken potpie, smoked mahi mahi, and pizza. $–$$

### Robert Is Here
9200 SW 344th St
Tel: 305-246-1592
B, L & D daily Nov–Aug
This fruit stand is way out in the country at the turnoff from US 1 to the national park. Tropical fruit shakes are made in front of your eyes. Try the key lime shakes or refreshing mango. Florida fruit, veggies, salsa, and other goodies are available. Robert – a larger-than-life character who has been in business here since 1960 – is on hand. $

## Ochopee

### Joannie's Blue Crab Café
39395 Tamiami Trail
Tel: 239-695-2682
Daily 9am–5pm
A real Everglades experience, this highway café is on the Tamiami Trail in blink-and-you'll-miss-it Ochopee. It's classic backwoods cuisine: alligator fritters, Indian fry bread and salsa, and homemade sangria. You'll also find the eponymous blue crab soup, fruit smoothies, and a salad of fresh grilled veggies, bananas, and salsa. $

**RIGHT:** the Ivey House offers tasty food and comfortable lodging in Everglades City.

# EVERGLADES ECOLOGY

**The 'River of Grass' sustains a combination of tropical and temperate species found nowhere else in the United States**

The Everglades ecosystem is entirely dependent on the subtropical cycle of dry (winter) and wet (summer) seasons. The fauna and flora of the region have adapted to these alternating seasons, often moving from one part of the Everglades to another according to the fluctuations in water level – the lifeblood of this vast, mysterious wilderness.

## EVERGLADES HABITATS

The Everglades consists of a variety of habitats, each vital to the health of the overall ecosystem.
- **hardwood hammocks**: tree islands that stand above the high-water level and support mahogany, cabbage palms, and other trees, and provide a refuge for mammals such as raccoons in the wet season.
- **bayheads**: small, shallow islands dominated by bay trees growing on rich, organic soil.
- **willows**: wispy vegetation that grows in the deep water near hammocks – generally in the shape of a doughnut with a gator hole at the center.
- **sawgrass prairie**: covering much of the Glades, sawgrass grows on a thin layer of soil formed by decaying vegetation on the region's limestone base.
- **freshwater sloughs**: channels of freshwater that help plants and animals survive the harsh conditions of the dry season.
- **pinelands**: found in the few areas where the elevation is over 7 ft (2 meters). Fire is vital to their existence because it clears out competing vegetation.
- **cypress swamps**: areas where the water is deepest and the layer of soil extremely thin. Cypress trees are among the few species that tolerate such water-logged conditions.
- **coastal prairie**: contains salt-tolerant plants like cactus.
- **mangrove**: a dense tangle of mangrove trees that thrive along the southwestern coast. They play a vital role in protecting the shoreline against rough seas and act as a nursery for marine animals such as blue crab, shrimp, and molluscs.

**ABOVE:** alligators are vital to the ecology of the Everglades. During the wet season, they use their feet and snout to dig holes that store water during the dry months and serve as an oasis for many animals, including turtles and birds.

**RIGHT:** epiphytes, also known as air plants, are nonparasitic plants that grow on trees but get water and nutrients as they run down the bark and gather in crooks and hollows. Among the most distinct epiphytes found in the Everglades are Spanish moss and orchids.

**LEFT:** the Florida panther is a subspecies of the cougar that has adapted to a subtropical climate. This shy cat lives in the most remote areas of the Everglades, particularly in Big Cypress Swamp The panther is endangered: only 30 to 50 survive in the wild.

## SAVING THE EVERGLADES

About 30 percent of the Everglades has been lost thanks to human interference throughout the 20th century. Roads, canals, and dikes (such as Hoover Dike, above) impede the water's normal flow and the seasonal fluctuations in water levels. Much land has been drained for farming, while expanding urban areas on the coast have drained precious water for their washing machines and swimming pools. The dependence of industrial agriculture on chemical fertilizers has taken a heavy ecological toll as well. Especially disruptive is phosphorus, which encourages the growth of exotic plants such as cattails that have choked vast areas of marshland.

The campaign to save the Everglades took a giant leap forward in 2008 when Governor Charlie Crist announced the state's intention to purchase 187,000 acres (76,000 hectares) from the US Sugar Corporation. The deal will not only take a huge swath of land out of intensive agricultural production but help restore the natural flow of water from Lake Okeechobee south across the Everglades.

**ABOVE AND RIGHT:** the Everglades' rich bird life includes the endangered white ibis (above) and roseate spoonbill and the distinctive anhinga (right), often seen drying its feathers at water's edge. Birds of prey include the osprey and rare southern bald eagle.

**ABOVE:** apple snails are the sole diet of the endangered snail kite – a dependency typical of the Everglades.
**LEFT:** a great expanse of sawgrass, punctuated by tree islands known as "hammocks," is the classic Everglades landscape.

# FLORIDA KEYS

**A string of islands off the state's southern tip beckons travelers with beautiful beaches, crystal clear waters, and some of Florida's best snorkeling and scuba diving**

he Florida Keys are a ragged skein of some 800 islands formed of ancient coral reefs transformed into limestone bedrock. Only about 80 of them have names. The 20-plus islands that lie in a direct line were strung together first by an improbable railroad and later by the southernmost portion of US 1 dubbed the **Overseas Highway**, a 125-mile (200-km), 43-bridge exercise in forced linear travel, passing through each Keys community in unalterable sequence. The entire coastline – 2,800 sq nautical miles – is a designated National Marine Sanctuary.

The road through the Keys may appear to be a tacky strip lined with seedy storefronts, billboards, and gas stations. In many places, that's exactly what it is – but stifle your disappointment. Like the Everglades, the Keys do not dazzle the casual tourist who stays behind the windshield. Park the car. Get on a bicycle or boat. Suck in the sweet, clean air. Gape at the immense canopy of sky and the mounds of whipped clouds. Can you see the curve of the earth in the distance, where the sea turns from aqua to azure? Put on a mask, snorkel, and fins. Rent a rod and reel. You'll soon be overcome by Keys Disease.

## Biscayne National Park

Although not officially on the Keys, **Biscayne National Park ❶** (tel: 305-230-1275; www.nps.gov/bisc), a few miles east of **Homestead**, encompasses the northernmost portion of the region. Most of the park's 173,000 acres (70,000 hectares) are

inaccessible by car. It's a watery world of living coral reefs, mangrove shoreline, and tropical lagoons, inhabited by an astoundingly varied array of creatures ranging from manatees and parrotfish to pelicans. At the **Dante Fascell Visitor Center** on Convoy Point, visitors can opt for glass-bottom boat tours, scuba and snorkeling excursions, and boat rentals.

## On to the Keys

There are two ways to drive to the Keys from mainland Florida. The slower but more scenic route is US 1 south to Route

**Main attractions**
BISCAYNE NATIONAL PARK
PENNEKAMP STATE PARK
DOLPHIN COVE
FLORIDA KEYS WILD BIRD
   REHABILITATORS
THEATER OF THE SEA
DOLPHIN RESEARCH CENTER
BAHIA HONDA STATE PARK
LOOE KEY NATIONAL
   MARINE SANCTUARY
NATIONAL KEY DEER REFUGE

**LEFT:** Pennekamp State Park.
**BELOW:** a patient at the Turtle Hospital.

*Feeding an ailing dolphin at the Dolphin Cove Research & Education Center.*

**TIP**

Chamber of Commerce information centers along US 1 offer numerous money-saving coupons for Keys attractions.

997 just south of Florida City. A column of tall Australian pines graces the path to the Card Sound toll bridge. On either side of the bridge, clumps of red and black mangroves impersonate solid islands. The bridge ends on North Key Largo. A right on SR 905 leads through hammocks of Jamaica dogwood, loblolly, feathery lysiloma, and mahogany until the road runs directly back into US 1, the Overseas Highway.

The toll bridge and scenic detour can be avoided by continuing south on US 1 over Jewfish Creek and a sliver of road known as "Death Alley" until it was widened. Signs still advise drivers to be patient, because a passing zone is only minutes ahead – such signs are a recurrent feature throughout the Keys, as are frequent roadside memorials to accident victims testifying to the folly of impatience. When US 1 – and the road – eventually runs out, you've entered Key West.

## Key Largo

Humphrey Bogart, Lauren Bacall, and Edward G. Robinson confronted a killer hurricane on **Key Largo ②** in the movie of the same name. All that remains of those nostalgic Bogie days is the Caribbean Club Bar (MM 104), where a few scenes are rumored to have been filmed, and the original *African Queen*, cradled on davits and looking quite forlorn at a Holiday Inn just down the road.

The conch is queen of the Keys. Inside its shell – a familiar coffee-table ornament – the stalk-eyed blob is not among God's handsomest creations. But if you can put the conch's looks out of your mind, conch fritters, chowder, or salad make a tasty meal with a spicy kick (although today most of the conch eaten in the US comes from the Bahamas). For a close-up look at queen or horseshoe conchs in their natural habitat, visit **John Pennekamp Coral Reef State Park ❸** (MM 102.5; tel: 305-451-1202; www.pennekamppark.com; open daily), the country's first undersea park. Here, a 78 sq mile (200 sq km) coral reef extends 3 miles (5km) into the ocean, providing a home for a diverse community that includes nearly 600 species of fish. A park concession offers glass-bottom boat rides, sailing and snorkeling tours aboard a 38-ft (12-meter) catamaran, and kayak rentals. It also conducts scuba tours,

## Florida Keys

Recommended Restaurants and Bars on pages 154–5

ranging from a brief lesson followed by a non-certified dive that very afternoon to four-day classes earning PADI open water certification. Dive shops along US 1 offer similar packages. One of the highlights of a dive trip is a visit to **Key Largo Dry Rocks**, where the *Christ of the Deep*, a replica of Guido Galletti's statue *Christ of the Abyss* (in the Mediterranean Sea off Genoa, Italy) lies submerged in a natural valley surrounded by a coral reef in 21ft (7 meters) of water.

## Swim with dolphins

Two facilities within a few miles of each other provide an opportunity to learn about and swim with dolphins. **Dolphin Cove Research & Education Center** (MM 102; tel: 305-451-4060; www.dolphinscove.com; advance reservations; charge) offers bottlenose dolphin swims and encounters as well as eco-tours, sunset cruises, and flamingo trips. **Dolphins Plus** (MM 100; tel: 305-451-1993; www.dolphinsplus.com; open daily; charge), which offers a five-day dolphin therapy program for disabled people, also provides the opportunity to swim and interact with dolphins in structured or unstructured swims.

US 1 continues spectacularly through Rock Harbor to **Tavernier** ❹, once the site of a huge wrecking fleet that cruised the reefs claiming salvage from grounded ships. Today **Florida Keys Wild Bird Rehabilitators** (MM 93.6; tel: 305-852-4486, www.fkwbc.org; open daily) salvage and rehabilitate wild birds that have been injured by fish hooks, cars, and other human-related causes. Their outdoor facility is a wonderful place to learn about the birds of the Keys and is particularly fun at 3.30pm – pelican feeding time.

## South to the Purple Isles

Watch on the bay side for the **Rain Barrel Art & Craft Gallery** (MM 86.7; tel: 305-852-3084; open daily), a unique artisans' village. On **Windley Key** ❺ at the 125,000-year-old **Windley Key Fossil Reef Geological State Park** (MM 85; tel: 305-664-2540; visitor center open Thur–Mon 8am–5pm; charge) visitors are offered a rare opportunity to view fossilized specimens of ancient coral animals.

The 50-year-old landmark **Theater of the Sea** (MM 84.5; tel: 305-664-2431, www.theaterofthesea.com; reservation desk open daily 10am–5pm; charge) is host to

**TIP**

Addresses on the Keys are given as mile markers (MM). The markers begin just south of Florida City at MM 126 and end in Key West at MM 0. The Keys are divided into four sections: upper, MM 106-65; middle, MM 65-40; lower, MM 40-9; and Key West, MM 9–0. The designations B/S and O/S refer to bayside or oceanside locations.

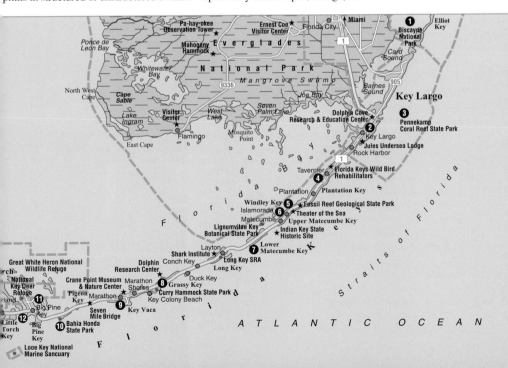

*Sunbathing in Marathon.*

**BELOW:** a Florida "wrecker" *c.*1858.
**BELOW RIGHT:** kicking back with a cold beer at a Key Largo bar.

sea lion and dolphin shows, glass-bottom boat rides, and even a shark pit. Reserve well in advance for the Dolphin Adventure package, which includes a swim with the dolphins.

The realization that vast seas completely surround these small tufts of land sinks in as you cross the bridge over Whale Harbor to **Upper Matecumbe Key**. Polished, armed-to-the-teeth fishing vessels lining the harbor trumpet the area's focus on sport fishing. The action revolves around **Islamorada ❻** (pronounced "eye-la-mo-rada"), which bills itself as the world's sport fishing capital. At the southern end of town, the **Hurricane Monument** (MM 81.6) commemorates 600 people who died in the Labor Day hurricane of 1935.

## Tarpons, spiders, dolphins

**Robbie's Marina** (MM 77.5; tel: 877 664-8498) on **Lower Matecumbe Ke ❼** is the embarkation point for a visit t **Lignumvitae Key Botanical State Park** accessible only by privately owned c charter boats (for reservations, tel: 305 664-9814; park open Thur–Mon, one-hou tours at 10am and 2pm). The tour include a visit to the 1919 Matheson House and stroll through a virgin tropical forest. Ren a glass-bottom kayak at Robbie's and pad dle out to **Indian Key**, an early "wreck ers'" settlement. Feeding the tarpons a Robbie's is a popular pastime.

From the Matecumbes, US 1 winds it way across increasingly breathtakin waterscapes to **Long Key State Recre ation Area**, with a beach, observatio tower, boardwalk and the Golden Or Weaver Nature Trail – named after th large but harmless spiders that spi sturdy, ornate webs in the trees.

On **Grassy Key ❽**, Flipper is the mos famous graduate of the **Dolphi Research Center** (MM 59; tel: 305-289 1121, www.dolphins.org; daily 9am–4.30pm charge), a serious nonprofit teaching an research facility that offers guided tours. ▶

## Wrecking Crew

It's difficult to imagine that abandoned and overgrown Indian Key was once a bustling settlement. It was the home port of Jacob Housman, one of the Keys' most notorious "wreckers," who bought the property in 1831 for $5,000. In an age before lighthouses, he was one of a hearty breed of seagoing salvagers who sailed out to distressed ships that had foundered on coral reefs to rescue passengers, and then strip the vessels of anything valuable. Wrecking was an honorable, legal, and profitable enterprise.

It was indeed profitable for Housman, who brought slaves to Indian Key to build him a mansion. There's speculation, however, about a dark side to his reputation: some wreckers were known to move navigation warning lights to assure they kept busy. It is known that Housman left the Keys under a cloud of suspicion.

Indian Key was devastated in the Second Seminole War, and it is believed that Housman died while working on a wrecker. Others of his profession fared better: In Key West, John H. Geiger's handsome home is now the Audubon House, and Asa Tift built the residence that Ernest Hemingway later made famous.

also possible to swim with resident dolphins at the center's Dolphin Encounter, but reservations must be made months in advance.

## Marathon

On the outskirts of **Marathon ❾**, the 10,000-acre (4,000-hectare) **Curry Hammock State Park** (MM 56; tel: 305-289-2690, www.floridastateparks.org/curryhammock; daily 8am–sunset; charge) encompasses five islands and the world's largest concentration of Florida thatch palms.

With a population of about 13,000, Marathon – primarily a cement strip of shopping centers and gas stations – is the main settlement in the Middle Keys. Numerous fishing charter boats depart from marinas here.

**Crane Point Museum and Nature Center** (MM 50.5; tel: 305-743-3900, www.cranepoint.org; Mon–Sat 9am–5pm, Sun noon–5pm;charge) offers a comprehensive overview of the Keys' history, wildlife, and ecology. Highlights include a wild bird center and a simulated tropical coral reef.

Yes, that really is a hospital for turtles in the center of town. And the **Turtle Hos-**

pital (MM 48.5; tel: 305-743-2552, www.turtlehospital.org; by reservation; charge) even has an ambulance to transport sea turtles during rescues and releases. The facility – the only state-certified veterinary hospital in the world for sea turtles – has been looking after its patients for more than 20 years. Guests who stay overnight at the adjacent Hidden Harbor Motel get a free tour of the hospital.

## Pigeon Key

Henry Flagler built housing on **Pigeon Key** to shelter workers he brought to

*A two-man band keeps patrons entertained at a waterfront bar.*

**BELOW:** sunset provides a spectacular backdrop to an evening meal.

*For a unique perspective on the National Key Deer Refuge, join a kayak tour led by naturalist Bill Keogh (tel: 305-872-7474; www.keyskayaktours.com).*

**BELOW:** jet skis are available throughout the Keys.

Florida to work on his Overseas Railroad (the nearby town earned its name when one of the workers referred to the project as a "marathon"). Several of the structures survived and are part of a tour that departs from the **Pigeon Key Visitors Center** (MM 48; tel: 305-743-5999, www.pigeonkey.net; departures at 10am, 11.30am, 1pm, 2.30 pm; charge). A film tells the fascinating story of Mr. Flagler and Flagler's Folly, the railroad he built from Miami to Key West in spite of huge obstacles.

## Seven Mile Bridge

The part of the highway that hops from Marathon to Big Pine Key is called **Seven Mile Bridge** and spans the longest between-island stretch you can drive in the Keys. Actually just a shade under 7 miles (11km) and built between 1979 and 1982, it runs over a channel between the Gulf of Mexico and the Straits of Florida. Paralleling it is the original bridge built for Flagler's railroad. The trains ran until the hurricane of 1935 ruined the roadbed and the Great Depression ruined the economy, making an automobile route a more practical alternative.

Just over the bridge, Big Pine Key is second in size only to Key Largo. **Bahia Honda State Park ⑩** (MM 37; tel: 305-872-2353, www.bahiahondapark.com; daily 8am–sunset; charge) has one of the best beaches on the Keys. You can rent a beach chair or explore the waters with rented dive equipment or a kayak. The highlight of a visit is a snorkeling tour out to **Looe Key National Marine Sanctuary**, whose 5-mile (8-km) stretch of reef is one of the world's most sensational aquatic showcases.

*Recommended Restaurants and Bars on pages 154–5*

## Big island, little deer

**Big Pine Key** ⓫ is home to the **National Key Deer Refuge** (visitor center at MM 30.5; Big Pine Shopping Center, 28950 Watson Blvd; tel: 305-872-0774, fws.gov/nationalkeydeer; park open daily sunrise–sunset). The colony of diminutive deer, a subspecies of the Virginia whitetail, grow to about 30 inches (75 cm) tall and 38 inches (95 cm) in length. In earlier days, hunters, developers, and automobiles reduced the population to less than 50, but efforts at the refuge – including strictly enforced speed limits – have boosted their numbers into the hundreds.

Turn right near MM 30 onto Key Deer Boulevard to the **Blue Hole**, a flooded quarry that attracts deer and alligators.

## The final keys

Farther down US 1, the **Torch Keys** ⓬ are named after their flammable trees. A short distance off **Little Torch Key** is a private island that houses the secluded and exclusive **Little Palm Island Resort and Spa**. Accessible by a ferry from Little Torch Key, the resort's villas cater to an elite clientele. The restaurant, however, is open to the public.

**Summerland Key** offers scenic side roads, and **Cudjoe Key** has modern campsites for large trailers. On **Sugar Loaf Key** ⓭, named for an Indian midden that looked like loaves of old-fashioned sugar, turn right just past MM 17 to view **Perky's bat tower**, built in 1929 as a boardinghouse for bats. The local businessman imported them in the hope they would swallow the island's mosquito problem, but once released from the tower, they never returned.

The **Saddlebunch Keys** are little more than a series of mangrove outcroppings. Big Coppit, Rockland, and East Rockland house the servicemen of the US Naval Air Station on **Boca Chica** (Little Mouth) **Key** ⓮. Stock Island, once a center for cattle herds and pigpens, serves as a suburb of Key West and is the home of the **Tennessee Williams Performing Arts Center** (tel: 305-295-7676, www.twstages.com).

Before crossing the next bridge, prepare yourself for the short hop into another, very different, world. You have literally reached the end of the road. This is Key West. ❑

**TIP**

Some people refer to the Keys as a 126-mile (203-km) traffic jam, which is at its worst on weekends. Try to plan your arrival and departure on a weekday.

**BELOW:** Bahia Honda State Park.

# RESTAURANTS AND BARS

## Restaurants

Prices for a three-course dinner per person, excluding tax, tip, and beverages:

**$** = under $20
**$$** = $20–45
**$$$** = $45–60
**$$$$** = over $60

### Big Pine Key

### Rob's Island Grill
31251 Avenue A (MM 31)
Tel: 305-872-3022
L & D Wed–Mon
With wall-to-wall TVs and two high-def big screens, this is *the* place for sports fans during college and pro games. Rob's offers American pub fare as well as a raw bar and more ambitious entrees such as prime rib on Friday and Saturday nights. $

### Islamorada

### Chanticleer South
81671 Overseas Hwy (MM 81.5)
Tel: 305-664-0640
D Tue–Sun
Chef Jean-Charles Berruet, for 35 years one of the premier restaurateurs of Nantucket, Massachusetts, has brought his considerable skill and creativity to the Keys. The contemporary French menu has a heavy emphasis on seafood, and because there are just 16 tables – 12 inside and 4 outside – he cooks almost all entrees by himself. Desserts, such as chocolate soufflé and apple tart with calvados, range from $14 to $17. $$$

### Islamorada Fish Company
81532 Overseas Hwy (MM 81.5)
Tel: 800-258-2559
L & D daily
Dine on the waterfront patio or in the original Island Conch House eatery, where stone crab and dynamite fish sandwiches get top billing. The historic and handsomely furnished Zane Grey Lounge hosts live music on weekends. $

### Lazy Days Oceanfront Bar & Grill
Overseas Hwy (MM 79.9)
Tel: 305-664-5256
L & D daily
Chef Lupe whips up tasty homemade soups, terrific fish sandwiches, and sublime coconut fried jumbo shrimp. And if you bring in your own fresh-caught seafood, she'll cook it to order. The outside patio overlooks the water. Happy hour from 4pm–6pm brings three-for-$1 appetizers. $–$$

### Marker 88
88000 Overseas Hwy (MM 88)
Tel: 305-852-9315
L & D daily
Sit back with a key lime martini and an appetizer of blackened tuna sashimi and enjoy the fabulous sunset over Florida Bay. All the fish on the menu is fresh from local waters; for the undecided, there's a seafood platter served over pasta. $$$–$$$$

### Key Largo

### Ballyhoo's Island Grille
97860 Overseas Hwy (MM 97.8 Median)
Tel: 305-852-0822
L & D daily
Although it's right on Route 1, this venerable restaurant in a 1930s conch house was once part of a fishing camp and evokes a feeling of stepping back in time. The all-you-can-eat fish and stone crab claw specials can't be beat, and there's a very cheerful happy hour from 4pm to 7pm. $

### The Fish House
102401 Overseas Hwy (MM 102.4)
Tel: 305-451-4665
L & D daily
Fresh fish is delivered right to the kitchen door and filleted on the spot at this Conch-style eatery which specializes in … fish. Next door, the Fish House Encore has a sushi bar, all-you-can-eat specials, and piano music Friday and Saturday evenings. $–$$

### Key Largo Conch Restaurant & Coffee Bar
100211 Overseas Hwy (MM 100.2), Oceanside Key
Tel: 305-453-4844
B, L & D daily
There's a full roster of homemade treats, including terrific lobster bisque and freshly prepared seafood. Patrons can access wi-fi, and pets are welcome. $

**LEFT:** both kids and adults enjoy Mrs Mac's Kitchen.
**OPPOSITE:** fresh seafood is a staple of Keys cuisine.

## Mrs Mac's Kitchen

99336 Overseas Hwy
(MM 99.5)
Tel: 305-451-3722
B, L & D Mon–Sat
Terrific Keys fare is served
in a funky diner atmos-
phere. All the standard
American favorites are
here, along with more
ambitious offerings pre-
pared with a Caribbean
flair. House specialties
include conch salad and
chowder, crab cakes, and
fish of the day with homemade Tijuana sauce. Wine
and beer are served, and
there's a kid's menu. $

## Snook's Bayside Restaurant

99470 Overseas Hwy
(MM 99.9)
Tel: 305-453-3799
L & D daily, Br Sun
Overlooking the Gulf of
Mexico, this informal spot
with an outdoor tiki bar
offers a creative menu
featuring mahi-mahi tacos
and pistachio-crusted yellowtail snapper. Tapas,
served from 3pm, range in
price from $7 to $14.
There's nightly entertainment, a Thursday night pig
roast with dancing, and a
Sunday brunch buffet. $$$

Little Palm Key

## Dining Room at Little Palm Island

28500 Overseas Hwy
Tel: 305-872-2551
B, L, D daily, Br Sun
Reserve well in advance
for this island resort
restaurant, which serves
sophisticated French and
pan-Latin cuisine.
Patrons (16 years of age
and older, please) can
opt for the elegant can-
dlelit waterfront dining
room or a table on the
beachfront terrace. $$$$

Little Torch Key

## Parrotdise Waterfront Bar and Grille

83 Barry Ave (MM 28.5)

Tel: 305-872-9989
L & D Wed–Sun
"You hook it, we cook it"
is the motto here. But
for the fishing-chal-
lenged, there are tasty
treats such as lobster
macaroni and cheese,
smoked dolphin dip, and
cashew grouper. Happy
hour is 3–7pm daily, and
the mellow sounds from
solo acoustic guitar
music entertain patrons
Thursday, Friday, and
Sunday. $–$$

Marathon

## Farella's Village Café

Overseas Hwy (MM 50.5)
Tel: 305-743-9090
B, L & D daily
For 20 years this has
been Marathon's favorite
destination for Italian
food. Pizza, pasta, home-
made soups, and a salad
bar share the menu with
fish specialties, including
shrimp scampi and bouill-
abaisse. On Sunday there
are breakfast and dinner
buffets. There's live
music and dancing on
weekends, and Wednes-
day is Latin night. $–$$

## Island Fish Company

12648 Overseas Hwy
(MM 54)
Tel: 305-743-4191
L & D daily
She-crab chowder,
freshly-shucked oysters,
and stone crab claws are
among the house
specialties. Tex-Mex
choices include seafood
quesadillas and grilled
shrimp tacos. And for
dessert – fried key lime
pie. $–$$

## Keys Fisheries Market & Marina

3502 Gulf View Ave (MM 49
at the end of 35th St)
Tel: 305-743-4353
B, L & D daily
It's flopping-fresh
seafood all the way at
this dockside fish mar-

ket, marina, and restau-
rant. House favorites
include blackened mahi-
mahi and Cajun snapper,
but the lobster Reuben
tops the charts. Music at
the tiki bar begins at
3pm. $

## 7 Mile Grill

1240 Overseas Hwy
(MM 47.5)
Tel: 305-743-4481
B, L & D daily
For more than 50 years a
Keys favorite for freshly
prepared, moderately
priced American fare.
Many items on the menu
are priced under $10,
including the fried oyster
sandwich and stuffed
crabs. $

## Bars

Big Pine Key

## No Name Pub

N. Watson Blvd
Tel: 305-872-9115 $
Since 1936 tourists have
been getting lost trying
to find their way here,
and they keep on
looking. Perhaps it's
because this is one of
the Keys' few remaining
untarted-up restaurants,
a place where locals
come to quaff a beer or
down a tasty burger or
cheesesteak sub. It's
right next to the No
Name Bridge ... ask a
local for directions. $

Grassy Key

## The Wreck & Galley Grill

58835 Overseas Hwy (MM 59)
Tel: 305-743-8282
A lively sports bar with
indoor and outdoor tiki
dining and daily all-you-
can-eat specials
including Monday frogs
legs, Thursday BBQ pork
ribs, Friday prime rib, and
Saturday crab. $

Islamorada

## Whistlestop

Overseas Hwy (MM 82.5)
Tel: 305-664-2623
This popular and mellow
sports bar offers a wide
range of pub and comfort
fare, including meatloaf
and brick-oven pizza. At
happy hour (4–6pm) the
game room is a boister-
ous and clubby spot. $

Stock Island

## Hogfish Bar/Grill

6810 Front St
Tel: 305-293-4041
A bustling but laid-back
spot on the waterfront
adjacent to the marina
that served as head-
quarters for the Bay of
Pigs operation. House
specialties include a
"Killer" hogfish sand-
wich on Cuban bread
and lobster BLTs. Live
weekend entertainment
and a mellow atmos-
phere make this a
favorite local hangout. $

# FLORIDA'S LIVING CORAL REEF

**Coral reefs have been described as underwater tropical forests. They teem with wildlife, from sea slugs to swarms of brilliantly colored fish**

The Florida Keys are fringed by the only true living coral reef in the continental US, stretching for some 200 miles (320km) from Miami to the Dry Tortugas. The reef is particularly rich in the Upper Keys, where it harbors around 500 species of fish and over 50 types of coral.

### THE REEF AS HABITAT

A coral reef is an efficient and diverse habitat. Every source of nutrients is used and recycled through a variety of food chains. Each chain starts with algae, which is either loose in the water or living inside corals. Small fish graze on corals, and in turn they are preyed upon by large fish.

Inner or "patch" reefs develop in shallow waters and feature delicate corals and colorful residents such as angelfish, tang, and spiny lobster. Farther out is the main barrier reef, with larger stands of hardier coral, where predatory fish such as barracudas and sharks cruise around and moray eels lurk in caves.

### A SENSITIVE ENVIRONMENT

Coral looks rock hard but is, in fact, very fragile, and sensitive to the slightest change in conditions. It grows only in shallow, clean, salt water, where the temperature is at least 68°F (19°C). Since coral needs sunlight to grow, if the water level rises too much it will die. The water must also be low in nutrients; an excess of nutrients causes algae to flourish until it eventually smothers the coral.

Florida's reef has been under intense ecological pressure. The main threats are pollution (from agricultural run-off, oil, and sewage), overfishing, and tourism. John Pennekamp Coral Reef State Park attracts over a million visitors annually. The reef is damaged by clumsily driven boats and by careless divers who touch or step on the coral. A reef takes thousands of years to form, and new growth of coral does not keep pace with the rapid die-off.

**RIGHT**: the stinging tentacles of a sea anemone target all sorts of small creatures that float past, including fish and shrimp.

**ABOVE**: Like other soft corals, sea fans have a flexible skeleton rather than a rigid casing. They thrive in the inner reefs, where they are less likely to be damaged by wave action

**LEFT**: The slender body of the queen angelfish allows it to slip through narrow gaps in the reef.

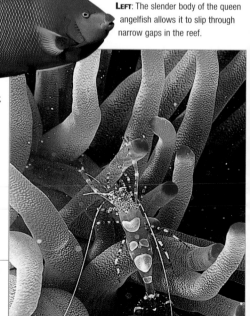

## HOW CORAL IS FORMED

Every coral is a colony of hundreds of soft-bodied animals called polyps, each of which usually measures about a quarter of an inch (5mm) across.

By extracting calcium from the sea water, each polyp constructs a skeleton of limestone that forms a protective casing; together these skeletons make up a coral. Most of the reef consists of the casings of dead polyps, which build up on top of one another over many thousands of years. Only the top surface of the reef is alive.

Until around 200 years ago, people commonly believed that polyps were plants. They are, in fact, related to jellyfish and sea anemones, and have tentacles, a mouth, and a stomach. During the daytime, the polyp extends its stinging tentacles around the mouth (as in the picture of brain coral at the top) in order to catch phytoplankton in the surrounding sea water; they close again at night.

Most corals grow in partnership with algae, which exist inside them. Polyps get oxygen and nutrients from the algae and, in return, the algae extract carbon dioxide for photosynthesis. Algae also give coral its color. The manner and rate at which a coral grows depends on its species and water conditions.

**ABOVE**: stripes and other patterns make it difficult for predators to spot prey. Fish like grunts also seek safety in numbers.

**LEFT**: although they resemble plants, sponges – like coral – are stationary aquatic animals that feed on bacteria, phytoplankton, and other tiny organisms by filtering water through their pores.

*Recommended Restaurants and Bars on pages 166–7*

# KEY WEST

At the state's southernmost tip is the 'Conch Republic,' a gathering of free thinkers with a laid-back attitude and a penchant for good times

Orlando
Florida
Miami
Key West

The gateway to **Key West** ⓰ – the southernmost point in the continental United States – is as prosaic as any in Florida. US 1 on the outskirts of town is littered with the detritus of modern life – an unbroken chain of shopping centers, hotels, car dealers, and fast-food restaurants. However, as you proceed south into the town center, the character of the place changes quickly: the American flavor of fast-food emporiums and strip malls evaporates in an ambience that's not quite Bahamian, not quite Cuban, not quite nautical – just very Key West.

Here homes and businesses – some restored, some crumbling – meld in a collage of discordant color that somehow suits this city. The people who blend into this bizarre landscape are as incongruous as the colors: long-haired survivors of the hippie era, gay couples, leather-faced fishermen, jet-setters and yachters, and, of course, an enormous number of tourists. Only in Key West could so much that is so different seem so right.

## The early days

The inimitable character of Key West derives in large part from its history as a haven for transients. Its proximity to the American mainland and the West Indies has introduced many different influences, but the city has transformed those influences into something totally its own.

Somehow, the Calusa Indians managed to get to this speck 100 miles (160km) from the Florida peninsula, 90 miles (145km) from Cuba, 66 miles (106km) north of the Tropic of Cancer. The Spanish were the first Europeans to explore the waters and build settlements here, but Indians and pirates made life dangerous. In fact, a young Spanish cavalryman, granted Key West by his governor in 1815, gladly sold it six years later for just $2,000 to Alabama businessman John Simonton. The settlement became part of the US in 1821 when Florida was ceded by Spain. In 1845 the government began constructing a Naval Base (now called **Truman Annex**) and in 1866 completed **Fort Zachary Taylor** ⓐ

**LEFT:** a classic Conch house.
**BELOW:** a "pirate" greets visitors.

*The 2,000 to 3,000 free-range chickens that peck their way through the streets of Key West descend from the mid-1800s when residents kept the birds for cock fights and food. Many townspeople take pride in their gypsy livestock, extending their "live free" philosophy to the birds. Others consider them a pestilence. The Chicken Store, at 1229 Duval Street, is dedicated to keeping the flock safe, often sending out the Rooster Rescue Team to aid orphaned and injured birds.*

(Southard St; tel: 305-292-6713, www.floridastateparks.org; daily 8am–sunset; charge), now a museum of Civil War artifacts, to defend the coastline. The **East Martello Museum and Gallery** (3501 S. Roosevelt Blvd; tel: 305-296-3913, www.kwahs.com; daily 9am–5pm; charge) was one of two towers that were begun – but never completed – and meant to help defend the fort. Today it houses local-history exhibits.

## Mixed fortunes

For many years the business of "wrecking"– the salvaging of ships that foundered on treacherous offshore reefs – was a boon to the economy. By 1888 Key West was the largest city in Florida and had become the richest city per capita in the US, a distinction that lasted into the early 1900s. Towards the end of the 19th century, lighthouses had reduced the need for wreckers, but Cuban migrants had imported cigar-making along with their rich culture, and sponge fishermen also prospered.

Completion of the Overseas Railroad in 1912 added another dimension to the booming economy: tourism. Yet by 1930

Key West faced collapse. The stock market crash of 1929, coupled with the closing of the US naval station, disease in the sponge beds, and labor troubles that forced cigar makers to Tampa, began a decline that reached rock bottom with the destruction of the railroad in the 1935 hurricane.

World War II provided a catalyst when the Navy reclaimed its island facilities and President Harry S. Truman established his **Little White House** ❸ (111 Front St; tel: 305-294-9911, www.trumanlittlewhitehouse .com; daily 9am–4.30pm, tours every 20 minutes; charge) on the base. The disastrous Bay of Pigs invasion followed by the Cuban Missile Crisis during John F. Kennedy's presidency brought another brief wave of military money. While not as visible as in the past, the Navy is still present in Key West, though nowadays tourism, shrimping, and restoration seem to be the city's major businesses.

## Getting Oriented

**Old Town**, the original part of the city, encompasses approximately 3,000 historic buildings, as well as Mallory Square and the Historic Seaport. There are a couple of ways to get an overview of the

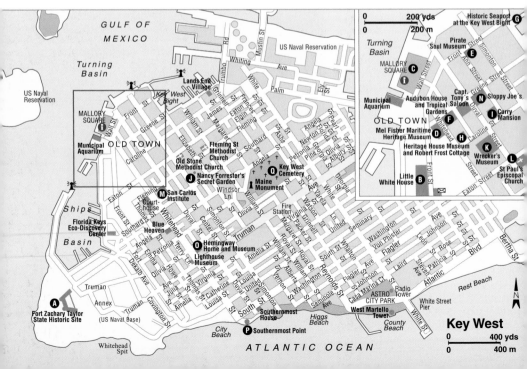

*Recommended Restaurants and Bars on pages 166–7*

island: the venerable **Conch Train** (tel: 305-294-5161, www.conchtourtrain.com) and its newer clone, the **Old Town Trolley** (tel: 305-296-6688, www.historictours.com). The trolley allows riders to disembark and reboard at several spots along the route. Both leave every 30 minutes from different locations around town, including Mallory Square.

If Old Town is the heart of Key West, **Mallory Square ⓒ** is its commercial soul – the spot around which the city grew and lately the place around which its renaissance has revolved. Throngs of tourists gather here every evening for the famous **Sunset Celebration**. The sun doesn't just set here. On the contrary, the shiny orange orb gets an extraordinary send-off from an astonishing assortment of jugglers, fire-eaters, acrobats, and peddlers. It's such a popular event that the Westin Resort hired the hugely popular Dominic and his Flying House Cats to move from the Mallory Square pier to their own pier to perform. The miniature Mardi Gras occasionally upstages even the main attraction. A sunset that teases the sky with a pink streak before torching it aflame in reds and

oranges can elicit standing ovations from the assembled crowd.

## Of pirates and painters

Many of the main attractions are within walking distance of Mallory Square, and most of them tell a story about the area's rich history. The **Mel Fisher Maritime Heritage Museum ⓓ** (200 Greene St; tel: 305-294-2633, www.melfisher.org; Mon–Fri 8.30am–5pm, Sat–Sun 9am–5pm; charge) displays treasures from the Spanish ships

*The East Martello Museum is housed in a structure built – but never used – as a defensive tower.*

**BELOW LEFT:** music man in Mallory Square. **BELOW:** Little White House.

### Harry's Hideaway

There was once a famous part-time resident who loved this town even though he was the last person anyone would have diagnosed with Keys Disease. "I've a notion," he once remarked, "to move the capital to Key West and just stay."

Harry S. Truman used to duck out of Washington whenever he could and settle in, loud Hawaiian shirts and all, at the former commandant's quarters at the Key West naval station. He brought plenty of work with him, but there was always time for fun. One of the highlights of a tour of the Little White House Museum is a poker table on the downstairs veranda, where Truman would stay up late with naval officers and civilian aides, playing hand after hand in a mellow matrix of bourbon, conversation, and cigar smoke. For lunch he would walk over to Pepe's on Caroline Street.

Other presidents have also found Key West to be a salubrious and sometimes strategic spot. President Kennedy set up his command post here during the Bay of Pigs Invasion in 1961, and many of the 125,000 Cubans who arrived in the 1980 Mariel boatlift landed here.

*Colorful shops and cottages line Duval Street.*

**BELOW:** crowds and entertainers gather for the daily Sunset Celebration in Mallory Square.

(524 Front St; tel: 305-292-1113, www.piratesoul.com; daily 9am–7pm; charge) recreates piracy's golden age from 1690 to 1730; displays include the world's only authenticated pirate treasure chest.

John James Audubon (1785–1851) usually heads the lists of painters associated with Key West. In fact, the naturalist-artist spent only a short time here while sketching Florida's birds, but that tenuous connection with the city didn't stop entrepreneurs from renovating and reopening the 1830 house where he stayed. The **Audubon House and Tropical Gardens** ❶ (205 Whitehead St; tel: 305-294-2116, www.audubonhouse.com; daily 9.30am–4.30pm; charge) showcases the artist's original folio of *Birds of America*.

*Nuestra Señora de Atocha* and *Santa Margarita*, which sank in the waters west of Key West during a fierce hurricane in 1622, as well as accounts of the hunt and dramatic salvage operation.

Pirate lore, Ernest Hemingway's bloodstained World War I uniform, and fanciful paintings by folk artist Mario Sanchez are among the permanent exhibits at the nearby **Museum of Art & History** (281 Front St; tel: 305-295-6616, www.kwahs.com; daily 9.30am–4.30pm; charge), in the 1891 Custom House.

Pat Croce's **Pirate Soul Museum** ❶

## Historic Seaport

Once home to the island's shrimping fleet, the **Historic Seaport at the Key West Bight** ❶ is today home port of most of the island's charter fishing and touring boats, as well as the **Harborwalk** that connects a number of popular restaurants and bars, including **Turtle Kraals** and **Half Shell Raw Bar**. A visit to the city isn't complete without a voyage on its waters,

*Recommended Restaurants and Bars on pages 166–7*

and schooners such as the 80-ft (24-meter) *Liberty* (tel: 305-292-0332; www.libertyfleet.com) offer a magnificent opportunity.

The **Key West Express** (tel: 888-539-2628; www.seakeywestexpress.com) to Fort Myers Beach, Marco Island, and Miami also sails from here.

## Old Town ramble

Key Westers have indulged an infatuation with restoring their homes, a hobby that has transformed the island into a live-in architectural museum, and the best way to savor Old Town is on foot.

Start on Caroline Street, with several fine old mansions. The **Heritage House Museum and Robert Frost Cottage** ❶ (410 Caroline St; tel: 305-296-3573, www.heritagehousemuseum.org; Mon–Sat 10am–4pm; charge) at No. 410 is typical of Bahamian styles. The **George A.T. Roberts House** at No. 313, with its spacious veranda and gingerbread trim, exemplifies Conch architecture. The **Curry Mansion** ❶ at No. 511, which admits visitors (tel: 305-294-5349; charge), is also a guest house, as is the 1887 **Conch-style Cypress House** at No. 601.

Other highlights include **Nancy For-**rester's Secret Garden ❶ (Free School Lane, just past 521 Simonton; tel: 305-294-0015, www.nancyforrester.com; open daily 10am–5pm; charge), a lush rainforest with orchids, palms, and tropical birds; writer Shel Silverstein's Greek Revival home and studio on the 600 block of William Street; the Octagon House at 712 Eaton Street once owned by clothing designer Calvin Klein; and poet Elizabeth Bishop's home at No. 624 White Street.

## The Duval Crawl

**Duval Street**, which stretches from the Gulf to the Atlantic, has an iconic status in Key West. It's where the bars are – not all of them, but enough for a slow promenade down this bright, boisterous avenue where the music begins in the afternoon and continues into the wee hours at places like **Jimmy Buffet's Margaritaville** and the **Hog's Breath Saloon**.

The lower end of Duval, toward Mallory Square, has a slew of souvenir shops selling lewd T-shirts and shot glasses. Wade past them to No. 322, the Oldest House Museum, also known as the **Wrecker's Museum** ❶ (tel: 305-294-9501, www.oirf.org; Thu–Sat 10am–2pm;

**TIP**

One of Key West's newest attractions is the $6-million Florida Keys Eco-Discovery Center (accessed through Truman Annex at the end of Southard St; tel: 305-809-4750). The environmental education facility showcases the Keys' underwater and upland habitats, and exhibits include a walk-through version of the Aquarius Undersea Lab, a manned underwater research habitat off Key Largo.

**BELOW LEFT:** Museum of Art & History. **BELOW:** Audubon House.

charge), the 1829 home of a sea captain who made his money from wrecking; **St Paul's Episcopal Church**  at No. 401, which offers free organ and piano concerts on weekdays beginning at noon; and some of the city's finest art galleries. At No. 516 the **San Carlos Institute** (tel: 305-294-3887; Fri–Sun noon–6pm), a theater, museum and cultural center, caters to the Cuban emigrant community.

## Papa's place

At the corner of Greene and Duval streets is one of Key West's most famous bars, **Sloppy Joe's**, touted as one of Ernest Hemingway's favorite watering holes when he lived here from 1931 to 1940 with his wife Pauline. Purists will want to quench their thirst at **Captain Tony's Saloon** (428 Greene St) – the original Sloppy Joe's and the oldest licensed saloon in Florida. The interior, wallpapered in business cards and newspaper clippings, will take you back to the time when Hemingway relaxed here with a drink after a hard day at the typewriter.

He would stroll down from his home, now preserved as the **Hemingway Home and Museum** (907 Whitehead St; tel: 305-294-1136, www.hemingwayhome.com; daily 9am–5pm; charge). His writing studio out back appears as it did when he worked here on such novels as *To Have and Have Not*, which is set in Key West. Descendants of his six-toed cats still have the run of the place and drink from a fountain that once served as the urinal at Captain Tony's.

## The southern tip

Across the road from Hemingway's house is the **Key West Lighthouse and Keeper's Quarters Museum** (938 Whitehead St; tel: 305-294-0012, www.kwahs.com; daily 9.30am–4.30pm; charge). Built in 1847 and decommissioned in 1969, the lighthouse has been restored and visitors can climb the 88 steps for incredible views.

A rather smaller beacon is the **Southernmost Point**, at the corner of Whitehead and South streets. While it has lost its title as southernmost point in the US to a spot on the Big Island of Hawaii, this landmark is still 755 miles (1,215km) south of Los Angeles. Nearby is the 1896 **Southernmost House** (1400 Duval St; tel: 305-296-3141, www.south

*The Hemingway Home is decorated with hunting trophies and other objects from the author's many adventures.*

**BELOW:** Southernmost House.

*Recommended Restaurants and Bars on pages 166–7*

ernmosthouse.com; open daily; charge), which exhibits documents, including autographs of George Washington and Thomas Jefferson, and memorabilia from former Key West residents Hemingway and Tennessee Williams (who lived at 1431 Duncan St).

## Bahama Village

In **Bahama Village** on the western edge of Old Town, the city's Caribbean atmosphere is at its strongest, with modest, colorfully painted wooden houses, restaurants, and shops. On Thomas Street, Hemingway sometimes boxed at the **Blue Heaven** restaurant back when it was a saloon. Jazz trumpet legend "Fats" Navarro lived at No. 828.

## Key West Cemetery

Even 20-acre (8-hectare) **Key West Cemetery ⓞ**, established in 1847, has fascinating sights. Among them are a statue of a lone sailor that commemorates the 252 men who died aboard the battleship *Maine*, which sank in Havana in 1898, and epitaphs reading "I told you I was sick" and "Devoted fan of singer Julio Iglesias." The cemetery has been the center of a controversy because of the local custom of recycling graves.

## Off key

For all of its air of "that's all there is, there ain't no more," Key West isn't the last of the Florida Keys. To reach the westernmost of the islands, you have to travel by boat or seaplane to the Dry Tortugas, 68 miles (109km) beyond Duval Street's last bar.

Romantic as it sounds today, the name merely told 16th-century mariners that the island was "dry," meaning there was no freshwater; *tortugas*, Spanish for turtles, meant there was no fresh meat. There wasn't much else until 1846. That was when the US government started laying bricks on the Tortugas' Garden Key to create the largest masonry structure in the Western Hemisphere. The hexagonal Fort Jefferson – the "Gibraltar of the Gulf" – was built to provide a safe haven for American vessels pausing near

the entrance to the Gulf of Mexico for repairs or provisioning. Never completed and abandoned by the Army in 1874, in 1992 the fort became **Dry Tortugas National Park ⓰** (for ferry information, tel: 305-292-6100, www.fortjefferson.com; departures daily at 8am, return at 5pm; charge). Today, the appropriate line for the place might be "ye shall beat your swords into snorkels." The waters beneath the fort's walls are ideal for exploring the coral reefs that are one of the Keys' most famous attractions. ❏

*Sloppy Joe's, one of Ernest Hemingway's favorite bars, has been in business for more than four decades.*

**BELOW:** Key West Lighthouse and Keeper's Quarters Museum.

# RESTAURANTS AND BARS

## Restaurants

Prices for a three-course dinner per person, excluding tax, tip, and beverages:
**$** = under $20
**$$** = $20–45
**$$$** = $45–60
**$$$$** = over $60

### A&B Lobster House
700 Front St
Tel: 305-294-5880
D daily
The caviar is delivered fresh daily, and lobsters are flown in from Maine. House specialties include grouper Oscar, Brazil nut snapper, and farm-raised baby conch sautéed in rum butter sauce. But the beef here also measures up, with offerings such as filet mignon Béarnaise. The waterfront view is spectacular from the wrap-around balcony, and a stop at the property's Berlin's Cocktail & Cigar Bar for a nightcap rounds out a perfect evening. $$$–$$$$

### Alice's Restaurant
1114 Duval St
Tel: 305-292-5733
Br, L & D daily
Chef Alice Weingarten, "the queen of Key West cuisine," describes her food as "New World fusion confusion." But don't let her fool you; she knows exactly what she's cooking up – dishes like crispy lacquered duck, macadamia coconut crusted shrimp, and spicy pink vodka conch bisque. Small and large plates are available. Start off with a pomegranate cosmopolitan cocktail, and finish up with Alice's terrific cappuccino bread pudding or tropical fruit shortcake. $$$

### Blue Heaven
729 Thomas St
Tel: 305-296-8666
B, L & D daily
Journalist Charles Kuralt said of the scallop sauce here: "[it] would make cardboard taste good." The breakfasts, including shrimp and grits and made-from-scratch pancakes, are delicious. The lunch and dinner menu relies heavily on Caribbean influences, with specialties including Caribbean barbecue shrimp and yellowtail snapper. There's a lovely outdoor patio. $–$$

### B.O.'s Fish Wagon
801 Caroline St
Tel: 305-294-9272
L & D daily
Many consider this rustic, open-air spot to be a defining Key West dining experience. Get in line for delicious, if somewhat pricy, fish sandwiches, chili, conch fritters, and homemade fries. Live entertainment. No credit cards. $

### Café Marquesa
Marquesa Hotel,
600 Fleming St
Tel: 305-292-1244
D daily
This is a popular spot for an elegant and romantic meal. The sophisticated New American menu emphasizes seafood and might include macadamia-crusted yellowtail snapper or Nantucket scallop lasagnetta with blue crab and porcini sauce. $$$–$$$$

### Café Solé
1029 Southard St
Tel: 305-294-0230
D daily
Chef John Correa combines his extensive knowledge of French sauces with local seafood to create a unique menu that might include bouillabaisse or conch carpaccio – Bahamian conch sliced thin and served with virgin olive oil and lime juice. But his signature dish – hog snapper with a red pepper zabaglione – is a culinary standout. $$$

### Commodore Waterfront Restaurant
700 Front St, Historic Seaport
Tel: 305-294-9191
D daily
When you're tired of grouper and snapper and looking to sink your teeth into a succulent hunk of prime rib or a New York sirloin with melted Roquefort cheese and cream, head over to this bustling, open-air waterfront spot. There are, however, loads of fresh fish items on the menu, including Florida lobster tails. Three-course prix fixe menus are offered. $$$–$$$$

### El Siboney Restaurant
900 Catherine St
Tel: 305-296-4184
L & D daily

**RIGHT AND LEFT:** a cool drink and a tasty bite on the patio at the Blue Heaven.

Here's a Key West treasure: a Cuban restaurant with great ambience and ample portions of well-prepared, reasonably priced food. Order a sangria and perhaps the daily special, which might be grilled grouper fillet, *masas de puerco fritas* (fried pork chunks), or *bistec de Palomilla*. All entrees are served with rice, black beans, sweet plantains, and Cuban bread. $

### Martin's Fine European Dining
917 Duval St
Tel: 305-295-0111
D daily, Br Fri–Sun
Expect fine European dining with an accent on German cuisine served in elegant, contemporary surroundings. House specials include marlad confit, weiner schnitzel, and jager schnitzel with homemade spaetzle. Brunch selections include a handsomely prepared seafood crepe and lobster Benedict. $$$–$$$$

### Paradise Café
1000 Eaton St
Tel: 305-296-5001
B & L Mon–Sat
As advertised, the "home of the monster sandwich" serves up terrific sandwiches on Cuban bread toasted on a press, along with half-pound burgers, homemade soups, Cuban cooked pork, breakfast sandwiches, and terrific key lime pie. Indoor and outdoor seating is limited, but the waterfront is just a short walk away. $

### Pepés Café and Steak House
806 Caroline St
Tel: 305-294-7192
B, L & D daily
The oldest restaurant in

the Keys (established in 1909) isn't resting on its laurels: the food is excellent and still served in the outdoor enclosed courtyard where Harry Truman loved to dine. Hand-cut steaks are a house specialty, as are fresh oysters and key lime pie. Sunday night BBQ packs in the crowds. $$–$$$

### Pisces Seafood Restaurant
1007 Simonton St
Tel: 305-294-7100
D daily
For 25 years this intimate, candlelit restaurant has been one of the most popular destinations for award-winning seafood. In their signature dish, "tango mango," shelled Maine lobster medallions and shrimp are flambéed in cognac. Original works by Andy Warhol are on display. $$$–$$$$

### Turtle Kraals Restaurant & Bar
Margaret St and Historic Seaport
Tel: 305-294-2640
B, L & D daily
The large and diverse menu at this waterfront eatery features classic fried seafood platters, chowders, and dishes prepared with a Southwestern flair. It opens at 7am for breakfast and stays open until the wee hours. $–$$

### Bars
### Aqua Nightclub
711 Duval St
Tel: 305-294-0555
Gays and straights turn out to party at this club that has one of the island's largest dance floors and best sound systems. Tuesday to Sunday nights at 9pm the popular drag performers, the Aquanettes, take the

stage. Monday is karaoke night, and on other nights DJs and/or live performers entertain.

### Bull & Whistle Bar
224 Duval St
Tel: 305-296-4565
A three-tiered establishment with something for almost everyone: The Bull, an open-air bar with live entertainment; The Whistle, with a wrap-around balcony overlooking Duval Street action below; and the Garden of Eden, a clothing-optional rooftop bar.

### Fogarty's Flying Monkey's Saloon
227 Duval St
Tel: 305-294-7525
A favorite watering hole for Key West 20-somethings attracted by the 22-ounce key lime margaritas, $1 Jell-O shots, and "Howlers" – a lethal potion of grain alcohol, vodka, and lemonade. The food here is surprisingly good, too.

### Green Parrot
601 Whitehead St
Tel: 305-294-6133
The first and last bar on US 1 has been a popular watering hole since 1890. Tourists and locals pack in to listen to blues on the legendary jukebox as well as for the live weekend entertainment.

### Hog's Breath Saloon
Duval and Front sts
Tel: 305-296-4222
A Key West institution featuring live entertainment; happy hour daily 5–7pm; a raw bar; and Coney Island hot dogs.

### Virgilio's
524 Duval St
Tel: 305-296-8118
A classic cocktail lounge with live music, dancing, Monday night $5 martinis, and a varied clientele dressed in everything from Carhartts to Chanel. La Trattoria, in front of the bar, provides a late-night dining menu.

# ATLANTIC COAST

The sun and sea that lured early tourists to Florida's east coast are still a big attraction, but there are also fascinating historic sites, including the oldest continuously occupied city in the US

D riving Florida's Atlantic coast retraces the route that funneled early "tin-can" tourists toward the seaside playgrounds of Miami and Fort Lauderdale. Strung along the coast are dozens of towns and cities, each with a distinct personality and its own slice of the tourism market.

Fort Lauderdale, on the southern end of the "Gold Coast," which starts just north of Miami, is perhaps best known for hard-partying college-age visitors, though the city has worked hard to refashion itself into a family-friendly destination. Palm Beach and Boca Raton, on the other hand, are favored by the upper crust, who inhabit lavish waterfront mansions and exclusive country clubs.

To the north is the Space Coast, site of the Kennedy Space Center. Nearby are the brackish lagoons and pristine beaches of Merritt Island National Wildlife Refuge and the old-time seaside town of Cocoa Beach, popular with surfers.

The pace quickens dramatically a little farther north at Daytona Beach, which is notable as both a spring break destination and as the home of Daytona International Speedway, site of the Daytona 500 and other auto races. Historic St Augustine, the oldest continuously inhabited city in the US, operates at a decidedly slower pace and contrasts sharply with Jacksonville, Florida's largest city, with a revitalized downtown, numerous museums, and active port.

Motorists on the Atlantic coast have a choice of routes. A1A is slow and narrow but usually within tantalizing sight of the ocean; US 1 is somewhat speedier but tends to be clogged with local traffic, though it's not a bad option for short drives; and I-95 is, predictably, the fastest and least scenic but is still a sensible choice if you need to cover the greatest distance in the least time. ❑

---

**PRECEDING PAGES:** a quiet inlet on Amelia Island.
**LEFT:** there's nightly entertainment at the Trade Winds Lounge in St Augustine.
**TOP:** a kitschy architectural detail at the Magic Beach Motel in Vilano Beach.
**ABOVE RIGHT:** the Apollo/Saturn V Center at the Kennedy Space Center.

*Recommended Restaurants and Bars on pages 180–1*

# FORT LAUDERDALE

The party scene has mellowed a bit – the town
fathers are cultivating a family-friendly image –
but the Strip remains a popular destination
for those in search of sun, surf, and sand

I t seems almost inconceivable that **Fort Lauderdale's ❶** beautiful beaches and resorts were a dismal swamp less than a century ago. A wooden fort built here during the Seminole Wars rotted for two decades after troops left in 1857. The only significant development during this period was the construction of a House of Refuge for shipwrecked sailors. For the most part, it remained a waterlogged hideaway for escaped slaves and army deserters.

Once again, Henry Flagler's railroad changed everything. In 1911, the city was incorporated. The swampy coast kept construction off the famous beach, and, as a result, the sands were kept open to the public, and hotels and businesses were situated on the far side of Route A1A.

## Beach party

Known as the **Strip**, the city's palm-lined, 2-mile (3-km) beachfront was romanticized as a spring-break destination in the 1960 beach-party movie and song *Where the Boys Are*. For much of the 1970s, the Strip was the site of what seemed like one big drunken beach party. A crackdown in the 1980s put an end to the brawls and other alcohol-infused disruptions. New bars that were not part of hotels were banned, as was public consumption of liquor. Arrests for violations were common. By 1990, many spring-break revelers had decamped to Daytona Beach.

Kids still come for a glimpse of the Strip, but their numbers are smaller and their behavior has been tempered; you'll find many more families these days. The once-notorious **Elbo Room** bar ❹, made famous in the movie, is still open, but even the bartenders admit that it's not what it used to be. Although toned down a bit, Fort Lauderdale still has a lively bar scene, with much of the action along Commercial and Las Olas boulevards and the banks of the Intracoastal Waterway.

Over the next several years, the Strip will undergo a major transformation as numerous high-rise condominiums and luxury hotels open for business. Among those hoping to strike gold are the Atlantic Hotel & Spa, Hilton Fort

**Main attractions**
THE STRIP
RIVERWALK
MUSEUM OF ART FORT LAUDERDALE
MUSEUM OF DISCOVERY AND SCIENCE
DANIA JAI-ALAI
SEMINOLE HARD ROCK HOTEL AND CASINO
LOXAHATCHEE NATIONAL WILDLIFE REFUGE

**LEFT:** the beach at Las Olas Boulevard.
**BELOW:** tropical blossom at Butterfly World.

Lauderdale Beach, Trump International Hotel & Tower, and the W Fort Lauderdale Hotel.

## The waterfront

Fort Lauderdale is heralded as the "Yachting Capital of the World," and more than 44,000 yachts are registered here. Many tie up at **Bahia Mar Yacht Basin B** at the southern end of town. Fans of John D. MacDonald's Travis McGee novels may recognize the marina as home of the fictional detective's houseboat, *The Busted Flush*.

Just to the north, the **International Swimming Hall of Fame C** (1 Hall of Fame Dr; tel: 954-462-6536, www.ishof.org; daily 9am–5pm; charge), a showplace for water sports, houses two pools, a diving well, and a swimming flume, as well as Olympic memorabilia.

## The Strip's northern end

At the northern end of the beach, hidden behind seagrape trees, **Bonnet House Museum and Gardens D** (900 N. Birch Rd; tel: 954-563-5393, www.bonnethouse.org; guided tours Tue–Sat 10am–4pm, Sun noon–4pm; charge) is perhaps

the city's most curious sight. Built in 1920 by the late Evelyn and Frederic Bartlett, both artists, it is a lyrical mansion of artistic whimsy, decorated with unusual antiques and an odd collection of knickknacks. Descendants of Mrs Bartlett's beloved Brazilian monkeys still inhabit the manicured grounds of the 35-acre (14-hectare) estate, now listed in the National Register of Historic Places.

Across the way, at the 180-acre (70-hectare) **Hugh Taylor Birch State Recreation Area E** (3109 E. Sunrise Blvd; tel: 954-564-4521; daily 8am–sunset; charge), visitors can swim, hike, and rent canoes to explore the lagoons.

## The Venice of America

When developer Charles Rodes was faced with transforming acres of mangrove swamp into prime real estate in the 1920s, he resorted to "finger-islanding" – dredging up a series of parallel canals and using the fill to create long peninsulas between them. It was the same system used in a certain Italian city. Rodes dubbed his creation **The Isles F**, and Fort Lauderdale earned the nickname "Venice of America." The Isles have

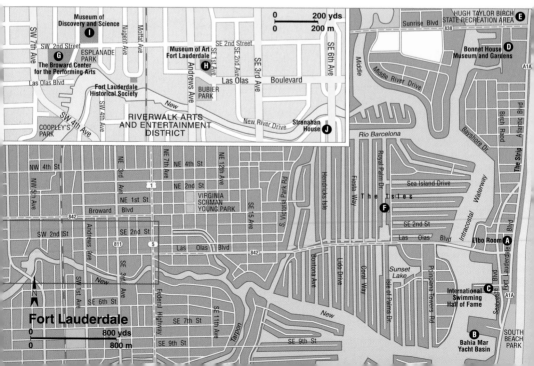

more than 300 miles (484 km) of canals, inlets, rivers, and bays, and along their frontage ornate mansions sit cheek-by-jowl with tiny cracker boxes awaiting the wrecking ball.

Numerous companies offer narrated tours of The Isles' "millionaire's row." The somewhat worn but serviceable *Jungle Queen* (tel: 954-462-5596, www.jungle-queen.com), an old-fashioned riverboat, sails from a dock just off Seabreeze Boulevard, next to Bahia Mar. The three-hour cruise includes a 45-minute stop at Jungle Isle, home to several lethargic alligators and an overpriced snack bar; the evening cruise includes an all-you-can-eat barbecue on the island. The *Carrie B* (Las Olas Blvd at SE 5th Ave; tel: 954-768-9920, www.carriebcruises.com), a replica 19th-century paddle-wheeler, offers 90-minute narrated cruises. Riders pay a one-time fare for unlimited trips aboard the **Water Bus** (tel: 954-467-6677, www.watertaxi.com), which cruises the waterways and includes stops at many downtown attractions.

## Riverwalk

Gas-lit Las Olas Boulevard, peppered with shops, restaurants, and galleries, is the major thoroughfare from the beach to downtown's **Riverwalk Arts and Entertainment District** (tel: 954-462-0222, 800-249-ARTS, www.stay4stars.com). Many of the city's top attractions are here, linked by a promenade along the New River.

On the western end, **The Broward Center for the Performing Arts** **G** (201 SW 5th Ave; tel: 954-462-0222, www.browardcenter.org) hosts a full roster of concerts, dance, opera, and ballet.

At the **Museum of Art Fort Lauderdale** **H** (1 E. Las Olas Blvd; tel: 954-525-5500, www.moafl.org; Wed–Mon 11am–7pm; charge) is an impressive col-

*Fort Lauderdale's party scene isn't as wild as it used to be, but it's still a popular destination for college-age beachgoers.*

**BELOW:** a Riverwalk restaurant.

**TIP**

Is it a circus? Is it a flea market? With elephants, clowns, and more than 12 million visitors each year, the 80-acre (32-hectare) Swap Shop of Fort Lauderdale (3291 W. Sunrise Blvd; tel: 954-791-7927; www.floridaswapshop.com) is a bit of both.

lection that includes works by Picasso, Calder, Dalí, Warhol, and William Glackens. There's also an extensive exhibit of European Expressionists from the late 1940s and '50s, the so-called CoBrA works by artists from Copenhagen, Brussels, and Amsterdam.

Nearby, the **Museum of Discovery and Science ❶** (401 SW 2nd St; tel: 954-467-6637, www.mods.org; Mon–Sat 10am–5pm, Sun noon–6pm; charge), South Florida's largest science museum, has more than 200 hands-on educational exhibits and the region's only IMAX 3D/PSE theater.

The **Fort Lauderdale Historical Society** (219 SW 2nd St; tel: 954-463-

4431, www.oldfortlauderdale.org; Tue–Sat 10am–5pm, Sun noon–5pm; charge), housed in the New River Inn, oversees several historic properties. At the promenade's eastern end is **Stranahan House ❿** (Las Olas Blvd at 335 SE 6th Ave; tel: 954-524-4736, www.stranahanhouse.org; tours daily 1pm, 2pm, and 3pm; charge), the restored turn-of-the-19th-century home of Fort Lauderdale pioneer Frank Stranahan and Broward County's oldest structure.

## A sea of slots

Numerous cruise ships with onboard casinos set sail from **Port Everglades ❷** in the southern part of the city. SeaEscapes Cruises (tel: 877-SEA-ESCAPE, www.seaescape.com) specializes in day and evening cruises; Imperial Majesty Cruise Line (tel: 954-453-4625, www.imperialmajesty.com) is host to two-night cruises to Nassau in the Bahamas.

## Jai-alai, fishing, butterflies

Five miles (8km) south of Fort Lauderdale, in **Dania ❸**, is the **John U. Lloyd Beach State Recreation Area ❹** (tel: 954-923-2833; daily 8am–sunset;

charge), with 244 acres (99 hectares) of barrier island and a stunning beach. It is also home to the **International Fishing Hall of Fame and Museum** (300 Gulf Stream Way; tel: 954-927-2628, www.igfa.org; Mon–Sat 10am–6pm, Sun noon–6pm; charge). But most folks visit to catch the live sports action at **Dania Jai-Alai** (301 E. Dania Beach Blvd; tel: 954-920-1511, www.betdania.com; games Tue–Sat at 7pm; Tues, Sat, and Sun matinees; charge).

Just to the west, in **Davie**, **Flamingo Gardens ❺** (3750 S. Flamingo Rd; tel 954-473-2955, www.flamingogardens.org; daily 9.30am–5.30pm; closed Mon June–Sept; charge) encompasses an historic home, 60 acres (24 hectares) of rare plants, and a wildlife and bird sanctuary.

## Hollywood

Continue south to **Hollywood ❻**, which was founded by a Californian but bears no resemblance to its West Coast namesake. The major draw is the 2-mile (3-km) oceanfront boardwalk and its entertainment complex of restaurants, bars, shops, and cinemas. Hollywood Beach is a favorite winter vacation spot for tens of thousands of French Canadians, transforming it into a bilingual community.

Just inland, on SR7, attractions at the **Seminole Indian Native Village ❼** (tel: 954-961-4519) include alligator wrestling shows, a poker casino and bingo hall, and a history museum. The nearby **Seminole Hard Rock Hotel and Casino** (tel: 954-327-7625, www.seminolehardrockhollywood.com; open 24 hrs) is one of the state's most modern gambling halls.

*The Museum of Discovery and Science features interactive exhibits designed to educate and entertain.*

**LEFT:** Dania Jai-Alai offers parimutuel betting.
**BELOW:** a peacock, Flamingo Gardens.

vegetables – along with pickles from New York, bagels, and fresh-baked treat – are sold at the farmers' market at th **Festival Flea Market Mall** (2900 W Sample Rd; tel: 954-979-4555, www festival.com; Mon–Fri 9.30am–5pm, Sat Sun 9.30am–6pm), which has more tha 500 vendors.

At Coconut Creek's **Butterfly World** (3600 W. Sample Rd; tel: 954-977-4400 www.butterflyworld.com; Mon–Sat 9am 5pm, Sun 11am–5pm; charge), visito can view more than 5,000 butterflie representing some 50 species that f freely in aviaries at the world's large facility of its kind.

## Up the coast

The beach drive north from Fort Lauderdale is particularly rewarding. The oceanfront strip of A1A through Lauderdale-by-the-Sea is lined with small, moderately-priced motels and inexpensive restaurants. From here the road brushes the shoreline Intracoastal Waterway.

Although it has grown rapidly as a resort, **Pompano Beach** ❽ – "swordfish capital of the world" – is still a major agricultural center. The area's fruits and

## Boca Raton

When architect Addison Mizner built th Cloister Inn in 1926 on 356 prime acre (144 hectares) in **Boca Raton** ❾, h envisioned the entire area becoming resort, with a fleet of gondolas romanti cally plying a canal through town. Th waterway was never completed; instea the filled-in ditch became the Camin Real, where tall palms grace the route t his inn, now the **Boca Raton Resort** (te 561-447-3000). The **Boca Raton His**

**rical Society** (tel: 561-395-6766, www.
>cahistory.org) offers tours.

Mizner's dream was partially realized.
oca today is one of Florida's most
oscale villages, with elegant boutiques,
iic restaurants, and a first-rate museum.
he **Boca Raton Museum of Art** (501
laza Real, Mizner Park; tel: 561-392-
500, www.bocamuseum.org; Tue–Fri
0am–5pm, Wed to 9pm, Sat–Sun noon–
pm; charge) exhibits works by artists
anging from Matisse and Modigliani to
/arhol, as well as pre-Columbian and
frican art.

Boca's posh veneer even surpasses that
f Palm Beach in one respect: it is home
f the **Royal Palm Polo Sports Club**
8000 Jog Rd; tel: 561-994-1876;
harge), "the winter polo capital of the
orld." Matches are open to the public
undays at 3pm Jan–mid-Apr.

## elray Beach

elray Beach ⑩ is an inexpensive alter-
ative to the resorts to the north and south.
he nearby **Morikami Museum and**
**apanese Gardens** (4000 Morikami Park
d; tel: 561-495-0233, www.morikami.org;
ue–Sun 10am–5pm; charge) is an

unusual find, a tribute to the culture of a
colony of Japanese immigrants.

It is well worth making the trip 10
miles (16km) inland to the **Loxahatchee**
**National Wildlife Refuge ⑪** (tel: 561-
734-8303; www.fws.gov/loxahatchee; refuge
open daily sunrise–sunset; visitor center open Wed–Fri 9am–4pm, Sat–Sun
9am–4.30pm; charge), which contains
the most northerly part of the Everglades.
Wildlife ranges from alligators to a great
variety of birds.                          ❏

*The Seminole Hard
Rock Hotel and
Casino has
nightclubs,
restaurants, a spa,
rock concerts, and, of
course, gambling.*

**BELOW:** civil rights
protestors, 1963.

## African-American History

**F**ort Lauderdale's $14 million African Amer-
ican Research Library and Cultural Center
(2650 Sistrunk Blvd; tel: 954-625-2800;
Mon–Thu 10am–9pm, Fri–Sat 10am–6pm,
Sun 1pm–5pm) is one of the country's three
such public research facilities, and the only
one that includes Caribbean as well as African
cultures. Today the local black population is
growing rapidly, due largely to the arrival of
Caribbean immigrants. But the area was not
always quite so welcoming. Segregation was
a way of life well into the 1960s. Many citizens remember the days when
they could swim only on holidays at John Lloyd State Park and had to attend
segregated schools. The Old Dillard School (1009 NW 4th St; tel: 754-322-
8828) was built in 1924 to serve as the first school for black children in
Broward County. Known as the "colored school," the 10-classroom building
is now a museum and education center.

Today Fort Lauderdale is a melting pot: Latinos, Asians, and immigrants
from a host of other nations are settling here, and the ethnic diversity is
creating a cosmopolitan atmosphere unusual for a city of its size.

# RESTAURANTS AND BARS

## Restaurants

Prices for a three-course dinner per person, excluding tax, tip, and beverages:

**$** = under $20
**$$** = $20–45
**$$$** = $45–60
**$$$$** = over $60

## Boca Raton

### Henry's
16850 Jog Road
Tel: 561-638-1949
L Mon–Sat, D daily
Care for a glass of champagne with your meatloaf? This "country club row" restaurant's impressive wine list accompanies a menu of gourmet comfort food. Diner aficionados will be happy to see standard classics along with more upscale offerings for discriminating palates. $$

### Jake's Stone Crab Restaurant
514 Via De Palmas
Tel: 561-347-1055
D daily, L Fri–Sun
King crab is given the royal treatment, as is the restaurant's namesake stone crab and a huge selection of fish delivered daily. House specialties include Bahamian conch chowder and she-crab soup. $$$–$$$$

### Mark's Mizner Park
344 Plaza Real, Mizner Park
Tel: 561-395-0770
L & D daily, Sun Br
Chef Mark continues his award-winning contemporary American formula in a spacious, ultrachic spot with an al fresco patio. In addition to pizza and handcrafted pasta, signature dishes include black spaghetti with clams, mussels, shrimp, and scallops, and oak-grilled veal chop. $$

## Dania

### Le Petit Café de Dania
3308 Griffin Rd
Tel: 954-967-9912
L Tue–Fri, D Tue–Sun
French-born chef Christian le Padellac combines some of Brittany's tastiest treats with contemporary American touches. Luncheon crepes with fillings such as Swiss cheese, shrimp, and garlic butter are ethereal. Dinner entrees range from frogs' legs with garlic and herbs to veal cordon bleu. And for dessert? La crêpe, naturellement. $$–$$$

## Fort Lauderdale

### Aruba Beach Café
1 E. Commercial Blvd
Tel: 954-776-0001
L & D daily, B Sun buffet
A diverse menu and live entertainment keep this waterfront spot hopping. The broiled seafood platter tops $30, but burgers, salads, and conch fritters are always on the menu. $–$$

### Canyon
1818 E. Sunrise Blvd
Tel: 954-765-1950
D nightly
Reservations for this popular, intimate Southwestern bistro? "No way – forget about it," warns the website. But patrons stoically wait in line for an opportunity to relax in one of the intimate, draped booths, sip prickly-pear margaritas, and graze on specialties such as masala-dusted bison skewers and jalapeño panko-crusted jumbo shrimp. $$$

### Capital Grille
Galleria Mall,
2430 E. Sunrise Blvd
Tel: 954-462-0000
L & D daily
The steakhouse chain that originated in Washington, DC, specializes in dry aged beef, with specialties such as Kona-crusted sirloin and porcini-rubbed Delmonico steak. The atmosphere is akin to a gentlemen's club, with dark wood and stuffed animal heads. $$$$

### Casablanca Café
3049 Alhambra St
Tel: 954-764-3500
L & D daily
Although it bills itself as an American piano bar and restaurant, the menu at this romantic beachside spot ranges from spanakopita to fettuccine con pollo. Live entertainment Wednesday, Friday, and Saturday evenings features jazz and contemporary pop. $$

### Chima Brazilian Steakhouse
2400 E. Las Olas Blvd
Tel: 954-712-0580
L Tue–Sun, D daily
Bring a big appetite to this fixed-price, all-you-can-eat Brazilian barbecue, where gaucho-costumed waiters dart about the elegantly

**LEFT:** Riverwalk has more than a dozen eateries.
**OPPOSITE:** the Quarterdeck is good for a casual meal.

decorated room with huge skewers of more than 15 different cuts of meat. A large and diverse salad bar is included. $$$$

### Eduardo de San Angel
2822 E. Commercial Blvd
Tel: 954-772-4731
D Mon–Sat
*Gourmet* magazine has rated Eduardo Pria's restaurant one of the best in the US, and indeed the Mexican-born chef has put together a menu that may be unique north – and south – of the border. Fresh flowers and crisp linen table-cloths set the mood for elegantly-prepared dishes such as slow roasted crispy duck with spicy guava syrup and ancho chile-flavored crepe with cuitlacoche, serrano chiles, and onions. $$$

### Grille 66 and Bar
Hyatt Regency Pier 66,
2301 SE 17th St
Tel: 954-728-3500
L & D daily
You've got to respect a place that features "The Baked Potato," sea-salted, with Vermont butter, smoked bacon bits, and chive sour cream. It works because it's delicious, as is the 24-ounce porterhouse with truffle butter and the veal Milanese with arugula salad. And somehow it all tastes better because your table overlooks the intracoastal waterway. The wine list features more than 400 vintages. $$$–$$$$

### Quarterdeck
2933 E. Las Olas Blvd
Tel: 954-525-2010
Daily 11am–2am
This is a Florida chain decorated in nautical paraphernalia and serving burgers, seafood, sandwiches, and other

hearty staples. The bar attracts a young, lively crowd. $–$$

### River House
301 SW 3rd Ave
Tel: 954-525-7661
L & D daily, Sun Br
Housed in three historic buildings along the scenic Riverwalk, the specialty here is "day boat" fish – freshly caught and delivered to the kitchen door. Many of the dishes reflect a fusion of Caribbean, Asian, Mexican, Mediterranean, and American influences. Sunday brunch includes a raw bar and carving stations. $$–$$$

### Thai Spice
1514 E. Commercial Blvd
Tel: 954-771-4535
L Mon–Fri, D daily
Traditional and original Asian dishes, with an emphasis on fresh seafood, in three intimate dining rooms. There's a fine wine list and an unusually lengthy desert menu. $$

Lake Worth
### Bizaare Avenue Café
921 Lake Ave
Tel: 561-588-4488
D Tue–Sat
There are two floors in this renovated 1926 building. Patrons dine upstairs on a traditional American bistro menu while watching "beautiful and bizarre images" on a 6-ft (2-meter) screen. Downstairs they lounge in easy chairs and order tapas, wraps, and light fare. $$$

Oakland Park
### Catfish Dewey's
4003 N. Andrews Ave
Tel: 954-566-5333
L Mon–Sat, D daily
The ambience – complete with sea horse chandelier and stuffed fish – is old-time Florida, as are the reasonable prices. Nightly

all-you-can-eat specials feature farm-raised catfish, fried sea scallops, barbecue ribs, and stone crabs in season. $–$$

Pompano Beach
### Darrel & Oliver's Café Maxx
2601 E. Atlantic Blvd
Tel: 954-782-0606
D daily
For more than 20 years one of the area's most highly regarded restaurants has been serving its own version of eclectic New American dishes, creating treats such as blue cheese and pine nut-crusted rack of lamb and mango jerk-glazed pork tenderloin. There's a superb wine list as well as a full bar. $$$–$$$$

### Bars
Boca Raton
### Gatsby's
Shoppes at Village Point,
5970 SW18th St
Tel: 561-393-3900
The place to watch a Gators game, play some pool, and chow down on classic pub grub. The Sushi Room is open Wed–Sat evening.

Delray Beach
### Blue Anchor
804 Atlantic Ave
Tel: 561-272-7272
There's Guinness on draft (served ice cold, Florida style) and a menu of authentic dishes such as steak and kidney pie and roast beef with Yorkshire

pudding at this beachfront British pub. Live entertainment Thur–Sat.

### City Limits
19 NE 3rd Ave
Tel: 561-279-8222
Don't look for bar snacks and pizza. This place is all about the music. The club's sound system pumps out some of the area's best live entertainment, from blues to funk to Latin Thur–Sat night.

Fort Lauderdale
### O'Hara's Music Café
722 E. Las Olas Blvd
Tel: 954-524-1764
A favorite for weekday happy hour and live music ranging from jazz and R&B to classic rock. The outdoor patio is a prime spot for people-watching.

### Village Pump Bar
4404 El Mar Dr
Tel: 954-776-5840
One of Fort Lauderdale's oldest bars is always hopping. But when Boston's favorite baseball team is playing, the "home of Red Sox Nation" really rocks.

### Waxy O'Connor's Irish Pub & Eatery
1093 SE 17th St
Tel: 954-525-9299
Huge digital screens are tuned into current sports matches at this Irish pub. Patrons begin to pack the outdoor patio beginning at happy hour at 4pm and stay into the wee hours as live bands rock.

*Recommended Restaurants and Bars on pages 194–5*

# PALM BEACH

There are Mediterranean-style mansions, classy shops and restaurants, pristine nature preserves, and several fine cultural venues in and around this sanctuary for the super-rich

The joke has it that Mother Nature would have built **Palm Beach ❶** if she had enough money. And indeed, the sweet aroma of dollars permeates the entire length of the 4½-mile (7-km) island, a living tableau of over-the-top opulence. Fortunately, plans floated by locals over the years (including one requiring residents to have ID cards to enter) sank, and the roads into – and out of – one of the country's wealthiest towns are open to all.

You can leave Florida – and enter Palm Beach – by proceeding north on Route A1A. You can't miss it. The garish shopping centers and neon hotel signs vanish. Clean, uncluttered streets take over. The structures behind the high walls of concrete and ficus hedges aren't museums; they're the trophy homes of the ultrarich.

## Palm Beach takes root

There seem to be various stories as to the origins of the city's signature palm trees. The most popular relates how a boatload of Spanish sailors transporting 100 cases of wine stumbled upon the barren strand in 1878. They sold their cargo, including 20,000 coconuts, to a shrewd islander for $20. The islander sold two coconuts for a nickel to his neighbors. They planted them in the sand and, voilà, the beach got its palms.

In the 1890s, Rockefeller partner Henry Flagler visited the area. He liked it, built a winter home (Whitehall), and transformed Palm Beach into a personal playground for himself and his wealthy, fun-loving friends. Astors and Vanderbilts and assorted dukes and duchesses followed Flagler into town. They stayed at Flagler's Royal Poinciana Hotel, one of the largest wooden buildings ever constructed and the largest resort hotel of its time. With more than a touch of the era's characteristic racism, black men once pedaled guests around the grounds aboard "Afromobiles," and a feature attraction was Cakewalk Night, when black dancers competed for a big white cake, then entertained richly dressed guests with spirituals. The hotel burned down several

**Main attractions**

THE BREAKERS
WORTH AVENUE
SOCIETY OF THE FOUR ARTS
FLAGLER MUSEUM
CITYPLACE
NORTON MUSEUM OF ART
KRAVIS CENTER
PALM BEACH GARDENS
SINGER ISLAND
JUPITER
HOBE SOUND
SAVANNAS PRESERVE

**LEFT:** downtown Palm Beach.
**BELOW:** relaxing on the beach.

**TIP**

Make sure the kids pack
their bathing suits for a
visit to the Palm Beach
Zoo (1301 Summit Blvd;
tel: 561-533-0887;
www.palmbeachzoo.org),
just off I-95. They can
cool down in the dancing
fountain after touring the
23-acre (9-hectare) zoo,
where exhibits include
more than 400 animals
and an $18-million re-
creation of a Central and
South American rainfor-
est. Lunch and refresh-
ments are served at the
lakefront Tropics Café.

**BELOW:** Society of
the Four Arts.

times and eventually was reborn as **The Breakers Ⓐ** (1 S. County Rd; tel: 561-655-6611, www.thebreakers.com), but its ghost lingers on – fortunately, minus the Afromobiles and tasteless entertainment.

Palm Beach's next transformation began when New York architect Addison Mizner came to visit in 1918. He stayed on, adding his ostentatious flourishes to existing Spanish structures, creating a fanciful yet functional self-contained world of spires, courtyards, plazas, and arcades that contribute greatly to the town's present-day charm and distinctive appearance. Visitors can see his designs along many of the manicured avenues.

## The season

In his enlightening literary portrait, Palm Beach resident and author John Ney told the story of a young Junior Chamber of Commerce type bragging at a Palm Beach party. "I'm one of those under-40 millionaires!" the man boasted, startling a long-time resident who quickly replied, "I was a millionaire before I was born!" The moral of the story is that it's impossible to ride into Palm Beach and blend in with the surroundings, so don't even try.

Unless you prefer to gape at empty mansions undergoing beauty treatments and garden manicures, visit during the "social season" – an indeterminate period of time that falls between Thanksgiving and Easter. That's when you'll see the pretty people who actually live in the palatial dwellings. The annual migration of the moneyed class ignites a round of galas, charity balls, and political cocktail parties in election years. People willing to pay $1,000 or more per plate can get invited to some of the prestigious balls. But it may take a larger donation to get into one of the exclusive political gatherings.

## Touring the town

The centerpiece of "downtown" Palm Beach is **Worth Avenue Ⓑ**. It has been likened to London's Bond Street, Paris' Faubourg St Honoré, and Rome's Via Condotti. Here a multitude of art galleries, boutiques, antique shops and jewelry stores – many housed in buildings designed by Mizner – open onto courtyards and winding vistas. Mizner's 1920s Town Hall and Casa de Leoni (450 Worth Ave), which hints at a Venetian Gothic influence, also exemplify his style.

*Recommended Restaurants and Bars on pages 194–5*

The cultural hub of Palm Beach is **The Society of the Four Arts** Ⓒ (2 Four Arts Plaza; tel: 561-655-7226, www.fourarts.org; gallery open Mon–Sat 10am–5pm and Sun 2pm–5pm, gardens open daily 10am–5pm; charge), a nonprofit cultural organization founded in 1936. The campus, on the intracoastal waterway, encompasses an art gallery, auditorium, two libraries, and botanical gardens.

Continue down Cocoanut Row to Whitehall, built in 1902 and now open to the public as the **Flagler Museum** Ⓓ (1 Whitehall Way; tel: 561-655-2833, www.flaglermuseum.us; Sun noon–5pm, Tue–Sat 10am–5pm; charge), the top single attraction in Palm Beach. Flagler and his third wife lived in this great Beaux Arts mansion, dubbed the "Taj Mahal of North America," for only four years. The rooms and most original furnishings have been restored, and one of Flagler's railroad cars is on display in the garden. Highlights inside include the Marble Hall, with its painted ceiling and elegant staircase, and the master bathroom, with a wonderful onyx washstand. The decor in some of the bedrooms was very innovative in the Flaglers' day. Nearby is the

Royal Poinciana Chapel and Sea Gull Cottage, which were built by Flagler in 1886 to be his first winter home.

The Breakers has weathered booms, busts, and even two fires, but it remains one of the nation's first-class resorts. Stately Venetian arches lead into the lobby, comfortable sofas and Persian carpets line the rambling hallways, and the Circle Dining Room has a vast skylight, cathedral windows, and a bronze chandelier. The Flagler Steak House is one of the town's power restaurants. Another cavernous old hotel, **The Biltmore** (north of Royal Poinciana Way), func-

*Worth Avenue is the centerpiece of Palm Beach's tony shopping district.*

**BELOW:** Bethesda-by-the-Sea Episcopal Church was built in Gothic style in 1925.

*CityPlace has more than 65 shops and restaurants, plus nightclubs and a movie theater.*

**BELOW:** patio dining at the elegant Café Boulud.

of late cereal heiress Marjorie Merriweather Post, a National Historic Landmark. It's now **Mar-A-Lago E**, owned by entrepreneur Donald Trump, who bought the 17-acre (7-hectare) property in 1985, turned it into a spa and country club, and opened membership to anyone who could afford the $150,000 initiation fee. It was here, in 2004, that "The Donald" married supermodel Melania Kauss.

At No. 126 is the estate Addison Mizner built in 1919 for cosmetics mogul Estée Lauder. Nearby is El Mirasol, a home built by Mizner and formerly owned by John Lennon ("Imagine no possessions …"). Next door stands a house that once belonged to Woolworth Donahue, heir to the dime-store fortune. One of "The Donald's" homes, on 7 acres (3 hectares) of oceanfront, recently went on the market for $125 million.

On North Ocean Boulevard is the former estate of the Kennedys. It became known as the "Winter White House" in the 1960s when John F. Kennedy first wintered here, but John Ney wrote of a local prejudice against this neighboring "royal family." It was here, in 1992, that Kennedy's nephew, William Kennedy

tions at the moment as a condominium.

Show up at least a half-hour before noon to get a courtyard table at the elegant **Café Boulud** (*see listing page 194*) in the Brazilian Court Hotel just a short walk from Worth Avenue. Younger heirs gravitate to **Ta-boo** (*see listing page 194*), right on the Avenue. The Esplanade, at the eastern end, is a two-story clutch of shops surrounding a courtyard with another popular lunch spot, **Café L'Europe**.

## Mansion Row

Known as Mansion Row, South Ocean Boulevard runs past the Moorish estate

Smith, was charged with raping a young woman he had met in a Palm Beach bar. After a televised trial, Smith was found not guilty.

If you keep driving north on Ocean Boulevard you will eventually run out of road. Park in a metered space, if you can find one, and take the short hike to the wooden clock on the **Palm Beach Inlet**. If you make it early enough you will witness a sunrise all the money around you can't buy.

## The sport of kings

With champagne hawked from a canopied cart instead of hot dogs and beer, it's obvious that polo is not like a Sunday afternoon baseball game. Palm Beach's pet sport is played at the nearby **Palm Beach Polo and Country Club** (11199 Polo Club Rd, West Palm Beach) and Boca Raton's **Royal Palm Polo Sports Club**. Here, some of the top matches in the world have attracted players such as Great Britain's Prince Charles. You must be either rich or have a wealthy sponsor to participate. But it costs little to watch from your car. More than 20 area polo fields host matches from October to July.

## The other Palm Beach

Across Lake Worth, the city of **West Palm Beach** ⑦ was conceived as a satellite by its rich patron, Flagler. It was reserved for servants, gardeners, and other workers who toiled to keep Palm Beach from crumbling while their employers partied, shopped, played polo, and acquired more money. In fact, parts of the city are still in need of major repairs. But **CityPlace**, an upscale shopping, dining, and entertainment complex, has changed the face of downtown. Centennial Square, at the top of Clematis Street, has a new, $2 million interactive

*Formerly a church, the Harriet Himmel Theater for Cultural and Performing Arts is the centerpiece of CityPlace.*

**BELOW:** The Breakers has a staff of 1,800.

**SHOP**

In Palm Beach Gardens, the Gardens Mall (3101 PGA Blvd; tel: 561-775-7750, www.thegardens-mall.com) is one of the area's finest upscale shopping complexes. It's anchored by Nord-strom's, Saks, and Bloomingdale's, and houses numerous restaurants and a multi-screen cinema.

**BELOW:** the Cuillo Centre for the Arts on Clematis Street is a performing-arts venue.

fountain, and is host to a free concert series – Clematis By Night – every Thursday.

One very good reason to come to West Palm Beach is to visit the **Norton Museum of Art ⑥** (1451 S. Olive Ave; tel: 561-832-5196, www.norton.org; Tue–Sat 10am–5pm, Sun 1pm–5pm; charge), which has an outstanding permanent collection. Among its most vaunted possessions are works by French Impressionists and Post-Impressionists from Cézanne to Picasso, as well as fine 20th-century American works, including some by Georgia O'Keeffe, Edward Hopper, and Andy Warhol, plus lovely Chinese artifacts.

The **Raymond F. Kravis Center for the Performing Arts ⑭** (701 Okeechobee Blvd; tel: 561-832-7469, www.kravis.org) is a major venue for a wide variety of performing artists and groups, ranging from the Monterey Jazz Festival to Gregorian Masters.

## Palm Beach Gardens

Much of Palm Beach County around Lake Okeechobee is given over to sugar cane; construction, real estate, and banking are other big industries. **Palm Beach Gardens ②**, a burgeoning upscale suburb north of Palm Beach, is headquarters of the Professional Golfers Association (PGA), which has given its initials to one of that town's main thoroughfares. The PGA operates numerous championship golf courses and a Hall of Fame.

Twenty miles (32km) west of downtown West Palm Beach in the town of **Loxahatchee** is **Lion Country Safari ③** (2003 Olion County Safari Rd; tel: 561-793-1084, www.lioncountrysafari.com; daily 9.30am–5.30pm; charge), the area's top family attraction, where you can drive along 4 miles (6km) of jungle trails past nearly a thousand roaming animals. The well-fed lions seem to have grown rather lazy, but it's thrilling to watch one lead a parade of cars or see a giraffe peering in at you; keep your windows closed, though. There are also safari boat rides, a petting and feeding area for small animals, and a reptile and dinosaur park.

## Jupiter and Singer Island

Route A1A curves back to the beach over Blue Heron Boulevard. You can follow it through the high-rises of **Singer Island ④** (home of John D. MacArthur Beach, one

of the state's best) all the way to **Jupiter** ❺. This town once was a terminal for the Celestial Railroad, which took its name from the stations it served – Juno, Neptune, Mars, and Venus, as well as Jupiter. Flagler's railroad bypassed this peninsula, so it remains less developed. A monument in Jupiter marks the site of the abandoned Celestial track.

Just off Route A1A, visitors can climb the 105 steps of the restored 1860 brick **Jupiter Inlet Lighthouse and Museum** (tel: 561-747-8380, www.jupiterlight-house.org; Tue–Sun 10am–5pm; charge). The reward is a fabulous view of the Gulf Stream – a veritable river in the Atlantic Ocean. Cross the bridge to tour the museum's **Dubois Pioneer Home**, the oldest in Palm Beach County, then quench your thirst at **The Crab House**, just up the road.

Jupiter is perhaps most famous as the hometown of actor Burt Reynolds, whose dad once served as the town sheriff. The **Burt Reynolds and Friends Museum** (100 N. US Hwy 1; tel: 561-743-9955; http://burtreynoldsmuseum.org; Fri–Sun 10am–4pm; charge) houses his collection of film memorabilia.

The mansions of Jupiter Island house millionaires who aren't fond of Palm Beach, but the owners are equally wary of tourists. You will find no hotels, convenience stores, or gas stations here. Police pull over any vehicles that stray off public roads into narrow, private drives. Still, it's worth a look. Turn off US 1 to SR 707 through an archway of overhanging trees.

Australian pines, palms, and fuchsia hide most homes. Yachts huddle along the shore. In 1961 a circuit court judge upheld restrictive zoning laws when he

*The Kravis Center encompasses a 2,200-seat concert hall, a playhouse, and an outdoor amphitheater.*

**BELOW:** the Norton Museum includes works by 19th- and 20th-century European and American artists.

*John D. MacArthur Beach State Park on Singer Island is a favorite destination for swimming, kayaking, fishing, and nature walks.*

**BELOW:**
Savannas Preserve State Park.

said of Jupiter Island, "Many people would consider it dead – but it is very much alive with genteel living, friendship, and compatibility. The town doesn't want what many others have, but many others would be better off if they had more of what this town has and wants to keep – seclusion, solitude, and tranquility."

### Into the wild

Just north of Jupiter off US 1 in **Hobe Sound**, **Jonathan Dickinson State Park ❻** (tel: 772-546-2771, www.floridastateparks.org; daily 8am–sunset; charge)

preserves the last wild river in southeast Florida. You can rent a canoe or kayak and paddle along the upper Loxahatchee River past alligators and rarities like bald eagles. The park rolls through tall sand dunes that peak at Hobe Mountain, an 86-ft (26-meter) sand pile with an observation deck. It is the highest point in South Florida.

The park encompasses the restored homestead of Trapper Nelson, a folk hero who opened a zoo where he wrestled alligators and devoured raw possum. After health officials closed the zoo, he retreated into isolation. When police found him dead with a bullet in his head, some suspected foul play because he had been holding up a multimillion-dollar land deal. The Trapper Nelson Interpretive Site is accessible only by a boat tour with park staff.

Farther north, you cross the St Lucie Canal, which, together with the Caloosahatchee River, forms the Okeechobee Waterway linking the east and west coasts. It is used by thousands of craft annually. In **Stuart ❼**, naturalist Nancy Beaver offers two-hour trips into the Indian River Lagoon on **Sunshine Wildlife Tours** (her boat

leaves from Finn's Waterfront Grill; tel: 800-517-7207, www.sunshinewildlifetours.com; charge). Bottlenose dolphins and manatees are often spotted aboard the cruise, which includes a visit to Bird Island, one of the state's top bird rookeries.

## On the beach

East of Stuart is **Jensen Beach**, where turtles are a big attraction. Large loggerheads and green sea turtles crawl out of the ocean at night each May to lay eggs in the sand. Nearby, on the rocky shores of **Hutchinson Island 8**, you'll find two fascinating properties owned by the Historical Society of Martin County (825 NE Ocean Blvd; tel: 772-225-1961, www.elliott museumfl.org; Mon–Sat 10am–4pm, Sun 1pm–4pm; charge). **The House of Refuge at Gilbert's Bar** is the last of 10 houses built more than a century ago for shipwrecked sailors and travelers. **The Elliot Museum**, named after inventor Harmon Elliot, contains all manner of wonderful things, from Elliot's wacky inventions to a mini-circus and re-creations of early 20th-century shops.

**Savannas Preserve State Park 9** (tel: 772-398-2779, www.floridastateparks.org;

daily 8am–sunset; charge), a freshwater marsh that stretches for 10 miles (16km) from here to Fort Pierce, has habitats similar to those of the Everglades. The park's education center is in Port St Lucie. The drive up Route A1A to **Fort Pierce** is particularly scenic.

## Driftwood and Disney

**Vero Beach 10** has miles of lovely beaches, plus the Indian River Island Sanctuary, which can be reached by a footbridge at the end of Dahlia Lane. Another chief landmark is the rickety looking **Driftwood Resort** (www.thedriftwood.com) on Ocean Drive. Eccentric entrepreneur Waldo Sexton fashioned it from just that. Newer additions have gone condo, but visitors can snack in the dining room or stroll through this architectural jumble perched like a shipwreck at the tide line. So improbable is the construction, it looks as if a simple tug might bring the whole thing down. Yet it has withstood high waves and fierce hurricanes ever since the 1930s.

The **Ocean Grill** (lunch Mon–Fri, dinner nightly), also created by Sexton, is a short stroll up the beach. Its bar extends

**TIP**

The 56-acre (23-hectare) Florida Oceanographic Coastal Center (Hutchinson Island; tel: 772-225-0505; www.floridaoceanographic.org), between the ocean and Indian River lagoon, offers guided nature walks along a one-mile trail Mon–Sat at 11am and Sun at 2pm, immediately after the stingray program and feeding.

**LEFT:** Savannas Preserve State Park.
**BELOW:** outdoor dining at Vero Beach.

# Hobe Sound
## National
## Wildlife Refuge

**U.S. FISH AND WILDLIFE SERVICE**
**DEPARTMENT OF THE INTERIOR**

*Hobe Sound provides habitat for 30 threatened and endangered species as well as sea turtle nesting sites.*

over the water, where windows mist with sea spray.

Another major presence here is **Disney's Vero Beach Resort** (www.dvc. disney.go.com), a sprawling, elegant complex with several restaurants.

**Pelican Island National Wildlife Refuge** is the oldest wildlife sanctuary in the US, established in 1905. Rent a boat for a close look, but obey signs warning you to "Stay off the island."

## Sebastian Inlet

Thirteen miles (21km) north is **Sebastian ⑪**. **Sebastian Inlet State Park** (tel: 321-984-4852; www.floridastateparks.org; charge), on the ocean, is excellent for fishing and swimming. At the southern

**BELOW:**
Juno Beach.

end of the park, the **McLarty Treasure Museum** (daily 10am–4.30pm; charge) is on the site of an old Spanish salvage camp. It deals mainly with the loss of a Spanish Plate Fleet during a hurricane in 1715; about 700 sailors perished. The displays include coins, jewelry, and many domestic objects. Archaeologists believe an Indian mound nearby may contain the skeletal remains of some of Florida's first European settlers. Some claim that shipwreck survivors may have lived with the Ais tribe even before the founding of St Augustine in 1565.

Sebastian Inlet is popular among surfers. Florida's best, and virtually only, surfing action is on the east coast. (The Gulf of Mexico caters to windsurfers.) Most non-wind enthusiasts hang out in the regions between Sebastian Inlet and Daytona Beach.

On Route 1, **Mel Fisher's Treasure Museum** (1322 US Hwy 1; tel: 772-589-9875; www.melfisher.org; Tue–Sat 10m–5pm, Sun noon–5pm; charge), exhibits the astounding finds that "The World's Greatest Treasure Hunter" and his crews salvaged from numerous sunken ships. ❑

# Lake Okeechobee

**Water-management schemes and agriculture have taken a heavy toll on the lake, though restoration plans offer a glimmer of hope**

It was once a mythical lake, unknown to whites until 1837, when Colonel Zachary Taylor stumbled upon it during the Second Seminole War. People of the Mayaimi and Tequesta cultures, and later the Seminoles, lived on its margins, paddling out to the lake to fish. At 730 sq miles (1,890 sq km), Lake Okeechobee (from the Seminole *oki chubi*, or "big water") is the largest lake in Florida. For 6,000 years, it has been the canary in the coal mine for the ecological health of the Everglades.

The Kissimmee River fed the lake, flushing the central Florida prairie country through a broad, winding floodplain to the limestone basin that impounds the lake. During the wet season, the 20-ft-deep (3-meter) lake self-regulated by spilling its banks, sending a sheet flow trickling into the sawgrass wetlands of the Everglades. During the dry season, the lake shrank, exposing littoral bulrush marshes that supported apple snails, the principal diet of birds called snail kites. Nature's polarities – large and small, fast and slow, wet and dry – were all embraced by the complex ecosystem. It was a marvel of natural engineering, unique in the world.

Starting with Howard Disston in 1881 and Governor Napoleon Broward in 1905, irrigation schemes began to drain the Everglades and tame Lake Okeechobee, leading to new towns, dairy farming, ranching, citrus growing, and sugar cane plantations. Hurricanes in 1926 and 1928, which killed more than 2,500 people when a wall of water from Lake Okeechobee flooded towns, led to the creation of the 20-ft-high (18-meter) Herbert Hoover Dike. The 110-mile (180-km) dike is part of the 1,400-mile (2,250-km) Florida National Scenic Trail and popular with hikers, bicyclists, and birdwatchers.

In 1948, Congress authorized the Central and South Florida Project, creating 1,800 miles (2,900km) of roads, canals and levees designed to provide flood protection for urban and agricultural lands and preservation of fish and wildlife habitat. In 1971, the US Army Corps of Engineers channelized the Kissimmee River, opening up lands for ranching. On the south, sugar plantations pumped back runoff into the lake to keep cane beds dry. Lake levels dropped to 12ft (4 meters).

For the Everglades, it's been an ecological disaster. Fifty percent of the original wetlands are gone. Wading bird populations have been reduced by 90 percent. Fourteen animal species are listed as endangered. Lake Okeechobee has become a dumping ground, its bottom sediments overloaded with phosphates from agricultural runoff, arsenic, and pesticides that must be disposed of as hazardous waste. And there has been an outcry on the tourist-dependent Gulf and Atlantic coasts as polluted freshwater releases into the Caloosahatchee and St Lucie estuaries have created red tides and disturbed the delicate ecosystem of oyster and crab hatcheries.

A $7.8 million rescue plan, signed into law in 2000, has offered a glimmer of hope. Work has begun on a new reservoir and stormwater treatment areas, and the Kissimmee River has been returned to its original floodplain. The state took a huge leap forward in 2008 when it proposed to purchase 187,000 acres (75,700 hectares) from US Sugar Corporation, the country's largest sugar producer. The land is critical in restoring the southward flow of water from the lake through the Everglades. ❑

**RIGHT:** crop dusting near Lake Okeechobee.

# RESTAURANTS AND BARS

## Fort Pierce
**Mangrove Mattie's**
1640 Seaway Dr
Tel: 772-466-1044
L & D daily, Sun Br
A prime location overlooking the Fort Pierce inlet
plus all-you-can-eat spe-
cials (summer only) and
terrific seafood make this
one of the area's most
popular dining choices.
The outdoor patio is
delightful when there's a
breeze, and the wine list
is surprisingly thoughtful
for a casual spot. $

## North Palm Beach
**Ruth's Chris Steak
House**
700 S Rosemary Ave,
City Place
Tel: 561-514-3544
D daily
Prime Midwestern corn-
fed beefsteak seared at
1800°F and served on
plates heated to 500°F.
Some argue that this is
the best of the premium
beef chains. Heretics can
opt for seafood, lamb, or
pork. There are also locations in Fort Lauderdale,
Coral Gables, and Boca
Raton. $$$$

## Palm Beach
**Café Boulud**
Brazilian Court Hotel,
301 Australian Ave
Tel: 561-655-6060
B, L & D daily, Sat–Sun Br
Renowned French chef
Daniel Boulud re-creates
his New York City suc-
cess at this "secret gar-
den of elegance, charm
and comfort" just a few
steps from Worth
Avenue. The three-course
prix fixe luncheon bistro
menu, which changes
daily, is an excellent way
to test the waters. Jack-
ets required at dinner.
$$$$

**Flagler Steakhouse**
The Breakers,
313 Worth Ave
Tel: 561-835-1600
L & D daily
Only 5 percent of all beef
is awarded the distinc-
tion of prime, and we're
pretty sure that much of
that is consumed in this
elegant dining room over-
looking The Breakers'
golf course. It's aged,
hand cut, and served in
the restaurant's signa-
ture colossal prime rib
chop, steak au poivre, or
a myriad of other dishes
that may include broiled
twin lobster tails. $$$$

**Hamburger Heaven**
314 S. County Road
Tel: 561-655-5277
B, L & D Mon–Sat
Here's proof that even
the rich like a good
burger, a thick, creamy
milkshake, and a wedge
of freshly baked choco-
late cake. And it all
seems to taste better at
the counter of this sim-
ple, old-fashioned spot
just a few steps from
tony Worth Street. $

**Ta-Boo**
221 Worth Ave
Tel: 561-835-3500
L & D daily, Sun Br

How many restaurants
can claim to have served
the Duke and Duchess
of Windsor, Jimmy Buf-
fet, and Donald Trump?
More than 60 years old,
this institution is where
people come to be seen
and overheard – a chic
American bistro with the
ambience of a British
gentlemen's club. Much
of the food is unpreten-
tious – pizza and
cheeseburgers are on
the menu, along with
veal Milanese. Bloody
Marys and espresso
martinis are specialties
at the weekend piano
bar. $$–$$$

## Palm Beach Gardens
**Seasons 52**
11611 Ellison Wilson Road
Tel: 561-625-5852
L & D daily
New American food
served up with a guaran-
tee: every dish weighs in
under 475 calories and
contains no butter or
transfats. Many are
grilled over an open fire,
which works particularly
well with dishes such as
Thai lemongrass grilled
chicken skewers. Patrons
with a sweet tooth may
want to order a couple of
the desserts – tasty
treats such as tiramisu
and key lime pie served
in shot glasses at $2.25
each. There's live enter-
tainment at the sophisti-
cated wine bar. $$

## West Palm Beach
**Havana**
6801 S. Dixie Hwy
Tel: 561-547-9799
L & D daily
A casual spot with ample
portions of some of the

area's best Cuban fare. The mojitos are frosty, the *bistec especial Havana* with *chicichuri* sauce spicy, and the hospitality warm and inviting. The coffee – best with a creamy flan – is not to be missed. For more than a decade the 24-hour walk-up window has been one of the busiest spots in town during the wee small hours. $–$$

### Marcello's La Sirena
6316 S. Dixie Hwy
Tel: 561-585-3128
D daily
Marcello Fiorentino's parents opened this intimate, 60-seat Italian restaurant in 1986, and he's ably carried on their tradition of serving deftly prepared classic treats such as *vongole al forno* and *saltimbocca alla Romana*. The restaurant serves only wine, but its list – heavy on Italian vintages – is excellent. $$$–$$$$

### Mark's City Place
700 S. Rosemary Ave
Tel: 561-514-0770
D daily
Mark Militello's fourth South Florida location offers the same innovative contemporary American fare that has won him a host of national awards. Although the menu changes daily, favorites include duck leg confit, pan seared pork loin, and Australian kobe short ribs. $$$

### Sushi Jo
319 Belvedere Rd
Tel: 561-868-7893
L & D Mon–Fri, D Sat–Sun
American-born Jo Clark has been working in

restaurants since the age of 13 and trained under some of this country's finest sushi chefs. He combines his knowledge and passion for the cuisine to turn out terrific sushi in one of the area's trendiest restaurants, just across from the Biba Bar *(see below)*. There are outposts in Palm Beach Gardens and Manalapan. $$

### Spoto's Oyster Bar
125 Datura St
Tel: 561-835-1828
L & D daily
Seafood lovers will have a field day at this cool, contemporary restaurant and lounge. Start with a platter from the raw bar or a bowl of oyster stew, then dig into a selection of grilled specialties. The patio is pleasant on a warm, breezy evening. $$

## Bars
### Palm Beach
### The Leopard Lounge
Chesterfield Hotel,
363 Cocoanut Row
Tel: 561-659-5800
L & D daily
Everything is spotted, from the carpets and the waiters' vests to the occasional celebrity. Don't expect many of the local wildlife to show up, however. The nightly entertainment ranges from classical guitar to show tunes.

### West Palm Beach
### Biba Bar
Hotel Biba,
320 Belvedere Road
Tel: 561-832-0094
One of the country's first motor lodges has been retrofitted with vibrantly colored eclectic furnishings and now boasts an Asian-inspired outdoor

garden where the young and chic gather to sip vintage wine and champagne and listen to house music.

### Blue Martini
Okeechobee Blvd, City Place
Tel: 561-835-8601
James Bond might not recognize his beloved libation in one of its many new guises: a "sex in the city" or "mango madness." But this popular spot with outposts throughout the state offers more than 20 variations, along with sophisticated bar snacks and live entertainment nightly.

### E.R. Bradley's Saloon
104 Clematis St
Tel: 561-833-3520
This is a waterfront restaurant by day, but by night it is one of the town's liveliest venues, where DJs and live bands crank up the music. It is said that a Bradley bloody Mary works wonders on

those who overimbibed the night before.

### Respectable Street
518 Clematis St
Tel: 561-832-9999
This is one of the area's major live music venues. Wednesday to Sunday nights, local folks mix with tourists to dance the night away to tunes by DJs and performances by regional and touring bands.

### Palm Beach Gardens
### Club Safari
4000 RCA Blvd
Tel: 561-622-8888
The rumble in the jungle is at the hotel on the highway. It's as if Walt Disney had been commissioned to overdesign a nightclub, and the customers – drawn heavily from Marriott guests – love the video wall where videos from the 1970s and 1980s are broadcast. The hits of the 1950s–1980s are spun by local DJs Thur–Sun.

**LEFT:** Café Boulud at the Brazilian Court.
**RIGHT:** Ta-Boo is a favorite of Palm Beach socialites.

*Recommended Restaurants on page 207*

# THE SPACE COAST

Kennedy Space Center, at the heart of NASA's
launch pad to the heavens, tells the story
of America's adventures in space

The gun must be fired perpendicularly to the plane of the horizon, that is to say, toward the zenith. Now the moon does not traverse the zenith except in places between 0° and 28° of latitude." With those parameters in mind, members of the Observatory of Cambridge in Jules Verne's 1873 book *De La Terre à la Lune* advised that their manned projectile *Columbiad* should begin its journey to the moon from either southern Texas or southern Florida.

In the book, Texans were aghast, arguing that Florida, "a mere peninsula confined between two seas," could never sustain the shock of the discharge, that it would "bust up" at the very first shot.

"Very well, let it bust up!" replied the Floridians. And on December 1, 1873, before a vast assemblage of 5 million people, "the discharge of the *Columbiad* was accompanied by a perfect earthquake. Florida was shaken to its very depths." But it didn't bust up in the book – or in real life.

The National Aeronautics and Space Administration (NASA) continues to shake up Florida's Atlantic coast each time it launches rockets from Kennedy Space Center, just about 100 miles (160km) from the spot the prescient Mr Verne chose to launch the fictional *Columbiad*. The center is at the heart of the Space Coast, a 40-mile (65-km) swath of land that stretches from its northern terminus in Titusville through Cocoa Beach and south to the Melbourne-Palm Bay area.

## Center of operations

Cape Canaveral has been associated with the space program ever since NASA's manned flights began in the early 1960s. Space Coast nomenclature can get a bit confusing, however, and some clarification is in order. Cape Canaveral has long been the name of the peninsula that extends south from Merritt Island and east of the Banana River. (Its name was changed to Cape Kennedy after the president's 1963 assassination but was changed back to Canaveral in 1973.) It's the site of the Cape Canaveral Air Force

**Main attractions**
KENNEDY SPACE CENTER
IMAX THEATER AT THE
  KENNEDY SPACE CENTER
APOLLO/SATURN V CENTER
ASTRONAUT HALL OF FAME
MERRITT ISLAND NATIONAL
  WILDLIFE REFUGE
CANAVERAL NATIONAL
  SEASHORE
COCOA BEACH PIER

**LEFT:**
shuttle launch.
**BELOW:** moon
gravity simulation.

**TIP**

When in orbit the space shuttle travels at 17,500mph (28,200kph) about 10 times faster than a bullet.

Station, where the earliest experimental American military rockets were launched. **Kennedy Space Center ❶** (NASA Pkwy; tel: 321-449-4444; www. ksc.nasa.gov; daily 9am–6pm, center may be partially or completely closed on launch days), including launch pads for the space shuttles, is on Merritt Island. It lies, in fact, within Merritt Island National Wildlife Refuge.

Although the space center is a government facility, the **Visitor Complex** is operated by a private company without the benefit of taxpayer funds. The complex sprawls across a landscaped campus, incorporating nearly a dozen buildings and several outdoor exhibits. Begin by getting oriented at **Information Central**, where a multimedia presentation introduces the themes and attractions within the complex. Use the schedule for films, live events, and tours posted here to plan your day.

### The red planet and beyond

**Robot Scouts**, located in another wing of the main building, is a walk-through exhibit that takes a whimsical look at the role of robot probes in interplanetary

exploration. At the opposite end of the main building is the venue for **Astronaut Encounter**. Here guests get the chance to discuss space travel with NASA astronauts. Representing the fewer than 500 men and women who have flown in space, the astronauts answer questions, narrate videos, and invite a young audience member onto the stage to become part of the presentation.

**Mad Mission to Mars** opposite is the title of a live-action stage show using theme-park techniques and 3-D computer animation to teach an audience of "astronaut trainees" essential facts about physics, rocketry, and living in space. The show is aimed at kids, but adults come away with a better understanding of what will be involved in the first interplanetary journey.

At the **Nature and Technology** exhibit, visitors are brought back to Earth – in fact, to the diverse environment in which the space center is located. Some 5,000 alligators make their home in Merritt Island National Wildlife Refuge – they've been known to loll alongside the 15,000-ft (4,600-meter) runway where space shuttles land – and this exhibit

**BELOW:** Mad Mission to Mars is a stage show that takes the audience on a voyage through the cosmos.

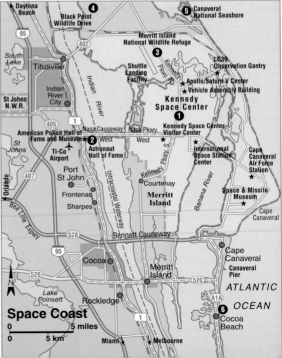

*Recommended Restaurants on page 207*

explains how an almost primeval environment coexists alongside a realm of advanced technology.

To get up close and personal with one of the space-traveling elite, make a reservation to have **Lunch with an Astronaut**. Offered at 1pm Monday through Friday, this extra-cost option (about $23 for adults, $16 for children) is exactly what it says it is: an opportunity to join a crew member for a multicourse lunch, complete with a briefing, conversation, and photo-

and-autograph session. (As occasionally astronauts are not available, it's advisable to make reservations well in advance.)

Anyone who remembers listening to a live report of Alan Shepard's 1961 suborbital flight on a tinny transistor radio or black-and-white television knows that space exploration, though only a recent development, has a remarkably rich and vivid history. At the **Early Space Exploration** exhibit, visitors can watch a recreation of a Project Mercury launch, see

*In the Rocket Garden are rockets that propelled Mercury, Gemini, and Apollo astronauts into space.*

**TOP LEFT:** lunch with an Astronaut. **BELOW LEFT:** space suit. **BELOW:** control room simulation.

## Kennedy Space Center – Tours and Tickets

The standard admission charge to the Kennedy Space Center Visitor Complex includes entry into the Astronaut Hall of Fame (*see page 204*); the standard KSC bus tour, which stops at the LC39 Observation Gantry, the Apollo/Saturn V Center, and the Space Station Facility; and admission to all the attractions at the Visitor Complex, including Mad Mission to Mars and the outdoor exhibits.

For those who want to see more of the Kennedy Space Center, there are two other visitor tours. NASA Up Close (2 hours) stops at the A/B Camera Stop, the closest you can get to the shuttle launch pads; the Shuttle Landing Facility; and the enormous Vehicle Assembly Building. Cape Canaveral Then and Now (2½ hours) tours the base's first launch sites, which were used in the early Mercury and Apollo moon-landing programs, and includes a visit to the Air Force Space and Missle Museum. Both tours cost $21 and must be booked in advance.

flight possible. Here are the Redstone, Atlas and Titan models, including an example of the Mercury-Atlas engine that blasted John Glenn into orbit in 1962. The one horizontal specimen is a Saturn 1B, an enormous vehicle designed by NASA (the others were adapted from military rockets) and originally built as a rescue vehicle rocket for Skylab astronauts in the 1970s; it later served as a backup for the Apollo-Soyuz project.

By the way, if you're still around the Visitor Complex at dusk, head over to the Rocket Garden for a look at the dramatic lighting display.

The space center is home to the only back-to-back **IMAX theaters** in the world. Two films are shown throughout the day on 5½-story screens: *Space Station* is a remarkable 3-D look at the shape, character, and challenges of life in the international space station. *Walking on the Moon 3D* combines archive footage of the first lunar explorers with 3-D IMAX technology to amazing effect, giving the audience an opportunity to share in the awesome experience of walking on the moon and highlighting the dangers these brave astronauts faced.

*Audio-visual displays, interactive exhibits, and numerous artifacts chronicle the development of the US space program.*

**BELOW:** visitors get a view of mission control.

the mission control-room consoles used by ground crews during Mercury and Gemini missions, and even examine the interiors of the tiny capsules from those pioneering days.

## Heavy lifting

Just outside is the **Rocket Garden**, resembling nothing so much as a display of stark modern sculpture. Eight rockets, all but one mounted vertically as if ready to soar skyward, trace the evolution of the technology that made manned space

*Recommended Restaurants on page 207*

**Exploration in the New Millennium** takes a slightly more serious approach to the next phase of space exploration. The presentation starts with terrestrial voyages of discovery such as the Vikings' adventures in Greenland and Iceland a thousand years ago, then speculates on the logistics of travel to Mars and beyond. A small chunk of Mars, incidentally, is on the premises: this is the only place in the world where it's possible to touch an actual piece of the Red Planet, which fell to Earth as a meteorite. Afterwards, you can send a bit of your own identity Mars-ward, by creating an electronic signature to be stored on a microchip that will one day make the interplanetary journey.

## Shuttle mission central

Another impressive outdoor display dominates the opposite corner of the campus. This is **Explorer**, a full-size replica of a space shuttle that includes an accurate mockup of the flight deck. Climbing aboard is as close as most space enthusiasts will come to sitting inside a real shuttle. Near the shuttle are the familiar orange fuel tanks and twin solid rocket boosters used in the early stages of launch. The boosters, incidentally, are recovered after being jettisoned; boats dedicated to this function are moored in the Banana River nearby.

If clambering through Explorer whets your appetite for information on the real-life shuttle, head next door to the **Launch Status Center**, which offers live briefings on recent launches and missions in progress. If a shuttle is in orbit at the time of your visit, you'll be able to watch live images broadcast from space.

From the Launch Status Center, it's a short walk to the **Astronaut Memorial**, dedicated in 1991 to honor Americans who lost their lives in service to the space program. Elegant in conception, the memorial consists of a highly polished, 50-ft (15-meter) granite space mirror in which the astronauts' names are engraved. The granite surface reflects passing clouds, so names appear to float in the heavens.

The **Shuttle Launch Experience** (minimum height: 48in/122cm) was created shortly after Epcot's Mission: SPACE *(see page 241)*. This is a much tamer ride, but the concept is exactly the same: to let you feel just what the astro-

*Though the shuttle is playing a key role in the construction of the International Space Station, NASA plans to retire its entire fleet by 2010, leaving duties to other countries' space agencies. New missions to outer space will revert to the systems used for the Moon missions: a reusable module atop a large, disposable rocket.*

**BELOW LEFT:** Apollo/Saturn V Center. **BELOW:** Apollo 14 command module.

**TIP**

**BELOW:** "crew members" are given a pre-launch briefing before boarding the Shuttle Launch Experience.

nauts feel when a space shuttle is launched. The biggest difference between the two rides is that you do not feel heavy G-forces as there is no spinning involved. The pre-show here also pays more attention to the science of what actually happens in a real shuttle launch, explaining the physics of getting into outer space in one piece. Compared to Orlando's motion simulators, this ride is rather mild, allowing visitors who are not exactly fans of thrill rides to get a taste of what it takes to get into space.

On your way to the bus tours, have a quick look at the floating 9-ton granite sphere in **Constellation Square**. Somehow water pressure keeps this ball afloat, allowing you to find your favorite constellation by spinning it around.

### Restricted area tour

After touring the Visitor Complex, board a bus for a narrated tour of outlying space center facilities that play a vital part in NASA operations. (Itineraries may be altered or tours suspended, depending on mission schedules).

The route passes the **Orbiter Processing Facility**, where shuttles spend several months for maintenance and repair. This is one of the few places, outside of space itself, where shuttle cargo doors can be opened and closed. The spacecraft are then transported to the 525-ft-tall (160-meter), 8-acre (3-hectare) **Vehicle Assembly Building**, the largest building by volume in the world. This is where shuttles are outfitted with twin solid rocket boosters and an external fuel tank. Nearby is the **Launch Control Center**, familiar from television coverage of final countdowns.

Equally impressive, if only for their sheer size, are the **Crawler Transporters**, two 6-million-pound (2.7-million-kg) tracked vehicles built to carry assembled shuttles along the 3½-mile (5½-km) route to the launch pads. In service for more than 30 years, the Crawlers travel at 1mph (1.6kph) when carrying a shuttle, boosters, and a fuel tank.

The first stop is at the **LC 39 Observation Gantry**, a 60-ft (18-meter) platform that affords a sweeping view of the launch pads, Vehicle Assembly Buildings, and the surrounding area. On exhibit is a 7,000-lb (3,200-kg) shuttle main engine, and a model re-creation of a launch count-

down. A 6-minute film presents a briefing by astronaut Marsha Ivins on how a shuttle is prepared for launching.

**Launch Pads 39A** and **39B** are historic structures – they were used for the Apollo moon launches – now adapted to the needs of the shuttle program. With their service structures towering alongside, the massive concrete pads are rivaled only by the spacecraft themselves as emblems of modern space exploration.

The tour continues to the **Apollo/Saturn V Center**, dedicated to the men and machines whose work culminated in the moon landings of 1969 and 1971. A video presentation reviews the early phases of the Apollo program, prior to a re-creation of an Apollo launch in the firing room. Still the main attraction here is a re-creation of the July, 1969, Apollo 11 landing presented in the **Lunar Theater**. The Center houses the original **Lunar Module** and **Command Service Module** and one of only three Saturn V rockets still in existence. When the first of the rockets was fired in 1967, it created the loudest noise ever made by human beings.

## Viewing a launch

For many travelers, the high point of visiting the Space Coast is viewing an actual launch. There is truly nothing like it. You stand amid an expectant throng, listening to a radio or loudspeaker, or just waiting, as the countdown clock ticks off the remaining minutes. Miles away stands a gleaming white space shuttle, with a large rust-colored external tank. It releases clouds of vapor like a dragon about to wake from a deep slumber. Then, as the anticipation becomes almost unbearable, the countdown reaches its final seconds.

There is a burst of fire from the shuttle's main engines, and for a few long

*A high-definition screen gives visitors a view of the International Space Station as it appears from the shuttle.*

**BELOW:** the Shuttle Launch Experience is an elaborate simulator ride.

*The Astronaut Hall of Fame pays tribute to the men and women of the US space program.*

**BELOW:** a G-force simulator similar to those used in astronaut training allows visitors to experience 4Gs.

seconds the beast stays where it is, its engines building up thrust, billowing clouds of steam and smoke. Finally, the two solid rocket boosters ignite with a flame so bright that it seems to rival the sun, and the shuttle quickly leaves the Earth. The cheers of the crowd are soon drowned out as the roar of the shuttle's engines reaches you while the magnificent flying machine heads for space.

## A place to watch

How can you experience this cosmic departure? Like thousands of others, you can simply find a spot along US 1 in Titusville or Route A1A in Cape Canaveral

or Cocoa Beach. Or, if you're going to be at the Kennedy Space Center on launch day, purchase a Launch Viewing ticket (first-come, first-served), which allows you to ride a bus to a viewing site about 6 miles (10km) from the launch pad. Don't forget to bring a pair of binoculars.

If you're coming to the space center specifically to view a launch, it's a good idea to plan on staying a few extra days in case there's a delay. There are no guarantees, however; launches are sometimes postponed for weeks. Call 321-449-4444 for information or buy launch tickets online at www.ksctickets.com.

## Astronaut Hall of Fame

"[T]he surface was beautiful, beautiful … Magnificent desolation." So wrote Buzz Aldrin in a 1972 letter describing how it felt to walk on the moon. The document, on exhibit at the **Astronaut Hall of Fame** ❷ (6225 Vectorspace Blvd, Titusville; tel: 321-269-6100; daily 10am–6.30pm) about 6 miles (10km) west of the Kennedy Space Center, is just one artifact among thousands that are gathered here to tell the story of the American experience in space.

But there's a lot more here, including a Mercury trainee capsule, the command module from Apollo 14, and wheels from the moon rover. One of the highlights is the state-of-the-art **Simulator Station** interactive area, where visitors can experience firsthand a variety of astronaut-training devices. Among them is a G-force centrifuge that creates the sensation of gravity four times that on Earth, a moon walk simulator, and a shuttle simulator that allows visitors to test their piloting skills. Special activities are arranged for viewing shuttle launches, and astronauts occasionally drop by for a visit.

## Back to nature

In contrast to all this high-tech adventure are two nearby nature preserves. At the 140,000-acre (57,000-hectare) **Merritt Island National Wildlife Refuge** ❸ (PO Box 6504, Titusville; tel: 321-861-0667; www.fws.gov/merrittisland; daily dawn–dusk, closed several days before launches), adjacent to Kennedy Space Center, endangered West Indian manatees loll peacefully in brackish lagoons, sea turtles waddle ashore to lay eggs on pristine beaches, and alligators bask in

the sun on creek banks. The refuge lies along a prime migratory flyway, and the sky is filled in early spring with warblers and shorebirds while, on the ground, egrets and herons are in breeding plumage, wood storks and ospreys build nests, and bald eaglets test their wings.

The mild climate and varied environment of marshes, hardwood hammocks, pine forest, scrub, and coastal dunes sustain more than 500 species of wildlife, including more than 20 on the Endangered or Threatened Species List. This is one of the most important nesting areas in the country for loggerhead, green, and leatherback turtles. Much of the wildlife can be spotted along 7-mile (11-km), one-way **Black Point Wildlife Drive** ❹, a self-guided auto tour through salt- and freshwater marshes. The entrance is on SR 406, a mile east of the intersection with SR 402. Manatees, most prevalent in the spring and fall, can best be viewed from the observation area near Haulover Canal Bridge on SR 3.

The best time to visit the refuge is during the off-season, when wildlife populations are at their highest and mosquitoes, high temperatures, and thunderstorms are

**TIP**

Canaveral National Seashore is also home to the Eldora Statehouse, a reminder of the challenges faced by early settlers along the "Mosquito Lagoon." Tel: 386-428-3384 for more information.

**BELOW LEFT:** more than 300 bird species inhabit Merritt Island, including great blue herons.
**BELOW:** a leatherback hatchling swims out to sea.

## Tule Walks

It's one of the most riveting beachside spectacles served up by nature: a 600-pound (270-kg) loggerhead sea turtle trudges ashore in the moonlight and, in a grueling act of devotion that can last as long as two hours, digs a sandy nest in which she deposits as many as 100 Ping-Pong-ball-sized eggs. Rear flippers working counterpoint to cover up her handiwork, then carving out a shallow, false nest to trick yolk-hungry predators, the turtle finally crawls back to the ocean.

To see this or maybe even the hatchlings emerge two months later, there's no better place than Canaveral National Seashore. While it is a violation of federal law to harm a sea turtle or disturb its nest – the beach is zealously patrolled during nesting season to make sure the curious keep their distance – the park sponsors occasional evening turtle walks. After locating a female that has already begun laying eggs and is not likely to be spooked, rangers escort small groups to witness the ritual.

Tours start around 8pm and last until midnight. Reservations can be made in May or June by calling 386-428-3384, ext. 18.

*An osprey nests within sight of the Kennedy Space Center.*

**BELOW:** a dolphin surfs the wake of a research boat on the Banana River.

least likely to present a problem. The Visitor Information Center, 5 miles (8km) east of US 1 in Titusville on SR 402, has wildlife displays, educational resources, fishing information, and trail maps. Nearby **Pelican Island National Wildlife Refuge** is accessible via a boardwalk over the ocean which offers stunning views of the island (tel: 772-562-3909; www. fws.gov/pelicanisland; daily 7.30am–sunset). This bird rookery – the nation's first National Wildlife Refuge – was established in 1903.

## Beauty and the beach

Adjacent to the wildlife refuge is the 57,000-acre (23,000-hectare) **Canaveral National Seashore ❺** (212 S. Washington Ave, Titusville; tel: 386-428-3384; daily 6am–6pm winter, to 8pm in summer; visitor center daily 9am–5pm), whose miles of barrier dunes and sea-swept beaches are a haven for beachcombers and nature lovers. Two of the beaches, **Apollo** and **Playalinda**, at the northern and southern tips of the park, have restrooms, boardwalks and, from May 30 to September 1, lifeguards. In between, the landscape

remains untouched. Portions of the seashore may be closed before shuttle launches or when parking lots are full.

Another word of caution, or recommendation, as the case may be: Canaveral is the destination of choice for Florida's nude sunbathers, who are constantly at odds with local authorities. The legal wrangle over whether Florida's laws against public nudity can be enforced on federal land has been going on for years. If you want to chuck your clothes, you'll have plenty of company. But there's no guarantee that a deputy sheriff won't slink out of a palmetto thicket and slap you with a citation.

Those who prefer beaches in a more developed setting will find **Cocoa Beach ❻** to their liking – an old-time seaside town with chain motels, restaurants, and souvenir shops, as well as first-rate beaches. The biggest attraction is the **Ron Jon Surf Shop** (4151 N. Atlantic Ave, Cocoa Beach; tel: 321-799-8888; daily 24 hours), a neon-lit palace devoted to bikinis, boogie boards, surfboards, and scuba gear. Famous surfers occasionally drop in for autograph sessions; scuba diving and surfing lessons are also available. ❑

# RESTAURANTS

## Restaurants

Prices for a three-course dinner per person, excluding tax, tip, and beverages:

**$** = under $20
**$$** = $20–45
**$$$** = $45–60
**$$$$** = over $60

### Cocoa Beach

### Cocoa Beach Pier
401 Meade Avenue, ½ mile north of SR 520, off A1A
Tel: 321-783-7549
Daily L & D
You could do a lot worse than ending your trip to the Space Coast on the pier at Cocoa Beach. Walk to the end of the pier and you can see the launch pads with your naked eye. It's no secret that this is prime launch-viewing real estate. On the pier itself are three places to eat: the Atlantic Grille is the fanciest option, the Boardwalk is a cheap and cheerful bar serving fish sandwiches and burgers, and Marlin's Good Times Bar and Grill splits the difference. Any of the choices affords a great view of the Atlantic and the surfers trying to ride it. The Tiki Bar at the end of the pier is a great place to enjoy an ice-cold beer or frozen daquiri while the sun is setting. $–$$$

### The Fat Snook
2464 S. Atlantic Ave
Tel: 321-784-1190
Daily D
This tastefullly airy and arty restaurant does something others in Cocoa Beach dare not: feature locally caught seafood. It is amazing that most other seafood restaurants on this stretch of coast seem obsessed with telling you how far the seafood has come. Not here. Local produce is featured in every course. $$$

### Gregory's Steak and Seafood Grille
900 N. Atlantic Ave
Tel: 321-799-2557
Daily D
This family-run restaurant's signature 12oz baseball-cut steak is the best bit of beef on the beach. If you have room for starters or afters, there is a fine selection of seafood nibbles and salads. Vegetarians are given little solace here, but those who eat fish will have plenty of dishes to choose from so long as they don't dwell on the ironies of indulging in North Atlantic fish while on the South Florida coast. Groucho's comedy club is just upstairs. $$$

### Mango Tree Restaurant
118 N. Atlantic Ave
Tel: 407-799-0513
Tue–Sun D
A romantic, tropical setting of fresh flowers, wicker furniture, and white linen sets the tone for this quirky little restaurant. Inside, a tropical aquarium, extensive butterfly collection, and pianist provide a relaxing backdrop. The menu features fine Italian-American cuisine and several fresh seafood specialties. The Indian River Crabcakes should be celebrated as it is one of the few indigenous seafood dishes on any Cocoa Beach menu. $$$

### Punjab
White Rose Shopping Center, 285 W. Cocoa Beach Cswy
Tel: 321-799-4696
Daily L & D
Unfortunately located in a characterless shopping center, Punjab is still worth a visit for its fine Indian cuisine. Budget travelers take note: the lunch menu featuring soups and curries is an absolute bargain. The evening menu is more extensive and features Tandoori and seafood and lamb specialties. $$

### Silvestros Italian Restaurant
Banana River Square, 2039 N. Atlantic Ave
Tel: 321-783-4853
Daily D
It would be very easy to miss Silvestros; the nondescript storefront does not scream out "fine Italian dining" to anyone. But they've done a great job of turning this corner of Banana River Square into a continental welcome. The menu is what you'd expect from any trattoria – carpaccio, saltimbocca, veal scaloppini, and an array of pasta dishes – but the extensive list of Italian wines makes Silvestros worth the visit. $$$

**RIGHT:** a burger joint in Cocoa Beach.

# KENNEDY SPACE CENTER

**This is where the Apollo moon missions began and where space shuttles blast off. Millions of visitors come every year to learn about the US space program**

Plan to devote a whole day to the Kennedy Space Center. Divide your time between the Visitor Center, where you can walk around indoor and outdoor exhibits, and the rest of the complex, which can be explored on bus tours.

IMAX movies are the big attraction here: *Magnificent Desolation: Walking on the Moon 3D*, narrated by Tom Hanks, features rare film of the lunar surface. *Space Station 3D* explores life aboard the International Space Station. The giant five-story screen and 3D effects reputedly simulate the sensation of floating in space.

Other attractions here include the Space Shuttle Plaza and Rocket Garden, a display of massive rockets. The Early Space Exploration exhibit focuses on the Mercury and Gemini missions, including the original Mercury Mission Control Center. Taking a cue from the folks at Disney World, the Shuttle Launch Experience uses simulator technology to re-create the sensation of blasting off on the back of a rocket, and Mad Mission to Mars is a humorous multimedia show with live actors and a battery of digital effects .

**KSC TOURS**

Space center tours run daily from 9.30am to 3.45pm. Their routes include a visit to Launch Complex 39, a 60-ft (18-meter) observation tower overlooking the space shuttle launch pad; the International Space Station Center, with full-scale re-creations of station modules; and the Apollo/Saturn V Center, which explores the moon missions of the 1960s and '70s with multimedia shows, hands-on exhibits, and a reconstructed control room.

**LEFT**: a replica of the space shuttle, an external fuel tank, and rocket boosters are displayed at the Space Shuttle Plaza.

**ABOVE**: *Discovery* orbits Earth with its cargo bay doors open. *Discovery* has completed more than 30 space flights, more than any other shuttle

**ABOVE**: a space shuttle crew is welcomed home by the public after landing in Florida.

**LEFT**: an astronaut prepares to be submerged in a neutral buoyancy tank during a training exercise. His suit – an Extravehicular Mobility Unit – is used for spacewalks outside the space shuttle and space station.

## PREPARING FOR LIFT-OFF

❶ The shuttle is assembled in the Vehicle Assembly Building. Two solid booster rockets, which separate from the shuttle two minutes after lift-off (and fall to earth to be re-used), and the external fuel tank (which detaches after eight minutes but then disintegrates on re-entering the Earth's atmosphere) are put in place here.
❷ The shuttle is moved on vast Crawler Transporters along the 3.5-mile (5-km) Crawlerway to the launch pad, moving along at just 1 mile (1.6 km) per hour.
❸ After the shuttle is in place, the astronauts board via the service tower.
❹ When the engines ignite at lift-off, a flame trench in the launch pad channels the burning gases away from the shuttle and is flooded with cooling water – producing dramatic clouds of steam.

**ABOVE AND RIGHT:** the space shuttle undergoes maintenance prior to launch.

**ʙᴠᴇ:** an astronaut snaps a photo of himself during a cewalk outside the International Space Station.
**ᴏᴡ:** the Space Station passes over South Florida.

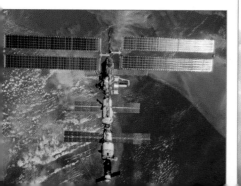

Recommended Restaurants on pages 226–7

# DAYTONA BEACH TO JACKSONVILLE

From the site of America's premier auto race to its oldest continuously inhabited city, Florida's northeast coast encompasses high-speed thrills, big-city attractions, charming historic precincts, and, of course, miles of beautiful beaches

n 1903 automakers Alexander Winton and Ransom E. Olds, the father of the Oldsmobile, raced along the sands just north of **Daytona** ❶ in the first official time trial in motor-sports history. Drivers feeling the need for speed have flocked to the area ever since. In the 30-odd years that followed, 15 land-speed records were set on Daytona's 23 miles (37km) of hard-packed quartz sand, culminating with a 1935 run by English racer Sir Malcolm Campbell that clocked in at a stunning 276.82mph (445.49kmh). The National Association of Stock Car Auto Racing, aka NASCAR, was founded here in 1947. And in 1959 NASCAR president William "Big Bill" Henry Getty France, once a beach stock-car driver, opened the Daytona International Speedway.

## Motor city

These days NASCAR fans converge on Daytona in early February for a marathon of racing and revelry that culminates in the annual **Daytona 500**. Motorcycles take over several weeks later during **Bike Week**, which – along with **Biketoberfest** in, yes, October – is one of the world's largest motorcycle events. But Daytona offers plenty to entertain racing enthusiasts any time of year.

Come into the city from I-95 along International Speedway Boulevard and the storied raceway looms large to the right. At the adjacent visitor center, the **Daytona 500 Experience** ❷ (1801 W. International Speedway Blvd; tel: 386-947-6800; www.daytona500experience.com;

daily 9am–7pm; charge) is an interactive, multimedia attraction that includes historical exhibits, simulation rides, a pit-stop challenge, an IMAX movie, and a trolley tour around the speedway's steep banks.

Those with a low NASCAR tolerance will probably be satiated with a walk around the extensive welcome center and gift shop, but for a significant extra fee diehard fans can take three laps around the track riding shotgun with a professional driver. If after all that you haven't had enough cars, head over to the **Living Legends of Auto Racing Museum**

**LEFT:** Lightner Museum.
**BELOW:** Colonial Spanish Quarter.

*The Daytona 500 Experience features a 45-minute, 3-D IMAX movie about the race, cars, and drivers.*

**BELOW:** originally powered by a kerosene lamp, the Ponce de Leon Light could be seen 20 miles (32km) out to sea.

**B** (2400 S. Ridgewood Ave; tel: 386-763-4483, www.livinglegendsofautoracing.com; Mon–Sat 10am–5pm; free) for more racing memorabilia, vintage autos, and photos.

## Spring Break, USA

Separated from the mainland by the Halifax River and reached via a series of high bridges, Daytona's famous beachfront is anchored by the historic **Main Street Pier C**. At 1,000ft (305 meters), it's the longest pier on the East Coast, and while it's seen better days – in 1999 it was hit hard by Hurricane Floyd – it does boast fantastic panoramic views of the beachfront strip and the bright blue ocean from its observation tower and sky lift. Also at Main Street is the **Salute to Speed** exhibit of more than 30 granite plaques documenting the beach's racing heritage.

Nowadays the scene on the sands is less rowdy than its "party hearty" heyday as a spring-break destination for thousands of college students – many of whom have moved on to places like Panama City and South Beach – but it's still festive, crammed with hot dog vendors and boogie-board rentals. Private cars are also allowed on certain strips of

the beach, accessible (for a $3 fee) from designated ramps. But go easy on the gas pedal – the 10mph (16kmh) speed limit is strictly enforced.

## Beyond the beach

Daytona wasn't always full of fast cars and drunk students. Glimpses of quieter days can be found at the city's excellent **Museum of Arts and Sciences D** (352 S Nova Rd, State Route 5A; tel: 386-255-0285, www.moas.org; Mon–Sat 9am–5pm, Sun 11am–5pm; charge). Inside, the Center for Florida History tracks the story of the state's development from prehistory to modernity. The star of the exhibit – and a big hit with kids – is the 13-ft-tall (4-meter) skeleton of a giant ground sloth. The largest and most complete ever discovered in North America, it was excavated in 1975 from a site known as the Daytona Bone Bed by a pair of amateur paleontologists. Outside, an interpretive nature walk winds through the dense hardwood forest of pretty **Tuskawilla Park**.

A few miles south of the Daytona strip sits the meticulously restored **Ponce de Leon Lighthouse E** ( 4931 S. Peninsula Dr; tel: 386-761-1821, www.ponceinlet.org

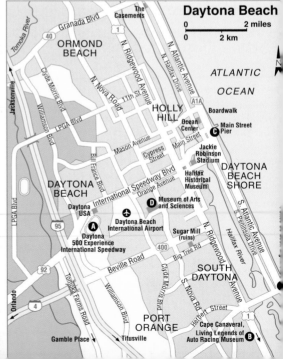

Daytona Beach

aily 10am–6pm; charge). Completed in 887, it is, at 175ft (53 meters), the llest lighthouse in Florida, not to men-on one of the best maintained in the ountry. The lighthouse keeper's resi-ence and other outbuildings are full of xhibits on Daytona's maritime history nd the development of lighthouse tech-ology through the years.

## rmond Beach

s Route A1A North winds along the hore toward St Augustine it'll take you hrough the former "Millionaire's 'olony" of **Ormond Beach ❷**, site of 1at legendary first time trial in 1903. )riginally home to Timucuan Indians – nd known as "Nocoroco" – the area was olonized by the British in the 18th cen-1ry. Settlers established vast indigo and ice plantations such as the 20,000-acre 3,000-hectare) Mount Oswald plantation, un by Scotsman Richard Oswald and ow the site of **Tomoka State Park ❸**.

When Spain took control of Florida in 1e early 19th century, King Ferdinand ffered land grants to planters living in 1e Bahamas. Ormond Beach is named or British sea captain James Ormond,

who received a grant of 2,000 acres (800 hectares) to develop his plantation on the Halifax River. Other early settlers included Charles Bulow; the ruins of his vast plantation – destroyed in the Sec-ond Seminole Indian War – are preserved at **Bulow Plantation Ruins Historic State Park ❹** (CR 2001; www.florida stateparks.org/bulowplantation; Thu–Mon 9am–5pm; charge) about 3 miles (5km) west of Flagler Beach.

Railroad magnate Henry Flagler extended the Florida East Coast Railroad to Ormond Beach in the late 1800s, and by the turn of the last century the area

*Packed sand at Daytona Beach is ideal for automobiles; driving on the beach (in designated areas only) is a long tradition.*

**BELOW:** the Daytona 500 Experience captures the thrill of the actual race.

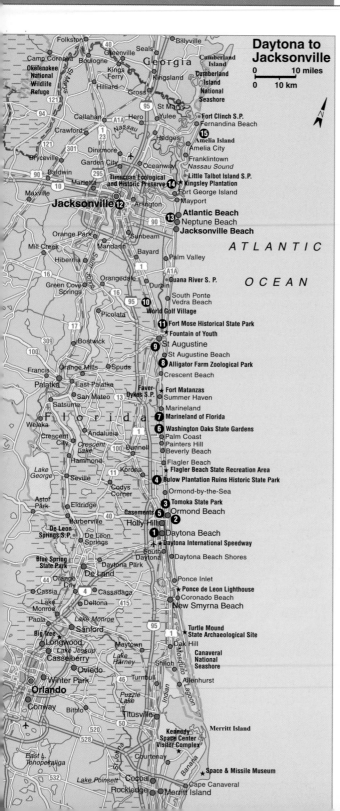

**Daytona to Jacksonville**

0          10 miles

0          10 km

was the summer playground for wealthy society folk with names like Astor and Vanderbilt, who stayed at the posh Ormond Hotel. Wealthy industrialists like Standard Oil titan John D. Rockefeller made it their winter home. Rockefeller wintered for more than 20 years in Ormond Beach, where he was famous for his golf game and his habit of passing out dimes to his neighbors. When he died in 1937, at 97, the *New York Times* noted that "his spare figure was a familiar sight" in the community. His home, the **Casement ❺**, named for its many casement windows, is now a museum and cultural center (25 Riverside Dr; tel: 386-677-7005; www.obht.org/casements.htm; guided tours Mon-Sat, call for hours; charge).

## Up the coast road

If you've got time en route to St Augustine, take a detour just north of Ormond Beach to drive **The Loop** – a scenic 23 mile (37-km) stretch of road shaded by ancient live oaks and curtains of Spanish moss. Take Highbridge Road west from A1A, past tranquil salt marshes full of herons and egrets, to Walter Boardman Road, then head south on the Old Dixie Highway, which passes both Bulow Plantation Ruins State Park and **Bulow Creek State Park** – home of the towering, 400-year-old Fairchild Oak – before curving back toward Ormond Beach.

Back on the road to St Augustine, A1A passes through the quiet communities of **Flagler Beach**, **Painters Hill** and **Palm Coast**, home of **Washington Oaks State Gardens ❻** (6400 N Oceanshore Blvd; tel: 386-446-6780; www.floridastateparks.org/washingtonoaks; daily 8am–sunset; charge), notable for its acres of formal gardens showcasing both indigenous and exotic flora.

Two miles (3km) north is **Marineland of Florida ❼** (9600 Oceanshore Blvd; tel: 904-471-1111; www.marineland.net; open daily 8.30am–4.30pm; charge), the world's first oceanarium. Originally built as an underwater film stage and research center, the aging facility closed after being badly damaged by Hurricane Frances in 2004. One $10-million rehab later, it

*Recommended Restaurants on pages 226–7*

reopened as the home of a **Dolphin Conservation Center**, where kids and adults alike can interact and swim with 11 Atlantic bottlenose dolphins.

For yet another close encounter with Florida wildlife, stop just outside of St Augustine proper at the **Alligator Farm Zoological Park** ❽ (999 Anastasia Blvd; tel: 904-824-3337, www.alligatorfarm.com; daily 9am–5pm, extended summer hours; charge). Opened in 1893, it's home to scores of alligators and crocodiles and claims to have one of the largest bird rookeries in Florida.

## St Augustine

Though Pensacola and Jacksonville can lay claim to European settlers before **St Augustine** ❾ was established in 1565, both earlier colonies quickly fell victim to famine, plague, and war – making this pretty, historic city on Matanzas Bay the oldest continuously occupied settlement in the United States. First founded by the Spanish 42 years before the British staked a claim to Virginia's Jamestown Island, St Augustine endured thanks to a series of forts that helped the settlers defend against repeated attacks by Semi-

noles, various pirates, and the British.

The last of these fortresses, **Castillo de San Marcos** ❻ (1 S. Castillo Dr; tel: 904-829-6506; www.nps.gov/casa; daily 8.45am–5.15pm; charge) still looms at the edge of the bay. Built of coquina, a limestone made from bits of shell and coral that's indigenous to northern Florida, the Castillo withstood repeated bombardments thanks to the soft rock's unique ability to absorb cannon blasts. It was ceded to the British in 1763, returned to the Spanish in 1784, then turned over to the newly formed United

*Castillo de San Marcos has stood guard over Matanzas Bay for more than three centuries.*

**BELOW:** historic reenactors prepare to fire a cannon from Castillo de San Marcos.

The Oldest Wooden Schoolhouse is one of dozens of historic structures in St Augustine's colonial district.

**BELOW:** a stained-glass panel in the Cathedral-Basilica of St Augustine recounts scenes from the life of the city's patron saint.

States in 1821. It served as a Union prison (under the name Fort Marion) during the Civil War and was retired from active duty in 1901. Along with a reconstructed section of the defensive earthwork that once surrounded it, the Castillo is now a national monument, the only extant 17th-century fort in the country.

St Augustine proudly celebrates its tempestuous history, noting that five flags have flown over the city: Spanish, British, Spanish again (under a new flag), Confederate, and US. And though there are many ways to explore the town – including trolley, horse-drawn carriage, and a plethora of ghost-themed excursions – a walk through downtown may give the best sense of the scope of its heritage.

## The old city

A short walk from the **Visitor Center G** at 10 S. Castillo Drive (www.ci.st-augustine.fl.us; daily 9am–5.30pm) takes you

past the crumbling Huguenot Cemetery to the gate of the colonial district, a pedestrian-friendly strip of historically significant buildings and exhibits interspersed with shops selling everything from Spanish-inspired pottery to Thomas Kinkade paintings.

Just past the gate is the **Oldest Wooden Schoolhouse ⊕** (14 St George St; tel 888-653-7245; www.oldestwoodenschoolhouse.com; open daily; charge), built in the early 18th century. Originally a bachelor's home, it was converted to a one-room school in 1788. Nearby is the **Colonial Spanish Quarter ⊙** (53 S George St; tel: 904-825-6830, www.historicstaugustine.com/csq/history.html; daily 9am–5.30pm; charge), a living-history museum where costumed guides lead visitors through the daily life of a typical 18th-century Spanish colonial village. Down this street, the reconstructed **Spanish Military Hospital ⊙** (3 Aviles St; tel: 904-827-0807; www.spanishmilitaryhospital.com; Mon–Sat 10am–5pm Sun noon–5pm; charge) gives a glimpse of the grimmer side of colonial life.

At the south end of the district, the **Oldest House Museum Complex ⓚ** (27

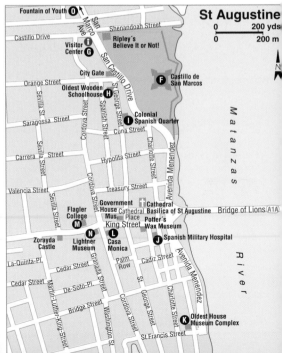

*Recommended Restaurants on pages 226–7*

Charlotte St; tel: 904-824-2874, www.stau-gustinehistoricalsociety.org; daily 9am–5pm; charge), operated by the St Augustine Historical Society, includes Florida's oldest surviving dwelling from the Spanish colonial period. The site has been occupied since the 1600s, but the current structure dates to the early 1700s. It combines British, Spanish, and American architectural influences, with thick coquina walls on the first floor and a second floor made of wood. Inside are antique furnishings and exhibits detailing the workings of a colonial household. The complex includes several other buildings full of exhibits on the cultural and military history of St Augustine and the state of Florida, plus a traditional garden, an 18th-century detached kitchen, and a museum shop.

## Henry Flagler's heyday

Head west up King Street to a trio of buildings built by railroad man Henry Flagler, a figure arguably as pivotal in Florida's development as the Spanish. All three were formerly luxury hotels, though only the crenellated **Casa Monica** Ⓛ (95 Cordova St; tel: 904-827-1888, www.casamonica.com), built in 1888,

still serves in that capacity. The 400-room **Hotel Ponce de Leon**, a sparkling example of Spanish Renaissance architecture, is now the main residence hall for private **Flagler College** Ⓜ (74 King St; tel: 904-829-6481, www.flagler.edu; charge for tour), a four-year liberal arts school with a student body of about 2,500. Only part of the building is open to the public.

Across the street, what was once the Hotel Alcazar is now the **Lightner Museum** Ⓝ (75 King St, tel: 904-824-2874; www.lightnermuseum.org; daily 9am–5pm; charge). Chicago publisher Otto Lightner bought the building in 1946 to house his impressive and eclectic collection of Gilded Age ephemera, which includes everything from Tiffany glass and Art Nouveau furniture to mechanical musical instruments, needlework, buttons, and curiosities like a mummy and shrunken head. Be sure to check out the ceramic statuette of a newsboy in the stairs to the third-floor gallery:

*St George Street leads through the heart of the historic district.*

**BELOW:** Flagler College was originally the opulent Hotel Ponce de Leon.

*Tiffany glass at the Lightner Museum.*

he's holding a copy of *Hobbies*, the magazine that made Lightner's fortune.

## Heading north

On the edge of town, San Marco Avenue, the road leading back to I-95, is lined with antique shops and trolley-tour outfits. A garish sign points the way to the **Fountain of Youth** (11 Magnolia Ave; tel: 904-829-3168; www.fountainofyouthflorida.com; daily 9am–5pm; charge) a 15-acre (6-hectare) archaeological park on the site of the Timucuan village where Ponce de Leon first claimed Florida for the Spanish crown. It's free to drink from the titular natural spring.

There's not a lot on the interstate between St Augustine and Jacksonville save for outlet malls and the **World Golf Village**, a golf resort encompassing two courses, the **World Golf Hall of Fame** (Mon–Sat 10am–6pm, Sun noon–6pm; charge), and an IMAX theater.

Back on Route A1A, about 2 miles (3km) north of the city lies the site of Gracia Real de Santa Theresa de Mose, better known as **Fort Mose** (pronounced *mo-say*), the first free community of former slaves in the United States. A century before the Emancipation Proclamation, enslaved African-Americans fleeing South Carolina plantations journeyed to this sanctuary where, if they pledged allegiance to the Spanish king and converted to Catholicism, they were guaranteed freedom. The fort had its own militia and served as the northernmost defense of St Augustine during the Revolutionary War. It was abandoned in 1763 and is now contained within **Fort Mose Historical State Park** (15 Saratoga Blvd; tel: 904-823-2232, www.floridastateparks.org/fortmose; daily 8am–sunset).

## Jacksonville

Sprawling across the St John's River, **Jacksonville** is an odd hybrid. Neither a big tourist draw nor a center of industry, it is nonetheless Florida's most populous city and, thanks to its consolidated city-county government, the largest city in terms of sheer land mass in the United States. Founded in 1791 as Cowford – after the shallow, narrow part of

*Recommended Restaurants on pages 226–7*

the St John's across which farmers led cattle – it was later renamed for Old Hickory himself, Andrew Jackson, then governor of the Florida territory.

An important port for both Union and Confederate forces during the Civil War, the little city emerged relatively unscathed from that conflict, only to be essentially destroyed on May 3, 1901. The Great Fire of that year started in a mattress factory and razed more than 2,000 buildings over 146 city blocks, as devastating in scope as the Great Chicago Fire 30 years earlier. Legend has it that the glow from the inferno could be seen from as far away as Savannah, Georgia. Still, the city rebuilt quickly, as architects and designers flocked to town to make their mark. Ten years later it was again a major naval and shipping hub, while the extension of rail lines to the area made it, like St Augustine and Ormond Beach, a popular resort destination for moneyed Northerners. Drawn by the mild climate, the nascent movie industry moved in as well; by 1916 Jacksonville had more than 30 studios, making it the winter film capital of the world. It was also, perhaps most notably, a vital

player in the development of an African-American film industry, thanks to directors like Richard Norman, whose Jacksonville-based Norman Studios produced a series of feature films depicting black characters as heroes and romantic leads at a time when parts for black actors were limited to villains and bumpkins.

Like many American cities, Jacksonville suffered in the latter part of the 20th century as sprawl decentralized the civic core and investment moved out of town. But today traffic over Jack-

*Colonial cannon are on display at the Fountain of Youth.*

**BELOW:** World Golf Village.

*Andrew Jackson was the first US governor of Florida and Jacksonville's namesake.*

**BELOW:** Jacksonville Landing on the St John's River.

sonville's magnificent bridges testifies to its continued vitality. The port remains a busy shipping center; a few miles north, at the mouth of the St John's, massive aircraft carriers and other vessels dock at the **Mayport Naval Station**, outside the fishing village of Mayport. And thanks to some aggressive urban planning, not to mention the investment generated when the city hosted the Super Bowl in 2005, parts of a once-distressed downtown have been successfully refashioned as a tourist-friendly entertainment zone.

## The rebirth of downtown

**Jacksonville Landing**, a pedestrian marketplace of shops, nightclubs, and restaurants on the north bank of the St John's, anchors the revitalized downtown. Nearby, at 128 Forsyth Street, is the lavish **Florida Theatre**. Designed in high Moorish style to resemble a starlit courtyard, it opened in 1927 as a luxury vaudeville and movie palace and is, perhaps most famously, the site of Elvis Presley's first-ever concert appearance. Extensively rehabbed in the 1980s, it's now a cornerstone of the downtown arts renaissance; see www.floridatheatre.com for programming.

Also downtown are the **Museum of Science and History** (1025 Museum Circle; tel: 904-396-7062; www.themosh.org; Mon–Fri 10am–5pm, Sat 10am–6pm, Sun 1pm–6pm; charge), full of exhibits on Jacksonville's history and ecology, and the new **Museum of Contemporary Art Jacksonville** (333 N. Laura St; tel: 904-366-6911; www.mocajacksonville.org; Tue–Sat 10am–4pm, Wed to 9pm, Sun noon–4pm; charge). Originally founded in 1924, "MOCA Jax" moved to its new digs in the renovated Western Union Telegraph Building in 2003. Both the permanent collection and the changing exhibit galleries showcase a broad spectrum of work by contemporary artists.

The free "First Wednesday" art walk is another popular way to take the measure of the city's art scene. The self-guided gallery hop encompasses a range of venues in six downtown blocks and happens the first Wednesday of every month from 5pm to 9pm. You can pick up a map at Jacksonville Landing or MOCA Jax.

A few other attractions lie north of downtown. The **Jacksonville Zoo** (370 Zoo Pkwy; tel: 904-757-4463, www.jax-zoo.org; daily 9am–5pm; charge) report-

*Recommended Restaurants on pages 226–7*

edly has one of the largest exotic animal populations in the South, with everything from Florida box turtles to four massive African elephants. Nearby, the **Anheuser-Busch Brewery** (111 Busch Dr; tel: 904-696-8373, www.budweisertours.com; Mon–Sat 10am–4pm) offers free tours – and complimentary samples – to those interested in learning where their Budweiser comes from.

## Into the neighborhoods

Across Main Street Bridge is the chic neighborhood of **San Marco**, whose business district was designed in the 1920s to mimic Venice's Piazza San Marco. At 1996 San Marco Boulevard, the Art Deco **San Marco Theatre** anchors an upscale commercial strip of boutiques, wine bars, cafés, and art galleries. Showing first-run movies and serving food and beer, it's a popular destination for young professionals and families.

Just southwest of downtown are genteel **Avondale** and up-and-coming **Riverside**, full of vintage 19th-century homes and soaring oaks and magnolias. One neighborhood landmark is the **Cummer Museum of Art and Gardens** (829

Riverside Ave; tel: 904-356-6857, www.cummer.org; Tue 10am–9pm, Wed–Sat 10am–5pm, Sun noon–5pm; charge). Inside, 13 galleries showcase traveling and permanent exhibits covering an 8,000-year span of art history. The Cummer is open late on Tuesdays, and admission is free from 4pm to 9pm. Behind the museum, beautiful formal gardens – one Italian, one English – slope down to the St John's River.

Tourists seeking more pop thrills may want to make a pilgrimage to Riverside's

*A marble archer takes aim at the sky in the gardens of the Cummer Museum of Art.*

**BELOW AND BELOW LEFT:** the Cummer Museum of Art and its riverside gardens.

*Powerboats and other pleasure craft are berthed at a Fernandina Beach marina.*

**BELOW:** American Beach.
**BELOW RIGHT:** Fernandina Beach is a popular destination for charter fishing.

**Robert E. Lee High School**, whose strict former gym teacher, Leonard Skinner, unwittingly gave his name to Jacksonville's favorite sons, the rock band Lynyrd Skynyrd, thanks to his habit of suspending the band members for having long hair. After the grave of front man Ronnie Van Zant was vandalized in 2000, his remains were moved and interred in the family plot in Riverside Memorial Park Cemetery.

Riverside's historic **Five Points** district offers a cluster of hip restaurants and funky shops around the intersection of Park, Lomax, and Margaret streets. The center of young, artsy Jacksonville, Five Points is a great area for a leisurely afternoon of window shopping. Check out the eclectic offerings in the 1928 **Park Arcade Building**, one of Jacksonville's earliest commercial structures and once home to Florida's first indoor-outdoor miniature golf course.

Built in the 1920s as an exclusive subdivision, adjacent Avondale is a bit more upscale. On the central strip of St John's Avenue you'll find everything from Lilly Pulitzer boutiques to jazzy bistros. Side streets offer blocks of beautifully restored Mediterranean Revival homes and an array of welcoming parks. Much of Riverside/Avondale was designated a historic district in 1997.

Jacksonville's southernmost neighborhood of **Mandarin** has a fascinating history all its own thanks in large part to the influence of Harriet Beecher Stowe, who wintered in the small farming community from 1867 to 1884. Following the success of *Uncle Tom's Cabin*, Stowe owed her publisher another book. Rather than write a second novel, she lovingly documented the landscape and culture of northern Florida in *Palmetto-Leaves*. The

## A Beach of Their Own

In 1935, at the height of Jim Crow, African-Americans were forbidden to use Florida's beaches. So it was a monumental day when businessman Abraham Lincoln Lewis, president of the Afro-American Life Insurance Company, bought 200 acres (80 acres) of Amelia Island and founded American Beach, the country's first African-American resort.

In its heyday, middle-class black northerners traveled more than 1,000 miles (1,600km) through the segregated South to vacation on Amelia Island. Black families thronged to the beach on weekends, and jazz greats like Louis Armstrong and Cab Calloway drew packed crowds to the clubs. Ironically, the gains of the Civil Rights era took a toll on the community – black tourists finally had other options – but a determined core hung on and fought hard against encroaching development, refusing to sell to those who would turn the area into yet another golf course or gated community. Today only 120 of the original 200 acres remain, but its historic significance has finally been recognized. In 2002 American Beach was placed on the National Register of Historic Places.

collection of sketches about fishing on the St John's River and picnicking under live oaks laden with Spanish moss is considered some of the earliest unintentional promotional writing about Florida and was instrumental in enticing tourists to the south. In 1872 Stowe helped found a racially integrated school in Mandarin; the building still stands today as home to the preservation-minded **Mandarin Community Club** at 12447 Mandarin Road. Across the street a plaque marks the site of the former Stowe cottage.

## By the sea

The pretty shore communities of **Atlantic Beach** and **Neptune Beach** ⓭ lie about 20 minutes due east of Jacksonville. The white sand beaches may not offer the hedonistic pleasures of Daytona – the sand's softer, so no driving, and Jacksonville, lying north of Florida's tropical zone, actually has four seasons, so the water can be gray and choppy. But if all you want to do is soak in the sun, you should be fine most of the year.

Where Atlantic Avenue hits 1st Street and the beachfront, there's a strip of restaurants and shops. **Pete's Bar**, at 117

First Street, is a local landmark, popular for both the cheap beer and pool. Novelist John Grisham is a regular, and the watering hole features prominently in his 2000 novel *The Brethren*, set in and around Neptune Beach. A bit farther south, **Jacksonville Beach** offers a bikini-friendly strip of surf shops and bars popular with college students and others looking to party down.

## North to Amelia Island

Up A1A from Jacksonville's beaches are the resort communities of **Amelia Island** and **Fernandina Beach**. They're an easy day trip from downtown on the interstate or, if you're coming up the coast road, via the ferry from Mayport to Fort George Island. The brief crossing costs $5, and boats run every 30 minutes.

A half mile from the ferry dock is the **Kingsley Plantation** (11676 Palmetto Ave; tel: 904-251-3537, www.nps.gov/timu; daily 9am–5pm; charge) in the **Timucuan Ecological and Historic Preserve** ⓮, a 46,000-acre (18,600-hectare) expanse of

*A friendly tavern in Fernandina Beach.*

**BELOW:** Amelia Island.

*Recommended Restaurants on pages 226–7*

*Leave room for a sumptuous dessert at the Amelia Island Plantation Resort.*

**BELOW:** Segways are a fun and speedy way to explore Amelia Island Plantation.

woods and wetlands. Built in 1798, the plantation house is the oldest in the state. Merchant and planter Zephaniah Kingsley settled here in 1814 with his Senegalese wife, Anta Mdgingine Jia (or "Anna," as she was known), whom he had purchased as a slave in Cuba and consequently freed. Their vast estate produced cotton, indigo, and sugar cane and was home to 80 enslaved Africans until 1837, when, faced with increasingly oppressive laws restricting the rights of "persons of color," Kingsley moved his family and 50 freed slaves to Haiti. A self-guided tour of the restored grounds and buildings, which include both the large main house and the tiny slave quarters, offers a fascinating glimpse into an earlier way of life.

## Seaside resorts

Just south of the Georgia border, A1A crosses the Intracoastal Waterway to beautiful **Amelia Island** ⑮, 32 miles (51km) northeast of Jacksonville. Amelia is famed as a posh escape for the wealthy, who congregate at the vast and exclusive **Amelia Island Plantation Resort** and the lavish **Ritz-Carlton**. But the island has plenty to offer those outside the Forbes 500.

The quaint town of **Fernandina Beach**, on the island's northern tip, dates back to the 1850s and looks it. From the Victorian courthouse (now the post office) to the gracious frame homes bearing gingerbread balustrades, turrets, and gables, the town is a snapshot of another moment in time. In the late 19th century, Fernandina was a busy, affluent shipping port, and the state's first resort destination for the rich Yankees who later moved south to St Augustine, Ormond Beach, and beyond. A walking tour of the historic district's 40 blocks takes visitors past a fantastic array of Gothic, Queen Anne, and late Victorian architecture.

One building worth a particular look is the **Tabby House** at 27 S. Seventh Street. Made from a traditional cement mixture of crushed oyster shells called "tabby," the lacy, intricate Victorian home was designed by R.S. Schuyler and is now on the National Register of Historic Places.

The **Amelia Island Museum of History** (233 S. Third St; tel: 904-261-7378, www.ameliamuseum.org; Mon–Sat 10am–4pm, Sun 1pm–4pm; charge), housed in the former Nassau County jail, offers a quick and comprehensive overview of the area's evolution from Timucuan village to Spanish mission, Civil War port, and Victorian-era playground, and continues up to the current day.

East of Fernandina Beach you'll find **Fort Clinch State Park** (2601 Atlantic Ave; tel: 904-277-7274, www.florida stateparks.org/fortclinch; daily 8am–sunset; charge). Construction of this fort at the mouth of the St Mary's River was begun in 1847 but never completed. It served as a military post during the Civil War, the Spanish-American War, and World War I, and became one of the state's first parks in 1935. Nowadays visitors can tour the barracks, preserved in their Civil War state, as well as hike, camp, and picnic on the dunes or along the freshwater ponds and salt marshes that provide a habitat for birds, turtles, alligators, and a multitude of other Florida wildlife. Across the sound you can see the heel of Georgia's Cumberland Island, a national seashore from tip to toe. □

# Cumberland Island

**Just over the border in Georgia is an island frozen in time, where nature plays a dominant role and wild horses roam the beaches**

Georgia's largest and southernmost barrier island, Cumberland Island captures the diversity of the coastal ecosystem in one 17-mile-long (27-km) package. Sand dunes and an uninterrupted stretch of beach line the eastern shore, where loggerhead turtles creep ashore at night to lay their eggs. Inland are quiet hardwood forests of oak and pine and freshwater ponds hospitable to gators; to the west, tidal marshes harbor fiddler crabs and myriad birds. It's a peculiarly magical place, thanks to one simple fact: though humans have inhabited the island through the years, there have never been so many as to significantly alter or endanger the natural environment.

For centuries the island was a seasonal fishing destination for Timucuan Indians. Later, Spanish and then British settlers established military outposts. In the 18th century, Revolutionary War hero General Nathanael Green bought land on the island, and in time his widow and heirs built a four-story tabby mansion and named the estate Dungeness. By the middle of the 19th century, the island supported 15 plantations and small farms – and about 500 slaves.

Union troops held the island during the war, but after emancipation times were tough. Farms failed and plantations shut down. Up on the north end of the island, a small settlement was the locus of a community of former slaves. The tiny, rustic First African Baptist Church – best known as the site of the 1996 wedding of John F. Kennedy, Jr, and Carolyn Bessette – still stands today.

Then, in the late 19th century, industrialist Thomas Carnegie, brother of Andrew, bought two defunct plantations, including Dungeness, and built an even grander home on the foundation of the old mansion. Thomas died in 1886, but his wife, Lucy, and their nine children remained on the vast estate, eventually building several additional houses on the island for the Carnegie daughters. With Vanderbilts and Duponts as their guests, they entertained in high Gilded Age style.

When Lucy Carnegie died in 1916 her will dictated that her horses be turned loose. Today about 200 wild horses, descendants of the Carnegie herd, roam the island freely. Visitors probably won't get close enough to see them, but they're often visible by boat, as they amble down a deserted beach.

In the 1970s, a Hilton Head developer endeavored to turn land bought from the Carnegie heirs into a resort, complete with marina and golf course. Happily, those plans were abandoned, and most of Cumberland Island is now preserved in perpetuity as a National Seashore, though private citizens still have rights to some tracts of land, which are held in trust by the Park Service.

Island visitors are limited to 300 a day via a twice-daily ferry from the village of St Mary's, about an hour's drive from Jacksonville. Cars are forbidden to all but Park Service personnel and permanent residents. The exclusive Greyfield Inn is the only lodging on the island that doesn't require a tent. A day trip allows for about four hours of sightseeing – enough time to tour the otherworldly ruins of the Dungeness estate and walk a loop through the salt marshes and up the hard-packed beach of the Atlantic shore before ducking back through the mossy forest to the western shore and the ferry dock, where the *Cumberland Queen* waits to take you back to the real world.  ❑

**RIGHT:** a wild horse grazes at the ruins of Dungeness.

# RESTAURANTS

## Amelia Island

**Ocean Grill**
Amelia Island Plantation
6800 First Coast Hwy
Tel: 888-261-6161
D Tue–Sat
Expect high-end dining at this elegant resort restaurant with ocean views, an extensive wine list, and superior Continental cuisine. $$$$

## Atlantic Beach

**Ragtime**
207 Atlantic Blvd
Tel: 904-241-7877

L & D daily
Finely crafted beers and Cajun-inspired seafood make this brewpub a busy – and relatively classy – spot on the beach strip. Gumbo and beignets are as good as you'll get in New Orleans; a children's menu features homemade root beer. $$

## Fernandina Beach

**La Bodega Courtyard Café**
19 S. 3rd St
Tel: 904-321-1922
L Mon–Sat, D Tue–Sat
With wrought-iron fences and tinkling fountains, the romantic courtyard may be what draws you in, but the kitchen at this quaint Amelia Island spot delivers on the plate. The menu showcases con-

temporary Southern cuisine strong on fresh seafood and other local, seasonal ingredients. Reservations recommended. $$$

**Lulu's Bra and Grill**
11B S. 7th St
Tel: 904-261-7123
L & D Tue–Sat, Sun Br
No, it's not a typo. This casual, Latin-inspired café tucked away off Centre Street works its whimsical theme to the hilt with walls decorated with ladies undergarments. Pressed sandwiches, including a savory Cuban, and creative entrees like crab cakes with key lime mustard sauce make it a local fave. $$

## Jacksonville

**Al's Pizza**
1620 Margaret St
Tel: 904-388-8384
L & D daily
With five locations in town and at the beach, this local minichain has a lock on ultracasual dining. Pizzas are fresh and ample and available in "New York-style" thin- and Sicilian thick-crust versions. $

**BB's**
1019 Hendricks Ave
Tel: 904-306-0100
L Mon–Fri, D Mon–Sat, Br Sat
Popular with both business lunchers and soccer moms, this casually modern sibling of Biscotti's *(see below)* offers a range of glob-

ally inspired bistro fare from fried calamari and wood-oven pizzas to prosciutto-wrapped pork chops. $$

**Biscotti's**
3556 St John's Ave
Tel: 904-387-2060
L & D daily, Br Sat–Sun
A regular on "Best of Jacksonville" lists, this much-loved Avondale institution offers consistently excellent café fare and creative daily dinner specials, not to mention some of the city's best cheese grits. Ask for a tour of the cake case. $$–$$$

**Bistro Aix**
1440 San Marco Blvd
Tel: 904-398-1949
L Mon–Fri, D daily
The night-out destination of choice for hip Jacksonville, this laid-back French-Mediterranean spot in chic San Marco dishes up sophisticated seasonal dishes like fork-tender organic short ribs and a devastating penne spiked with spicy sausage and goat cheese. The primo wine list has many pours available by the glass and half-bottle. $$$

**The Brick**
3585 St John's Ave
Tel: 904-387-0606
L & D daily, Sat–Sun Br
This spacious and airy eatery on Avondale's historic St John's Avenue is a reliable choice for Kobe beef burgers or a French

**LEFT:** a bartender at Mi Casa pours a long tall beer.
**RIGHT:** a tasty entree at the Ocean Grill, Amelia Island.

dip, but it's even more popular as a nightspot. There's live jazz nightly and the bar is usually buzzing. $$–$$$

**Clark's Fish Camp**
12909 Hood Landing Rd
Tel: 904-268-3474
L Sat–Sun, D daily
A kitschy local institution, this ramshackle former bait shop is as famous for its amazing collection of taxidermy as for its epic range of seafood. Daring diners go for the "Swamp Fest" platter, which includes fried bites of gator tail, soft shell crab, frog legs, conch, catfish, and squid. $$

**The Fox**
3580 St John's Ave
Tel: 904-387-2669
B & L daily, Sat–Sun Br
Hipster owned and operated, this vintage Avondale diner is wildly popular for weekend brunch. Waffles and French toast are some of the best in town; late risers can tuck into lunch specials like homemade meatloaf and chicken potpie. $

**Mossfire Grill**
1537 Margaret St
Tel: 904-355-4434
L & D Mon–Sat
Named for the blaze that devastated the city in 1901, popular Mossfire offers a mash-up of contemporary American and Southwestern flavors – fish tacos, giant burritos, and an excellent shrimp quesadilla doused with red chili vinaigrette. Go off menu and try the gut-busting Texas Pete cheese fries if you dare. $$

Neptune Beach
**Mezza Luna Ristorante**
110 First St
Tel: 904-249-5573

D Tue–Sun
No peel-and-eat-shrimp here: casually upscale Mezza Luna has been dishing up Mediterranean-inspired dishes like ahi tuna tartare and savory wood-fired pizzas for more than 20 years. $$$

**Pete's Bar**
117 First St
Tel: 904-249-9158
A local landmark since 1933, Pete's lays claim to the first liquor license in Duval County. Rowdy and grimy, the beachfront dive features 25-cent pool and ice-cold Pabst and is a favorite haunt of novelist John Grisham.

**Sliders Seafood Grille**
218 First St
Tel: 904-246-0881
L Sat–Sun, D daily
Seafood fresh off the boat and prepared to order is the signature at this casual, dog- and kid-friendly spot near the beach. Thursday happy hour specials knock fresh shucked oysters even further down from an already ridiculously low price. $$

Ormond by the Sea
**Betty's A1A Café**
1900 Oceanshore Blvd
Tel: 386-441-8131
L & D Wed–Mon
This friendly diner just north of Daytona on Route A1A offers all the standards, specials like meatloaf and gravy, and an unparalleled parking-lot view of the ocean. $

St Augustine
**Cap's on the Water**
4325 Myrtle St
Tel: 904-824-8794
L Fri–Sun, D daily
With an award-winning wine list, a raw bar, and a menu of creative but classic seafood, Cap's is a textbook example of

rustic Florida elegance. The deck, shaded by massive live oaks, offers sunset views of the Intracoastal Waterway. Kids, dogs, and boaters are welcome. $$–$$$

**Columbia**
98 St George St
Tel: 904-824-3341
L & D daily
In the heart of St Augustine's historic district, Columbia's gracious courtyard and dining rooms ooze old-world Spanish charm. The menu is laden with Iberian classics, from tapas and sherry to three takes on paella, the house specialty. Reservations recommended. $$$

**Mi Casa Café**
69 St George St
Tel: 904-824-9317
L daily to 5pm, Sat to 11pm
A laid-back spot in the historic district for beer and a bite. The menu has a few Spanish and vegetarian dishes. The shady patio is perfect for a midday break. There's live music Sat–Sun. $–$$

**Mill Top Tavern and Listening Room**
19½ St George St
Tel: 904-829-2329

L & D daily
Head up above the working water wheel of this rustic former gristmill to the breezy deck overlooking the Castillo de San Marcos. The menu is basic coastal pub grub, but try the Mill Top Special: one pound of shrimp, 15 barbecued wings, and all the fixings. There's live folk music nightly. $–$$

**Outback Crab Shack**
8255 CR 13 North
Tel: 904-522-0500
L & D daily
The sign says it all: "No shirt, no shoes, no problem." For $55 you can dine family-style from a heaping platter of boiled or fried sea critters; $40 nets you 5lbs (2kg) of crawfish boil. Boaters welcome. $$

Wilbur by the Sea
**Boon Docks**
3948 S. Peninsula Dr
Tel: 386-760-9001
L & D daily
This place is so casual they forgot the walls. The cabana-esque Boon Dock's – perched above a marina on the Halifax River – is a local favorite for ultrafresh fish and seafood prepared simply and well. $

# CENTRAL FLORIDA

Theme parks are the order of the day, but there are also gardens, museums, and even a few nature preserves where you can escape the crowds

The lake-studded, river-creased terrain of Central Florida has long lured tourists seeking an escape from reality. Initially they came to walk in gardens hung with Spanish moss and brimming with flowers, gaze at tropical fish through crystalline spring water, and encounter birds, alligators, and other exotic wildlife. Then a famous Hollywood mouse set up shop in the neighborhood. The resulting expansion of tourist attractions was unmatched in volume and variety and, despite the stunning white sands and aquamarine waters of the coast, visitors headed inland in droves. They flocked to Central Florida to experience self-contained pleasure domes that use new technology to tease and tantalize the senses. Simple pleasures like fishing, swimming, and lazing in the sun have been elbowed aside by hi-tech "imagineers" who can resurrect long-dead presidents and animal trainers who teach killer whales to play basketball.

Inevitably, Walt Disney World Resort remains king of Central Florida's theme parks and thus merits a whole chapter to itself, beginning with a little background information and progressing through attraction-packed accounts of each of the Disney theme lands. The other major theme parks – Universal Orlando, SeaWorld, Wet 'n' Wild, Cypress Gardens, and other more modest (though, in some cases, no less endearing) attractions – are covered in "Orlando and Its Other Worlds."

Since the theme-park explosion, Orlando itself, synonymous with Disney World in many people's minds, is now a thriving modern city with more hotel rooms than Miami Beach. Examples of Art Deco and Belle Epoque architecture survive among the high-rises and shopping centers, and suburban, well-off Winter Park is a pleasant place in which to touch base with reality. Art museums have sprung up, too, which just goes to show that Orlando can appeal to those interested in both high and low culture. ❏

---

**PRECEDING PAGES:** Dueling Dragons are twin roller coasters at Universal's Islands of Adventure. **LEFT:** Hard Rock Cafe. **TOP:** a SeaWorld orca show. **ABOVE RIGHT:** Seuss Landing at Islands of Adventure is modeled after the colorful, lopsided worlds imagined by beloved children's book author Theodor Seuss Geisel, aka Dr Seuss.

# WALT DISNEY WORLD RESORT

**Fantasy continues to thrive here, just as Walt imagined. The 'World' remains a magnet for millions of starry-eyed visitors, both young and old**

I f you're under the impression that **Walt Disney World Resort ❶** (www.disneyworld.com) is nothing but an overgrown amusement park, think again. Situated off Interstate 4 about 16 miles (26km) from downtown Orlando, Disney World is a city in its own right. Encompassed within its 47 sq miles (111 sq km) – an area twice the size of Manhattan – are four of the most elaborate theme parks ever constructed as well as two water parks, two nighttime entertainment districts, five golf courses, three spas, a sports complex, 16 hotels and over 100 restaurants.

The "World" has its own police force, fire and sanitation departments, power plant, and water treatment facility, and an average daily population of more than 110,000 people. It even has quasi-governmental status, thanks to a deal Walt Disney and brother Roy cut with the state of Florida creating the Reedy Creek Improvement District, a "public corporation" that gives the Disney company powers that are usually reserved to municipalities, such as issuing bonds, levying taxes and establishing building codes. It can even build an airport or a nuclear reactor, if the need arises.

The motivation behind Disney World's expansiveness is to provide an all-in-one vacation experience that induces visitors to stay longer and spend more. Indeed, many people find that one visit isn't nearly enough; they return year after year, with or without children, and never feel as if they've run out of things to do.

## Survival strategies

For the uninitiated, visiting Disney World can be a bewildering experience – or worse. The so-called "happiest place on Earth" takes on a very different aspect when you're waiting in line, sweat trickling down your back, and your kids – exhausted from a day of overly ambitious touring – are whining like police sirens.

How do you prevent your dream vacation from degenerating into a nightmare? The first thing you need to know is that Disney World is not the kind of place that

**LEFT:** Epcot by night.
**BELOW:** Mickey and Minnie at the Magic Kingdom.

# Walt Disney World

Universal Studios

Buena Vista Lake

HAWK'S LANDING GOLF CLUB ★

Marriott Orlando World Center ★

International Drive South

Greeneway

Central Florida

535

Saratoga Spring Resort & Spa ★

P DOWNTOWN DISNEY ❻

Buena Vista Lagoon

P

536

Buena Vista Drive

Lake Buena Vista

LAKE BUENA VISTA GOLF COURSE

4

Disney's Typhoon Lagoon

❼

Gaylord Palms Resort & Convention Center ★

Tampa

Port Orleans- Riverside ★

Port Orleans French Quarter ★

Old Key West Resort ★

Buena Vista Drive

Bonnet Creek

Epcot Center Drive

Vista Boulevard

EAGLE PINES GOLF COURSE

Bonnet Creek Road

Epcot Center Drive

Caribbean Beach ★

Buena Vista Drive

Pop Century ★

Disney's Wide World of Sports ➤

Disney's Fort Wilderness Resort & Campground ★

P

Epcot ❸

World Showcase Lagoon

Epcot Main Entrance/ Toll Plaza

Beach Club Villas ★

BoardWalk Resort & Villas ★

Walt Disney World ❶

P

Magic Kingdom Main Entrance/ Toll Plaza

Vista Boulevard

Monorail

Yacht and Beach Club ★

Dolphin Hotel ★

Swan Hotel ★

Disney's Hollywood Studios/ Main Entrance/ Toll Plaza

Osceola Parkway

World Drive

Disney's Hollywood Studios ❹

All-Star Music Resort, All-Star Movies Resort ➤

West Buena Vista Drive

Coronado Springs Resort ★

P

Disney's Blizzard Beach ❽

Bay Lake

Discovery Island

Wilderness Lodge & Villas ★

Contemporary Resort ★

Ticket and Transportation Center

P

All-Star Sports Resort ★

Animal Kingdom Main Entrance/ Toll Plaza

P

Disney's Animal Kingdom ❺

❷ Magic Kingdom

Seven Seas Lagoon

Grand Floridian Resort & Spa ★

Polynesian Resort ★

MAGNOLIA GOLF COURSE

Shades of Green ★

World Drive

Disney's Animal Kingdom Resort ★

US Highway 27

## Walt Disney World

1mile

1 km

0

0

ewards spontaneity. Planning is essential, and reservations – for hotels, rental cars, and restaurants – are a must.

Timing is equally important. The two biggest gripes tourists have about Disney World are the crowds and the prices. You can minimize both by traveling off-season, when the theme parks aren't quite so mobbed and hotels and airlines offer sizable discounts. Time of day is a consideration, too. In general, attendance at the theme parks peaks between the hours of 10am and 4pm. The best strategy, therefore, is to arrive as early as possible, take a break in the afternoon for shopping and a sit-down meal (or, if you're staying at an on-site resort, sneak back to your hotel for a snooze and a swim), then pick up the trail in the late afternoon or evening.

Keep in mind that the gates at Disney World sometimes open 30 to 60 minutes earlier than the scheduled times. Granted, dragging yourself out of bed at 7am to get to the parks by 8am is hardly appealing, but you can often do more in the first couple of hours, when lines are short, temperatures are mild, and you're feeling fresh, than in the remainder of the day.

Attitude is a key element, too. Resist the temptation to be too ambitious. The tendency among most visitors is to squeeze as much as possible into the shortest period of time. This seems like sound economics: you paid a bundle to get in and now you want your money's worth. But before committing yourself to an elaborate touring plan, consider the hazards of trying to do too much. Unrealistic expectations will lead only to disappointment and exhaustion.

Unless you enjoy running frantically from one attraction to another, forget about cramming everything into a short visit or even following some preordained schedule. Instead, select three or four "must-dos" for each day and fill in with other attractions as time allows.

## Magic Kingdom

The **Magic Kingdom** ❷ (tel: 407-824-4321; daily, hours vary, see www.disney-world.com; charge) is Disney World's oldest park and the one closest to Walt's original vision of a "timeless land of enchantment." Though attractions have been updated over the years and a few are targeted at seasoned thrill-seekers,

**TIP**

FastPass allows guests to avoid long lines at some of Disney World's most popular attractions. Insert your ticket in a FastPass turnstile, get a ride time, and return later with little or no waiting.

**BELOW LEFT:**
costumed characters roam the park greeting guests.

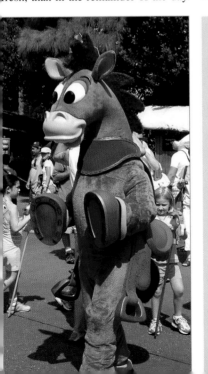

## Behind the Scenes

If you're curious about those secret corridors under the Magic Kingdom, want to learn about the art and history of Disney animation, or yearn to swim with the fish in Epcot's Living Seas aquarium, sign up for one of the resort's Behind the Scenes tours, which grants you special access.

There are about 15 tours in all, guided by enthusiastic cast members or staff experts. Among the most popular are the five-hour Keys to the Kingdom tour, limited solely to the Magic Kingdom; Backstage Magic, a daylong excursion through the Magic Kingdom, Disney-MGM Studios and Epcot; Wild by Design, which traces the planning and development of Animal Kingdom; Gardens of the World, a study of plants at Epcot's World Showcase; Disney's Architecture, a look at how Disney "imagineers" design and construct the parks' whimsical buildings; and Backstage Safari, which includes a visit to a wildlife housing area and veterinary hospital at Animal Kingdom. Although most tours require that participants be at least 16 years old, Disney's Family Magic, a two-hour interactive exploration of the Magic Kingdom, is open to visitors of all ages.

Tours vary in price, frequency, and duration. Some require the purchase of separate park admission, and those lasting more than four hours include lunch. All require an advance reservation. For information, call 407-939-8687.

**TIP**

The resort is very popular as a honeymoon destination, and you can get married here too. No-frills ceremonies are available, but if you have the cash to spare, you can invite all your favorite Disney characters.

**BELOW RIGHT:** a young visitor in a festive mood.

the park remains a gentle, almost quaint place whose power to enchant lies more in extravagant design (what the Disney people call "imagineering") than in thrill rides or special effects. This is, at heart, a children's park, although the painstaking detail, good humor and whimsy with which Walt's vision is brought to life rarely disappoints even the most jaded traveler.

## Main Street

Setting the stage at the entrance to the park is **Main Street, USA**, a picture-perfect evocation of an American town. Although there are no rides or shows here, there are more than a dozen shops and restaurants as well as a fleet of double-decker buses, horse-drawn trolleys, and old-fashioned fire trucks. The **City Hall** to the left has maps and information and can book meals. It also contains the park's Lost and Found office. At the top of Main Street, housed in a stately Victorian-style building near the entrance, is the **Walt Disney World Railroad**, which takes passengers on a 20-minute circuit around the park in vintage steam engines. To the right of the

main entrance is the tucked-away **Town Square Exposition Hall**. When not being used for conventions or presentations, the auditorium shows continuous reels of classic Disney films. This quiet and cool retreat on the fringes of the park is almost always empty.

Otherwise, Main Street is meant to be explored. In addition to the highly decorated souvenir shops there are such gems as the barber's shop with a barbershop quartet and the **Main Street Watchmaker**, which sells timepieces featuring Disney characters. Main Street leads to a roundabout known as the Hub, beyond which is **Cinderella's Castle**, the visual anchor of the park and a Disney icon second only to Mickey himself: its Forecourt Stage is home to **Dream Along with Mickey**, the park's newest live show. Pathways radiate from this central plaza into five distinct "lands," starting on the left (as you face Cinderella Castle) with **Adventureland**, a mélange of fantasy architecture and lush plantings meant to evoke such exotic locales as the South Seas and the Amazon. The attractions here are a mixed bag. **Pirates of the Caribbean** is the best of the lot – an

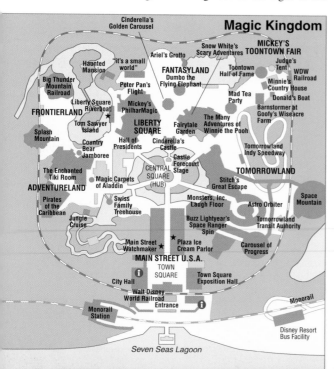

*Recommended Restaurants on pages 253-5*

audio-animatronic romp through the Spanish Main with rum-swilling buccaneers and lots of yo-ho-ho high spirits. This ride was recently updated to include Johnny Depp's character from the movie of the same name.

The other attractions in Adventureland serve to entertain kids with time to spare. These include the **Magic Carpets of Aladdin**, a basic hub-and-spoke ride; the **Swiss Family Treehouse**, a free play area based on the Robinsons' fictional home; **The Enchanted Tiki Room**, a short show featuring animatronic birds which provides a chance to cool off, if not much else); and **Jungle Cruise,** a 10-minute boat ride featuring animatronic animals and a hokey narration. Check them out if lines are short; otherwise, troll over to Frontierland, where the theme is the Old West and the rides are more interesting.

## Frontier fantasy

The two biggies at **Frontierland** are **Splash Mountain** and **Big Thunder Mountain Railroad**. The first is a log flume ride with a *Song of the South* theme and a drenching, five-story finale –

enough to elicit screams without inducing real terror. The other is a roller coaster in an elaborate red-rock setting. Scenes of ramshackle mining camps whiz by as your runaway train careens through canyons and caverns and over rickety bridges. Though this is hardly a kiddie ride, it's a piece of cake compared to the big coasters at other Orlando parks.

Opposite Big Thunder Mountain you can hitch a ride on one of the rafts that crosses the so-called Rivers of America (actually a circular lagoon) to **Tom Sawyer Island**, a refreshingly low-tech attraction where kids explore caves,

*Strollers are convenient for much needed naps.*

**BELOW:** Cinderella appears in Cinderellabration, a live stage show at the Magic Kingdom.

## Arriving at the Magic Kingdom

If you are not staying at a Disney Resort, allow plenty of time to get to and from your car to the Magic Kingdom's entrance. Trams from the parking lot drop guests off at the Ticket and Transportation Center, where you can buy your ticket and then board a boat or the monorail to reach the main entrance. From here you join the other crowds that have been directly deposited from their Disney Resort transportation. Other Disney parks operate similarly, but there the tram from the parking lot will deliver you, more or less, to the park's main entrance. Guests again enjoy an advantage as their transportation (monorail, bus, or boat) will bring them there from the front of their lodging.

**TIP**

The Galaxy Palace Theater in Tomorrowland features Disney characters and live bands seasonally. Check the entertainment schedule for performance times.

trails, and a pioneer fort under their own steam. Best of all, mom and dad can enjoy a cool glass of lemonade on the porch of **Aunt Polly's Dockside Inn**, an out-of-the-way spot for sandwiches, ice cream and cold drinks.

Another big attraction in Frontierland is the **Country Bear Jamboree** – a 16-minute hillbilly revue starring a cast of animatronic bears. Though it's been a crowd-pleaser for nearly three decades, the cornball humor isn't everybody's cup of tea.

The Wild West melds into colonial America in **Liberty Square**. The most popular attraction here – and perhaps the best in the park – is the **Haunted Mansion**. Visitors board a "doom buggy" for a tour of the house, visiting a library full of "ghost writers," a haunted ballroom and, in a clever bit of "astral projection," an apparition that appears in your car. The holographic effects – cutting edge when the ride opened some 25 years ago – hold up pretty well. On the opposite side of Liberty Square, the **Hall of Presidents** is an animatronic show with a true-blue American theme. The high point is a roll call of all US presidents, followed by remarks by th[e] current president and Abraham Lincoln. [If] you're looking for a quick way to rest you[r] feet, head over to the Liberty Squar[e] Riverboat, a vintage Victorian steamboa[t] that tours the Rivers of America.

## For the youngest among us

The next two areas, **Fantasyland** an[d] **Mickey's Toontown Fair**, are intende[d] for the preschool crowd. Kiddie ride[s] such as **Dumbo the Flying Elephan[t]** and **Cinderella's Golden Carouse[l]** will be familiar to anyone who has bee[n] to a county fair, although Disne[y] dresses them up beautifully. "Dar[k] rides" like **Snow White's Scar[y] Adventures** recap Disney's most mem[-] orable films and songs.

Notable, too, is the **Mad Tea Party** [–] what folks in the amusement-park bi[z] call a "spin-and-barf" ride – which whirl[s] you around in a "teacup" mounted o[n] whirling discs. And then there's **"it's [a] small world,"** the ride that Disney critic[s] love to hate, featuring scores of anima[-] tronic dolls in folksy costumes singing [a] chirpy melody. Love it or hate it, yo[u] can't say you've experienced the Magi[c]

**BELOW:** a crowd gathers for a parade down Main Street.

Kingdom without riding it at least once. Across from here are two of Fantasyland's finest children's attractions. **Peter Pan's Flight** is a fantastic dark ride over the streets of London to Neverland. Your pirate ship flies past key scenes from the classic Disney film before touching down. **Mickey's PhilharMagic** plays on vintage films, too, incorporating countless songs and characters into a so-called 4-D movie aimed at young children (most other 4-D films in Orlando are much too scary for the little ones). Meanwhile, **The Many Adventures of Winnie the Pooh** is a ride that is worth no one's time, as it feels in every way a poor imitation of the slow, child-friendly rides Disney normally does so well. Quieter times are to be had at the **Fairytale Garden** between Cinderella's Castle and the entrance to Tomorrowland, where Belle from *Beauty and the Beast* tells stories; at **Ariel's Grotto**, home of the Little Mermaid; and at **Pooh's Playful Spot**, a playground for younger children.

The charm of **Mickey's Toontown Fair** lies in the loopy, toon-ish set design and the freedom with which young visitors can explore their surroundings.

Three attractions – **Mickey's Country House**, **Minnie's Country House**, and **Donald's Boat** – invite kids to explore at will. Look inside Minnie's refrigerator and check for messages on her answering machine, wander through Mickey's garden, peruse the baby pictures in his bedroom, or get soaked aboard Donald's leaky boat, the *Miss Daisy*, a play area where just about everything drips, sprays or splashes.

There's only one ride in this section of the park, the **Barnstormer at Goofy's Wiseacre Farm**, a roller coaster styled like an old-fashioned biplane and scaled down for young riders and their parents. Mickey himself greets visitors in the red-and-white-striped **Judge's Tent**, and an all-star lineup of Disney characters hang out at the **Toontown Hall of Fame**. There's often a separate line for those who prefer to hobnob with Disney's best – that is, worst – villains.

## Tomorrow's world

Wrap up your visit to the Magic Kingdom at **Tomorrowland**, a confection of chrome-and-neon architecture inspired by such disparate sources as H.G. Wells

**TIP**

The FastPasses for Space Mountain run out by midday, so get one quick if you plan to ride it at all.

**BELOW:** Main Street was inspired by Walt Disney's recollection of his boyhood Missouri hometown.

## How to Cut in Line – the Official Way

The biggest gripe people have about theme parks is the long lines. Both Disney and Universal have heard your grumbles and now offer programs that greatly reduce the amount of time you'll spend staring at the back of another person's head. The FastPass system allows you to collect a timed ticket for Disney's most popular attractions. As the day goes on, the time between ticket issue and your redemption window continues to grow. Some rides may run out of FastPass tickets before lunchtime.

You are allowed to hold two "waiting" FastPasses at any time so long as they are for different rides. For the big thrill rides, Single Rider lines offer a wait nearly as short as the FastPass system, but your party will be split up.

*Walt Disney and his most famous creation are commemorated near Cinderella's Castle in the Magic Kingdom.*

**BELOW:** small bronze statues of Goofy, Minnie, and other classic Disney characters are arranged around the Magic Kingdom's central hub.

and Fritz Lang's *Metropolis*. **Space Mountain** is an indoor roller coaster replete with whiz-bang visual effects, including scary stretches of inky darkness. The ride is bumpy enough to rattle your innards without the loop-the-loops of the mega-coasters at other parks. **Buzz Lightyear's Space Ranger Spin** is fun, too – a cross between a dark ride and a shooting arcade that lets you zap "aliens" with a laser gun while being whisked around an indoor track. If you arrive at Tomorrowland from Fantasyland you will pass the noisy **Tomorrowland Indy Speedway**, a souped-up go-cart track that takes many of the controls out of the drivers' hands. How it ties into "Tomorrow" is anyone's guess.

At **Walt Disney's Carousel of Progress**, the audience sits in a rotating theater that chronicles the way technology has changed the lives of an animatronic family. Old folks seem to enjoy the show. Teens and young adults find it a snooze.

Everyone will enjoy **Monsters, Inc. Laugh Floor**, an interactive show that lets guests submit jokes to be retold by the Monsters themselves. **Stitch's Great Escape** features the mischievous alie getting loose and treating the audience t some special sights, sounds, and smell

## Parades and fireworks

No journey to the Magic Kingdom i complete without taking in one of th star-studded parades or finding you prefered spot for the nighttime firework display. The **Disney Dreams Com True Parade** (afternoons daily) is th lesser of the Magic Kingdom's tw parades but still brings the park to standstill and is a big hit with youn children who can't get enough of wav ing at famous characters. This parade i not worth planning for; in fact, if yo have teens this would be the perfec time to take advantage of short waitin times and take a couple of spins o Space Mountain. **SpectroMagic** (mos evenings) is well worth planning fo especially as it is always followed b Wishes, the park's fireworks show. I addition to standard-issue characters an music, this show employs spectacula lighting technology on the floats – th Magic Kingdom is even plunged int darkness to heighten its effects. If yo

## Disney's Hometown

Epcot was originally conceived by Walt Disney as an experiment in urban planning – an Experimental Prototype Community Of Tomorrow inhabited by real citizens. His father had helped build an exhibit at the 1893 World Columbian Exposition in Chicago, and Disney himself had been a longtime advocate of inner urban planning and city beautification projects. The plan was abandoned after Walt's death in favor of an unimaginative "world's fair," but the dream wasn't permanently forgotten. It was resurrected in 1994 in the form of Celebration, a town designed from the ground up by Disney "imagineers."

With about 8,500 residents, the town has the manicured look of a theme park, featuring a spotless downtown and houses designed by some of the most notable architects in the business. Despite Celebration's commercial success, the experiment hasn't all been smooth sailing. Some residents chafed at the restrictive bylaws, and the school's progressive agenda provoked the wrath of parents and county supervisors.

So, is Disney's experiment in "new urbanism" a success? You can judge for yourself. Celebration is 5 miles (8 km) south of Disney World near the intersection of US 192 and I-4. Special events include a Great American Pie Festival in February, a Beach and Seafood Festival in April, and vintage car shows in March and September. For information, call 407-566-2200.

*Recommended Restaurants on pages 253-5*

are planning to see **Wishes** afterwards, try to claim a patch on the right side of the hub facing Cinderella's Castle before the parade starts. This will provide excellent viewing for both the parade and the fireworks without your needing to navigate the crowds again. Wishes (most evenings) is one of the most spectacular fireworks displays you are likely ever to see, and the choreography of live action, music, and explosions is flawless – even Disney cynics are likely to be converted by the finale. To get the full effect you must have a clear view of the front of Cinderella's Castle. This makes the hub and the Plaza Restaurant very popular as showtime approaches.

## Epcot

Opened in 1982, Disney World's second theme park, **Epcot** ❸ (daily, see www.disneyworld.com for details), is modeled loosely on a World's Fair. The park is laid out in two circular areas. The first, **Future World**, anchored by that monumental silver golf ball called **Spaceship Earth**, is devoted to science and technology. Its attractions are housed in pavilions that contain rides, shows, and

exhibitions sponsored by big corporations. Inside Spaceship Earth, for example, is a dark ride sponsored by AT&T that transports passengers through a series of animatronic tableaux chronicling the history of communications from the Stone Age to the Space Age.

To the left of Spaceship Earth (in the outer ring of World Showcase) is **Universe of Energy**, sponsored by ExxonMobil. The main attraction here, a combination film and dark ride called **Ellen's Energy Adventure**, is a comedic take on the issue of energy use. Plodding and poorly scripted, the show isn't worth seeing on your first visit.

The next pavilion houses Epcot's most thrilling ride. Dubbed **Mission: SPACE**, it delivers an "astronaut-like" experience, simulating a rocket lift-off and the weightlessness of space. Disney hired NASA consultants to design the ride. It's so realistic that barf bags are available. Disney recently added a tamer version for those not wanting to experience the G-force of take-off.

The next attraction, **General Motors Test Track**, features six-person vehicles that undergo a series of "tests" –

**KIDS**

Children can make masks and kites and do other craft projects at Kidcot Fun Spots. There's one at each country in World Showcase.

**BELOW LEFT:** Spaceship Earth looms over the entrance to Epcot.

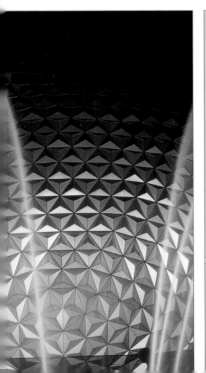

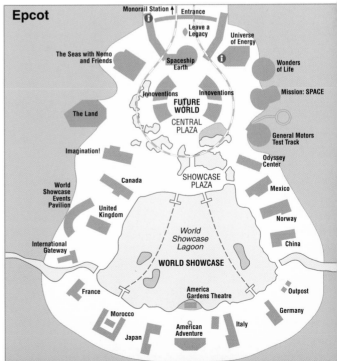

Epcot

*Ice cream stands and other food vendors are situated throughout the parks.*

**BELOW:** IllumiNations lights up the sky over Epcot.
**BELOW RIGHT:** an Epcot visitor.

little patience for slow-moving adults

On the opposite flank of Future World is a trio of pavilions, each worth a visit given enough time. **The Seas with Nemo & Friends** takes you down under in your ride vehicle – a clammobile – before delivering you to **Living Seas**. The centerpiece is a huge saltwater aquarium containing an artificial coral reef populated by tropical fish, sharks, sea turtles, and an occasional scuba diver. Dolphins and manatees are given their own tanks, where visitors can get a close-up view.

## Life and land

The strongest environmental message in the whole park is sponsored by Nestlé and found inside **The Land** pavilion. The **Circle of Life** features characters from *The Lion King* who are persuaded by Simba to stop the needless destruction of their native habitat for a useless holiday resort – a paradoxical sentiment for Disney to endorse by anyone's standards. **Living with the Land** is an intriguing, slow boat ride through different exhibits about maximizing agricultural production without destroying

acceleration, road handling, suspension, crash – that simulate the course at a GM proving ground.

From the Test Track, it's a short walk to a pair of low-slung buildings that bracket Future World's central plaza. This is **Innoventions**, an exposition of new products developed by companies like Motorola and IBM. A perennial favorite is a section devoted to Sega's latest video games. One problem with Innoventions: the coolest gizmos are often monopolized by kids who have

*Recommended Restaurants on pages 253-5*

atural habitat. You will see many of the rops grown here on the menu at the arden Grill.

One unqualified success in The Land **Soarin'** a hang-gliding simulator that kes you over various sights of outanding beauty in California.

The big draw over at the **Imagination! avilion** is a 3-D movie, **Honey, I hrunk the Audience**. The story line is lly, but the effects are amazing. The ark ride in this pavilion, called **Journey to Your Imagination**, is one of Epcot's isfires; skip it your first time around.

## World Showcase

ome children may consider World Showase – a quick tour through 11 nations of e world – a bore, but most adults, at least ose that like to shop, eat, or drink, will nd it interesting. Each pavilion gives ou the chance to experience a nation's onsumables without actually visiting the ountry. As this half of Epcot usually ays open later than Future World, a ouple could easily make a romantic, if arly, night of it here. In some ways it's ven better than Downtown Disney as e food is more varied and the atmos-

phere, especially at night, is less hectic.

Top of the romantic destination list would be **Mexico's** dimly lit **San Angel Inn Restaurante**, set under a re-created Mayan temple. The only ride in Mexico is the **Gran Fiesta Tour Starring the Three Caballeros**, a poor dark ride featuring Donald Duck touring various Mexican landscapes. The land of the Vikings is retold in **Maelstrom**, a slow boat ride with unexpected turns and drops that finishes with a short film about the Norwegian way of life. The main features of **Norway** are a re-created stave church and a Norwegian castle that houses the **Akershus Royal Banquet Hall**.

**China** features one of the best shops in World Showcase, a fine restaurant in the **Nine Dragons**, and an enjoyable Circle-Vision (the screen wraps completely around the audience) film called **Reflections of China**. Set in a re-created temple, it takes you from the Great Wall of China to Hong Kong and shows some of the most amazing natural environments, not just in China but the world. There are no proper attractions at **Germany**, but with a year-round Oktoberfest atmosphere and several fine German beers on

**TIP**

IllumiNations is a spectacular fireworks show with lasers and fountains displayed in and above the World Showcase Lagoon.

**BELOW:** Mission: SPACE is an astronaut simulator ride and one of Disney's newest attractions.

offer, no one ever really seems to notice. The **Biergarten Restaurant** is the main attraction here, but shops in half-timber houses also sell some fine Christmas ornaments and quality wooden toys for younger children. Designer labels, fine wines, and even ashtrays are for sale in the **Italy** pavilion, which is a collage of Venetian architecture that includes the Doge's Palace and the Campanile from St Mark's Square. Italian cuisine is served up **in L'Originale Alfredo di Roma Ristorante**.

## Patriotic fervor

Portraying one's own country in a theme park full of sweeping generalizations was always going to make interesting viewing for outsiders. No one will be surprised by the patriotic nature of the attractions, but the **Spirit of America Fife and Drum Corps**, the **Voices of Liberty**, and even the **American Adventure** film do their best to explain this patriotism to foreign guests. The film, which features an animatronic Ben Franklin and Mark Twain among others, does its best to provide a balanced view of American history by

**BELOW:** a torii gate welcomes visitors to Epcot's Japan Pavilion.

including the destruction of Native American cultures and the horrors of slavery. By the end, though, emotive patriotism replaces historical accuracy. Even more disappointing is that with America's rich culinary scope, from Cajun cornbread to New England clam chowder, Disney chose for the **Liberty Inn** to serve burgers and fries.

Just like the real country, many people could come to **Japan** just to shop. There is a huge selection of smartly designed sushi plates and knives, silk garments, eccentric toys, and other delicate trinkets. Though the quick-service restaurants here serve fine sushi, the **Teppanyaki Dining Rooms** is the best place for a sit-down meal. The **Morocco** pavilion has some of the finest faux architecture in World Showcase. You can even have a go at getting lost in the warren of shops selling Middle Eastern art and dress, including fine rugs and bronze work. The country's cuisine is summed up at **Restaurant Marrakesh**.

It should be no surprise that you get two fine restaurants, **Chefs de France** and **Bistro de Paris**, and an accomplished patisserie in France. There is

also a fine wine shop and, in the ultimate sign of good taste, a store selling Insight Guides.

**Impressions de France** is a panoramic film shown throughout the day that takes you on a sweeping journey over the French countryside. Get your gourmandizing done before you leave France – fish and chips are the main fare in the **UK**. This little Britain has everything from Blighty, including a Beatles cover band at the **Rose and Crown Pub**.

America's neighbor gets a rugged interpretation with mountainous terrain and the Circle-Vision Film, **O Canada!** The signature restaurant **Le Cellier Steakhouse** serves meals hearty enough for any lumberjack.

## Disney's Hollywood Studios

Dedicated to the "Hollywood that never was and always will be," **Hollywood Studios** ❹ (daily, see www.disneyworld.com for details) is, in many respects, Disney World's most satisfying park. An unabashed attempt to compete with Universal Studios, the park combines some of Disney's best rides with a behind-the-scenes look at movie making.

Upon entering the park, visitors are immediately transported back to the golden age of Hollywood. Lining either side of **Hollywood Boulevard** – the park's main staging area – are replicas of iconic Tinseltown buildings, most housing shops stocked with Disney merchandise. This is also the first place you'll encounter costumed characters, including actors playing stock Hollywood "types" (a struggling actress, an imperious director, and so forth) who do street skits.

Towering over a plaza at the end of Hollywood Boulevard is a 12-story **Sorcerer's Hat** like the one worn by Mickey in *Fantasia*. Kiosks beneath the hat review highlights in Disney history – not worth the time if you're on a schedule.

Behind the Sorcerer's Hat, in a replica of Graumann's Chinese Theater, is **The Great Movie Ride**, a Magic Kingdom-style dark ride through sets from classic film scenes, from the romantic ending to *Casablanca* to scarier scenes from *Alien*.

Hollywood iconography continues on **Sunset Boulevard**, which veers off to the right of the plaza. About halfway down, in a roofed amphitheater modeled

*Street performers at Disney's Hollywood Studios bring back the golden age of motion pictures.*

**BELOW:** Johnny Weissmuller and Maureen O'Sullivan in *Tarzan*, an MGM classic featured in The Great Movie Ride.

## A Sporting Place

Sports fans should make a point of checking the schedule at Disney's Wide World of Sports, a $100-million, 200-acre (80-hectare) complex with a baseball stadium, a 5,000-seat basketball fieldhouse, 12 tennis courts, and facilities for about 30 other sports.

The complex is host to scores of amateur and professional competitions including the Atlanta Braves' spring training. The Multi-Sports Experience features baseball, football, and other activities.

Other events include training programs for high school and college baseball, lacrosse, soccer, softball, and gymnastics as well as tournaments ranging from Little League baseball and inline hockey for kids to the US Men's World Cup Soccer Team.

The complex is on Victory Way near Hollywood Studios, just west of I-4. For a list of upcoming events, call 407-939-1500. Admission is charged for premium events.

For fans of water sports, the Walt Disney World Resort has a web of waterways connecting lakes large and small, and almost all its resorts are on a lake or canal, with their own landing places or marinas. Dozens of different types of pleasure craft can be rented. For sailing, conditions are best at two big lakes – Seven Seas Lagoon and Bay Lake at the Magic Kingdom Resorts.

**BELOW:** Rod Serling welcomes visitors to the Twilight Zone at the Tower of Terror.

after the Hollywood Bowl, is **Beauty and the Beast Live on Stage.** This condensed version of the Disney film is a big hit with children. It lacks the *wow* factor and air conditioning of other live shows, but often fills up prior to showtimes.

## The big show

A few steps away is the entrance to a second open-air venue, the Hollywood Hills Amphitheater. This is the site of **Fantasmic,** Hollywood Studios' big finale, which plays nightly just before closing. The special-effects crew pulls out all the stops, dazzling the audience with lasers, fountains and fireballs in a show that pits Mickey Mouse against Disney's nastiest villains.

The structure hulking over the end of Sunset Boulevard is the **Twilight Zone Tower of Terror,** housed in what appears to be an abandoned hotel. Inside, you're ushered into an "elevator" that hurtles through space – up, down, up, down – with a few pauses for creepy, heart-stopping views. This is decidedly not an experience for those with shaky stomachs or a fear of heights.

The excitement continues over at the

**Rock 'n' Roller Coaster Starring Aerosmith,** an indoor coaster with enough twists to satisfy hard-core thrill seekers. The launch is especially riveting, achieving a speed of 60mph (97kph) in less than 3 seconds. A word of warning: this is not a ride for lightweights. If you thought Space Mountain was a challenge, this one will knock you for a loop.

## Around Echo Lake

Return to the Sorcerer's Hat and explore the area on the opposite side of the plaza around Echo Lake. The big draw here is the **Indiana Jones Epic Stunt Spectacular,** starring stuntmen who reenact scenes from *Raiders of the Lost Ark,* then explain how it's done. There are gunfights, fistfights and other feats of derring-do, not to mention a couple of searing explosions. Across the way is **Sounds Dangerous,** a comedy in which Drew Carey plays a reporter trailing a smuggler. Most of the action takes place in the dark, while the audience listens in with headphones. The script is inane, but the show illustrates how sound can advance a story.

An Imperial walker, one of those spacey war machines that sprang from the mind of George Lucas, stands in front of **Star Tours,** the park's only simulator ride. Here you're ushered into a "star-speeder" for a madcap journey through the cosmos. The ride isn't particularly frightening, but it does give passengers a good shake.

The atmosphere takes on an urban, brick-and-mortar quality as you drift into the area around New York Street. Here you'll find a statue of Miss Piggy standing in front of a theater showing Jim Henson's **Muppet Vision 3-D,** a raucous 25-minute romp with Kermit, Piggy, and the rest of the muppet crew.

Next, wander over to **New York Street,** a backlot rendition of the Big Apple. Take a few moments to appreciate the extraordinary detail that went into its construction. The subtle street sounds – a distant siren, car horns, a jackhammer – are an especially nice touch.

A side street leads to the **Honey, I**

*Recommended Restaurants on pages 253-5*

**Shrunk the Kids Movie Set Adventure**, a super-sized playground designed from an insect's point of view. Kids zoom down slides on a blade of grass, explore tunnels in a giant mushroom and get a good soaking around a leaky "hose." A word to the wise: the playground is sweltering on a hot day, there's not much room for adults to sit, and once children disappear into the tunnels it takes a while to find them, much less convince them that it's time to leave. Nearby, **Lights, Motors, Action!** is a car-, motorcycle- and JetSki-stunt show that will put you on the edge of your seat. Fans of cars spinning around and making noise will love this type of thing, but for anyone else, this show is a complete waste of time. The Indiana Jones stunt show is much better.

## Backlot tour

It's a quick stroll down **Commissary Lane** and across the central plaza to **Mickey Avenue**. To the far left is the **Backlot Tour**, a 35-minute tram ride with glimpses of the wardrobe department, scenery workshop, and what appears to be a quiet suburban street

lined with trim little houses. The buildings are only shells, of course, used in television commercials and programs. Later, the tram pulls into Catastrophe Canyon, which you're told is a movie set for a film currently under production. Within moments the earth begins to shake, an oil tanker explodes and a flash flood comes barreling toward you. The tour ends with an exhibit of showbiz memorabilia at the American Film Institute Showcase.

At the end of Mickey Avenue in a little plaza called the Animation Courtyard

*Star Tours takes riders on a virtual adventure in space.*

**BELOW:** Indiana Jones, originally played by Harrison Ford, is brought to life in a popular stunt show.

**TIP**

Mickey's Jammin' Jungle Parade at Animal Kingdom features costumed characters, stylized floats, rolling drums and a lively call-and-response theme. The parade starts in Africa and circles Discovery Island. Check the entertainment schedule for times.

**BELOW:** Miss Piggy and Kermit the Frog star in Muppet Vision 3-D.

is **The Magic of Disney Animation**, a tour of a working animation studio, including a presentation by an artist and a couple of interesting films, one featuring the unlikely team of actor Robin Williams and newsman Walter Cronkite. The last two shows – **The Voyage of the Little Mermaid** and **Playhouse Disney – Live on Stage** – are sweet and schmaltzy, and intended mostly for families with small children.

## Animal Kingdom

Disney World's newest and largest theme park, **Disney's Animal Kingdom ❺** (daily, see www.disneyworld.com for details), is essentially a state-of-the-art zoo dressed up in extravagant style. You realize you're in for something special the moment you walk through the front gates into an area known as **The Oasis** – a tropical garden laced with trails that lead past alcoves containing river otters, anteaters, sloths, and other small animals.

Emerging from The Oasis, you're greeted by a view of the **Tree of Life**, an artificial banyan-like tree that rises 14 stories above **Discovery Island**, set in a large lagoon connected by bridges to the

park's four main "lands." What looks at first like the tree's gnarled bark are actually carved animal figures – more than 300 in all – swirling around the trunk and limbs. Showing in a theater in the base of the tree is a 3-D film, **It's Tough to be a Bug!**, based loosely on the Disney-Pixar movie *A Bug's Life*. The story involves seeing the world from an insect's point of view. You experience what it's like being on the receiving end of a fly swatter and encounter several noxious members of the insect family, including an acid-spraying termite and a stinkbug with, shall we say, a bad case of gas.

Walking around Discovery Island in a clockwise direction, the first bridge on the left leads to **Camp Minnie-Mickey**, designed in Adirondack style and devoted to live shows. The big attraction here is **Festival of the Lion King**, an uplifting 30-minute pageant based loosely on the animated film, with song, dance, acrobatics, and flamboyant costumes. The other show, **Pocahontas and Her Forest Friends**, is a morality tale on the importance of caring for the natural world, with the Indian princess, a talking tree, and a cast of skunks, oppos

## The Mouse at Sea

Launched in 1998, the Disney Cruise Line sails two ships, *Disney Magic* and *Disney Wonder*, modeled after the luxury liners of the 1920s. Week-long land-and-sea packages include 3 or 4 days at a Disney resort and the remainder at sea. Ships sail from Port Canaveral, an hour east of Orlando, to Nassau, Freeport and Castaway Cay in the Bahamas. Seven-day cruises alternate between the eastern Caribbean (St Maarten, St John and St Thomas) and the western Caribbean (Key West, Grand Cayman and Cozumel), with a stop at Castaway Cay. This last destination, a tiny island, was a notorious hideout for drug smugglers until Disney transformed it into a private getaway.

Shipboard amenities range from lavish stage shows and first-run movies to fitness rooms, spas, and a choice of swimming pools. Passengers rotate among several theme restaurants. One restaurant aboard each ship is reserved for adults and serves romantic, candlelight dinners.

Douglas Ward, author of the influential *Berlitz Complete Guide to Cruising and Cruise Ships*, describes the Disney ships as "a sea-going never-never land" providing "a highly programmed, strictly timed and regimented experience." Security, he adds, is very good, with children provided with ID bracelets and parents given pagers for emergencies.

For information, call 800-951-3532, or contact a travel agent.

*Recommended Restaurants on pages 253-5*

sums, snakes, rats, and other live animals. Sappy even by Disney standards, the show appeals mostly to preschoolers. Children get a kick out of the four **Character Greeting Trails**, which lead back to pavilions housing costumed characters who spend a few minutes posing for pictures, signing autographs, and joshing around with little ones and adults.

## Out of Africa, into Asia

Return to Discovery Island and cross the first bridge on your left to **Africa**, where you immediately find yourself amid a clutch of shops and restaurants called **Harambe**, modeled loosely on a real-life Kenyan village. Next to an enormous, artificial baobab tree is the entrance to the park's most popular attraction, **Kilimanjaro Safaris**. Here visitors board safari vehicles for a 20-minute ride across a re-created patch of African veldt. This being Disney, merely seeing lions, giraffes, zebras, and other wildlife isn't enough. About halfway through the tour, your driver learns that poachers are threatening an elephant mother and calf, and off you go on a wild ride to rescue the threatened beasts and catch the bad guys.

It's only a few steps from the safari exit to the **Pangani Forest Exploration Trail**, a nature walk where you can view endangered species like black-and-white colobus monkeys, as well as hippos, gorillas, and meerkats. A research center harbors a colony of naked mole rats and a cleverly disguised aviary.

If you're looking for a break from the crowds, you might consider a side trip to **Rafiki's Planet Watch**, an area for environmental education. The journey starts with a ride on the Wildlife Express, a replica of a vintage steam locomotive that passes through the not-terribly-scenic "backstage" area. At the end of the line is the **Conservation Station**, a veterinary facility with exhibits on conservation and animal care. Skip both if pressed for time.

Next door to Africa is **Asia**, a pastiche of thatched huts, stone spires, and palace walls inspired by the traditional architecture of Thailand, Nepal, and India.

Asia encompasses four main attractions. To your left as you enter is the Caravan Stage, presenting **Flights of Wonder**, a 20-minute show featuring hawks, falcons, parrots, and more than a dozen other birds. Also here is **Kali River Rapids**, a whitewater ride with a jungle setting and an environmental message. The third stop in Asia is the **Maharajah Jungle Trek**, a nature walk with views of Bengal tigers, fruit bats, and exotic birds. Disney's newest thrill ride, **Expedition Everest** feels like a decrepit mountain train scaling its way up the side of the world's tallest peak, and includes a steep backward drop when you come to the "end of the track." As if that weren't enough to frighten you, there is always the chance that the Yeti might surprise you as well.

Return again to Discovery Island and cross the first bridge on the left to **DinoLand, USA**. You'll notice a more campy, carnival-like atmosphere here,

*A giraffe wanders the savanna at Animal Kingdom.*

**BELOW:** King Louie from Disney's *Jungle Book.*

*The Guitar Gallery is one of several shops at Downtown Disney.*

**BELOW:** ferries cruise across the Seven Seas Lagoon near the Grand Floridian Hotel.

injecting a welcome dose of humor into the mostly straight-faced approach elsewhere in the park. Just past an elaborate kid's play area called **The Boneyard**, you'll find signs to **Dinosaur**, DinoLand's biggest thrill ride.

The conceit here is that you're a visitor at the Dino Institute, a facility dedicated to "Exploration, Excavation and Exultation" and, you soon learn, the developer of a time machine that is about to transport you back to the Age of Dinosaurs. Your mission: save the last surviving *Iguanodon* before an asteroid collides with Earth. What follows is a jolting ride through a misty Jurassic forest that's being pelted by a barrage of meteors. Dinosaurs abound, of course, not the least of which is a *Carnotaurus*, a ferocious predator with razor-sharp teeth and a sour disposition. The experience is quite intense, so exercise discretion when visiting with young children.

Next on the agenda is **Chester & Hester's Dino-Rama**, a mini-carnival, with midway games and a couple of amusement-park rides: **Primeval Whirl** and **TriceraTop Spin**. A large shop, **Chester**

**& Hester's Dinosaur Treasures**, is packed to the rafters with dino-related toys and novelties – a good place to pick up gifts for the folks back home. **Finding Nemo – the Musical** is the Animal Kingdom's newest production, and it's poor. The technique of using live actors carrying puppets is confusing, and at times this seems more of a college theater workshop than the highly accomplished production that is the norm for Disney.

## Downtown Disney

**Downtown Disney ❻** is an entertainment complex on Lake Buena Vista about a mile east of Epcot. It's divided into three sections – West Side, Pleasure Island and Marketplace – and is intended mostly for an adult audience.

The **West Side** is the least defined of the three areas, a mixed bag of restaurants, shops and showplaces anchored on one end by **Cirque du Soleil**, a wildly imaginative theater troupe combining circus art and stagecraft, and on the other by **Planet Hollywood**, the well-known theme restaurant. In between are a few more restaurants,

including **Wolfgang Puck** and **House of Blues**. You'll also find a place called **DisneyQuest**, a sort of pinball arcade on steroids, with cutting-edge video games and virtual-reality rides. Loud and crowded, it has limited appeal for the post-pubescent. Nearby is a **Virgin Megastore**, with acres of floor space and dozens of listening stations. Several more specialty shops – ranging from cigars to guitars – are situated in a building next door, which also houses a 24-screen movie theater.

Sometimes called "Disney for adults," **Pleasure Island** was originally conceived as a nightclub district but is presently undergoing a complete overhaul. Most of the nightclubs will be closed in favor of family-friendly shops, restaurants, and attractions.

Among the venues that will remain open is the **Raglan Road Irish Pub and Restaurant**, which attempts to re-create an Irish pub. They've succeeded if you're looking for the atmosphere of Dublin's Temple Bar during a tour-group party; in other words it looks much like any other "authentic" Irish pub in America. Many shades of stout and ale are on

offer alongside a fine selection of whiskey, and live Irish folk music takes you through the night.

Also staying in Pleasure Island is a **Harley-Davidson** shop. The merchandise here is dominated by leather jackets, T-shirts, hats, and assorted knickknacks plastered wth the Harley logo, though actual motorcycles – most bristling with chrome and other custom adornments — are also on display.

If you're a surfer – or just want to look like one – make a point of checking out **Curl by Sammy Duval**, a high-end surf shop with an extensive selection of surfer-dude clothing, gear, and accessories. There are even a few surfboards.

## Shopping zone

**Marketplace** occupies the eastern portion of Downtown Disney and is devoted to shopping and eating. In addition to the world's largest Disney store are shops carrying home furnishings, sporting gear, and toys. Far more interesting is the **LEGO Imagination Center**, if only for the Lego sculptures displayed around the store. For eats, there's the Ghirardelli Soda Fountain & Chocolate Shop, a

**TIP**

You can sign up for a 90-minute surfing lesson at Typhoon Lagoon. Lessons are offered Tuesday and Friday at 6.30am. The fee is about $135.

*Shoppers, diners, and revelers crowd the walkways of Downtown Disney at night.*

**BELOW:** Planet Hollywood at Downtown Disney.

giant McDonald's, and a Rainforest Cafe, ensconced in what appears to be a smoldering volcano.

## Disney's BoardWalk

You'll find a second and smaller entertainment complex at the **BoardWalk**. Diners have a couple of good choices here. The Flying Fish Cafe, serving seafood, and Spoodles, specializing in Mediterranean cuisine, are both highly regarded, though sports fans may prefer the ESPN Club, a sports bar outfitted with more than 70 TV screens. Drinkers can sample handcrafted suds at the Big River Grille & Brewing Works or join the singalong crowd at Jellyrolls, which features a raucous dueling pianos act. Dancers can boogie at the Atlantic Dancehall, modeled after the classic dancehalls of the 1930s and 40s. DJs and live bands lay down the groove; wallflowers can take advantage of dance lessons offered most nights.

## Disney's water parks

Water parks aren't for everybody, but if you're reasonably spry, don't mind hordes of rambunctious teens, and aren't self-conscious about walking around half naked, you'll have a blast flying down the various chutes and flumes or bobbing peacefully on one of the gentle "river trips."

Disney World has two water parks to choose from. A good fit for teenagers and young adults is **Typhoon Lagoon ❼** (tel: 407-560-4141; 10am–5pm, extended hours summer and holidays; charge). Here you'll find a selection of high-speed slides as well as an enormous surf pool, a snorkeling trail where you can fin through the water with tropical fish and harmless sharks, and a 45-minute raft trip through rainforest grottoes and waterfalls.

**Blizzard Beach ❽** (tel: 407-560-3400; same hours as Typhoon Lagoon; charge) is Disney's largest water park and offers the hairiest rides, including Summit Plummet, which zips riders down a 350-ft (107-meter) ramp at speeds close to 60mph (97kph). In addition, there are at least a dozen other slides, as well as the world's longest whitewater raft ride, in which five passengers bob through 1,200ft (360 meters) of standing waves and roaring cataracts. ❑

# RESTAURANTS

## Restaurants

Prices for a three-course dinner per person, excluding tax, tip, and beverages:

**$** = under $20
**$$** = $20–45
**$$$** = $45–60
**$$$$** = over $60

## Magic Kingdom

### Cinderella's Royal Table
Cinderella's Castle
B & L daily
Though the food at this restaurant is far below the standard you'd expect at this price, its setting at the heart of Cinderella's Castle can't be beaten. Children can have their picture taken with Cinderella before lunch, and other fairytale princesses visit while they are eating. In addition to the Fairytale Lunch, there is a Once Upon a Time Breakfast Buffett. Reservations must be made far in advance. $$$

### Tony's Town Square Restaurant
Main Street, USA
L & D daily
With decor inspired by the classic film *Lady and the Tramp*, this restaurant serves up Italian fare in a light and airy environment. Be warned of Disney's tomato sauce. This oregano-laden concoction is definitely not to everyone's taste but is served throughout the park, finding its way onto everything from the posh pasta here to kiddie's spaghetti meals in other restaurants. $$

## Epcot

### Akershus Royal Banquet Hall
Norway Pavilion
B, L & D daily
In addition to its character breakfast featuring Disney princesses in a castle setting, this restaurant offers a fine lunch and dinner menu, with a choice of good fish dishes and other Norwegian specialties. There's a smorgasbord of cheeses, pickled fish, and rustic breads. $$

### Biergarten Restaurant
Germany Pavilion
L & D daily
This buffet-style restaurant set in a dimly lit mock-timber house serves uninspired German fare. There is, of course, a healthy selection of beers to wash it down with, and the accordion player will catch up with you eventually. $$

### Bistro de Paris
France Pavilion
D daily
The signature restaurant for France is poorly appointed, with a dining area that feels not unlike a convention luncheon setting. The lengthy wine list and fine view could help you forget this, but you'd expect more from a Disney restaurant charging this much. $$$

### Chefs de France
France Pavilion
L & D daily
A faithful re-creation of a typical Parisian café. The cooking may not be up to Michelin-star status, but it is very good, and you can dine under a faux Eiffel Tower. $$

### Coral Reef Restaurant
The Seas with Nemo and Friends
L & D daily
This seafood restaurant is situated alongside the aquarium at The Seas with Nemo and Friends, providing dreamy views into the largest inland saltwater environment ever built. The food is fine dining at Disney's best, and it's hard to beat the setting. $$$

### Garden Grill
The Land Pavilion
L & D daily
A revolving restaurant overlooking scenic ecosystems and a boat ride, its

Reservations for any of Disney's restaurants can be made at any resort's reception desk, any park's information office, or by telephoning 407-939-3463.

menu includes salads and vegetables grown in The Land greenhouses. The "Full Country Breakfast" stars Mickey, Minnie, and Chip 'n' Dale. $$

### Le Cellier Steakhouse
Canada Pavilion
L & D daily
Americans like their steak as much as their northern neighbors, and if you plan on having dinner here you must book in advance even during the slow periods. The wine cellar could make a romantic setting if you are lucky enough to get a table. $$

Prices for a three-course dinner per person, excluding tax, tip, and beverages:
**$** = under $20
**$$** = $20–45
**$$$** = $45–60
**$$$$** = over $60

### L'Originale Alfredo di Roma Ristorante
Italy Pavilion
L & D daily
Colorful, festive offshoot of the famous Roman restaurant. The specialty is fettuccine Alfredo. All pastas are made fresh. Strolling musicians entertain guests. $$

### Restaurant Marrakesh
Morocco Pavilion
L & D daily
After experiencing the fantastic warren-like architecture of the Morocco pavilion, you can't help but be disappointed by the lack of authenticity at Restaurant Marrakesh. The interior beyond the guest services desk seems bare, and although some of the food excels, most of it is a poor Ameri-

canized version of Middle Eastern food. This must be the only Moroccan restaurant in the world without a standard tagine dish. On a more positive note, the live music and belly dancing add a touch of Moroccan flare. $$

### San Angel Inn Restaurante
Mexico Pavillion
L & D daily
Authentic Mexican food served in a faux environment – under the shadow of a Mayan temple and a smoldering volcano. The dim lighting makes a good option for couples hoping for a bit of romance. $$

### Teppanyaki Dining Rooms
Japan Pavilion
L & D daily
Reservations are usually necessary to get a seat around one of the five teppanyaki grills. Diners encircle the chef as he creates stir-fry creations, which are shared around the table. $$

## Animal Kingdom

### Rainforest Café
Oasis; tel: 939-9100;
www.rainforestcafe.com
L & D daily
This is one of the most highly themed restaurants in Disney. Many will be familiar with this chain and its use of animatronic animals and faux decor to re-create a rainforest canopy. Unfortunately, the theme stops at the food. Instead of an iguana burger and plantains, expect large portions of typical American food. Waits of an hour or more are not uncommon without reservations. $$

## Hollywood Studios

### 50s Prime Time Café
Echo Lake
L & D daily
This reincarnation of mom's kitchen has a certain fetish appeal. Waiters discipline anyone who does not clean their plate or is caught with elbows on the table. And at times they behave like mom's children, too, becoming tattletales and pests just the same. The food is what you'd expect from mom and includes meatloaf, peas, and indulgent desserts you choose from a retro Viewmaster toy. $

### Hollywood Brown Derby
Hollywood Boulevard
L & D daily
This re-creation of the legendary Hollywood restaurant features fine food at fine prices. Of course, the only celebrities you are likely to see here are in photos on the walls. $$$

### Mama Melrose's Ristorante Italiano
Streets of America
L & D daily
This cozy Italian restaurant serves child-friendly

favorites such as pizza and lasagna. $$

### Sci-Fi Dine-In Theater
Commissary Lane
L & D daily
This is Hollywood Studio's best dining experience. Every party gets to take a seat in an old Chevy or other vintage car and watch classic sci-fi films on the drive-in screen. The food plays second fiddle to this theme and features burgers, sandwiches, and pasta dishes. Reservations are essential here, even during the slow seasons. $$

## Downtown Disney

### Bongos Cuban Café
Westside
L & D daily
The brainchild of pop star Gloria Estefan and her husband Emilio. A giant pineapple sprouting from the roof sets the tone of the place, which throbs with Latin music and brilliant colors. Aficionados of Cuban cuisine may have better luck elsewhere. $$

### Fulton's Crab House
Pleasure Island
L & D daily
Downtown Disney's lagoon provides a berth for this replica of a Mississippi riverboat. Inside is one of Disney's finer restaurants. The menu offers a bounty of seafood with a few beef, poultry, and pasta dishes to keep everyone in the party happy. The Alaskan king crab claws are bigger than most men's hands, and there is a wine selector to help choose an appropriate vintage. $$$

### House of Blues
Westside
L & D daily

**LEFT:** movie memorabilia fills Planet Hollywood.

Founded by original Blues Brother Dan Aykroyd and done up like the kind of ramshackle wharfside warehouse you might find in the Mississippi Delta. The food is surprisingly good for a chain, with southern favorites like fried catfish, seafood gumbo, jambalaya, and bread pudding dribbled with brandy sauce. If you're traveling with kids, consider booking a table for the Sunday Gospel Brunch. You'll jump up for Jesus and chow down on all the southern vittles you can eat. $$

## Wolfgang Puck
Westside
L & D daily
The cavernous rooms and chatty clientele aren't exactly conducive to an intimate conversation; the atmosphere is all color and energy, with open kitchens, video monitors showing chefs at work, and a bustling wait staff. The menu runs the gamut from sushi and gourmet pizza to lamb chops and seafood, all prepared with the celebrity chef's Californian flair (except perhaps the Wiener schnitzel). The upstairs dining room is quite expensive. The downstairs café is cheaper and more casual. $$

## Planet Hollywood
Westside
L & D daily
Every inch of the dome-shaped dining room is jammed with movie props, memorabilia, and other eye candy. The good news is that the food has improved since the company's brush with bankruptcy in 1999. The bad news? The wait can be terribly long, especially when the theaters let out, so make reservations well in advance. $$

## Portobello Yacht Club
Pleasure Island
L & D daily
First-rate northern Italian cuisine and seafood specialties fill the menu here, while diners cram the floor in a restaurant that could be a fine-dining experience if the spacing wasn't so similar to cafeteria seating. $$$

## Rainforest Café
Marketplace
L & D daily
The smoke you've been seeing billowing in the distance is from a smoldering volcano that sits atop the Rainforest Café, a cavernous restaurant with an extravagant jungle setting. Even with priority seating, you'll have a good long wait. $$

Disney Resort Dining
*Magic Kingdom resorts*
## Artist's Point
Wilderness Lodge, 901 Timberline Dr, Lake Buena Vista
D daily
Inspired by national-park lodges, this hotel restaurant features salmon, rainbow trout, elk chops, venison, bison, and other hearty dishes associated with the American west. The wine list features labels from the Pacific northwest. $$$

## California Grill
Contemporary Resort, 4600 North World Dr
D daily
Views of the Magic Kingdom are spectacular from this refined restaurant on the 15th floor of the Contemporary Resort. The menu changes seasonally but usually includes entrées like oak-roasted chicken and pork tenderloin prepared with a light California touch. Don't pass up the appetizers, an eclectic mix of sushi, salads,

and pasta. Ask to be seated in time for the fireworks. $$$

## Narcoossee's
Grand Floridian Resort and Spa, 4401 Grand Floridian Way, Lake Buena Vista
D daily
With a sweeping lakeside setting, this is the Grand Floridian's "casual" offering. Its inventive cuisine uses fresh ingredients and lots of seafood. Softshell crabs and Prince Edward Island mussels in white wine and garlic are signature dishes. $$$

## Victoria and Albert's
Grand Floridian Resort and Spa; 4401 Grand Floridian Way, Lake Buena Vista
D daily
Disney spins a Victorian fantasy at this prix-fixe restaurant. The seven-course meal is served by a white-gloved butler and maid (Albert and Victoria) in a romantic, domed dining room. The menu features some of the finest Continental cuisine in town. Very expensive but, fans say, worth the money. $$$

*Epcot resorts*
## ESPN Sports Club
Disney's BoardWalk
L & D daily
Jocks will love this theme restaurant crammed with all things sporty, including more than 70 television screens; there's even one in the restroom, lest you miss a minute of the big game. Bring a big appetite. Entrées, including hamburgers, hot dogs, sirloin, and grilled chicken, are oversized. Desserts are big and yummy. $$$

## Flying Fish Café
Disney's BoardWalk
L & D daily
One of Disney's best restaurants, in a whimsi-

cal setting with a busy stage kitchen. It serves potato-wrapped yellowtail snapper and other creative dishes. There's chocolate lava cake for dessert. $$$

## Il Mulino New York Trattoria
Swan Hotel, 1200 Epcot Resorts Blvd
D daily
Is this the classiest restaurant at Disney World? The illuminated wine bar is tops for sure, and it has a good selection of fine wines. The cuisine is based on classic Italian bistro recipes. The seafood dishes stand out the most. $$$

## Kimono's
Swan Hotel, 1200 Epcot Resorts Blvd
D daily
The sushi chefs here are not shy and are happy to prepare their beautiful creations in front of your eyes. For those who prefer their fish cooked, there are hot dishes and tempura available as well. There's karaoke in the evening. $$$

## Todd English's bluezoo
Dolphin Hotel, 1200 Epcot Resorts Blvd
D daily
Presentation is king at this fine-dining restaurant, from the sleek backlit bar and minimalist design to the plates of seafood with a wedge of lemon. There is a kids' menu here, but do yourself a favor and leave the little ones behind so you can enjoy this very grown-up restaurant. $$$

Reservations for any of Disney's restaurants can be made at any resort's reception desk, any park's information office, or by telephoning 407-939-3463.

Recommended Restaurants on pages 273–7

# ORLANDO AND ITS OTHER WORLDS

Beyond the gates of Disney is a wide array
of destinations, ranging from elaborate
theme parks and first-class museums
to alligator farms and wilderness areas

Orlando
Florida
Miami

**W**alt Disney World Resort's chief competitor is Universal Orlando (www.universalorlando.com), a complex of two theme parks, three hotels, and an entertainment district about 9 miles (15km) down I-4. Hipper than Mickey, with a knowing pop sensibility, Universal is especially appealing to teenagers and young adults who like big roller coasters, loud music, and action movies.

## Universal Studios

Universal's flagship property is **Universal Studios Florida ❶** (tel: 407-363-8000; daily, hours vary, see www. universalorlando.com; charge), a theme park inspired by the art and science of Hollywood movies. Sprawling across more than 400 acres (160 hectares), the park is laid out in a by-now familiar pattern: six themed "neighborhoods," each with its own rides and shows, arranged around a lagoon. As Universal likes to remind us, this is a working production facility. Sections of the park double as movie sets.

The top thrill ride is **Revenge of the Mummy**, an indoor roller coaster that takes you through fireballs and skeletal warriors. **Terminator 2 3-D** thrusts the audience into the action with Arnold Schwarzenegger. **Shrek 4-D** uses the same cinema technology, but is much more suitable for small children. **Twister… Ride It Out** gives audiences the chance to experience the awesome power of a tornado. Nature is sent to

scare you some more in **Disaster** – a simulated San Francisco earthquake – and **Jaws** – a gentle boat ride along the New England coast that is violently disrupted by the great white horror. The top family ride is undoubtedly the **ET Adventure**, set in an area called **Woody Woodpecker's Kidzone** devoted entirely to young children, which includes the **Nuthouse Coaster**, the water-soaked **Curious George Goes to Town** playground, **Fievel's Playland**, and two live shows: **A Day in the Park with Barney** and **Animal Actors on**

**Main attractions**
UNIVERSAL STUDIOS
ISLANDS OF ADVENTURE
SEAWORLD
DISCOVERY COVE
DOWNTOWN ORLANDO
ORLANDO SCIENCE CENTER
WINTER PARK
GATORLAND

**LEFT AND BELOW:**
costumed
characters greet
visitors to Universal
Orlando.

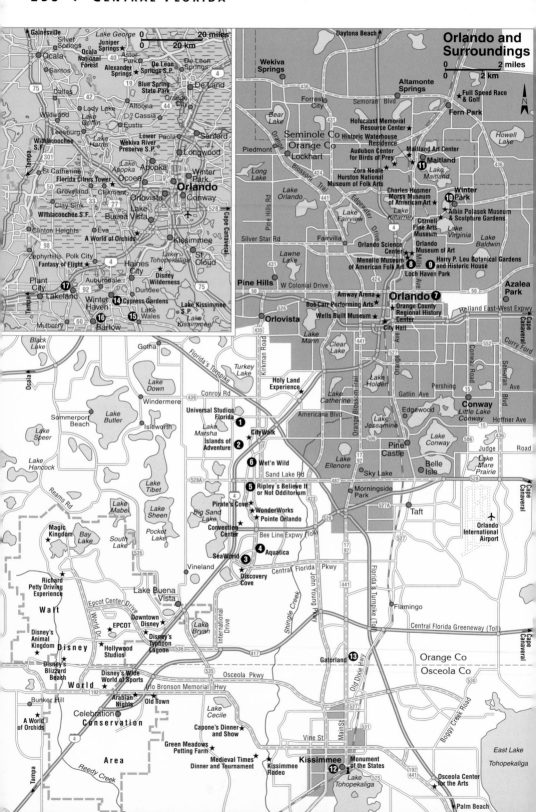

**Location**. Kids will also love Universal's newest attraction: **The Simpsons Ride**, a wild journey through Krustyland.

The combination of humor and nostalgia is crucial to the success of shows like **Beetlejuice's Graveyard Revue** and **Blues Brothers**. In **Fear Factor Live**, which is based on the hit reality show, audience members are selected at random to try hair-raising (and sometimes harebrained) stunts.

## Islands of Adventure

Universal's newest theme park, **Islands of Adventure** ❷ (daily, hours vary, see www.universalorlando.com; charge), isn't really made up of islands but five elaborately themed zones arrayed around a central lagoon known as the Inland Sea. Children's books, cartoons and comic strips provide themes for rides, shops, and restaurants, and costumed characters such as Popeye, Bullwinkle, and Spider-Man make appearances. The five "islands" are **Seuss Landing**, inspired by the beloved children's books of Theodor Seuss Geisel, aka Dr. Seuss; the **Lost Continent**, a sort of medieval fantasyland; **Jurassic Park**, a dinosaur-

themed area based on Stephen Spielberg's 1993 film; **Toon Lagoon**, dedicated to cartoon characters from TV and the funny papers; and **Marvel Super Hero Island**, which brings to life the world of Marvel Comics.

What makes the park special, however, are the high-tech thrill rides. **The Amazing Adventures of Spider-Man**, for example, combines simulator technology and 3-D visuals. Along the way you encounter a small army of evildoers who send your tram into wild spins and lurches. The tour culminates in what feels like a headlong plunge into the city streets below, only to be saved at the last moment by – who else? – your friendly neighborhood Spider-Man. On **The Jurassic Park River Adventure** you dodge amazingly lifelike dinosaurs before taking a stomach-flipping, 85-ft (26-meter) plummet, while in the **Discovery Center** you can witness baby raptors hatching from ostrich-sized eggs. But if it's more water action you're after, head to **Toon Lagoon** for **Dudly Do'Rights Ripsaw Falls** or **Popeye and Bluto's Bilge Rat Barges**. Kids will love exploring **Me**

**TIP**

Universal's newest show is the acclaimed **Blue Man Group**. You do not have to buy a theme park ticket to see this show. Tickets start at $59 for adults and $49 for children.

**BELOW:** a cast member at Islands of Adventure poses with visitors after a show.

## Universal's Express Expense

The Universal Express system, similarly to Disney's FastPass (*see page 239*), allows visitors priority access to the most popular rides by letting them avoid the long lines. Unlike Disney's FastPass, which is free to all guests; you have to pay for this privilege if you are not a guest at one of Universal Orlando's resorts (the Hard Rock Hotel, Portofino Bay, Royal Pacific). The cost is $50.99 for one park or $55.99 for two. The pass is valid for only one day. Though this price is very steep, Universal Express is a quicker system than Disney's FastPass. Guests do not need to wait for a time slot, just show up at the attraction and you'll be accommodated almost straight away, and you can do the same ride as many times as you like.

Universal's, if not Orlando's, biggest new attraction begins. In 2009 the **Wizarding World of Harry Potter** will take over the Lost Continent. This fully immersive Harry Potter environment will include Hogwart's Castle, Hogsmeade, and the Forbidden Forest.

## CityWalk

Before leaving Universal, drop in on **CityWalk**, where a dozen restaurants and nightclubs keep the party rolling long after the kiddies have gone to bed. **The Red Coconut Club** features signature martinis, a happy hour, and live music daily, while at **Bob Marley: A Tribute to Freedom** reggae bands perform in an open-air courtyard that re-creates Marley's Jamaica home. Other nightspots include **Pat O'Brien's** and its dueling pianos, the sophisticated **City Jazz Club**, and the world's largest **Hard Rock Cafe**, as well as the theme-laden **Jimmy Buffet's Margaritaville**.

*Shooting the rapids at Popeye & Bluto's Bilge-Rat Barges.*

**BELOW:** nightlife on CityWalk's Plaza.
**BELOW RIGHT:** T. rex at the Jurassic Park River Adventure.

**Ship, the Olive**, where from a dry platform they can shoot water cannons on unsuspecting barge riders below.

Daredevils make a beeline for two roller coasters. Passengers on **Dueling Dragons** choose one of two coasters that ride on intertwining tracks devilishly engineered for several near misses at speeds in excess of 55mph (90km/h). **The Incredible Hulk Coaster** catapults you up a tunnel with the same force as a fighter jet, before turning upside down seven times.

The Lost Continent is about to have a spectacular makeover as construction on

Themes dominate the eating side of things, too, with restaurants dedicated to pro basketball and auto racing. Emeril's, created by TV chef Emeril Lagasse, is the only place for fine dining.

## SeaWorld, Discovery Cove and Aquatica

The other don't-miss theme park in Orlando is **SeaWorld** ❸ (tel: 407-351-3600; www.seaworld.com; daily, hours vary, see website; charge). Its name sums up what it has to offer. The world's largest marine park is the home of dancing penguins, prancing seals, people who ski on the backs of dolphins, and much, much more. The star of the show is Shamu the killer whale, who takes part in crowd-thrilling stunts. Other popular shows include bottlenose dolphins and pseudorcas (false killer whales) playing with their trainers and interacting with the audience; Clyde the otter and Seamore the sea lion cavorting around a pirate ship; and Odyssea, a fascinating Cirque du Soleil-style production. In addition to the shows, there are marine exhibits, including areas where you can touch the animals and a tunnel that leads you through a pool of sharks.

SeaWorld has a couple of big thrill rides, too. The more benign is **Journey to Atlantis**, a cross between a log flume and a roller coaster. There's a story behind the ride involving the emergence of Atlantis, but with two 60-ft (18-meter) plunges, several smaller dips, and a non-stop barrage of laser lights, you won't have a chance to follow along. Only hard-core thrill-seekers should consider riding **Kraken**, a "floorless" roller coaster with a drop of 144ft (44 meters), seven inversions, three subterranean passages, and a top speed of 65mph (105kph).

Adjacent to SeaWorld is a new and very different sort of theme park. SeaWorld calls it **Discovery Cove**, and it's more akin to a tropical resort than an amusement park. For starters, admission is limited to 1,000 people per day, and guests pay a flat fee that includes just about everything they'll need – food, towels, snorkeling equipment and more. What you get for your money is the freedom to roam a beautifully landscaped 32-acre (13-hectare) property where you can snorkel around an artificial coral reef stocked with tropical fish, float down a tropical river, splash in waterfalls, or simply lounge beneath a palm tree on a white sandy beach.

For most visitors, the highlight of Discovery Cove is an opportunity to swim with a dolphin. "Swim" may not be

**TIP**

If viewing sharks through acrylic isn't thrilling enough, consider getting into the water with them. SeaWorld's new Sharks Deep Dive program ($150) puts guests into a diving cage for a swim in the shark tank.

**BELOW:** an underwater viewing area gives visitors a unique perspective on one of SeaWorld's biggest stars.

*A dolphin encounter is a highlight of a day at Discovery Cove.*

entirely accurate. What you do is interact with the animal under the watchful eye of a trainer, who teaches you hand signals that cue the dolphin to roll over, wave flippers, exchange kisses, and tow you along.

SeaWorld's latest addition is the nearby **Aquatica ❹**. This new water park leaves its Orlando rivals trailing in its wake by combining the traditional flume and tube rides with the sealife SeaWorld is famous for. The Dolphin Plunge is the most popular attraction. Its clear plastic slide dips through a pool inhabited by black and white Commerson's dolphins.

## I-Drive

Running alongside I-4 for about 10 miles (16km) between Disney World and downtown Orlando is **International Drive**, a tourist strip with hotels, restaurants, shopping plazas and, for lack of a better term, several "roadside attractions." Typical of this last category is **Ripley's Believe It or Not Odditorium ❺** (8201 International Dr; daily 9am–1am; tel: 407-354-0501; www.ripleys.com; charge), a takeoff on Robert Ripley's famous books of oddities, with exhibits on such sideshow staples as two-headed calves and curiosities like a Rolls-Royce constructed of matchsticks.

Along the same lines is **Wonder-Works** (9067 International Dr; tel: 407-351-8800; www.wonderworksonline.com; daily 9am–midnight; charge), although the emphasis here is on high-tech games and science-related exhibits. It's worth driving by just to see the extraordinary building, which looks like a neoclassical temple that's been turned upside-down. This is also home to the **Outta Control Magic and Comedy Dinnershow**. WonderWorks also runs the **Magical Midway** (7001 International Dr; tel: 407-370-5353; www.magicalmidway.com; Mon–Thur

*Recommended Restaurants on pages 273–7*

2pm–10pm, Fri 2pm–midnight, Sat 10am–midnight, Sun 10am–10pm; charge). At **Pirate's Cove** (8501 International Dr; tel: 407-352-7378; daily 9am–11.30pm; charge), miniature golf fans have two courses to get their licks on the links. Captain Kidd's course is good for beginners while the more difficult Blackbeard's Challenge is popular among the more serious duffers. There is another location at 12545 SR 535 in Lake Buena Vista near Disney World Resort (tel: 407-827-1242).

The **Marching Mallards** at the Peabody Orlando hotel (9801 International Dr; tel: 407-352-4000; www.peabodyorlando.com) is the best free show in town. You can see their grand entrance to John Philip Sousa's "King Cotton March" each morning and their return march each afternoon. **Wet 'n' Wild ❻** (6200 International Dr; tel: 407-351-1800; www.wetnwildorlando.com; daily, hours vary, see website for details; charge), yet another water park, is at the northern end of International Drive just across from (and owned by) Universal Orlando and has a reputation for some of the hairiest slides in Orlando.

## Nearer my Lord to thee

Under the heading "Only in Orlando" comes the **Holy Land Experience** (4655 Vineland Rd, tel: 407-872-2272; www.holylandexperience.com; Mon–Sat 10am–5pm, Sun noon–6pm; entrance fee), a "Bible-believing, Christ-centered" theme park situated just beyond International Drive. The brainchild of Jewish-born Baptist minister Marvin Rosenthal, the park re-creates ancient Jerusalem with scaled-down replicas of Herod's Temple, the Wilderness Tabernacle, Calvary Garden Tomb, and a street bazaar. Elaborate multimedia shows and outdoor dramas feature actors in period costumes. A Scriptorium houses an impressive collection of Biblical antiquities with hundreds of scrolls, manuscripts, and religious artifacts.

International Drive is a prime area for shopping, too. **Pointe Orlando** (9101 International Dr; tel: 407-248-2838; www.pointeorlando.com; Mon–Sat 10am–10pm, Sun 11am–9pm, many restaurants and bars stay open later) is an attractive upscale retail complex, with live entertainment, bars, restaurants, and a 21-screen cineplex with an IMAX theater.

**TIP**

Public transportation along International Drive is provided by the I-Ride Trolley, which runs daily 8am–10.30pm. A single fare is $1. A one-day pass is $3.

**BELOW:** visitors cool off at Wet 'n' Wild water park.

*Zora Neale Hurston remembered her Florida birthplace in her autobiography,* Dust on the Tracks.

**BELOW AND BELOW RIGHT:** Orlando Science Center.

## Downtown Orlando

The downtown area of **Orlando ❼** is a hub for business and the arts, with shops, galleries, and restaurants as well as gracious public spaces like **Lake Eola Park**, a 20-acre (8-hectare) oasis with an amphitheater, walking trails and paddleboats. **Church Street Station**, an entertainment complex in a restored 19th-century train depot, is in the midst of a slow revival. Orange Avenue, named for the city's most illustrious export, connects these two and has become the main drag for downtown life. At its southern base is the **Westin Grand Bohemian** (325 S. Orange Ave, Orlando; tel: 407-313 9000; www.theboheme.com), a top-class hotel that includes the **Boheme**, one of the city's finest restaurants *(see page 276)*, and the **Grand Bohemian Gallery** (Grand Bohemian Hotel, 325 S. Orange Ave., Orlando; tel: 407-581 4801; www.grandbohemian-gallery.com; Mon 10am–5.30pm, Tue–Sat 10am–8pm, Sun 10am–3pm; free), which

features a fine collection of European and American art.

From Church Street to Washington Street, there is a medley of bars that would seem more appropriate on a college campus than in a business center. But there is culture here, too. At 29 S. Orange Avenue is the **Cityartsfactory** (tel: 407-648 7060; www.cityartsfactory.com; gallery hours vary; free), now housed in the old Philips Theater. This is the center for the Downtown Arts District and features a large exhibition space and several commercial art galleries.

North of Central Boulevard is **Wall Street Plaza**, a bar and restaurant complex with happy-hour specials to lure office workers. Most nights feature live music in one of the bars. Walk through Wall Street Plaza to Heritage Square. In the stately 1927 Orange County Courthouse is the **Orange County Regional History Center** (65 E. Central Blvd; tel: 407-836-8500; www.thehistorycenter.org; Mon–Sat 10am–5pm, Sun noon–5pm; charge). Here four floors of exhibits chronicle the history of central Florida, starting with the region's native inhabitants and running through the arrival of

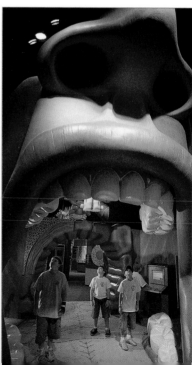

*Recommended Restaurants on pages 273–7*

European settlers, the development of the citrus industry, and the growth of tourism. Changing exhibits focus on a variety of topics, ranging in recent years from the "rogues and rascals" of Florida's pioneer period to the area's rock 'n' roll history.

Ella Fitzgerald and Duke Ellington are just two of the luminaries who stayed at the Wells Built Hotel, erected in 1929 by William Monroe Wells, Orlando's first African-American physician. Opened as the **Wells' Built Museum of African American History and Culture** (511 W. South St; tel: 407-245 7535; www.pastinc.org; Mon–Fri 9am– 5pm; charge), it houses exhibitions on life in the segregated South.

African-American culture is also the subject of the tiny **Zora Neale Hurston National Museum of Fine Arts** (227 E. Kennedy Blvd; tel: 407-647-3307; www.zoranealehurstonfestival.com; Mon–Fri 9am–4pm; free) in nearby Eatonville, the first black township in the United States, founded in 1887. Raised in Eatonville, Hurston later became a prominent figure in the Harlem Renaissance, authoring books such as *Their Eyes Were Watching God* and *Of Men and Mules*. The gallery feaures work by African-American artists; an annual festival is held in Hurston's honor.

Just northwest of downtown is Centroplex, home to the **Bob Carr Performing Arts Center** venue and **Amway Arena**. This is Orlando's main entertainment complex, hosting the Philharmonic orchestra, theater productions, and the Orlando Magic basketball team.

## Loch Haven Park

Just north of downtown in lovely **Loch Haven Park ❽** is a cluster of cultural institutions. The **Orlando Science Center** (777 E. Princeton St; tel: 407-514-2000; www.osc.org; daily 10am–6pm, Fri–Sat until 9pm; observatory Fri–Sat 6pm–9pm; charge) encompasses 10 halls filled with interactive exhibits that, among other things, lead visitors on a journey through the human body, back to the Age of Dinosaurs, and across the cosmos. An

eight-story domed theater, said to be the largest in the world, shows big-screen films, and sky shows are presented in the planetarium.

On the opposite side of the park is the **Orlando Museum of Art** (2416 N. Mills Ave; tel: 407-896-4231; www.omart.org; Tue–Fri 10am–4pm, Sat–Sun noon–4pm; charge), whose permanent collection of ancient American and African art and works by American painters such as Maurice Prendergast and Georgia O'Keeffe is

Below the Dam *by Maurice Prendergast at the Orlando Museum of Art.*

**BELOW:** a glass sculpture by Dale Chihuly at the Orlando Museum of Art.

**TIP**

Special events at Leu Gardens include a summer concert series featuring the Orlando Philharmonic Orchestra.

**ABOVE:** Harry P. Leu Botanical Gardens.
**BELOW:** a painting by self-taught artist Earl Cunningham at the Mennello Museum.

supplemented by traveling exhibitions. Special events are held on the first Thursday evening of every month, with live music and a sample of cuisine from local restaurants.

So-called "outsider art" is the focus of the **Mennello Museum of American Folk Art** (900 E. Princeton St; tel: 407-246-4278; Tue–Sat 10.30am–4.30pm,

Sun noon–4.30pm; entrance fee), also in the park. In addition to traveling exhibitions, the museum shows works from its permanent collection, largely dedicated to the "primitive" paintings of Earl Cunningham, a self-taught artist whose brightly colored canvases have been acquired by several major museums, including the Metropolitan Museum of Art and the Smithsonian Institution.

## Center stage

The area's two best theaters are also in Loch Haven. The **Orlando Shakespeare Theater** (812 E. Rollins St; tel: 407-447-1700; www.orlandoshakes.org) began nearly 20 years ago as a month-long festival and has since grown into a year-round theater; it has now partnered with the University of Central Florida, which provides further educational resources. Of course, the season is dominated by the Bard's works, but there is room for modern playwrights, too. The Rep (1001 E. Princeton St; tel: 407-896-7365; www.orlandorep.com) pays special attention to providing affordable productions suitable for a younger audience and the entire family by transferring

*Recommended Restaurants on pages 273–7*

classic fairy tales and children's books to the stage. Weekend matinees are especially popular.

It's a short drive from Loch Haven Park to the **Harry P. Leu Botanical Gardens and Historic House** ❾ (920 N. Forest Ave; tel: 407-246-2620; www.leugardens.org; daily 9am–5pm; charge), where paths meander through 49 acres (20 hectares) of specialty gardens, including one of the South's largest collections of roses and camellias and areas devoted to palms, herbs, tropical plants, and wetlands. Short tours of the historic Leu House are offered throughout the day.

## Winter Park

To the north of Orlando is **Winter Park** ❿, an upscale suburb with a gracious, old-money atmosphere. Park Avenue is a good place for strolling when the tourist trails lose their charm. It is lined with places for adults to enjoy such pleasures as a quiet glass of wine and a fine meal – and there is not a themed restaurant in sight. At the southern end of Park Avenue, on the trim Mediterranean-style campus of Rollins College, is the

**Cornell Museum of Fine Arts** (1000 Holt Ave; tel: 407-646-2526; Tue–Sat 10am–5pm, Sun 1pm–5pm; charge). Though quite small, it is one of the finest and oldest art museums in the Southeast. Each year, the Cornell stages six to eight exhibitions drawn from its holdings of more than 6,000 European and American works of art. The collection encompasses paintings, drawings, and sculpture from the 1450s to the 1990s. At the start of the school year, one gallery is dedicated to exhibiting work by contemporary local artists.

Also associated with Rollins College is the **Charles Hosmer Morse Museum of American Art** (445 N. Park Ave; tel: 407-645-5311; www.morsemuseum.org; Tue–Sat 9.30am–4pm, Sun 1pm–4pm; charge), a few blocks away. Though the museum's holdings include paintings by such notable American artists as George Inness, John Singer Sargent, and Thomas

**ABOVE AND BELOW LEFT:** the Charles Hosmer Morse Museum features an extensive collection of Tiffany stained glass.

## Dinner Theater

One of Orlando's unique entertainment options is a night at one of its many dinner theater shows. These sometimes cheesy affairs focus on big productions accompanied by standard fare. Some are most definitely better than others. One of the best is Arabian Nights (3081 Arabian Nights Blvd, Kissimmee; tel: 407-239-9223). This enchanting dinner show stars 50 Arabian, Lippizaner, palomino, and quarter horses that are put through their paces by skilled riders in an enormous arena. Dolly Parton's Dixie Stampede (82511 Vineland Ave, Orlando; tel: 866-443-4943) continues the horse theme. Guests are divided between Union and Confederates and the rivalry begins. Equestrianism is also on display in the Medieval Times Dinner and Tournament (4510 W. Irlo Bronson Hwy, Kissimmee; tel: 888-WE-JOUST). Set in the 11th century, it features a well-executed jousting tournament.

Other theme dinners include The Outta Control Magic Comedy Dinner Show (9067 International Dr; tel: 407-351-8800), which offers hand-tossed pizza and unlimited beer, wine, and soda. Entertainment is a mixture of comedy, improv, and magic that promises to "tickle your funny bone every eight seconds." Pirate's Dinner Adventure (6400 Carrier Dr; tel: 407-248-0590) is an action-packed evening of swashbuckling. Sleuth's Mystery Dinner Show (8267 International Dr; tel: 407-363-1985) is perfect for fans of murder mystery weekends and whodunits.

The vision of a single artist is in evidence a few miles north at the **Maitland Art Center** (231 W. Packwood Ave; tel: 407-539-2181; www.maitlandartcenter.org; Mon–Fri 9am–4.30pm, Sat–Sun noon–4.30pm) in suburban **Maitland ⑪**. Founded as an art colony in the 1930s by visionary artist and architect André Smith, the museum is designed in an idiosyncratic Aztec style on 6 acres (2½ hectares) of gardens and courtyards. Still an active center, it offers instruction, concerts, and exhibitions.

walk from Rollins College. The collection is dominated by the figurative sculpture of Albin Polasek, the Czech-American artist who lived and worked here before his death in 1965. Works by Augustus Saint-Gaudens and other American sculptors are also on display.

## Maitland museums

The vision of a single artist is in evidence a few miles north at the **Maitland Art Center** (231 W. Packwood Ave; tel: 407-539-2181; www.maitlandartcenter.org; Mon–Fri 9am–4.30pm, Sat–Sun noon–4.30pm) in suburban **Maitland ⑪**. Founded as an art colony in the 1930s by visionary artist and architect André Smith, the museum is designed in an idiosyncratic Aztec style on 6 acres (2½ hectares) of gardens and courtyards. Still an active center, it offers instruction, concerts, and exhibitions.

When William H. Waterhouse settled in Maitland at the end of the 19th century, he was a pioneer. By the time he'd completed his home here, he had become one of the area's most in-demand builders. The **Historic Waterhouse Residence and Carpentry Shop Museums**

*The Charles Hosmer Morse Museum has a fine collection of 19th- and early 20th-century paintings and decorative arts.*

Hart Benton, the big attraction is an unmatched collection of stained glass by Louis Comfort Tiffany. The highlight of the collection is a reconstruction of the Tiffany Chapel, designed for the 1893 World Columbian Exposition in Chicago.

Sculpture is the focus of the **Albin Polasek Museum and Sculpture Gardens** (633 Osceola Ave; tel: 407-647-6294; www.polasek.org; Tue–Sat 10am–4pm, Sun 1pm–4pm; charge), a short

**BELOW:** Albin Polasek Museum.

*Recommended Restaurants on pages 273–7*

(820 Lake Lily Dr; tel: 407-644-2451; Thur–Sun noon–4pm; charge) have been fully restored to show how he and his family would have lived on the shores of Lake Lily. Waterhouse built this house himself using basic tools like those found in the carpentry shop. Staff hold demonstrations and workshops that let you try the tools out for yourself. The house is viewed by tour only, but the tour guide is a very enjoyable gentleman who brings the house and the community alive with his insight. There is also a self-guided tour through a traditional Victorian herb garden.

Several hundred wounded eagles, hawks, ospreys, and other raptors are rescued and rehabilitated by the **Audubon of Florida's National Center for Birds of Prey** (1101 Audubon Way; tel: 407-644-0190; Tue–Sun 10am–4pm; charge) on Lake Sybelia. Although recuperating birds are kept in an isolated facility to minimize human contact, visitors can view members of about 32 species that are too severely injured to be returned to the wild.

A more somber experience awaits visitors at the small **Holocaust Memorial**

**Resource and Education Center of Central Florida** (851 N. Maitland Ave; tel: 407-628-0555; www.holocaust-edu.org; Mon–Thur 9am–4pm, Fri 9am–1pm, Sun 1pm–4pm; free). One room tells the history of the Holocaust with multimedia displays. Another offers changing exhibits on various aspects of the Nazi extermination campaign.

## Kissimmee

South of Orlando, a short drive from Disney World, is **Kissimmee** ⑫, a small town chock-full of chain motels, fast-food joints, and second-string attractions, most clustered around US 192, also known as Irlo Bronson Memorial Highway.

Before Disney there was **Gatorland** ⑬ (14501 Orange Blossom Trail; tel: 800-393-5297; www.gatorland.com; daily 9am–5pm; charge), an old-fashioned tourist attraction that's managed to survive the development of modern theme parks by sticking with a simple formula: if one alligator is good, thousands

*An alligator wrestler at Gatorland demonstrates his unique skills.*

**BELOW LEFT:** all tied up at Gatorland.
**BELOW:** Renaissance art at the Cornell Museum.

*The waterskiing spectacular is a longstanding tradition at Cypress Gardens.*

## Polk County

**Cypress Gardens** ⓮ (6000 Cypress Gardens Blvd, Winter Haven; tel: 863-324-2111; www.cypressgardens.com; daily, hours vary, see website; charge) had a 67-year run before old age forced its closure in 2003. But Georgia businessman Kent Buescher and the state of Florida came to the rescue, and this signature park reopened in late 2004. In addition to the southern belles and water-ski shows of yesteryear, Buescher has added four roller coasters, carnival rides, and a concert schedule in an effort to modernize the attraction and make it more competitive.

are better. Visitors can view breeding pens and nurseries, stroll through a cypress swamp, see monkeys, snakes, and other exotic wildlife, and sample down-home delicacies like smoked gator ribs and deep-fried gator nuggets. Two shows keep visitors entertained: the Gator Jumparoo Show, in which alligators leap out of the water to snatch a chicken from a trainer's hand, and the Gator Wrestling Show, featuring a wrangler who manhandles one of the big reptiles.

**Fantasy of Flight** (1400 Broadway Blvd SE, Polk City; tel: 863-984-3500; www.fantasyofflight.com; daily 10am–5pm; charge) offers a trip down aviation's memory lane, beginning with the early years when pilots went skydiving because they had no other choice. In addition to a realistic flight simulator, the attraction has a number of aircraft on display. Biplane and hot-air balloon rides also are available.

Some visitors looking for an uplifting morning head to **Orange Blossom Balloons** (tel: 407-894-5040; www.orange

## Discount Shopping

**S**hopping in Orlando is dominated by enormous discount malls. For international travelers the discounts are even bigger thanks to the weakened dollar. Some of the best options include Festival Bay (5250 International Dr; tel: 800-481-1944), which contains such heavily themed stores as Vans Skatepark, with a 25,000-sq-ft (2,000-sq-meters) street course, and a Ron Jon Surf Shop. Florida Mall (8001 S. Orange Blossom Trail; tel: 407-851-6255) is a destination in itself. There are six department stores, 18 jewelry stores, 22 shoe stores, over 53 clothing stores, and a hotel.

With so many supermalls in Orlando, it's easy to overlook the Lake Buena Vista Factory Stores (15657 State Road 535; tel: 407-238-9301) east of I-4, but its bargains would stand out anywhere else. The Gap and Reebok outlets offer some of the best discounts in Orlando, while the S&K Men's Store has unbelievable bargains for tailor-made suits, shirts, and pants. Premium Outlets (8200 Vineland Ave; tel: 407-238-7787) has 110 discount stores and is one of the largest malls in Florida. Designer names include Polo, Ralph Lauren, Hugo Boss, Dior, Burberry, Armani, Diesel, Calvin Klein, and The Gap. Little Me and OshKosh cater to children. Prime Outlets (4951 International Dr; tel: 407-352-9600) currently houses over 100 stores, but an expansion is under way. Factory outlets include Nike, Gap, Adidas, Reebok, Tommy Hilfiger, and Neiman Marcus.

blossomballoons.com; daily flights, weather permitting; charge) for a bird's-eye view of the area, complete with champagne toast and breakfast.

**Full Speed Race & Golf** (5720 W. US 192; tel: 407-397-7455; www.full speed.cc; Mon–Fri noon–midnight, Sat–Sun 10am–midnight; charge) features six NASCAR simulators that use three-sided screens to put you in the heat of a stock-car race. The attraction also has an 18-hole, black-lighted miniature golf course with a racing theme.

Gardeners should stop at **A World of Orchids** (2501 Old Lake Wilson Rd; tel: 407-396-1887; Mon–Sat 9.30am–4.30pm), a conservatory brimming with lush tropical plants, including thousands of orchids, some of them quite rare. Those who prefer nature in a, well, natural setting should visit the Nature Conservancy's **Disney Wilderness** (2700 Scrub Jay Trail; tel: 407-935-0002; Mon–Sat 9am–5pm; charge), a 12,000-acre (4,800-hectare) preserve with 7 miles (11km) of hiking trails through wetlands and pine flatwoods ecosystems. Guided walks and off-road "buggy" tours are available.

## Orange country

Next to sunshine, sand, and sea, Florida prompts thoughts of citrus: the state still grows over 70 percent of the nation's oranges. Citrus stands flourish along the backroads, and sweet-smelling orange blossoms saturate the air in spring. On a clear day, you can see 2.7 million orange trees, about a third of Florida's crop, from the top of the **Florida Citrus Tower** (141 N. Highway 27; tel: 352-394-4061; www.citrustower.com; Mon–Sat 8am–5pm; charge) on US 27 near

*Founded in 1936, Cypress Gardens is often billed as Florida's first theme park.*

**BELOW:** hiking among cypress trees in the Disney Wilderness.

*Despite the quick pace of growth in the Orlando area, there are still some untrammeled natural spaces.*

**BELOW:** Florida accounts for more than 70 percent of the US orange crop.

**Clermont**, 20 miles (32km) west of Orlando. You can buy fruit and will learn that the sweetest oranges aren't necessarily orange.

## South of Orlando

One hundred miles south of Orlando, **Lake Wales** ⓯, at 250ft (76 meters) above sea level, is one of the highest places in the state and the southern anchor of Orlando's cultural corridor. The **Lake Wales Museum and Cultural Center** (325 S. Scenic Highway; tel: 863-678-4209; Mon–Fri 9am–5pm, Sat 10am–4pm; charge) in the railroad depot displays vintage railcars, antiques and exhibits about the area's turpentine, lumbering, railroading and citrus industries. The entire downtown region is in the National Register of Historic Places. Even higher is the 205-ft (62-meter) Singing Tower in **Bok Tower Gardens** (1151 Tower Blvd; tel: 863-676-1408; daily 8am–6pm; charge), just north of town. The tower's 53-bell carillon rings out daily.

**Spook Hill** haunts Fifth Avenue in Lake Wales. Turn off your car motor at the bottom of the steep drive, put it into neutral, and your car will appear to roll back uphill. The place to dine and sleep in the area is **Chalet Suzanne**.

Fifteen miles (24km) west of Lake Wales is **Bartow** ⓰, the center of an industry that has boosted the economy but taken a toll on the environment. SR 60 takes you past lunar landscapes of sand mountains and craters filled with stinking water. This is Bone Valley, heart of the phosphate mining industry. Draglines often dig up fossils of mammoths and giant sharks – hence the name. Florida produces 75 percent of the US's phosphate, a key ingredient in fertilizer.

## An unexpected gem

**Lakeland** ⓱ is another blue-collar city. The main source of interest to visitors is **Florida Southern College** at McDonald Street and Ingraham Avenue, southwest of downtown. Students here study within the world's largest collection of buildings designed by Frank Lloyd Wright (1869–1959). Maps available from the Visitor Center (Mon–Fri 10am–4pm) provide a self-guided tour of these functional works of art – the oldest of which is the **Annie Pfeiffer Chapel**, built in 1938. ❑

# RESTAURANTS

## Restaurants

Prices for a three-course dinner per person, excluding tax, tip, and beverages:

**$** = under $20
**$$** = $20–45
**$$$** = $45–60
**$$$$** = over $60

## Celebration and Kissimmee

### Azteca's Restaurant
809 N. Main St, Kissimmee
Tel: 407-933-8155
L & D daily
There's nothing pretentious about this local favorite. The walls are decorated with eclectic hangings, and the menu includes Mexican standards such as burritos, enchiladas, and nachos for starters. All Mexican beers are available. $$

### Café D'Antonio Ristorante Celebration
691 Front St, Celebration
Tel: 407-566-2233
L & D daily
This upscale Italian restaurant serves an extensive selection of pastas but an even wider selection of meat and chicken dishes, with several veal selections. Its wine list includes fine Italian wines and a healthy selection from California. There is also a location in Maitland that includes a deli and café (see below). $$$

### Columbia Restaurant
649 Front St, Celebration
Tel: 407-566-1505
L & D daily
The Columbia restaurant

chain dates to 1905 when its original outlet opened in Tampa's Ybor City. This classy restaurant serves Spanish cuisine that has amalgamated Cuban and Mexican influences while in Florida. The result for anyone who likes a bit of spice is a winner. There is flamenco dancing in the evening. $$$

### Market Street Café
701 Front St, Celebration
Tel: 407-566-1144
B, L & D daily
This classic American diner serves breakfast all day, which includes everything from a posh crab omelette to buttermilk pancakes. Dinner selections are varied and include burgers, meatloaf, and stir-fry. There is also an old-fashioned soda fountain serving ice-cream treats. $$

### Plantation Room
Celebration Hotel, 700 Bloom St, Celebration
Tel: 407-566-6002
B, L & D daily
Affordable, gourmet, nouvelle Florida cuisine, including master dinners featuring everything from 'gator to kangaroo. Breakfast is lovely and an excellent value. $$$

### Sherlocks
715 Bloom St, Suite 130, Celebration
Tel: 407-566-1866
B, L & D daily
This little bit of England has nestled quietly into Disney's hometown. A

combination teahouse, deli, and restaurant, it is open all day for quick cups of Earl Grey to Champagne Tea. Live music plays most weekend evenings. $$

## Universal Studios

### Finnegan's Bar and Grill
New York
Tel: 407-224-3613
L & D daily
Meant to be a hometown Irish pub in New York City, Finnegan's has a very friendly wait staff and serves fish and chips, corned beef, and, of course, Irish stew. Guinness is on tap. $$

### International Food and Film Festival
Universal Studios, World Expo
Sample fast-food versions

of Mexican, Italian, Chinese, and American dishes, though you may want to skip the main course and head directly to the ice-cream bar for banana splits and gooey sundaes. Food-related movie clips play on various video monitors that are stationed around the eatery. $$

### Lombard's Seafood Grille
San Francisco/Amity
Tel: 407-224-3613
L & D daily
Lombard's serves the best food at Universal Studios. The clam chowder pays homage to the east coast, while the fresh seafood and tasty pastas have a more Californian feel. Either way, you're likely to leave happy. $$

**Confisco Grille**
Port of Entry
Tel: 407-224-4012
B, L & D daily
Decorated as an exotic wharfside tavern, Confisco Grille offers ethnic dishes ranging from fajitas and pad thai to barbecued ribs. Drinks are available at the Backwater Bar, which has a small patio perfect for people-watching. The restaurant also hosts the daily character breakfast. $$

**Green Eggs & Ham Cafe**
Islands of Adventure, Seuss Landing
A dream come true for Seuss fans if not for culinary critics, with burgers, fries and green-egg-and-ham sandwiches tinted with minced parsley. $$

**Mythos**
Lost Continent
Tel: 407-224-4012
L & D daily
The park's best restaurant is ensconced in a regally appointed cavern with sculpted walls, purple upholstery, and lagoon views. Entrées include wood-roasted lobster with wild mushroom risotto, cedar-planked salmon with orange-horseradish mashed potatoes, and wood-fired pizza, plus other child-friendly dishes. $$$

**Bob Marley: A Tribute to Freedom**
Tel: 407-224-3663
L & D daily
You can chow down on yucca chips, jerk chicken, and plenty of Red Stripe beer while jammin' to reggae. The exterior is modeled after Marley's home in Kingston, Jamaica. Inside, photos and other artifacts chronicle his life and career. Live bands perform nightly on the courtyard stage. $$

**Emeril's Restaurant Orlando**
Tel: 407-224-3663

L & D daily
Featuring the creations of television chef Emeril Lagasse. Assertive Creole flavors bubble up through artfully prepared specialties like grilled pork chop with caramelized sweet potatoes. Wine connoisseurs can choose from more than 10,000 bottles. The desserts are equally glorious; homey favorites like root beer floats and banana cream pie become decadent masterpieces. $$$

**Hard Rock Cafe Orlando**
Tel: 407-224-3663
L & D daily
When it comes to theme restaurants, the big daddy of 'em all is the Hard Rock Cafe. With seating for 600 in the restaurant and 3,000 in the concert hall, this is the largest Hard Rock in the world, and, like its humbler brethren, its walls are plastered with gold records, album covers, flashy costumes, and instruments that have been strummed and drummed by some of the rock world's biggest names. A pink Cadillac revolves over the bar; a Sistine Chapel-like mural featuring a heavenly host of dead rock stars adorns the ceiling; and stained-glass panels pay tribute to a trinity of rock legends – Elvis Presley, Chuck Berry, and Jerry Lee Lewis. It's a bit much to take in over a meal, which is why the Hard Rock offers free tours in the afternoon. $$

**Jimmy Buffet's Margaritaville**
Tel: 407-224-3663

L & D daily
For a laid-back beach bum, Jimmy Buffet is quite the entrepreneur. Decked out in beachy, tropical style, this restaurant leans toward Caribbean flavors – conch fritters, seafood chowder, grilled fish – with a sprinkling of American standards, including the inevitable "cheeseburger in paradise." $$

**Latin Quarter**
Tel: 407-224-3663
L & D daily
Both the food and the music are spicy at the Latin Quarter, dedicated to the culture and cuisine of 21 Latin American nations. After dinner, an orchestra and dance troupe take the stage. Dance instructors initiate neophytes into the wonders of merengue, salsa, and the mambo. $$

**Pat O'Brien's Orlando**
Tel: 407-224-3663
L & D daily
An older crowd inhabits Pat O'Brien's, a replica of a landmark New Orleans watering hole. The singalong crowd loves the dueling pianos, and foodies enjoy jambalaya, muffeletta, and other Big Easy specialties. Wash it down with a Hurricane, O'Brien's signature rum drink. $$

**Bice Ristorante**
Portofino Bay Hotel, 5601 Universal Blvd
Tel: 407-503-1415
D daily
The clean, simple lines of this upscale trattoria make way for a fine Italian dining experience. The Bice chain began in

**LEFT:** the sound of New Orleans at Pat O'Brien's.
**RIGHT:** Mythos is set in a cavern-like dining room.

Milan and is famed as much for its hospitality as its food. $$$

### Emeril's Tchoup Chop
Royal Pacific Resort, 6300 Hollywood Way
Tel: 407-503-3000
L & D daily
Emeril's second restaurant on Universal Orlando's property is dedicated to the delicate flavors of Asian and Polynesian cuisine. The restaurant's seductive decor is created using palm trees, bamboo, and waterfalls. $$$

### Mama Della's Ristorante
Portofino Bay Hotel, 5601 Universal Blvd
Tel: 407-503-3463
D daily
As heavy on themes as on the stomach. The hearty Italian fare is accompanied by fine wines and strolling entertainment, including singers and guitarists. Mama herself makes an appearance, too, insisting that everyone eats up. $$$

### Palm Restaurant
Hard Rock Hotel, 5800 Universal Blvd
Tel: 407-503-7256
D daily
Carnivores can slice into slabs of beef at this knock-off of the famous New York steakhouse – a favorite with the meat and martini crowd. Like the original, there are celebrity caricatures on the wall and a whiff of testosterone in the air. $$$

International Drive and Lake Buena Vista

### Bergamo's Italian Restaurant
Festival Bay Mall, 5250 International Dr
Tel: 407-352-3805
D daily

Bergamo's has earned kudos for an attractive ambience and beautifully-prepared pasta, steak, and seafood (thankfully not overcooked, as is so often the case in Orlando). It also has the largest list of Italian wines in the city, and the wait staff, all talented vocalists, sing everything from operatic arias to Neapolitan folk songs every evening. $$$

### B-Line Diner
Peabody Hotel, 9801 International Dr
Tel: 407-345-4460
24 hours daily
A cozy, 1950s-style diner that's open 24 hours a day, it features thick sandwiches, griddle cakes, and a jukebox with vintage tunes. The corned-beef hash and eggs for breakfast is about as good as slop can get. $$

### Bola Ristorante
8148 International Dr
Tel: 407-345-8884
L & D daily
This Italian restaurant has the classiest interior on I-Drive and would not look out of place on South Beach. The cuisine is classic Italian fare, with a lighter touch. Chefs take pride in creating simple dishes using the finest ingredients. The bar has a happy hour between four and seven, with half-priced drinks and appetizers. $$$

### Cala Bella
Rosen Shingle Creek, 9939 Universal Blvd
Tel: 407-996-3663
D daily
Located at the out-of-the-way Rosen Shingle Creek Resort, this Italian restaurant has a reputation for well-presented basic Italian dishes like risotto,

fresh pasta, steak, seafood, and Tuscan bean soup. $$

### Capital Grille
Pointe Orlando, 9101 International Dr
Tel: 407-370-4392
D daily, L Mon–Fri
Dry-aged steak is the centerpiece of the Capital Grille's menu, one that is not kind to vegetarians but does offer a few seafood options. The wine cellar has over 5,000 bottles from around the world. $$$

### Capriccio Grill Italian Steakhouse
Peabody Orlando, 9801 International Dr
Tel: 407-345-4450
L & D daily
A show kitchen is the center of attention at this upscale, marble-clad restaurant specializing in gourmet pizza, grilled meats and seafood, heaping bowls of pasta, and other Italian dishes. $$$

### Ciao Italia Ristorante Italiano
6149 Westwood Blvd
Tel: 407-354-0770
D daily
This family-run restaurant has a warm, welcoming setting combined with fine food. The standard

menu is basic, but evening specials offer more adventurous entrées, and the wine list has a fine selection of Italian wines. $$$

### Dux
Peabody Hotel, 9801 International Dr
Tel: 407-345-4550
D Tue–Sat
Elegant restaurant with innovative American cuisine. Starters include Osetra caviar and lobster and potato salad. Entrées focus on fish, but there are steaks and lamb for those craving meat. One of Orlando's finest dining experiences. $$$

### A Land Remembered
Rosen Shingle Creek, 9939 Universal Blvd
Tel: 866-996-9939
L & D daily
This steakhouse is named after a novel written by Patrick Smith, which focuses on Florida's history and landscapes. So it should be no surprise that alligator appears on the menu. Otherwise, the fine-dining menu is varied, with several seafood options available for those not wanting steak. The wine list will leave no one disappointed. $$$

## Ming Court

9188 International Dr
Tel: 407-351-9988
L & D daily
Interior koi ponds and gardens set the stage at this fine Chinese restaurant. The chefs cook up specialties of several provinces and even produce fine sushi as well as a delectable dim sum menu. Ask for a table near the open kitchen. $$

## Norman's

The Ritz-Carlton Grande Lakes, 4012 Central Florida Prkwy
Tel: 407-393-4333
D daily
Norman Van Aken's New World Cuisine is defined by dishes created when European tradition encounters the native cultures of the Caribbean, Central America, and Florida. Sommeliers offer advice on which vintages best accompany these dishes, and the setting is elegance all the way. $$$

## The Oceanaire Seafood Room

Pointe Orlando, 9101 International Dr, Suite 1002
Tel: 407-363-4801
D daily
Decorated like a 1930s ocean liner, this sleek diner serves "ultra-fish" seafood, which means that it has arrived that day and was probably in the sea the day before. Such ideals deserve celebration, especially in a city where such sourcing of ingredients often plays second fiddle to grand themes. Hence the menu changes daily but often includes oysters, simple and tasty fish entrées, and a fine wine list with stewards to guide your selection. Still, it's a pity that in the heart of Florida so much is flown in from New England and Alaska instead of making the best of the bounty of two nearby coasts. $$$

## Primo

Ritz-Carlton Grande Lakes, 4040 Central Florida Prkwy

Tel: 407-393-4444
D daiy
Chef Melissa Kelly creates this "sensible" Italian menu based upon locally sourced ingredients, making the most of the varied citrus fruits and seafood available in Florida. $$$

## Venetian Room

Caribe Royale, 8101 World Center Dr
Tel: 407-238-8060
D Tue–Sat, jackets suggested
The Caribe Royale's flagship restaurant adds a touch of class to this corporate hotel. The fine-dining menu here features European favorites such as foie gras and cheese platters, with an extensive wine list containing some of California's most renowned winemakers. $$$

SeaWorld

## Seafire Inn Restaurant

L & D daily
This sprawling restaurant serves Caribbean-style food during the daily Music Maestro lunch show. Reservations are required for the Makahiki Luau, a Polynesian-themed dinner theater. $$

## Sharks Underwater Grill

Near Sharks Encounter
L & D daily
Set beside the enormous Sharks Encounter aquarium, one entire wall of the Underwater Grill's dining room is exposed to the tank, letting you sit in awe of the magnificent creatures swimming past. The food here, mostly seafood, is exquisite; the restaurant can easily produce one of the best meals you'll have at a theme park. $$$

Downtown and Loch Haven Park

## The Beacon

The Sanctuary, 100 S. Eola
Tel: 407-841-5444
D daily, Br Sat–Sun, bar open daily to 2am
This trendy tapas bar has breathed new life into the nightlife scene of Thornton Park, though you have to have a thick wallet to enjoy its extensive wine list, chic interior, and gourmet tapas. This is the place to rub elbows with Orlando's upper crust. $$$

## The Boheme

Grand Bohemian Hotel, 325 S. Orange Ave
Tel: 407-313-9000
B & D daily, L Mon–Sat
This is one of Orlando's best restaurants, and as each year passes another award is received. A recent addition, the Bohemian Wine Room, allows parties of up to 14 guests to enjoy a private dining room and exclusive service for the evening. $$$

## Gargi's Lakeside Italian Ristorante

1414 N. Orange Ave
Tel: 407-894-7907
L & D Mon–Sat, D Sun
Located on Lake Ivanhoe in the heart of downtown Orlando, this family-run restaurant has grown over the years from a tiny bistro. The menu features veal, steaks, and seafood, all served with fresh pasta. In addition to a sturdy wine list, there is a wide selection of martinis to choose from. $$

## The Globe

27 Wall Street Plaza
Tel: 407-849-9904
Café 11am–11pm, bar to 2am

**LEFT:** Hard Rock Cafe. **RIGHT:** Luma on Park in Winter Park allows patrons to sample half-glasses of wine.

As it's located in the downtown Wall Street Plaza nightlife area, The Globe serves two purposes: a quick bite for office workers and a quick meal of pizza, sandwiches, or salads before heading on to more serious drinking elsewhere. There are sushi and cocktail specials Mon–Fri for happy hour, when live music is played on the patio. $$

### The Harp Restaurant
25 S. Magnolia Ave
Tel: 407-481-2927
L Mon–Fri 11am–2pm, D Mon–Sat
Could this be Orlando's first gastropub? The attached Celt Irish Pub has a lively atmosphere, while The Harp serves meaty entrées from a limited menu in sedate surroundings. The prices are far too high for pub grub, but neither the atmosphere nor the food exceed those standards. $$$

### Harvey's Bistro
390 N. Orange Ave
Tel: 407-246-6560
L & D Mon–Fri, D Sat
A little European style goes a long way at this welcoming bistro, popular with business lunchers and nighttime revelers. Even pot roast and meatloaf are something special, not to mention more ambitious choices such as seared calf liver, crab cakes, roasted duck, and a variety of nicely done pasta dishes. $$$

### Hue Restaurant
629 E. Central Blvd
Tel: 407-849-1800
D daily
Hue makes the most of local produce in creating familiar American fare such as wood-grilled filet mignon. The designer interior has a cozy,

Scandinavian vibe, with crisp lines accented by warm lighting and candles. The happy hour is very popular. $$$

### Little Saigon
1106 E. Colonial Dr
Tel: 407-423-8539
L & D daily
This no-nonsense family-run restaurant is a welcome addition to a town that celebrates simulation over authenticity. Traditional Vietnamese dishes range from delicate spring rolls and rice noodles to big bowls of soup and fiery stir-fries. $–$$

### White Wolf Café
1829 N. Orange Ave
Tel: 407-895-5590
L & D Mon–Sat
This tiny slice of Bohemia is a breath of fresh air in theme-crazed Orlando. The service isn't exactly snappy, but the atmosphere is friendly, and the menu – ranging from egg salad sandwiches to wild mushroom lasagna – has enough creative quirks to sustain your interest. $

### Winter Park and Maitland

### Antonio's la Fiamma
611 S. Orlando Ave, 2nd floor, Maitland
Tel: 407-645-1035
L & D Mon–Fri, D Sat
Another branch of the fine Antonio's restaurant chain serving pasta, risotto, and authentic Italian meat and fish entrées. $$$

### Brio Tuscan Grille
480 N. Orlando Ave, Suite 108, Winter Park
Tel: 407-622-5611
L & D daily
This dark-wood-lined Italian chain restaurant could make a good setting for a romantic evening, but one suspects business lunches are more common in this

branch, part of the Winter Park Village shopping complex. The menu emphasis is on pork and steaks, but there are hand-tossed pizzas and other lighter touches available for vegetarians or children. $$

### Café de France
526 Park Ave, South Winter Park
Tel: 407-647-1869
L & D Tue–Sat
Start your meal with foie gras, escargot, or the daily selection of pâté before enjoying a fine selection of soups and salads and entrées that include lamb, pork, and a fish of the day. A fine wine list is available to accompany your meal. $$$

### Houston's
215 S. Orlando Ave, Winter Park
Tel: 407-740-4005
L & D daily
You are not likely to stumble across this restaurant, as it is tucked away from

Orlando Avenue with not much else around it to draw visitors. This makes its setting on the edge of one of Winter Park's numerous lakes feel even more secluded. The menu varies from pricey five-star burgers to gourmet steaks and seafood. $$$

### Luma on Park
290 S. Park Ave, Winter Park
Tel: 407-599-4111
D daily, lounge from 4pm
This is perhaps the finest dining experience in the buzzing Park Avenue restaurant scene. The menu features a lot of seafood, from scallops to barramundi, and there are steaks and chops, too. The wine list consists of boutique winemakers, mostly from California, and there is a "flight" available that provides samples of their bottles. Uniquely, half-glasses are available for those who would like to change wines for each course yet remain upright. $$$

# GULF COAST

**Beautiful beaches lure travelers to the west coast, but you'll also find vibrant urban neighborhoods, fine museums, an elaborate theme park, and, in a few quiet corners, a slice of Florida as it used to be**

**T**he Gulf of Mexico caresses the fine, bleached sand of Florida's western shores. Its warm waters undulate gently or, sometimes, not at all, often flat as a sheet of glass on humid summer days. Shells of every color and shape are washed up on the sands to the endless delight of beach-combing vacationers.

Such tranquil scenes stand in sharp contrast to the clamor on the shores. Newcomers and developers have laid siege to this once placid part of Florida. From the metropolitan Tampa-St Petersburg nucleus, one of the fastest growing conurbations in the US, north to New Port Richey and south to Fort Myers, the Gulf Coast has begun to resemble the waterfront wall of windows characteristic of the Miami-to-Palm-Beach strip on the Atlantic Coast. Here you'll find retirement farms, condo complexes, and stucco mansions. With them have come professional sports, massive malls, traffic jams, and urban sprawl.

And like the rest of Florida, the Gulf Coast is a place for indulging the imagination. St Petersburg delves into the surreal at the Salvador Dalí Museum, containing one of the most comprehensive collections of Dalí's work in the world, while the glittering domain of the circus is celebrated in Sarasota and Venice, where circus impresario John Ringling left a legacy of theaters, museums, schools for the performing arts, and festivals.

When it comes to theme parks, Tampa's Busch Gardens competes with the best of Orlando's attractions. A great swath of land has been turned into a miniature Africa, complete with big game and a jungle cruise.

But the old Gulf Coast lingers in the fishing villages around Cedar Key and spots south of Naples, and Latino color still enlivens Tampa's Ybor City, founded by a wealthy Cuban tobacco merchant in the late 19th century and now, with its specialty shops, bars, and museum, a tribute to Florida's once thriving cigar industry. Art Deco, too, may still be encountered in downtown Tampa, proving this architectural renaissance is not confined to sunny Miami Beach. ❏

---

**PRECEDING PAGES:** a vintage train station is preserved at Heritage Village near Clearwater. **LEFT:** people – and pelicans – gather at Naples Pier. **TOP:** teeing off on Gasparilla Island near Fort Myers. **ABOVE RIGHT:** Ringling Museum, Sarasota.

*Recommended Restaurants on pages 290–1*

# TAMPA

The largest city on the Gulf Coast has numerous cultural attractions, a historic Cuban neighborhood, and one of Florida's best theme parks

I t's December at the Henry Plant Museum, housed in the 1891 Tampa Bay Hotel on the University of Tampa campus. The annual **Christmas Stroll**, a much-loved tradition, is in full swing. Spiced cider and cookies are served on the verandah. Carolers sing *We Wish You a Merry Christmas* around a Christmas tree. And shoppers squeeze into the gift shop, hoping to find a unique present that echoes Christmas past.

It may be 75°F (24°C) outside, but families strolling the **Henry Plant Museum ❶** (401 W. Kennedy Blvd; tel: 813-254-1891; Tue–Sat 10am–4pm, Sun noon–4pm; charge) are dressed in their brightest holiday outfits and buoyed by Christmas spirit. They peer into 14 former guest rooms, each a "cabinet of curiosities" from around the world collected by railroad magnate Henry Plant and his wife Margaret and brought to the $3-million resort on Plant's railroad cars.

## Holiday cheer

At Christmas, rooms are trimmed with trees and antique holiday accessories connected to a theme. One shows alligator hunting and fishing on the adjoining Hillsborough River and other outdoor pursuits. Another re-creates a Victorian children's Christmas with porcelain dolls and train sets. Still others depict Tampa Bay Hotel's 40-year history, from the arrival of the Plant Rail System in 1884 to the resort's rapid decline after Plant's death, and its purchase by the City of Tampa for use as a university and history museum in 1933.

The Victorian love of travel inspired the Moorish design of this national historic landmark. Constructed from reinforced concrete, the 6-acre (2-hectare) hotel building has six minarets, four cupolas, and three domes on the roof, totaling 13, the number of months in the Islamic calendar. One of six Florida hotels built by Plant, the 511-room Tampa Bay Hotel was the most modern resort of its day, with private baths, electric lighting, elevators, and telephones in every room. It had a beauty shop, barbershop, florist, grand salon, sanitarium,

**Main attractions**
HENRY PLANT MUSEUM
YBOR CITY
RIVERWALK
TAMPA BAY PERFORMING ARTS CENTER
TAMPA MUSEUM OF ART
TAMPA BAY HISTORY CENTER
FLORIDA AQUARIUM
BUSCH GARDENS
MUSEUM OF SCIENCE AND INDUSTRY
LOWRY PARK ZOO

**LEFT:** downtown Tampa.
**BELOW:** *Immigrant Statue,* Ybor City.

*Old-time cigar shops
are part of Ybor
City's Cuban heritage.*

dining room, solarium, and ballroom with orchestra. Landscaped grounds covering 150 acres (60 hectares) of waterfront included 21 buildings, an 18-hole golf course, tennis courts, croquet courts, a boathouse, stables, a racetrack, kennels, a bowling alley, a casino with a 1,500-seat auditorium, a swimming pool, even a zoo.

Yankee-born Henry Bradley Plant made his fortune by consolidating the bankrupt railroads of the South after the Civil War. A self-made man who got his start delivering express packages, Plant helped spearhead winter tourism in Florida. And the swampy waterfront of 400-sq-mile (1,000-sq-km) Tampa Bay, whose name may derive from the Timucuan Indian word *Tanpa*, meaning "sticks of fire," was one of the unlikely beneficiaries.

Set at the mouth of the Hillsborough River, this blue-collar port – the seventh largest in the US – is an industrial power-house, transporting over 50 million tons of cargo annually, including phosphate from nearby mines, citrus, cattle, seafood, even yachts. Still, while "Industrial Chic" appeals to many – and it certainly is fascinating to visit the Twiggs Street docks and watch the banana boats unloading – it can

be a headache for casual tourists navigating the sprawling city to visit attractions like Busch Gardens, the Lowry Park Zoo, the Museum of Science and Industry, Ybor City, and the Florida Aquarium.

Thankfully, that's starting to change. Inspired perhaps by the grand vision of Plant himself, the City of Tampa is working to create new cohesion within the city. Distinct neighborhoods, such as the Cuban cigar capital of **Ybor City** and the historic upscale dining and shopping mecca of **Hyde Park/SoHo**, on either side of downtown, are now connected by inexpensive streetcar and tram service. You'll still need to hop on I-275 to visit Busch Gardens, the Lowry Park Zoo, and the Museum of Science and Industry. But Tampa is beginning to feel like a manageable destination, worthy of more than a quick stop en route to Gulf beaches.

## Downtown Tampa

Symbolic of Tampa's ambitious revitalization project is the **Riverwalk** cultural corridor taking shape on the east bank of the Hillsborough River opposite the Plant Museum. At the north end, the five-theater **Tampa Bay Performing Arts Center ②**

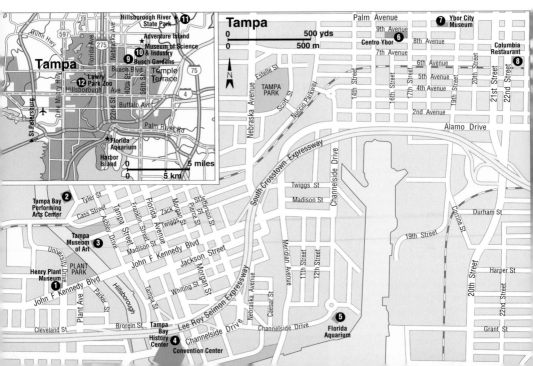

813-229-STAR), the largest cultural center south of Kennedy Center in Washington, DC, is already a major destination for theater productions, classical concerts, and the arts. Anchoring the southern end, the **Tampa Museum of Art ❸** (tel: 813-274-130; Tue–Sat 10am–4pm, Sun noon–pm; charge) is re-emerging as a state-of-the-art facility. The new museum will have two-story atrium, glass ceilings, stone floors, and a boxlike, cantilevered structure sheathed in a metal skin and programmable LED lighting that will mirror changes in the surrounding environment. TMA's wide-ranging art collection includes classical antiquities and regional contemporary art, such as a photo exhibit on Mexican artist Frida Kahlo and glass art displayed in a light-filled river terrace.

## Then and now

**Tampa Bay History Center ❹** (225 S. Franklin St; tel: 813-228-0097; Mon–Fri 9am–5pm; charge), in the Tampa Convention Center Annex, is a small museum telling the story of Tampa from prehistoric times to the present. Tampa's strategic importance during a succession of wars is examined, starting with nearby

Fort Brooke, the 1824 military outpost used by the US Army during the Second and Third Seminole Wars (1835–55) and occupied by the Confederate Army during the Civil War. Tampa's important national role as a major mobilization point for US troops during the Spanish-American War in 1898 was reprised in World War II, when 15,000 servicemen were stationed at McDill Air Force Base. In 1910, the Ybor and Sparkman channels, connecting the east side of Hillsborough Bay with the old channel running from the Hillsborough River to

*Moorish domes cap the Henry Plant Museum – formerly the Tampa Bay Hotel – at the University of Tampa.*

**BELOW LEFT:** Ybor City. **BELOW:** "pirates" storm the city during the annual Gasparilla Invasion.

## Pirates of the Caribbean

Tampa's rites of spring occur every February when its businessmen and bigwigs exchange their suits and briefcases for puffed-sleeved shirts and buckled boots and board the *José Gasparilla*, which leads the annual Gasparilla Invasion. Pirates climb the three masts to the crow's nests, blast cannons, and set off for the mouth of the Hillsborough River flanked by hundreds of smaller craft with their own swashbuckling crews. Upon landing, pirates swarm the streets of downtown Tampa, where hundreds of thousands of spectators watch them lead a parade. The first Gasparilla Invasion was held in 1904. It grew out of the Gulf Coast's reputation as a haunt for blood-thirsty buccaneers, particularly a legendary character named José Gaspar, who was believed to have lived on Gasparilla Island near Charlotte Harbor and plundered his way along the Gulf Coast. History books sometimes refer to Gaspar, but no records prove his existence. One theory holds that Gaspar was the invention of a fisherman who, in the 1870s, claimed to have sailed with Gaspar in order to boost his business in treasure maps.

*Decorative lights illuminate Seventh Avenue near Centro Ybor.*

**BELOW:** a shark prowls the waters of the Florida Aquarium.

Tampa Harbor, were constructed, allowing Tampa to develop into a major port.

## Water world

The biggest visitor attraction in the Port of Tampa is the soaring **Florida Aquarium ❺** (tel: 813-273-4020; daily 9.30am–5pm; charge) in the Garrison Seaport Center on Channelside Drive. This attractive aquarium is one of the best in the country. A carefully crafted interpretive theme tying together exhibits on three floors lets you follow a drop of Florida water from its source to the sea, passing through different habitats. Allow plenty of time to enjoy the many inter-

active exhibits, which include the Bay and Beaches and the very popular Coral Reef, a simulated Key West dive site contained within a 500,000-gallon (2-million-liter) tank filled with 1,500 tropical fish. Throughout the day, divers jump into the tank and answer visitor questions via intercom. This is the only aquarium in the country where, for a fee, kids six years old and over can don scuba gear and "Swim with the Fishes" in the coral reef. You can also board a boat outside the aquarium for a Wild Dolphin Ecotour, which allows you to look for some of the 400-plus dolphins that live in Tampa Bay. Bring binoculars!

## Ybor City

About the time Plant was building his rail system, steamship lines, and hotels, Vicente Martinez Ybor was planning to move his cigar factory from Key West due to labor problems. Just northeast of downtown, near the train tracks, Ybor City, which grew to prominence as the "Cigar Capital of the World," no longer pulsates with the color and excitement of its Cuban heyday when crowds gathered at cockfights and to hear Cuban freedom fighter José Martí make fiery speeches, and Teddy Roosevelt rode into town ahead of the Rough Riders and headquartered at the Tampa Bay Hotel alongside Clara Barton, founder of the Red Cross. Ybor City today has received a facelift and is now a popular New Orleans–style shopping and nightclub district, bustling with activity into the wee hours.

The building around which the enclave grew, Ybor's 1886 cigar factory is the centerpiece that spurred the restoration of other classic buildings in Tampa. Once upon a time, cigar workers sat in rows tediously rolling cigar while a "reader," employed by the workers, entertained them with Spanish-language selections from poetry, books, and newspapers. Entrepreneurs rescued Martinez's handsome building, restored it iron grillwork and oak interiors, an cleaned its red-brick exterior. They hav added restaurants and shops and now ca it **Centro Ybor ❻**, where you can sti

*Recommended Restaurants on pages 290–1*

buy a good cigar or treasures from Tampa attics. You can lunch with businessmen at the rustic Rough Riders restaurant under old photos of Teddy and his men, and you can see *puros* (cigars) made by hand.

Start any visit by touring **Ybor City Museum ⑦** (1818 9th Ave; tel: 813-248-3712; Mon–Sun 9am–5pm; charge). The museum complex includes three restored cigar workers' homes, historic photos, and artifacts of the cigar industry; guided tours of Ybor City are also available. The streetcar travels along **Seventh Avenue** (known as La Setima), the main strip, with shops selling cigars and lacy Spanish fabric. For lunch, sample a "hot, pressed Cuban" (a pork sandwich, not a Latino hunk in a hurry) at **La Tropicana**, considered the best in the city. Don't miss dinner at the landmark **Columbia Restaurant ⑧** on the corner of 22nd Street. The family-run Columbia, built in 1905, is the real deal. Sit back and enjoy the flamenco show, strolling violinists, and the gracious black-jacketed waiters serving classic Spanish dishes like paella and garbanzo bean soup. There are other branches but none as authentic as the original.

## Wild kingdom

Started in 1959 as a family zoo of exotic animals and tropical gardens for visitors to the Anheuser-Busch Brewery, **Busch Gardens ⑨** (Busch Blvd and 40th St; tel: 813-987-5000; open daily; charge) has matured into one of Florida's top three theme parks. It combines the best of everything you'll find in Orlando: a superb Africa-themed conservation zoo, professional concerts and seasonal shows, landscaped grounds, and 10 rides, from super-soaking water rides to state-of-the-art roller coasters, featuring gravity-defying inversions, barrel rolls, and intertwining tracks.

The park's 335 acres (136 hectares) include 10 distinct areas: Morocco, Crown Colony, Edge of Africa, Serengeti Plain, Egypt, Nairobi, Timbuktu, Congo, Stanleyville, and Bird Gardens. Entering through Morocco, get an overview of the whole park by boarding the skyway ride, which begins at Crown Colony in the southeast and ends at Congo in the northwest, or riding the delightful miniature train, which puffs its way slowly around

*The birds in Busch Gardens' aviary are especially friendly.*

**BELOW LEFT:** Ybor City Museum.

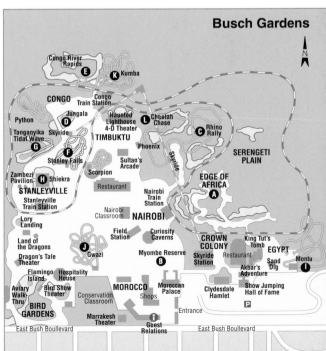

Busch Gardens

**TIP**

One day at Busch Gardens wasn't enough? Inquire about a free or discounted next-day ticket at Guest Relations before you leave the park.

**BELOW:**
hieroglyphics adorn the highly stylized entrance to Montu, one of Busch Gardens' state-of-the-art roller coasters.

the 65-acre (26-hectare) Serengeti Plain on the park's east side, with stops at Nairobi, Congo, and Stanleyville. The southwest corner, the original roadside attraction of tropical gardens, flamingos, snakes, and exotic animals, is more slow-paced. It has toddler rides, bird shows, walk-through aviaries, and pleasant shaded pathways.

Plan your visit to this huge park carefully and pace yourself: there are few shortcuts between attractions, so you'll be on your feet for the better part of the day. A two-day pass lets you dedicate one day to learning about the 2,700 animals that live in naturalized environments in the park and another to rides. If rides are the main draw, and you're short on time, the best strategy is to knock off a few rides in the morning and use the restful animal exhibits for downtime in between. Busch Gardens' rides load very quickly, typically half the time of Orlando parks. Remember, though: African wildlife is more active in the cooler morning hours and sleeps in the afternoon. This can be a problem in a park where enclosures are large and so natural it can be hard to see the animals.

## African safari

The park's hottest tickets for animal lovers are five daily **Serengeti Safaris** (limit 20 people, first-come, first-served) that start at Crown Colony and truck out onto Serengeti Plain to view rhinos and zebras and feed giraffes. If you're keen, head there first and sign up for a tour. If it's sold out, the next best thing is the **Edge of Africa** ❶ exhibit, which features nose-to-nose encounters with baboons, Nile crocs, hippos, a lion and lioness, hyenas, vultures, and meerkats. Rangers holding "animal ambassadors," such as monkeys and snakes, stroll the park. They are trained wildlife biologists, and you'll learn a lot from them. Brass plaques have wildlife conservation messages that can be rubbed and collected in a free wildlife guide. Other displays mimic a biologist's field diary. Some of the best can be found in the entrancing **Myombe Reserve** ❷ gorilla exhibit in Nairobi, one of the most satisfying of Busch's animal exhibits.

## Wild ride

It may seem odd to have "rides" in a wildlife park, but in the race for tourist dollars, Busch Gardens is determined to

keep up with frontrunners like Disney and SeaWorld. Hot on the heels of Disney's Animal Kingdom, **Rhino Rally ⓒ**, a simulated Jeep ride, premiered at Busch in 2001. **Jungala ⓓ**, a new attraction in the revitalized Congo, has a zipline experience, a climbing area, a jungle village, and Bengal tigers, orangutans, and other residents of the former Claw Island. Congo also has the popular **Congo River Rapids ⓔ**, which simulates a white-water ride, while next door, in Stanleyville, two other water rides – the **Stanley Falls ⓕ** flume ride and **Tanganyika Tidal Wave ⓖ** chute – guarantee a good drenching.

But it is for its roller coasters that Busch Gardens leads the pack. The latest, **Shiekra ⓗ**, North America's first dive coaster, is a floorless monster that climbs 200ft (60 meters) up, then rockets 90 degrees down in a simultaneous loop and roll. **Montu ⓘ**, one of the tallest and longest inverted roller coasters in the world, reaches a G-force of 3.85 at 60mph (100kmh). The deafening clatter of **Gwazi ⓙ**, an old-fashioned double wooden coaster that is the Southeast's fastest and largest, is half the reason this ride seems so scary. Terrifying **Kumba ⓚ** spirals 360 degrees through one of the world's largest vertical loops. A height limit on the big rides prevents young kids from boarding. For them, there's **Cheetah Chase ⓛ**, a five-story "wild mouse" style coaster. With a top speed of 22mph (35kmh), it's a perfect first coaster ride.

## Wet and wild

After a steamy day in the jungle, refresh yourself in the body flumes, lagoons, and waterfalls of adjoining **Adventure Island** (10001 McKinley Dr; tel: 813-987-5600; open seasonally; charge). A combo ticket allows you to visit both parks. Another of Tampa's top attractions – the **Museum of Science and Industry ⓾** (4801 E. Fowler Ave; tel: 813-987-6000; daily 9am–5pm; charge) – is also nearby. MOSI contains a vast array of lively science exhibits, a butterfly pavilion, Florida's first IMAX cinema, and

hands-on contraptions that allow you to learn how your body works. One of the most popular attractions is Gulf Coast Hurricane, a re-created 75-mph (120-kmh) wind tunnel that pitches you into the eye of a storm.

It's not all man-made hoopla. **Hillsborough River State Park ⓫** (daily 8am–sunset; charge), 15 miles (24km) from downtown, has a large campground and hiking trails and is a prime spot for canoeing. **Lowry Park Zoo ⓬** (7350 N. Blvd; daily 9.30am–5pm; charge), just before Busch Gardens, has been named the top family-friendly zoo in the US. It has wooden walkways that wind through 56 acres (23 hectares) and seven exhibit areas, including Asian Gardens and Primate World, a petting park, and a free-flight aviary. One highlight is the manatee hospital, where you can watch recuperating manatees swimming from above and below. Interestingly, Lowry Park Zoo started as a mini-zoo of raccoons, alligators, exotic birds, and other indigenous animals next to Henry Plant's Tampa Bay Hotel in the 1930s. After outgrowing Plant Park, it was moved to Lowry Park in 1959. ❑

**TIP**

Canoe Escape (tel: (813-986-2067) organizes a variety of canoe trips through Hillsborough River State Park. Call for reservations.

**BELOW:** the so-called Mystic Sheiks of Morocco march through the Zagora Cafe.

# RESTAURANTS

## Ashley Street Grille
200 N. Ashley Dr
Tel: 813-226-4400
B, L & D daily
Turning out original takes on American classics, this quiet riverside restaurant allows fine ingredients to shine, using only the best seafood, heirloom vegetables, fine cheese, and a subtle, sure hand in the kitchen. It has tasting menus in addition to the standard tariff. Home-baked breads are particularly good, as are other bakery items. $$$

## Bean There Traveler's Coffee House
3203 Bay-to-Bay Blvd
Tel: 813-837-7022
B & L daily
A great place to know about if you're traveling between Tampa and St Petersburg, this South Tampa coffee shop serves all-day breakfast, strong coffee, and sandwiches. It's on the right side of the road, just past McDill Avenue. $

## Bern's Steak House
1208 S. Howard Ave
Tel: 813-251-2421
D daily
The baroque decor has been likened to that of a funeral parlor, but the selection of beef and wines is what brings people to award-winning Bern's, one of Tampa's most famous restaurants. The menu gives the vital statistics of every cut of meat, up to a 60-ounce (2-kg) sirloin that serves six. But vegetarians and pescatarians are well covered, too, with organic veggies pulled from the restaurant's own garden and a tank of live fish. Over one-half million bottles of wine, representing some 6,000 varieties, fill the cellars – thought to be the largest on-hand stock of wines kept by any restaurant in the world. $$$$

## Byblos Café
2832 S. MacDill Ave
Tel: 813-805-7977
L & D Mon–Sat
Authentic Lebanese food, including baba ghanoush, hummus, and tabouleh, anchor the menu of this family-owned Mediterranean cafe, named for a city in ancient Phoenicia. An adjoining market will sell you the fixings to make it yourself at home. $$–$$$

## Caffe Paradiso
4205 S. Macdill Ave
Tel: 813-835-6622
D Mon-Sat
Italian classics win raves from native-born diners at this family-run storefront café. Try the delectable salmon-stuffed ravioli or the tender osso buco alla Milanese – just like your mamma used to make. $$$

## Cephas
1701 E. 4th Ave
Tel: 813-247-9022
L & D Mon–Sat
Jerk chicken and curried goat are on the menu at this sweet little West Indian restaurant run by Jamaica-born Cephas Gilbert. Portions are huge, cheap, and cheerful. $

## City's Gourmet Deli
514 Tampa St
Tel: 813-229-7400
B & L Mon-Fri
They roast their own meats and use European chocolate in their brownies at this upmarket deli. Soups, salads, and sandwiches are all homemade. $

## Columbia Restaurant
2117 E. 7th Ave
Tel: 813-248-4961
L & D daily
Founded in 1905 as a corner café by Cuban immigrant Casimiro Hernandez, Sr, the block-long Columbia Restaurant in Ybor City is the oldest continuously operated restaurant in Florida and is still family owned. A perennial award winner for its Iberian meat and seafood cuisine, as well as its extensive wine list, this landmark eatery features an old-fashioned cigar bar, two floors of majolica-tiled dining rooms, and excellent nightly flamenco dinner shows. Signature dishes,

**LEFT:** Columbia Restaurant specializes in Spanish and Cuban fare. **OPPOSITE:** a sidewalk café in Ybor City.

served by elegant waiters of the old school, include the house "1905" salad, tossed at your table; paella; Cuban black bean soup; shrimp *al ajillo*; red snapper Alicante; pompano *en papillote*; and the famous Cuban shredded beef dish, *ropa vieja*. There are sister branches in Celebration, Sarasota, Clearwater, St Augustine, and on the pier at St Petersburg. $$$

### Dish
1600 E. 8th Ave
Tel: 813-241-8300
L & D daily
The other not-to-be-missed Ybor City restaurant, Dish is located in Centro Ybor and offers grilling stations throughout the restaurant where you can make up your own plate. A hugely popular place. $$

### Jackson's Bistro-Bar-Sushi
601 S. Harbour Island Blvd
Tel: 813-277-0112
L & D daily, Sun Br
The bustling downtown waterfront location is the big draw at this restaurant, which covers all the bases, offering sushi, bistro classics, and an extensive wine list. It can get busy when there are conventions in town. $$$

### Mise en Place
442 W. Kennedy Blvd
Tel: 813-254-5373
D Tue–Sat
A leading proponent of Floribbean cuisine, a fusion of fresh Florida seafood and Caribbean spices, this longtime chef-owned restaurant pleases both foodies and the style-conscious without being too full of itself or overdressed. The eclectic dishes include such heavy hitters as mustard pecan-encrusted rack of lamb with bour-

bon shallot demi-glace and creole grilled salmon with crawfish and southern fixins' like collard greens. There's a full-blast tasting menu for the adventurous. $$$–$$$$

### Oystercatchers
2900 Bayport Dr
Tel: 813-874-1234
L & D daily, Sun Br
Fresh, line-caught, wild seafood, simply prepared on the grill, and organic produce highlight the menu of this Italian restaurant in the Grand Hyatt Tampa Bay hotel, which is also rated one of the best places in Tampa for Sunday brunch. Newly remodeled in soothing pale woods, stone, and light tones, the restaurant is very relaxing, allowing signature dishes like fresh crab cakes to shine. Adjoining Armani's offers a fine-dining atmosphere for evening dinner. Both restaurants are overseen by Tampa-born chef de cuisine Kenny Hunsberger, seen on the PBS program *Great Chefs of the South*. $$$$

### Pelagia Trattoria
4200 Jim Walter Blvd
Tel: 813-313-3235
B, L & D daily
New Mediterranean cuisine, as envisioned by a talented Turin-born chef, makes this casual bistro a winner for breakfast, lunch, or dinner. Even the most health-conscious diner will be delighted by the creative menu, which has many starred low-carb, low-cholesterol, and other interesting options. Try Mediterranean salad with warm pancetta and feta and roasted salmon with balsamic-green apple sauce and broccoli rabe in sweet garlic. Finish with golden delicious apple tart, rosemary-

almond cream, and caramel sauce for a decadent treat. Everything is made from scratch daily and receives Chef Fabrizio's creative touch. $$$–$$$$

### Restaurant BT
1633 W. Snow Ave
Tel: 813-258-1916
L & D Mon–Sat
In the mood for something different? This Vietnamese restaurant offers the fresh herb-sparked flavors of French-inspired Asian food with many personal touches. $$$

### Seven 17 South
717 S. Howard Ave
Tel: 813-250-1661
L Mon–Fri, D Mon–Sat
Italian and Pacific Rim influences highlight the award-winning menu at this old tavern, where you'll encounter such interesting dishes as sake-infused catch of the day and crab wontons. $$$–$$$$

### Side Berns
2208 W. Morrison Ave
Tel: 813-258-2233
D Mon–Sat
The sassy younger sibling of Bern's has achieved its well-deserved awards with a quite different take on cuisine from its famous parent. The fusion food runs heavily toward spiced seafood dishes and exotic game meats like ostrich. Desserts are works of art. $$$$

### Vizcaya Restaurante and Tapas Bar
10905 N. Dale Mabry Hwy
Tel: 813-968-7400
L & D Mon–Sat
Superb tapas win raves from locals at this family-run Basque restaurant. Try the sea bass, paella, and other mini-dishes with some excellent Spanish wine. $$–$$$

### Wine Exchange
1611 W. Swan Ave
Tel: 813-254-9463
L & D daily, Br Sat–Sun
Located in tony Hyde Park, this hip place is all about the wine. Each entrée on the fairly straightforward menu of pizzas, pastas, and sandwiches, supplemented by attractive daily specials such as Dijon-encrusted salmon and grilled Delmonico steak, is paired with individual wine suggestions, by the bottle or glass. Patio dining is lovely. No reservations taken; expect a line. $$$$

### Yacht StarShip
603 Channelside Dr
Tel: 813-223-7999
Br, L & D cruises
This well-reviewed dinner cruise aboard an $8-million yacht plies the waters of beautiful Tampa Bay while you strut in all your finery and enjoy well-executed four-star Continental cuisine, dance to live music, and watch the sunset. A 25 percent locals discount is a big draw. $$$–$$$$

Recommended Restaurants on pages 302–3

# ST PETERSBURG TO CEDAR KEY

Having shed its reputation as a retirement haven, this city by the bay – home of the Dalí Museum and other cultural attractions – is a gateway to gorgeous beaches, unspoiled fishing villages, and crystal clear rivers where manatees swim

**W**hat makes the perfect beach? Florida geologist Dr Stephen Leatherman, aka Dr Beach, thinks he knows. Using criteria such as sand softness, number and size of waves, color and condition of water, presence of wildlife and pests, and human use and impacts, Leatherman annually scrutinizes 650 US beaches before announcing his Top Ten.

Leading contenders every year are the white-sand beaches edging the barrier islands, or "keys," that buffer the Gulf of Mexico side of **St Petersburg** and the **Pinellas Peninsula**. In 2005, **Fort De Soto Park ❶**, a huge county park, campground, and boat launch encompassing five barrier islands at the southern tip of the peninsula, was ranked America's Best Beach. In 2006, **Caladesi Island State Park ❷**, a boat-in-only beach on an island north of Clearwater, took second place. **Clearwater Beach ❸**, popular with overseas visitors, is perennial winner of top City Beach in the Gulf region.

Thousands of lodgings, from historic hotel resorts to vacation condos, along with neighborhood restaurants serving fresh grouper, stoneclaw crab, and other local seafood, crowd the seafront the length of Gulf Boulevard, the main thoroughfare linking beaches. Each beach community is joined to the "mainland" by a causeway that crosses the tranquil Intracoastal Waterway between the mainland and the barrier islands. From here, you're just minutes from US 19, which links the 26 communities of the Pinellas Peninsula, and Interstate 275, linking Tampa and Sarasota via Tampa Bay bridges.

## Gulf shore

With record sunshine and turquoise waters lapping 35 miles (56km) of shoreline, the gulf is mesmerizing. Walk for miles on these super-clean beaches, swim or kayak in shallow gulf waters, go fishing and scuba diving, watch seabirds and other wildlife, take boat tours to undeveloped island refuges, or just soak up the sun. **Long Key**, at the south end, boasts **St Pete Beach ❹**,

---

**Main attractions**

FORT DE SOTO PARK
CALADESI ISLAND STATE PARK
ST PETE BEACH
CLEARWATER AQUARIUM
SUNCOAST SEABIRD
  SANCTUARY
MUSEUM OF FINE ARTS
SALVADOR DALÍ MUSEUM
FLORIDA HOLOCAUST MUSEUM
WEEKI WACHEE SPRING
CRYSTAL RIVER
CEDAR KEY

**LEFT:** Don CeSar Beach Resort.
**BELOW:** Clearwater canine.

*A pedicab trawls for passengers on the Clearwater beachfront.*

home to the bright pink historic Don CeSar Resort, and **Passe-a-Grill Beach**, with its low-rise historic district and quaint shops. On the quieter north end, the busy beachfront at **Clearwater Beach ❺** has kid-flavored distractions, including Captain Memo's Pirate Cruise (25 Causeway Blvd, Dock 3; tel: 727-446-2587; open daily), a two-hour cruise where parents relax while kids do activities.

Nestled in a residential waterfront neighborhood is **Clearwater Marine Aquarium** (249 Windward Passage; tel: 727-447-0980, www.cmaquarium.org; Mon–Fri 9am–5pm, Sat 9am–4pm, Sun 11am–4pm; charge) quietly carries out award-winning work as a marine rescue and release center. Enclosures hold recuperating sea turtles, otters, dolphins, and other sealife, all injured or otherwise impacted by human carelessness. CMA's star attraction is Winter, a bottlenose dolphin who lost her tail to a crab trap and, while waiting for a prosthetic tail to be fitted, is learning to swim sideways. There are regular enrichment exercises with dolphins in the main pool and reserved times to feed a dolphin and have your photo taken (additional fee; visitors provide the camera). Multimedia presentations about CMA's work take place in an attractive circular theater.

Not far away, in **Indian Shores ❻**, is another important animal hospital that deserves your support. **Suncoast Seabird Sanctuary** (18328 Gulf Blvd; tel: 727-391-6211; open daily; free) was founded by bird-lover Ralph Heath. Donations allow Heath to care for 500-plus injured and crippled cormorants, pelicans, sandpipers, white herons, and other seabirds.

Several miles inland, **Pinewood Cultural Park ❼** (Walsingham Rd and 125th St North, Largo), encompasses a trio of worthy attractions: the **Florida Botanical Gardens** (tel: 727-582-2100; daily 7am–7pm), with 120 acres of theme gardens and natural areas; the **Gulf Coast Museum of Art** (tel: 727-518-6833; Tue–Sat 10am–4pm, Sun noon–4pm), which shows contemporary art and fine craft objects by Southeastern artists; and **Heritage Village** (tel: 727-582-2123; Tue–Sat 10am–4pm, Sun 1pm–4pm), a living-history compound with two dozen vintage structures from the 1850s to the early 1900s.

## St Petersburg

**St Petersburg ❽** is beginning to overcome its reputation as a retirement haven (fostered by the movie *Cocoon*, filmed at the St Petersburg Shuffleboard Hall of Fame). A regenerated waterfront, top museums, a major-league baseball team, year-round festivals, and activities geared to an outdoor lifestyle are attracting a younger demographic. Shuffleboard is even becoming hip, thanks to in

part, to a popular free St Pete Shuffle every Friday night at the historic courts.

Tampa Bay was originally home to the Tocobaga, Timucua, and Manasota cultures. Villages, dugout canoes, and shell mounds have been excavated at **Weedon Island Preserve Cultural and Natural History Center 9** (1800 Weedon Island Dr; tel: 727-453-6500, www.weedonisland-center.org; Wed–Sun 10am–4pm; charge), a natural area of marshes and backwaters crisscrossed by hiking trails on the Pinellas Peninsula side of Tampa Bay. Spanish explorers Panfilo de Narvaez in 1528, followed by Hernando de Soto in 1539, named the peninsula Punta Pinal, or "Point of Pines," later Pinellas. De Soto found the only mineral springs on the peninsula near a large Tocobaga village in Safety Harbor.

European diseases wiped out 98 percent of Florida's native people by 1700. They were replaced by Creek Indians, dubbed Seminoles, who settled Florida, displacing black slaves who had sought sanctuary from brutal plantations in the South. The US government waged three Seminole Wars to remove the Seminoles and bring in white settlers, building forts throughout Florida that today have become towns and cities.

In 1875, 1,600 acres (650 hectares) of what would eventually become St Petersburg, were purchased and settled by General John Williams of Detroit. Williams made a deal with exiled Russian nobleman Peter Demens to bring the railroad to Pinellas Peninsula. Demens overcame yellow fever and flooding to expand a short logging track on the peninsula into Henry Plant's Orange Belt Line, joining the gulf with citrus groves in Sanford in central Florida. The port prospered until the disastrous citrus freeze of 1894-5, when Plant bought the branch railroad for a song. In 1914, St Petersburg again made transportation history when Tony Jannus piloted a flying airboat called the *Benoist* 21 miles (34 km) over Tampa Bay, the world's first commercial flight.

*A wildlife rehabilitator at the Suncoast Seabird Sanctuary introduces visitors to one of her patients – a double-crested cormorant.*

## Art and history

Folksy **St Petersburg Museum of History A** (335 2nd Ave NE; tel: 727-894-1052, www.stpetemuseumofhistory.org; Tue–Sat 10am–5pm, Sun 1pm–5pm; charge), at the foot of the commercial pier complex, has exhibits on local his-

**BELOW:** Fort De Soto Park is often ranked as one of America's best beaches.

*Salvador Dalí's Nature Morte Vivante is on display at the Dalí Museum in St Petersburg.*

**BELOW:**
the Arts Center.

Beach Dr NE; tel: 727-96-2667, www.fine-arts.org; Tue–Sat 10am–5pm, Sun 1pm–5pm; charge). Founded by Margaret Acheson Stuart to house her private art collection, the museum has the atmosphere of a stately home showcasing family treasures, from masterpieces by Berthe Morisot, Claude Monet, Paul Cezanne, and other French Impressionists to pre-Columbian pottery and sacred Asian art. The new Hazel Hough Wing, scheduled to open in 2008, doubles the size of this popular museum. Also new in 2008 is the country's largest collection of glassworks by modern master Dale Chihuly at the nearby **Arts Center** ❶ (719 Central Ave; tel: 727-822-7872, www.theartscenter.org; Tue–Sat 10am–5pm). Artists can rent studio space and display their works in this complex, one of the largest glassblowing facilities in the Southeast.

tory, including a Tocobaga dugout canoe and a full-scale replica of the *Benoist* airboat. The story of St Petersburg's historic African-American community is well told here and at the **Dr Carter G. Woodson Museum of African American History** ❷ (2240 9th Ave South; tel: 727-323-1104, www.woodsonmuseum.org; Mon, Wed and Fri 11am–2pm daily; free).

One block west of Straub Park is the elegant **Museum of Fine Arts** ❸ (255

By far the most famous cultural attraction here is the **Salvador Dalí Museum** ❺ (1000 3rd St South; tel: 727-823-3767, www.salvadordalimuseum.org; Mon–Wed 9.30am–5.30pm, Thu 9.30am–8pm, Fri 9.30am–6.30pm, Sat 9.30am–5.30pm, Sun noon–5.30pm; charge), a world-class institution that seems oddly out of place

in this sun-loving vacationland. The gift of the Morse family – personal friends of Salvador and Gala Dalí – the collection features 1,300 diverse works. The core of the collection is six enormous commissioned masterworks by the surreal artist, but the early Dalí landscapes of Spain, filled with lush Impressionist influences, are unexpectedly charming. Docent tours of the museum are highly recommended to understand the complex psychological references buried in Dalí's paintings. The gift shop is a must for Dalí fans. It even sells dripping clocks!

Two other museums round out the cultural offerings. **Florida International Museum ⑤** (244 Second Ave North; tel: 727-822-3693, www.floridamuseum.org; Mon–Sat 10am–5pm, Sun noon–5pm; charge) is affiliated with the Smithsonian and stages traveling exhibitions that attract thousands of visitors. Past topics have included Princess Diana and the Treasures of the Tsars. The Kennedy Gallery, a permanent exhibit, includes re-creations of the West Wing and Oval Office and more than 600 personal items once owned by the Kennedy family.

More somber is the **Florida Holo-** caust Museum ⑥ (55 5th St South; tel: 727-820-0100, www.flholocaustmuseum.org; Mon–Sun 10am–5pm; charge), third largest in the country. Florida was the first state in the nation to mandate Holocaust education in schools. This museum's central exhibit is a railroad car used to transport Jews to concentration camps.

## Dunedin

The historic communities of Pinellas Peninsula are just a short drive away. Or, if you're feeling ambitious, you can bike, rollerblade, jog, or hike the popular

*A docent demonstrates old-fashioned kitchen utensils at Heritage Village in Pinewood Cultural Park.*

**BELOW LEFT:** a Roman statue of Aphrodite at the Museum of Fine Arts. **BELOW:** Mirror Lake Park.

## The St Pete Shuffle

Shuffleboard is popular in Florida, where shuffleboard courts are found at many vintage motels. Players use cues to push weighted pucks down a narrow elongated court, with the aim of positioning them in a marked scoring area. The game, reputedly invented in England and played at the court of Henry VIII, is related to bowling, croquet, billiards, and shove ha'penny, a table-top pub version using coins. Organized in 1924, the

**Historic Mirror Lake Shuffleboard Complex** (559 Mirror Lake Dr North; tel: 727-822-2083) in downtown St Petersburg gained fame as the world's largest shuffleboard club in its postwar heyday, with a membership of 5,000 using 110 courts. Today, there are only 65 courts, but the historic shuffleboard complex is still going strong. It has a Shuffleboard Hall of Fame and tournaments, and attracts young families to free special events on Friday nights, dubbed the St Pete Shuffle. Themed events have included a Harry Potter night, an ice-cream social, a fashion show, a Hurricane Katrina fund-raiser, and an India night with yoga, belly-dancers, a street bazaar, and music.

*The collection at the Museum of Fine Arts ranges from Greek and Roman antiquities to 19th- and 20th-century European and American paintings.*

**BELOW:**
Gulf Coast sunset.

**Pinellas Trail**, a paved north-south urban trail on the former railroad tracks that starts in St Petersburg and ends 37 miles (60 km) away in the Greek fishing community of Tarpon Springs.

North of Clearwater, on US 19, **Dunedin ⑩**, famous for its March Celtic Festival, owes its name to Scottish merchants who arrived with the railroad in 1889. This pretty waterfront town is a great place to stroll or bicycle and visit unique boutiques and homespun galleries. Time your visit to coincide with the Friday morning **Green Market** and mingle with residents buying fruits and vegetables, homemade bread, Caribbean foods, organic coffee, local honey, organic salsa, cheese, and other goodies. These make great gifts or picnic fixings if you decide to head over the causeway to **Honeymoon Island State Park ⑪** (1 Causeway Blvd; tel: 727-469-5942; daily 8am–sunset; charge), where rustic cabins

became popular among honeymooners in the 1940s. Tiny **Dunedin Museum of History** (349 Main St; tel: 727-736-1176; Tue–Sat 10am–4pm; charge), in the former railroad station, offers historic walking tours and an exhibit of souvenirs from couples who vacationed on Honeymoon Island. To fulfill your own desert-island fantasies, hop aboard a ferry from Honeymoon Island, the only way to reach **Caladesi Island State Park** (tel: 727-460-5942; open daily 8am–sunset; charge).

## Tarpon Springs

Celtic influences give way to Greek ones in **Tarpon Springs ⑫**, which sprang up on the banks of the Anclote River with the railroad. Key West "Conchs" cornered the sponge business in the late 1800s, but around 1900, with Key West's sponge beds dwindling, businessman John Corcoris summoned family and friends from the Aegean Islands to test the beds around Tarpon Springs. They found them rich in sponges, including grade A "wool" types and decorative "finger sponges." Corcoris pioneered the use of copper-helmeted diving suits for sponging in deeper waters, replacing the

## The Sunken Gardens

Plumber George Turner, Sr, an avid gardener, created the 6-acre (2-hectare) **Sunken Gardens** (1825 4th Street North; tel: 727-551-3102) in St Petersburg in 1903 by draining a lake and using the resulting fertile muck as the foundation for waterfalls, lush tropical plantings, and hundreds of vibrant plants lining tranquil walkways. The gardens became so popular that Turner began charging admission. Three generations tended the gardens before they were sold in 1999 to the City of St Petersburg, which now offers daily admission, horticultural workshops, and a wedding venue. The children's science museum Great Explorations occupies the restored 1926 Mediterranean Revival building next door, making this a popular family destination.

*Recommended Restaurants on pages 302–3*

old-time "hookers" who rowed out to shallow waters, locating sponges by looking through a glass-bottomed bucket and "hooking" them with a hooked rod. Weighing up to 200 pounds (90 kg), diving suits were frequently death traps for the young Greeks who wore them, as they dived deeper and suffered the fatal effects of nitrous-oxide build-up, commonly known as the bends.

The multimillion-dollar sponge business began to ebb in the 1940s, when red tide disease killed off the sponges. The introduction of inexpensive, synthetic sponges virtually shut down the industry. Nowadays, the sponge market has faded, but the epic story of Tarpon Springs' sponge divers lives on, kept alive by community pride, business know-how, and tourists eager to experience something real amid Florida's artifice.

In Tarpon Springs, you'll hear Greek spoken everywhere, see knots of older men passing the time on street corners, and enjoy moussaka, kebabs, baklava, and other Greek delicacies in family-run, Mediterranean–tiled cafés like **Mykonos** and **Hella's**. Tourism is concentrated along the sponge docks on white-washed

**Dodecanese Boulevard**, now sadly devoid of its piles of sponges and savvy buyers. Nearby are warehouses where sponges are still washed, dried, hand-trimmed, and sold to luxury bath stores and home improvement centers for use in faux paint effects.

## Sponge divers

Numerous cruises to beaches on Anclote Key depart from the docks, but only a few old-time spongers like George Billiris of **St Nicholas Boat Lines** (tel: 727-942-6425) still demonstrate sponge-diving on a real sponge boat. The 1907 **Sponge Exchange** is now a shopping arcade, where you can buy sponges in cool, dark shops smelling of the ocean. Tarpon's history is told on a plaque outside the Exchange and at **Spongearama** (tel: 727-942-3771; charge), which has items and photos from earlier sponging days. On the dock is a statue of a sponge diver – a heroic, Adonis-like figure gazing back to a glorious past, helmet in hand.

Greek youths in Tarpon still have their rites of passage. On the Feast of Epiphany in January, the Greek Orthodox archbishop blesses local waters and

*A sponge diver in Tarpon Springs shows off an old-fashioned deep-water diving suit.*

**BELOW:** though the sponge industry has declined since its heyday in the early 1900s, some sponges are still processed in Tarpon Springs and sold as luxury items.

*A Cedar Key gallery features the work of local artists.*

tosses a crucifix into **Spring Bayou**. Boys aged 16 to 18 dive into the chilly waters to retrieve it and earn extra blessings for themselves and their families. A white dove, symbolizing the Holy Spirit, is released to begin a glendi, or festival, with Greek food, music, and dance. **St Nicholas Greek Orthodox Cathedral** (36 N. Pinellas Ave), built in 1943 in downtown Tarpon, is a replica of St Sofia Cathedral in Constantinople. Its neo-Byzantine walls are full of icons. One – a statue of the Blessed Mother – is said to shed tears.

## Mermaids and manatees

North of Tarpon Springs is another remnant of a glorious past: the 1940s roadside attraction known as **Weeki Wachee Spring** ⓭ (US 19/SR 50; tel: 352-596-2062; www.weekiwachee.com; daily in summer 10am–4pm, limited hours in other seasons; charge). Named by Indians for the "winding waters" of its snaking river, Weeki Wachee had waters so clear that Navy frogman Newton Perry used them to stage underwater shows. He taught young women the technique of breathing through hoses so they could remain far below the surface for long periods of time.

Then he dressed them in mermaid costumes, and a famous attraction was born. The Weeki Wachee mermaids perform strenuous acrobatics about 16ft (5 meters) underwater, which visitors watch through plate-glass windows. The park offers a river cruise past a rainforest (where sprinklers provide the precipitation) and a pelican orphanage for recovering patients from the Suncoast Seabird Sanctuary.

When old-time sailors first encountered the gentle manatees that congregate at Florida's crystalline springs in winter, they mistook them for real-life mermaids. On closer inspection, these slow-moving, torpedo-shaped "sea cows" proved whiskery and a tad rotund but just as entrancing. You're guaranteed a sighting of manatees at **Homosassa Springs State Wildlife Park** ⓮ (4150 S. Suncoast Blvd; tel: 352-628-5343, www.homosassasprings.org; daily 9am–5.30pm; charge), just west of US 19, which has an underwater viewing point as well as a boardwalk area where resident manatees gather for a carrot from a ranger. You can swim with manatees at **Crystal River National Wildlife Refuge** (SE Kings Bay Dr; tel: 352-563-2088, www.fws.gov/crystalriver; open daily; charge)

*Recommended Restaurants on pages 302–3*

in nearby Crystal River, where 100-plus springs feed into King's Bay. **Crystal River State Archaeological Site ⓑ** (3400 N. Museum Point; tel: 352-795-3817, www.crystalriverstateparks.org; daily 8am–sunset; charge) preserves a huge ceremonial ground used by Indians 2,000 years ago. An on-site museum displays artifacts.

## Cedar Key

A 25-mile (40-km) drive on SR 24 crosses several bridges to reach the quiet fishing resort of **Cedar Key ⓰**. During and after the Civil War, the five islands that made up Cedar Keys formed the largest port city in the state, linked to Fernandina by Florida's first major railroad, the work of politicians Augustus Steele and David Levy Yulee. Cedar Key's main industry was the manufacture of pencils from local cedar trees. Denied investment in Cedar Key's prosperity, Henry Plant built a rival railroad to Tampa in 1884, which, along with a devastating hurricane in 1896, led to Cedar Key's decline. Railroad service continued until 1932, and a type of whisk brush made from palm fiber was manufactured in a large Cedar Key factory in 1910 by its inventor, a dentist named Dr Andrews.

Cedar Key is now known for bird rookeries on surrounding **Cedar Keys National Wildlife Refuge** (SR 24; tel: 352-493-0238, www.fws.gov/cedarkeys; charge) and as a weekend getaway for seafood lovers. **Cedar Key State Museum Park** (12231 SW 166th Court; tel: 352-543-5350; Thu–Mon 1pm–4pm; charge) documents the port's short-lived prominence and displays an incredible collection of seashells. **Cedar Key Historical Society Museum** (7070 D St; tel: 352-543-5549, www.cedarkeymuseum.org; Sun–Fri 1pm–4pm, Sat 11am–5pm; charge) displays historical artifacts from the town, including the original heart-cedar Andrews Home and fiber brush factory. There is an exhibit on famed naturalist John Muir, who recuperated in Cedar Key in 1867, at the end of a 1,000-mile (1,600-km) walk from Wisconsin.

Unique art galleries and boutiques occupy historic buildings on 2nd Street.

Some are slated to be converted into a spa and wellness resort. Cedar Key's oldest and most famous building is the 1859 **Island Hotel** (372 2nd St; tel: 352-543-5111), a moody hostelry that has suitably creaky floorboards and is rumored to be haunted. The Neptune Bar is a popular watering hole. The restaurant is known for its fine continental dining, including palm salad, a unique starter invented by a former owner that improbably mixes fresh hearts of palm with a nutty ice cream topping.

Local oysters, clams, and stoneclaw crabs are reliably good in Cedar Key. With the 1995 ban on gill nets, fishermen began hatching clams and oysters in the shallow gulf waters around the salt marshes aided by specialists from the University of Florida in Gainesville. **Southern Cross Sea Farms** (12170 SR 24; tel: 352-543-5980) offers daily tours of a clam hatchery. The **Cedar Key Seafood Festival** brings thousands of seafood lovers to Cedar Key each October. Book ahead. ❏

*The historic Island Hotel has been feeding hungry visitors to remote Cedar Key for more than a century.*

**BELOW:** in many parts of the Cedar Keys, boats are more common than cars.

# RESTAURANTS

## Restaurants

Prices for a three-course dinner per person, excluding tax, tip, and beverages:

**$** = under $20
**$$** = $20–45
**$$$** = $45–60
**$$$$** = over $60

## Cedar Key

### Blue Desert Café
12815 SR 24
Tel: 352-543-9111
D Tue–Sat
This funky little restaurant is near the bridge over the estuary into Cedar Key. There's no fried food here, and the wait can be long for the fresh Southwest and Mediterranean fare. Popular dishes include Greek pizzas, Italian calzones, Mexican burritos, and fresh local crab. Well worth the wait. $

### Island Hotel Restaurant
224 2nd St at B St
Tel: 352-543-5111
B, L & D daily
The best fine dining in Cedar Key is at a pleasant corner restaurant in the gracious Island Hotel. Expect rich Continental cuisine, emphasizing fresh seafood done every which way but plain. Starters include the famous palm salad (combining hearts of palm, ice cream, and pistachio nuts), which was invented here. Breakfast and lunch are available, as well as dining in the tiny Neptune Bar. $$–$$$

## Dunedin

### Black Pearl of Dunedin
315 Main St
Tel: 727-734-3463
D Mon–Sat
For a fancy night out in

Dunedin, this upscale New American restaurant is hard to beat. Elegant dishes like New Zealand rack of lamb, Maryland crab imperial, Long Island duck, and baked Florida oysters with spinach, pancetta, and Pernod are highlights. $$$

### Casa Tina
369 Main Street
Tel: 727-734-9226
L & D Mon–Sat
Here's something you don't find every day – a Mexican restaurant emphasizing healthy and authentic cuisine. But that's what this brilliant cantina in downtown Dunedin is all about. It wins raves from diners as far away as St Petersburg and Tampa. Recipes are authentic and made fresh daily. Sample a wide array of traditional moles, salsas, poblanos, and burritos, and South of the Border hits like *pescado a la Veracruzana*, using the catch of the day. $–$$

### Walt's Seasonal Cuisine
1140 Main St
Tel: 727-733-1909
L & D Tue–Sat
There's lots of buzz over this unpretentious new bistro. Chef Walt, a Dunedin native with Cordon Bleu training, plans his menu around what's fresh, local, and seasonal each day. Look for pompano, grouper, sea scallops, and a surf and turf with crab cakes at dinner. Light and tasty

items such as seafood chowder, poached shrimp and mango salad, and seared ahi tuna are available at weekday lunch for under $10 each. $–$$$

## Homosassa Springs

### Riverside Crab House
5297 S. Cherokee Way
Tel: 352-621-5080
L & D daily
The river views at this restaurant adjoining the Riverside Resort in Homosassa Springs are just lovely. The food is typical: lots of grouper, shrimp, and crab. $$

## Clearwater Beach

### Bob Heilman's Beachcomber
447 Mandalay Ave
Tel: 727-442-4144
L & D daily
For 60 years, this landmark restaurant has served reliable all-American favorites like dry-aged prime rib and steaks, fried chicken, and surf and turf. There's even fried chicken livers! Soups, salads, sandwiches, and burgers are on the lunch menu. $–$$$

### Caretta on the Gulf
500 Mandalay Ave
Tel: 727-441-2425
L & D daily
High-end, beachfront dining at the Sandpearl Resort features haute cuisine with Latin American and Caribbean influences, plus a sushi bar, wood-burning oven, and extensive wine list. $$$–$$$$

**LEFT:** a tasty snapper dish at Caretta on the Gulf.

### Crabby Bill's

5100 Gulf Blvd
Tel: 727-360-8858
L & D daily

You can wear your sandy flip-flops to this fun, ultra-casual, and very popular seafood shack, which serves the freshest and best-priced grouper, crab, and other seafood from its own boats daily. Seating is family style at picnic tables and booths. There are no reservations, so expect a line, but service is speedy. There's another branch in Indian Rocks Beach. $–$$

### The Hurricane

807 Gulf Way
Tel: 727-360-9558
L & D daily

One of the most durably popular restaurants on the Gulf Coast, with multiple bars, commendable seafood, and the clincher – great sunset views. $–$$

### Bella Brava

515 Central Ave
Tel: 727-895-5515
L & D Mon–Sun

This upmarket Italian-American hot spot is the place to be seen. A new chef and a recently revamped menu now includes locally sourced and organic items. One hit: grilled prosciutto-wrapped Florida grouper on a bed of charred corn kernels, asparagus, and pasta tossed with roasted pepper butter. $$–$$$

### Café Alma

260 1st Ave South
Tel: 727-502-5002
L & D Mon–Sat

Café Alma is the kind of chic, European-style, white-tablecloth eatery that works just as well as an upmarket lunch bistro in the daytime and a casually elegant night-club offering dinner, small plates, and a full bar until the wee hours. The international menu emphasizes healthy Mediterranean cuisine and includes many vegetarian and seasonal items. There's a patio, bar, and nightly DJ. $–$$$

### Central Café and Organic

243 Central Ave
Tel: 727-824-0888
B, L & D Mon–Sat

A local favorite, this downtown all-organic soup-salad-sandwich-dessert place has healthy and inexpensive takeout. Try the chicken salad and "cosmic cookies." $

### Ceviche Tapas Bar

10 Beach Dr
Tel: 727-209-2302
D daily

Spanish-style small plates, or tapas, are the focus here. They're the perfect food to share in this intimate, candlelit setting. Good for a light bite or full mix-and-match meal. $$

### Marchand's Bar and Grill

501 Fifth Ave NE
Tel: 727-894-1000 $$$
L & D Mon–Sat

Specializing in Mediterranean-style seafood, the elegant Marchand's is located in the remodeled historic Renaissance Vinoy Resort overlooking Safety Harbor just north of downtown. Go for the creative antipasto plate and seared dayboat scallops on a bed of saffron couscous accompanied by baby bok choy and shallot truffle marmalade. $$$

### Moon Under Water

332 Beach Dr NE
Tel: 727-896-6160
L & D daily

Hot curry, enough to make you break into a sweat, is the specialty of this waterfront pub serving British-Indian food. On the menu are classics like shepherd's pie, cornish pasty, fish and chips (with traditional malt vinegar), burgers, a variety of lighter Mediterranean-inspired salads and sandwiches, and some very good British ale. There's live music on weekends. A great place for a swift pint and some nosh. $–$$

### Parkshore Grill

300 Beach Dr
Tel: 727-896-9463
L & D daily

The location of this welcoming New American grill, opposite Straub Park in downtown St Petersburg, is unbeatable. And so is the food. The large menu has a selection of steaks, chops, light takes on seafood, and several vegetarian options. Sidewalk dining offers great people watching. $$

### Red Mesa

4912 4th St North
Tel: 727-527-8728
B, L & D Mon–Sat

Classic dishes from Mexico and the Southwest shine here. Look for *Divorciados* at breakfast (two fried eggs with separate sauces, chorizo-potato hash, and chipotle cactus salsa) and wild mushroom quesadillas and Southwest tuna sashimi at lunch and dinner along with elegant specials. *Muy sabroso*! $–$$

### Savannah's Cafe

113 Central Ave
Tel: 727-388-4371
L & D Mon–Sat

This family-run gem does Southern and Caribbean food right and has a loyal following. The menu includes all the jambalaya, fried catfish, plantains, collard greens, and other Creole dishes of your dreams. $–$$

### Roy's

100 1st Ave SW
Tel: 352-498-5000
L & D daily

On the banks of the Steinhatchee estuary, Roy's has been pleasing diners since 1969. Fried food features heavily, including fried chicken, coconut shrimp, and catfish. You'll also find local Apalachicola oysters, soft shell crab, and grouper. A popular Sunday lunchtime place for day-trippers. $$

### Hella's

735 Dodecanese Blvd
Tel: 727-945-7865
L & D daily

Gaily painted Hella's offers dockside dining right across from the historic sponge docks in Tarpon Springs. The family-owned restaurant offers excellent spanakopita, gyros, moussaka, and other Greek delicacies. Save room for heavenly baklava and other honey-drenched sweets baked in the adjoining bakery. $

### Mykonos

628 Dodecanese Blvd
Tel: 727-934-4306
L & D daily

One of the Greek fishing port's most popular restaurants, Mykonos is the real deal. Don't pass up its traditional specialties, including the signature Greek salad loaded with finely chopped parsley and dill as well as kalamata olives, tomatoes, onions, feta, and tangy dressing. $

# BEAUTIFUL BEACHES

**Beaches account for more than 1,300 miles of Florida's Atlantic and Gulf of Mexico coastlines and are among the best in the continental US**

Broad ones, narrow ones, busy ones, quiet ones: beaches in Florida come in all shapes and sizes, and wherever you are in the state you should find one to suit your tastes. Furthermore, even if you are not staying on the coast, the sea is never far away. Sports facilities are often excellent in the resorts, whether you want to muck about playing volleyball or go parasailing.

The Atlantic Coast has the best waves, while the water in the Gulf of Mexico is warmer and calmer and therefore better for children. Many beaches lie on barrier islands, which ring much of the Florida peninsula, and an impressive number are protected as state or federal parks.

### THE BEST OF THE BEST

Florida's beaches, along with those of Hawaii, dominate lists of the top US beaches, which take into account everything from the softness of the sand to ease of access. Many of the best are on the Gulf Coast, where gorgeous sunsets are an added bonus. Everyone has his or her favorite beach, but below is a list of the beaches that are consistently praised. They are suitable for families and chosen from all areas. Even those within protected areas offer facilities.

● **Southeast**: Crandon Park, Bill Baggs, South Beach (Greater Miami); Bahia Honda State Park (Keys).
● **Atlantic Coast**: John Lloyd Beach State Recreation Area (Dania); Anastasia Beach (St Augustine).
● **Gulf Coast**: Caladesi Island State Park (Dunedin); Siesta Beach (Sarasota); Fort de Soto Park (St Petersburg).
● **Panhandle**: St George Island (Apalachicola); St Andrews (Panama City Beach); Grayton Beach; Port St Joe.

**LEFT**: it is the human scenery rather than the quality of the sand and water that makes South Beach so popular. Rollerbladers, models, and men with pumped-up bodies come here to see and be seen.

**ABOVE:** Daytona Beach is one of Florida's busiest and most unpretentious resorts. It is also well-known for its long tradition of auto racing and for allowing motorists to drive on its broad, hard-packed sands.

**LEFT:** Florida's protected beaches will appeal to those in search of a more peaceful and uncrowded experience. Lovely, undeveloped beaches are found in state and federal parks all over Florida, sometimes in close proximity to heavily traveled resorts.

**LEFT:** you can surf all along Florida's Atlantic Coast. You'll find a few posers in Miami, but the stretch from Sebastian to Melbourne is best.

## SAFETY BY THE SEASIDE

Most people will enjoy a completely trouble-free time on the beach, but there are dangers to be aware of.

● Sunburn: this tops the danger list; you should use plenty of sunscreen, wear a broad-brimmed hat, and stay out of the midday sun.

● Sea currents: the waters off Florida are not dangerous as a rule, but you can encounter rough surf and strong currents, particularly along the Atlantic Coast. Most deaths occur when exhausted swimmers drown after trying to swim against a riptide or undertow. Riptides are the cause of 80 percent of lifeguard rescues in the US. If caught in either, do not panic – swim across the current rather than against it.

● Marine life: if you brush against a jellyfish in the water, you will receive only a short-lived sting. But stingrays, which move close to shore in August and September to mate, can deliver a very nasty sting. Seek medical help if the barb stays in the skin.

All popular beaches have lifeguards, who can advise on conditions. There is also a warning system of color-coded flags:

☞ green: good swimming conditions.
☞ yellow: caution.
☞ red: danger from currents, winds or lightning.
☞ blue: hazardous marine life (eg jellyfish).

**ABOVE:** the Panhandle is known for its blindingly white beaches of quartz sand, which has washed down from the Appalachian Mountains over the centuries.

**BELOW:** beaches along Florida's central Atlantic coast are a critical nesting site for sea turtles, which return every year to lay their eggs in the sand.

**LEFT:** tourists started coming to Florida in the late 1800s, but the last thing they wanted to do was get a suntan. It was only after the 1920s that swimming in the sea and sunbathing took off in a big way.

*Recommended Restaurants on pages 320–1*

# SARASOTA TO NAPLES

**Wonders abound on this stretch of the Gulf Coast, ranging from the extravagant winter home of circus magnate John Ringling to the "sugar sand" beaches and abundant bird life on countless barrier islands**

n the late 1800s, the 225-mile (360-km) stretch of coastline between Sara-sota and Naples was a roadless outpost of fishing villages that sprang up along huge estuaries where the Hillsbor-ough, Manatee, Myakka, Peace, and Caloosahatchee rivers meet the Gulf of Mexico and a chain of offshore islands, or keys. The intermingling of coastal waters, nearshore wetlands, subtropical mangrove swamps, and upland island hammock forests created a blessed ecosystem, home to unimaginable numbers of creatures, from wading birds, dolphins, and manatees to black bears, panthers, and other wildlife.

## Changing hands

For millennia, this rich environment had been ruled by the powerful Tocobaga and Calusa cultures. They built cool, open-sided, thatch-roofed, chickee-hut compounds atop shell mounds and fished for shark, redfish, mullet, and pinfish on the coast, and bass, bream, and garfish in the marshy rivers and lakes of the interior. In the 1700s, Seminoles moved onto lands vacated by vanishing Florida tribes. They were harassed by the US government through three wars of attrition in the mid-1800s, leaving just a handful of holdouts in the Everglades by century's end.

Even this impenetrable watery fortress was under siege, as entrepreneurs set their sights on developing southwest Florida. Among the first to arrive was inventor Thomas Edison, who built a home and laboratory in Fort Myers in

1886. Edison beautified Fort Myers by planting palm trees (hence its nickname: City of Palms). His efforts attracted a former employee, the young automaker Henry Ford, who bought the home next door. The families vacationed together, took camping trips into the Everglades, and planted banyan trees, rubber and other exotics for use in tire making and other commercial ventures.

Not far away, in Naples, a streetcar advertising salesman named Barron Gift Collier set his sights even higher. Collier bought 1 million acres (400,000 hectares)

### Main attractions
ANNA MARIA KEY
SOUTH FLORIDA MUSEUM
ST ARMAND'S CIRCLE
MOTE MARINE AQUARIUM
SELBY BOTANICAL GARDENS
MYAKKA RIVER STATE PARK
RINGLING MUSEUM OF ART
EDISON AND FORD WINTER
  ESTATES
SANIBEL AND CAPTIVA ISLANDS
J.N. "DING" DARLING
  NATIONAL WILDLIFE REFUGE
NAPLES
MARCO ISLAND

**LEFT:** Cà d'Zan.
**BELOW:** Sanibel Island sunbather.

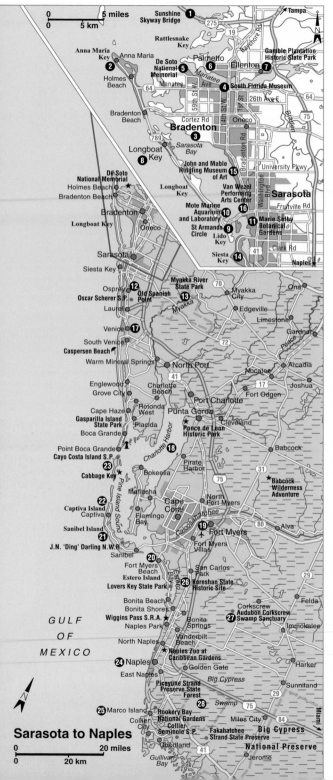

in the western Everglades, anticipating a boom in real estate once canals diverted and controlled Everglades water slowly spreading across the landscape to the nearby Ten Thousand Islands region of the Gulf. Collier's major contribution to the county that bears his name was the construction of US 41, the Tamiami Trail, linking Naples to Miami.

In the drier Sarasota Bay area, development moved more quickly. In 1911, Midwest circus impresario John Ringling purchased 66 acres (27 hectares) on Sarasota Bay as a winter home for his wife Mable and, over the next decades, created a splendid Venetian-style estate, built a bridge to St Armand's Circle, and helped promote Sarasota as a winter destination. Among Ringling's neighbors were wealthy Chicago widow Bertha Potter Palmer, who ranched on 30,000 acres (12,000 hectares) east of her home at Old Spanish Point, and Marie Selby, whose beloved garden estate near downtown Sarasota is now an orchid research center.

## First, relax!

Southwest Florida's natural beauty remains unrivaled in the Southeast. But if you are expecting a desert island atmosphere, you'll be disappointed if you visit between January and May, when lodgings (including Florida's immaculate campgrounds) charge their highest prices of the year and are sold out months in advance; traffic gridlocks the skinny highways; beaches are packed; and major attractions heroically try to cater to the needs of thousands of frazzled visitors, most of them retirees from the North, or "snowbirds."

Consider vacationing here in the shoulder seasons (May–June and October–December), when temperatures are pleasant and things are quiet. You could also stay on one of the islands accessible only by boat or floatplane, such as Cabbage Key or Cayo Costa Island. Boating is the most relaxed way to get an intimate look at this watery region, whether paddling a kayak on an estuary "blue highway" or steering a cabin cruiser on intracoastal waterways.

*Recommended Restaurants on pages 320–1*

## Across the bridge

Drive south on I-275 over Tampa Bay, passing through St Petersburg, and continue south into Manatee County via the **Sunshine Skyway Bridge ❶** ($1 toll). Arching its 4-mile-long (6-km) back like a metal cat – the better to allow large boats under its span – the bridge is impressive and more than a bit scary, with dropaway sides and large center cables. South of the bridge, I-275 joins I-75 and historic Tamiami Trail (US 41). Head west on SR 64 to the relaxed Gulf island of **Anna Maria Key ❷**, an ideal place for weary visitors to decompress before exploring farther afield.

Just beyond **Bradenton ❸**, at the mouth of the Manatee River, lovely Anna Maria Key is one of the least developed Gulf islands. Park the car and ride the free trolley or use a bicycle or scooter to really feel like a local. The gorgeous white-sand beaches of Anna Maria, Holmes, Bradenton, and Coquina line narrow Gulf Drive, which has a good choice of beachfront vacation cottages, condominium resorts, and a popular bed-and-breakfast inn. Fine dining is excellent on this island, but you'll also find seafood

shacks specializing in stone crab and beach cafés serving all-you-can-eat pancakes. Islanders are involved in conservation efforts protecting endangered sea turtles, which crawl ashore nightly from May to October to lay ping-pong-ball-size eggs on the beaches. For information and guided tours of nesting sites, call 941-778-5638 or visit www.islandturtles.com.

Bradenton's **South Florida Museum ❹** (201 10th St W; tel: 941-746-4131; Mon–Sat 10am–5pm, Sun noon–5pm; closed Mon May–June and Aug–Dec; charge) offers an excellent introduction to South Florida's natural and cultural history. Opened in 1947 and recently upgraded, this well-interpreted museum is renowned for its Tallant Collection of Native American Artifacts, featuring 15,000 Indian artifacts dating from between AD 300 and 1725. Unearthed by amateur archaeologist Montague Tallant from 130 sites across Florida, much of the collection is now in the Smithsonian's Museum of the American Indian. Look for the gold crocodile god pendant that is the museum's logo.

Snooty, the oldest manatee in captivity, lives in the museum's Parker Manatee

*Folks gather on a pier on Anna Maria Key for a sunset view of the Gulf of Mexico.*

**BELOW:** a mastodon fossil at the South Florida Museum.

*A roller rink lights up the night at St Armand's Circle.*

**BELOW:** Mote Marine Aquarium and Laboratory.

Aquarium. He shares the pool with other manatees injured in boating incidents in Florida waters (manatees don't form long-term bonds – every poolmate is a new best friend). Twice-daily presentations about Snooty and his pals are a huge draw for grandparents and kids. There are also live, narrated star shows in the Bishop Planetarium, where you can learn about the seasonal movements of constellations across Florida's clear skies.

Small but fascinating, **De Soto National Memorial ❺** (3000 75th St NW; tel. 941-792-0458, www.nps.gov/deso; visitor center open daily 9am–5pm; free) commemorates the place where Spanish conquistador Hernando de Soto came ashore in 1539. This well-run National Park Service site has a visitor center, interpretive film, exhibits, bookstore, and ranger talks. Kids enjoy the living-history presentations at Camp Uzita, which re-creates 16th-century Spanish Florida and demonstrates how to fire a crossbow and an arquebus. There is also a small beach, a nature trail through a mangrove swamp and other ecosystems, and a picnic area.

Another popular local hangout is **Emerson Point Preserve** (5801 17th St West) in nearby **Palmetto ❻**. Located just beyond a quiet residential area, this bayfront archaeological site preserves the area's largest shell mound, now hidden in thick woods Another hidden treasure is **Gamble Plantation Historic State Park ❼** (3708 Patten Ave; tel: 941-723-4536; daily 8am–sunset; free) in **Ellenton**. It preserves an antebellum home on a mid-1800s sugar plantation and was used as a refuge by Confederate official Judah P. Benjamin who later escaped to England.

## Sarasota's islands

Returning to the barrier islands west of Bradenton, Gulf Drive meanders through well-heeled **Longboat Key ❽** to **St Armand's Key**. Laid out around a central plaza, **St Armand's Circle ❾** (300 Madison Dr; tel: 941-388-1554) is among the most pleasant retail experiences in Florida. Boutiques specializing in walking shoes, beachwear, books, and local art, among other things, are interspersed with sidewalk cafés offering everything from crab cakes to hearty breakfasts, homemade ice cream, and lattes.

Just a few minutes away, **Mote Marine Aquarium and Laboratory ❿**

(1600 Ken Thompson Pkwy; tel: 941-388-4441; daily 10am–5pm; charge) is fun and educational. Founded in 1955 by shark researcher Dr Eugenie Clark, Mote has grown into a 10-acre (4-hectare) aquarium, lab, and research center, displaying over 100 marine species in exhibits showcasing the laboratory's cutting-edge research. Watch a device tracking sharks in the Gulf, sidle up to real sharks in an enormous tank, or experience a simulated shark attack. Touch tanks allow kids to pet rays, wriggly horseshoe crabs, and other creatures.

Housed nearby is the excellent **Marine Mammal Research and Rehabilitation Center**. Enclosures contain recuperating sea turtles, and a pair of spotted and spinner dolphins named Moonshine and Harley live in a large pool, where they play with each other and interact with keepers. You can get even closer to the two long-time resident manatees, Hugh and Buffett, whose huge tank offers eyeball-to-eyeball encounters with these gentle torpedo-shaped giants.

The adjoining **Dolphin and Whale Hospital** is the premier marine mammal rescue facility on the South Florida coast.

## The upper crust

Like Dunedin to the north, Sarasota was pioneered by Scottish immigrant businessmen in the 1880s. John Hamilton Gillespie, an aristocratic lawyer and businessman, built historic Desoto Hotel on Main Street and Sarasota's first golf course, and was named Sarasota's first mayor in 1902. Soon afterwards, wealthy Northerners started to settle in town.

**Marie Selby Botanical Gardens** ⓫ (811 S. Palm Ave; tel: 941-366-5731, www.selby.org; daily 10am–5pm; charge), south of downtown, was the home of Marie and Bill Selby. Voted one of Florida's top botanical gardens, it has a Zen theme, with plaques featuring Asian brush paintings and quotes, Buddha statues, and koi ponds amid peaceful pathways. There are native and seasonal plantings, Marie's beloved rose garden, spectacular banyan trees, a bamboo grove that Marie planted to screen out Sarasota's high-rises, and a popular gift shop and nursery. The greenhouse has many examples of the hothouse orchids and bromeliads (air

*Asian art is displayed throughout the Marie Selby Botanical Gardens.*

**BELOW:** the Selby mansion houses exhibits of botanical art and photography.

*More than 20 large-scale artworks are on display along Sarasota's bayfront.*

**BELOW:** the Renaissance-style gardens of the Ringling Museum of Art are filled with fountains and sculpture.

plants) for which the gardens are known. The Selbys' former home is now a tranquil tea house.

South of Sarasota, Bertha Potter Palmer's estate at **Old Spanish Point ⓬** (337 N. Tamiami Trail, Osprey; tel: 942-966-5214; Mon–Sat 9am–5pm, Sun noon–5pm; charge) is used by local schools as an archaeological and environmental education center. It has an interesting exhibit called "Window to the Past," which allows you to see inside an excavated Indian shell midden.

Mrs Palmer was an innovative rancher, crossing native cracker cows with other cattle on her Meadowsweet Pastures Ranch. The former ranch, 15 miles (24km) south of Sarasota, is now **Myakka River State Park ⓭** (13208 SR 72; tel: 941-361-6511, www.myakkariver.org; daily 8am–sunset; charge), Florida's largest state park and a good place to enjoy kayaking, hiking, and camping. The rustic cabins make a great alternative to busy beach hotels for outdoor lovers and those on a budget. But if the beach is what you want, Old Spanish Point and Myakka River State Park is not far from **Siesta Key ⓮**, renowned for its pretty sandy

beaches, low-rise development, and quiet, old-fashioned resorts.

## Three-ring circus

Sarasota's star attraction is, of course, the **John and Mable Ringling Museum of Art ⓯** (5401 Bayshore Rd; tel: 941-359-5700; daily 10am–5.30pm; charge), north of downtown. Devote a whole day. As well as the art museum, the estate includes Historic Asolo Theater, the Ringling winter home, the circus museum, landscaped grounds, and a restaurant serving light Italian and American fare. Docent-led tours take place hourly.

Flush with profits from his "Greatest Show on Earth" and lucrative investments in oil, railroads, and real estate, John Ringling was a modest man with a grand vision. He brought artisans, red tile, stone, and art from around the world to create his estate. **Cà d'Zan** (House of John) was inspired by the Doge's Palace in Venice and was completed in 1926. You can tour the inside, where rooms feature tapestries and antiques, but it is the exterior, with its intricate terra-cotta decoration and boat landing, that makes this a unique American dream home.

John and Mable loved to travel and collect art. Their personal art museum, built in 1931 and now the state art museum, contains one of the most important collections of works by the Flemish painter Peter Paul Rubens (1577–1640). Along with exceptional Baroque art, the museum displays Asian and American works and a magnificent replica of Michelangelo's *David*, which dominates a formal courtyard of allées lined with topiaries. The 18th-century **Asolo Theater** (tel: 941-360-7399), built in Italy, sits near Cà d'Zan. The interior was dismantled piece by piece at a castle in Asolo, then shipped to Sarasota in 1950 and reassembled. The theater is host to a year-round roster of events, including dance and theatrical performances, chamber music concerts, art lectures, and a film series.

A less imposing building houses the 1948 **Ringling Museum of the American Circus**. It has memorabilia, including

*Recommended Restaurants on pages 320–1*

rare posters, from Ringling's three-ring circus extravaganza. Don't miss the 3,800-sq-ft (350-sq-meter) miniature replica of Ringling Circus. It took model-maker Howard Tibbals 50 years to complete.

Another venue for dance and music is the **Van Wezel Performing Arts Center** ⑯ (777 N. Tamiami Trail; tel: 800-826-9303, www.vanwezel.org), a shell-shaped building on the waterfront just south of Ringling Museum. Both the Asolo and Van Wezel theaters host films during the **Sarasota Film Festival** in April.

## From Venice to Fort Myers

Sarasota's circus legacy spilled over into **Venice** ⑰, a seaside community 20 miles (32km) south along US 41, which served as home to the Ringling Clown College until the 1990s. Venice's main claim to fame is as the "Sharkstooth Capital of the World." Tiny fossilized shark's teeth wash up on undeveloped **Caspersen Beach**, the longest beach in Sarasota County. They lure fossil collectors to an annual festival every August, the highlight of which is a popular seafood contest among local restaurants.

Things are quieter in the retirement communities around **Charlotte Harbor** ⑱, where the Peace River opens into an enormous bay. With little in the way of attractions, **Punta Gorda** and **Port Charlotte** provide a change of pace from the rapid growth to the north and south. Legends of pirates and explorers are rife along the coast, culminating on Gasparilla Island, the so-called "kingdom" of the colorful but imaginary José Gaspar, who is celebrated in Tampa's annual Gasparilla Festival. **Boca Grande**, mid-island, offers a peek at the lifestyles of the rich and famous at an historic resort.

One of the few things that draws people

*Visitors take in the view from the top of Cà d'Zan, John and Mable Ringling's waterfront mansion.*

**BELOW:** the Ringling Museum is filled with precious art and furnishings gathered during Ringling's annual visits to Europe in search of new circus acts.

*Bird-watchers flock to the J.N. "Ding" Darling National Wildlife Refuge on Sanibel Island.*

**BELOW:** Gasparilla Island golf course.

## Paradise Coast

Farther south, in **Fort Myers** ⓳, the **Edison and Ford Winter Estates** (2350 McGregor Blvd; tel: 239-334-7419, www.efwefla.org; daily 9am–5.30pm; charge) spans both sides of McGregor Boulevard, the moneyed avenue leading into downtown. After moving here for his health at the age of 39, Thomas Edison lived to the age of 84. He produced some of his greatest inventions in his Florida laboratory, including phonographs and motion pictures. After his death, Edison's widow Mina bequeathed the estate to the city, as a shrine to her husband.

Overlooking the broad Caloosahatchee River, Edison's Seminole Lodge and its Guest Wing were among the first prefabricated buildings in the US, constructed in Maine and brought to Fort Myers by schooner. Tropical gardens engulf the homes. Native Florida palms, satin leaf figs, calabash trees from South America, cinnamon trees from India and Malaysia, and the largest banyan tree in Florida – some 6,000 species were collected by Edison at a cost of $100,000. In this idyllic setting, he entertained famous friends like President Herbert Hoover,

inland is **Crescent B Ranch**, the largest working ranch east of the Mississipi. Purchased from the Babcock family by a private company in 2006, 80 percent of this pristine western Everglades landscape is wilderness, an important wildlife corridor between Lake Okeechobee and the Gulf; 20 percent will be developed as an environmentally sustainable community. **Babcock Wilderness Adventures** (tel: 800-500-5583; reservations required) offers swamp-buggy tours of Babcock Ranch and Telegraph Cypress Swamp, where you might see cracker cattle, wild turkeys, alligators, and possibly panthers. The ranch is 40 miles (65km) northeast of Fort Myers on SR 331.

Recommended Restaurants on pages 320–1

Harvey Firestone, and automan Henry Ford, whose modest vacation bungalow, **The Mangoes**, is part of the tour. Edison offered to light up his new town with electric installations, but the townspeople refused for fear the lights would keep their cattle awake at night.

Visitors peer through plexiglass into the furnished rooms of Edison's **Seminole Lodge** and **Guest Wing**, which have recently undergone an award-winning restoration. You can also visit Edison's **Little Office**, the **Caretaker's House**, the **Moonlight Garden**, the **Rock Fountain**, and the **Swimming Pool Complex**. Edison's 1928 Botanic Research Corporation Laboratory, adjoining the visitor museum, gift store, café, and research garden across the street, is worth the wait to get in: it looks like the great man has just popped out for lunch, mid-experiment.

**Fort Myers Beach** ⓴, the lively resort town on **Estero Island**, attracts mainly families in the high season but becomes an attractive, old-fashioned island community the rest of the year, when locals stroll at sunset in undeveloped **Lovers Key State Park**, on the south end of the island.

## Sanibel and Captiva

Just west of Fort Myers Beach, a toll bridge leads to two exclusive island retreats – **Sanibel** ⓴ and **Captiva** ⓴ – where you can commune with nature and still buy a deli sandwich for lunch. The main attractions here are sandy beaches and the millions of shells that turn up on them, luring thousands of collectors. Just about everything related to molluscs – from classification to art to medicine – is covered in the **Bailey-Matthews Shell Museum** (3075 Sanibel-Captiva Rd; tel: 239-395-2233, www.shellmuseum.org; daily 10am–5pm; charge), a good place to spend an hour figuring out your murexes from your junonias.

In 1974, Sanibel seceded from Lee County, set up its own city government, and put a near halt to the runaway development threatening to ruin its beautiful environment. Buildings here may not rise higher than a palm tree and must blend with the scenery, so, even though the island is amply supplied with lovely homes, pricey hotels and restaurants, shopping centers, schools, and the like, natural beauty dominates. Less regulated than Sanibel, Captiva is undergoing construction and, sad to say, mini-mansions are gradually creeping in, threatening the quiet island ambience. Gift shops, island-style cafés, and vacation rentals are crammed into a village on the far end, close to a popular public beach.

Sanibel has many protected areas, the most notable being the outstanding **J.N. "Ding" Darling National Wildlife Refuge** (off Sanibel-Captiva Rd; tel: 239-472-1100, www.fws.gov/dingdarling; daily 7.30am–sunset, Wildlife Drive closed Fri; charge), named for the famous cartoonist and conservationist who made his home on Sanibel and helped develop the National Wildlife Refuge system.

These are some of the most productive wetlands for wildlife in Florida. The best birding is in winter, when early-morning low tides lure huge numbers of birds to the mudflats. At the entrance to the 5-mile (8-km) **Wildlife Drive**, look for roseate spoonbills (the only naturally

> *There is only one Fort Myers, and 90 million people are going to find it out.*
>
> Thomas Edison, 1914

**BELOW:** Sanibel Island is famous for the number and variety of seashells on its beaches.

*Fishing is excellent in the Gulf Coast's many bays and inlets.*

**BELOW:** luxury condos overlook the Gordon River in Naples.

pink-hued birds; flamingoes turn pink because of the crustaceans they eat); several species of herons, including little and great blues and tricoloreds; white and brown pelicans; curve-billed ibis; long-necked anhinga "snake" birds; and other wading birds. The most eco-friendly way to see the refuge is to take one of the excellent tram tours with a trained naturalist; ride a bicycle or walk through the refuge; or paddle a kayak with concessionaire **Tarpon Bay Explorers** (tel: 239-472-8900). Binoculars come in handy.

**Cayo Costa Island State Park ㉓**, north of Captiva, is one of Florida's most unspoiled barrier islands. It has terrific birding and 9 miles (14km) of dune-backed beaches, and you can spend the night in one of the island's rustic cabins or camp out. You'll need to take a boat here, bring supplies, and expect only basic facilities (there's no hot water or electricity).

Another option is to take a boat or float-plane to the **Cabbage Key Inn and Restaurant** (tel: 239-283-2278) from Captiva Island, Pine Island, or Punta Gorda. Historic Cabbage Key was built in the 1930s by the famous publishing family of author Mary Holt Rinehart.

Today, it's a rustic island getaway, with wood-paneled cabins in the woods and an inn atop a shell mound whose funky bar is papered with dollar bills. Things get lively when boaters tie up for hearty meals in the restaurant. Reserve well ahead.

## Naples and environs

The pretty resort town of **Naples ㉔**, at the edge of the Everglades, is easy on the eyes but hard on the purse. Even so, like an Italian tenor with a voracious appetite for life – and a rapidly expanding waistline – Naples revels in its outstanding natural beauty while, behind the beautiful facade, a long history of real estate speculation (the infamous Golden Gate Estates boondoggle took place here in the 1960s) threatens the delicate balance of its fragile Everglades ecosystem. Elegant seafront resorts, an emphasis on the arts and fine living, and abundant outdoor activities are a powerful lure for tourists and residents alike.

But there are signs of trouble in paradise, as Naples becomes a haven of wealth and conspicuous consumption. It boasts the largest number of billionaires and golf courses in the country; over-

*Recommended Restaurants on pages 320–1*

scaled mega-resorts along the beaches of Naples and nearby **Marco Island ㉕** continue to spring up; and every month new roads, strip malls, and residential areas are carved out of the swamp. In a sad irony, the names of these Las Vegas–style gated communities seek to celebrate the very threatened flora and fauna they are supplanting: panthers, big cypress, and other disappearing Everglades species.

Excessive development is especially evident on Marco Island, which has little of the charm of the Gulf Coast's other islands. The northernmost and largest of the Ten Thousand Islands, Marco became a popular tourist destination when Captain William Collier moved his family to the north end of the island in 1871 and offered guests rooms in his home for $2 a night. It's said that the enterprising Collier (no relation to Barron Collier) was responsible for rumors of pirates on the Gulf Coast.

Sadly, most of the island was sold for development during the real-estate boom of the 1960s. Today, after you cross the bridge to the island via North Collier Boulevard from Naples, you run slapbang into anonymous beachfront high-

rise resorts, condo complexes, quiet residential areas, and a snazzy marina.

For casual visitors, Marco's attractions are all nature-oriented. **Rookery Bay National Estuarine Research Reserve** (300 Tower Rd; tel: 239-417-6310, open daily), at the turnoff for southern Marco Island from US 41, interprets wildlife in Naples Bay and Ten Thousand Islands National Wildlife Refuge. It has a popular **Southwest Florida Birding and Wildlife Festival** in January and offers guided birding tours to many locations, including **Tiger Tail Beach Park** (tel: 239-642-8414; parking fee) at the end of Hernando

*Naples Pier was originally built in 1888 as a passenger dock and is now a popular gathering spot for sunset views.*

**BELOW LEFT:** Naples' Third Street shopping district.
**BELOW:** a Koreshan model of the universe.

## The World Within

Florida has attracted many unusual pioneers, but none are as strange as physician Cyrus Reed Teed, founder of the faith of Koreshanity, who, in 1894, brought followers from Chicago to Estero to build the village of New Jerusalem. The colony, known as the Koreshan Unity, believed that the universe existed within a giant, hollow sphere, with the sun in the center and life covering the inner walls. The restored 11-building village at **Koreshan State Historic Site ㉖** (Corkscrew Rd; tel: 239-992-031; open daily; charge) demonstrates how Teed "proved" his theories and how his commune shared property and practiced celibacy. The 250-person colony faded after Teed's death in 1908, when Teed failed to reincarnate as predicted. In 1960, the last four members deeded the property to the state. Today, visitors fish, picnic, boat, and hike where Teed's visionaries once carried out survey experiments to prove that the horizon curves upward. Tours of the settlement are available. **Mound Key Archaeological State Park**, a 120-acre (50-hectare) island in Estero Bay created by the Calusa Indians, is nearby.

*Stan's Idle Hour is a tiny slice of Old Florida on Marco Island, now largely given over to condos and commercial development.*

**BELOW:** a Marco Island marina.

entertainment on Thursdays. **Fifth Street South** has undergone a renaissance in recent years and is now a pedestrian-friendly hangout with a dynamic mix of theater, boutique hotels, shops, and restaurants. The popular **Naples National Art Show** takes place here in February, around the corner from the **Von Liebig Art Center** (585 Park St; tel: 239-262-6517). There is plenty of parking near beach access points. A small historic complex includes the 1895 **Palm Cottage** (137 12th St S.), which has exhibits on local history. It sits at the foot of **Naples Pier**, a small fishing pier that once served as Naples' only transportation access.

## Zoo with a mission

For evidence of strong community spirit in Naples, look no farther than **Naples Zoo at Caribbean Gardens** (1590 Goodlette-Frank Rd; tel: 239-262-5409; daily 9.30am–5.30pm; charge), set amid 45 acres (18 hectares) of historic botanical gardens. It started as a family operation in 1967, when "Jungle Larry" Tetzlaff moved his zoo from Ohio to these spectacular gardens, which had been planted in 1919 by conservationist Dr Henry

Drive on Marco Island, prime viewing for both shoreline and wetland birds.

For curiosity value alone, consider visiting **Goodland**, a funky little fishing village on the island's east side, where you'll find **Stan's Idle Hour Seafood Restaurant** (221 Goodland Dr West; tel: 239-394-304) on the waterfront. Every Sunday afternoon, Stan's is the site of a raucous outdoor dance party featuring seafood, lots of alcohol, and a live band.

Naples is much more sedate. The historic old town, a few blocks from the beach, has been thoughtfully preserved and is a wonderful place to linger. **Third Street South** has many historic Craftsman bungalows, more than 100 distinctive shops, galleries, and restaurants, and free

*Recommended Restaurants on pages 320–1*

Nehrling and restored in 1952 by Julius Fleischmann, heir to the yeast empire.

Parlaying a passion for wildlife into a job with animal collector Frank Buck, Tetzlaff and his wife Nancy (aka "Jungle Jane") offered more than another roadside attraction. They emphasized wildlife conservation, using live animal shows as teaching tools. In 2007, the City of Naples bought the zoo and gardens, but the Tetzlaffs still oversee daily operations.

Specializing in big carnivores, Naples Zoo is unique in Florida for exhibiting all of Africa's top predators – leopards, lions, spotted hyenas, and wild dogs – and rare Indonesian tigers. The zoo donates a portion of sales in its gift shop to wildlife conservation organizations. Among the ventures personally overseen by Conservation Director Tim Tetzlaff is a lemur project in Madagascar that involves local people in conserving habitat. At Naples Zoo, lemurs live free, alongside monkeys and apes, on an island in an alligator-filled lake. They can be viewed on daily boat tours.

Two cat exhibits are memorable. With only a thick glass barrier as protection, the Leopard Rock exhibit allows you to sit inches from curious leopards (look for the gorgeous black leopard, mistakenly called a black panther). Panther Glade, a joint project with the National Wildlife Federation, offers a look at an animal you may never see in the wild: the endangered Florida panther. The zoo is currently raising funds for its new Black Bear exhibit, which will house Florida black bears in a replica of an Old Florida homestead.

## Natural wonders

Some 80 percent of Collier County is protected in parks and other preserves. Twelve sites are part of the south section of the Great Florida Birding Trail. At the top of every birder's list is **Audubon Corkscrew Swamp Sanctuary** ㉗ (375 Sanctuary Rd West; tel: 239-348-9151; daily 7am–5.30pm, extended hours Apr–Sept), northeast of Naples. It preserves the last old-growth bald cypress forest and the largest nesting site in the world for endangered wood storks.

Less well known is **Picayune Strand Preserve State Forest** ㉘ (tel: 239-348-7557), where, directed by new laws to manage water for more natural, slow sheet flows for Everglades wildlife and habitat, the South Florida Water Management District is removing decades-old canals and roads and improving culverts through US 41, at the south end of the preserve. One of the first such projects, the preserve is worth visiting for its environmental value. The only visitor services are a developed equestrian campground and a trail at the main entrance on the north side. Drive east of Naples and cross I-75 to enter the preserve. ❑

*Relaxing on a Naples beach.*

**BELOW:** Naples Zoo at Caribbean Gardens.

# RESTAURANTS

## Anna Maria Key

**Beach Bistro**
6600 Gulf Dr
Holmes Beach
Tel: 941-778-6444
D daily
Chef Sean Murphy's sumptuous but airy Beach Bistro, one of Florida's most lauded restaurants, is nestled in the bottom of a condo complex at the north end of Anna Maria Key, but the pilgrimage to reach it only sharpens the anticipation for diners. Murphy and his talented

staff use fresh, local produce to create playful, French-influenced Floribbean cuisine. Try any dishes featuring tastebud-exploding local plum tomatoes and community farm veggies. Classics include three different sizes of Gulf bouillabaisse, a sinfully rich foie gras with brioche and Iowa lamb, tiny poached Nova Scotia lobster claws, beef tenderloin, island-style grouper, and an artisan cheese plate to finish. There's a casual bar serving a full menu. $$$$

**Sun House Restaurant**
111 Gulf Dr South
Bradenton Beach
Tel: 941-782-1122
L & D daily
Centrally located at Bradenton Beach, Sun

House is popular for sunset dining on laid-back Anna Maria Key. The sunny, fruity Floribbean food is inspired by island living. At lunch, items like jerk chicken amp up sandwiches and salads. At dinner, try the catch of the day grilled, blackened, jerked, or fried, or crowd-pleasers like teriyaki ahi tuna and Key West chicken Oscar. $$$–$$$$

## Captiva Island

**Bubble Room**
15001 Captiva Dr
Tel: 239-472-5558
L & D daily
If the idea of eating amid a brightly colored cornucopia of bric-a-brac from the 1930s appeals to you, then this unique restaurant is a must, if only for a drink and some appetizers. $–$$

**Key Lime Bistro**
11509 Andy Rosse Lane
Tel: 239-395-4000
B, L & D daily
This casual café in front of the Captiva Island Inn is a popular choice for a quick meal before or after the beach. The emphasis is on packing in a big crowd, so service tends to be perfunctory. But you'll find a large menu that will fuel you up for the day, including substantial egg dishes at breakfast, fried grouper sandwiches, burgers, and good salads. $–$$$

**Mucky Duck**
11546 Andy Rosse Lane
Tel: 239-472-3434
L & D Mon–Sat, L Sun

You can eat pub-style food right on the beach at this popular tavern, a fixture on Captiva since the 1970s. $

## Fort Myers

**Cru**
2262 First St
Tel: 239-466-3663
D daily
A dead cert for the martini crowd, Cru is a chic, urbane eatery that produces light, fresh Florida Fusion-style fare. A beguiling menu includes free-range chicken, Colorado bison, freshly caught pompano, tiger prawns, and organic veggies such as golden beets and heirloom tomatoes from the farmers' market in Centennial Park. There are small plates and an extensive wine list. $$$$

**Prawnbroker Restaurant and Fish Market**
13451-16 McGregor Blvd
Tel: 239-489-2226
D daily
Catch of the day is the specialty at this casual restaurant and market. Patio dining is available. It gets busy, so make reservations. $$–$$$

**The Veranda**
2122 Second St
Tel: 239-332-2065
L Mon–Fri, D Mon–Sat
Southern regional cuisine is the focus of this great little restaurant, which occupies two 1902 homes in downtown Fort Myers. The chef offers gourmet versions of down-home specialties like grits, fried chicken, crab

**LEFT:** grilled scallops at the Naples Tomato.

cakes, and fritters, the traditional accompaniments to grouper and other fresh seafood. $$$$

## Longboat Key

### Euphemia Haye
5540 Gulf of Mexico Dr
Tel: 941-383-3633
D daily
Euphemia Haye doesn't have a long menu, but it's a perfectly chosen one, with duck taking center stage, along with imaginatively prepared fresh seafood, steak, poultry, pasta, and vegetarian options. The more casual upstairs Haye Loft has entertainment and longer hours. It serves an abbreviated version of the downstairs menu, along with thin-crust pizza, a daily sandwich special, and the killer pies for which the restaurant is known. $$$$

## Marco Island

### Olde Marco Restaurant
100 Palm St
Tel: 239-394-3131
D daily
Bite into 124 years of history when you dine at this venerable restaurant. Continental dining at its finest includes fresh grouper, rack of lamb, and dramatically flambéed shrimp. $$$$

## Naples

### Bistro 821
821 5th Ave South
Tel: 239-261-5821
D Mon–Sat
Pacific Rim-influenced Floribbean cuisine with classic French styling soars at this sprightly restaurant in the heart of downtown Naples. Rock lobster is paired with a satay sauce. Uptown macaroni and cheese includes shrimp and prosciutto. Sea bass is roasted in a miso-sake jus. There's even elk tenderloin for the adventurous. Desserts are outrageous and include profiteroles and créme caramel. $$$$

### Naples Tomato
4700 Tamiami Trail North
Tel: 239-598-9800
L & D Mon–Sat
This attractive Neapolitan-style restaurant is far out in Naples' north end in an unassuming strip mall. But that doesn't faze foodies: Naples Tomato is one of the most popular restaurants in the area. Pasta is made fresh daily, zucchini and eggplant are locally grown, and the menu includes wild salmon and perhaps the world's juiciest free-range chicken breast. The eponymous tomatoes are sourced locally in season; the tomatoes that provide the zing in the restaurant's signature tomato bisque and pasta and pizza dishes are San Marzanos from Naples, prized for their bright, rounded flavor. Help yourself to wines from the self-serve Enomatic system while you soak up the good cheer. $$$$

### Shula's Steakhouse
5111 N. Tamiami Trail
Tel: 239-430-4999
D Mon–Sat
In the Hilton Naples, this steakhouse was started by the popular NFL coach and is highly rated for its Black Angus steaks. $$$$

## Sanibel Island

### Mad Hatter
6467 Sanibel-Captiva Rd
Tel: 239-472-0033
L Tue–Sat, D daily (D only Mon–Sat in the low season)
It may have only 12 tables, but this jewel on the Gulf is the best place on Sanibel for sunset dining. The New American cuisine rises to the challenge of its surroundings, with interesting variations on classics such as shrimp Wellington and sesame ahi tuna with Thai peanut satay sauce. $$$$

### Timbers Restaurant and Sanibel Grill
703 Tarpon Bay Rd
Tel: 239-472-3128
D daily
Set near the J.N. "Ding" Darling National Wildlife Refuge, the Timbers is a two-in-one: Sanibel Grill, a raw bar and grill with a sports bar atmosphere, and more formal service in the Timbers dining room. $$$–$$$$

## Sarasota

### Bijou Café
1287 First St
Tel: 941-366-8111
L Mon–Fri, D Mon–Sun (closed Sun in summer)
This elegant European-style bistro has been winning kudos from diners for over 20 years. An engaging, internationally flavored menu created by the chef-owner, who is French-South African, includes local and organic produce and an array of homemade soups, salads, charcuterie, and artisan cheese plates, and Southern specials like jambalaya. Award-winning wine list. $$$$

### Blue Dolphin Café
470 John Ringling Blvd
Tel: 941-388-3566
B & L daily
A hands-down favorite for all-day breakfast, Blue Dolphin scores big by serving fabulous egg dishes made with local eggs. A good place for preshopping fortification in St Armand's Circle. $

### Michael's on East
1212 East Ave
Tel: 941-366-0007
L Mon–Fri, D Mon–Sat
Chic and always busy, Michael's has long been one of Sarasota's most lauded restaurants. The supper-club atmosphere is perfect for enjoying fine New American dining, with creative takes on steaks, seafood, and other classics. $$$$

### Tommy Bahama's Tropical Café
300 John Ringling Blvd
Tel: 941-388-2888
L & D daily
This popular upmarket chain restaurant believes that life is one big party. The eclectic but well-executed menu features tropically-tinged seafood and meat entrées, such as Tortola chicken tortilla soup, coconut shrimp, mahi mahi, and sea bass, which you can wash down with plenty of margaritas. There's even piña colada cake for dessert. A good place to wear a Hawaiian shirt and get your Jimmy Buffett on. $$$$

## Siesta Key

### Broken Egg
140 Avenida Messina
Tel: 941-346-2750
B & L daily
A popular breakfast and lunch spot, whether you eat on the sunny patio or in the bright dining room. Healthy options include whole-wheat pancakes and turkey sausage. $

### Miguel's
6631 Midnight Pass Rd
Tel: 941-349-4024
D Mon–Sat
Its name to the contrary, Miguel's specializes in traditional French cuisine, served in a homey dining room. You'll find all kinds of Gallic faves here, including escargot, crevette, and coquille St Jacques, as well as filet mignon, sole meunière, and duck. $$$$

# SPRING TRAINING

**The 'boys of summer' get an early start in Florida, where baseball fans can watch some of their favorite players and teams getting in shape for the upcoming season**

Balmy temperatures and the chance to rendezvous with old friends are two great reasons to travel to Florida in February, March, and April for a late winter vacation. Another is to get a preview of the upcoming major league baseball season during spring training. Spring training in Florida is now a century-old ritual that offers relaxed practice time for players, tryouts for new recruits, and professional-level games at low cost for fans between big-league teams like the Boston Red Sox and Minnesota Twins.

### THE GRAPEFRUIT LEAGUE

Eighteen teams play in 17 venues throughout Florida in what's dubbed the Grapefruit League. Most begin their workouts in mid-February, then play a series of games against other spring-training teams and minor league, college, and local teams in March and the first week of April. The first to arrive are usually the pitchers and catchers, followed by position players. Games are held at popular venues like Legends Field in Tampa and Roger Dean Stadium in Jupiter, which also offer special events such as bat and T-shirt giveaways and visiting sports mascots. The athletes often come over and meet fans after the games – an extra thrill for autograph-seeking kids. In 2008, a record-breaking 1.6 million fans attended 259 games in Florida stadiums, recording an average attendance of 6,478 fans per game.

Tickets go on sale as early as December and range from $5 for bleacher tickets to $15 for reserved seats. Ticket information can be obtained by calling the team's Florida venue (see Travel Tips, page 379) or by calling TickCo Premium Seating (tel: 800-279-4444; www.tickco.com). For information about Florida's Grapefruit League, go to www.floridagrapefruitleague.com.

**ABOVE:** fans gather for autographs around Philadelphia Phillies pitc Jamie Moyer at Bright House Networks Field in Clearwater.

**ABOVE:** a trainer helps a ballplayer work out his winter kinks. Spring training gives veterans an opportur to shape up for the regular season

**LEFT:** the New York Mets are put through their paces during a workout at 7,160-seat Tradition Field in Port St Lucie on Florida's Atlantic Coast. The minor league St Lucie Mets play at the stadium during the regular season.

**LEFT:** a Phillies fan watches his favorite team take the field. Spring training is especially fun for kids, who often have a chance to meet their heroes close-up.

## THE BIRTH OF A TRADITION

Spring training as an annual Florida ritual traces its origins to 1913, when player-manager Johnny Evers brought the Chicago Cubs to Tampa for training, after the team slid to a disappointing third place in the league. In February, the Cubs played the first of a three-game series against the Havana Athletics, a team of Cuban hot shots, most of whom had played American college baseball. Some 6,000 fans packed Plant Field – many of them Cuban cigar factory workers from Ybor City and West Tampa whose employers let them out early from work to attend the games. The Chicago Cubs trounced the Athletics in all three matches, then played several intra-team games and even a local team on Egmont Key. Tampa fell in love permanently with baseball.

By 1914, other Florida towns were working hard to attract major-league baseball teams. Among them was Jacksonville, which hosted the league champions, the Philadelphia Athletics, in 1914. Their manager was Connie Mack, grandfather of Florida Senator Connie Mack III, who had played for the Washington Senators in 1888 and been the first to skipper the Athletics for an entire season in Jacksonville in 1903. Over the years, improved train and auto connections brought more players to the Sunshine State, and, with the exception of the World War II years, when trains were commandeered for troops, spring training has been an annual ritual throughout Florida ever since.

**ABOVE:** Lou Gehrig (left) and Bob Shawkey with a mess of trout that Shawkey caught and brought to show his teammates at the Yankees' training camp at St Petersburg in 1927.

**ABOVE:** peanuts, popcorn, and Cracker Jacks are perennial favorites, though some stadiums offer more ambitious fare.

**BELOW:** the Grapefruit League encompasses 18 major league teams playing more than 30 games each.

CAUTION
MANATEE AREA

REAL ESTATE
INFO
BARNETT
REALTY
(352) 400-0401

# NORTH FLORIDA

In this lightly traveled corner of the Sunshine
State are historic cities, pristine beaches, colorful
seaside villages, and a vast inland wilderness

I n the middle of a sprawling expanse of pine forest in
North Florida, a billboard tells the story of this largely
undeveloped region. "Florida's Last Frontier," proclaims
the sign, put there by a real-estate man eager to sell land to
modern pioneers. If the billboard gives the impression that
the northern reaches of the Sunshine State are a little old-
fashioned and move at a slower pace than the rest of Florida,
perhaps it is correct. And if the sign means that some of the state's last hidden
treasures – unsullied beaches, meandering rivers, and inland wilderness –
await discovery here, that's true as well.

But if the billboard implies a place without a past, then it is woefully mis-
leading. For it is these piney woods that attracted Florida's first Spanish settlers, that resounded with gunfire during colonial and
Indian conflicts and the American Civil War, and that
helped some men amass fabulous wealth but seldom
allowed them to keep it.

Pensacola, for example, is now a thriving metropolis,
but the city over the years has been the possession of
five different nations. There were places like Magnolia
and Saint Joseph and New Port, once prosperous communities with fancy hotels and lavish mansions, now
greatly diminished by disaster, disease, or economic
downturns. Madison's Southern charm and Gainesville's
air of academia have roots dating back before the Civil
War. Indeed, the heritage of this entire region is written in overnight success
– in booms of lumber, cotton, and citrus, followed by busts so total that little remains of the glory days.

And what of North Florida today? It is a land of contrasts, cosmopolitan in
the cities of Pensacola and Tallahassee but overwhelmingly rural in the spaces
that stretch between them. Like the rest of the state, it has its vibrant seaside
communities. But there are fewer of them here than elsewhere, and many
more stretches of pristine beach – known collectively as the "Forgotten Coast,"
white and powdery as sugar, without a hint of a high-rise building. ❑

---

**PRECEDING PAGES:** Steinhatchee, on the Nature Coast. **LEFT:** a back-porch view of
the Gulf of Mexico from a Seaside beach house. **TOP:** a docent in period costume
at Historic Pensacola Village. **ABOVE RIGHT:** Saint Mark's National Wildlife Refuge.

Recommended Restaurants on page 337

# GAINESVILLE AND NORTH CENTRAL FLORIDA

**Tourists often overlook this area, which encompasses one of the nation's largest universities, Florida's scenic horse country, several historic waterways, and the lightly traveled Nature Coast**

For 50 years, zoology professor Archie Carr commuted from his home in Micanopy to the University of Florida campus in Gainesville via **Payne's Prairie**, a 50-sq-mile (130-sq-km) limestone sinkhole reminiscent of the Everglades, with its changing wetlands, luxuriant sea of grasses, and extraordinary wildlife. "To a taste not too dependent upon towns, there is always something," marveled Carr in his 1964 essay *The Bird and the Behemoth*. "If only a new set of shades in the grass and sky or a round-tail muskrat bouncing across the blacktop or a string of teal running low with the clouds in the twilight in front of a winter wind. The prairie is a solid thing to hold to in a world all broken out with man."

## Green at heart

Thanks to the efforts of Carr and wife Marjorie, Payne's Prairie (named after Seminole chief King Payne) was recognized in 1971 as Florida's first state preserve. Today, it's one of Florida's most important natural resources: a major recharge for the Floridan Aquifer, which provides drinking water for millions; a sanctuary for wildlife such as wild horses, bison, cattle, alligators, and Florida's largest population of sandhill cranes; and a beloved greenbelt for Gainesville residents, who flock to its six trails.

The Carrs were not alone in their passion for north-central Florida's subtle wetlands and the independent souls who lived there. Naturalist William Bartram traveled here by steamboat in 1774 and

wrote so inspiringly about Payne's Prairie, poet Samuel Taylor Coleridge used the descriptions in his poem "Kubla Khan." And in 1928, New York writer Marjorie Kinnan Rawlings moved to an old home amid citrus groves on Orange Lake, where she thrived until her death in 1959. Kinnan Rawlings' stories about life among the fish camps of Cross Creek brought worldwide attention to this Florida backwater and won her a Pulitzer Prize for the classic tale of a boy and his fawn, *The Yearling*. The sleepy homestead she restored, now a beautifully

**Main attractions**

UNIVERSITY OF FLORIDA
FLORIDA MUSEUM OF
  NATURAL HISTORY
HARN MUSEUM OF ART
KANAPAHA BOTANICAL
  GARDENS
MARJORIE KINNAN RAWLINGS
  HISTORIC STATE PARK
OCALA
SILVER SPRINGS
SUWANEE RIVER
NATURE COAST

**LEFT:** Gainesville's historic area. **BELOW:** Florida Museum of Natural History.

*Exhibits at the Samuel P. Harn Museum of Art range from ancient to modern.*

tended state park, is the very symbol of Old Florida, a must for anyone who has ever been inspired to write.

## Gators in the swamp

North-central Florida is a huge area, encompassing Alachua and neighboring counties between the hill country around Ocala to the south; the spring-fed Santa Fe River to the north; the St John's River, Lake George, and Ocala National Forest to the east; and the legendary Suwannee River to the west. To see it, consider basing yourself in Gainesville and making day trips to surrounding sights.

An interesting cultural mix of city and country, rich and poor, brainy and brawny,

Gainesville ❶ grew up around the citrus, turpentine, phosphate, and cattle industries in the mid-1800s, when the Cedar Key–Fernandina railroad opened east coast markets. As these businesses faded, a new opportunity presented itself. In 1906, a public university was founded in Gainesville, merging a seminary and agricultural college. A century later, 51,000 students attend the **University of Florida Ⓐ**, the country's third largest. Famous for its Gators football team, which plays in a stadium dubbed the "Swamp," this public university excels as a research institution, with regular breakthroughs in neurology, food science (Gatorade and other commercial products were developed here),

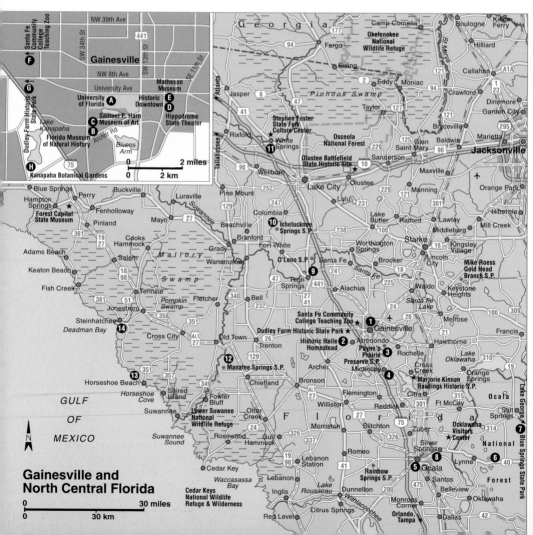

**Gainesville and North Central Florida**

0         30 miles

0         30 km

and agriculture. Archie Carr was one of UF's most popular professors until his death in 1987. To honor Carr's lifetime research and restoration work with endangered sea turtles across their range, the Archie Carr Center for Sea Turtle Research was founded in 1986 to continue his conservation work.

## Natural history

The best way to learn about Carr's passion for sea turtles is to read his many inspiring books and to visit the **Florida Museum of Natural History ❸** (SW 34th St and Hull Rd; tel: 352-846-2000, www.flmnh.ufl.edu; Mon–Sat 10am–5pm, Sun 1pm–5pm; charge), housed in an airy modern building in the UF Cultural Plaza. Kid-friendly, intelligent exhibits include fossils from the last 65 million years and the role of water as it flows through a hardwood hammock, bog, limestone cave, and other habitats. Florida's first peoples are well interpreted, with walk-through exhibits that include a replica Calusa Indian hut.

The hot ticket here is the **Butterfly Rainforest**, a 6,400-sq-ft (600-sq-meter) screened vivarium filled with tropical plants and living butterflies. A Wall of Wings displays thousands of stunningly beautiful butterfly specimens.

Flowing water and Zen-like tranquility greet visitors to the **Samuel P. Harn Museum of Art ❻** (SW 34th St and Hull Rd; tel: 352-392-9826, www.harn.ufl.edu; Tue–Fri 11am–5pm, Sat 10am–5pm, Sun 1pm–5pm; charge) next door. This teaching museum contains 7,000 examples of world-class art, from traditional Asian and African crafts to a large collection of modern masterpieces, including works by Claude Monet and photographs by Ansel Adams. Downstairs, the chic **Camelia Court Café** is a lunch spot offering light entrées, fresh roasted coffee, and free wireless Internet. It's open to 10pm on Thursdays for **Museum Night**, so if you're attending one of a performance at the **Phillips Center for the Performing Arts** (tel: 352-392-1900) across the plaza, you're in luck.

East of the university, the **Historic**

**Downtown** is still regenerating. Neighborhoods here are a mix of converted warehouses, turn-of-the-century brick buildings, shotgun shacks, and Victorian mansions slowly reviving as bed-and-breakfasts, restaurants, boutiques, and professional and government offices.

You can't miss the **Hippodrome State Theater ❹** (25 SE 2nd Pl; tel: 352-375-HIPP, http://thehipp.org) in the former Federal Building, a glorious 1911 Beaux Arts building with six white corinthian columns. A local favorite, the "Hippo" has stage performances and movies every night of the week. On Wednesday afternoons, **Gainesville Farmers' Market** is a good place to mingle with residents, listen to live music, and buy organic produce, raw dairy products, free-range meat, fresh roasted coffee beans, European bakery items, even arts and crafts.

On the edge of Sweetwater Park, just east of downtown, is the **Matheson Museum ❺** (13 E. University Ave; tel: 352-378-2280; Tue–Fri 9.30am–1.30pm, Sun 1pm–5pm; charge), where you can learn about Alachua County and tour the elegant 1863 **Matheson House**, the second oldest home in Gainesville.

*Century Tower rises 157ft (48 meters) above the University of Florida campus.*

**BELOW:** an Asian butterfly alights on a flower in an indoor "rainforest" at the Florida Museum of Natural History.

*A boardwalk leads visitors into Payne's Prairie Preserve State Park.*

**BELOW AND BELOW RIGHT:** Marjorie Kinnan Rawlings Historic State Park preserves the author's humble homestead.

Among the family-friendly attractions on the rural outskirts of Gainesville are the **Santa Fe Community College Teaching Zoo** ❸ (3000 NW 83rd St; tel: 352-395-5604, daily 9am–2pm, call for appointment; charge), a unique small zoo that teaches zookeeping skills; and the **Dudley Farm Historic State Park** ❹ (18730 W. Newberry Rd; tel: 352-472-1142, Wed–Sun 9am–5pm; charge), in Newberry, where costumed interpreters demonstrate pioneer life on a working family farm. Activities in the 18 historic buildings include tending heritage variety crops and livestock and cane grinding for a functioning cane syrup facility.

**Kanapaha Botanical Gardens** ❺ (4700 SW 58th Dr; tel: 352-372-4981; Mon–Wed, Fri 9am–5pm, Sat–Sun 9am–dusk; charge) is the second largest botanical garden in Florida. Named for the adjoining Kanapaha Lake (*Kanapaha* is a Timucua Indian word meaning "palmetto leaf house"), this 62-acre (25-hectare) garden features 1½ miles (2.5km) of trails that meander through 14 plant collections. Highlights include Florida's largest bamboo collection, the largest herb garden in the Southeast, and a water garden. Gardeners will enjoy the plant nursery and popular spring garden show. There's also a terrific gift shop, which sells unique nature-themed items. Look for a memoir by Kanapaha's colorful founder, Don Goodman, in which he recounts how he lost his right arm to a vicious alligator.

The **Historic Haile Homestead** ❷ (8500 Archer Rd; tel: 352-336-9096; reserved tours on weekends only; charge) on the former Kanapa Plantation southwest of town, was a working farm of a different order. A cotton plantation and an antebellum home were built in 1854 by black slaves who accompanied the Haile family from South Carolina. One feature of the homestead is its Talking

## Cross Creek Memories

**B**orn in Washington, DC, in 1896, Marjorie Kinnan Rawlings moved to the Cross Creek homestead in 1928, intending to write and live off the land. Along with a traditional Cracker home, she inherited an orange grove, two cows, two mules, 150 chicken coops, two chicken brooders, a planter, reaper, cultivators, and an old Ford truck. Her first husband didn't take to backwoods life, and the couple divorced in 1933, the year her first novel about Cross Creek appeared. Rawlings stayed on with her black maid, who later wrote a memoir about their relationship entitled *The Perfect Maid*. In 1941, Rawlings married Ocala hotelier Norton Baskin, and the couple split their time between Cross Creek and a home near St Augustine. Rawlings wrote nine books, including a cookbook (she was a passionate cook), the memoir *Cross Creek*, and *The Yearling*. Her publishing career was nurtured by legendary New York editor Maxwell Perkins, who was the first to suggest she write about her neighbors.

She died in St Augustine in 1953. Cross Creek was donated to UC Florida and became a state park in 1970.

Walls, unpainted surfaces where the Hailes recorded reflections on their lives.

## Across the prairie

Sweetwater Branch Creek, on Gainesville's southeast side, drains into **Payne's Prairie Preserve State Park** ❸ (tel: 352-466-3397; daily 8am–sunset; charge). Trails leave from the 15th Street preserve entrance. The 3-mile (5-km) **La Chua Trail** begins at historic La Chua cattle ranch, passes Alachua Sink, where giant alligators loll menacingly in the muck below, and continues to an observation deck. Binoculars are helpful if you want to glimpse some of the 800 species of plants, 271 species of birds, and 430 species of vertebrates living in 25 diverse natural communities. To reach the main visitor center, drive south on US 441 and watch for signs. The center offers an interpretive film, exhibits, a bookstore, and ranger talks, and a trail leads to an observation tower. There's also a good observation platform on the east side of US 441.

Continue south to reach **Micanopy** ❹, founded as a fort during the Seminole Wars and the oldest inland town in the state. Stop at the former warehouse that houses the **Micanopy Historical Society Center** (tel: 352-466-3200; open daily; charge) to view folksy exhibits and pick up a historic walking-tour booklet for the quiet main street. Many buildings house bed-and-breakfasts, antique shops, cafés, and unique stores like Mosswood, a purveyor of back-to-the-land goods with a tiny farmers' market on Sundays.

Micanopy substituted for Ocala in the 1981 film *Cross Creek*, loosely based on Marjorie Kinnan Rawlings' memoir of the same name. **Marjorie Kinnan Rawlings Historic State Park** (18700 South County Road; tel: 352-466-3672; open daily; no tours Mon–Wed or in Aug; charge) is southeast of US 441, off CR 325. You can self-tour the sleepy farmyard, where chickens peck around the barn, oranges ripen on trees, and a vintage car awaits its former owner under an awning. Female rangers, dressed in 1940s house dresses, give tours of the home, a classic dog-trot building designed to maximize breezes in the days before air conditioning. With their colorful tales and passion for the writing life, these custodians evoke the feisty spirit of Rawlings, one of a breed

> **TIP**
>
> People from miles around make pilgrimages to Blue Highway Pizzeria (204 NE US 441; tel: 352-466-0062) in Micanopy to enjoy unpretentious food and family atmosphere. The owners buy local produce, which keeps prices down and guarantees freshness. Try the Greek-inspired Blue Highway salad and vibrant Margherita pizza made with homemade mozzarella, tomato sauce, and fresh basil.

**BELOW:** a historic Micanopy inn.

Daphnis and Chloe
(c.1882) by Elizabeth
Jane Gardner at
Ocala's Appleton
Museum of Art.

**BELOW:** park
rangers in period
costume illustrate
life in the 1880s at
Dudley Farm
Historic State Park.

of woman writers and artists who exited the cities in the early 1900s to live life on their own terms in the country. Bring a picnic – there's a pleasant park next door.

## The great outdoors

Heading south to **Ocala ❺**, the landscape shifts to a pastoral scene of rolling hills, grazing horses, and picturesque barns. No surprise, then, that Ocala is the "Horse Capital of the US," with more than 900 horse farms. A few stables offer tours, but there are horse-themed events throughout the year, including Horse Shows in the Sun in February and the Ocala Shrine Rodeo in August. Just east of the historic downtown is the **Appleton Museum of Art** (4333 NE Silver Springs Blvd; tel: 352-236-7100; Tue–Sat 10am–5pm, Sun noon–5pm; charge), a neoclassical building housing a wide-ranging collection and traveling exhibitions.

**Ocala National Forest ❻** abounds with hiking trails and opportunities for camping, boating, and bird watching on adjoining **Lake George**. The multi-agency **Ocklawaha Visitors Center** (3199 NE CR 315, Silver Springs; tel: 352-236-0288) has information on out-

door activities in Marion County. Lake George is fed by the **St John's River**, an important travel corridor for Florida's earliest canoe cultures and later steamboat travelers. The location of the St John's River, flowing north to meet the Atlantic at Jacksonville, led to the development of riverbank communities like **Enterprise** and **Palatka**. Thriving tourist centers during the Victorian period, they are now mere shadows of their former selves.

Your best bet for canoeing or tubing are **Alexander and Juniper Springs**. It's better to come on weekdays when attendance is light. The largest recreation area in the forest is **Salt Springs** on SR 40 and 314, with a canoe path from **Lake George** to the St John's River.

Snorkeling in crystal springs at **Blue Spring State Park ❼** (2100 W. French Ave, Orange City; tel: 386-775-3663; daily 8am–dusk; entrance fee) and **Lower Wekiva River Preserve State Park** (1800 Wekiwa Cir, Apopka; tel: 407-884-2008; daily 8am–dusk) are also popular. At the start of the paved **West Orange Trail**, you can hire bikes and rollerblades and cruise for 19 miles (30km) around Lake Apopka to Winter Garden.

Florida's bird population was decimated by steamboat travelers shooting egrets, herons, storks, and other birds living on the forested banks. Famed naturalist John James Audubon collected specimens for his research in 1834, but others shot birds for their valuable plumes. The state's oldest theme park, **Silver Springs ❽**, just east of Ocala, harkens back to the steamboat era on the Oklawaha River, a tributary of the St Johns. It has wonderful old glass-bottom paddleboats that allow you to look down into Florida's deepest natural springs. The animals along these riverbanks live protected lives, and the area around the springs has remained so natural it was used in *Tarzan* films.

## Springs eternal

"Springs are bowls of liquid light," wrote famed conservationist Marjorie Stoneman Douglas. That's certainly true of the hundreds of springs that percolate

*Recommended Restaurants on page 337*

through Florida's underlying limestone. North of Gainesville, they feed the Santa Fe River and its tributaries, then merge with the Suwannee River. The farther north you drive toward the Georgia border on US 441, the more "southern" it gets. Historic towns like **Alachua** and **High Springs ❾**, which grew up with the railroad, have reinvented themselves as genteel rural villages, complete with historic bed-and-breakfasts, antique shops, and restaurants serving field-fresh greens. Canoeing and tubing are the preferred ways to beat steamy hot summers in this neck of the woods, where almost every household has a boat in its yard, and there's a canoe launch every few miles.

At **Ichetucknee Springs State Park** ❿ (12087 SW US Hwy 27; tel: 386-497-4690; daily 8am–sunset; charge), 4 miles (6½km) northwest of Fort White, rent a tube or canoe, park your car at the south entrance, board a tram to the north entrance, and float back down the crystalline Ichetucknee River to the parking lot at a leisurely pace (allow 2–3 hours). There are no alligators in the 72°F (22°C) water but plenty of basking turtles on logs (laughingly

referred to as "shell stations" by a ranger). Small fish among the eel grass form the main diet of elegant snowy egrets and beady-eyed herons that stand motionless in the shallows, waiting to pounce. Park authorities protect water quality by banning water, food, and tobacco on the river, so eat a hearty meal and hydrate yourself beforehand. Life doesn't get much better than a canoe ride on the Ichetucknee in winter. Temperatures are pleasant, tubing is

*Pointy "knees" grow from the roots of cypress trees in river wetlands.*

**BELOW:** Silver Springs has an assortment of exotic wildlife.

*The Nature Coast has a decidedly down-home and folksy atmosphere compared to the more developed parts of the state.*

**BELOW:**
Steinhatchee is a remote fishing village at the mouth of the Steinhatchee River.

restricted to the south entrance, and you'll have the river to yourself.

The Santa Fe River joins the **Suwannee River** near Branford. The Suwannee rises in Georgia and meanders across northern Florida, finally entering the Gulf near the town of Suwannee. It forms a cultural corridor that flows through Florida, carrying with it the echoes of generations of people working and playing on its banks and looking to it for moments of inspiration. Stephen Foster, composer of the 1851 song *Old Folks at Home*, never saw the Suwannee, but his lyrics so evoked the way of life here that Florida adopted the tune as its state song in 1935.

You can learn more at **Stephen Foster State Folk Culture Center** (US 41; tel: 386-397-2733; daily 9am–5pm; charge) in **White Springs ⓫**, north of Lake City. Among the attractions are rides on a riverboat and a carillon that rings out Foster favorites like *O Susannah* and *Camptown Races*. There's a **Florida Folk Festival** here every May, and you'll see baptisms in the river, eat black-eyed peas, and hear storytellers and folk singers perform.

## Nature Coast

West of Chiefland, the Suwannee loses energy and meanders into Gulf waters in one of the largest undeveloped river delta-estuary systems in the United States. Protected as the 52,935-acre (21,422-hectare) **Lower Suwannee National Wildlife Refuge** (SR 347; tel: 352-493-0238), this area of scenic tidal marshes, coastal islands, and cypress groves is a coastal region below the Panhandle variously called the Big Bend, Hidden Coast, or Nature Coast. The refuge fronts 26 miles (42km) of Gulf coastline and protects 250 bird species. There are 40 miles (64km) of trails and 50 miles (80km) of forested back roads, but it's easiest to travel by boat. Kayakers can put in at **Shell Mound** and paddle the estuary or do three different river loops from the town of **Suwannee**.

Forgot your boat? **Lower Suwannee River Tours** in **Manatee Springs State Park ⓬** (SR 320; tel: 352-493-6072; daily 8am–sunset; charge) offers river rides. This lovely park has a huge campground that makes a great base for explorations. Swim in the springs and walk a boardwalk to the observation point at the mouth of the spring run, a slam dunk for sighting manatees drifting in the slow currents in winter.

North of Suwannee is **Horseshoe Beach ⓭**, a retirement community so remote it feels like you're on an island. Most popular is **Steinhatchee ⓮**, a fishing village that attracts retirees and tourists. **Steinhatchee Landing Resort** offers activities for the whole family, and the pleasant waterfront has boat rentals, gift shops, and restaurants. Nearby **Keaton Beach** is one of the few settlements with a tiny patch of sand and slides for the kids.

By anyone's reckoning, the Nature Coast is Florida's most unspoiled region. Sunsets are extraordinary. Seafood is freshly caught. And the pace of life feels like another era altogether. Unless your children are easily amused, this area may not hold their interest for long. But for anyone looking to retreat from the modern world or write that novel, a vacation cottage on stilts overlooking the Gulf may be your ticket to paradise. ❑

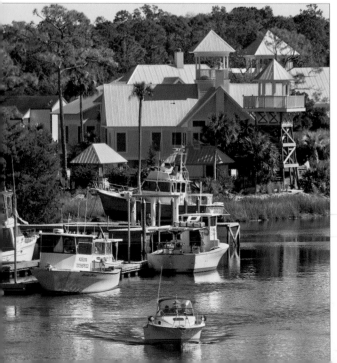

# RESTAURANTS

## Restaurants

Prices for a three-course dinner per person, excluding tax, tip, and beverages:

**$** = under $20
**$$** = $20–45
**$$$** = $45–60
**$$$$** = over $60

## Alachua

### Deneno's Restaurant
14960 Main St
Tel: 386-418-1066
L & D daily
This excellent North Italian restaurant uses local greens, and all dishes, whether meat, fish, or pasta, have a light touch. A perfect end to a day of kayaking or tubing on the Santa Fe River. $$$

## Cross Creek

### The Yearling Restaurant
14531 E. County Rd 325
Tel: 352-466-3999
D Thu–Sun, L Sat–Sun
This no-frills backwoods restaurant is right on Cross Creek down the road from "Miz Rawlings'" former home. It is legendary for its down-home cuisine, the type local people hunted, fished, or trapped for themselves, then fried up for dinner. Look for frogs' legs, alligator, venison, quail, and land turtle, with hush puppies, collard greens, grits, and other fixings. $$

## Gainesville

### Mildred's Big City Food
3445 W. University Ave
Tel: 352-371-1711
L & D daily
Chef-owner Bert Gill is one of Florida's most visible promoters of fresh, local eating. He buys organic produce from local farm-

ers and seafood fresh off the boat in Cedar Key. The menu changes daily and includes imaginatively prepared specials like mushroom soup with truffle oil, sweetbreads with poached egg, braised venison with Florida butter beans, and pan-seared grouper on tomato risotto. Lunch features quiche, sandwiches, soups, and salads. $$–$$$$

### New Deal Café
3445 W. University Ave
Tel: 352-371-1711
Tel: L & D daily
Under the same ownership as Mildred's, this café offers lighter and less expensive fare. Choose from grassfed burgers, salads, soups, flatbread pizzas, paninis, and one-dish entrees like pecan-crusted chicken with vanilla whipped potatoes. $–$$

### Ti Amo
12 SE 2nd Ave
Tel: 352-378-6307
L & D daily
Set in an historic brick warehouse, Ti Amo is a late-night restaurant serving Mediterranean-style small plates. The menu changes daily and offers all kinds of tasting treasures. $$–$$$

### Booklover's Café
505 NW 13th St
Tel: 352-374-4241
Daily 10am–9pm
This café inside an antiquarian bookstore serves cheap vegan food – bliss

**RIGHT:** roadside stands sell local pecans.

for thrifty bibliophiles with a health-conscious bent. $

### Paramount Grill
12 SW 1st Ave
Tel: 352-378-3398
L Mon–Fri, D Mon–Sat, Br Sun
All blond woods and white tablecloths, the lovely Paramount Grill is one of Gainesville's top fine dining picks. Chef-owner Clif Nelson is devoted to local produce, and his New American cuisine combines elegance and freshness. Sunday brunch is popular. $$–$$$$

### Manuel's Vintage Room
6 S. Main St
Tel: 352-375-7372
L & D Tue–Sat
This intimate Italian restaurant has oodles of charm. The menu offers Italian classics such as veal piccata and make-your-own pasta dishes. Nontraditional choices include snails as a starter, grouper in cognac sauce, and chicken breast sautéed with habanero peppers in a white wine butter sauce. $$–$$$$

### Dragonfly Sushi and Sake Company
201 SE 2nd Ave
Tel: 352-371-3359

L & D daily
This upscale sushi bar serves high-quality sushi in a hip atmosphere, complete with plasma TVs showing old Japanese movies and hypnotic techno music. $$

## High Springs

### Floyd's Diner
615 NW Santa Fe Blvd
Tel: 386-454-5775
B, L & D daily
You can't miss this shiny vintage diner. The classic dishes on the large menu are very good, and there's even a separate menu for dogs who get to share food with their owners on the patio. A great local hangout. Full bar. $

## Newberry

### Flour Pot Bakery
13005 SW 1st Rd #137
Mon-Fri 7am–6pm, Sat 9am–5pm, Sun 9am–2pm
In the new Tioga Town Center, just west of downtown Gainesville, this European-style bakery turns out authentic French baguettes and other breads, pastries, cakes, and cookies. You can order homemade sandwiches, salads, quiches, and savory croissants to eat in their café or take with you. $

*Recommended Restaurants pages 354–5*

# TALLAHASSEE AND THE PANHANDLE

The capital is a gateway to a 'Forgotten Coast'
of gleaming white beaches, turquoise
waters, and sleepy seaside villages

n the early 19th century, most of Florida was a thick jungle. Settlement was concentrated in the northern tier, and Pensacola and St Augustine were the largest communities. Travel between these two territorial "capitals" was daunting and slow; trails through the interior were poorly marked, and pirates and storms plagued the ocean route. Each wanted to be the seat of territorial government, but the Territorial Legislative Council quickly realized that a more central location was necessary.

In 1823 two members of a site selection committee – one from Pensacola, the other from St Augustine – met at St Marks on Apalachee Bay to inspect the region selected by the council. This region was located between the Suwannee and Ochlockonee rivers; the two committee men moved north toward an old Indian village that the Creeks and Seminoles called "Tallahassee," meaning "old town" or "old fields."

Both men were enamored with the rolling hills and fine orchards of the Tallahassee area. One feature in particular seemed especially charming, a glittering waterfall that graced a prominent hillside. The settlement that grew here kept the Indian name.

## Government town

Tallahassee ❶ has undergone many changes since then, but it's still a government town. The skyline is dominated by the high-rise capitol soaring 22 stories above a steep hill, but high-rise resi-

dential condos are now beginning to challenge the capitol's dominance.

Of those employed in the city, almost half work for local, state, or federal government. But don't let visions of boring bureaucrats frighten you. Tallahassee is one of the best-kept secrets in Florida. A friendly community, the city has done an excellent job of preserving its landmarks, its natural beauty, and a small-town flavor that belies its burgeoning growth rate.

All this adds up to a metro-area population of about 159,000 who live amid a pleasing blend of old and new. It is a city

**Main attractions**
FLORIDA STATE CAPITOL
MISSION SAN LUIS
WAKULLA SPRINGS
ST MARKS NATIONAL
  WILDLIFE REFUGE
APALACHICOLA
PANAMA CITY BEACH
SEASIDE
FORT WALTON BEACH
GULF ISLANDS NATIONAL
  SEASHORE
HISTORIC PENSACOLA VILLAGE

**LEFT:** beach in the Panhandle.
**BELOW:** Florida Supreme Court.

rich in Old South town houses and plantation mansions that have been restored to their former grandeur. Oaks dripping with gray moss line picturesque streets, and dogwoods and azaleas bloom with vibrant spring color.

An elevator ride to the 22nd-floor observation deck of the **Florida State Capitol** **Ⓐ** (S. Monroe St and Apalachee Pkwy; tel: 850-488-6167; Mon–Fri 8am–5pm) will give you a bird's-eye view of the city, awash in a sea of trees. The **Old** **Capitol**, restored to its 1902 condition, is a museum piece that sits at the foot of its high-rise successor. The state legislature sits for just 60 days a year. If you visit in April or May, you can watch representatives and senators in action.

For some background, visit the **Museum of Florida History** **Ⓑ** (500 S. Bronough St; tel: 850-245-6400; Mon–Fri 9am–4.30pm, Sat 10am–4.30pm, Sun noon–4.30pm; free). This fine museum provides an overview of Florida's history, with exhibits ranging from a 12-ft (4-meter) tall mastodon to Spanish treasure and war relics.

## In the beginning

In 1539, Spanish conquistador Hernando de Soto came to this area in search of the gold that he never found. While wintering here he celebrated the first Christmas in America. He explored the area around **Lake Jackson** north of town, but remains of his main camp were found at a site near downtown. Today, Lake Jackson is a favorite fishing spot, but it's known as the "disappearing lake" because of a sinkhole that periodically empties the lake in dramatic fashion.

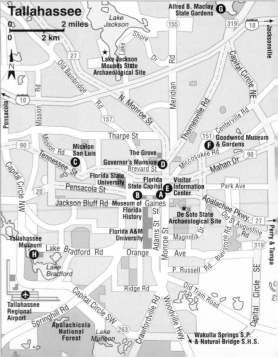

In the 17th century, Tallahassee became the western capital of Spanish colonial Florida. A string of Franciscan missions ran between St Augustine and Tallahassee; the largest and most important of these was **Mission San Luis** **C** (2021 Mission Rd; tel: 850-487-3711, www.missionsanluis.org; tours Tue–Sun 10am–4pm; free), which today is re-created on the original site and is an archaeological park.

## Magnificent mansions

Wealth isn't new to the city, which has an array of restored homes built by prominent citizens in the years immediately before and after the Civil War. The most outstanding of these is **The Grove** (N. Adams Street), former home of territorial governor Richard Keith Call. Next door, at No. 700, is the more ornate **Governor's Mansion** **D** (tel: 850-488-4661; Mar–May, Mon, Wed, and Fri 10am–noon; free), which was modeled on General Andrew Jackson's plantation home in Tennessee. Access to the governor's house is limited, but tours are available by appointment. Other historic residences can be seen on guided tours arranged through local hotels or the city's

**Visitor Information Center** **E** (106 E. Jefferson St; tel: 850-606-2305).

The real wealth, however, sparkles north of town in the form of 71 former plantations and 300,000 acres (120, 000 hectares) that now serve as exclusive hunting preserves. In fact, the Tallahassee area boasts the largest concentration of plantations in America. Some of these estates are held by private owners, but there are a couple of exceptions. **Goodwood Museum and Gardens** **F** (1600

*Tallahassee's Kleman Plaza serves as a civic hub near the state capitol.*

**BELOW LEFT:** Mission San Luis. **BELOW:** the Old Capitol.

set; charge). New York financier Alfred B. Maclay fashioned a garden of camellias, azaleas, palmettos, and other native and exotic plants around a tiny lake. Guided tours are available, and you can swim, fish, picnic, and go boating.

Tallahassee retained its rural Southern flavor longer than many other Florida communities of its size. The **Tallahassee Museum** **H** (3945 Museum Dr; tel: 850-576-1636; www.tallahasseemuseum.org; Mon–Sat 9am–5pm, Sun 12.30pm–5pm; charge) pays homage to its not-so-distant past. Here a wonderful working farm depicts Florida pioneer life in the late 19th century, and nature trails wind through the grounds, where bears, bobcats, and alligators reside. Other exhibits include the restored home of Napoleon's nephew, Prince Achille Murat; a one-room schoolhouse; and a grist mill. The museum is on the shores of Lake Bradford near Tallahassee Regional Airport, 4 miles (6 km) southwest of downtown Tallahassee.

*The Panhandle has miles of undeveloped coastline and quiet fishing towns.*

Miccosukee Rd; tel: 850-877-4202; main house open Mon–Fri 10am–2pm; free) underwent a major restoration in 2001 and a replica of the plantation's 1911 Carriage House was completed in 2008. You can explore the gardens and take tours inside the main house, which has original features such as marble fireplaces and a mahogany staircase.

You can also visit **Alfred B. Maclay State Gardens** **G** (3540 Thomasville Rd; tel: 850-487-4556; daily 8am to sun-

## Memories of war

Although Florida's role in the Civil War was mainly to supply men and food for

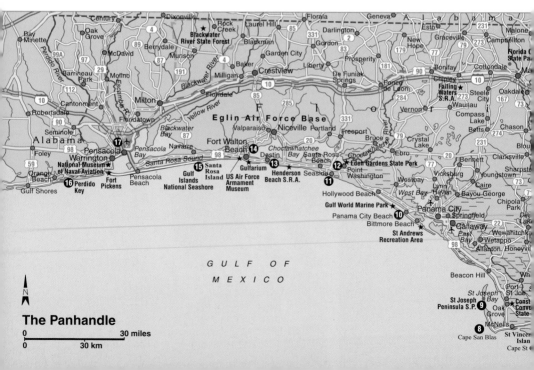

**The Panhandle**

0 _____ 30 miles

0 _____ 30 km

Recommended Restaurants pages 354–5

battles raging farther north, it did not completely miss the action. As the war entered its final month, Union troops landed near St Marks intending to take the fort there as well as Tallahassee itself. But attempts to cross the St Marks River were met with disaster at Natural Bridge, a spot southeast of Tallahassee where the river dips underground for 50 yards before resurfacing. Strongly entrenched Confederates – militia, old men, and teens – were ready for them. The Confederates inflicted heavy casualties on the Union soldiers and beat them back, making Tallahassee the only Confederate capital east of the Mississippi to resist capture.

The battlefield is preserved as the **Natural Bridge Battlefield State Historic Site** (7502 Natural Bridge Rd; tel: 850-922-6007, www.floridastateparks.org/natural-bridge; daily 8am–sunset; free), about 10 miles (16km) southeast of the city. There is an annual reenactment of the famous battle on or about March 6.

## The real Black Lagoon

From Natural Bridge, backtrack to Route 363 and head south to SR 267. Proceed west to **Wakulla Springs State Park** ❷ (550 Wakulla Park Dr; tel: 850-926-0700; daily 8am–sunset; charge). The park encompasses a large virgin hardwood and pine forest, but the main attraction is the spring after which the park is named, one of the largest in the world, pumping more than 687,000 gallons (2.6 million liters) of water a minute into a vast pool. You can swim in the clear spring waters or take a ride on a glass-bottomed boat. There are boat trips upriver, where alligators laze on the shores and anhinga birds dry their wings on cypress branches. The classic 1954 horror film *The Creature from the Black Lagoon* was filmed here.

If you want to dig in for a longer stay, consider booking a room at the gracious **Wakulla Springs Lodge** (1 Springs Dr, Wakulla Springs; tel: 850-224-5950), with its rare Spanish tiles adorning the Moorish-style doorways. Note the ceiling beams in the lobby. They were etched with Aztec and Toltec Indian designs by a German

*Shoppers will find a mixture of treasures and trash at antique shops and knickknack stores throughout the region.*

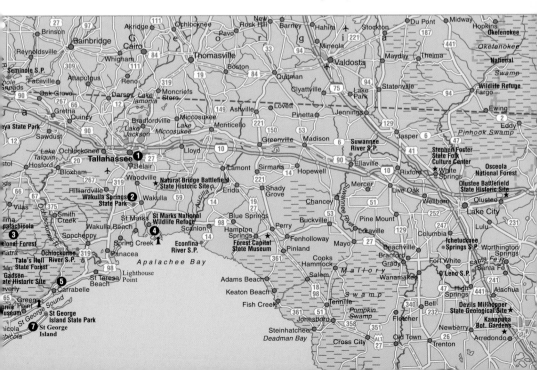

*Historic inns throughout the Big Bend region preserve the spirit of old-time Florida.*

hark back to the days when lumbermen and turpentine folks eked out a sparse living in the sandy woods. Wander through the **Apalachicola National Forest** ❸ (tel: 850-643-2282) just west of Tallahassee and **Tate's Hell State Forest** (290 Airport Rd, Carrabelle; tel: 850-697-3734) near Carrabelle and you'll see how wild Old Florida used to be.

Ecotourism has taken root in this region, which is rich in opportunities for hiking, biking, fishing, kayaking, and canoeing. Bird-watching is especially popular. Birders come from far and wide to see the bird life of **St Marks National Wildlife Refuge** ❹ (1200 Lighthouse Rd, St Marks; tel: 850-925-6121; visitor center 8am–5pm, park 6am–8pm), a salt marsh that attracts some 300 bird species, including elegant, watchful hawks, noisy ducks, and numerous shorebirds.

immigrant reputed to have once painted castles for Kaiser Wilhelm.

## The Panhandle

The Florida Panhandle is a world apart. In contrast to the theme parks, crowds, and craziness of the I-4 corridor in central Florida, the Panhandle is laid back, shady, and more of what Old Florida used to be like.

West of Tallahassee, the inland areas are covered in vast tracts of forest that

## Big Bend

There are a couple of ways to explore the Panhandle. If you are in a hurry to get to Pensacola, take I-10 west from Tallahassee. You'll get there in less than four hours but miss a scenic drive along the **Big Bend**, where the Panhandle dips into

the peninsula. While it makes for a longer drive, US 98 and its side roads are the only way to experience the essence of the region. Several roads in Leon, Wakulla, and Franklin counties are part of what is called the **Big Bend Scenic Highway**, 200 miles (320km) of scenic roads that lead motorists around Apalachicola National Forest to St George Island State Park.

South of Tallahassee, US 98 leads past a string of small fishing towns. Among the most prominent is **Carrabelle ❺**. During the post-Civil War years it was a booming place, when lumber and turpentine were king, and stately schooners carried goods up North. The railroad also brought industry to Carrabelle and allowed salted mullet to be shipped north.

World War II brought another boom in the form of Camp Gordon Johnston, a gigantic training base for amphibious soldiers bound for Europe and the Pacific. Carrabelle later became a commercial fishing port, and, in recent years, a sportsman's paradise. What makes Carrabelle different from other coastal areas in this part of the Big Bend is its

"true" beach – a rare commodity in a region noted more for its estuaries, tidal creeks and rivers.

## To hell and back

Carrabelle is set near Tate's Hell Swamp, which sprawls over most of Franklin County. The name is connected to the legend of Cebe Tate, a hunter who vanished into the swamp almost a century ago. According to local lore, he entered the wilderness in search of a panther that

*Panhandle beaches are known for fine white "sugar sand" and clear blue water.*

**BELOW:** nautical paraphernalia fill roadside shops on and around the Big Bend Scenic Highway.

*Miniature golf in Panama City Beach.*

**TIP**

Test your fish-flinging skills at the annual St George Island Mullet Toss in June.

**BELOW:** the calm waters of the Gulf of Mexico are excellent for kayaking.

had been killing his livestock. It took him a week to find his way out, but not before suffering a snakebite that ultimately proved to be fatal.

Tate's Hell drains into another vast domain with remote nooks and crannies of its own, Apalachicola National Forest. Covering 557,000 acres (225,400 hectares), this is the largest of Florida's three national forests. It encompasses pine forest, swamps, and rivers, and has numerous recreational facilities.

The lower end of the Ochlockonee River meanders through Apalachicola National Forest, providing canoeists with pristine rowing through woodlands rife with wildlife. A canoe trail begins 20 miles (32km) west of Tallahassee and continues downriver for 67 miles (108km) to **Ochlockonee River State Park**, south of **Sopchoppy**.

## Florida's oyster capital

Twenty miles (32km) west of Carrabelle is the old cotton port of **Apalachicola** ❻. Oystermen from this area provide at least 90 percent of Florida's oysters, which are cultivated in the shallow waters of Apalachicola Bay.

Seafood isn't Apalachicola's only claim to fame. One of the city's early physicians made the world more bearable by inventing refrigeration and air conditioning. While trying to control malaria in the region in the late 1840s, Dr. John Gorrie succeeded in building an ice machine that kept his patients' rooms cool. Gorrie got a patent for the machine, but no credit for his work until long after his death in 1851. The **John Gorrie State Museum** (6th St and Ave D; tel: 850-633-9347, www.floridastateparks.org/johngorrie museum; Mon, Thu, Fri, Sat, Sun 9am–5pm; charge) has a replica of the first ice machine (the original is in the Smithsonian Institution in Washington, DC).

## Calm before the storm

Connected by a toll bridge to US 98 is **St George Island** ❼, part of which is protected as **St George Island State Park** (1900 E. Gulf Beach Dr, St George Island; tel: 850-927-2111; daily 8am–sunset; charge), with 9 miles (14km) of undeveloped beach and woods that are a favorite nesting place for ospreys. The park was

*Recommended Restaurants pages 354–5*

damaged during Hurricane Dennis in 2005, but all-new facilities have been built and the beach is open for business.

Next door, but accessible only by boat from Apalachicola, is St Vincent Island, a nirvana for wildlife enthusiasts, who come to see loggerhead turtles, wild turkeys, and non-native sambar deer, originally from India.

Back on the mainland, you can detour along SR 30E to sample the magnificence of **Cape San Blas** ❽. Sunset is a particularly moody time to sit on the sand dunes and gaze out over the Gulf of Mexico, but be sure to take insect repellent. To the north is **St Joseph Peninsula State Park** ❾ (8899 Cape San Blas Rd; tel: 850-227-1327, www.floridastateparks.org/stjoseph; daily 8am–sunset; charge), with miles of beautiful beaches and an excellent hiking trail, plus rental cabins and a basic campground.

Heading north on the mainland, you'll find **Port St Joe**, which burst into existence in the 1820s. In those days it was a major cotton-shipping port replete with warehouses, casinos, and sprawling mansions. Yellow fever swept the town in the early 1840s, killing more than two-thirds of the population. The town boomed

again in the early 20th century due to the railroad and export lumber business.

## Party town

To the northwest is **Panama City Beach** ❿. All the beaches in this area received a severe battering from hurricanes Erin and Opal in 1995 and hurricane Ivan in 2004; the scars left by Ivan are healing and the pristine white beaches still sparkle. In fact, this part of the Gulf Coast has some of the world's most beautiful beaches.

*A recreational fishing boat is equipped for a day of angling on the Gulf.*

**BELOW:** bikers at the beach.

Panama City Beach – the "Spring Break Capital of the South" – is currently undergoing a sweeping revitalization. It's still a party town, but old buildings have been razed to make way for new museums, galleries, parks, homes, and shopping malls. **Pier Park** (Front Beach Rd at Pier Park Dr; tel: 850-236-9974; Mon–Sat 10am–9pm, Sun noon–6pm) is touted as the premier shopping destination; and the new Panama City-Bay County International Airport, expected to open in 2009, will undoubtedly boost visitation significantly.

While in Panama City Beach, stop at Zoo World (9008 Front Beach Rd; tel: 850-230-4839, www.zoo-world.us; open daily; charge), which has more than 20 endangered species as well as one of Florida's better petting zoos; or catch the sea lion and dolphin shows at **Gulf World Marine Park** (15412 Front Beach Rd; tel: 850-234-5271; daily from 9am; charge), also on the seafront.

## An architectural interlude

Between Seagrove Beach and Grayton Beach is **Seaside** ⓫, one of the state's most unusual communities. Built in the 1980s, this experiment in urban planning attempts to re-create a Victorian resort. It has tidy streets lined with quaint wooden cottages complete with gingerbread detailing and picket fences. Seaside is worth a peek (and there's a beach, of course), but as with many modern planned communities, there is a sense of surreal conformity. Little wonder that it was chosen as the setting for *The Truman Show*, the 1998 movie with Jim Carrey as a man living in a made-for-TV world.

You'll find rather more authentic grace inland at **Eden Gardens State Park** and the **Wesley House** (off US 98 and CR 295 in **Point Washington** ⓬; tel: 850-231-4214, www.floridastateparks.org/Eden Gardens; tours hourly Thu–Mon 10am–3pm; charge), where a stately old Southern mansion is set in lovely ornamental gardens. The white-columned home was built of heart-pine and cypress in the late 1800s by a local lumber baron.

## The Emerald Coast

Next on US 98 is **Destin** ⓭, a fishing town where marlin and sailfish test their strength and cunning against fishermen.

While there aren't as many commercial fishing boats and shrimp boats as there used to be, the Gulf water is just as green and clear as the day it was created. That's why the area between Port St Joe and Pensacola is called the Emerald Coast. Here, dozens of charter boat captains begin their day at 5am loading barrels of ice in anticipation of the day's catch. Closer to land, the "big game" fish is mullet – one of the most exciting of the inshore catches. Fishermen use long, narrow skiffs in their search, the better to pole shallow bayous favored by the fish. It's often the main course at local seafood joints and is usually served with coleslaw or baked beans, grits, and hush puppies.

Just across from Destin is **Fort Walton Beach ⓮** and **Niceville**, home to the vast **Eglin Air Force Base**. Eglin is the largest base of its kind in the US, encompassing some 724 sq miles (1,875 sq km) of land and more than 97,000 sq miles (250,000 sq km) of airspace. The base employs some 20,000 people who contribute considerably to the local economy. The **US Air Force Armament Museum** (100 Museum Dr; tel: 850-651-1808;

Mon–Sat 9.30am–4.30pm; free), just outside Eglin near Valparaiso, will interest fans of military aviation. The gift shop is full of models and other curiosities.

## Gulf Islands

There are numerous small beach communities west along US 98, but the best route is SR 399, which veers south at Navarre onto **Santa Rosa Island ⓯**. Here you can revel in miles of billowing dunes topped by miniature magnolias.

*A dolphin trainer works with one of her "pupils" at Gulf World Marine Park in Panama City Beach.*

**BELOW:**
Fort Walton Beach.

*Architectural details add charm and character to Pensacola's historic downtown.*

The strip's promoters claim the sands are the whitest in the world.

This part of the coast is all part of **Gulf Islands National Seashore**, which protects 150 miles (240km) of pristine coastline that runs west as far as Gulfport in Mississippi. Visitors can stop at park sites and enjoy a day in the sun. There are campsites and nature trails as well as picnic areas and other facilities. Another gorgeous section of the National Seashore is on **Perdido Key** ⓰, a 30-minute drive southwest of Pensacola, with lovely beaches and salt marshes rich in bird life.

## Pensacola

Finally, more than 200 miles (320km) from Tallahassee, is **Pensacola** ⓱, a coastal city that is a mixture of Old South charm, Spanish heritage, and Navy bravado. The city has taken steps to preserve its 400-year-old heritage in two historic districts near downtown as well as in museums, battle sites, and forts. And it isn't just in museum pieces that the city's history lives. It's in streets with names such as Intendencia, Zaragoza, and Cervantes, and it moves in the wind at St Michael's Cemetery, where tombstones bearing Spanish inscriptions date back to the 1700s. The area also has beautiful beaches – miles and miles of undeveloped coast where sand dunes (not condominiums) rise high above blue seas.

## Contested territory

Don Tristan de Luna was the first to attempt establishing a settlement in the area in 1559, six years before St Augustine. But de Luna and the 1,500 colonists who came with him abandoned the settlement two years later. It wasn't until 1752 that a permanent settlement was established at Pensacola, though the

*Recommended Restaurants pages 354-5*

Spaniards had tried again in 1698 and 1722. Since its founding, Pensacola has flown the flags of five countries in Plaza Ferdinand VII. The city celebrates its proud history each spring with the **Fiesta of Five Flags**. There are parades, art shows, and a reenactment of de Luna's landing in 1559.

The British occupied Pensacola during the Revolutionary War but lost the city to the Spanish in 1781 after a month-long siege. The victory cut off British access to the fledgling American states and buoyed the hopes of colonists fighting for independence farther north.

Four decades later, Andrew Jackson marched into Pensacola to claim Florida for the United States. Jackson, the first territorial governor of Florida, tried to convince the Spaniards to clean up streets he found "filthy and disgusting." Fed up, he packed up and went home after two months.

## Historic Pensacola Village

Today, the original town square near Pensacola Bay is the centerpiece of the **Seville District**, a 37-block section of restored homes, shops, and old-time eateries that is Pensacola's crowning achievement in historic preservation. The square and nearby streets are a pleasant place to spend an afternoon strolling around. Several museums and some lovely restored homes in this district have been gathered together under the name Historic Pensacola Village. **Tivoli House**, (205 E. Zaragoza St; tel: 850-595-5985, www.historicpensacola.org), dispenses tickets and information and organizes guided tours.

One of the most notable restored houses in the neighborhood is "the Oldest House" on Church Street, known as the **Lavalle House**. The exact construction date of Lavalle House is unknown, but historians consider it typical of the French Creole cottages of the 18th century. Other fine houses are the nearby **Dorr House**, at the corner of Church and Adams streets, and the so-called **Steamboat House**, on Government Street.

There are several good museums. On Zaragoza Street is the **Museum of Commerce** and **Museum of Industry** (201 E. Zaragoza St; tel: 850-595-5985; Mon–Sat 10am–4pm). The nearby **T.T. Wentworth Jr. Museum** (330 S. Jef-

*Pensacola is a sizable city, with a metropolitan population of 402,000, seven colleges and universities, a fine airport, a distinctive downtown, an educated work force, fine hospitals, and centers of research and technology.*

**BELOW LEFT AND BELOW:** Historic Pensacola Village.

*Vacation houses – many available to rent – have views of the Gulf and direct beach access.*

**BELOW:**
cypress swamp.
**BELOW RIGHT:**
Fort Barrancas.

array of artworks ranging from pre-Columbian pottery to modern painting.

**Seville Quarter**, billed as Pensacola's premier entertainment and dining complex, is in a restored 19th-century building on Government Street, on the fringe of Seville Square. It's a good place for a night out, with a wide range of bars and restaurants.

## Pensacola's other districts

For background on Pensacola's role in the Civil War, the **Civil War Soldiers Museum** is worth a visit (108 S. Palafox Pl; tel: 850-469-1900; Tue–Sat 10am–4pm; charge) in the **Palafox District** – a cluster of early 20th-century residences at the southern end of Palafox Street.

The city's third historic district takes you back to the days of Pensacola's lumber boom. Residents built big houses and made big money. Today, dozens of houses from the era still stand in a 50-block area called the **North Hill Preservation District**, north of Wright Street. Thanks to preservationists who set out to save the decaying neighborhood, many of the handsome homes have been

ferson St; tel: 850-595-5990; Mon–Sat 10am–4pm) is a fine Spanish Renaissance Revival building with a fascinating collection of Florida memorabilia. Other old houses have been turned into antique stores and restaurants serving deli sandwiches, wine and cheese, and gourmet ice cream. Here too is the **Pensacola Museum of Art** (407 S. Jefferson St; tel: 850-432-6247, www.pensacolamuseumofart.org; Tue–Fri 10am–5pm, Sat–Sun noon–5pm; charge), which has an eclectic

## The Inland Empire

Most tourists in the Panhandle focus on the coastal region, but lovers of nature will find the interior equally enticing. For example, in an isolated spot on the Apalachicola River just south of I-10 is Torreya State Park (2576 NW Torreya Park Road; tel: 850-643-2674). The park encompasses more than 13,000 acres (5,200 hectares) of the state's most diverse geography and is home to a rare species of the Torreya tree. To the west, 3 miles (5km) north of Marianna off SR 167, is Florida Caverns State Park (3345 Caverns Rd; tel: 850-482-9598), one of a few parks with air-filled caves, replete with spellbinding limestone formations. On the surface are trails for hiking and horseback riding. A canoe trail runs 52 miles (84km) south to Dead Lakes, north of Wewahitchka on SR 71, where a forest of cypress, oak, and pine is drowned by the natural overflow of the Chipola River.

Closer to Pensacola, I-10 skims the edge of Blackwater River State Forest (11650 Munson Hwy; tel: 850-957-6140), a vast woodland with hiking and camping. The tannin-stained Blackwater River winds through the forest and is excellent for canoeing.

Recommended Restaurants pages 354–5

restored. Visitors must content themselves with a view from outside, as most are private residences.

## Defending Pensacola

Across the bay, **Fort Pickens** (tel: 850-934-2635; open daily; charge), a pentagonal stronghold with a bastion at each corner, took five years to build and accommodated as many as 600 men.

In the early days of the Civil War, Union soldiers at Fort Pickens on the western tip of Santa Rosa Island engaged Confederate troops at **Fort Barrancas** (Pensacola Naval Air Station; tel: 850-455-5167) on the mainland. Pickens guarded the harbor entrance and prevented the Confederates from using the shipyard and adjacent railyard. Some historians believe the first shots of the tragic conflict may have actually been fired here, not at Fort Sumter in South Carolina. In the end, the Yankee invasion of Tennessee in 1862 forced Confederate leaders to move their manpower north, and Pensacola was abandoned. The town stayed in Union hands for the rest of the war. In the 1880s the fortress was famous for its imprisonment of Apache chief Geronimo. Both forts can be toured; Fort Pickens has a campground.

## High flying

The area is also home to the **Pensacola Naval Air Station**, the nation's largest, founded in 1914. All Navy training for land and sea is headquartered at the base. According to the Pensacola Chamber of Commerce, the Department of Defense is a powerful economic engine here. The military employs some 20,000 active duty personnel and other federal workers and contributes more than $2.77 billion in annual wages.

The base is also the headquarters of the famous precision-flying team, the Blue Angels, who put on two shows here each year. You may see them training over Sherman Field.

The **National Museum of Naval Aviation** (1750 Radford Blvd; tel: 850-452-3604, www.naval-air.org; daily 9am–5pm; free) exhibits more than 150 restored aircraft, ranging from a World War II airship to four former Blue Angels Skyhawks. There is also an IMAX theater and flight simulators. ❑

*Docents in period costume "interpret" 19th-century life at Historic Pensacola Village.*

**BELOW:** Blue Angels exhibit at the National Museum of Naval Aviation.

# RESTAURANTS

## Restaurants

Prices for a three-course dinner per person, excluding tax, tip, and beverages:
**$** = under $20
**$$** = $20–45
**$$$** = $45–60
**$$$$** = over $60

### Apalachicola

**Boss Oyster**
123 Water St
Tel: 850-653-8139
L & D daily
Here's where to find the local delicacy – world-famous Apalachicola Bay oysters, shrimp, crayfish, and barbecue. Dine inside, or outside on the open-air porch. $$$

### Destin

**Graffiti and the Funky Blues Shack**
Village of Baytowne Wharf,

707 Harbor Blvd
Tel: 850-654-2764
D daily
An expansive menu filled with gourmet pasta and pizza is served in a casual setting decorated with folk art. The Funky Blues Shack bar is open to 2am. $$

**Rutherfords 465 at Regatta Bay**
465 Regatta Bay Blvd
Tel: 850-337-8888
L daily
Set at a country club, Rutherfords offers a variety of salads and sandwiches. There's also a full bar. $$

### Eastpoint

**That Place on 98**
500 US 98
Tel: 850-670-9898
L & D daily

A colorful waterfront eatery right on US 98 in a sleepy oyster village. You can accompany your meal of crab cakes, Panhandle chowder, crab claws, and smoked fish dip with a splendid view of Apalachicola Bay. $$

### Grayton Beach

**Criolla's**
170 E. Scenic Hwy 30-A
Tel: 850-267-1267
D Mar–Aug Mon-Sat, Sep–Feb Tue–Sat
Criolla's features an Australian chef who specializes in dishing up plates of Down Under fare, from lemon myrtle-infused sorbet to kangaroo served mid-rare. Plank grilling is a house specialty that produces a smoke-enhanced flavor. $$$$

### Panacea

**Angelo & Son's Seafood Restaurant**
US 98
Tel: 850-984-5168
L & D daily
Commonly called Angelo's, this popular family-owned restaurant was all but destroyed during Hurricane Dennis in 2005 but has since been rebuilt high up on stilts. Angelo's – which benefits from having its own fishing fleet – features house specialties such as bulldozer lobster, grouper, and escargot. There are always creative, daily chalkboard specials. $$$

### Panama City Beach

**Another Broken Egg**
11535 Hutchison Blvd
Tel: 850-249-2007
B & L daily, Sun Br
Another Broken Egg is a great place to take the family. It has something for everyone, all in a cozy French country atmosphere. Tasty omelettes, crisp salads, and delicious sandwiches. The perfect spot for a nice Sunday brunch or a quick bite before hitting the beach. $

**Montego Bay Seafood House**
4920 Thomas Dr
Tel: 850-234-8686
473 Beckrich Rd
Tel: 850-233-6033
L & D daily
Craving raw oysters or a great seafood platter? Head over to this beach-side seafood house and raw bar. There's something on the extensive menu for all tastebuds, including award-winning seafood gumbo, appetizers, large salads, juicy ribs and burgers, perfectly seasoned chicken, and fresh fried seafood. $$

### Pensacola

**Dharma Blue**
300 S. Alcaniz St
Tel: 850-433-1275
L & D Mon–Sat
Set in a "vibrant coastal atmosphere," Dharma Blue offers the finest sushi bar in Florida, a cocktail bar, indoor and outdoor seating, and savory lunch favorites

**LEFT:** the ambience at Dharma Blue is casual and arty.
**OPPOSITE:** Boss Oyster specializes in a local delicacy.

such as fried grouper sandwiches, seared crab cake sandwiches, and fried green tomato clubs. $$

## Jackson's Restaurant
400 S. Palafox St
Tel: 850-469-9898
D Mon-Sat
Jackson's is an award-winning, upscale treat. It's housed in a 19th-century building, with a sophisticated but not stuffy atmosphere and an efficient wait staff. The kitchen is often best when it does the least, allowing the natural flavors of fresh seafood to play the dominant role. Elsewhere on the menu, Southern standards are given gourmet treatment. Be sure to leave room for the sumptuous desserts. $$$$

## McGuire's Irish Pub
600 E. Gregory St
Tel: 850-433-6789
L & D daily
Located in Pensacola's 1927 Old Firehouse, McGuire's is famous for its fine corned beef and cabbage, shepherd's pie, rosemary scented Irish lamb stew, and mushroom pie, along with great local seafood and steaks. $$

## The Melting Pot of Pensacola
418 E. Gregory St #500
Tel: 850-438-4030
D daily
For a change of pace from the coastal surf 'n' turf eateries, try the Melting Pot, a fondue restaurant that won the Wine Spectator Award of Excellence four years in a row. $$$

## Seville Quarter
130 E. Government St
Tel: 850-434-6211
L & D daily

Pensacola's premier dining and entertainment complex started in 1967 as the dream of Bob Snow, a multitalented entrepreneur who fell in love with Pensacola while in the Navy. Today there are four themed restaurants gathered here in historical surroundings: Rosie O'Grady's, Apple Annie's, Lili Marlene's World War I Aviator's Pub, and the Palace Oyster Bar. $

## Blue Parrot Oceanfront Café
68 W. Gorrie Dr
Tel: 850-927-2987
L & D daily
Situated right on the beach, the Blue Parrot features generous indoor and outdoor seating – and for those chilly evenings, the patio even has heaters. There's a well-rounded, surf 'n' turf menu that includes items such as conch fritters, seafood gumbo, burgers, salads, and Apalachicola Bay oysters raw, baked, or Rockefeller style. $$$

### St Teresa
## Summer Camp Beach Restaurant
108 Sea Pine Dr
Tel: 850-697-2200
L daily
This new eatery does a delicious meal that's off the beaten path. A view of the Gulf awaits, but the food is the main attraction, with a menu of the region's freshest food – fish, oysters, clams, scallops, shrimp, and more. All dishes are presented simply but artfully. $$

### Tallahassee
## Andrew's Capital Grill and Bar
228 S. Adams St
Tel: 850-222-3444

L & D Mon–Sat, Sun Br
Andrew's is a local landmark, located downtown near the seat of Florida's political power. Andrew's was noted as "Best Outdoor Dining" by *Tallahassee* magazine and offers burgers, sandwiches, salads, and more ambitious entrées. $$

## Café Huston Oven & Grille
3197 Merchants Row Blvd #110
Tel: 850-877-7833
L & D daily
This is a quick-serve restaurant with an upscale atmosphere, and a great place to socialize and catch a game on TV. American cuisine is made from scratch, including homemade pizza, gourmet salads, and char-grilled burgers, chicken, and grouper. $$

## Harry's Seafood Bar & Grille
301 S. Bronough St
Tel: 850-222-3976
L & D daily
Harry's will remind diners of the Big Easy. It serves a wide variety of New Orleans-style cuisine including fresh seafood, salads, sandwiches, desserts, and more. $$

## La Lanterna
2766 Capital Circle NE
Tel: 850-878-9738
L & D Mon–Sat
This is an authentic Italian restaurant and a family-owned market and deli, featuring a wide array of Italian grocery items, meats, and cheeses. The food is freshly prepared for takeout, including bread, pasta, lasagna, cannoli, gelato, sandwiches, and salads. $$

## Mellow Mushroom
1641 Pensacola St
Tel: 850-575-0050
L & D daily
This Italian-American restaurant features a variety of specialty pizzas, like the mega-veggie, the mighty meat, and the Hawaiian. Hoagies, calzones, salads, garlic and stone-baked pretzels, cookies, hummus, and seasonal soups round out the tasty menu. $

## Morelia Mexican Dining
1400-35 Village Square Blvd
Tel: 850-907-9173
L & D daily
This casual, award-winning Mexican restaurant serves up classic dishes such as tacos, tostadas, fajitas, burritos, and enchiladas. $$

# INSIGHT GUIDES

## TRAVEL TIPS

# FLORIDA

# T RANSPORTATION

# GETTING THERE
# AND GETTING AROUND

## GETTING THERE

### By Air

Most major US and international carriers serve Florida. Fare prices are competitive, so shop around before buying a ticket; it's usually cheaper to travel midweek. A variety of discount fares and "package deals," which can significantly cut round-trip rates to and from Florida, are also available. Special Internet-only deals can be found easily online.

Florida has 14 international airports, but the state's major hubs are Miami, Orlando, Fort Lauderdale, and Tampa, all of which are efficient, safe, and easy to get around. Miami International Airport is the state's largest. It is also a major jumping-off point for flights into the Caribbean and Latin America. In addition, there are connections to regional airports, which include Daytona Beach, Fort Myers, Jacksonville, Key West, Marathon, Melbourne, Naples, Palm Beach, Panama City, Pensacola, St Petersburg-Clearwater, Sarasota-Bradenton, Gainesville, and Tallahassee.

Many scheduled services are supplemented by charter flights. A lot of package flights land at Orlando-Sanford Airport, 30 miles (48km) north of Orlando. In summer, this small airport is jammed with tourists, and lines at immigration can be long. Furthermore, the extra distance can be costly, especially if you plan to use public transportation to reach Orlando. A rental car is essential if you arrive at a distant airport.

**Special Note**: Expect delays departing US airports due to new Homeland Security anti-terrorism rules. These are apt to change, so

check before flying. Pack items in both carry-on and checked luggage in clear bags, leave gifts unwrapped, and take laptops out of bags for inspection by Transportation Security Administration (TSA) personnel. Consider wearing slip-on shoes as all footwear must be removed and scanned by x-ray machines. Passengers are allowed *one* carry-on resealable 1-quart (1-liter) clear plastic bag, which can contain liquids, gels, and aerosols in containers of 3 ounces or less. The contents in the plastic bag must be sealed and may be subjected to x-ray inspection separate from the carry-on bag.

The telephone numbers of the main airports are:
Miami International Airport (MIA), tel: 305-876-7000
Fort Lauderdale/Hollywood International Airport (FLL), tel: 954-359-1200
Orlando International Airport (MCO), tel: 407-825-2001
Orlando-Sanford Airport, tel: 407-322-7771
Tampa International Airport (TPA), tel: 813-870-8700

#### International and Domestic Airlines

Major airlines serving Florida:

America West: tel: 800-235-9292; www.americawest.com
American: tel: 800-433-7300; www.aa.com
British Airways: tel: 800-47-9297; www.british-airways.com
Continental: tel: 800-525-0280; www.continental.com
Delta: tel: 800-221-1212; www.delta-air.com
Frontier: tel: 800-432-1359; www.flyfrontier.com

JetBlue: tel: 800-538-2583; www.jetblue.com
Lufthansa: tel: 800-645-3880; www.lufthansa/usa.com
Northwest-KLM: tel: 800-225-2525; www.nwa.com
Southwest: tel: 800-435-9792; www.southwest.com
Spirit: tel: 800-772-7117; www.spiritair.com
TED: tel: 800-225-5833; www.flyted.com
United Airlines: tel: 800-864-8331; www.ual.com
US Air: tel: 800-428-4322; www.usairways.com
Virgin Atlantic: tel: 800-862-8621; www.virginatlantic.com

### By Train

**Amtrak** (tel: 800-872-7245; www.amtrak.com) offers leisurely service from the Midwest, Northeast, and South – and connecting service from points west – to 13 Florida cities. Silver Service is available between New York City and Florida, with major stops in Jacksonville, Orlando, Tampa, and Miami. The Palmetto does the same route but has business-class service. For those who want to take their car, Auto Train service from Lorton, Virgina, near Washington DC, to Sanford, north of Orlando, is an option.

### By Bus

**Greyhound** (tel: 800-231-2222; www.greyhound.com) provides bus service to Florida and all over the state. Intercity service includes many out-of-the-way stops en route and can be slow; try to use "Express" buses, which stop in fewer places. Bus terminals are often in run-down areas of town, so take care when traveling to or from stations.

## By Ship

Florida is surrounded by water, so it's quite easy to travel to or from the state by sea. Fort Lauderdale is the state's largest transatlantic harbor. Florida offers year-round cruises into the Atlantic, Caribbean, or Gulf of Mexico.

For a complete overview, ask a travel agent, check the travel ads in any Sunday newspaper, or check on the Internet at sites like www.cruise.com. Packages vary, with cruises lasting from a few hours or a day to over two weeks. Three-day jaunts to the Bahamas are popular. So, too, are the one-day or one-night trips that don't stray too far from the coast, which, for some people, are simply an opportunity to gamble. Casinos are illegal in Florida, except on the Seminole reservation, but the law does not apply in international waters.

## GETTING AROUND

### Public Transportation

Cities with walkable historic downtowns, such as Tampa, Key West, St Augustine, Orlando, and St Petersburg, encourage visitors and residents to use inexpensive trams and light rail to get around. Florida's abandoned railway beds have found new life as countywide trails linking historic communities under the Rails-to-Trails program. Most offer bicycle and rollerblade rentals. For a list of public transportation in Florida, log onto www.apta.com/links/state_local/fl.cfm.

### Trains

**Amtrak** serves 13 cities in Florida. A high-speed rail link between Miami and Orlando was approved by Florida voters but is still in the planning stages. **Tri-Rail** service (tel: 800-874-7245; www.tri-rail.com) links Miami and West Palm Beach. It is geared to commuters but can be useful for reaching places like Fort Lauderdale and Boca Raton. Trains run hourly, with reduced weekend service. Several cities, including Tampa, have light rail service throughout the downtown and adjoining tourist areas.

### Buses

Greyhound bus service links cities throughout Florida. Once there, inexpensive city bus lines can be an excellent and inexpensive way of getting around.

### Taxis

Taxis are available in all the main tourist centers. They tend to be expensive, and you usually have to telephone for pick up. Your hotel can call for you, otherwise numbers are listed in the Yellow Pages. Don't stand by the side of the road, even in Miami, and expect to hail a passing cab. Water taxis are available on the intracoastal waterway in Fort Lauderdale, a fun way to sightsee.

### Driving

A car is the most convenient way to travel around Florida. More than 20 million visitors enter the Sunshine State by car every year – about twice as many as those entering by plane. One of the reasons for the reliance on the car is that it is virtually essential to have a car once you arrive. Bus, train, and taxi service within Florida are quite irregular, unreliable, and slow to cover the state's vast distances.

Traffic has grown exceptionally dense on Florida's highways, reflecting the large numbers of new residents and growing tourism. Speed limits are strictly enforced. Drive with care and allow plenty of time to get to your destination. Avoid rush hour while traveling in metro areas. Whenever possible, it's quickest to drive on interstates, the largest and fastest of the highways, which link major metro areas, with spurs to local expressways.

I-75 connects northern Florida with Gulf of Mexico cities and Miami; I-95 is the main east coast route. I-10 is an east-west route across the Panhandle. I-4, Florida's Fantasy Highway, links Tampa to Daytona Beach with exits at Seaworld, Disneyworld, Celebration, and various other attractions. The Florida Turnpike, a toll road, begins its slash across central Florida from I-75 near Wildwood, south of Ocala, and ends at Florida City. A shorter toll route is the Bee Line Expressway between Orlando and the Space Coast. Carry plenty of quarters and dollar bills; some highways do not have manned toll booths to give change.

US highways cross large chunks of Florida – US 1 runs all the way down the east coast to Key West – but are not fast through-routes. They are heavily trafficked and often lined with stores and interrupted by traffic lights. State routes are normally the same size as US highways. County roads are secondary roads that are better for enjoying the scenery.

### Private Transportation

#### Car Rental

Most rental agencies require you to be at least 21 years old and have a valid drivers license and a major credit card. Many take debit cards, too, and some will take cash in lieu of a credit card, but this might be as high as $500. Foreign travelers will need to produce a drivers license from their own country.

You will find rental car companies in most cities and airports. Available rental vehicles range from modest economy cars to luxury convertibles, vans, and 4WD vehicles. Rates are cheap both by US and international standards, but you should still shop around, preferably online, for the best rates and features. Smaller local rental firms outside the airports are often less expensive than the large national companies because they don't charge high airport fees. When choosing a vehicle, take into account gas prices, which, although cheap by European standards, add up on long-distance drives.

It's cheaper to arrange car rental in advance. Check with your airline, bus, or rental agent, travel agent, or the Internet for special package deals that include a car: rental rates can be reduced by up to 50 percent if you buy a so-called "fly-drive" deal. Be wary of offers of "free" car rental: such cars do not include extras like tax and insurance.

Go over the insurance coverage provisions carefully with the agent before signing the rental agreement. Loss Damage Waiver (LDW), or Collision Damage Waiver (CDW), is essential. Without it, you'll be liable for any damage done to your vehicle in the event of an accident, regardless of whether or not you are to blame. You are advised to pay for supplementary liability insurance on top of standard third-party insurance. Insurance and tax charges can add a lot to an otherwise inexpensive rental, so take it into account in your budgeting. Also be sure to walk around the rental car slowly, check it for existing damage, and make a careful note of any dents or dings before leaving the lot.

### Boat Rental

Floridians have an intimate relationship with water, and the state's coastal areas, intracoastal waterways, and rivers allow many residents to park a boat right next to their house. Guided sightseeing, fishing, and diving cruises are available in many areas; you'll even find water taxis. In some places, such as Key West and more remote barrier-island communities on the Gulf of Mexico, a boat is almost a necessity to get around. Rentals are available in many places. Don't leave Florida without getting out on its sparkling waters at least once.

# A CCOMMODATIONS

# HOTELS, YOUTH HOSTELS, BED & BREAKFASTS

### Choosing Lodgings

Accommodations in Florida range from luxury resorts, which cater to your every last need, to modest mom-and-pop motels; cozy, antiques-filled bed-and-breakfasts and small historic inns; and budget lodgings in youth hostels and campgrounds beside the ocean or in the forest.

Although rather anonymous, chain motels and hotels are usually reliable and in some places, such as Gainesville, are your main option if you don't want to go the bed-and-breakfast route. Family-owned motels, many built close to popular roadside attractions of the 1940s and 1950s, are usually acceptable if you're on a budget; a quick check online for photos and reader reviews can sometimes head off problems. In major tourist areas like Orlando, Kissimmee, and Miami Beach, the quality and variety of tourist accommodations is particularly good. Bedrooms are often large and normally come with two double or queen-sized beds.

Florida's beach communities and theme-park destinations like Orlando and Kissimmee also have a huge selection of self-catering vacation rentals, an often overlooked option. Most are either in modern housing estates called "subdivisions," or in self-catering complexes, consisting of privately owned individual properties, or condominiums. The former, though usually in residential areas, are generally the best choice: homes are often large and have a pool and excellent facilities. Major tour operators offer self-catering accommodations. If you don't want to go completely self-catering, consider staying in one of the excellent new all-suites hotel

chains or in a motel room with a kitchenette, known as an efficiency.

Beachfront vacation rentals offer the best of both worlds. Many are right on the beach within small resort complexes that have swimming pools, laundry, barbecue grills, and gear for beach activities. In remote undeveloped areas along the Gulf, vacation rentals predominate.

### Reservations and Prices

Reservations are generally required in advance. If you are traveling in the high season, book several months in advance if you have your heart set on a particular hotel – or if you want to stay inside Walt Disney World. Room rates vary enormously between high tourist season in the winter months and the off-season months of May and June and September to early December; the cost can rise by 30 percent or more during peak tourist months. Ask for a discount if you are staying for a week or more, or if you are visiting during the off season, which for many hotel proprietors is an extremely lean time. Florida imposes a resort tax in addition to the usual sales tax, which is added to the price of the rooms. It varies from county to county and ranges from 2 to 5 percent.

### Chain Hotels and Motels

These are ubiquitous throughout the United States and have many fans. Some people dislike chains because they offer no variety, lack a personal touch, and are often located in the most commercial, nondescript areas of town next to busy highways. The advantage is that once you've been to a hotel run by a particular chain, even though these are usually a

franchise, you can bank on certain facilities and a standard of service wherever you are in the US. For travelers wanting to focus on their vacation, this can be a boon.

### Bed-and-Breakfasts

Bed-and-breakfasts vary greatly in terms of price and quality, but the one thing they have in common is that they are almost invariably in a private and/or historic home. Old towns such as Key West, St Augustine, and Gainesville are known for their historic bed-and-breakfast accommodations; in outlying rural areas, bed-and-breakfast might be offered in a modern private home on several acres. Few have restaurants, and facilities will not be as extensive as in a regular hotel. Privacy can be an issue in older inns, but some have separate cottages with self-catering facilities, allowing you to come and go as you please. Hosts are usually a mine of information about local sights, and this can be a great way to make lifelong friends. For those travelers who enjoy the personal ambience – not to mention the afternoon teas, wine and cheese happy hours, and wonderful home-cooked breakfasts found in such places – bed-and-breakfasts are a great choice.

### Camping

Over 100,000 campsites at some 700 campgrounds all over Florida offer ample choice of outdoors accommodations – from simple areas for tents and sleeping bags to elaborate villages with utility hook-ups for recreational vehicles (RVs), restaurants, pools, mini-golf courses, and planned activities.

## Private Campgrounds

Private campgrounds have blossomed around popular tourist attractions and usually have vacancies. Central Florida seems to have the majority of these facilities to accommodate the droves of Disney tourists. Walt Disney World is southwest of Orlando, in Kissimmee, an area that is surprisingly rural and densely forested. If you avoid the main commercial strip, which is noisy and heavily trafficked, camping can be a good option.

A nationwide network of private campgrounds, called Kampgrounds of America (KOA), has around 30 members in Florida. They offer good-quality facilities, including swimming pool, restaurant, laundry, etc. Most accept reservations. Contact KOA at PO Box 30558, Billings, MT 59114-0558; tel: 406-248-7444; www.koa.com.

To obtain information about private campgrounds in Florida, contact Florida Association of RV Parks and Campgrounds, 1340 Vickers Drive, Tallahassee, FL 32303; tel: 850-562-7151; www.floridacamping.com. The association will send you the Florida Camping Directory, which lists hundreds of campgrounds representing nearly 50,000 campsites in Florida divided by region and with details of amenities. You can make reservations using toll-free numbers listed in the brochure.

## Camping in State Parks

Florida's state parks – blessed with incredibly scenic settings such as barrier-island beaches, natural springs, and inland forests – have twice won the government Gold Medal for best in the nation. Many have campgrounds where campsites can be rented for up to 14 days and excellent, clean facilities, including showers, laundry, etc. They are hugely popular, especially among Florida residents, so book well in advance to avoid disappointment. Reservations are accepted up to 60 days in advance of check-in: call the park where you plan to camp. In addition, parks normally hold back some spaces for people who arrive on the day.

Arrive early morning in the most popular areas to get a site. The base fee, usually $16–25, depending on location, covers up to four people; up to eight people may stay at any site. At least one person, 18 years or older, must be in each group. There is a small charge for extra cars and electricity. Only pets on handheld leashes are allowed in state park picnic areas; no pets are allowed in the campgrounds or on public beaches. Fees tend to be higher in the Florida Keys, and only Florida residents may obtain an annual camping permit. Most state park campsites are booked solid in the busy late winter and early spring seasons.

For more information, contact Florida Department of Natural Resources, 3900 Commonwealth Boulevard, Tallahassee, FL 32399-3000; tel: 850-488-9872; www.floridastateparks.org.

## Camping with Mickey

Fort Wilderness Resort inside Walt Disney World has more than 800 campsites. You can rent trailers, which have air conditioning, color TV, radio, cookware, and linens, and sleep up to six people. The resort is located amid 650 acres (263 hectares) of woods and streams on Bay Lake, east of the Magic Kingdom.

For information and reservations, contact Walt Disney World Central Reservations, P.O. Box 10,000, Lake Buena Vista, FL 32830; tel: 407-934-7639; www.bookwdw.reservations.disney.go.com.

---

ACCOMMODATION LISTINGS

# WALT DISNEY WORLD AND ORLANDO

## Magic Kingdom

**Contemporary Resort**
4600 N. World Drive,
Lake Buena Vista, FL 32830
Tel: 407-824-1000
The monorail passes through the middle of this 15-story A-frame built over a quarter-century ago. Most rooms have two queen-size beds and a daybed. Tower rooms have private balconies overlooking the Magic Kingdom or Bay Lake; those in the Garden Wings have nice views but are somewhat distant from the central property. There are several bars and restaurants, including the elegant California Grill – a popular spot for watching Magic Kingdom fireworks. Amenities include a supervised evening children's program, salon, water activities, a health club and tennis center, several swimming pools, and a video arcade. **$$$**

**Grand Floridian Resort & Spa**
4401 Grand Floridian Way,
Lake Buena Vista, FL 32830
Tel: 407-824-3000
The Victorian era in all its splendor is re-created at Disney's flagship property, an elegant confection of glistening white, wooden buildings with red shingled roofs, gracious verandas, and turrets. Open-cage elevators in the plant-filled, five-story, chandeliered lobby serve second-floor shops and restaurants. Most rooms in the four- and five-story lodge buildings have two queen-size beds and a daybed; many overlook the Seven Seas Lagoon. Amenities include some of Disney's finest dining experiences at Victoria and Albert's and Citricos, and a fine waterside restaurant, Narcoossee's; several bars, a supervised evening children's program, the Grand Floridian Health Club and Spa, several swimming pools, and water activities. **$$$**

**Polynesian Resort**
1600 Seven Seas Drive,
Lake Buena Vista, FL 32830
Tel: 407-824-2000
One of Disney's most authentic theme hotels re-creates a Pacific Islands retreat. The centerpiece is the Great Ceremonial House, a tropical extravaganza of plants and waterfalls. Rooms, in 11 two- and three-story "longhouses," vary in size, but most have two queen-size beds, a daybed, and balconies. Those overlooking the Seven Seas Lagoon afford front-row seats for Magic Kingdom fireworks. There are several restaurants and bars, two pools, a playground, supervised evening

children's programs, and water activities. **$$$**

**Wilderness Lodge and Villas**
901 W. Timberline Drive,
Lake Buena Vista, FL 32830
Tel: 407-824-3200
A skillful blending of wood and stone replicates the "rustic architecture" associated with early national park lodges. The eight-story lakefront dwelling appears rustic but its 728 rooms are large and comfortable, with two queen-sized beds, sitting areas, and balconies. The 181 villas, in a five-story adjoining tower, range from efficiencies to two-bedroom units with kitchens, dining areas, whirlpool tubs, and DVD players. Boats sail to the Magic Kingdom. **$$$–$$$$**

### Epcot

**Disney's Boardwalk and Villas**
2101 N. Epcot Resorts Boulevard,
Lake Buena Vista, FL 32830
Tel: 407-939-5100
Elaborately detailed buildings with brightly colored facades and twinkling lights re-create an East Coast boardwalk circa 1920 in Epcot. The 372 rooms are spacious, with two queen-sized beds, daybeds, and ceiling fans. The 520 villas are Disney Vacation Club time-share units that sleep four to 12 people and have kitchens, a laundry, whirlpool tub, and DVD player. Nightclubs, restaurants, games, and shops line the boardwalk. Ferry boats and buses serve the parks. **$$$–$$$$**

**Caribbean Beach**
900 Cayman Way,
Lake Buena Vista, FL 32830
Tel: 407-934-3400
Each of the five areas at this vibrant, 2,112-room resort that circles 45-acre (18-hectare) Barefoot Bay re-creates a Caribbean Island and has its own pool, beach, and laundry. A food court and several restaurants offer casual dining. Family-friendly activities include water sports, bicycle rentals,

video arcade, playgrounds. Easy access to Epcot and Disney's Hollywood Studios. **$$–$$$**

**Dolphin Hotel**
1200 Epcot Resorts Boulevard,
Lake Buena Vista, FL 32830
Tel: 407-934-4000
Two 56-ft (17-meter) -high dolphins and hundreds of seven-story banana leaves festoon the facade of this 27-story, triangular, turquoise hotel with four nine-story wings. The lobby has a circus theme, and the spacious rooms, with turquoise and peach furnishings, have two queen-size beds, desks, and chairs. Some have balconies. There is a supervised evening children's program. In addition to the seashell-shaped pool there are several restaurants and lounges on the property, which is within walking distance of Epcot and the BoardWalk. **$$$**

**Old Key West Resort**
1510 N. Cove Road,
Lake Buena Vista, FL 32830
Tel: 407-827-7700
Although it's miles from the ocean, this hotel's color scheme and architecture bear an uncanny resemblance to buildings in the seaside resort towns far to the south. Studios have two queen-size beds, tables and chairs, small refrigerators, microwaves, and coffeemakers. One-bedroom villas have king-size beds in the main bedroom and queen-size sleeper sofas in the living room. Two- and three-bedroom villas have full kitchens and porches or balconies. All units except studios have private whirlpool tubs. There are grills and picnic tables, several restaurants, a health club, swimming pools, shopping, tennis courts, a video arcade, and playgrounds. **$$$**

**Port Orleans-French Quarter**
2201 Orleans Drive,
Lake Buena Vista, FL 32830
Tel: 407-934-5000
This moderate hotel is reminiscent of New

Orleans, and its landscaping makes it very suitable for couples wanting to get away as there are many quiet, romantic spots in which to linger. On the other hand, kids will love the Doubloon Lagoon pool with its colorfully themed attractions that include alligator and dragon slides. **$$**

**Port Orleans-Riverside**
1251 Riverside Drive,
Lake Buena Vista, FL 32830
Tel: 407-934-6000
The former Dixie Landings has been renamed but retains the feel of the Old South. Accommodations are in two- and three-story buildings divided into "parishes." All rooms are the same size, and most have two double beds. Mansion rooms are in antebellum-style "estates," while Bayou rooms are in rustic-appearing buildings surrounding Man Island, a sprawling water complex. Only mansions have elevators. Amenities include six swimming pools, a restaurant and food court, shops, bars, bike and boat rentals, and fishing excursions. **$$**

**Swan Hotel**
1200 Epcot Resorts Boulevard,
Lake Buena Vista, FL 32830
Tel: 407-934-3000
Just across the road from the Dolphin is this Westin property, topped by two 47-ft-tall (14-meter) swans. Rooms in the 12-story main building and two seven-story towers are a bit smaller in size than those in the Dolphin (see listing above), but similar in color and amenities. There's a pool as well as several restaurants and bars, including the fine Il Mulino's and Kimono sushi bar, and a supervised evening children's program. **$$$**

**Yacht and Beach Club and Beach Club Villas**
1800 Epcot Boulevard,
Lake Buena Vista, FL 32830
Tel: 407-934-7000 (Yacht Club) and 407-934-8000 (Beach Club)
Each of the three

properties overlooking a 25-acre (10 hectares) lake has a distinct theme, but they share many facilities. Yacht Club rooms are finished in a nautical motif; those in the Beach Club are reminiscent of a private seaside retreat. Most, however, have either one king-size or two queen-size beds (some with daybeds), ceiling fans, and a table with chairs. The studios and one- to three-bedroom villas sleep up to eight. The resort's highlight is Stormalong Bay, an elaborate swimming area with whirlpools, water slides, and a private beach. In addition, there are several pools, a miniature golf course, a health club, restaurants and bars, boating, a supervised evening children's program, a salon, tennis courts, a video arcade, and shops. **$$$**

### Animal Kingdom

**All-Star Movies, Music, and Sports**
1991 W. Buena Vista Drive,
Lake Buena Vista, FL 32830
Tel: 407-939-7000 (All-Star Movies), 407-939-6000 (All-Star Music), 407-939-5000 (All-Star Sports)
This was Disney's only budget complex until the Pop Century (see listing below) opened. It has 30 three-story buildings divided by themes. Each has a distinctive facade, but aside from a few decorative touches, the size and decor of most rooms are identical: they're 260 sq ft (24 sq meters), have two double beds, small bureaus, a table with chairs, and bathrooms with separate vanity areas. Popular with families, the resort has a game room, playground, outdoor pool, shopping, and food court. Buses transport guests to the parks. **$$**

**Disney's Animal Kingdom Lodge**
2901 Osceola Parkway,
Lake Buena Vista, FL 32830
Tel: 407-938-3000

A 1,293-room, Africa-themed resort on a 33-acre (13-hectare) savannah teeming with wildlife. A four-story observation window in the elaborate lobby overlooks the savannah, as do many of the rooms, which have balconies, handcrafted furniture, and traditional tapestries. Amenities include three restaurants, a health club, shops, playground, video arcade, and outdoor pool. **$$$–$$$$**

## Hollywood Studios

**Coronado Springs Resort**
Lake Buena Vista, FL 32830
Tel: 407-939-1000
The American Southwest and Mexico are re-created at this 1,921-room lakefront complex with fountains, a Mayan pyramid, and the country's largest ballroom. Each of the three buildings evokes a different setting – oceanfront, the city, the countryside – with rooms decorated accordingly. Standard rooms have two double beds. Pools, health club and spa, playground, video arcades, shops, restaurant, food court, bars, and water sports. **$$–$$$**

**Pop Century**
901 Century Drive,
Lake Buena Vista, FL 32830
Tel: 407-938-4000
Encompassing 20 four-story buildings, this resort is divided into two sections: the Legendary Years, depicting the first 50 years of the 20th century, and the Classic Years, depicting the second 50 years. Statues representing various aspects of pop culture are used to carry the themes. Rooms, smaller than at other Disney properties at 260 sq ft (24 sq meters), have two double beds, bathrooms with a separate vanity area, and small dressers, tables, and chairs. Each section has a food court, swimming pool, playground, shopping area, and video arcade. **$$**

## Other Disney Resorts

**Buena Vista Palace**
1900 Buena Vista Drive,
Lake Buena Vista, FL 32830
Tel: 866-397-6516
www.buenavistapalace.com
Located across the lagoon from Downtown Disney, the Palace's rooms are all very well appointed in sleek modern furnishings and pillow-top beds. Most have outdoor balconies, and some even offer a view of the lake. The Island Suites provide more space than the smallish rooms. The resort has a large spa and pool facilities and six restaurants to choose from. **$$**

**Grosvenor Resort**
1850 Hotel Plaza Boulevard,
Lake Buena Vista, FL 32830
Tel: 407-828 4444
www.grosvenorresort.com
One of several hotels on Disney property but not actually operated by the Disney Company, the Grosvenor is a middle-of-the-road lakeside resort with convention facilities and comfortable, if not lavish, rooms. A variety of recreational facilities and restaurants is available. There is also the Murderwatch Mystery Theater dinner show on Saturday night. Free transportation to the parks is provided for all guests. **$$$**

**Hilton**
1751 Hotel Plaza Boulevard,
Lake Buena Vista, FL 32830
Tel: 407-827-4000
www.hilton-wdwv.com
Within walking distance to Downtown Disney, this large hotel is set among 23 acres (9 hectares) of tropical landscaping. Hotel guests receive similar benefits as Disney Resort guests, including Extra Magic Hours, an on-site Disney Character breakfast, free transportation to the parks, and access to five Disney golf courses. Several grades of suite are available for those needing more space. All rooms have Hilton Serenity Beds to provide extra comfort and

an MP3 compatible clock radio. **$$$**

**Perri House**
10417 Centurion Court,
Lake Buena Vista, FL 32836
Tel: 407-876-4830
A chance to get away from it all without leaving the Disney grounds. This small country inn is secluded on a quiet 16-acre (7-hectare) nature reserve adjacent to Walt Disney World. **$$$**

**Royal Plaza Hotel**
1905 Hotel Plaza Boulevard,
Lake Buena Vista, FL 32830
Tel: 407-828-2828
www.royalplaza.com
Located near Downtown Disney, the Royal Plaza was refurbished in 2007. Its standard rooms are the largest in the Downtown Disney area, are appointed with subtle contemporary decor and furnishings, and have all the modern amenities you'd expect. Suites are also available. The pool is nothing to shout about, but being this close to Disney, you may not find time to use it. **$$**

## Celebration and Kissimmee

**Celebration Hotel**
700 Bloom Street, Celebration,
FL 34747
Tel: 407-566-6000 or
888-499-3800
Located in downtown Celebration, this 115-room boutique hotel evokes old Florida. Hand-painted murals and hand-tinted historic photos of orange groves, wildlife, and other scenes decorate the quiet lobby. The terrace has rocking chairs and overlooks the pool, lake, and adjoining workout room. Rooms have pinstriped wallpaper, and reproduction antique furnishings. Each has a CD player, TV, and DSL. Guest privileges at Celebration's 18-hole golf course and the Fitness Center at the hospital are included. On-site restaurant. **$$$**

**Celebrity Resorts**
2800 N. Pioinciana Boulevard,
Kissimmee, FL 34746
Tel: 866-507-1429
This timeshare

establishment has several different sizes of accommodations, from standard rooms to three-bedroom villas. All are quite affordable and available for short stays. The resort has tennis, basketball, and racquetball courts, a fitness center, three outdoor pools and one indoor pool, and a playground. The rooms and suites are well designed, making the most of their space. **$$**

**Holiday Inn Hotel and Suites-Maingate East**
5678 W. Irlo Bronson Memorial Highway (US 192), Kissimmee,
FL 34746
Tel: 407-396-4488 or
800-366-5437
This large, family-oriented hotel near the Magic Kingdom, with 614 rooms and suites, has pools, children's entertainment, and special "kid's suites." **$$**

**Hyatt Regency Grand Cypress Resort**
One Grand Cypress Boulevard,
Orlando, FL 32836
Tel: 407-239-1234 or
800-554-9288
This luxury resort has a lush garden setting near Downtown Disney. Amenities include golf, a racquetball club, windsurfing on a lake, a "Kid's Club," and an equestrian center, as well as convention facilities. 750 rooms and suites. **$$$$**

**Mystic Dunes Resort and Golf Club**
7900 Mystic Dunes Lane,
Celebration, FL 34747
Tel: 407-226-9501 or
877-747-4747
www.mystic-dunes-resort.com
Located on 600 acres (245 hectares) of meticulously landscaped grounds, this timeshare resort makes for a grand short-term retreat.

### PRICE CATEGORIES

Price categories are for a double room for one night in high season (Jan–Apr):
**$** = less than $75
**$$** = $75–150
**$$$** = $150–200
**$$$$** = more than $200

The sleekly furnished, one- to three-bed villas all have a fully equipped kitchen, washer and dryer, and a whirlpool bath. Resort amenities include the Mystic Dunes Golf Club, four heated swimming pools (one of which has a two-story water slide and children's wading pool), mini-golf, tennis, and basketball courts. **$$$**

**Omni Orlando Resort at ChampionsGate**
1500 Masters Boulevard, ChampionsGate, FL 33896
Tel: 407-390-6664
www.omniorlandoresort.com
Southwest of Celebration along the I-4 corridor, this luxury resort is surrounded by 36 holes of golf designed by Greg Norman. It is also home to the David Leadbetter Golf Academy. No prizes for guessing what brings most guests here. For those not wanting to golf, there is a big pool with a water slide, a lazy river, and seven restaurants to keep you busy. **$$$**

**Orange Lake Resort and Country Club**
8505 W. Irlo Bronson Memorial Highway (US 192), Kissimmee, FL 34747
Tel: 407-239-0000 or 800-877-6522
www.orangelake.com
This handsomely constructed lakeside resort complex has several pools set in beautiful landscaped grounds. The two- and three-bedroom suites feel spacious and inviting and have all the amenities you'd require on holiday, even a kitchenette. There is also a small lazy river to float down, and the Splash lagoon pool has a water slide to entertain children. For bigger boys and girls there are four championship golf courses to choose from. **$$$**

**Palm Lakefront Hostel**
4840 W. Irlo Bronson Highway (US 192), Kissimmee, FL 34747
Tel: 407-396-1759
www.orlandohostels.com
The only place in Orlando that properly caters to the backpacking crowd: you can get a bed for less than 20 bucks at times, and a

public bus connects it directly to Disney and other theme parks. Of course this isn't luxury lodging, but it's not bad. With a clean pool and a lakeside view, it is more than serviceable. **$**

**Ramada Resort Maingate**
2950 Reedy Creek Boulevard, Kissimmee, FL 34737
Tel: 407-396-4466 or 800-365-6935
Comfortable, family-friendly lodging near the Magic Kingdom, with swimming pools and tennis courts. 278 rooms. **$$**

**Seralago Suites-Maingate East**
5678 W. Irlo Bronson Memorial Highway (US 192), Kissimmee, FL 34746
Tel: 407-396-4488 or 800-366-5437
www.seralagosuites.com
The concept behind this large, family-oriented hotel near the Magic Kingdom is a winner: "kidsuites" and two-room suites that cost less than $100 dollars a night – ideal if you are on a budget and insist on putting little ones to bed in a different space. The quality of the hotel, though, is no better than you'd expect for these prices. The rooms are as dull and dreary as any Motel 6 chain, the kidsuites are only one room with a fort built around the children's bunk beds, and even the 2-room suites feel a bit cramped (though they are still the best bargain in the area). The pool not only lacks any unique design but is also missing the most essential quality for most families: shade. There is shuttle service to the park once a day. **$**

### Universal Orlando

**Hard Rock Hotel**
5800 Universal Boulevard, Orlando, FL 32819
Tel: 407-503-7625
The accommodations at this Mission-style hotel range from comfortable standard rooms to opulent suites worthy of a rock star. Eclectic rock 'n' roll memorabilia is displayed around the building. The

huge pool has a beach, water slide, and underwater sound system. Restaurants, bars, fitness rooms, indoor play area, and Hard Rock store. **$$$$**

**Portofino Bay Hotel**
5601 Universal Boulevard, Orlando, FL 32819
Tel: 407-503-1000
A beautiful re-creation of the seaside village of Portofino, Italy, this expensive resort is worth every penny. Rooms are sumptuous, and there are three elaborate pools, a spa, an indoor children's play area, and restaurants, including the elegant Delfino Riviera. Free water taxis transport guests between Universal's theme parks and the hotel. Guests at on-site hotels are given express access to most rides and attractions. **$$$$**

**Royal Pacific Resort**
6300 Hollywood Way, Orlando, FL 32819
Tel: 407-503-3000
Attempting to re-create the South Pacific in central Florida, this resort is centered around a lagoon-like pool fringed with palm trees, waterfalls, a sandy beach, and cabanas. It's less expensive than the other two Universal hotels, but the quality is as good. There are six restaurants and bars, a children's activity room, a fitness room, and convention facilities. **$$$$**

### I-Drive, SeaWorld and Kissimmee

**Arnold Palmer's Bay Hill Club & Lodge**
9000 Bay Hill Boulevard, Orlando, FL 32819
Tel: 888-422-9445
www.bayhill.com
Duffers are in heaven at this golf resort, where they can play two championship courses or brush up their technique in the Arnold Palmer Golf Academy. The atmosphere at the wood-and-stone lodge is low-key and clubby, with nicely appointed rooms. Arnie is often in residence during the winter months. **$$$**

**Caribe Royale**
8101 World Center Drive, Orlando, FL 32819
Tel: 800-823-8300
www.cariberoyale.com
This enormous resort has over 1,200 suites and over 100 villas. Each suite has either two queen beds or one king, a wet bar, microwave, refrigerator, and coffeemaker. Each suite has a full kitchen, washer and dryer. The main pool has a 75-ft (23-meter) water slide. Other amenities include tennis courts, a video arcade, fitness center, basketball court, and free transportation to Disney World. Their flagship restaurant, The Venetian Room, offers fine Italian cuisine. **$$**

**Castle DoubleTree Resort**
8629 International Drive, Orlando, FL 32819
Tel: 407-345-1511
www.doubletreecastle.com
Spires, mosaics, banners, and rich purple-and-gold drapes and bedspreads give this mid-range hotel a touch of medieval whimsy. Amenities include two restaurants, a fitness center, free shuttles to the theme parks, and a pleasant courtyard pool. **$$**

**Clarion Suites**
7675 W. Irlo Bronson Memorial Highway (US 192), Kissimmee, FL 34747
Tel: 407-396-4000
Popular with families, this five-story hotel is close to major theme parks. **$$**

**Enclave Suites at Orlando**
6165 Carrier Drive, Orlando, FL 32819
Tel: 407-351-1155 or 800-457-0077
www.enclavesuites.com
Just off of International Drive, this all-suites hotel offers a lot more than the average chain. All rooms include a fully equipped kitchen, and the Kid Suites are decorated in theme-park style. There are two outdoor pools and one indoor pool, two kiddie pools, and a playground to keep everyone busy. **$$**

**Four Points Hotel Sheraton by Lakeside**
7769 W Irlo Bronson Memorial Highway (US 192), Kissimmee,

FL 34747
Tel: 407-396-2222 or
800-848-0801
A 651-room resort with a
choice of eateries, a pool,
miniature golf, tennis, and
paddleboats. **$**

**Gaylord Palms Resort &
Convention Center**
6000 W. Osceola Parkway,
Kissimmee, FL 34746
Tel: 407-586-0000
www.gaylordpalms.com
As the name suggests, this
is one of Orlando's best
convention hotels, with a
large amount of its
sprawling grounds devoted
to meeting spaces.
Families may feel a bit out
of their element here, but
there is so much space you
should be able to avoid the
suits if need be. The
expansive glass atrium
recreates various
destinations in Florida from
St Augustine to Key West.
The rooms carry on this
theme. The Canyon Ranch
Spa may be on site to help
execs de-stress, but after a
long vacation in Orlando
mom and dad may need to
use its services as well. **$$$**

**Grand Cypress Resort**
One Grand Cypress Boulevard,
Orlando, FL 32819
Tel: 407-239-1234
www.grandcypress.hyatt.com
This luxurious resort has a
lush garden setting near
Downtown Disney.
Amenities include the
famous Grand Cypress Golf
Academy and four exclusive
Jack Nicklaus-designed golf
courses on property, a
racquet club, windsurfing
on the lake, a "Kids' Club,"

**BELOW:** Universal's Hard
Rock Hotel.

and an equestrian center,
as well as convention
facilities. **$$$**

**International Plaza Resort
and Spa**
10100 International Drive, Orlando,
FL 32819
Tel: 407-352-1100 or
800-327-0363
www.intlplazaresort.com
This 17-story mock Spanish
tower at the center of this
sprawling hotel complex
resembles an old
Californian mission on
growth hormones. Set on
28 acres (11 hectares) of
tropical landscaping, it has
three pools and two kiddie
pools, plus 60,000 sq ft
(5,600 sq meters) devoted
to meeting spaces. And it's
within walking distance of
SeaWorld. Other amenities
include three pools and
miniature golf. A
refrigerator and
coffeemaker are in each
room. **$$$**

**Peabody Orlando**
9801 International Drive, Orlando,
FL 32819
Tel: 407-352-4000 or
800-732-2639
An elegant, 27-story
landmark hotel in the
tourist corridor, with an
Olympic-size pool and
convention center. Known
for its twice-daily "March of
the Peabody Ducks" and
afternoon tea Monday to
Friday. 891 rooms and
suites. **$$$$**

**Renaissance Orlando
Resort**
6677 Sea Harbor Drive, Orlando,
FL 32821
Tel: 407-351-5555 or
800-327-6677
Across the street from
SeaWorld and Discovery
Cove, and 15 minutes from
Disney World and Universal
Orlando, this elegant, 10-
story tower and convention
complex will suit business
travelers as well as
families. Rooms are huge
and well appointed; service
is excellent. The lobby is a
sunny atrium with glass
elevators, marble floors,
waterfalls, goldfish ponds,
shops, and restaurants.
Amenities include a pool,
exercise room, spa, tennis
courts, and more than 40
meeting rooms. A great

value. **$$$**

**Ritz Carlton Orlando
Grande Lakes**
4012 Central Florida Parkway,
Orlando, FL 32837
Tel: 407-206-2400
www.ritzcarlton.com
Located to the east of
International Drive, this
luxury resort is designed to
resemble a grand Italian
palazzo. The rooms feature
marble baths, are
generously sized, and are
impeccably appointed.
Amenities include a
40,000-sq-ft (3,700-sq-
meter) spa and a Greg
Norman-designed golf
course. **$$$**

**Rosen Shingle Creek**
9939 Universal Boulevard, Orlando,
FL 32819
Tel: 866-996-9939 or
407-996-9939
www.shinglecreekresort.com
This enormous resort
seems to come out of
nowhere. Though it is
situated near I-Drive, it
stands alone and requires
transportation to reach
anything else. The rooms
here are very well
appointed and generously
oversized compared to the
average Orlando hotel
room. Two fine restaurants,
Cala Bella and A Land
Remembered, can keep
guests more than happy on
site. Among the other
amenities are four heated
pools, including a child's
wading pool and a lap pool,
the award-winning Shingle
Creek Golf Club, and the
Shingle Creek Spa. **$$$**

**Sheraton Safari Hotel**
12205 Apopka-Vineland Road,
Orlando, FL 32836
Tel: 407-239-0444 or
800-423-3297
www.sheratonsafari.com
This African-themed hotel
has elaborate decor inside
and out, with an over-the-
top swimming pool that has
a 79-ft python water slide,
a lobby filled with
indigenous sculpture, and
animal print fabrics
decorating every room.
Free transportation to all
Disney parks. **$$**

**Sheraton Studio City
Resort**
5905 International Drive, Orlando,
FL 32819

Tel: 407-351-2100 or
800-327-1366
Across from Universal
Orlando, this economical,
21-story round hotel has
302 rooms that evoke the
Hollywood of the 1940s
and 1950s. **$$**

**Wyndham Resort**
8001 International Drive, Orlando,
FL 32819
Tel: 407-351-2420
www.wyndhamorlandoresort.com
One of the best of the many
choices along International
Drive, this is a vast,
sprawling and at times
confounding place, yet it's
surprisingly quiet, with more
than 1,000 spacious rooms
and pleasant swimming
pools. **$$$**

## Downtown Orlando

**Courtyard at Lake Lucerne**
211 N. Lucerne Circle East,
Orlando, FL 32801
Tel: 407-648-5188
www.orlandohistoricinn.com
This is actually four B&Bs
located alongside each
other in downtown Orlando.
Three are fully restored
historic houses, including a
sprawling old plantation
home; the fourth is
Orlando's finest surviving
Art Deco building. In all of
the houses, the rooms are
well appointed and have a
welcoming air that you will
never find in a hotel.
Breakfast is, of course,
included, as is a free
cocktail in the evening. **$$$**

**Eö Inn**
227 N. Eola Drive, Orlando,
FL 32801
Tel: 407-481-8485
www.eoinn.com
This historic inn was built in
1923 and overlooks Lake
Eola in the prestigious
Thornton Park area. It was
converted into a fine
boutique hotel in 1999.
With only 17 rooms, the
service is always

**PRICE CATEGORIES**

Price categories are for a
double room for one night
in high season (Jan–Apr):
**$** = less than $75
**$$** = $75–150
**$$$** = $150–200
**$$$$** = more than $200

personable, and the decor is chic and spacious. With the Urban Spa on site, this hotel feels as much a retreat as a place to stay. **$$$**

**Orlando International Youth Hostel**
4840 W. Irlo Bronson Memorial Parkway, Orlando, FL 32801
Tel: 407-396-8282 or 800-909-4776
Sitting across from downtown's Lake Eola, this hostel is in a beautiful old house with 40 private and

shared rooms, kitchen facilities, and park. Kids welcome. **$**

**Orlando Marriott Downtown**
400 W. Livingston Street, Orlando, FL 32801
Tel: 407-843-6664 or 800-574-3160
A 15-story downtown hotel with 290 rooms, across from the Orlando Arena and the Carr Performing Arts Center. Casual dining, signature sports bar. **$$$**

**Veranda Bed and**

**Breakfast**
115 N. Summerlin Avenue, Orlando, FL 32801
Tel: 407-849-0321 or 800-420-6822
Five 1920s homes in downtown Orlando have been turned into a delightful bed-and-breakfast inn, with hardwood floors and period furnishings. **$$**

**Westin Grand Bohemian Hotel**
325 S. Orange Avenue, Orlando, FL 32801
Tel: 407-313-9000 or

800-GRAND-123
This 250-room artisan hotel displays 100-plus works by European artists like Gustav Klimt and Egon Schiele and one of only two Imperial Grand Bosendorfer pianos in the world. Sumptuous rooms and suites are furnished in dark Java wood tones, red and purple velvet fabrics, silver paint, Tiffany-style lamps, and luxury bed linens. The Boheme Restaurant is one of the best in downtown Orlando. **$$$**

## CENTRAL FLORIDA

### Lake Wales

**Chalet Suzanne Restaurant and Country Inn**
3800 Chalet Suzanne Drive, Lake Wales, FL 33853
Tel: 863-676-6011 or 800-433-6011
Chalet Suzanne, owned by the Hinshaw family since 1931, is like a vacation with a fussy Swiss aunt. Thirty classic guest rooms surround the chateau-style inn, decorated in sunny yellows and creams and furnished with antiques, lace, quilts, and rockers. The sprawling inn overlooks tiny Lake Suzanne, and its orange grove has a renowned restaurant

serving rich Continental cuisine. There's a private airstrip, pool, ceramics studio, and gift shop selling Chalet Suzanne's famous cream soups. **$$$$**

### Maitland

**Thurston House Bed and Breakfast**
851 Lake Avenue, Maitland, FL 32751
Tel: 407-539-1911 or 800-843-2721
www.thurstonhouse.com
Set on the shores of Lake Eucalia, this Victorian farmhouse is a reminder of days long gone in central Florida. One thing that hasn't changed is you can

still sit in a rocking chair on the veranda and watch the osprey dive for fish in the lake. The rooms have all the modern amenities you'd expect in a small hotel and some you wouldn't, such as original fireplaces filled with candles. **$$**

### Sebring

**Santa Rosa Inn**
509 N. Ridgewood Drive, Sebring, FL 33870
Tel: 941-385-0641
This is a well-run, friendly, historic hotel with 25 beautifully furnished rooms and suites, and wonderful home-cooked meals. **$**

### Winter Park

**Park Plaza Hotel**
307 S. Park Avenue, Winter Park, FL 32789
Tel: 407-647-1072 or 800-228-7220
A quiet and intimate bed-and-breakfast hotel built in the 1920s, with 27 beautiful rooms and lots of southern charm. **$$–$$$**

## TAMPA BAY AREA

### Bradenton and Gulf Islands

**Harrington House**
5626 Gulf Drive, Anna Maria Island, FL
Tel: 941-778-5444
www.harringtonhouse.com
An attractive beachfront B&B. Four houses and two bungalows contain 17 large rooms, many of which have balconies, fireplaces, and whirlpool tubs. Amenities include full breakfast in the dining room, a lounge, pool, kayaks, bicycles, and beach gear. **$$–$$$$**

**Holiday Inn Riverfront**
100 Riverfront Drive West,

Bradenton, FL 34205
Tel: 941-747-3727 or 800-HOLIDAY
A Mediterranean-style motor inn near the Manatee River, with 153 rooms, pool, restaurant, and lounge. **$$**

**Tortuga Inn Beach Resort**
1325 Gulf Drive North, Bradenton Beach, FL 34217
Tel: 941-778-6611 or 877-TORTUGA
www.tortugainn.com
An airy six-building complex with one-, two-, and three-bedroom hotel rooms, suites, and apartments facing the Gulf or bay. Amenities include full kitchens, two pools,

WiFi, laundry, barbecue grills, private dock, and beach. Pet-friendly. **$$–$$$$**

**Tradewinds Resort**
1603 Gulf Drive North, Bradenton Beach, FL 34217
Tel: 941-779-0010 or 888-686-6716
www.tradewinds-resort.com
Choose from 34 one-bed, one-bath pastel-hued cottages and a two-bed unit in this lovely palm-lined island resort. Amenities include full kitchens, pools/spas, barbecue grills, laundry, WiFi, private dock, and beach. Pet-friendly. **$$$–$$$$**

### Clearwater/ Clearwater Beach

**Belleview Biltmore Resort**
25 Belleview Boulevard, Clearwater, FL 33756
Tel: 727-442-6171 or 800-237-8947
www.belleviewbiltmore.com
The only one of railroad magnate Henry Plant's

luxury hotels still operational in this area, this 350-room grande dame resort has golf, tennis courts, pools, boats, and fishing. **$$$$**

**Clearwater Beach Hotel**
500 Mandalay Avenue,
Clearwater Beach, FL 33767
Tel: 727-441-2425 or
800-292-2295
www.clearwaterbeachhotel.com
A beachfront hotel with 150-plus rooms and efficiencies, pool, restaurant. Pets allowed. **$$**

**Green Gables Bed and Breakfast**
1040 Sunset Point Road,
Clearwater, FL 33755
Tel: 727-442-8722
www.greengables.us
Clearwater's only bed-and-breakfast, this romantic 1910 inn is set amid lush gardens on the waterfront. Three rooms with private baths. Ten minutes from downtown Dunedin. **$$**

**Sheraton Sand Key Resort**
1160 Gulf Boulevard,
Clearwater Beach, FL 33767-2799
Tel: 727-595-1611 or
800-325-3535
A huge resort on the beach. Many of the 390 rooms have Gulf views. Pool, tennis, sailboats, umbrellas, beach chairs. **$$$**

### Indian Rocks Beach

**Sarah's Seaside**
306 Gulf Boulevard,
Indian Rocks Beach, FL 33785
Tel: 727-596-8063 or
800-597-8063
www.gulfsideresorts.com
The seven weekly vacation rentals in this tropical-themed complex on a quiet beach are charming. One-, two-, and three-bedroom villas and a studio cottage have many personal touches, and all have modern kitchens and appliances, sitting rooms with TV and DVD player, queen or king beds, and decks. Extras include a pool, laundry, barbecue grills, WiFi, sea kayaks. Check in at 810 Gulfside, the sister property. No pets. Weekly rates are available. **$$$$**

### St Pete Beach

**Colonial Gateway Inn**
6300 Gulf Boulevard,
St Pete Beach, FL 33706
Tel: 727-367-2711
This property overlooks the beach, with 200 tastefully decorated rooms, including efficiencies. Popular with families. **$$**

**Don CeSar Beach Resort**
3400 Gulf Boulevard,
St Pete Beach, FL 33706
Tel: 727-360-1881 or
800-637-7200
This fuchsia-colored 1920s resort on the beach has 277 super-deluxe rooms that attract celebrities. There's a pool, private beach, tennis courts, fitness center, and restaurant, plus sailing, windsurfing, and scuba lessons. **$$$$**

**Island's End Resort**
1 Pass-A-Grille Way, St Pete Beach, FL 33706
Tel: 727-360-5023
www.islandsend.com
Five one-bedroom fully equipped cottages and a three-bedroom home sit dockside near historic Pass-a-Grille Beach shops and activities. Tropical foliage, gazebos, wooden walkways, and light breakfast. **$$$-$$$$**

### St Petersburg

**Bayboro House Bed and Breakfast**
1719 Beach Drive SE,
St Petersburg, FL 33701
Tel: 727-823-4955
A charming Victorian inn overlooking Tampa Bay with three cozy rooms, generous breakfasts, and an airy veranda. **$$**

**Renaissance Vinoy Resort & Golf Club**
501 Fifth Avenue NE,
St Petersburg, FL 33701
Tel: 727-894-1000, 800-468-3571
When it opened in 1925, this was the first US hotel with steam heat in every room. Now it's a lush restored resort, with excellent restaurants, golf course, tennis courts, fitness center, private marina. Guided tours of the haunted nooks and crannies. **$$$$**

### Safety Harbor

**Safety Harbor Resort & Spa**
105 North Bayshore Drive,
Safety Harbor, Fl 34695
Tel: 727-726-1161 or
888-237-8772
This spa resort has a unique Florida attraction: mineral springs prized by early Indians. Enclosed since 1944, the springs are part of a comprehensive health and wellness program. There's an Aveda Concept spa, complimentary Aveda toiletries in guest bathrooms, and light New American cuisine in the on-site restaurant. Many of the 175 upgraded guest rooms and suites overlook Tampa Bay. **$$$$**

### Sarasota

**The Cypress – A Bed and Breakfast**
621 Gulfstream Avenue, Sarasota, FL 34236
Tel: 941-955-4683
www.cypressbb.com
This graceful, two-story inn is built entirely of cypress wood and has lovely architectural features as well as a terrific setting across from the bay. Amenities in the four guest rooms include air conditioning, TVs, oriental rugs, fresh flowers, and ceiling fans. Gourmet breakfast and afternoon hors d'oeuvres. **$$-$$$$**

**Gulf Beach Resort Motel**
930 Ben Franklin Drive, Sarasota, FL 34236
Tel: 941-388-2127 or
800-232-2489
www.gulfbeachsarasota.com
This is a casual motel that attracts European families and others who return every year. There are 48 rooms, private gardens, kitchens, pool, shuffleboard, and fine Gulf views. **$$**

**Hyatt Sarasota**
1000 Boulevard of the Arts,
Sarasota, FL 34236
Tel: 941-953-1234 or
800-233-1234
Modern downtown hotel with views of Sarasota Bay, 297 rooms, pool, sauna, health club, sailing,

restaurants, and bars. **$$-$$$**

**Surf View Resort Motel**
1121 Ben Franklin Drive, Sarasota, FL 34236
Tel: 941-388-1818 or
800-833-1818
www.surfviewresort.com
A clean, comfortable motel right on the beach with 27 rooms, pool, and playground. **$-$$**

### Tampa

**Casita de la Verdad**
1609 E. 6th Avenue, Tampa, FL 33605
Tel: 813-654-6087
www.yborcityguesthouse.com
There are just two rooms in this restored 1908 cigar maker's home in Ybor City, but both are beautiful, with either an antique sleigh bed or four-poster bed and clawfoot tub. **$$$-$$$$**

**Don Vicente de Ybor Historic Inn**
1915 Avenida Republica de Cuba, Tampa, FL 33605
Tel: 813-241-4545 or
866-206-4545
A boutique hotel with 16 rooms in a building constructed in 1895 by the founder of Ybor City. The lobby features a dramatic staircase. Rooms have wrought-iron balconies and antiques. **$$$**

**Economy Inn Express**
830 W. Kennedy Boulevard, Tampa, FL 33602
Tel: 813-253-0851
Located near the Henry Plant Museum and the University of Tampa, this budget motel covers the basics, with 50 rooms and free HBO. **$**

**Hilton Garden Inn**
1700 E. 9th Avenue, Tampa, FL 33605
Tel: 813-769-9267 or
800-221-2424
This 95-room hotel, the first new hotel to be built in historic Ybor City in 100

years, is a good place to stay while enjoying Ybor City's nightlife and has "cooked-to-order" breakfasts. **$$**

**Holiday Inn Busch Gardens**
2701 E. Fowler Avenue, Tampa, FL 33612
Tel: 813-971-4710 or 800-HOLIDAY
Family-oriented motel with 399 rooms, free transport to nearby Busch Gardens, pool, sauna, and exercise room. **$-$$**

**Hyatt Regency Tampa**
2 Tampa City Center, Tampa, FL 33602
Tel: 813-225-1234 or

800-233-1234
A modern high-rise hotel in the heart of downtown Tampa's business district. There are 521 rooms, a swimming pool, and an exercise room. **$$-$$$**

**Saddlebrook Resort**
5700 Saddlebrook Way, Wesley Chapel, FL 33543
Tel: 800-729-8383
A relaxing 480-acre (195-hectare) resort, 12 miles (19km) north of Tampa. Renowned for its Arnold Palmer Golf Academy, it has year-round golf clinics on two 18-hole championship golf courses.

The 800 luxury guest rooms and one-, two-, and three-bedroom suites all have kitchens and overlook greens. Olympic pool, luxury spa, wellness center, five restaurants, 45 tennis courts, and meeting facilities. **$$$-$$$$**

**Tahitian Inn**
601 S. Dale Mabry Highway, Tampa, FL 33609
Tel: 813-877-6721 or 800-876-1397
A rare non-chain hotel in Tampa, this classic 1950s inn is a good value. It has tropical decor throughout and 79 comfy rooms.

Heated outdoor pool, spa, and workout room. **$-$$**

### Tarpon Springs

**Spring Bayou Inn**
2 West Tarpon Avenue, Tarpon Springs, FL 34689
Tel: 727-938-9333
www.springbayouinn.com
Five antique-filled rooms and one efficiency each have a private bath, WiFi, and other amenities in this lovely two-story 1900s home in downtown Tarpon Springs. Small fridges in some rooms. Home-cooked gourmet breakfast. **$$**

# SOUTH FLORIDA

### Charlotte Harbor and Gulf Islands

**Banana Bay Waterfront Motel**
23285 Bayshore Road, Port Charlotte, FL 33980
Tel: 941-743-4441
www.bananabaymotel.com
A cute motel with rooms, suites, and efficiencies overlooking Charlotte Bay. DSL, pool, shuffleboard court, and fishing pier, plus kayak rental. Pet-friendly. **$$**

**Boca Grande Club**
5000 Gasparilla Road, Boca Grande, FL 33921
Tel: 941-964-2211
Gorgeous beachfront resort on Gasparilla Island specializing in romantic getaways. One-, two-, and three-bedroom condos have all you need. Restaurant, bar, pool, fitness club, tarpon fishing, and other activities. **$$-$$$$**

**Captiva Island Inn**
11508 Andy Rosse Lane, Captiva Island, FL 33924
Tel: 239-395-0882 or 800-454-9898
www.captivaislandinn.com
Large and small restored cottages surround a tropical-style bed-and-breakfast inn in the heart of historic Captiva Island. Some cottages have kitchens and fireplaces; rooms, suites, and lofts in main inn. Restaurants and shops nearby. **$$-$$$$**

**Carousel Inn on the Beach**
6230 Estero Boulevard, Fort Myers Beach, FL 33931
Tel: 239-463-6131 or 800-613-9540
www.carouselbeachinn.com
The 27 spacious one-bedroom suites and efficiencies at this quiet beachfront inn on Estero Island have full kitchens and are popular with families. Pool, barbecue grills, shuffleboard court. **$$-$$$$**

**Casa Ybel Resort**
2255 W. Gulf Drive, Sanibel Island, FL 33957
Tel: 239-472-3145 or 800-276-4753
www.casaybelresort.com
A secluded 1890s resort on 23 acres (9 hectares) of undeveloped beachfront. The 114 one- and two-bedroom suites have Gulf views and sleeper sofas. Pool, restaurant, café/bar, spa services, golf, basketball/volleyball, and bicycle rentals. **$$$$**

**Days Inn – Port Charlotte**
1941 Tamiami Trail, Port Charlotte, FL 33948
Tel: 941-627-8900 or 800-329-7466
The highest-rated Days Inn in the system, this modern motel sits among moss-covered oak trees and is centrally located. All rooms have fridges and free WiFi; business rooms also have microwaves. Free continental breakfast. **$$**

**McCarthy's Inns on the Beach**
2550 N. Beach Road, Englewood, FL 34223
Tel: 941-474-1582
These attractive one- and two-bedroom vacation rental homes are located on the beach on tranquil Manasota Key. Fishing, hiking, shops, and a restaurant are nearby. Fully equipped. Laundry. **$$**

**West Wind Inn**
3345 W. Gulf Boulevard, Sanibel Island, FL 33232
Tel: 239-472-1541 or 800-824-0476
www.westwindinn.com
A casual resort on Sanibel Island with miles of clear, white sand for shelling. Rooms come with fridges or kitchens. Nearest motel to the wildlife refuge. **$$**

### Fort Myers

**Ramada Inn**
2500 Edwards Drive, Fort Myers, FL 33901
Tel: 941-337-0300 or 800-833-1620
Modern, high-rise downtown hotel with 416 rooms, pool, tennis, boat docks, and exercise room. **$$-$$$**

### Naples

**Hotel Escalante**
290 Fifth Avenue South, Naples, FL 34102
Tel: 239-659-3466 or

877-485-3466
www.hotelescalante.com
An intimate, Mediterranean-style hotel with 10 rooms on a garden estate in old Naples. One- and two-bed rooms and suites have Plantation-style mahogany armoires, king beds with creamy linens, irons, ceiling fans, and Molton Brown bath amenities. Facilities include a courtyard with pool and hot tub; a library with large-screen plasma TV, wines, and ports; and spa services. Breakfast and lunch in hotel restaurant Thur–Sun. **$$$-$$$$**

**Inn on Fifth**
699 Fifth Avenue South, Naples, FL 34102
Tel: 239-403-8777 or 888-403-8778
www.innonfifth.com
This Irish-owned boutique hotel in old Naples exudes European elegance. Amenities in its 87 rooms, suites, and efficiencies include whirlpool tubs and WiFi. Roof-top pool, hot tub, fitness center, spa packages, golf privileges, two on-site restaurants

(one featuring Irish food) and full breakfast. **$$$$**

**Naples Courtyard Inn**
2630 Ninth Street North, Naples, FL 34103
Tel: 239-261-3870 or 800-432-3870
www.naplescourtyardinn.com
This tropical-flavored inn a couple of miles from the beach is a fantastic deal. Serene rooms and suites have granite vanities, king or double beds, fridges, coffeemakers, and WiFi. There's a fitness center and pool and breakfast in the Chickee Hut in the lush gardens. **$$–$$$**

**Vanderbilt Beach Resort**
9225 N. Gulfshore Drive, Naples, FL 33963
Tel: 941-597-3144 or 800-243-9076
www.vanderbiltbeachresort.com
A pleasant motel right on the beach with 50 rooms and efficiencies and a pool. **$$**

## Marco Island

**Marco Island Lakeside Inn**
155 First Avenue, Marco Island, FL 34145
Tel: 239-394-1161 or 800-729-0216
www.marcoislandlakeside.com
Zen-like tranquility pervades this peaceful inn near Marco Island beaches. The 19 one- and two-bedroom suites and studios include kitchen facilities, WiFi, washer/dryer, and irons. On-site laundry, pool, sushi bar, and steakhouse. **$$$–$$$$**

**Olde Marco Island Inn & Suites**
100 Palm Avenue, Marco Island, FL 34145
Tel: 239-394-3131 or 877-475-3466
www.oldemarco.com
This 1883 inn is built on a Calusa Indian shell mound. It has 58 modern and very spacious one-, two-, and three-bedroom suites and penthouses, with full kitchens, sitting rooms with sleeper sofas, and screened lanais. Pool, fitness center, golf, fishing, and nature tours. An award-winning gourmet restaurant is on-site. **$$$$**

## The Everglades – West Side

**Everglades Spa & Lodge**
201 W. Broadway, Everglades, FL 34139
Tel: 239-695-3151
www.bankoftheeverglades.com
This unusual inn occupies the 1923 building of the former Bank of the Everglades. Some of the six one-bed rooms, suites, and efficiencies have kitchens. Amenities include WiFi, spa services, and daily continental breakfast. **$$–$$$$**

**Glades Haven Cozy Cabins**
801 S. Copeland Avenue, Everglades City, FL 34139
Tel: 239-695-2746 or 888-956-6251
A resort with 24 rustic but comfy cabins that will appeal to outdoors lovers. Duplex cabins (some with screened porches) sleep four; full-size cabins have kitchens. All have a/c, heat, and TVs. Amenities include a lounge, pool, boat ramp, marina, and gear rentals. **$$$**

**Ivey House Bed and Breakfast**
107 Camellia Street, Everglades City, FL 34139
Tel: 239-695-3299 or 877-567-0679
www.iveyhouse.com
This historic landmark inn was built in 1928 to accommodate workers constructing the Tamiami Trail. Owned by the Haraden family, it offers bed-and-breakfast accommodations in 18 luxurious poolside rooms in the new inn; 11 rustic but air-conditioned rooms with shared baths in the original lodge; and two bedrooms in a cute cottage. Buffet breakfast is served daily. The inn is well known for its excellent naturalist-guided kayak tours into the Ten Thousand Islands. **$–$$$$**

**River Wilderness Waterfront Villas**
210 Collier Avenue, Everglades City, FL 34139
Tel: 239-695-4499
www.river-wilderness.com
Built on stilts, the 14 one- and two-bed villas and apartments at this resort

on the river in Everglades City are perfect for independent travelers. All have kitchens, microwaves, fridges, and screened porches. On-site amenities include a pool, barbecue grill, dock, canoes, and continental breakfast. **$–$$$**

**Rod & Gun Lodge**
205 Broadway, Everglades City, FL 34139
Tel: 239-695-2101
www.evergladesrodandgun.com
Founded with Everglades City on the Barron River in 1864, the historic Rod & Gun Lodge was purchased by area promoter Barron Collier in 1922 and has hosted presidents, rock stars, and film stars. It has its own marina, and there are 17 cottages and a dark-paneled main building with a cocktail lounge, restaurant, and covered patio. An atmospheric and comfortable base for Everglades explorations. **$$**

## The Everglades – Southeast Side

**Note:** Due to hurricane damage, Flamingo Lodge, the only overnight lodging in Everglades National Park, is closed until further notice. The closest motel accommodations are in Florida City.

**Best Western Florida City/Homestead Gateway to the Keys**
411 S. Krome Avenue, Florida City, FL 33034
Tel: 305-246-5100 or 800-937-8376
www.bestwestern.com
This national chain motel has a pool, and some of the 114 rooms have microwaves and fridges. **$$**

**Everglades International Hostel**
20 SW 2nd Avenue, Florida City, FL 33034
Tel: 305-248-1122 or 800-372-3874
www.evergladeshostel.com
A friendly youth hostel located in a 1930s boardinghouse with six-bed dorms and private double rooms with baths. Kitchen, garden, Internet access, laundry. **$**

**Ramada Inn Florida City Hotel**
124 E. Palm Drive, Florida City, FL 33034
Tel: 305-247-8833
www.hamptoninnfloridacity.com
This chain lodging is superior to any other lodging in Florida City. It's super-clean, has crisp white duvets on king-size beds, and some of its 123 rooms have fridges and sleeper sofas. Hot breakfast, DSL, pool. Book ahead; it's popular. **$$–$$$**

## Miami

**Biltmore Hotel**
1200 Anastasia Avenue, Coral Gables, FL 33134
Tel: 305-445-1926
www.biltmorehotel.com
This 1926 grande dame flaunts her Mediterranean style with the largest pool in the US and 150 acres (60 hectares) of tropical landscaping. The 276 rooms and suites have stone floors, European bedding, and lovely views. Nine restaurants, a golf course, tennis courts. **$$$$**

**Everglades Hotel**
244 Biscayne Boulevard, Miami, FL 33132
Tel: 305-379-5461 or 800-327-5700
www.miamigate.com/everglades
A 376-room high-rise hotel in the heart of downtown Miami, with a pool and restaurants. **$$**

**Hotel Inter-Continental**
100 Chopin Plaza, Miami, FL 33131
Tel: 305-577-1000 or 800-327-3005
www.interconti.com
A soaring, high-rise hotel with 639 rooms, gourmet restaurants, pool, skyline views, fitness center, and jogging track in the center of downtown Miami. **$$$**

**Hotel Place St Michel**
162 Alcazar Avenue, Coral Gables, FL 33134

### PRICE CATEGORIES

Price categories are for a double room for one night in high season (Jan–Apr):
**$** = less than $75
**$$** = $75–150
**$$$** = $150–200
**$$$$** = more than $200

Tel: 305-444-1666 or 800-848-HOTEL
www.hotelplacestmichel.com
This historic hotel in downtown Coral Gables has 27 rooms with antiques galore and an elegant French restaurant. **$$$**

**Miami River Inn**
118 SW South River Drive, Miami, FL 33130
Tel: 305-325-0045 or 800-HOTEL-89
www.miamiriverinn.com
A beautifully restored 40-room inn by the Miami River in Little Havana with pool and Jacuzzi. **$$**

**Omni Colonnade Hotel**
180 Aragon Avenue, Coral Gables, FL 33134
Tel: 305-441-2600 or 800-533-1337
www.omnihotels.com
A prestigious hotel in downtown Coral Gables with 157 rooms, pool, shopping complex, Jacuzzi, lounge, and small gym. **$$$**

### Miami Beach

**Cardozo on the Beach**
1300 Ocean Drive, Miami Beach, FL 33139
Tel: 305-535-6500 or 800-782-6500
www.cardozohotel.com
An oceanfront Art Deco hotel in the heart of the historic district of South Beach, with 44 beautifully decorated rooms. **$$–$$$**

**Clay Hotel and Miami Beach International Hostel**
1438 Washington Avenue, Miami Beach, FL 33139
Tel: 305-534-2988
www.clayhotel.com
A very popular, 200-bed youth hostel with dormitory

**BELOW:** a South Beach hotel.

rooms and kitchen facilities in the Art Deco district of South Beach. **$**

**Fontainebleau Hilton Resort and Towers**
4441 Collins Avenue, Miami Beach, FL 33140
Tel: 305-538-2000 or 800-548-8886
This is an opulent and extensively renovated 1,206-room hotel built in the 1950s. Facilities include a pool with waterfalls, tennis courts, a health club, restaurants, nightclubs (with famous Latin floorshow), shopping, and activities for children of all ages. **$$$**

**Hotel Chelsea**
944 Washington Avenue, Miami Beach, FL 33140
Tel: 305-534-4069
www.thehotelchelsea.com
A hip hotel for the budget challenged, rooms here have stripped-down elegance, with futon-style beds. DJ in the lobby on weekends. Front patio overlooks the avenue. Free nightly cocktail. **$$–$$$**

**Hotel St Augustine**
347 Washington Avenue, Miami Beach, FL 33140
Tel: 305-532-0570 or 800-310-7717
www.hotelstaugustine.com
European chic pervades this new hotel in an Art Deco building in SoFi (South of Fifth). Spare rooms are cozied up with quilts on the beds and nice details. **$$$$**

**National Hotel**
1677 Collins Avenue, Miami Beach, FL 33139
Tel: 305-532-2311 or 800-327-8370
An elegant landmark Art Deco hotel with all the necessary modern amenities, beautifully renovated, and on the ocean. Its long, narrow pool is unique. **$$–$$$**

### Florida Keys

**Cheeca Lodge**
8101 Overseas Highway (MM 82), Islamorada, FL 33036
Tel: 305-664-4651 or 800-327-2888
One of the most popular resorts in the Keys, with 203 rooms, tennis, golf,

pools, fishing pier, private beach, diving, and snorkeling. **$$$**

**Curry Mansion Inn**
511 Caroline Street, Key West, FL 33040
Tel: 305-294-5349 or 800-253-3466
www.currymansion.com
A grand Victorian-style mansion turned into a charming 28-room inn with pool and lush gardens. **$$$**

**Cypress House**
601 Caroline Street, Key West 33040
Tel: 800-525-2488
www.cypresshousekw.com.
This elegant but unpretentious 1895 B&B is a fine example of Bahamian architecture. Rooms in the inn and two nearby historic buildings are well appointed, with TVs and a/c; two on the first floor share a bath. Expanded continental breakfast buffet and afternoon cocktails by the secluded lap pool. **$$$–$$$$**

**Dove Creek Lodge**
147 Seaside Avenue (MM 94.5), Key Largo, FL 33037
Tel: 800-401-0057
www.dovecreeklodge.com
The emphasis at this refined waterfront lodge is on service. Rooms are large, with balconies, DVD players, large-screen TVs, and DSL. Staff can arrange activities, including deep-sea fishing, launching from outside the front door. Snapper's, a popular restaurant and bar with live entertainment, is next door. **$$$$**

**Hawk's Cay Resort**
61 Hawks Cay Boulevard, Duck Key, FL 33050
Tel: 305-743-7000 or 800-432-2242
www.hawkscay.com
A rambling, Caribbean-style resort that pampers guests, with 176 rooms, swimming pool, tennis courts, restaurants, bars, boat rental, scuba lessons, marina, and a good breakfast buffet. **$$$**

**Holiday Inn Sunspree Key Largo Resort**
Overseas Highway (MM 100), Key Largo, FL 33037
Tel: 305-451-2121 or 800-843-5397

A modern, tropical resort with 132 rooms, swimming pool, marina, bars, as well as spectacular ocean views. **$$$**

**Holiday Isle Resort**
84001 Overseas Highway (MM 84), Islamorada, FL 33036
Tel: 305-664-2321 or 800-327-7070
www.holidayisle.com
A comfortable, modest holiday hotel resort with a choice of four hotels and five restaurants, pools, beach, water sports, and marina. **$$–$$$**

**Island City House Hotel**
411 William Street, Key West, FL 33040
Tel: 305-294-5702 or 800-634-8230
www.islandcityhouse.com
Off the main strip, this tropical garden hotel has 24 suites, with kitchens, swimming pool, and Jacuzzi. **$$$**

**Jules Undersea Lodge**
51 Shoreland Drive (MM 103.2), Key Largo, FL 33037
www.jul.com
Experience underwater living in this extraordinary subaquatic hotel. **$$$**

**Pier House Resort & Caribbean Spa**
1 Duval Street, Key West, FL 33040
Tel: 305-296-4600 or 800-327-8340
www.pierhouse.com
A luxury 142-room resort that feels like it's on its own island, with pools, private beach, bars, and cabanas. **$$$**

**Pines and Palms Resort**
80401 Old Highway, Islamorada, FL 33034
Tel: 800-624-0964
www.pinesandpalms.com
Classic, family-friendly, Keys lodgings. Oceanfront and oceanview cottages and suites have one, two, or three bedrooms, full kitchens, living areas, patios or balconies, and a/c. The freshwater pool is a delight. **$$–$$$$**

**Southernmost Motel**
1319 Duval Street, Key West, FL 33040
Tel: 305-296-6577 or 800-354-4455
www.southernmostresorts.com
A comfortable motel with 127 rooms, pool, and full-service concierge. **$$–$$$**

# CENTRAL EAST COAST

## Bay Harbor

**Bay Harbor Inn**
9660 E. Bay Harbor Drive,
Bay Harbor Islands, FL 33154
Tel: 305-868-4141
www.bayharborinn.com
This comfortable
waterfront hotel has 45
rooms, two excellent
restaurants, a pool, and
boat docks. $$$

## Boca Raton

**Boca Raton Resort and
Club**
501 E. Camino Real, Boca Raton,
FL 33431
Tel: 561-395-3000 or
800-327-0101
A plush and historic hotel
with golf course, pools,
tennis courts, and health
spa, among other
amenities. $$$

## Boynton Beach

**Golden Sands Inn**
520 SE 21st Avenue,
Boynton Beach, FL 33435
Tel: 561-732-6075
Twenty-four rooms in the
downtown area not far
from the beach.
Restaurant with takeout
service only. $

## Deerfield Beach

**Carriage House Resort
Motel**
250 S. Ocean Boulevard,
Deerfield Beach, FL 33441
Tel: 954-427-7670 or
800-303-6009
www.carriagehouseresort.com
This is a tidy and friendly
beach motel with 30
rooms, pool, and
shuffleboard court. $$

## Fort Lauderdale

**Howard Johnson Oceans
Edge Resort**
700 N. Atlantic, Fort Lauderdale,
FL 33304
Tel: 954-427-7670 or
800-446-4656
More than 100 beachfront
rooms with pool, lounge,
24-hour food, and shuttle
service. $$$
**Marriott's Harbor Beach
Resort**
3030 Holiday Drive,
Fort Lauderdale, FL 33316
Tel: 954-525-4000 or
800-222-6543
A high-rise, seafront resort
with 624 comfortable
rooms, pool, cabanas,
tennis courts, health club,
shopping, and
windsurfing. $$$

**Riverside Hotel**
620 E. Las Olas Boulevard,
Fort Lauderdale, FL 33301
Tel: 954-467-0671 or
800-325-3280
www.riversidehotel.com
Located in the downtown
shopping district, this
historic hotel has 117
antique-furnished rooms,
swimming pool, restaurants,
and lounge. $$$
**Tropic Seas Resort**
4616 El Mar Drive,
Lauderdale-by-the-Sea, FL 33308
Tel: 954-772-2555 or
800-952-9581
www.tropicseasresort.com
A 1950s motel on the beach
just north of Fort Lauderdale
with 16 rooms, swimming
pool, shuffleboard, and
barbecue. $$

## Madeira Beach

**Shoreline Island Resort**
14200 Gulf Boulevard,
Madeira Beach, FL 33708
Tel: 727-397-6641 or
800-635-8373
www.shorelineresort.com
A great hangout place, this
property with one- and two-
bedroom efficiencies is on
a quiet waterfront and
restricted to guests 21
years and over. $$

## Palm Beach

**Brazilian Court**
301 Australian Avenue,
Palm Beach, FL 33480
Tel: 561-655-7740 or
800-552-0335
www.braziliancourt.com
An old tropical hotel with
103 rooms and suites,
lush gardens, pool,
restaurant, bar, and
afternoon tea. $$$
**The Breakers**
1 S. Country Road, Palm Beach,
FL 33480
Tel: 561-655-6611 or
888-BREAKERS
www.thebreakers.com
One of the grand old
hotels of the 1920s, this
oceanfront landmark has
572 luxurious rooms,
pools, beach, croquet,
tennis courts, golf course,
health club, restaurants,
boutiques, and night
clubs. $$$

# NORTHEAST COAST

## Cocoa Beach

**Cocoa Beach
Oceanside Inn**
1 Hendry Avenue, Cocoa Beach,
FL 32931
Tel: 321-784-3126 or
800-874-7958
www.cocoabeachoceansideinn.com
This inn has 40 rooms on
the beach, with fishing, a
pool, a restaurant, and
shuttle bus service.
$$–$$$
**Comfort Inn and Suite
Resort**
3901 N. Atlantic Avenue,
Cocoa Beach, FL 92931
Tel: 321-783-2221 or
800-228-5150
Ninety-four rooms on the
beach with restaurant,
lounge, pool. $–$$
**Ron Jon Resort**

1000 Shorewood Drive,
Cape Canaveral, FL 32920
Tel: 866-854-4835
www.ronjonresort.com
Ron Jon has two quirky
advantages: it is the
closest oceanfront resort
to most Orlando
attractions and is the
nearest place outside the
Kennedy Space Center to
watch a launch. This
property is primarily for
timeshare owners, but its
unique location makes it
well worth checking out for
a night or two on the
coast. Kids will love the
elaborate pools, lazy river,
and water slide. The
suites aren't big, but
remain comfortable
enough to accommodate
for a night or two. $$

## Daytona Beach

**Adam's Mark Resort**
100 N. Atlantic Avenue,
Daytona Beach, FL 32118
Tel: 386-254-8200 or
800-444-2326
www.adamsmark.com/daytonabeach
This large hotel's
distinctive architecture and
oceanfront site make it
perennially popular.
Multiple restaurants,
lounges, health club, spa,
and 437 rooms. $$–$$$
**Beach Quarters Resort**
3711 S. Atlantic Avenue,
Daytona Beach, FL 32118
Tel: 386-767-3119
www.thebeachquarters.com
A mid-rise hotel with
antique furniture in 26
suites, plus kitchens, pool,
and cozy restaurant. $$

**Daytona Beach Hilton**
2637 S. Atlantic Avenue,
Daytona Beach, FL 32118
Tel: 386-767-7350 or
800-HILTONS

### PRICE CATEGORIES

Price categories are for a
double room for one night
in high season (Jan–Apr):
**$** = less than $75
**$$** = $75–150
**$$$** = $150–200
**$$$$** = more than $200

TRANSPORTATION

ACCOMMODATIONS

ACTIVITIES

A – Z

A towering hotel with 214 rooms overlooking the beach, plus swimming pool, Jacuzzi, sauna, fitness center, and kid's playground. **$$–$$$**

**Plaza Resort and Spa**
600 N. Atlantic Avenue, Beach Shores, FL 32118
Tel: 386-255-4471
www.plazaresortandspa.com
This oceanfront property offers family-oriented amenities, including in-room fridges and a fitness center. **$$**

## New Smyrna Beach

**Ocean Air Motel**
1161 N. Dixie Freeway, New Smyrna Beach, FL 32168
Tel: 386-428-5748
A modest but pleasant motel located 5 minutes from the beach with 14 rooms, pool, and picnic tables. **$**

**Riverview Hotel**
103 Flagler Avenue, New Smyrna, FL 32169
Tel: 386-428-5858 or 800-945-7416
A landmark hotel overlooking the intracoastal

waterway, with 18 beautifully furnished rooms, pool, and restaurant. **$$**

## St Augustine

**Casa de Solana B&B Inn**
21 Aviles Street, St Augustine, FL 32084
Tel: 904-824-3555
www.casadesolana.com
Small, gracious, antiques-filled inn with four comfortable suites and homemade breakfasts. **$$**

**Casa Monica**
95 Cordova Street, St Augustine, FL 32084
Tel: 904-827-1888 or 800-648-1888
www.casamonica.com
This historic landmark was built in 1888 and beautifully restored in 1999. The property has a huge lobby, pool, fountains, art galleries, high-end shops, four-star restaurants, and luxurious rooms with fine linens and amenities. **$$$–$$$$**

**La Fiesta Oceanside Inn**
810 Beach Boulevard (Hwy A1A),

St Augustine, FL 32084
Tel: 904-471-2220
www.lafiestainn.com
This beachfront inn sits on a private boardwalk and has a variety of rooms and suites, with fridges, microwaves, balconies, and/or patios. **$$–$$$$**

**Pirate Haus**
32 Treasury Street, St Augustine, FL 32084
Tel: 904-808-1999
www.piratehaus.com
Known for its "pirate pancake breakfast," this European-style budget hostel in downtown boasts clean rooms, a large kitchen, rooftop barbecue, laundry, bike rentals, Internet access, and an innkeeper who's a real local character. **$**

**St Francis Inn**
279 St George Street, St Augustine, FL 32084
Tel: 904-824-6068 or 800-824-6062
www.stfrancisinn.com
This is an 18th-century historic home reborn as a B&B inn. There are 11 rooms and suits with old-

fashioned fans, plus a pool. **$$**

## Jacksonville

**Comfort Suites Hotel**
8333 Dix Ellis Trail, Jacksonville, FL 32256
Tel: 904-739-1155 or 800-228-5150
www.comfortsuiteshotel.net
In the heart of the shopping and restaurant district, this 128-room hotel has full kitchenettes, a pool, and health spa. **$–$$**

**House on Cherry Street**
1844 Cherry Street, Jacksonville, FL 32205
Tel: 904 384-1999
An antiques-filled riverside inn with four cozy rooms and hearty, homemade breakfasts. **$**

**Radisson Riverwalk Hotel**
1515 Prudential Drive, Jacksonville, FL 32207
Tel: 904-396-5100 or 800-333-3333
A 321-room resort hotel with tennis courts, pool, restaurant, and shops. **$$–$$$**

# NORTH CENTRAL FLORIDA

## Alachua

**Comfort Inn**
15920 NW US Highway 441, Alachua, FL 32615
Tel: 386-462-2414 or 877-424-6423
A modest and clean 60-room inn, with restaurant and lounge near the highway. **$**

## Cedar Key

**Dockside Motel**
11 Dock Street, Cedar Key, FL 32625
Tel: 352-543-5432
www.dockside-cedarkey.com
The town's only harborside motel. **$**

**Island Hotel**
373 2nd Street, Cedar Key, FL 32625
Tel: 352-543-5111
www.islandhotel-cedarkey.com
This is an 1859 hotel in the former General Store. Ten spotless rooms exude "shabby chic," with quilts on four-poster beds, antiques, hand-cut wooden walls and floors, ceiling fans, air conditioning, and private bathrooms with showers (some have clawfoot tubs). Rooms access a wraparound second-floor balcony. No phones or TVs. Full breakfast. Popular restaurant and bar. **$$**

**Old Fenimore Mill Condominiums**
P.O. Box 805, Cedar Key, FL 32625
Tel: 352-543-9803 or 800-767-8354
These one-, two-, and three-bed vacation rentals are built on stilts overlooking the tranquil bay and are on

the south end of downtown. Amenities include private beach, fishing dock, pool, hot tub, barbecue grills, picnic area, laundry. **$$$$**

## Gainesville

**Hilton University of Florida Conference Center**
1714 SW 34th Street, Gainesville, FL 32607
Tel: 352-371-3600 or 800-HILTONS
www.ufhotel.com
Set on 9 acres (4 hectares) across from UF Cultural Plaza, this attractive seven-story Hilton was built in 2000 and has 248 deluxe rooms with two queen beds, ergonomic work stations, DSL, computer games, and Web TV. Restaurant, pool, hot tub, fitness center, buffet breakfast. **$$$$**

**Magnolia Plantation Inn and Cottages**
309 SE Seventh Street, Gainesville, FL 32607

Tel: 352-375-6653 or 800-201-2379
www.magnoliabnb.com
This Victorian B&B is surrounded by landscaped grounds and has five second-floor guest rooms with queen beds, gas fireplaces, private baths with clawfoot tubs. Sitting parlors and a dining room are on the ground floor. Seven one- to three-bedroom cottages have fireplaces, Jacuzzis, kitchens, and sitting rooms. Full breakfast. **$$–$$$$**

**Paramount Plaza Hotel & Conference Center**
2900 SW 13th Street, Gainesville, FL 32607

Tel: 352-377-4000 or
877-992-9229
www.paramountplaza.com
Located on Bivens Arm
Lake Nature Preserve, this
four-story lakefront hotel is
very reasonably priced. It
has 192 double, queen-,
and king-size rooms and
seven suites, all with
balconies, pillow-top
mattresses, down pillows,
WiFi, cable TV, video
games, phones, and desks.
There's also a restaurant,
pool, fitness center, and
business center. **$–$$**

**Sweetwater Branch Inn**
625 E. University Avenue,
Gainesville, FL 32607
Tel: 352-373-6760 or
800-595-7760
www.sweetwaterinn.com
A picture-perfect 1885 B&B
in downtown with 12 guest
rooms and five cottages, all
with showers and clawfoot
tubs. The owner's family
antiques, vintage teapots,
and romantic furnishings
grace rooms and public
spaces. The pretty gardens
and adjoining McKenzie
House are popular wedding
venues. Hot buffet
breakfast and afternoon
wine and cheese. **$$–$$$$**

## High Springs

**Grady House**
420 NW First Avenue,
High Springs, FL 32655
Tel: 386-454-2206
www.gradyhouse.com
This lovely Arts and Crafts
B&B on the main highway in
High Springs was built in
1917 as a railroad
boardinghouse. Its five color-
themed rooms have period
details, antiques, and
artworks; a two-bedroom
cottage sleeps four.
Gardens, ponds, gourmet
breakfast, and friendly
dalmatians. **$$–$$$$**

**High Springs Country Inn**
520 NW Santa Fe Boulevard,
High Springs, FL 32643
Tel: 386-454-1565
www.highsprings.com/cinns
Located on US 441, near
downtown, this clean
budget motel has 16
renovated rooms with one
or two beds, private baths,
phones, cable TV, fridges,
coffeemakers, and WiFi. **$**

**Rustic Ranch Inn**
5529 NW State Road 45,
High Springs, Florida 32643
Tel: 386-454-1223
www.rusticinn.net
Set on 9 acres (4
hectares), this six-room
ranch-style inn is a great
place to unwind. Nature-
themed rooms are
spacious and have king or
queen beds with carved
headboards, baths,
fridges, microwaves,
coffeemakers, private
decks, and views. Pool.
Delivered continental
breakfast. Packages
include lodging, canoe
rental, and dinner in High
Springs. **$$–$$$**

## Keaton Beach

**The Eagle's Nest at Dekle Beach**
5960 Potts Still Road, Perry,
FL 32348
Tel: 850-584-7666
www.eagles-nest-vacations.com
These three attractive
seafront stilted vacation
rentals between Keaton
Beach and Perry are great
getaways. They are fully
equipped with kitchens,
three bedrooms, a private
deck, pier, boat ramp, fish-
cleaning station, and
laundry. **$$$$**

## Micanopy

**Herlong Mansion**
402 NE Cholokka Boulevard,
Micanopy, FL 32667
Tel: 352-466-3322 or
800-437-5664
www.herlong.com
This B&B in Micanopy
originated as a pioneer
home and became a
colonial-style family home in
1910. It has 10 fireplaces
and 11 Arts and Crafts-style
rooms, suites, and cottages
with high ceilings, antique
beds and dressers,
gleaming wood floors, rugs,
and private baths. Full
breakfast and afternoon
wine and cheese included;
dinner optional. **$$–$$$$**

## Ocala

**Heritage Country Inn**
14343 W. Highway 40, Ocala,
FL 34481

Tel: 352-489-0023 or
888-240-2233
www.heritagecountryinn.com
Each of the six historic-
themed rooms on this
peaceful ranch in horse
country has a private
entrance, fireplace, TV,
phone, Jacuzzi, and
shower. Full breakfast.
**$$–$$$**

**Ritz Historic Inn**
1205 E. Silver Springs Boulevard,
Ocala, FL 34470
Tel: 352-671-9300 or
888-382-9390
A romantic 1925 inn amid
fountains, courtyards, and
gardens. Suites have king
or queen beds, sleeper
sofa, cable TV, phone,
fridge, microwave,
coffeemaker, and DSL.
Other amenities include a
mosaic pool, Jacuzzi,
massage, business center,
continental breakfast. **$$**

**Seven Sisters Inn**
820 SE Fort King St, Ocala,
FL 34471
Tel: 352-867-1170 or
800-250-3496
www.7sistersinn.com
Two adjoining 1880s
Victorian houses have
been transformed into an
exotic themed inn with 13
rooms, period antiques,
private baths, full
breakfast, and afternoon
tea. **$$**

## Palatka

**Azalea House**
220 Madison Street, Palatka,
FL 32177
Tel: 386-325-4547
www.theazaleahouse.com
This elegant 1880 Victorian
gabled B&B in Palatka's
regenerating historic district
has many links to the St
John's River's storied past.
It has six charming guest
rooms with central a/c and
heat. Homemade pastries
at breakfast. Pool, gardens,
decks, and parlor. **$$**

## Steinhatchee

**Steinhatchee Landing Resort**
203 Ryland Circle, Steinhatchee,
FL 32359
Tel: 352-498-3513 or
800-584-1709
www.steinhatcheelandingresort.com
This 35-acre (14-hectare)
resort features vacation
rentals inspired by old
Florida. The one- to four-
bedroom cottages are fully
equipped and have screened
porches, barbecues, and
views. Pool, Jacuzzi, petting
zoo, vegetable garden,
shuffleboard court, swings,
bicycles, and other
equipment rental. Pets up to
28 pounds allowed in some
cottages. **$$–$$$$**

**BELOW:** Magic Beach Motel, Vilano Beach.

# THE PANHANDLE

## Apalachicola

**Gibson Inn**
51 Avenue C, Apalachicola,
FL 32320
Tel: 850-653-2191
www.gibsoninn.com
This venerable 1907 B&B occupies a Victorian structure with a tin roof and wraparound porches. Thirty chintz-laden rooms and suites have antique beds, private baths with clawfoot tub, WiFi. Restaurant, lounge. Pet-friendly.
**$$–$$$$**

**Old Saltworks Cabins**
P.O. Box 526, Port St Joe, FL 32457
Tel: 850-229-6097
www.oldsaltworks.com
Looking for a cabin in the woods? The 11 rustic one- and two-bedroom family vacation hideaways at this old Civil War saltworks on St Joseph Bay are just the ticket. Fully equipped. Play fort, mini museum, nature trails. Two-night minimum.
**$$–$$$$**

**Witherspoon Inn**
94 Fifth Street, Apalachicola,
FL 32320
Tel: 850-653-9186
www.witherspooninn.com
A tastefully renovated former sea captain's residence in the historic district of Apalachicola, this homey historic B&B has four guest rooms with an Old Florida feel. Great homebaked goodies. **$$**

## Fort Walton Beach

**Aunt Martha's Bed and Breakfast**
315 Shell Avenue SE,
Fort Walton Beach, FL 32548
Tel: 850-243-6702
www.auntmarthasbedandbreakfast.com
A beautiful faux-Victorian B&B with comfortable rooms, library and grand piano, porch, and feng shui

## PRICE CATEGORIES

Price categories are for a double room for one night in high season (Jan–Apr):
**$** = less than $75
**$$** = $75–150
**$$$** = $150–200
**$$$$** = more than $200

gardens. Bountiful breakfasts. **$$**

**Best Western Fort Walton Beach**
380 Santa Rosa Boulevard,
Fort Walton Beach, FL 32548
Tel: 850-243-9444, 877-243-9444
Not your grandmother's Best Western chain lodging, this place is a shrine to pop art, with snazzy color themes and retro details. **$$–$$$**

## Panama City Beach

**Casa Loma**
13615 Front Beach Road,
Panama City Beach, FL 32407
Tel: 850-234-1100 or
888-460-9336
www.casalomapcb.com
The emphasis is on Mexico in this Gulf of Mexico mid-rise hotel. The 100 spacious guest rooms and two-room suites all have tiled floors, tropical furnishings, and *mañana* ambience. All rooms overlook the beach and have balconies; some have kitchenettes. **$–$$$$**

**Driftwood Lodge**
15811 Front Beach Road,
Panama City Beach, FL 32413
Tel: 850-234-6601, 800-234-6601
www.driftwoodpcb.com
A family motel on the beach with a selection of rooms, suites, efficiencies, and cabanas. There's lots to do, from shuffleboard and volleyball to lazing by the pool. **$–$$$$**

**Marriott's Bay Point Resort**
4200 Marriott Drive,
Panama City Beach, FL 32411
Tel: 850-234-3307 or
800-874-7105
This is an elegant resort with antique furnishings, Asian rugs, and beautiful views. There are 355 rooms and suites, restaurants, bars, pools, golf, tennis, a marina, and sailboat rentals. **$$–$$$**

## Pensacola

**Hilton Garden Inn**
12 Via de Luna Drive, Pensacola,
FL 32502
Tel: 850-916-2999
A new post–Hurricane Ivan beachfront hotel with the

trademark airy feel, large pool, and luxurious rooms for which Hilton is known.
**$$$$**

**New World Inn**
600 S. Palafox Street, Pensacola,
FL 32502
Tel: 850-434-7736
This boutique hotel is located halfway between downtown Pensacola and the waterfront. Its 15 period rooms offer understated elegance and amenities. There's also a lovely courtyard. **$$–$$$**

**Pensacola Grand Hotel**
200 E. Gregory Street, Pensacola,
FL 32501
Tel: 850-433-3336 or
800-348-3336
www.pensacolagrandhotel.com
A historic train station serves as the lobby of this 15-story hotel, with restaurant and health club. **$$**

**Pensacola Victorian Bed and Breakfast**
203 W. Gregory Street, Pensacola,
FL 32501
Tel: 850-434-2818 or
800-370-8354
www.pensacolavictorian.com
A restored ship's captain's home, this attractive B&B has four comfy rooms with private baths, phones, TV, and WiFi. Gourmet breakfast and treats. **$$**

## St George Island

**Buccaneer Inn**
160 W. Gorrie Drive,
St George Island, FL 32328
Tel: 850-927-2585 or
800-847-2091
This gulf-front motel has 100 spacious, light-filled rooms, some with kitchenettes. **$$–$$$**

**St George Inn**
135 Franklin Boulevard,
St George Island, FL 32328
Tel: 850-927-2903 or
800-322-5196
www.stgeorgeinn.com
A lovely three-story inn with pleasant rooms opening onto wraparound porches. Huge curving pool. **$$–$$$**

## Tallahassee

**Doubletree Inn Tallahassee**
101 S. Adams Street, Tallahassee,
FL 32301

Tel: 850-224-5000
One of many chains in Tallahassee, this 243-room high-rise hotel is clean, convenient, and aimed at business travelers. **$$**

**Governors Inn**
209 S. Adams Street, Tallahassee,
FL 32301
Tel: 850-681-6855 or
800-342-7717
www.govinn.com
This boutique hotel near the state capitol has 41 rooms and suites with private baths, antiques, four-poster beds, TV, WiFi. Continental breakfast, afternoon cocktails. **$$$**

**Little English Guesthouse**
737 Timberlane Road, Tallahassee,
FL 32312
Tel: 850-907-9777
www.littleenglishguesthouse.com
An authentic English B&B with the London owner's antiques and two sweet rooms. Cups of tea, English bath goodies, and a golden retriever complete the old world charm. **$$**

**McFarlin House Bed and Breakfast**
305 E. King Street, Quincy,
FL 32351
Tel: 850-875-2526 or
877-370-4701
www.mcfarlinhouse.com
A restored Victorian inn, 16 miles (28km) from Tallahassee, with eight antique rooms, private baths with showers or clawfoot tubs, TV, phone, and DSL. Full breakfast.
**$$–$$$**

**The Inn at Park Avenue**
323 E. Park Avenue, Tallahassee,
FL 32301
Tel: 850-222-4024
www.innatparkave.com
This B&B is near the state capitol and has an old-fashioned ambience, with high ceilings, hardwood floors, parlor, and four guest rooms with baths and showers. **$$–$$$**

# ACTIVITIES

# THE ARTS, FESTIVALS, SPORTS, AND SHOPPING

## THE ARTS

Entertainment in Florida is not an unadulterated diet of kitsch and theme park razzmatazz nor is it just laid-back Jimmy Buffet music on the beach and neighborhood arts and crafts shows. The state has a surprisingly vibrant cultural scene, with everything from Broadway shows and modern dance to high-quality performances of opera, classical, and rock music starring the most famous musicians and singers in the world. As far as the performing arts are concerned, the majority of top-quality shows are staged during Florida's popular winter high season, between October and April, although there is plenty to choose from year-round. The best performances tend to be focused in southern Florida and the Gulf in cities like Miami, Fort Lauderdale, Tampa, Sarasota, and Naples and in Orlando in central Florida. Below is a list of some of the main venues by region.

### Miami

**Adrienne Arsht Center for the Performing Arts of Miami-Dade County**, 14th Street and Biscayne Boulevard; tel: 305-949-6722; www.miamipac.com. A stunning new center that is host to national and international ballet, symphony, and opera companies.
**American Airlines Arena**, 601 Biscayne Boulevard; tel: 786-777-1000; www.aaarena.com. Miami's main entertainment venue for basketball games and major pop and Latin music concerts.
**Coconut Grove Playhouse**, 3500 Main Highway, Coconut Grove;

tel: 305-442-4000; www.cgplayhouse.com. A cozy, restored theater that features Broadway-bound plays and musical acts.
**Florida Grand Opera**, tel: 305-854-7890; www.fgo.org. Miami's resident opera company features internationally prominent and regional singers and performs in various venues in Dade and Broward counties.
**Gusman Center of the Performing Arts**, 174 E. Flagler Street; tel: 305-374-2444; www.gusmancenter.org. An ornate historic theater that offers drama, dance, and musical productions.
**Jackie Gleason Theater of the Performing Arts**, 1700 Washington Avenue, Miami Beach; tel: 305-673-7300. An ultra-modern 1,800-seat theater that stages Broadway plays.
**Miami City Ballet**, tel: 305-929-7012; www.miamicityballet.org. Latin-flavored classical ballet company with hints of jazz and modern dance. Various South Florida locations.
**New World Symphony**, tel: 305-673-3330; www.nws.org. First-rate repertoire of classical music performed at various Miami area theaters, but mainly the Lincoln Theater in Miami Beach and the Gusman Center for the Performing Arts.
**Teatro de Bellas Artes**, 2173 SW 8th Street; tel: 305-325-0515. A Spanish-language theater in Little Havana that offers live drama, comedy, and musical events.

### East Coast

**Bankatlantic Center**, 1 Panther Parkway, Sunrise; tel: 954-835-7000; www.bankatlanticcenter.com. A modern entertainment center near Fort Lauderdale that hosts major concerts.

**Broward Center for the Performing Arts**, 201 SW 5th Avenue, Fort Lauderdale; tel: 954-522-5334; www.browardcenter.org. This 2,700-seat waterfront theater is the top venue for cultural events in Fort Lauderdale.
**Caldwell Theater Company**, 7901 N. Federal Highway, Boca Raton; tel: 561-241-7432; www.caldwelltheatre.com. A professional regional theater.
**Jacksonville Symphony Orchestra**, tel: 904-354-5479; www.jax symphony.org. Variety of classical music performed throughout the Jacksonville area.
**Kravis Center**, 701 Okeechobee Boulevard, West Palm Beach; tel: 561-832-7469; www.kravis.org. A major performing arts center with theater, dance, and musical productions.
**Parker Playhouse**, 707 NE 8th Street, Fort Lauderdale; tel: 954-764-1441. Broadway plays, musical events, and dance troupes.
**Surfside Playhouse**, 300 Ramp Road, Cocoa Beach; tel: 321-783-3127; www.surfsideplayers.com. A community theater with first-rate performances.

### Buying Tickets

The easiest way to reserve and pay for tickets is simply to call up the relevant box office or go to the venue's web site and pay by credit card. Sometimes, however, you will be required to make reservations through Ticket-master, a ticket agency that runs a pay-by-phone operation and also has outlets in certain music and discount stores. Be warned that Ticketmaster charges a commission fee of $20 or more above the normal cost of a ticket.

## Central Florida

**Amway Arena**, 600 W. Amelia Street, Orlando; tel: 407-849-2000; www.orlandovenues.net. One of Orlando's main venues for evening events, sports, and concerts.
**Bob Carr Performing Arts Center**, 401 Livingston Street, Orlando; tel: 407-849-2001. A year-round community auditorium that hosts regional and national music, theater, and dance.
**Orlando Philharmonic Orchestra**, tel: 407-896-6700; www.orlandophil.org. Orchestra musicians present classics at the Carr Center and also accompany the Orlando Ballet.

## West Coast

**Asolo Center for the Performing Arts**, 5555 N. Tamiami Trail, Sarasota; tel: 941-351-8000; www.asolo.org. Nationally prominent multipurpose theater.
**Mahaffey Theater**, 400 First Street South, St Petersburg; tel: 727-892-5798. Municipal venue for traveling road productions.
**Philharmonic Center for the Arts,** 5833 Pelican Bay Boulevard, Naples; tel: 239-597-1111; www.thephil.org. Two theaters in a complex offering classical music and plays.
**Players of Sarasota**, 838 N. Tamiami Trail Sarasota; tel: 941-365-2494; www.players.org. A community theater that hosts comedy acts, dramas, and thrillers.

## At the Movies

The most famous movie theater in Florida is the Tampa Theatre, which is a restored 1926 movie house in downtown Tampa with a superb interior that was once described as an "Andalusian bonbon." The theater puts on a mix of classic and foreign films as well as special events. Another delightful venue for movies, plays, and other events is the Hippodrome, or Hippo, in downtown Gainesville, occupying the grand Beaux Arts building that once housed the Post Office.
Florida has several annual film festivals. The best known is the Miami Film Festival in mid-February, with screenings of foreign, American, and Florida films. Also look out for the South Florida Black Film Festival in April, which screens African-American films at various venues, and Sarasota's film festival in November.

**Ruth Eckard Hall**, 1111 N. McMullen Booth Road, Clearwater; tel: 727-791-7400; www.rutheckerdhall.com. National pop, jazz, classical, ballet, and dramatic acts.
**Sarasota Ballet**, 61 N. Pineapple Avenue, Sarasota; tel: 941-552-1032. A regional opera company that performs in its own historic theater.
**St Pete Times Forum**, 401 Channelside Drive, Tampa; tel: 813-301-6600; www.sptimesforum.com. This arena is home of the Tampa Bay Lightning pro hockey team and site for pop concerts and wrestling.
**Tampa Bay Performing Arts Center**, 1010 N. MacInnes Place, Tampa; tel: 813-229-7827 or 800-955-1045; www.tbpac.org. One of the largest performing arts centers in Florida, with both classical and popular entertainment on the schedule.
**Venice Little Theater**, 140 W. Tampa Avenue, Venice; tel: 941-488-1115; www.venicestage.com. Community theater showing musicals, dramas, and comedies.

## North Florida

**Northwest Florida Ballet**, Fort Walton Beach; tel: 850-664-7787; www.nfballet.org. Regional dance company performing across the Panhandle.
**Pensacola Little Theatre**, 400 Jefferson Street, Pensacola; tel: 850-432-2042; www.pensacolalittletheatre.com. Presents regional plays and musical performances.
**Pensacola Symphony Orchestra**, 18 E. Garden Street; tel: 850-435-2533; www.pensacolasymphony.org. A regional company that performs at several locations.
**Tallahassee Symphony Orchestra**, 1345 Thomasville Road, Tallahassee; tel: 850-224-0461; www.tallahassee symphony.org. A regional orchestra performing concerts at the university.

## FESTIVALS

The following festivals and other events are listed chronologically. Sports events are listed separately.

## Annual Events

### January

**Art Deco Weekend** (Miami). A celebration of Miami Beach's famous Art Deco architecture. Events include a street fair, music, and an art show. Early January. Tel: 305-672-2014.
**Feast of Epiphany Blessing** (Tarpon Springs). Young Greek men dive into Spring Bayou to compete for a

crucifix blessed by the Greek Orthodox priest. Early January.
**Zora Neale Hurston Festival** (Eatonville). The 20th-century writer is celebrated annually in the nation's oldest incorporated African-American community. Public talks, a street festival. Late January. Tel: 407-358-8108.

### February

**Florida Renaissance Festival** (Deerfield Beach). A medieval fair with jousting, classical music, and art. Early February. Tel: 954-776-1642.
**Edison Festival of Lights** (Fort Myers). An annual tribute to inventor Thomas Edison. Early February. Tel: 941-334-2999.
**Florida State Fair** (Tampa). The big daddy of Florida fairs, with livestock, agriculture, art, crafts, rides, food, and entertainment. Second week in February. Tel: 813-621-7821.
**Gasparilla Pirate Festival** (Tampa). A pirate invasion takes over downtown with music, food, and entertainment. Early February. Tel: 813-353-8108.
**Coconut Grove Arts Festival** (Miami). The largest art festival in the state. Mid-February. Tel: 305-447-0401.
**Seminole Tribe Fair** (Hollywood). American Indian arts, crafts, music, and foods. Mid-February. Tel: 954-967-3434.
**Las Olas Art Festival** (Fort Lauderdale). Street arts, crafts, music, and food. Tel: 954-472-3755.
**Greek Festival** (Fort Myers). Annual festival of Florida's Greek Orthodox community. Late February. Tel: 941-481-2099.
**Mardi Gras Parades** (Pensacola). Not as big as in New Orleans but still fun. Late February. Tel: 850-932-1500.

### March

**Carnival Miami**. A weeklong Hispanic heritage festival in Little Havana. Early March. Tel: 305-644-8888
**Florida Strawberry Festival** (Plant City). A tribute to strawberries with music, food, and entertainment, east of Tampa. First week in March. Tel: 813-752-9194.
**Medieval Fair** (Sarasota). Jousting, music, drama, Renaissance-era entertainment. Early March. Tel: 941-351-8497.
**Festival of States** (St Petersburg). Parades with school band music. Last week in March. Tel: 727-898-3654.
**Bonita Tomato-Seafood Festival** (Bonita Springs). Seafood, carnival rides, games, crafts, entertainment. Tel: 941-334-7007.
**Florida Film Festival** (Maitland). Documentaries, animation, short films. Late March. Tel: 407-629-0054.

## April

**Blessing of the Fleet** (St Augustine). Fishing boats get their blessing for the season. Easter Sunday. Tel: 904-829-5681.

**Indian Exposition and Pow Wow** (Fort Myers). American Indian arts, crafts, food, and music. Early April. Tel: 941-992-0311

**Jacksonville Landing Annual Folk Festival.** Folk music, art, and crafts. Early April. Tel: 904-353-1188.

**Conch Republic Celebrations (Key West).** Key West once again tries to secede from the state. Late April. Tel: 305-296-0213.

**Apalachicola Walk and Wine Festival**: art show, musicians, chef demonstrations, and wine tastings. Late April. Tel: 850-653-9419.

## May

**Sunfest West** (Palm Beach). Florida's largest music, art, and water sports festival. Tel: 561-659-5980.

**Florida Folk Festival** (White Springs). Folk music, crafts, and entertainment. Late May. Tel: 877-635-3655.

## June

**Billy Bowlegs Pirate Festival** (Fort Walton Beach). A tribute to the Seminole chief. First week in June. Tel: 800-322-3319.

**Goombay Festival** (Miami). Giant, colorful Bahamian street festival with live music, parades, and food. The festival is in Coconut Grove, whose inhabitants originate mainly from the islands. Early June. Tel: 305-372-9966.

**Fiesta of Five Flags** (Pensacola). Street festival with food and music memorializing the Spanish explorer Tristan de Luna. First week of June. Tel: 850-433-6512.

## July

**Hemingway Days** (Key West). A rowdy tribute to Hemingway and his work. The look-alike competition is a particular favorite, drawing middle-aged men with beards from far and wide. Late July.

**Florida International Festival** (Daytona Beach). Prestigious music festival featuring music from jazz to classical. Late July to early August. Tel: 386-252-1511.

## August

**Annual Wausau Possum Festival**: celebration in honor of the marsupial in the small town of Wausau near Panama City Beach. First Saturday in August.

## September

**St Augustine's Founding**

**Anniversary**. A reenactment of the first landing of the Spanish conquistadors in St Augustine in 1565. Saturday nearest September 8. Tel: 904-825-1010.

## October

**Fantasy Fest (**Key West). Wild and crazy Halloween celebrations that last all week. Late October. Tel: 305-296-1817.

**Halloween Horror Nights** (Orlando). Halloween fun on the grounds of Universal Studios. Tel: 407-22-HORROR.

**Guavaween** (Tampa). Latin-style Halloween celebration with a parade through Ybor City. Last Saturday in October. Tel: 813-621-7121.

## November

**Birthplace of Speed Celebration** (Daytona Beach). Mid-November. Tel: 386-677-3454.

**Riverwalk Blues Festival** (Fort Lauderdale). Music festival with hot rhythms and hotter Cajun dishes. Tel: 954-761-5985.

**St Petersburg Boat Show.** One of the South's largest boat shows at Bayfront Center. Tel: 954-764-7642.

**Roy Hobbs Baseball World Series** (Fort Myers). More than 100 teams vie for first place in this tournament named after a legendary baseball hero. Tel: 888-484-7422.

**Cine-Word Film Festival** (Sarasota). One of the top international film festivals in the US, drawing films and movie-makers from across the world. Tel: 941-364-8662.

**Fort Myers Beach Sandsculpting Contest**. A three-day event drawing amateur and professional sculptors. Tel: 239-332-2930.

**Miami Book Fair International.** This international congress of authors, publishers, and agents fills the city, hawking books. Also street vendors, entertainment. Tel: 305-237-3258.

## December

**Walt Disney World's Very Merry Christmas Parade** (Orlando). Disney does Christmas in typical over-the-top style. Mid-December. Tel: 407-824-4321.

**Lighted Boat Parade** (St Petersburg). A nautical-style Christmas parade in mid-December.

**Orange Bowl Parade** (Miami). Nation's top marching bands accompany amazing floats before the football bowl game. December 31. Tel: 305-341-4700.

**Caloosahatchee Cracker Festival and Civil War Reenactment** (Fort Myers). An historical reenactment of the southernmost Civil War battle. Tel: 941-461-7400.

# SPORTS

## Participant Sports

Florida is a great place in which to enjoy the outdoors and be active. Its large number of state parks, recreation areas, and nature preserves provide plenty of scope for walking, as well as swimming, fishing, cycling, boating, and so on. Being surrounded by water and with its numerous rivers, lakes, and springs, Florida has lots of activities that involve water. You can swim, either in the sea or in lovely freshwater pools. While not as good as California, there is surfing along the Atlantic Coast. Windsurfing is popular but not all resorts rent out equipment. Divers and snorkelers will have a wonderful time exploring the coral reef off the Florida Keys, and glass-bottom boat tours give those who don't want to get their feet wet a taste of the rich marine life. Horseback riding is not as popular as other parts of the US, but some parks have horses for rent and special trails. One of the best places to ride is the Payne's Prairie State Preserve near Gainesville.

## Boating

Florida's waterways are suitable for boats of every shape and size. For many people in Florida, having a boat is as normal as having a car. There are hundreds of marinas, from those on the coast that provide all amenities to more basic ones in the interior. They are listed in *Florida Boating*, which is available free from Florida Game and Fresh Water Fish Commission, 620 S. Meridian Street, Tallahassee, FL 32399-1600, tel: 850-488-6257. For salt water, you must contact Florida Marine Patrol, 3900 Commonwealth Boulevard, MS 650, Tallahassee, FL 32399, tel: 850-488-5600.

The Intracoastal Waterway, a natural but dredged channel that runs parallel to much of the east coast and parts of the west coast of Florida, is very popular among boaters – partly because in many places it is protected from the open water by barrier islands. Another popular route is the Okeechobee Waterway, which runs for 135 miles (217km) along the St Lucie Canal from Stuart, on the east coast, across Lake Okeechobee, and onto the west coast near Fort Myers via the Caloosahatchee River. Several marinas rent out houseboats for exploring inland waterways. These can be like mini-apartments, fully equipped with everything from microwave ovens to color TVs.

### Canoeing and Kayaking

You can canoe or kayak virtually anywhere in Florida, whether you want to paddle the testing Wilderness Waterway through the Everglades, paddle along the Blackwater River in the Panhandle, or explore the Peace River as it opens into Charlotte Harbor. You can rent canoes and kayaks in most parks, and there are plenty of private concessionaires, too. "Tubing" – floating down rivers on an inflated inner tube – has become a popular (and cheaper) alternative to canoeing and kayaking. One of the premier tubing spots is the Ichetucknee River in north-central Florida.

### Fishing

Fishing is more than a hobby for many Floridians. It is a way of life. Thousands of anglers travel from outside the state to enjoy the state's rich waters. **Saltwater fishing** requires no license, and there is no closed season on game fish. Florida's 8,000 miles (12,875km) of tidal coastline support over 600 varieties of saltwater fish. To catch them you can try anything from deep-sea fishing to surf casting or pier fishing. Grouper, amberjack, sea trout, mackerel, red snapper, sailfish, bonefish, and kingfish lurk in the deepest waters. In the late spring and summer, tarpon challenge deep-sea fishermen off Tampa Bay, Marathon, Boca Grande Pass, and Bahia Honda Channel. The Keys, the lower East Coast, and upper Gulf regions are home to blue marlin. **Freshwater fishing** is outstanding in Florida, with its 30,000 lakes and untold miles of rivers and streams, and licenses are inexpensive. Lake Okeechobee attracts few casual visitors, but it is very popular among anglers after bass. The St John's River is also big fishing territory. Angling is permitted in state parks and other preserves.

### Golf

Florida is one of the top golfing states in the country. It is said that one out of every 10 golf games in the US takes place in Florida, and few states have more courses. With over 1,000 golf courses spread across the state to choose from, you are never far from a tee. Many of the courses are private, but there are enough public courses for out-of-towners who don't have a friend at a local country club. And don't think that because Florida is flat its courses lack challenge and rolling beauty. Many courses were designed by experts who have created beautiful man-made undulations, ponds, and rolling hills amid the greens. Green fees vary from over $75 per person at the more exclusive private courses to less than $20 per person at the public courses. At many, the fees are higher in winter months, when Northerners flock to the state for the game. For information on locations of golf courses, fees, and regulations, call the Florida Sports Foundation,

tel: 850-488-8347, for a free copy of the *Official Florida Golf Guide*.

### Tennis

As a major sponsor of international tennis matches, Florida attracts players from the world over. Many hotels have their own courts, with tennis instructors who offer lessons. Several state, county, and city parks have courts available to the public for free or a small fee. For information on over 7,000 courts in the state, contact the Florida Sports Foundation, tel: 850-488-8347.

### Jogging/Running

Sweat-drenched and sunburned joggers and runners are very much a part of the Florida landscape. Hundreds of miles of designated pathways are dedicated to the sport, and the flat and regular roads lend themselves to those who are willing to brave the traffic. If you are from a colder climate, take it easy the first time you are out running in Florida; the humidity and heat can easily dehydrate a non-acclimatized runner. Be sure to wear a hat and sunscreen and carry water. A few major and minor races take place in Florida, most in winter. For information on clubs, races, and paths, write to the Florida Athletics Congress at 1330 NW 6th Street, Gainesville, FL 32601.

### Hiking

If you like to hike, you'll find numerous trails in city, county, and state preserves and parks throughout Florida. Trails are usually flat and sandy tracks surrounded by forests, lakes, rivers, and springs and, for some people, get a bit monotonous. The key is to learn about the natural history of the area you are in and watch for wildlife. Birding is particularly good along the coastline, especially the northwest Nature Coast, where trails have wider views over marshes and mudflats in the

**BELOW:** baseball fans watch pre-season action at Spring Training.

estuary to the Gulf of Mexico. Florida also has primitive and wilderness areas for hiking, such as Lake Wales Ridge and Disney Wilderness Preserve in central Florida, both run by The Nature Conservancy. And, of course, there are miles and miles of pristine sandy beaches, just perfect for long walks at sunset.

## Spectator Sports

### Football

Florida has three teams in the National Football League: the Miami Dolphins, the Tampa Bay Buccaneers, and the Jacksonville Jaguars. The Miami Dolphins have competed five times in the Super Bowl, although they haven't won since 1973. Tampa Bay, however, won the championship for the first time in 2003. The season runs from September to December. College games are also big news, and draw almost as many (highly partisan) fans as NFL matches. The best Florida teams are the Hurricanes of Miami, the Seminoles of Tallahassee, and the Gators from Gainesville. Tim Tebow, quarterback for the Florida Gators, won the 2007 Heisman Trophy, the first sophomore to win the prestigious college football award. The top college games take place around the new year, including the Orange Bowl in Miami, the Citrus Bowl in Orlando, and the Gator Bowl in Jacksonville.

### Baseball

Currently the official spring training grounds of 18 major league teams, from February through March, Florida is the place to watch your favorite players warm up for the regular season. Visiting teams also meet in friendly games in the so-called Grapefruit League, which draws big crowds. Florida's own major league baseball teams are the successful Florida Marlins and

### Learn Tennis in Style

Bradenton on the west coast of Florida is home to the famous Nick Bollettieri Tennis Academy, where stars such as Pete Sampras began their careers. Mere mortals can also have a go at nurturing their talent. As well as full-time courses, the Academy offers one-day sessions and also weekly training programs (for around $1,000). For more information, write to the Academy at 55000 34th Street West, Bradenton, FL 34210, or call 941-755-1000.

the Tampa Bay Rays. The season runs from April to August. For further information on games, contact the Florida Sports Foundation, 1319 Thomaswood Drive, Tallahassee, FL 32312, tel: 850-488-8347, or team websites.

### Polo

Horse racing is popular all over Florida, but polo is particularly big in southeast Florida, along the Gold Coast. The most famous polo clubs are in West Palm Beach, Boca Raton, and Lake Worth. The most prestigious tournament is the Challenge Cup, which takes place in Palm Beach in January. The season runs from December to April.

### Pari-Mutuels

**Thoroughbred Horse Racing**
Gulfstream Park, 901 S. Federal Highway, Hallandale, tel: 954-454-7000. January–March.
Hialeah Park, 2200 E. 4th Avenue, Hialeah, tel: 305-885-8000. March–May.
Calder Race Track, 21001 NW 27th Avenue, Miami, tel: 305-625-1311. May–June.
Tampa Bay Downs, 12505 Racetrack Road, Tampa, tel: 813-855-4401. December–April.

**Harness Racing**
Pompano Park, 1800 SW 3rd Street, tel: 954-972-2000. Year-round.

**Jai-Alai Frontons**
Fort Pierce Jai-Alai, tel: 772-464-7500. January–April.
Orlando Jai-Alai, tel: 407-339-6221. January–December.
Ocala Jai-Alai, tel: 352-591-2345. January–March and June–September.
Dania Jai-Alai, tel: 954-927-2841. Year-round.
Miami Jai-Alai, tel: 305-633-6400. Year-round.

**Greyhound Racing**
Daytona Beach Kennel Club, 2201 Volusa Avenue, Daytona Beach, tel: 386-252-6484.
Flagler Dog Track, 401 NW 38th Court, Miami, tel: 305-649-3000.
Jacksonville Greyhound Racing, Highway 17, Jacksonville, tel: 904-646-0001.
Palm Beach Kennel Club, 1111 N. Congress Avenue, West Palm Beach, tel: 561-683-2222.
Pensacola Greyhound Park, 951 Dogtrack Road, Pensacola, tel: 850-455-8595.
St Petersburg Kennel Club, 10490 Gandy Boulevard, St Petersburg, tel: 727-576-1361.
Sarasota Kennel Club, 5400

### Spring Training: Where to See Your Favorite Team

Below is a list of where US baseball teams do their spring training. Locations do change periodically, so phone to check.
**Atlanta Braves**, Walt Disney World, tel: 407-939-4263.
**Baltimore Orioles**, Fort Lauderdale Stadium, Fort Lauderdale, tel: 954-776-1921.
**Boston Red Sox**, City of Palms Park, Fort Myers, tel: 941-334-4700.
**Cincinnati Reds**, Ed Smith Stadium, Sarasota, tel: 941-954-7699.
**Detroit Tigers**, Marchant Stadium, Lakeland, tel: 863-686-8075.
**Florida Marlins**, Roger Dean Stadium, Jupiter, tel: 561-775-1818.
**Houston Astros**, Osceola County Stadium, Kissimmee, tel: 407-839-3900.
**Los Angeles Dodgers**, Holman Stadium, Vero Beach, tel: 772-569-6858.
**Minnesota Twins**, Lee County Sports Complex, Fort Myers, tel: 800-338-9467.
**St. Louis Cardinals**, Roger Dean Stadium, Jupiter, tel: 561-775-1818.
**New York Mets**, Port St. Lucie Complex, Port St. Lucie, tel: 772-871-2115.
**New York Yankees**, Legends Field, Tampa, tel: 813-879-2244.
**Philadelphia Phillies**, Jack Russell Stadium, Clearwater, tel: 727-442-8496.
**Pittsburgh Pirates**, McKechnie Field, Bradenton, tel: 941-748-4610.
**Tampa Bay Devil Rays**, Al Lang Field, St Petersburg, tel: 727-894-4773.
**Texas Rangers**, Charlotte County Stadium, Port Charlotte, tel: 941-625-9500.
**Toronto Blue Jays**, Dunedin Stadium, Dunedin, tel: 727-733-0429.

Bradenton Road, Sarasota, tel: 941-355-7744.
Tampa Greyhound Track: 8300 Nebraska Avenue North, Tampa, tel: 813-932-4313.
Washington County Kennel Club, Highway 79, Ebro, tel: 904-234-3943

### Sporting Events

#### January
**Orange Bowl** (Miami). The final game between Florida's two best college football teams. New Year's Day. Tel: 305-341-3000.
**Annual PGA Tour Golf Event** (Naples). Tel: 941-353-7767. Early January.
**Presidential Sailfish Tournament** (Islamorada). Tel: 305-664-2321. Late January.

**Speed Weeks** (Daytona Beach). Three weeks of racing that culminate in the Daytona 500 in January.

### February

**Islamorada Sport Fishing Festival**. Tel: 305-664-2321. Mid-February.

**Miami Beach International Boat Show**. Tel: 305-673-7311. Mid-February.

**Silver Spurs Rodeo** (Kissimmee). Tel: 407-847-4052. Late February.

### March

**Classics Day Vintage Motorcycle Races and Supersport AMA Road Races** (Daytona Beach). Tel: 615-851-3674. Early March.

**Doral Ryder Open Golf Tournament** (Miami). Tel: 305-223-7060. Late March.

**NASDAQ 100 Open** (Key Biscayne). Florida's top tennis tournament, tel: 305-446-2701. Mid-March.

**Naples Swamp Buggy Races**, tel: 800-897-2701. Early March.

**Florida Derby** (Gulfstream Park Racetrack). Tel: 954-454-7000. Early March.

**Tampa Bay Classic Equestrian Festival** (Tampa). Late March.

**Toyota Grand Prix of Miami**, tel: 305-230-7223. March.

### April

**Ron Jon/Duke Boyd Easter Surfing Festival** (Cocoa Beach). Early April.

**PGA Seniors Championship Golf** (West Palm Beach). Tel: 561-627-1800. Mid-April.

**Seven-Mile Bridge Run** (Marathon). Tel: 305-743-5417. Late April.

**Mount Dora Sailing Regatta**. Late April.

**Gulf Coast Offshore Powerboat Races** (Daytona). Tel: 954-618-2852. Late April.

### May

**Key West Fishing Tournament**. Tel: 800-970-9056. April–November.

**Flagler Beach Fishing Regatta**. Late May.

### June

**Annual Firecracker 5K and 10-Mile Beach Run** (Daytona Beach). Late June.

**Annual Ladies Billfish Tournament** (Pensacola). Tel: 800-453-4638. Late June.

### July

**Destin Shark Fishing Tournament**. Tel: 305-595-5911. Early July.

**International Billfish Tournament**. Tel: 850-453-4638. Early July.

**Central Florida Soap Box Derby** (Sanford). Tel: 407-330-5600. Mid-July.

**Port of the Islands Annual Shark**

**Tournament** (Naples). Tel: 239-672-3133. Late July.

### August

**King Mackerel Tournament** (Destin). Tel: 850-837-2506. Early August.

**Homasassa Ramblin River Raft Race**. Early August.

### September

**Labor Day Rodeo and Parade** (Okeechobee). Tel: 941-677-2604. Early September.

**Power Boat Racing** (Sanford). Late September.

**Triathlon** (Sarasota). Tel: 941-362-7339. Late September.

### October

**Annual Bonefish Tournament** (Marathon). Tel: 305-743-2821. Mid-October.

**Destin Shark Fishing Rodeo**. Tel: 850-837-6734. Early October.

**Airboat Races and Festival** (Okeechobee). Tel: 941-763-6464. Mid-October.

**Fort Lauderdale International Boat Show**. Tel: 954-765-4466. Late October.

**Breeders Cup** (Hallandale Race Track). Tel: 954-454-7000. Early November.

**Kissimmee Boating Jamboree**. Tel: 407-957-6236. Late October.

**World Championship Swamp Buggy Races** (Naples). Tel: 800-897-2701. Late October.

### November

**Marathon Sailfish Tournament**. Tel: 904-743-6139. Late November.

**St Petersburg Boat Show**. Tel: 727-892-5767. Late November.

### December

**Central Florida Sailfest** (Sanford). Early December.

**Sandy Claws Beach Run** (Sarasota). Tel: 941-951-5572. Early December.

## SHOPPING

### What to Buy

If you're into kitsch – plastic flamingo ashtrays, canned sunshine, orange perfume, and the like – you will find Florida a veritable treasure house. From roadside shacks to massive futuristic malls, stores carry plenty of traditional souvenirs. (Don't be surprised if your souvenir plate has a sticker on the bottom that says "Made in China.") And then, of course, there are the homegrown souvenirs like oranges, tangerines, limes, kumquats, and grapefruits that

can be shipped home for a small fee.

But if you look a little harder, Florida also has a variety of quality goods to take home from a trip. There are shops worth seeking out that sell designer clothing at discount prices (factory outlet malls), fascinating examples of Haitian art, Art Deco, and old Florida antiques, American Indian crafts, shells that forever smell of the sea, and folk art crafted from found objects. You'll find plenty of arts and crafts in remote rural island communities like Cedar Key, which has an assortment of art galleries selling everything from made-to-order handbags to painted cypress "knees," and the Greek sponge capital of Tarpon Springs, which sells local sponges as well as olive oil soap and other Mediterranean items in quaint harbor shops.

For more humdrum shopping, there is the usual array of convenience stores, drugstores, department stores, and supermarkets such as the Publix chain, which is found all over Florida. Many Floridians do their shopping in shopping malls, which contain the usual mix of department stores, boutiques, chain stores, and one-of-a-kind stores. The Gold Coast has the biggest choice of smart malls, particularly Miami, Fort Lauderdale, and Boca Raton. Just ask the staff in your hotel for details of the best malls in your area. Hours vary, but most shopping centers are open seven days a week.

Despite the abundance of citrus fruits, beef, fish, and other foods grown in Florida, much of it is exported out of the state and really good fresh, local food can be hard to find. There is now a Whole Foods in Winter Park and a Wild Oats in Tampa, but in many places, small business owners run health food stores at a loss and the cost of organic food can be prohibitively expensive. Most people either grow their own or patronize the growing number of farmers' markets, also called green markets, in communities throughout the state. In addition to selling locally grown, often organic produce, meat, dairy, flowers, honey, fair trade coffee and tea, and fresh salsas, green markets also often have booths offering hemp clothing and gifts. These markets are an easy and fun way to connect with locals and take the pulse of the community you are visiting. It's particularly good if you're staying in an efficiency or vacation rental and want to feel part of the local scene.

### Where to Shop

Here are just a few of Florida's most famous shopping spots.

### Cocoa Beach

**Ron Jon Surf Shop**, 4151 N. Atlantic Avenue, tel: 321-799-8888; 24 hours. Huge billboards along highways in central Florida advertise this local institution and beach bum's dream. Ron Jon sells bathing suits, surfboards, scuba equipment, suntan lotion, and lots of water toys.

### Fort Lauderdale

**Sawgrass Mills Factory Outlet Mall**, 12801 W. Sunrise Boulevard, tel: 954-846-2350; Mon–Sat 10am–9.30pm, Sun 11am–8pm. This is the largest factory outlet mall in the US, with about 300 stores, attracting around 20 million people a year. Shuttle buses ferry people from several Miami and Miami Beach hotels.

**Swap Shop of Fort Lauderdale**, 3291 Sunrise Boulevard, tel: 954-791-7927; Mon–Fri 7.30am–5pm Sat–Sun 7.30am–6.30pm. Not far from Sawgrass Mills, this is a bargain-hunter's paradise, with rows and rows of stalls selling jewelry, sunglasses, and much, much more at rock-bottom prices. The carnival and free circus is an added attraction.

### Fort Myers

**The Shell Factory**, 2787 N. Tamiami Trail, N. Fort Myers, tel: 941-995-2141; daily 9am–6pm. The world's largest collection of shells and coral in natural forms and transformed into jewelry, lamps, and baskets.

### Key West

**Key West Hand Print Fabrics**, 201 Simonton Street, tel: 305-294-9535; daily 9am–6pm. Watch as workers make brightly colored, hand-printed cotton and silk fabrics that are sold by the yard and as casual clothing.

**Fast Buck Freddies**, 500 Duval Street, tel: 305-294-2007; daily, extended Sat hours. A Key West institution, Freddie's is an emporium that specializes in the bizarre: sequined bikinis, battery-operated alligators, and fish-shaped shoes.

**Haitian Art Company**, 600 Frances Street, tel: 305-296-8932; daily 10am–6pm. One of the largest collections of paintings, sculptures, and papier-mâché art from Haiti in the US.

### Miami

**Bal Harbor Shops**, 9700 Collins Avenue, Bal Harbor, tel: 305-866-0311; Mon–Fri 10am–9pm, Sat 10am–7pm, Sun noon–6pm. An elegant shopping center with dozens of upscale boutiques.

**Bayside Marketplace**, 401 Biscayne Boulevard, tel: 305-577-3344; Mon–Thur 10am–10pm, Fri–Sat 10am–11pm, Sun 11am–9pm. A waterfront shopping and entertainment complex in downtown Miami with more than 150 shops.

**Loehmann's Fashion Island**, 18711 Biscayne Boulevard; Mon–Sat 10am–9pm, Sun noon–6pm. Miami is a great place to buy clothing, whether you are after designer labels or bargains. Loehmann's Fashion Island specializes in cut-rate designer clothes.

**Seybold Building**, 36 NE 1st Street, Miami, tel: 305-374-7922; Mon–Sat 9am–6pm. Downtown Miami is known for its discount jewelry and electronics, and the Seybold Building has one of the best selections of gold, diamonds, and watches.

**Streets of Mayfair**, 3390 Mary Street, Coconut Grove, tel: 305-448-1700; Mon–Thur 11am–10pm, Fri–Sat 11am–midnight, Sun 11am–10pm. A small, attractive mall in the heart of Coconut Grove, with mainly fashion boutiques.

### Orlando

**Belz Factory Outlet Mall**, 5401 W Oakridge Road, tel: 407-354-0126; Mon–Sat 10am–9pm, Sun 10am–6pm. Supposedly the most-visited "attraction" in Orlando after Walt Disney World, Belz is a bargain bonanza. This large, indoor mall is one of the best places in Florida to shop for designer clothes – Ann Klein, London Fog, Christian Dior, and many more – and for just about every brand of jeans, sneakers, and casual wear at discounts of up to 75 percent off retail prices.

**Mercado Mediterranean Village**, 8445 International Drive, tel: 407-345-9337; daily 10am–10pm. More than 60 specialty shops along a series of brick streets with an atmosphere of a Mediterranean village. Arts, crafts, jewelry, clothing, and leather goods.

**Orange World**, 5395 W. Irlo Bronson Memorial Highway, Kissimmee, tel: 407-396-1306; daily 8am–10.45pm. You can't miss this building: it's shaped like a gigantic orange. Inside is an assortment of freshly picked fruits, citrus candles, and orange blossom honey, all available to be shipped to friends and family back home.

---

**BELOW:** Third Street in Naples is known for tony boutiques.

# A HANDY SUMMARY OF PRACTICAL INFORMATION, ARRANGED ALPHABETICALLY

## **A** irport Taxes

Domestic flights include up to 20 percent in additional taxes to cover US Excise Tax (7.5 percent), post-9/11 security costs, and airport and facility fees. Airlines include this in the total for air fare.

## **B** anks and ATMs

Foreign visitors are advised to take US dollar travelers checks to Florida since exchanging foreign currency – whether as cash or checks – can prove problematic. An increasing number of banks, including First Union National Bank, Nations Bank, and Sun Bank chains, offer foreign exchange facilities, but this practice is not universal. Some department store chains offer foreign currency exchange. Most shops, restaurants, and other establishments accept travelers checks in US dollars and will give change in cash. Alternatively, checks can be converted into cash at the bank.

**Credit Cards** are very much part of life in Florida, as in other parts of the US. They can be used to pay for pretty much anything, and it is also common for car rental firms and hotels to take an imprint of your card as a deposit. Car rental companies may oblige you to pay a large deposit in cash if you do not have a credt card.

You can also use your credit card to withdraw cash from ATMs (Automated Teller Machines). Before you leave home, make sure you know your PIN number and find out which ATM system will accept your card. The most widely accepted cards are Visa, American Express, MasterCard, Diners Club, Japanese Credit Bureau, and Discovery Card.

### Budgeting for Your Trip

There has never been a better time for overseas visitors to travel in the United States. The dollar has plummeted to historic lows against the Euro and British pound, making the US an incredible bargain for European visitors.

Allow $80–100 a night for good-quality hotels for two people, although really memorable hotels and bed-and-breakfasts tend to run closer to $150 or more a night. At the other end of the spectrum, Florida has many gorgeous oceanside and forested campgrounds with full facilities for about $16 a night, and hostels and barebones motel lodgings can be found for less than $50.

You can probably get away with $30 a day per person for basic meals if you stick to diners, cafes, markets, and inexpensive restaurants and don't drink alcohol. Meals in better restaurants cost a lot more, but if you're determined to visit that famous high-end establishment and don't have the cash, one insider trick is to eat lunch there: you'll find many of the items on the dinner menu at much lower prices and still get to say you've eaten at a hip eatery.

Budget at least $4 per gallon for fuel for your rental car; most economy vehicles get over 30 miles per gallon. Trams, light rail, buses, and other public transportation in cities like Tampa and Miami are just a few dollars per ride, allowing you to get around for much less.

### Business Hours

US stores are often open seven days a week and tend to stay open into the evening, especially in tourist areas. Government offices are usually open only on weekdays from 8am or 9am to 4pm or 5pm. Post offices are usually open from 8am to 5pm and Saturday morning.

## Climate

### Temperature

The Sunshine State lives up to its name, with over 300 days of sunshine a year and mild winters. Having said that, Florida is equally well known for oppressive summer heat and humidity and extreme weather conditions, arising from its location in Hurricane Alley, the path of hurricanes forming in the Caribbean Ocean.

January is the coolest month, particularly in the north-central parts of the state, where even a slight change in elevation leads to a change in vegetation type and climate. At night, it can dip to 41°F (5°C) in Tallahassee in the Panhandle even as it stays at 66°F (18°C) in Key West. Many residents in the north have fireplaces to ward off the cool, damp conditions. Temperatures below freezing occur infrequently but can wreak havoc on the agricultural industry when they do. January highs climb to an average of 76°F (24°C) in Key West in winter and 61°F (16°C) in Apalachicola in the north. Due to the relatively mild winters, many South Florida homes do not have heating systems, and erratic winter weather in recent years (including occasional snow flurries in Miami) has caught residents unprepared.

In contrast, June through September, when high temperatures are mixed with high humidity, can be swelteringly hot and feel quite unpleasant away from air-conditioned homes, cars, and businesses. Sea breezes along the coast and daily thundershowers can create more bearable temperatures in north Florida cities in summer. The many bodies of water throughout Florida are, in fact, its hidden weapon in getting through the dog days of summer. Average summer temperatures are in the range of 86°–91°F (30°–33°C), with little variation from north to south. At night, temperatures "cool off" to between 70°F (21°C) and 80°F (26°C), which usually means you'll need to use air-conditioning or a fan to sleep in comfort.

### Rainfall

Florida's hottest months are also the rainiest. Thunderstorms occur with such regularity each day that you can set your watch by them. South Florida gets rain almost daily in June and July. The Everglades soak up nearly 9 inches (23cm) on average in June. In contrast with other parts of the US, there is little rain in November and December: only 2 inches (5cm) falls on average across the whole state.

## What to Do if a Hurricane Strikes

### During the storm

Stay indoors once the hurricane is buffeting your area. When the eye (the low-pressure area at the center of a hurricane) passes over, there will be a temporary lull in wind and rain for 30 minutes or more. Don't think it's over. When the eye has passed overhead, the storm will, in fact, resume – possibly with even greater force – from the opposite direction (hurricane weather systems rotate counterclockwise). Wait for word from the authorities before venturing out of your shelter.

### If ordered to evacuate

Most coastal communities have detailed evacuation procedures in place. Evacuation route signs are permanently located along highways in many of these areas. Follow instructions and designated routes as quickly as possible. Take blankets, flashlights, extra clothing, food, water, and medications. Leave behind pets (which are not allowed inside public shelters).

### After the storm passes

Drive with caution when told to return home. Debris in streets can be a hazard. Roads in coastal areas may collapse if soil has been washed from beneath them. Steer clear of downed or dangling utility wires. Stay tuned to radio stations for news of emergency medical, food, housing, and other assistance. If you have been staying in a rented home, re-enter the building with caution and make temporary repairs to correct hazards and minimize further damage. Open windows and doors to air and dry the house. Be careful when dealing with matches or fires in case of gas leaks.

### Lightning

Florida is unofficially dubbed the "lightning capital of the country." The state records an average of 10 deaths and 30 injuries from lightning each year. This dubious distinction is attributed to moist air that lies close to the ground and to unstable atmospheric conditions that exist mainly from May to September. Lasting just 1/1000th of a second, a bolt of lightning delivers a shock of 6,000–10,000 amps that can paralyze body functions. Even so, two-thirds of people hit by lightning in Florida have somehow survived. If you see dark clouds and lightning nearby, take cover. If you are riding in a car, stay inside until the storm passes. If you are at home or inside a building, don't try to "make a run for it." Many lightning victims are killed when getting in or out of their cars. Boaters should head for the nearest place they can tie up and evacuate the vessel.

### Hurricanes

The hurricane season in Florida usually runs from June 1 through November 30. The number of Atlantic hurricanes in a given year has ranged from as few as two to as many as 20, but on average one strikes Florida every two years. Still, the National Hurricane Center in Miami tracks each tropical storm very carefully, ready to issue evacuation orders if a hurricane is headed for the mainland. The average lifespan of a hurricane is 8 to 10 days. Florida's eastern and southeastern seaboards are the coastlines most vulnerable to hurricanes in August and early September, but patterns traditionally shift to the Caribbean later in September and October, endangering the Florida Keys, the Gulf coast, and the Panhandle.

In summer, tropical disturbances are common all over the tropics. It is from these that tropical depressions and then tropical storms develop, which can bring gales of up to 73 miles (117km) per hour and heavy rains. At this stage, the National Hurricane Center in Miami monitors developments very closely.

Florida's residents are well versed on precautions to be taken when a hurricane approaches. Newspapers run special sections on the subject at the start of each season, and most coastal communities publish evacuation plans and routes. People are encouraged to track the path of the storm on special charts, which are available in newspapers, on TV,

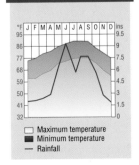

**CLIMATE CHART**

☐ Maximum temperature
■ Minimum temperature
— Rainfall

TRANSPORTATION
ACCOMMODATIONS
ACTIVITIES
A–Z

and even printed on the sides of grocery bags. Needless to say, tourists caught in Florida during an impending hurricane should drop plans to work on their suntans or visit tourist attractions and follow National Weather Service bulletins broadcast on radio and television.

Once a tropical storm has been upgraded to a named hurricane, this means that the National Hurricane Center has determined a hurricane may hit within 36–48 hours. It is time to begin taking final precautions against a direct hit: for example, checking that your vehicle's gas tank is full, gathering emergency supplies, sandbagging around houses, and boarding up windows. Stay tuned to the local radio or TV station for the latest storm information. A hurricane warning is issued when the storm reaches winds of at least 74mph (119km/h), and high water and storm surges are expected in a specific area within 24 hours. Warnings will identify specific coastal areas where these conditions may occur. Be ready to evacuate your home or hotel. Finish getting together the things you need to take to a shelter or anything else you will need if you stay home.

## Crime and Safety

Florida doesn't have a squeaky-clean reputation when it comes to crime, and attacks committed against tourists ruin the state's idyllic vacation-in-the-sun image periodically.

## Safety Tips for Motorists

When you first arrive, ask for advice from the car rental agent about the best route from the airport to your hotel. Better still, arrange to pick up your rental car from an agency near your hotel on the morning after you arrive, rather than tackle unfamiliar routes when very tired. Many car rental agencies will deliver your car to your hotel at no (or only a small) extra charge.

Use a map to plot your route before you begin any journey.

Ignore pedestrians or motorists who try to stop you, for example by indicating some supposed fault on your vehicle or even by ramming your car from behind.

Always keep your car doors locked, windows closed, and valuables out of sight while driving.

Avoid taking shortcuts in urban areas. If you get lost, drive to a well-lit and preferably busy area before stopping to look at your map.

The authorities have come up with various safeguards designed to protect visitors. Many of these are aimed at motorists, particularly in Miami, where a number of violent assaults have occurred when jet-lagged tourists disembarked long flights, missed the highway signs for Miami Beach, and found themselves in high-crime areas.

Car rental agencies have removed the special license plates that made rental cars an easy mark and have replaced them with standard-issue plates used by residents. In Miami, road signs have been improved and orange sunburst signs help guide visiting drivers along the main routes to and from the airport.

A little common sense goes a long way: Don't carry large sums of money or expensive video/camera equipment. Walk purposefully and don't make eye contact with unwelcome strangers or respond to come-ons. Don't travel alone at night. Ask the staff in your hotel for advice about areas that should be avoided.

## Currency

American dollars come in bills of $1, $5, $10, $20, $50, and $100, all the same size. The dollar is divided into 100 cents. Coins come in 1 cent (penny), 5 cents (nickel), 10 cents (dime), 25 cents (quarter), 50 cents (half-dollar), and $1 denominations. There is no Value Added Tax (VAT) in the US, but cities charge a sales tax, usually around 7 percent of the sale. Car rental companies charge both sales tax and service fees.

## Customs

You can bring into the US the following duty-free items: 1 liter of alcohol, if over 21 years of age; 200 cigarettes, 50 cigars (not Cuban) or 2kg of tobacco, if you're over 18; and gifts worth up to $100 ($800 for US citizens). Travelers with more than $10,000 in US or foreign currency, travelers checks, or money orders must declare these upon entry. Meats, fruits, vegetables, seeds, or plants (and many prepared foods made from them) are not permitted and must be disposed of in the bins provided before entering. For more information, contact US Customs & Border Protection (tel: 877-227-5511; www.cbp.gov).

## D isabled Travelers

Florida accommodations, attractions, restaurants, and parks welcome visitors with physical disabilities and

impairments. From ADA-compliant hotels to on-loan beach chairs and even mobility-assisted snorkeling and hang gliding, visitor services throughout Florida go to great lengths to make sure everyone enjoys barrier-free access to sun and fun. Under the Americans with Disabilities Act (ADA), accommodations built after January 26, 1995, and containing more than five rooms must be useable by persons with disabilities. Older and smaller inns and lodges are often wheelchair-accessible. For the sight-impaired, many hotels provide special alarm clocks, captioned television services, and security measures. To comply with ADA hearing-impaired requirements, hotels have begun to follow special procedures; local agencies may provide TTY and interpretation services. Check with the front desk when you make reservations to ascertain to what degree the hotel complies with ADA guidelines. Ask specific questions regarding bathroom facilities, bed height, wheelchair space, and availability of services. To find more about accommodations in Florida, visit www.visitflorida.com/planning/prop_finder, where you can narrow your search to ADA-compliant properties. Restaurants and attractions are required to build ramps for those with limited mobility. Many major attractions have wheelchairs for loan or rent. Some provide menus, visitor guides, and interpreters for hearing- and seeing-impaired guests. To search for ADA-compliant attractions, go to www.visitflorida.com/experience/attractions/listings.php.

For more information, read *Wheelchairs on the Go: Accessible Fun in Florida* by Michelle Stigleman and Deborah Van Brunt, www.wheelchairsonthego.com. For disability resources in Florida, contact the Clearinghouse on Disability (tel: 850-497-3423 or 877-232-4968). The Society for the Advancement of Travel for the Handicapped (tel: 212-447-7284; www.sath.org) publishes a quarterly magazine on travel for the disabled.

## E lectricity

The United States uses 110–120 volts AC (60 cycles). If visiting from outside North America, you may require an electrical adapter for any electronics or appliances you want to bring.

## Embassies

Foreign embassies are located in Washington, DC. Phone numbers include Britain (tel: 202-462-1340);

Germany (tel: 202-298-4000); France (tel: 202-944-6000); and Australia (tel: 202-797-3000).

## Emergency Numbers

In case of emergency, dial 911 to contact the police, fire, or ambulance service.

## Entry Regulations

Foreign travelers to the US (including those from Canada and Mexico) must carry a passport; a visa is required for visits of more than 90 days. A return plane ticket is also normally required. For the most current information, contact the U.S. Department of Homeland Security at www.dhs.gov.

## G ay and Lesbian Travelers

Florida is in the conservative Bible Belt, and rural destinations away from the cities may be less welcoming of gay travelers. Keep a low profile in such areas to avoid any problems. Gay travelers receive a huge welcome in gay-friendly locales like South Beach (Miami), Fort Lauderdale, and Key West and to a slightly lesser extent in Orlando, where the annual Gay Day at Walt Disney World is very popular. For more information, contact South Beach Business Guild in Miami (tel: 305-534-3336), the Gay and Lesbian Community Centers in Fort Lauderdale (tel: 954-463-9005), Key West (tel: 305-292-3223), and Orlando (tel: 407-228-8722). You'll find lots of information on GLBT activities in different parts of Florida at www.queeramerica.com. The Gay and Lesbian Yellow Pages (tel: 800-697-2812; www.glyp.com) offers regional information. Damron Company (tel: 415-255-0404 or 800-462-6654; www.damron.com) publishes guides aimed at lesbians and gay men and lists gay-owned and gay-friendly accommodations nationwide.

## H ealth

Most visitors to Florida will encounter no health problems during their stay: sunburn and mosquito bites in summer are the main nuisance. If you need medical assistance, ask the reception staff at your hotel or consult the Yellow Pages for the physician or pharmacist nearest you (in large cities, there is usually a physicians referral service number listed). The larger hotels may have a resident doctor. If you need immediate attention, go to a hospital emergency room (ER). Most emergency rooms are open 24 hours. There is nothing cheap about being sick in the US – whether it involves a simple visit to the doctor or a spell in a hospital. The initial fee charged by a good hospital might be $250, and that's before the additional cost of x-rays, medicines, examinations, and treatments have been added. Walk-in medical clinics are much cheaper than hospital emergency rooms for minor ailments. Foreign visitors are strongly advised to purchase travel insurance before leaving to avoid high urgent-care costs. Be sure you're covered for accidental death, emergency medical care, trip cancellation, and baggage or document loss.

### Health Hazards
#### Sunburn
An early overdose of sun can ruin in a few short hours a vacation that involved months of planning. One of the most common sights in Florida is that of the over-baked tourist painfully trying to sit or walk without rubbing against anything. If you are determined to get a suntan, do so gradually. Always wear a broad-brimmed hat, good-quality sunglasses, and use a high-factor sunscreen (30-plus) to protect your skin. The glare from Florida's azure seas and white sands increases the sun's intensity. Don't neglect to apply lotion on overcast days; the sun's ultraviolet rays penetrate the clouds, and the shade can lull you into staying outside too long. Florida's high heat and humidity can seriously tax the body's natural cooling systems. Dehydration and salt deficiency can lead to heat exhaustion, especially if you take medications or drink alcohol or strong coffee. It's best to moderate these, drink plenty of water, and take time to acclimate to the heat if you are not accustomed to it.

Long, uninterrupted periods of exposure to high temperatures can lead to heat stroke, which means that the body's core temperature rises to dangerous levels, and its normal cooling system – reddening and sweating – is overwhelmed. To head off problems, keep major arteries in your neck cool by wearing a wet bandanna or cotton shirt with a collar. If you feel dizzy and fuzzy-brained, feel muscle weakness and start to stumble, and your skin has become pale and dry rather than red and sweaty, immediately begin spraying yourself with water or, better yet, pour it on. This creates evaporative cooling and is the fastest way to recover.

You can also lie down in a dark room with a wet sheet over you and the air conditioning on. Whatever you do, don't jump into cold water in a pool or the ocean: it can send your body into shock. Heat stroke is a common problem for light-eyed, light-haired Europeans from northern climates and is a potentially serious condition, so don't ignore the telltale signs.

### Insects
People aren't the only creatures attracted to Florida's sun and sand. The state has many different types of insect, from mosquitoes to fleas, which bite and cause annoyance, if not discomfort.

**Mosquitoes:** Florida is infamous for its great swarms of mosquitoes, which can take the joy out of watching summer sunsets. Most big cities have mosquito control programs that have effectively curtailed the problem and reduced the potential for contracting West Nile virus carried by mosquitoes. Walt Disney World sends out teams to spray the whole park on a daily basis in summer. But pack a bottle of insect repellent, especially when venturing into backwoods areas like the Everglades. In truth, if you are more interested in the wildlife than anything else, you should visit in winter, when mosquitoes are rarely a problem. Sunrise and sunset are the worst times, so splash on plenty of repellent and cover up at these times.

**Love bugs:** Entomologists call them bibinoid flies, but to most Floridians they are simply known as love bugs because you will usually find them "flying united" right into your hair, face, or car's windshield. Love bugs don't bite. They are too busy mating. But they may cause trouble between May and September in various parts of the state. In moist, wooded hammock areas, black clouds of love bugs may hang over highways, slowing down traffic as they clog car radiators and splatter windshields.

**Fire ants:** If you are exploring off the beaten track, you might want to tread carefully, particularly when barefoot. Grassy fields are prime locations for mounds of fire ants. These tiny red ants inflict a burning sting and leave a reddish welt that turns into a blister. This can become infected if scratched. Some people are allergic to the sting of a fire ant and can suffer nausea or dizziness that needs prompt medical attention.

**Cockroaches:** Visitors new to tropical or subtropical regions may be startled by local cockroaches. Often called palmetto bugs, they grow to sizes unheard of in colder climates, usually resembling miniature armored patrol cars as they dart under carpets or disappear into cracks in the wall. They will eat virtually anything but steer clear of people.

**Sand flies**: Appropriately called "no-see-ums" by the locals, sand flies are another nemesis of the sunset beachgoer. They are what you feel but can't see, gnawing at your legs as you sink your toes into the sand. Repellent can help, and the herb pennyroyal, the active component in Avon's Skin So Soft cream, seems to work for some people.

## I nternet

The modems of many foreign laptops and handheld computers won't work in the US. You may need to purchase a global modem before leaving home or a local PC-card modem once you arrive in the US. For more information, log on to www.teleadapt.com. There are now numerous cyber cafés and business centers, such as Kinko's, in the US, where you can pick up e-mail. Most charge a fee for Internet access, either on their computer or your laptop. At Starbucks coffeehouses, for example, you must first purchase a T-Mobile Hot Spot pass (currently $9.95 day), before being able to log on; other coffeehouses and restaurants offer free Internet access as a customer incentive. You'll have fewer options in rural areas, but many lodgings offer dial-up high-speed (DSL) or Wireless Internet (WiFi) hot spots. Public libraries often offer free WiFi.

## M edia

### Television

All major cities have stations affiliated with major networks, local stations, and a vast number of cable hookups and satellite dish offerings. Hotel rooms usually have cable TV, but you often have to pay to watch movies (Pay Per View). Newspapers give daily and weekly information on TV and radio programs, and you can view an on-screen program guide for satellite TV.

### Newspapers

Daily newspapers roll off the presses in every large Florida city. The most widely read is the *Miami Herald*, but papers like the *Tampa Tribune* and *Orlando Sentinel* also have a reasonably wide circulation. There are several Spanish-language newspapers, and the *Miami Herald*

has a very popular Spanish language section, *El Nuevo Heraldo*. You can usually pick up *USA Today* from newspaper dispensers in the street or receive a free copy at certain hotel chains. Other national newspapers available in dispensers or good newsstands and bookstores include the *New York Times*, *Washington Post*, and *Wall Street Journal*. If you are planning on staying in a particular area, check out the local newspaper ahead of time for advance information. Most newspapers today have online equivalents.

## P ostal Service

The opening hours of federal post offices vary between central, big-city branches, and those in smaller towns or suburbs, but all are open Monday to Friday and some are also open on Saturday morning. Drugstores and hotels usually have a small selection of stamps. There are stamp-vending machines in the lobbies of most post offices as well as Automated Postal Centers that allow you to use a credit card to ship mail. As of May 12, 2008, first-class domestic rates are 42 cents for 1 oz with 17 cents for each additional ounce. Postcards are 27 cents each. Postage for overseas letters is 94 cents for 1 oz; 72 cents to Mexico and Canada. Postage for overseas postcards is currently 75 cents; 55 cents to Canada and Mexico.

Large envelopes over 13 ounces must now be sent by two- to three-day Priority Mail in the US or Media Mail, if the envelope contains printed materials. The fastest service offered by the post office is Express Mail, which guarantees next-day delivery to most destinations within the US, and delivery within two to three days to foreign destinations by Global Express Mail. Private courier services offering overnight and two-day delivery are usually the most reliable, although more expensive than the US Post Office. Ground delivery, taking an average of five days, is very popular. Telephone numbers for the main courier services are:
**FedEx**: 800-238-5355
**DHL**: 800-345-2727
**UPS**: 800-742-5877

## Public Holidays

Public holidays in the US include: New Years Day (January 1), Martin Luther King's Birthday (January 15), Presidents Day (third Monday in February), Memorial Day (last

Monday in May), Independence Day (July 4), Labor Day (first Monday in September), Columbus Day (second Monday in October), Veterans Day (November 11), Thanksgiving (fourth Thursday in November), and Christmas Day (December 25).

## T elephones

In this era of cell phones, you'll find fewer public telephones in hotel lobbies, restaurants, drugstores, garages, roadside kiosks, convenience stores, and other locations throughout the state. The cost of making a local call from a payphone for three minutes is 25–50 cents. To make a long-distance call from a pay phone, use either a prepaid calling card, available in airports, post offices, and a few other outlets, or your credit card, which you can use at any phone: dial 1-800-CALLATT, key in your credit card number, and wait to be connected. In many areas, local calls have now changed to a 10-digit calling system, using the area code. Watch out for in-room connection charges in the more upmarket hotels: it's cheaper to use a pay phone in the lobby.

### Cell phones

American cell phones use GSM 1900 or CDMA 800, a different frequency from other countries. Only foreign phones operating on GSM 1900 will work in the US. You may be able to take the SIM card from your home phone, install it in a rented cell phone in the US, and use it as if it's your own cell phone. Ask your wireless provider about this before leaving. Cell phones can be rented for about $45 a week in the US. Also available are GSM 1900 compatible phones with prepaid calling time, such as those offered by T-Mobile (www.t-mobile.com). Be aware that you probably won't be able to pick up a signal in remote rural areas, such as the Everglades and Keys in South Florida. Check the coverage before starting out.

## Tipping

Service personnel expect tips in Florida. The accepted rate for baggage handlers is $1 per bag. For others, including taxi drivers and waiters, 15–20 percent is the going rate, depending on the level and quality of service. Sometimes tips are included in restaurant bills when dining in groups. Moderate hotel tipping is around $1 per bag or suitcase handled by porters and bellboys, and 15–20 percent for room service. You should tip a doorman if he holds your car or performs other services. It is not necessary to tip chambermaids unless you stay several days, then budget about $1 a day.

## **V** isitor Information

Information is available from various outlets in Florida. Most cities have a Convention and Visitors Bureau (CVB), while elsewhere you must rely on the local chamber of commerce. State and national parks normally have excellent visitor centers, which dispense information and maps and offer ranger-guided talks and walks.

Below is a list of tourist information offices in Florida:

**Bradenton Convention and Visitors Bureau**
PO Box 1000, Bradenton,
FL 34206-1000
Tel: 941-729-9177
www.flagulfislands.com

**Daytona Beach Convention and Visitors Bureau**
126 E. Orange Avenue,
Daytona Beach, FL 32115
Tel: 800-544-0415
www.daytonabeach.org

**Everglades City Area Chamber of Commerce**
32016 Tamiami Trail East,
PO Box 130, Everglades City,
FL 34139
Tel: 941-695-3941

**Everglades National Park Headquarters**
40001 SR 9336, Homestead,
FL 33034
Tel: 305-242-7700
www.nps.gov/ever

**Big Cypress National Preserve Headquarters**
HCR 61, PO Box 110, Ochopee,
FL 34141
Tel: 941-695-4111 or 941-695-2000
www.nps.gov/bicy

**Greater Fort Lauderdale Convention and Visitors Bureau**
1850 Eller Drive, Suite 303,
Fort Lauderdale, FL 33316
Tel: 954-765-4466 or 800-227-8669
www.sunny.org

**Lee County Convention and Visitors Bureau**
P.O. Box 2445, Fort Myers, FL 33902
Tel: 239-338-3500 or 800-237-6444
www.fortmyers-sanibel.com

**Fort Myers Chamber of Commerce Visitor Center**
Edwards Drive, corner of Lee Street,
Fort Myers, FL 33901
Tel: 941-332-3624
www.fortmyers.org

**Emerald Coast Convention and Visitors Bureau**

PO Box 609, Fort Walton Beach,
FL 32549
Tel: 850-651-7122
www.destin-fwb.com

**Alachua County Convention and Visitors Bureau**
30 E. University Avenue, Gainesville,
FL 32601
Tel: 352-374-5260
www.visitgainesville.net

**Islamorada Chamber of Commerce**
MM 82.5, PO Box 915, Islamorada,
FL 33036
Tel: 305-664-4503
www.islamoradachamber.com

**Jacksonville and Jacksonville Beach Convention and Visitors Bureau**
201 E. Adams Street, Jacksonville,
FL 32202
Tel: 904-798-9111 or 800-733-2668
www.jaxcvb.com

**Key Largo Chamber of Commerce**
106000 Overseas Highway,
Key Largo, FL 33037
Tel: 305-451-4726
www.keylargo.com

**Florida Keys and Key West Tourism Development Council**
PO Box 1146, Key West, FL 33041
Tel: 305-296-1552 or 800-771-5397
www.fla-keys.com

**Key West Chamber of Commerce**
402 Wall Street, Key West, FL 33040
Tel: 305-294-2587
www.keywestchamber.org

**Marathon Chamber of Commerce**
MM 53, 12222 Overseas Highway,
Marathon, FL 33050
Tel: 305-743-5417 or 800-262-7284
www.floridakeysmarathon.com

**Greater Miami Convention and Visitors Bureau**
701 Brickell Avenue, Miami,
FL 33131
Tel: 305-539-3000 or 800-933-8448
www.miamiandbeaches.com

**Miami Beach Chamber of Commerce**
1920 Meridian Avenue, Miami,
FL 33131
Tel: 305-674-1300
www.miamibeach.com

**Art Deco Welcome Center**
1001 Ocean Drive, PO Box 190180,
Miami Beach, FL 33139
Tel: 305-531-3484

**Coral Gables Chamber of Commerce**
PO Box 347555, Coral Gables,
FL 33234
Tel: 305-446-1657
www.gableschamber.org

**Naples Visitor and Information Center**
895 Fifth Avenue South, Naples,
FL 34102
Tel: 239-262-6141
www.napleschamber.com

**Naples, Marco Island, Everglades CVB**
3050 N. Horseshoe Drive, Suite 218,
Naples, FL 34104
Tel: 239-252-2425
www.paradisecoast.com

**Orlando/Orange County Convention and Visitors Bureau**
6700 Forum Drive, Suite 100,
Orlando, FL 32821
Tel: 407-363-5800
www.go2orlando.com

**Walt Disney World Company**
PO Box 10000, Lake Buena Vista,
FL 32830-1000
Tel: 407-939-6244
www.disneyworld.com

**Palm Beach/West Palm Beach Chamber of Commerce**
45 Cocoanut Row, Palm Beach,
FL 33480
Tel: 561-233-3000
www.palmbeachfl.com

**Panama City Convention and Visitors Bureau**
17001 Panama City Beach Parkway,
Panama City, FL 32407
Tel: 800-PC-BEACH
www.800pcbeach.com

**Pensacola Visitor Information Center**
1401 E. Gregory Street, Pensacola,
FL 32501
Tel: 850-434-1234 or 800-874-1234
www.visitpensacola.com

**St Augustine Chamber of Commerce**
1 Riberia Street, St Augustine,
FL 32084
Tel: 904-829-5681

**St Petersburg/Clearwater Area Convention and Visitors Bureau**
14450 46th Street, Suite 108,
Clearwater, FL 33762
Tel: 727-464-7200
www.floridasbeach.com

**Sanibel and Captiva Islands**
Sanibel-Captiva Island Chamber of Commerce, 15159 Causeway Road,
Sanibel Island, FL 33957
Tel: 239-472-1080

**Sarasota Convention and Visitors Bureau**
655 N. Tamiami Trail (US 41),
Sarasota, FL 34236
Tel: 941-957-1877 or 800-522-9799
www.sarasotafl.org

**Stuart/Martin County Chamber of Commerce**
1650 S Kanner Highway, Stuart,
FL 34994
Tel: 772-287-1088

**Tallahassee Convention and Visitors Bureau**
106 E. Jefferson Street, Tallahassee,
FL 32302
Tel: 850-413-9200 or 800-628-2866
www.co.leon.fl.us/visitor/index.html

**Tampa/Hillsborough Convention and Visitors Bureau**
400 N. Tampa Street, Suite 2800,
Tampa, FL 33602
Tel: 813-223-1111
www.visittampabay.com

**Indian River County Tourist Council**
1216 21st Street, Vero Beach,
FL 32960
Tel: 772-567-3491

TRANSPORTATION

ACCOMMODATIONS

ACTIVITIES

A – Z

# WHAT TO READ

## Natural and Cultural History

**Birds of Florida** by Frances W. Hall, Great Outdoors (1994). The definitive guide to Florida's feathered inhabitants.

**Building a Company: Roy O. Disney and the Creation of an Entertainment Empire** by Bob Thomas, Hyperion (1999). An interesting look at the other Disney, Walt's big brother Roy, and his role as businessman and financier during the early days of the Disney company.

**The Celebration Chronicles: Life, Liberty, and the Pursuit of Property Values in Disney's New Town** by Andrew Ross, Ballantine Books (1999). A lucid evaluation of what went wrong – and right – at a company town designed by the Disney company.

**Diver's Guide to Florida and the Florida Keys** by Jim Stachowicz, Windward Publishing (1994). An excellent guide to underwater Florida.

**Dream State: Eight Generations of Swamp Lawyers, Conquistadors, Confederate Daughters, Banana Republicans, and other Florida Wildlife** by Diane Roberts, University Press of Florida (2004). The title of this engaging book by an NPR commentator and Florida native says it all!

**Everglades: River of Grass** by Marjorie Stoneman Douglas, Pineapple Press (1988). This seminal work describing the subtle magic of the Everglades, first published in 1947, contributed to the establishment of Everglades National Park.

**Florida Cookbook by** Jeanne Voltz and Caroline Stuart, Alfred A. Knopf (1993). The most readable of books about regional cuisine, full of anecdotes and historical nuggets.

**The Florida of the Inca** by Garcilaso de la Vega, University of Texas Press (1951). The story of the fateful expedition led by Hernando de Soto in the 16th century.

**The Florida Keys: A History and Guide** by Joy Williams, Random House (1988). A good read to enhance your enjoyment of the islands.

**ABOVE:** a Miccosukee Indian family in the Everglades.

**Florida Place Names** by Allen Morris, Pineapple Press (1974). The fascinating stories behind the names of Florida cities, counties, rivers, and so on.

**Life on Mars: Gangsters, Runaways, Exiles, Drag Queens and Other Aliens in Florida** by Alexander Stuart, Doubleday (1996). An entertaining look at Florida, giving an insight into the motley bunch of people who live there. Based on fact but with a touch of fiction.

**The Magic Kingdom: Walt Disney and the American Way of Life** by Steven Watts, University of Missouri Press (2001). A highly readable chronicle of Walt Disney's life and an interesting analysis of his remarkable influence on American, and world, culture.

**Married to the Mouse** by Richard E. Foglesong, Yale University Press (2001). A revealing examination of Walt Disney World's quasi-governmental status.

**Miami** by Joan Didion, Random House (1997). The famed California journalist turns her eagle eye on the Cuban community in Miami.

**A New History of Florida** by Michael Gannon, University Press of Florida (1996). The most readable history there is, and more up to date than others. Gannon's **A Short History of Florida** is also highly recommended.

**Kerouac in Florida: Where the Road Ends** by Bob Kealing, Arbiter Press (2004). This well-researched book examines the Beat author's secretive years in the College Park area of Orlando, where he wrote The Dharma Bums and Big Sur. Kerouac's former home is now a historical landmark used as a writer's residence.

**A Naturalist in Florida: A Celebration of Eden** by Archie Carr, edited by Marjorie Harris Carr, Yale University Press (1994). Poetic essays about Florida's extraordinary natural history by the famed sea-turtle researcher and UF professor.

The Orchid Thief by Susan Orleans. An entertaining account of the New Yorker magazine writer's travels into the Florida swamps with orchid collector John Laroche.

**Orange Blossom Trails: Walks in the Natural Areas of Florida** by Philip Manning, John Blair Publisher (1997). A non-native's look at Florida's parks and nature preserves.

**Snowbirds, Sand Castles and Self-Rising Crackers** by Al Burt, University Press of Florida (1997). A longtime reporter's look at the changing faces of residents and tourists.

**Some Kind of Paradise: A Chronicle of Man and the Land in Florida** by Mark Derr, University Press of Florida (1998). A fascinating history, with an emphasis on the impact of human society on the environment.

**Team Rodent** by Carl Hiassen, Ballantine Books (1998). A scathing rant against all things Disney, with emphasis on how the company manipulates the press, damages the environment, and strong-arms local government.

**Travels of William Bartram** by William Bartram, Dover Publications (1978). This diary was written by a Philadelphia-born botanist who traveled throughout Florida in the 1700s. It has wonderful accounts of fauna, flora, and indigenous people.

**Tropical Deco: The Architecture and Design of Old Miami Beach** by Laura Cerwinske and David Kaminsky, Rizzoli (1991). A good book for anyone interested in the Art Deco district of Miami.

**Visiting Small-Town Florida** by Bruce Hunt, Pineapple Press (1997). A look at 39 of the state's most interesting small towns – Florida's hidden side.

**The Wild Heart of Florida: Florida Writers on Florida's Wildlands** edited by Jeff Ripple and Susan Cerulean, University Press of Florida (1999). A superb natural history reader that will inspire nature lovers who think Florida's wild places are all gone.

## Fiction

**James W. Hall:** the author of excellent Florida-based thrillers, including Tropical Freeze, Bones of Coral, Hard Aground, and Mean Tide.

**Ernest Hemingway:** many of Hemingway's novels and short stories were written in the 10 years he lived in Key West, but To Have and Have Not is the only one set in the town (published in 1937). Sadly, it's not one of his best.

**Carl Hiassen:** a Miami Herald journalist, Hiassen writes excellent comic thrillers set in Florida. They include: Native Tongue (1992), which makes fun of theme parks; Skin Tight (1990), in which he turns his wit on plastic surgery in Miami; and Lucky You (1997), a twisted, wacky look at lottery winners. His book Strip Tease (1993) was made into a film, but his stories are best appreciated in print.

**Zora Neale Hurston:** one of Florida's leading 20th-century black authors, Hurston is best known for Their Eyes were Watching God (1937), about the devastating 1928 hurricane. Her life is commemorated at a tiny museum in the Orlando suburb of Eatonville, the first black township in the US, where she was born.

**James Weldon Johnson:** raised in Jacksonville, son of Florida's first black female teacher, Johnson was part of the Harlem Renaissance. His Autobiography of an Ex-Colored Man (Knopf, 1928), a fictional account of a biracial man, was originally published anonymously. Lift Every Voice and Sing (often called the "Black National Anthem") was written by Johnson and set to music by his brother in 1900.

**Elmore Leonard:** this internationally known thriller writer set several of his best novels in Florida. Try La Brava (1984), set in South Beach prior to its regeneration.

**John D. MacDonald:** one of Florida's most prolific novelists, MacDonald wrote many color-themed yarns about his detective Travis McGee –

## Send Us Your Thoughts

We do our best to ensure the information in our books is as accurate and up-to-date as possible. The books are updated on a regular basis using local contacts, who painstakingly add, amend and correct as required. However, some details (such as telephone numbers and opening times) are liable to change, and we are ultimately reliant on our readers to put us in the picture.

We welcome your feedback, especially your experience of using the book "on the road." Maybe we recommended a hotel that you liked (or another that you didn't), or you came across a great bar or new attraction we missed.

We will acknowledge all contributions, and we'll offer an Insight Guide to the best letters received.

Please write to us at:
**Insight Guides**
**PO Box 7910**
**London SE1 1WE**
Or email us at:
**insight@apaguide.co.uk**

including The Deep Blue Goodbye, The Dreadful Lemon Sky, Dress Her in Indigo, and The Empty Copper Sea.

**Thomas McGuane:** his Ninety-Two in the Shade (Random House, 1995) is a saga of treachery in which the sea and the seedy side of Key West play an integral role.

**Marjorie Kinnan Rawlings:** the tales in her 1942 work Cross Creek celebrate Rawlings' colorful neighbors in the backcountry hamlet of Cross Creek, where the former New Yorker found her literary voice and a much-loved haven. The Yearling (1939), the story of a boy and his fawn, won her a Pulitzer Prize.

**Frank Slaughter:** Storm Haven, East Side General, and In a Dark Garden are all novels with a Florida backdrop from another of the state's prolific tale-spinners. They were originally published in the 1940s and 50s.

**Harriet Beecher Stowe:** The famed author of the 1851 antislavery serial novel Uncle Tom's Cabin lived on the John's River in the late 1800s. Stowe's travel essays, published in the 1875 Palmetto-Leaves, boosted Florida tourism in the Victorian steamboat era.

## Other Insight Guides

Companion **Insight Guide** titles cover every major travel destination in North America, from Alaska to Arizona. City titles include Boston, New York, Philadelphia, Chicago, Orlando, Miami, San Francisco, and Washington DC. Regional titles include New England, New York State, and The New South.

These are complemented by a comprehensive range of easy-fold **Insight FlexiMaps**, laminated to make them durable and waterproof, and containing useful travel details. Local titles include Florida, Florida's Gold Coast, Miami, and Orlando.

A special Insight Guide, Cruising: All Questions Answered, shows first-time cruisegoers how to pick the right ship and cruise for them.

Two new series provide detailed information to US destinations in compact form:

● **Insight Step by Step Guides** provide precise itineraries and recommendations from a local, expert writer for dining, lodgings and sightseeing; titles include Las Vegas, New York and Orlando.

● **Insight Smart Guides** are packed with information, arranged in a unique A–Z format that helps you find what you want quickly and simply. Titles include Boston, Hawaii, Las Vegas, New York, Orlando, and San Francisco.

# ART & PHOTO CREDITS

Tony Arruza 11M, 47, 98, 105B, 127
Tony Arruza/Corbis 60
José Azel 83
Bancroft Library 29
Charles E. Bennett 20T, 24, 30T, 31, 33, 35
Bettmann/Corbis 42T
Steven Brooke/Museum of Contemporary Art, North Miami 105T
Busch Entertainment Corp. 78
Frederick Dau 32R
Everett Collection 245B, 246, 247T, 247B, 248
Fairchild Tropical Botanic Garden 111T, 111B
Najlah Feanny/Corbis 50
Ricardo Ferro 193
Florida Division of Tourism 43
Joe Gato/Miami City Ballet 61
Raymond Gehman/Corbis 51, 225
Greater Miami Convention & Visitors Bureau 107BR, 114
Clare Griffiths 207
Gavin Hellier/Robert Harding World Imagery/Corbis 172
Henry Morrison Flagler Museum 44
Historical Museum of Southern Florida/Tony Arruza 20B
J. Manning Strozier Library 22B
David Kadlubowski/Corbis 9ML
Catherine Karnow 102T
James Lemass 70, 74, 261, 263B
Library of Congress 22M, 27, 30B, 34B, 36, 37, 38, 39L, 39R, 40, 41, 42B, 44–45, 49B, 264T
Mennello Museum of American Folk Art 266B
Miami Herald 106BL
NASA/Kennedy Space Center 196, 199TL, 199BR, 202, 203T, 203B, 204T, 204B, 206T, 206B
Abraham Nowitz 2–3, 23B, 46, 52–53, 57, 84–85, 94, 96–97, 99, 100, 101, 102B, 104T, 104B, 106BR, 107BL, 107T, 108T, 108B, 109T, 109B, 110T, 110B, 112T, 112B, 113T, 113B, 118, 119, 121T, 121B, 122T, 122B, 123L, 123R, 124T, 124B, 125T, 125B, 126, 128, 182, 184, 186T, 186B, 187T, 188, 189T, 189B, 190B, 191BL, 195, 370
Richard Nowitz 1, 2, 4T, 4B, 5, 8B, 9T, 10B, 11T, 11B, 12–13, 14–15, 16–17, 18, 19T, 19B, 25, 26, 28, 32L, 54, 55, 56, 58, 64, 65, 66L, 66R, 67, 68, 69, 71, 72, 73, 75L, 75R, 79, 80, 81, 82, 86–87, 88–89, 90, 91T, 91B, 132, 133, 134, 135T, 135B, 136T, 136B, 137, 138, 139T, 139B, 140T, 140B, 141T, 141B, 142T, 142B, 143, 146, 147, 148, 150T, 150BR, 151T, 151B, 152T, 152B, 154, 155, 158, 159, 161T, 161BR,
161BL, 162T, 162B, 163L, 163R, 164T, 164B, 165T, 165B, 166, 167, 168–169, 170, 171T, 171B, 173, 175B, 177T, 177B, 178T, 178B, 179T, 179BL, 180, 197, 198, 199TR, 199BL, 200T, 200B, 201L, 201R, 205L, 210, 211, 212T, 212B, 213T, 213B, 215T, 215B, 216T, 216B, 217T, 217B, 218T, 218B, 219T, 219B, 220T, 220B, 221T, 221BL, 221BR, 222T, 222BR, 223T, 223B, 224T, 224B, 226, 227, 228–229, 230, 231T, 231B, 232, 233, 236, 237T, 238, 241, 242T, 242BL, 242BR, 243, 244, 249T, 249B, 250T, 250–251, 252T, 252B, 253, 254, 256, 259, 260T, 260BL, 262T, 262BL, 262BR, 264BL, 264BR, 266T, 267T, 267B, 268T, 268B, 269T, 269BL, 270T, 271T, 270-271, 272T, 272B, 274, 275, 276, 278–279, 280, 281T, 281B, 282, 283, 284, 285T, 285BL, 285BR, 286T, 286B, 287T, 287B, 288, 289, 290, 291, 292, 293, 294, 295T, 295B, 296B, 297T, 297BL, 298T, 298B, 299T, 299B, 300T, 300B, 301T, 301B, 302, 306, 307, 309T, 309B, 310T, 310B, 311T, 311B, 312T, 312B, 313T, 313B, 314T, 314B, 315, 316T, 316B, 317T, 317BL, 318T, 318B, 319T, 319B, 320, 324–325, 326, 327T, 327B, 328, 329, 330, 331T, 331B, 332T, 332BL, 332BR, 333, 334T, 334B, 335T, 335B, 336T, 336B, 337, 338, 339, 340T, 340B, 341T, 341BL, 341BR, 342, 343, 344T, 344B, 345T, 345B, 346T, 346B, 347T, 347B, 348, 349T, 349B, 350T, 350B, 351L, 351R, 352T, 352BL, 352BR, 353T, 353B, 354, 355, 356, 360, 373, 375, 378, 381, 382, 388
Palm Beach County Convention & Visitors Bureau 183, 187B, 194
Mike Parry/Tom Stack & Associates 205R
Timothy O'Keefe 269BR
Orange County Regional History Center 21B, 23T
Orlando Museum of Art 265T, 265B
Rubell Family Collection, Miami 59, 103T, 103B
Salvador Dalí Museum 296T
State Library and Archives of Florida 20M, 21T, 22T, 34L, 150BL, 179BR, 222BL, 297BR, 317BR
Universal Orlando 8T, 9B, 10T, 76, 77, 257, 260BR, 273, 277, 365
Gregory Wrona 153, 175T, 176, 181, 185T, 185B, 190T, 191BR, 192T, 192B, 358

# INDEX

*Numbers in italics refer to photographs*

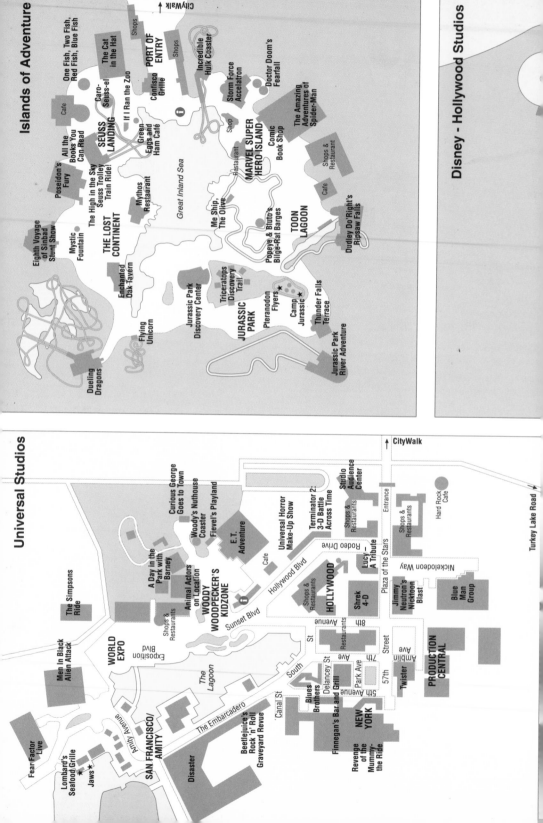

# Islands of Adventure

PORT OF ENTRY

Shops
Shops

Caro-Seuss-el
The Cat in the Hat
One Fish, Two Fish, Red Fish, Blue Fish
If I Ran the Zoo
Confisco Grille
Incredible Hulk Coaster
Storm Force Acceladron
Doctor Doom's Fearfall

↑ CityWalk

Cafe
All the Books You Can Read
SEUSS LANDING
Green Eggs and Ham Café
The High in the Sky Seuss Trolley Train Ride!

Poseidon's Fury

Shop
The Amazing Adventures of Spider-Man
MARVEL SUPER HERO ISLAND
Comic Book Shop

Shops & Restaurant

THE LOST CONTINENT
Mythos Restaurant
Great Inland Sea

Restaurant

Cafe

Eighth Voyage of Sinbad Stunt Show
Mystic Fountain

Me Ship, The Olive
Popeye & Bluto's Bilge-Rat Barges
Dudley Do-Right's Ripsaw Falls
TOON LAGOON

Enchanted Oak-Tavern

Flying Unicorn

Jurassic Park Discovery Center
Triceratops Discovery Trail
Pteranodon Flyers
Camp Jurassic
Thunder Falls Terrace

JURASSIC PARK

Dueling Dragons

Jurassic Park River Adventure

# Disney - Hollywood Studios

# Universal Studios

↑ CityWalk

The Simpsons Ride
Men In Black Alien Attack
Fear Factor Live

Curious George Goes to Town
Woody Woodpecker Coaster
Fievel's Playland
A Day in the Park with Barney
Animal Actors on Location

WOODY WOODPECKER'S KIDZONE

E.T. Adventure
Cafe
Universal Horror Make-Up Show
Terminator 2: 3-D Battle Across Time
Studio Audience Center

Entrance

Shops & Restaurants

Shops & Restaurants

Hard Rock Cafe

Rodeo Drive
Hollywood Blvd
HOLLYWOOD
Sunset Blvd
Shops & Restaurants
Lucy – A Tribute
Shrek 4-D
Plaza of the Stars
Jimmy Neutron's Nicktoon Blast
Blue Man Group

Nickelodeon Way

WORLD EXPO
Exposition Blvd
Shops & Restaurants

8th Avenue
St
Restaurants
Street
Ambin Ave
Twister
PRODUCTION CENTRAL

The Lagoon

South
5th Avenue
Delancey St
Park Ave
7th Ave
57th

Turkey Lake Road

Canal St
Blues Brothers
Finnegan's Bar and Grill
The Embarcadero
NEW YORK
Revenge of the Mummy- the Ride

Beetlejuice's Rock 'n' Roll Graveyard Revue
Disaster
SAN FRANCISCO/ AMITY

Amity Avenue

Lombard's Seafood Grille
Jaws